Trunch D/Ke 62

Em Ravoll
57

Rm Pearl

Timothy Lewis

D1443543

#85

Merry Christmas 1996!
to Ashley,

Hope you enjoy this.
Keep the faith
and continue to
dare to dream!

Your Mom and Dad
thought you'd like this.

Best wishes,
Jim O'Brien

DARE TO DREAM

The Steelers of
Two Special Seasons

By Jim O'Brien

Inside the Steelers locker room

This book is dedicated to my wife, Kathie O'Brien.

Copyright © 1996 by Jim O'Brien

James P. O'Brien — Publishing
P.O. Box 12580
Pittsburgh PA 15241
Phone: (412) 221-3580

First printing, September, 1996

Manufactured in the United States of America

Printed by Geyer Printing Company, Inc.
3700 Bigelow Boulevard
Pittsburgh PA 15213

Typography by Cold-Comp
810 Penn Avenue
Pittsburgh PA 15222

ISBN 1-886348-00-6

Acknowledgements

Writing is a lonely business, and publishing is a risky business, so you need a lot of people to lean on to gain the spirit and strength to succeed in these endeavors.

It all begins with my wife, Kathie, and our older daughter, Sarah, who read this manuscript and offered corrections and challenged me throughout, and our younger daughter, Rebecca, who helped me with the mechanics to complete the task. This book is a family affair.

My friend, Bill Priatko, a former pro football player, offered advice, encouragement and prayers, and Laird Stuart, a friend and Presbyterian minister who now serves in San Francisco, provided inspiration for the family album look of this book with a sermon he offered.

Thanks to my friends, Alex Pociask of Stevens Painton Corp., and Tom Snyder of Continental Design & Management Group, and John C. Williams and Peter P. Konczakowski of National City, for their loyal support. I am grateful to all my friends and patrons who have offered the financial backing so that I could continue writing and publishing books about sports achievement in Pittsburgh.

They include Steve and Charlie Previs of Waddell & Reed Financial Services, Richard J. Nesbit of Sutersville Lumber Co., Bill Baierl of Baierl Chevrolet, Barbara and Ted Frantz of Tedco, Inc., Thomas H. O'Brien and Gregory Fink of PNC Bank, Ed Harmon of Harmon Construction, Mike Ference of Ference Marketing & Communications, Andy Komer of Bowne of Pittsburgh, Frank B. Fuhrer, Frank Gustine Jr., Dick Swanson, Dave Brown, Jim Roddey, Jim Broadhurst of Eat'n Park, Ron Livingston of Babb, Inc., Frederick B. Sargent of Sargent Electric, Jack Perkins of Mr. P's, attorney Stanley M. Stein, Michael C. Linn of Meridian Exploration, Lloyd Gibson of North Side Bank, Larry Werner of Ketchum Public Relations, Dennis S. Meteny of Respironics, Inc., R. Everett Burns of E-Z Overhead Door Co., Jim Hesse of Wheeling-Pittsburgh Steel.

Thanks to the Steelers and their public relations department — Joe Gordon, Rob Boulware, Ron Miller, Mike Miller, Rene McNab — and Bob Labriola and Teresa Varley of *Steelers Digest*. The great photography was provided by Michael F. Fabus, George Gojkovich and Bill Amatucci, and the cover design was by Giuseppe Francioni of Prisma, Inc.

All the books in my series have been produced at Geyer Printing, where Stanley Goldmann, Bruce McGough and Tom Samuels have worked closely with me. A special tribute to Jerry Studeny, who retired after 36 years as production specialist at Geyer Printing and has nurse-maided all my books to press. Ed Lutz and Cathy Pawlowski of Cold-Comp Typographers were great to work with again. They truly care.

Thanks to my former colleague, Marty Wolfson, who helped get me started in the book business, and my mother, Mary O'Brien, who was looking forward to her 90th birthday at the end of 1996, who's always been there for me. My sister, Carole Cook, helps with the circulation area.

Herb Douglas, Jr., a 1948 Olympic Games bronze medal winner from my hometown of Hazelwood, prodded me, saying "You can't hope it will happen, you have to *make* it happen."

I am blessed to have all of them on my team.

Books By Jim O'Brien

COMPLETE HANDBOOK OF PRO BASKETBALL 1970-1971

COMPLETE HANDBOOK OF PRO BASKETBALL 1971-1972

ABA ALL-STARS

PITTSBURGH: THE STORY OF THE CITY OF CHAMPIONS

HAIL TO PITT: A SPORTS HISTORY OF
THE UNIVERSITY OF PITTSBURGH

DOING IT RIGHT

WHATEVER IT TAKES

MAZ AND THE '60 BUCS

REMEMBER ROBERTO

PENGUIN PROFILES

DARE TO DREAM

To order copies directly from the publisher, send $26.95 for hardcover edition. Please send $3.50 to cover shipping and handling costs per book. Pennsylvania residents add 6% sales tax to price of book only. Allegheny County residents add an additional 1% sales tax for a total of 7% sales tax. Copies will be signed by author at your request. Discounts available for large orders. Contact publisher regarding availability and price of all books in *Pittsburgh Proud* series, or to request an order form. Several of them are sold out; others are available only in hardcover editions.

Contents

95 LLOYD

Introduction
Iceballs, popcorn and peanuts

"He's such a sweetheart."
— Stella Kalaris
on Greg Lloyd

It was a bright sunny day in May, the last Thursday of the month, May 30, 1996, to be exact, and the Steelers were all set to start a minicamp in Pittsburgh the coming weekend. I had just come away from the clubhouse of the Steelers at Three Rivers Stadium, where I had spoken to some of the players and taken a few pictures. I was in the home stretch for completing this book.

I drove to West Park, not far from the stadium on the city's North Side. I went there to return some old newspapers that had been lent to me by Gus Karalis, a gregarious gentleman who was making ice balls under a rainbow-striped umbrella at his stand alongside the tennis courts of West Park.

His wife Stella was bagging popcorn and peanuts and dispensing them to customers. Gus and Stella Kalaris are part of the spring and summer and fall landscape on the North Side. They put their pushcart in the garage during the winter months and take it easy. Their stand is a Pittsburgh institution. The parents of Gus Kalaris, who immigrated to this country from Greece, had started selling from a similar pushcart in that same neighborhood in 1934.

The family had been friendly with Art Rooney and his family through the years. They came from the same neighborhood and had a similar zest for people and life. Gus and Stella are two of the nicest people you will ever meet between Pittsburgh and Athens. They have gotten to know many of the Steelers and Pirates and their families who have frequented their stand through the years. Gus, in fact, was the godfather for one of the sons of former Steelers offensive lineman John Brown, who became a PNC Bank executive.

"How's your book coming along?" Stella asked me soon after we had exchanged greetings, and I had given her husband his newspapers.

"I should have the writing done in about two weeks," I told her.

"Are you doing anything on Greg Lloyd?" she came back.

She caught me off guard with her inquiry. By coincidence, I had been working on the chapter about Greg Lloyd that very morning. Frankly, it was a difficult chapter to write. I wasn't sure I knew the real Greg Lloyd after spending two seasons with the Steelers while working on this book.

7

"He is such a sweetheart when he's here," said Stella. "He sits right there (she pointed to a high stool with a black cushion seat that stood alongside the popcorn and peanut compartment on the orange push cart). "I love to talk to him.

"You know, when he's in town, he goes to a Baptist church over in Manchester and teaches Bible school. He's got a nice wife and nice children. I asked him once, 'How come you're so mean when you're on the field?' He smiled at me, and he said, 'I have to. That's my image.' It's a shame, I think, because people get the wrong idea. He even gave Gus a Steelers' cap."

Gus Kalaris could get along with anybody, but, like his wife, he was a big fan of Greg Lloyd, and shared her consternation about Lloyd's public posturing.

"He usually orders a banana ice ball, sometimes cherry," recalled Kalaris, sidestepping the pigeons and squirrels that feed on the popcorn and peanuts that people drop near his stand. "He's unbelievable. He'll talk to the kids here; he'll pat them on the head. He's such a warm guy. I don't know why he's like he is down there at the stadium. That's hard to figure out."

Stella told me that she and Gus had gone to Christmas parties the past two years at the Rooney residence just a few blocks away. Dan and Pat Rooney had moved two years earlier from Mt. Lebanon back to his boyhood home, where his parents had lived all of their married lives, and had renovated it.

"Bill Cowher was there and he was very nice," said Stella. "Jim Leyland was there, too. He was nice, too, so different from the way he comes off when he's interviewed on television after the Pirates' games. He always seems so somber. It was a big surprise to see what he was really like."

Maybe, I thought, Lloyd and Leyland, and Rooney and Cowher as well, are all like those ice balls Gus scrapes out of blocks of ice, different colors, different flavors, sometimes icy, sometimes syrupy.

Nellie King called me on the telephone that afternoon, and I returned the call when I got home from West Park.

King, the former pitcher for the Pirates who once shared the team's broadcast booth with Bob Prince, has long been one of my favorite people on the Pittsburgh sports scene: a good man, a good story-teller. If they had a Hall of Fame in Pittsburgh for nice people, King and the Kalarises would be enshrined in it. He was calling to compliment me on a newspaper column I had written about my daughter Sarah's graduation at the University of Virginia. He had three daughters, so King could relate to my prideful reflections.

I mentioned Greg Lloyd to Nellie King and told him of my dilemma, about trying to discover and determine what the Steelers or any story subjects are really like. "I've met him at a couple of social events," said King, "and he came off well every time. He's a fiercely proud individual. I just think he's a warrior, and that he carries himself a certain way. He has an outlook on playing football the way a preacher has about God. It's just a calling, a way of life for him."

8

Like most media people, Myron Cope knew how difficult Lloyd can be. I spoke to Cope that day, too, and he also mentioned that wherever he appeared at banquets and such where Lloyd had been before him the reports on Lloyd were all positive. "He can turn on the charm when he wants to," said Cope.

This book is about players and people I came across during the 1994 and 1995 seasons. These were two of the greatest seasons in Steelers' history. They came so close to winning that elusive fifth Lombardi trophy — that "one for the thumb" ring. Its aim is to give you some insights into what the Steelers are all about, to give you a better appreciation for the players, coaches, administrators and others associated with the Steelers. They came up short both times, and maybe their fans did, too, in failing to appreciate their accomplishments.

I hope it will give you a better sense of the Steelers, as people, as someone else's children. There are some inspiring personal sagas here, some showing the triumph of the human spirit over a tragic past. Others show how they benefited by having good parents and caring people in their hometowns, good teachers, good coaches, good mentors. For some, there still rages a battle within to find their real selves.

Richard Wright, who came out of the Deep South and moved to Chicago and then New York, and wrote well-received books about his personal struggles as a young black man, such as *Native Son* and *Uncle Tom's Children*, once said in an interview, "I think the importance of my writing lies in how much *felt* life is in it. It gets its value from that."

I've always been interested in how people *felt* about their lives. I am a fan of Pittsburgh and all its sports teams. I have always been intrigued with people. They all have stories. I'm interested in where they came from and how they became what they became. I try to learn from it, I try to teach from it. I prefer to be positive in my approach. "It doesn't cost you anything to be nice," noted Nellie King. No, indeed, it does not. I strive to be fair and to write balanced portraits of these people. None of the offerings are the full story. No one ever knows the full story. They are simply sketches then, drawn from both short visits and long visits, sometimes a series of such, conversations with cohorts and fans and, hopefully, they will add to your enjoyment and understanding of the Steelers.

This is the first of two books about these Steelers of the '90s, so other players, coaches and personalities will be profiled in the next book, including Rod Woodson, Leon Searcy, Levon Kirkland, Tom Newberry, Joel Steed, Kevin Henry, C.J. Johnson, Andre Hastings, Eric Ravotti, Darren Perry et al., and some old-timers like Ernie Holmes, Elbie Nickel and Joe Zombek. They, too, have been a part of the Pittsburgh Steelers and their rich tradition.

9

"My characters start generally when they are at the worst place in their lives. To improve themselves, they struggle; they struggle to understand their condition. I like that in people. I like to see people pull themselves out of whatever holds them from their best selves. You know, everybody really has a best self and a worst self; some people never fight their way to the best self. That is one of the worst sins in the world — to see the best self, to know it is there and to fail to try to achieve it."

— Alice Walker, Author
The Color Purple

Under the big tent
Explaining what went wrong

"It's something that happened."
— Neil O'Donnell

There were less than two minutes remaining in Super Bowl XXX and the final result was already on the scoreboard. The Dallas Cowboys had beaten the Pittsburgh Steelers, 27-17. The Steelers were running out of time and miracles. That's when I left my seat in the last row of the auxiliary press box high above Sun Devil Stadium in Tempe, Arizona — it was a great seat as I could take in the complete surrealistic scene — and headed for the post-game interview tent set up outside the respective locker rooms.

The National Football League leaves no page unturned when it comes to coordinating everything associated with their showcase contest, and there was a series of runways designated for media use only. So it was easy to get from the top of the stadium to the base of the opposite end of the stadium, a matter of five minutes at best. There was no fighting the crowd to get from here to there.

A final roar came up from the crowd, and we later learned that Neil O'Donnell, the Steelers' quarterback, had yet another pass picked off by Brock Marion, a Cowboys' safety. This one didn't matter. The earlier two interceptions had cost the Steelers dearly. In truth, they had cost the Steelers the game, no debate there. O'Donnell had two errant throws to the sidelines picked off by Larry Brown. Brown was the only player near the ball on both occasions.

Brown had big runbacks on both interceptions and they set up short yardage touchdowns by Emmitt Smith, the star running back of the Cowboys. The Steelers had closed to within three points, trailing 20-17, and had the ball at their own 32 yard line with 4:15 on the clock, and had a chance to win or tie the game.

I recalled having breakfast with Tom Newberry, the Steelers' offensive guard, the day before the Steelers departed Pittsburgh for Phoenix, and he had said, "If we get the ball with four minutes to go, and we're close, we'll make the drive to win the game." He was right on the button, I thought.

Then O'Donnell's pass to Andre Hastings was hauled in by Brown, and the chance for a comeback victory by the underdog Steelers went up in smoke, or like the thousands of balloons that had been let loose in the spectacular halftime show.

I bumped into Bart Starr enroute to the interview area. He was being escorted to a get-away bus. I had played tennis with Bart and his wife at an NFL Owners Meeting in Maui in the early '80s — talk about a nice assignment — and he remembered me. So he slowed his pace and reflected on the game. Starr had been the MVP in the first two Super Bowls, before the NFL's championship contest was actually called the Super Bowl.

Starr suggested that O'Donnell got pressured on his first interception, and might have had a hand in his face and that he threw off his back foot, and that he and his receiver didn't read the defense the same way when the Cowboys blitzed O'Donnell on the second pickoff.

When Starr saw me pulling out my notebook, he smiled and hesitated. "Don't quote me on that because I'm not sure what happened, and I don't want to appear to be critical of O'Donnell. I don't know what really happened."

Starr agreed to assess the Steelers as a team, however, and put a positive spin on a disappointing setback for Pittsburgh fans. "They have a very bright future," said Starr. "I happened to be in Jacksonville earlier this season when they lost to that expansion team. To be in the situation they were in that day, and to finish up the season here in the Super Bowl is quite a story. It was a tremendous success story to come from that game to this game. For them to have turned their season around like that says a lot for the coach and his staff and the players. And O'Donnell was a big part of that."

Indeed, O'Donnell was voted the team's Most Valuable Player by his teammates at season's end. The scouting report on O'Donnelll had always been that he played a heady, conservative game, didn't make mistakes and didn't throw interceptions. It should have read that he didn't make many mistakes and didn't throw many interceptions. He picked the wrong day and the wrong setting and the wrong audience — there were 76,347 at Sun Devil Stadium and an estimated 135 million TV viewers, the most ever to watch a single event or show in history — to have a bad day.

O'Donnell did some good things in this game, once he settled down and quit throwing too soon, too hard and wide and high, but overall he clearly had a bummer of an afternoon. One newsman suggested shortly after the game that O'Donnell, not Larry Brown, was the Cowboys' MVP at Super Bowl XXX.

I had an opportunity to talk to another Hall of Fame quarterback before the Cowboys and Steelers started showing up for post-game interviews.

Sonny Jurgensen was among the 3,000 or so credentialed media present for the game. He was doing radio and TV commentary in Washington D.C. He had starred with the Eagles and Redskins, and could relate to what O'Donnell had done. He had his share of bad days, too.

"It looked like he had different problems on both of those passes that were picked off," said Jurgensen. "The first time he was on his heels when he threw it, and the ball just took off. On the second, it looked like the receiver didn't run where O'Donnell thought he would in a blitz situation.

"I thought it was a 'hot' read. O'Donnell didn't read it as a hot read and the receiver did, or something like that. He thought the inside guy (Hastings) was going to run a drag pattern and go outside. But he stayed inside. Hey, Dallas played a perfect game. No turnovers.

"Pittsburgh did a helluva job, too. They did a helluva job against Emmitt Smith. They held him to 49 yards rushing and Dallas to 56 yards rushing overall. They played well. They showed a lot of heart. I thought they made good adjustments in the second half. They did a great job against that big offensive line. They held them to 198 (net) yards passing. Against Aikman and those Dallas receivers, that's saying something. Bam Morris played well for Pittsburgh; they started off with (Erric) Pegram and he didn't do too much. It hurt them when they lost (Ernie) Mills to an injury early in the fourth quarter. It hurts when you lose some of your passing package."

"If it don't make dollars,
it don't make sense."
— Deion Sanders

When I covered my first Super Bowl game, for *The Miami News* in January of 1970, I remember the crush inside the clubhouse of the winning Kansas City Chiefs after they had defeated the Minnesota Vikings at old Tulane Stadium in New Orleans in Super Bowl IV. In those days, reporters were permitted into the dressing room for their post-game interviews. But the NFL soon outgrew that practice; there were too many media to even consider that as the Super Bowl became the biggest single sporting event in the world.

There was a white canvas tent that stretched about fifty or sixty yards long and about 25 yards wide where the post-game interviews were conducted outside Sun Devil Stadium. NFL public relations representatives from all the teams escorted players from the two teams into the tent. There were about 20 pedestals positioned along the walls of the tent. They were like open toll booths, or ticket booths at an amusement park. Players would stand on these pedestals with a fixed microphone in front of them, and would field questions from the media. It was as orderly and efficient a process as possible under the circumstances.

Announcements were made as each player picked for post-game interviews was about to enter the tent. "Kevin Greene of the Steelers will be at No. 10," someone would say over a p.a. system. And the media would scurry for the best possible position. The players remained at the pedestal as long as they chose to; the Cowboys all stayed a lot longer than the Steelers. Microphones and tape recorders and pads and pens were pressed up under the noses of the players. Some media folk held microphones at the end of lance-like poles to

13

make sure they got the best possible sound bites for their post-game reports. One of those microphones looked like it was covered with a raccoon tail. TV cameramen complained about it floating in front of the players being interviewed. It ruined the picture.

There was pushing and shoving, as is customary at such interviews, but few complaints from the media. I didn't see any arguments or outbursts, though all of us got smacked upside the head with a microphone or camera from time to time.

It was easy to run from one pedestal to another, trying to catch the interviews. If you couldn't get to any, the NFL took care of that, too. There were handouts with quotes from the Cowboys and Steelers available shortly after the game in the press box or at media headquarters in downtown Phoenix. Everything that is said by the Super Bowl participants is recorded in some manner, and available to all, thanks to the NFL's top-notch publicity mill.

Neil O'Donnell didn't like to be interviewed on the best of days, so he had to be a reluctant participant in this press appearance. He normally limited his availability to the media to one day during the preparation week, and then after the game. O'Donnell had come off well in both of his appearances before an assembly at the Doubletree Hotel ballroom during the week before the Super Bowl. He was most engaging.

The post-game grilling was a different challenge. He stood on the same stand that would later be utilized by Deion Sanders, the Cowboys' often outrageous commentator and cornerback. For Sanders, the pedestal was like a stage, though he declined a request to do a little dance. "If it don't make dollars, it don't make sense," said Sanders. For O'Donnell, the same space had to be more like a gallows platform. He remained about 15 minutes. Sanders would have stayed all night. "I want to take the Lombardi Trophy home and make love to it," Sanders said.

Sanders wore what could only be described as a zoot suit. He wore designer sunglasses and had a black derby with a little red feather tucked into the black band on the side. I once saw a black cast production of "Guys and Dolls" on Broadway, and Sanders looked like he could have fit in beautifully with that bunch. He looked like Nathan Detroit or Big Julie, two flashy-dressing Damon Runyon characters. Deion turns off a lot of people with his antics, but he plays to any assembled group the way Muhammad Ali once did.

He says whatever strikes his fancy.

"We did have an opportunity to win it."
— Neil O'Donnell

O'Donnell looked depressed, like he knew that he was already catching flak from the fans on the post-game hotline at WTAE Radio in

Pittsburgh. He was being blamed, fairly or unfairly, for the Steelers' loss to the Cowboys. How soon they forget? Wasn't it O'Donnell who'd rallied the Steelers to pull out a victory over the Indianapolis Colts? Wasn't it O'Donnell who directed the Steelers to 10 wins in 11 games after a 3-4 start? He could have had a perfect record if Yancey Thigpen, his best target all year long, hadn't dropped a touchdown pass in the end zone against the Green Bay Packers in the regular season finale.

O'Donnell did his best to answer questions that, naturally, centered on his disastrous moments. On his first interception, he said, "It just got away from me. The first one just slipped totally out of my hand. Those things happen. It was a turnover we didn't need then, but we bounced back to make it an interesting game."

On the second interception, he said, "It was a hot read. There was a little miscommunication between the receivers and the quarterback. But we're all in this thing together. You just can't single out one individual and say that was the reason why we lost this football game. That never was my style.

"I told everyone earlier in the week that it would be an exciting football game, that we would have a chance to win this one, and I think that it came true. I have to congratulate the Cowboys. They beat us even though we came in here and gave it our all.

"They were playing a lot of blitz zones, but we knew that coming in and it was not a surprise to us."

Someone was kind enough to note that O'Donnell got on a hot streak after his first interception. "That's one thing I do," declared O'Donnell. "You can't play this position and have it hanging over your head. You throw an interception, those things happen. It's not like it's a characteristic of Neil O'Donnell. I think I threw only seven this past year. It's something that happened, but we were going to take our chances. We didn't come in here just to play a close game; we wanted to take our shot."

Asked how he felt coming into the game, O'Donnell said, "I felt pretty relaxed. I really did, even coming out here. I slept well last night. A lot of people said you don't sleep well the night before. I slept fine. I got up this morning and felt great, and this is the best I've felt all week since I've been here. It's just too bad we fell a little short, because we did have an opportunity to win it.

"It was exciting to be here, but I felt very comfortable out there. I got hit a few times and that's all part of it. That doesn't rattle me at all. I'm just going to sit in the pocket and fire away. I'm just Neil O'Donnell. I'm just trying to make things happen out there. You just have to take your shots and take your chances. There's no tomorrow, and that's the tough thing about this. It's one game and if you win it, you're World Champions."

He said he didn't see Larry Brown at all on the interception that squelched the Steelers' chances for a late victory. "If I saw Larry, I don't think I would have thrown it there," said O'Donnell. He was trying to get the ball to Andre Hastings.

15

Asked to analyze where the mistake was made on that critical play, O'Donnell deferred. "I'm not going to comment on that. We're all in this together. We're all trying to win a championship, and those things happen. But I'm going to bounce back from it. I really am. It's my first Super Bowl. I learned a lot being here. We had a great year, we really did, and a lot of you people didn't give us a chance when we were 3-4. We came all this way, and we were in the game all the way until the last three minutes of the fourth quarter."

So he expected that he and the Steelers would profit from the experience, as disappointing as the final result might have been. Even O'Donnell conceded that "overall I think it was just a game that came down to two turnovers.

"I learned a lot. I learned a lot how to deal with you people, how to take things in stride. Being out there and playing in the big game. People can no longer ask me, 'Is this the biggest game you ever played in?' because I've been to the Super Bowl and I've started in one and played in one. So I've learned a lot and I'm very happy about my year and I just have to wait and see what happens next year.

"It was an experience and I hope to return, I really do, because I think this team is going to be extra hungry now and if we can just stay healthy, I think next year we really will be OK."

Pittsburgh Steelers/Michael F. Fabus

Pre-Super Bowl XXX fun in Sun Devil Stadium included Steelers' offensive line crew mugging for photographers. Up front, left to right, were Ariel Solomon, James Parrish, Dermontti Dawson, Emerson Martin and line coach Kent Stephenson. In rear, Justin Strzelczyk, Brenden Stai, Leon Searcy, Tom Newberry, John Jackson and Kendall Gammon.

Pause for thought
Who are these Steelers?

*"I learned a long time ago
that everyone who gets into
trouble is not a bad guy."*

I am a writer. When strangers ask me what I do, I feel good about telling them that I am a writer. It sounds good, it feels good. Writers have always been important to me. Books have always been important to me. I am proud of the books I have written about sports achievement in Pittsburgh.

I like to go out to schools to speak to students about writing and reading and how they might improve their communication skills, how they might find stories, how they might find themselves. I like to talk to them in the school library. All those books form a great backdrop for our discussion. I want to inspire them to read some of those books, to value books the way I did when I was their age. The way I do now.

I have been at this writing business since I was nine years old and bought an Ace printing press at the Variety Store in my hometown of Hazelwood, deep in the heart of Pittsburgh. I have been paid to write stories since I was 14 and became the sports editor of *The Hazelwood Envoy*, a bi-weekly. I was responsible for turning out a two page sports section in the local tabloid every two weeks. That blows my mind now, so much responsibility at such a young age, but it taught me how to be reliable, how to meet deadlines, how to beat deadlines.

This enabled me to become the sports editor of *The Pitt News*, the campus newspaper at the University of Pittsburgh, when I was a sophomore, to get a scholarship, to get a free college education. It opened up new worlds to me. My family couldn't afford to go on vacations when I was a kid. I had never been anywhere but Bridgeport, Ohio, my mother's hometown, before I went to Pitt. But I got to go to a lot of special places during my student days at Pitt, and it was the beginning of a lifetime of traveling to great places to watch and write about sporting events. I have met a lot of special people along the way, and a few jerks as well. But more good guys and girls than bad guys and girls. I have been blessed in that respect.

No one was more excited about flying in a big charter airplane with the Pittsburgh Steelers to Phoenix for Super Bowl XXX in January of 1996. It was still a nice way to make a living. I thought about all the Steelers fans who would have loved to have been with us, to share in the sunshine.

It all began in grade school. That's why I like to talk to young kids, from fourth to eighth graders, to impress upon them that they are old enough to start pursuing something they enjoy doing, to start thinking about college, and how they can get from here to there.

I get their attention when I tell them I have met and talked to Mario Lemieux, Muhammad Ali, Michael Jordan, Magic Johnson, Roberto Clemente, Joe Louis, Joe DiMaggio, Mickey Mantle and they ooh and aah when I tell them that one of my all-time favorite interview subjects was O.J. Simpson. Right up there with Dr. J. I have interviewed most of the famous athletes and coaches of the last 40 years, and, for the most part, it's been fun. A wild ride. It's more difficult these days; attitudes have changed about a lot of things.

The seventh graders at Gateway Middle School in Monroeville were smiling and laughing when I spoke to them on Friday, March 22, 1996, and told them stories about the Pittsburgh Steelers, and about what went into writing this book. It was my second visit to their school in as many months, my sixth in three years.

They especially liked the stories I told them about Bam Morris, the big running back of the Steelers, and his mother, Marie Morris of Cooper, Texas. I told them how one day in the Steelers' locker room Bam had dialed up his mother on his portable telephone, and had me talk to her. I told the students of our conversation; it was good stuff that provided real insight into her son, and how, as big and bad as he was on a football field, he was, in truth, a mama's boy. They got a kick out of that.

Morris called his mother frequently. He missed her and he liked to talk to her, tell her what was going on in his life, get some long-distance hugs and kisses to keep him going. I told the seventh graders stories about the Steelers when they were their age, and showed them pictures I had acquired from the parents of the players, pictures of the Steelers as little kids, one of Bam Morris as a nine-year-old Little Leaguer. He was a big kid with a big butt. Before Bam crashed in from the one-yard line to win the AFC title game for the Steelers, quarterback Neil O'Donnell was reputed to have told him, "Now get your big ass in the end zone!" Some sophisticated play call, huh?

I wanted the students to see that the Steelers once upon a time were just like them. That is a theme in this book, which is sort of a Steelers' family album.

When I was driving home from Monroeville after my day at Gateway Middle School, I was listening to WTAE Radio, the Steelers' station, when I heard a news bulletin at three o'clock that hit me like a stone between the eyes.

Bam Morris had been arrested in Dallas and charged with possessing more than five pounds of marijuana. He was arrested at 10:30 a.m. Central Standard Time after a traffic stop on Interstate 30, about 15 miles east of Dallas. Damn it, I muttered to myself, damn it.

Also arrested was a friend of his from Texas, Rodney Reynolds, who had been staying with Morris in Pittsburgh during part of the previous football season.

According to the arrest report, Morris was spotted weaving through traffic in his 1995 black Mercedes-Benz with Pennsylvania license plates, and was pulled over by police.

Morris gave police permission to search his leased automobile, something he was not required to do. Why would he let them do that if he knew the car was dirty with drugs?

Officer Mark Spears said he found a Reebok sports bag packed with what turned out to be six pounds of marijuana in the trunk of Morris' car. The report went on to say that Morris and Reynolds had been charged with third-degree felonies for possessing that much marijuana. They faced jail terms and up to $10,000 each in fines if convicted. Both originally said they had no knowledge of the marijuana. It sounded like a case of Dumb and Dumber.

I could see Bam Morris in my mind. See him as he looked when I spoke to him from time to time in the Steelers' locker room over the previous two seasons. I could see his mother, Marie Morris. I had met her the morning after Super Bowl XXX at a breakfast for the Steelers the day after a disappointing loss to the Dallas Cowboys.

What was Marie Morris thinking? How was she dealing with this revolting development? How could Bam be so stupid?

Bam was having huge homes built for both his mother and his sister back in Cooper. He wanted to take care of his family.

It didn't add up.

Marie Morris had talked to me on the telephone and at that Super Bowl breakfast. She had written letters to me, sent me photos and clippings about her baby, as she referred to him, the youngest of her ten children, and confided her feelings for him, the challenges he had offered her and her family along the way. She was so proud of her children, such a booster of Bam.

This had to hurt.

I felt compassion for Bam Morris. I didn't know what he was doing with so much marijuana. Smoking it would be the least possible offense. Smoking marijuana might be against the law, but it wouldn't make him the worst person in the world. Bam Morris had made a big mistake.

"He's not a bad guy," said one Steelers' official. "He may be lazy and he may not be that bright, but if you put everybody in jail who fell into that category it would get awfully crowded in a hurry."

He was coming into the final year of the contract he had signed after his outstanding career at Texas Tech. He had been one of the Steelers' bright lights in Super Bowl XXX. He could build on that and put himself into a position to make big, big money in the NFL, and be one of the league's most respected running backs.

Had Bam Morris blown his chances to be the richest man ever to come out of Cooper, Texas?

A man called one of the talk shows in Pittsburgh that same evening and said he had seen Morris over the two previous years in some of the city's more notorious night spots, questionable places where a smart professional athlete, or any clear-thinking adult, wouldn't be seen. The man said he had seen him more than once in the company of Eric Green at those same places. The man didn't explain what he was doing there himself.

Morris and his mother had provided me with what I regarded as one of my favorite chapters for this book. He had been one of the biggest football heroes in the history of high school football in Texas. He was a hometown hero in a state where football was a religion. And religion, the Baptist bent, was important to Marie Morris.

It upset me to hear this story. So many of the Steelers had gotten into scrapes with the law during the two years I had been following them and interviewing them to write this book.

Johnnie Barnes and Myron Bell had brushes with the local police, and Bell was apprehended with an unlicensed handgun in his possession. Deon Figures had caught a bullet in the knee while driving through Los Angeles near his home during the off-season. Yancey Thigpen had been robbed at gunpoint outside his home on the North Side. Joel Steed was suspended by the NFL for four games when he tested positive for steroid use early in the season. There had been negative stories about former Steelers Carlton Hasselrig, Glen Edwards, Terry Long and Joe Gilliam about alcohol and drug problems and misbehavior. There was a flap about Greg Lloyd during the playoffs when he blatantly swore during network television coverage of the clubhouse celebration after the AFC title game victory at Three Rivers Stadium. The season had started with a training camp controversy when Kevin Greene was criticized for the manner in which he had rejected the request of a young fan for an autograph. That was harsh talk show fodder for a few days.

There had been a reunion of the Steel Curtain's defensive line only the month before, in February, 1996, in Monroeville, and Joe Greene, L.C. Greenwood, Dwight White and Ernie Holmes had gotten together for the first time in 23 years. That also rekindled the stories about how Holmes once had an alcohol and drug problem, and a much-publicized shootout with police in a helicopter on the Ohio Turnpike. The Steelers managed to get Holmes out of that jam.

If the Steelers had succeeded in getting Holmes out of trouble, I thought, perhaps they would be able to get Morris out of this jam as well.

Couldn't the Steelers stay out of trouble? Should I be writing this book? That was the disturbing thought that came to mind as I was motoring my way home from Gateway Middle School. Who was I writing about? Who would be next to get into trouble?

It got worse the next day when a photo of a dismayed Bam Morris in orange jail garb, with a registration number across his chest, appeared on the front page of the Pittsburgh newspapers. It was the kind of photo that appeared when O.J. Simpson was arrested for the murder of his former wife, Nicole Simpson, and her friend, Ron Goldman. It was the kind of grim photo normally seen on "Most Wanted" lists in the local post office. It was sobering stuff.

Steelers' Morris arrested for drugs

Texas police find 5 lbs. of marijuana in trunk of his car

By Ed Bouchette
Post-Gazette Sports Writer

Bam Morris

Steelers running back Bam Morris could face up to 10 years in prison after he was arrested in Texas yesterday and charged with possessing more than 5 pounds of marijuana.

Morris had a prearraignment hearing and was released last night on 10 percent of his $25,000 bail after he was lodged in the Rockwall County Jail at noon. He was arrested at 10:30 a.m. CST after a traffic stop on Interstate 30, about 15 miles east of Dallas.

Rick Calvert, Rockwall County assistant district attorney, said Morris's case could be referred to a grand jury by Tuesday and, if probable cause is found, an indictment would be issued and the case turned over to 382nd District Court.

According to the arrest report, Officer Mark Spears spotted Morris weaving through traffic in his 1995 black Mercedes with Pennsylvania plates and pulled him over. Spears, of the Northeast Area Drug Interdiction Task Force, cited Morris. He then asked if he could search his car and was given permission.

Spears found a Peebok sports bag packed with more than 5 pounds of marijuana in the trunk of Morris' car. He then arrested Morris and his passenger, Rodney Reynolds, a friend from Texas who lived with Morris in Pittsburgh during part of last football season. Morris is a native of Cooper, Texas, a Dallas suburb.

Morris, 24, and Reynolds, 26, each has been charged with third-degree felonies for possessing between 5 and 50 pounds of marijuana. They face jail terms of between two and 10 years and up to $10,000 each in fines if convicted.

Both denied knowledge of the marijuana, police said. Morris listed his occupation as "pro football" and Reynolds as unemployed.

Morris, a third-round draft choice from Texas Tech in 1994, began last season as the Steelers' starting halfback, the heir to Barry Foster. But he lost that job to Erric Pegram midway through the season. He rushed for 559 yards, second on the team to Pegram, but led all runners

SEE **MORRIS**, PAGE A-2

Then news came out that Texas police, upon further search, also uncovered a packet of cocaine (1.5 ounces) under the ashtray of Morris' car. Now he was in even deeper trouble. Morris showed up in those orange overalls, looking like the Great Pumpkin, as one Pittsburgh sports broadcaster put it during a commentary, in TV reports that night. He was seen on TV being escorted into a court-room by police. He held a clipboard up to his face, shielding it from the cameras, the way criminals do.

It reminded me of seeing some boyhood friends of mine in similar circumstances on nightly news telecasts, and how I felt as I saw them being led in or out of the Downtown jail or courtrooms.

That same night there was a news report about Mario Lemieux scoring five goals and getting two assists as the Penguins beat the great Wayne Gretzky and the St. Louis Blues, 8-4, at the Civic Arena. Lemieux had been in a scoring slump, and he had been worried about his wife and newborn baby that week, and this was the way he bounced back when good news about his family came out of the hospital.

His wife, Nathalie, had given birth to their third child, their first son, Austin Nicholas Lemieux, three months premature. The baby weighed in at just barely over 2 pounds, and there was reason for great concern. This was the kind of story that sports writers and broadcasters loved to deal with, not the kind that was swirling about Bam Morris.

I had been around Bam Morris enough to know that he was not a bad guy. He did not always make good judgments, he had not demonstrated the discipline necessary to show a true commitment to keeping in shape to be at his best on the football field, and I had observed his cavalier and boorish response to TV and newspaper interviews. He had some bad habits; most of them could be chalked up to ignorance or immaturity.

When I first requested a 20-minute interview with Morris at the outset of this book-writing project, I was told by Steelers' public rela-tions officials that Bam said, "I don't talk to nobody for 20 minutes." Once we connected, though, he had all the time for me that I needed. I recall walking down the hallway in the Steelers' offices one day and seeing him seated in a dark room with the other offensive backs, watching game film. He spotted me, flashed a bright-eyed smile and waved to me, like a kid in a high school class. I had come a long way with Bam Morris, I thought at the time.

He went from being difficult to delightful in a short span.

During a four year stint as the assistant athletic director at the University of Pittsburgh from 1983 to 1986, I had dealt with and counseled many high-profile Pitt athletes after they had gotten into trouble for one reason or another. Most of the time it was a matter of bad judgment.

Athletes are pampered on every level, and learn that they can live by a different set of rules than the rest of the students, the rest of society. There were times I wanted to tell Bam something, suggest something — he needed some help — but it wasn't my job and I might have been out of line. I didn't want to ruffle anyone's feathers.

College coaches often complain that the NCAA rule books for the comportment of sports programs are too big and difficult to interpret and comprehend. In truth, the rules are quite simple. It is not too difficult to determine what's right and what's wrong, though most of us have stumbled in that regard. We have all made mistakes.

There was a hubbub the week before the Bam Morris incident, in the midst of March Madness, when a controversy developed because Georgetown University's basketball coach, John Thompson, had wanted to make a significant investment in a slot machine gaming operation in Las Vegas before school officials told him they didn't think that would be such a good idea. I have gone up and down on what I had thought of Thompson and his philosophies about sports through the years, but it blew my mind to think that Thompson thought it would be all right for a college basketball coach to be involved in a gambling casino operation, legal or not legal. Thompson should have known better. It was so contradictory to the message he has usually delivered from his well-worn soapbox.

When I was in Phoenix for Super Bowl XXX, I came across Pete Rose one day in my travels. He was sitting in a lobby of a downtown hotel. He wore dark sunglasses and I did not recognize him at first. When I covered the baseball beat back in the early '70s, Pete Rose was one of my favorite sports subjects. I liked his hustle, his enthusiastic approach to the game, his hitting and base running skills. Charlie Hustle. And he had time for everybody. The Cincinnati Reds were known as "The Big Red Machine, " and it was the best clubhouse in baseball for sportswriters to visit. Rose got into trouble because of his gambling habits, and had been banned from voting consideration for the Baseball Hall of Fame.

When I said hello and introduced myself to Rose in Phoenix, he couldn't have been nicer. I introduced him to some friends, Steelers' fans all, and he talked to them at length, signed some autographs, posed for pictures. Pete Rose had made some mistakes, but Pete Rose was not a bad guy. It was a shame he was not in the Hall of Fame.

I learned a long time ago, back in my hometown, that everyone who gets into trouble is not a bad person. Some are luckier than others.

Most of the people I have met in the sports world are pretty good people. It's no different in that regard from the rest of society. Despite the problems that some of the Steelers had gotten into, most of them were good citizens.

Some of them were exceptional people. They offered good success stories. Yes, there were some Steelers who would be great role models for youngsters. Their stories were worth telling. One can also learn lessons from the mistakes made by some of the Steelers.

The week before my appearance at Gateway Middle School, I made a similar visit on a Friday to do a day-long series of writing seminars with middle school students in Rochester, in Beaver County. It is a town that once turned out some great football players like Notre Dame's Jim Mutscheller and Alabama's Babe "Vito" Parilli.

One of the students proudly told me he was a second cousin of Tony Dorsett, from nearby Hopewell. Another said his aunt was dating Kevin Henry of the Steelers and that they planned to get married. Some seventh grade girls shrieked when they saw photos of Yancey Thigpen. They were happy to hear he was not married. They loved Yancey Thigpen, they said. There were signs in the school, just as there were at Gateway Middle School, calling attention to the school's support of the Steelers and other sports teams in the city, leftovers from Super Bowl XXX. These kids think the Steelers, the Penguins and the Pirates are the greatest.

There was a stocky young man at Gateway Middle School who reminded me of boyhood photos I had seen of the Steelers' Brentson Buckner, but he was wearing an authentic Steelers' game jersey with No. 95 and LLOYD across the shoulders.

"What do you like about Greg Lloyd?" I asked him.

"He's the meanest man in the NFL," he replied.

A youngster nearby said, "Yeah!"

They pick their own favorites.

Most of the kids put up their hands when I asked them who wanted to go to college someday. They had good penetrating questions. They wanted to know who was nice and who was not.

Some of them were so delightful. They had beautiful faces. Some of them had a gleam in their eye and looked like they had a chance at a good life. Some of them had eyes that are already glazed over. The light was not on. Why would a seventh grader regard himself or herself as someone who wouldn't want to go to college someday? I had two daughters in college at that time and I wanted these kids to have the same opportunities. I told them college was so much different from any educational experience they have ever had, that they would be on their own, and how some thrive and some perish with that newfound freedom.

One seventh grader wasn't as attentive as I would have liked. She squirmed and spoke in a whisper to her friends during my presentation. I learned later that both of her parents are in jail. I wondered how she got up in the morning and went off to school. How does a kid like that do her homework, pay attention in class, feel good about herself?

What would it be like to be a young girl, worrying about what your friends and classmates think of you in the best of circumstances, coming to school each day when your parents were in jail?

What was it like for Bam Morris to be sitting in a cell in the Rockwall County Jail? What was it like for his mother?

Bill Cowher
Focused on football

*"What Coach Cowher has done
is extraordinary."*
— Merril Hoge

During his first four seasons with the Steelers, Bill Cowher clearly demonstrated that he was an outstanding football coach, and certainly a worthy successor to Chuck Noll. They were the two most successful coaches in Steelers' history.

Noll set high standards for the Steelers, winning four Super Bowls in a six-year span in the '70s when the Steelers were heralded as "the team of the decade." Noll was not a tough act to follow, however, because his team qualified for the playoffs only once in his last seven seasons on the job, and the team's overall record during that same span was 52-61. He finished up his 23 seasons as head coach of the Steelers with a 7-9 team in 1991, and he was drawing criticism from the fans and media. They felt Noll and a new breed of athletes were no longer on the same page.

Noll used to like to say about an over-the-hill ballplayer that "it's time for him to get on with his life's work." Now Noll was getting the same sage advice, and he didn't like where it was coming from. It happens to the best of coaches as one of Noll's mentors, Don Shula of the Miami Dolphins, learned the hard way during the 1995 season.

Cowher came from Crafton, a middle class community on the outskirts of Pittsburgh and within 15 minutes of Three Rivers Stadium. So he knew well what Noll and the Steelers had accomplished in the '70s. That's the way Cowher recalled the Steelers, too, just like so many of the team's spoiled fans. So he knew it would not be an easy task, but he thought he was equal to the challenge of turning the team back into a perennial contender.

His dad had taken him when he was a child to see the Steelers play at Forbes Field and Pitt Stadium. So it seemed he would have a sense of history. What did he remember about those days, about the last game he'd seen at Pitt Stadium?

"I remember being at the game," said Cowher. "But I remember eating hot dogs and candy and everything else more than the game."

Cowher's first four teams all made the playoffs. His first team went 11-6. His third and fourth teams made it to the AFC championship game, and his fourth team made it all the way to Super Bowl XXX. Noll made it to the AFC championship game in his fourth year and the Super Bowl in his sixth year. His team's overall record of 17-2 in 1978 is the standard for success with the Steelers.

It is important to point out, however, that the 1994 and 1995 seasons were two of the outstanding seasons in Steelers' history. How's that? The overall records of 13-5 in 1994 and 13-6 in 1995 were the sixth and seventh best records (percentage-wise) in club history. Fans forget that before Noll came to Pittsburgh, the Steelers fielded mostly mediocre teams. The tenures of Noll and Cowher were clearly the best of times.

"There was a time," late owner Art Rooney often remarked, "when people didn't think we were smart enough to come in out of the rain."

In fact, the Steelers posted a winning season only three times in the team's first 25 years of operation, and only seven times in the first 37 years. The overall record during those 37 seasons was 164-268-19 — .380. That includes Chuck Noll's first season of 1969 when the Steelers were 1-13 — the worst record in Steelers' history. So Noll had the distinction of having the best and worst records.

Before Cowher came along, the Steelers had only three coaches who had winning records: Noll (209-156-1 — .572), Jock Sutherland (13-10-1 — .563), and Buddy Parker (51-48-6 — .514). During Parker's tenure, the Steelers traded off most of their top picks each year, and there was little or no excitement generated on Draft Day. Then again, no one made a fuss about Draft Day anywhere in the NFL back then. Cowher's record for his first four years was 46-25. Noll's record in his first four years was 24-34.

Cowher couldn't boast of a Super Bowl victory, but his success (.648 winning percentage) in his first four seasons on the job was unrivaled in club history.

"Maybe the time has come to carve Bill Cowher's chin on the side of the Clark candy building," wrote Dave Ailes, the sports editor of the *Tribune-Review*. "Cowher's carving a phenomenal start for himself as coach of the Steelers. A guy named Chuck Noll is revered in these parts, with good reason. He brought the franchise back from 40 years of oblivion, ascending to the NFL throne four times. Compared to Cowher's success ratio, though, Noll was a slow starter."

It is important, however, to keep in mind that Noll took the Steelers to four Super Bowls and won them all, a trick Cowher can never match. It would be hard enough just to get to four Super Bowls, and Cowher and his team came up short against the Dallas Cowboys, 27-17, in Super Bowl XXX. They had their chance. Cowher and the Steelers came within one scoring drive of winning it. No one could fault Cowher or his club for their effort.

Cowher came away from Phoenix a winner. Cowher had conducted himself well all week long at the Super Bowl XXX press conferences, smiled broadly and said all the right things and proved popular with the national media. He would have gotten an 'A' grade for his efforts if he had made sure his players appeared at all scheduled press conferences. There was a misunderstanding in respect to the team's obligations in that area, and the team drew a $25,000 fine from NFL headquarters. In the game itself, the most important of his tasks, Cowher showed his competitive fire and gutsiness in going for broke in the biggest game of his life. Had the Steelers won, they would still be applauding Cowher for his decision to go for an onside kick in the second half, a tactic that worked and kept the momentum clearly on the Steelers' side. Defensively, the Steelers made adjustments at the intermission, and made a comeback possible. Cowher succeeded where so many AFC coaches had failed in recent times by making the Super Bowl a bonafide contest.

"Maybe Cowher will never return to this stage," wrote Gene Collier of the *Pittsburgh Post-Gazette*, "but he'll do so in the knowledge that he coached the kind of game critics have begged for most of its glorious-despite-itself 30-year history.

"Cowher gambled at almost every opportunity across the green felt of Sun Devil Stadium," continued Collier, "and the fact that his Steelers lost Super Bowl XXX to a superior Dallas Cowboys team should never tarnish his daring and his accomplishments."

> *"If you're not talking about*
> *x's and o's, you can lose*
> *Bill's attention in a hurry."*
> — Kaye Cowher

Anybody who thought Noll was a focused coach — and he certainly was — might find it difficult to buy this observation, but Cowher might have been even more focused, or channeled, in relation to his football responsibilities. Noll prided himself on being a renaissance man, with keen interests in diverse areas. Noll loved to chat with the media in the hallways and the kitchen area at Steelers' headquarters, and he loved to share his thoughts on many subjects, especially non-football subjects. His eyes glazed over in a hurry when anyone wanted to probe him too deeply about his football philosophies. History, politics, piloting airplanes, scuba-diving, photography, fine wines, gourmet meals, education, history, child-rearing...these topics all appealed to Noll. Noll was often portrayed as a cold individual, but that was not the case. He was a charming, decent man; he simply fell short of being what some people wanted him to be. Sometimes the media wants to put everybody in a mold that would make their job easier. Noll was not always as interesting or colorful as they would have liked. He had a droll sense of humor. "I could never tell a joke," he confessed, which explained why his "Franco Who?" remark was mostly misunderstood. Noll was wary of the media, understandably, and was said to have made disparaging remarks about the media to his players behind closed doors, but he did not keep as much distance as Cowher from the regular beat guys.

Cowher was not comfortable with small talk. He seldom paused in the hallways to talk to members of the media. Some sportswriters said Cowher would lower his gaze as they approached him in the hallways at the stadium. It was easier to pass without a word that way. There were times he appeared paranoid about the press. For the most part, Cowher had received positive reviews during his initial four year run, and the Pittsburgh press had generally been less critical than that to be found in most major markets. Cowher had thrown up a lot of roadblocks to make their jobs more difficult, but he had given them little to criticize as far as performance was concerned.

The Steelers had been successful on the field, but had more than their share of off-the-field difficulties. What Noll used to term "distractions" became commonplace. No matter what happened, Cowher stayed the course. That was to his credit. Nothing seemed to keep Cowher and his club from moving forward. They were undaunted in that regard.

Cowher could have been more cordial; he could have lightened up in his personal approach. He often found it difficult just to say, "Hello." Or, "Good morning." It's a shame, because I saw him mix with people, and he could be downright charming and a wonderful ambassador for the Steelers and Pittsburgh. Noll assumed that role more after he retired.

Their styles could best be summed up by the way they handled their weekly press conferences. Noll sat at the end of a rectangular table in the midst of the media. It was like a card game. Cowher sat alone behind a table with the media sitting in student desks facing him in a classroom set-up. There was an imaginary moat between the two parties.

Cowher was not easy to get close to. I mentioned to his wife, Kaye, one day in the press box at Three Rivers Stadium that I found it difficult to get into any kind of casual conversation with her husband.

"If you're not talking about x's and o's," confided Kaye, "you can lose Bill's attention in a hurry."

Cowher concentrated on his job. No one could criticize him in that regard. The assistant coaches said he was extremely well organized. Former assistant coaches questioned his loyalty and fairness. Steve Furness, for one, felt he had done nothing to deserve being fired after his first two seasons looking after the defensive line. The former Steeler defensive standout seemed to have rubbed Cowher the wrong way. Ron Erhardt and Pat Hodgson had been with Cowher from the beginning, yet they were not rehired shortly after the team returned to Pittsburgh from its strong appearance in Super Bowl XXX. They were stunned. Where's the love, man? But few people who lose their jobs have much good to say about their former bosses, right?

Once asked what three words described him best, Cowher responded, "Loyal, dependable, confident."

Like everything else he had done since the Steelers hired him, Cowher did not look back or second-guess his decisions. He was so consistent in so many respects. That was the most impressive aspect of his approach. Cowher had an unrelenting resolve to keep on truckin'. He didn't dwell on past disappointments or setbacks. Like Satchel Paige, he didn't believe in looking back, somebody might be gaining on him. He was always looking forward to the next challenge. With him, taking a one-game-at-a-time approach did not sound like a cliche. It was a way of life. He was indomitable. He never seemed to waver from the philosophies he had picked up from the likes of Marty Schottenheimer and Sam Rutigliano, coaches he had worked for in his professional development days .

Merril Hoge, a holdover from the Noll days, played two seasons for Cowher before signing as a free agent with the Chicago Bears. He came back to Pittsburgh to serve as an analyst on WTAE Radio's coverage of Steelers games in 1995.

"I remember when he came in to replace Chuck Noll, and I was thinking, 'Man, I'm glad I'm not in his shoes.' But he did an amazing job," said Hoge. "He built an attitude that continues to this day. And that's taking nothing away from Chuck Noll. But what Coach Cowher has done is extraordinary.

"He always promised us as players that he would take care of us. 'If you give me everything you've got, I'll take care of you.' Coach Cowher is not only a great coach, he's a great friend. He's been able to toe that line. He does it from the heart. You can see how it works."

That was how he was able to rally a team that had gotten off to a frustrating 3-4 start in the 1995 season — there was second-guessing from the media then — and drive them to Super Bowl XXX, winning 10 of 11 games before the Steelers came up short against the Cowboys at Sun Devil Stadium. And the Steelers should have won that other game, as well, but didn't when normally sure-handed receiver Yancy Thigpen dropped a pass from Neil O'Donnell in the end zone on the final play at Green Bay. Cowher had the good sense to smile through that episode, hugging Thigpen as he came off the field. He did not want to end the regular season schedule on a negative note, so he made light of it, since it did not affect the Steelers' standing or playoff position. Some day, Cowher might check his career record and wish the Steelers had won the last game on the schedule in 1994 and 1995, which the media labeled "meaningless" games. In the end, there are no meaningless games.

During Super Bowl XXX week, Cowher discussed the Steelers, his personal philosophies about football, Pittsburgh and its special fans, Dan Rooney, his boss, and other related subjects. It provided some insights into Cowher, and his marvelous success since Rooney tapped him as the man to resurrect the Steelers and return them to their glory days.

Cowher was younger and more demonstrative than Noll. Cowher was 34 years old when he was hired, and Noll was nearing his

60th birthday when he retired. Free agency, agents and attorneys, big money and changing attitudes among athletes had all altered the pro sports scene, and Noll, like many of his contemporaries, found it difficult to deal with or accept many of the changes.

Cowher was certainly the equal of Noll when it came to demanding and receiving respect. He could freeze anyone with a steely glare. His face was more chiseled, and many noted his long chin, ear-to-ear mouth, and such features in characterizing the man.   The local editorial cartoonists had a lot of fun with his face, much to Cowher's chagrin. It was a caricaturist's dream. During his playing days, Cowher's nickname was "The Face." And if it's any consolation to Noll, Cowher can't tell a joke well, either.

"When Cowher is unhappy," wrote Alan Robinson of the Associated Press, "his eyes grow steel cold, his neck tightens, his jaw juts out and his voice hits a high decibel."

Bud Shaw, a columnist for *The Cleveland Plain-Dealer*, noted his fiery eyes and "a chin cut from brimstone." Shaw saw something else that characterized Cowher's approach to his position. "His news conferences are infomercials selling Pittsburgh to Pittsburgh," wrote Shaw. He credited Cowher for his promotional skills.

His approach to public relations and marketing was different from Noll. He appeared on radio and TV talk shows, had his own column in *Steelers Digest*, let NFL Films into his clubhouse before games and at halftime, was especially cozy with certain out-of-town writers, and appeared in print and TV commercials. Cowher became as identified with Pittsburgh as Iron City Beer, kielbasa and babushkas.

Cowher was always promoting Pittsburgh and the Steelers' special place in his hometown and the surrounding environs, and the fans lapped it up. They loved Bill Cowher. He was one of their own. They believed in Cowher Power? Who could blame them? When he wanted noise at the stadium — NFL rules to the contrary against such petitions — Cowher had a way of getting the word out and the fans always responded to his cheerleading. Sportscaster Myron Cope called for Terrible Towel demonstrations, and Cowher seconded the motion.

"Be loud," he said at the end of the press conference that preceded the AFC title game with Indianapolis. "Please be loud. We love the energy. We love the enthusiasm."

Cowher always complimented the crowd on its efforts.

"I think we have the best fans in America," Cowher often commented. "People here can relate to this football team. And we can relate to them. There's an appreciation, and I think there's a respect that typifies this city."

It is no wonder Cowher was so popular. He was twice honored as Pittsburgh's Man of the Year in Sports by the Dapper Dan Club and, in May of 1996, he was named Man of the Year at the annual YMCA Dinner that recognized the special achievements of hundreds of Pittsburgh area student athletes.

Bill Cowher accepts AFC championship trophy from Buffalo Bills owner Ralph Wilson as NBC's Greg Gumbel looks on at Three Rivers Stadium. Cowher is a coach with many faces as he goes about his business as the Steelers' field leader.

Photos by George Gojkovich

He was not a gifted athlete in his youth, but he had a message that made sense to young people who enjoyed playing sports and wanted somehow to be successful.

"When you grow up here," he said, "there is such a strong work ethic. I was never a great athlete. I've had to work hard for everything I've accomplished. Taking pride with the little ability I had and try to become the very best. It's something I was taught at an early age."

"He's a great communicator."
— Mike Tomczak

Cowher was aware of the team's rich tradition and its Hall of Fame history and while properly acknowledging the legacy he wanted everyone to know that it was a different era. To his credit, Cowher has always paid proper homage to Noll and his teams — "we haven't accomplished anything yet," he would say — and had wisely discouraged comparisons.

"I don't think it's anything to get caught up in," said Cowher at his first press conference upon becoming coach of the Steelers, when asked how he felt about succeeding Chuck Noll. "What the man has done for this city, for this organization, speaks for itself. No one can ever emulate him. All you can do is have the same kind of success.

"Chuck Noll is a legend. He's brought tradition, he has brought pride to the city. And that's the thing that I want to do also, in my own way. And I have no reservations about following Chuck Noll.

"We will bring back the pride and tradition that's long been associated with the Pittsburgh Steelers, and more appropriately, the great people of Pittsburgh." And Cowher kept his word.

Four years later, before Super Bowl XXX, he said, "The only pressure that we have is pressure we're putting on ourselves. And, really, I don't look at it as pressure. I mean, we have talked about a championship for four years and not just, you know, winning the division, getting to the playoffs, or getting to the Super Bowl. We have always talked about one thing: winning a championship.

"And so, while we have had that as our goal, I think it has been refreshing to see the city kind of resurrected again with a second generation of people that have come now and experienced the same excitement as they did with the teams of the '70s when they were kids. Now they're taking their kids to the games and talking to them about what it was like then. They've got their Terrible Towels twirling again. I think that is great. There is a bonding that is taking place in our city. When you can do that in a city, a city that's as special as Pittsburgh, it's very gratifying.

"You could see that at Three Rivers Stadium when we've been in the playoffs the past few years. I think that's what professional sports is all about. It's never been any more evident than in Pittsburgh."

Cowher has been complimented for being a players' coach, and extolled for his ability to relate to his charges.

"He's a great communicator," said quarterback Mike Tomczak. "He exhibits the personality of the city. He won't let us quit. He has that 'tough job, big chin' type of attitude. One time I made a mistake at camp, and he came marching across the field in my direction. He was still ten feet away from me and his chin was, like, right in my face.

"I played for Mike Ditka in Chicago. Like Bill, he grew up near Pittsburgh. There must be something about western Pennsylvania that gives coaches dramatic facial expressions and mustaches, that makes them disciplinarians. But the way I look at it, I played for one coaching legend in Ditka. Now I'm playing for an up-and-coming coaching legend."

Veteran linebacker David Little said of Cowher: "You can come in and talk to him about anything, like a father image. With Chuck, you always knew he was your boss." Little lasted just one season with Cowher.

Running back Bam Morris said, "Coach Cowher always tells us when you get the chance, you've got to make something happen."

Justin Strzelczyk, a holdover lineman from Noll's days, said, "Coach Noll was more intimidating. He was the Emperor. He was more like your grandfather. This guy is more like your uncle."

Linebacker Chad Brown wished Cowher could back up a bit when he was chewing somebody out. "You almost can't hear what he's saying because you're thinking, 'He's entirely too close to me right now.' Maybe it's a coaching thing, but I'm from California — we like our space — and I've never experienced anything like it."

Reserve running back Steve Avery said, "He's so emotional when he speaks to us that even his lips start shaking. Thank God, he doesn't have halitosis."

"Fortunately, I've never been on the end of one of his butt-chewings," said linebacker Kevin Greene. "But I hear they're quite exhilarating. You get that spray going. He's drooling, he's slobbering...head-butting...screaming. You got to love a coach like that."

Leon Searcy, an offensive tackle who departed Pittsburgh in favor of his home state of Florida as an unrestricted free agent after Super Bowl XXX, said of Cowher: "He's a player's coach. He's one you can trust, but one you can't take lightly. Because he's so intense with the game, when you go out and play, you better mean business."

Cowher was proud of his reputation as a players' coach. "I am very open with them," said Cowher. "I think you've got to be in this business. I think you respect people that not only tell you what you have to do, but why you have to do it. And I think that is the case in talking to them, not talking down to them.

"You try to create that sense where they feel comfortable displaying or expressing what they feel; at the same time, you are going to tell them how you feel, and not necessarily giving in. But I think if

33

they understand why you are doing things and the only prerequisite we ever use is what is in the best interest of the Pittsburgh Steelers to win a championship.

"They understand and respect that, and I have a great deal of respect for every player, and they understand that, so we communicate openly. We communicate at times maybe when there is a lot of emotion, but I think that is what this game is about, too. And I think there is a mutual respect between myself and the football team."

Defensive end Brentson Buckner said, "He lets players be themselves without getting carried away. But he'll never let anyone get bigger than the team."

Cowher said he was not a choreographed act on the sideline. What you see is the real Bill Cowher.

"I guess you've got to be yourself," said Cowher. "I have said before I am not very good at hiding my emotions. I am going to tell you how I feel; whether it is good or bad, and move on. I mean, I think in this business, if you try to harbor ill feelings, if you let things eat at you, you are not going to last very long.

"There are so many emotional ups and downs we go through every Sunday. You've got to enjoy it. You don't get too high with the highs; you don't get too low with the lows. It is such a great competitive form that we have in this business that you've got to enjoy it. And you know, I am not worried about getting burned out. Someone mentioned that to me before. I enjoy it. I can see doing this for a long time."

The crowning moment for Cowher had to come after the AFC championship game when he stood atop a hastily-assembled platform at midfield and accepted the championship trophy, along with Steelers' president Dan Rooney, from Buffalo Bills' owner Ralph Wilson. Cowher couldn't get over the scene, the continued cheering from the fans who filled the stadium and stayed around to witness the ceremony. Cowher kept holding the trophy on high to share it with all Steelers' fans and waving and saluting the faithful. It doesn't get any better for a hometown boy.

"I'm just happy the city can go through this," he said after the game. "That's why it's great. It unites everybody. It's like one big happy family. That's the way we are right now."

Cowher had tears in his eyes, and he didn't deny it. "I'm an emotional guy...I was feeling a sense of achievement."

Dan Rooney was a reminder of the rich heritage of Pittsburgh's NFL franchise, which dates back to 1933 when his father, Arthur J. Rooney, obtained the team for the purchase price of $2,500. The Rooneys remained constant in their mode of operation through different eras that presented different challenges. This was the first time Rooney was representing his family and the organization, rather than his father, for such a presentation. Rooney had recently undergone gallbladder surgery, and looked pale and underweight, but was boosted physically and spiritually by the warm response to what the

Steelers had achieved. Rooney should have been resting, but he wouldn't have missed this for the world.

"I think Dan is a unique individual," said Cowher at a press conference in Phoenix before Super Bowl XXX. "He is very down to earth. He is Pittsburgh. I mean this guy symbolizes the city. He has grown up there, and has inherited much from his father. I think with our football team he has created a very family-like atmosphere. It is important that he does things to create that. He makes an ongoing effort to do that.

"You know he is a guy that while he is there every day, very hands on, you never know it. He's not trying to coach the team. He is a great guy, and the one thing he has been to me for four years — in addition to being my boss — is my friend. He is a guy you can talk to, and he is a guy that cares just as much about that guy up at the top of the stadium as he does the ones in the private boxes, and I think that says everything about the man."

"Mike Ditka is a guy I've always respected."
— Bill Cowher

Pro Football Weekly graded NFL coaches in its New Year's issue of 1995 and gave Cowher an 'A' and called him a great motivator. Don Shula got a B, Bill Parcells an A-, Marty Schottenheimer a C+. Dave Wannstedt also got an A. Wannstedt, from the Pittsburgh suburb of Baldwin, and a former Pitt player under Johnny Majors in the mid-'70s, was a strong candidate for the Steelers' position when Noll surprised the team by retiring. The choice came down to Wannstedt and Cowher, and some in the organization wanted Wannstedt. Rooney chose Cowher. He had also named Noll in 1969, then an assistant under Shula at Baltimore, so he appeared to be two-for-two in picking the right coach to lead the Steelers. Wannstedt was with the Dallas Cowboys at the time, and was later chosen head coach of the Chicago Bears, succeeding Mike Ditka. Wannstedt had been interviewed for the Pitt job, too, but his alma mater went with Paul Hackett. That was a mistake, but it worked out for the best for Wannstedt.

Ditka, by the way, heaped praise on Cowher for "molding a no-nonsense team that the city of Pittsburgh wants."

Cowher had a chance to return the compliment when he participated in the Mike Ditka Celebrity Golf Classic at Beaver (Pa.) Lakes Country Club a week before training camp opened in 1995.

"It's an honor for me to be here," Cowher said. "Mike Ditka is a guy I've always respected and had a lot of admiration for. He's one guy who really exemplified western Pennsylvania."

Asked what accomplishment as an athlete he was most proud of, Cowher said it was playing five years in the National Football

League. He survived by scratching and clawing his way with the Philadelphia Eagles and Cleveland Browns. He was looking for players who wanted it just as badly, but had more talent than he did as a player.

Cowher was an emotional guy, much like Ditka. "It's one of the factors I considered a real plus," said Dan Rooney. "I think it had much to do with our selecting him as the head coach."

Tom Donahoe, the director of football operations, said of Cowher soon after he was hired:

"He's a coach with fire. He's going to be very demanding of the players. There's going to be one way to do it and there will not be any exceptions."

Donahoe had a history with Cowher. Donahoe was coaching the football team at South Park High School in 1975 when Cowher was in his last season as a player at Carlynton High School.

Cowher, in his final game at Carlynton, returned an interception 24 yards for a touchdown and caught two two-point conversion passes in a 47-7 victory over South Park on November 1, 1974. "He owes me," said Donahoe.

"The dignity of the team comes first."
— Dan Rooney

Chuck Noll and most of his players tell romantic tales of their days at training camp at St. Vincent College. Several said their best memories of their days with the Steelers were at the summer getaway when it was football 24 hours a day, and every one was in the same boat, or dormitory or dining hall. They enjoyed the camaraderie.

Randy Grossman, a reliable tight end on four Super Bowl winners, put it best: "Practice at the Stadium was like a 9 to 5 job, a more normal work day. At St. Vincent, we were completely removed from the real world. You were with a bunch of guys and you were sweating it out from morning till night. You didn't have to make your bed; somebody else did that for you. You didn't have to cook or make any schedule. You didn't have to worry about anything but football."

Cowher did not appear to care for camp as much as Noll. Maybe that had something to do with the fact that Cowher had an auto accident on his first trip to St. Vincent and had to have his car towed. That was no way to get initiated to the charms of the life in the Laurel Highlands.

"Training camp is one of those necessities you have to go through," said Cowher. "You have to hone up the skills, bring the football team together and develop a new chemistry. It's something you have to do. I'm not sure anybody likes it. It's just one of those things you have to go through during the course of the season."

Like Noll, Cowher did not care to discuss holdouts or players who were sidelined by injury when he was interviewed at his first camp: "We're going to coach the players who are here," said Cowher, cutting off any further discussion relating to holdouts. Writers paused in their note-taking to check to see which coach was addressing them.

"If you don't want to do what you're told, get out of here!" Cowher told the players at one heated camp session. The players circled around Cowher and Cowher read the riot act: "And that goes for everybody! You're here to play football! If you think otherwise, you'll be gone! Your job's on the line!" Cowher could have tied a Noll record there for most exclamations in a 30-second spiel.

Later, reflecting on the outburst, he said, "This football team will always know how I feel."

After Cowher became the coach, veteran offensive tackle John Jackson commented on the coaching change:

"I think everyone knew that we needed to make some changes after last season. I don't think anybody ever came out and said that Chuck should retire, but I have to admit that getting Bill has been a nice change for all of us."

Later, after a loss to New Orleans in pre-season, Jackson was surprised by Cowher's camp demeanor: "Chuck wouldn't have done it that way," said Jackson, perhaps having second thoughts on the subject. "Chuck would've just made us practice longer to let us know he was dissatisfied. Chuck never lost his temper on the practice field."

Like Noll, Cowher had said, "I don't concern myself with things I have no control over."

They shared some sentiments regarding player personnel. For example, neither he nor Noll cared for Jeff Graham, the wide receiver from Ohio State.

Cowher and Donahoe deep-sixed recalcitrant or problem players, getting rid of unhappy campers like Bubby Brister, Eric Green and Barry Foster, among others.

Under Cowher, assistant coaches were working longer hours, with days beginning shortly after daybreak and sometimes lasting beyond midnight. Cowher's coaches were not going down the road at night to bars and restaurants. When they went down the road it was for good. Coaches came and went during his first four years. It appeared it was either his way or the highway.

Dick Hoak had a chance to go elsewhere. He was offered the post as offensive coordinator by Tony Dungy at Tampa Bay soon after Super Bowl XXX, but declined to stay in his home area. Hoak grew up in Jeannette and lived in Greensburg, not far from the team's summer training camp at Latrobe.

Hoak, the only holdover assistant coach from the Noll era, said: "Camps are camps. You meet and you practice and you eat and you go to bed. The next morning you get up and do it again. Every day is the same. They just all run into each other."

Bryan Hinkle, a linebacker who had come up during the Noll regime and stayed for two seasons with Cowher before retiring, said, "Camp is more structured than Chuck's camps."

Bryan Hinkle liked Cowher's intensity: "He focuses on the positive rather than on the negative."

There were other more noticeable changes at training camp. Cowher put numbers on the players at camp, which was not the case when Noll was in charge. Noll used to stick two fingers between his teeth and whistle and wave the players to move. Cowher had Chet Fuhrman, the conditioning coach, set off an air horn to signal the start and finish of different drill sessions. Everything ran by the clock.

Cowher was more restrictive with the media, and where they could go and not go on the grounds. He moved media from between fields; he wanted no one to get in the path of his players. No one in the organization was permitted to chat with the media on the sideline during camp workouts. He drew the boundary lines his first year when he declined an invitation for him and his assistants to attend a pool party with the beat reporters in nearby Greensburg.

Noll and his assistants used to have a "happy hour" with the media immediately after the second practice session of the day. It was an "off-the-record" social time. I thought it was valuable time and that it helped establish a better working relationship between the coaches and media. Cowher discontinued the practice. Cowher was more concerned about spending time with his assistants and players.

He provided transportation for his players between the dormitories and the locker room and dining hall at St. Vincent College. He said he wanted to save their legs. Some insiders thought the camp was getting a lot softer, and that Cowher was pampering the players. Even some veteran players felt that way. It certainly made it more difficult for fans to get autographs between practice sessions.

Dan Rooney let Cowher do it his way. Noll was no longer the head coach at the camp. "He's not a ghost here," remarked Rooney.

Rooney realized he wouldn't have the same relationship, either, that he enjoyed for 23 years with Noll. "Bill Cowher is younger than three of my kids," said Rooney, who was 60 at the time. He could appreciate Cowher's appeal to the players. "He's young like they are and they like that. But that doesn't mean they're anti-Noll, either.

"When Chuck came in everybody said he worked for Don Shula, Paul Brown and Sid Gillman, so he was going to do this or that. But Chuck was himself and that's why he was a success. I think that's the biggest thing Bill Cowher has to be. He has to be himself. The dignity of the team comes first."

Strong as he appeared, Cowher did not always get his way. He wanted to shift Greg Lloyd from outside to inside linebacker and Lloyd balked at the idea and wanted none of it, and brought little effort and no enthusiasm to the experiment, so Cowher conceded and went back to the old way. Cowher said it was an "in-house matter" and declined further comment. It was easy to appreciate his discomfort with that one.

He has had outbursts with players, NFL officials, staff, even his own boss.

"If I need your attention, I usually know how to get it," said Cowher.

He said some of the same things Noll used to say: "We're going to do whatever it takes." Or, "We feel very much that we're going to find a way to win."

Cowher often spoke about "finding a way to win," which seemed to have become a standard motto among many coaches in pro and college sports in 1995.

Bobby April, his special teams coach in 1994 and 1995, left the team after the Super Bowl to return home to coach the New Orleans Saints. April had done a great job in turning a weakness into a strength, and he and Cowher seemed a lot alike in their emotional approach to the game.

"He's good because he gets the best out of players," said April. "His whole week of preparation is pretty technical. We have a psychological message and a motivational message. He likes to build up the team for the entire week, but he always speaks to them at least a couple of minutes a day.

"He bases everything we do on the Pittsburgh Steelers. He'll recognize an opponent, but his main concern is what we do and how we do it."

"I would love to spend years and years in Pittsburgh."
— Kaye Cowher

Cowher lived in Fox Chapel. Cowher never looked better than when his wife and their three daughters were at his side. They made for a handsome family. There were occasions, after a practice session at St. Vincent, or in the lobby at Steelers' headquarters, or some civic event, that Cowher had his daughters around him. He had three beautiful girls, Meagan Lyn, age 10, Lauren Marie, 8, and Lindsay Morgan, 5, during the 1995 season.

Cowher never looked happier. "I'm a very family-oriented person," he said.

His wife, Kaye, kept a more public profile than Marianne Noll, the wife of Chuck Noll. Kaye and her twin sister Faye had been outstanding basketball players at North Carolina State when Bill was playing football there, and they both played with the New York Stars of the Women's Professional Basketball League. The jubilant faces of Kaye and her kids and Bill's parents were frequently flashed on the TV screen during home games.

"I would love to spend years and years in Pittsburgh," said Kaye. "Bill's family is here; we have grandparents, uncles and aunts. It's a great situation for our children to have that family influence. It's not something that we've had in any other city."

His family was most important to Cowher.

Bill Belichick, then coach of the Cleveland Browns, came to Pittsburgh on a Monday night during the 1994 season to watch the Steelers play the Oilers. Cowher said he wouldn't be going to any games on the weekend when the Steelers had a bye.

"If I am, it would be the Carlynton Cougars," said Cowher, a 1975 Carlynton grad. "It won't be any professional team. I can guarantee you that.

"If I do it, it will be with my kids and wherever that takes me, that will be fine.

"If I was in my bye week and told my wife I was going to go watch an NFL game, she would shoot me."

Her husband had found a home in Pittsburgh once again. He could do no wrong with many of the team's fans. He quickly became a much-admired public figure.

A man with a drinking problem appeared at training camp one day. He came over and talked to Cowher for five minutes. He asked Cowher how he could turn his life around. Cowher conceded that stuff like that had happened before. He said he also got telephone calls from people seeking advice and counseling.

"I guess I look like a man with the answers," said Cowher, with a wide grin on his face.

Cowher could also break up people the way he sometimes expressed himself with some off-the-wall phrases or word choices. The media call them "Cowherisms."

One day at training camp, Cowher was discussing new rules in the NFL permitting offensive linemen to line up a step back of where they were once required to be, better to meet and arrest rushing linemen.

"They're trying to circumcise the rules," Cowher said.

Myron Cope caught that gaffe, and shot up, "What is this, some kind of Jewish plot? You mean 'circumvent,' don't you?"

Another time, Cowher said, "We've got to recapture a new chemistry." Or, after the AFC title game setback by San Diego, he said, "We have a good chemistry, but we may have to work on a new chemistry."

Another Cowherism: "I think it's important now that you step back and, you know, smell the snow."

He has a reputation for being too demanding, or indifferent to the feelings of so-called little people in the Steelers' organization. But he has been quite generous in sharing sports paraphernalia he's been given to those same people. Some say early success had spoiled him, and that he could be impossible to deal with.

Vic Ketchman covered the Steelers for 20 some years for the *Irwin Standard-Observer* before leaving the area to edit a house weekly newspaper for the expansion Jacksonville Jaguars. The year before

Kaye and Bill Cowher are proud of their three daughters (left to right), Lindsay Morgan, Lauren Marie and Meagan Lyn. The Cowhers are at home in the north suburban community of Fox Chapel.

he departed, Ketchman wrote a column on how Cowher's antics could wear thin on people:

"Cowher's natural personality is to scream and holler. He often makes his point to the media by raising his voice, and he has been known to raise his voice to even greater heights in other office dealings. His lack of people skills is the only threat to his coaching future.

"As long as he's winning, his forcefulness will be tolerated. However, all coaches experience losing at some point in their careers. That's when a coach needs friends; certainly not enemies."

Ed Bouchette, the beat writer for the *Pittsburgh Post-Gazette*, wrote: "The brick-sized chin juts out, eyes flash, angry words and saliva spew and a finger points sharply. When Wild Bill Cowher becomes upset, diplomacy takes a back seat."

Mike Ciarochi, the sports editor of the *Uniontown Herald-Standard*, had been on the Steelers' beat with Noll and Cowher as the coach. "You must understand," he wrote, "that Cowher is a man whose picture appears next to the definition of 'intense' in the dictionary."

Gerry Dulac of the *Pittsburgh Post-Gazette* wrote: "The venue doesn't always matter. He'll do it in the locker room or on the playing field. Doesn't matter if it's a player or coach. He gets that mouth all wrinkled and frothy and he starts delivering a spit-spewing message that very few ever forget.

"He is a strange mix of yuppie and pure Pittsburgh. He drives a black Saab convertible and wears Tommy Hilfiger sweaters, but he has that Western Pennsylvania tendency to butcher names like Norm Crosby and stumble into malaprops like Yogi Berra."

Tom McMillan, a sports talk show host for the Steelers' flagship station WTAE, wrote in *Steelers Digest:* "Cowher's basic philosophy never wavers, and that allows him to handle each situation forcefully and effectively without 'losing' his team ."

Cowher had some opinions about the media at large:

"I think it's too easy to sit here and second-guess and when you're sitting up on the 50-yard line about 100 yards up and you guys can see everything. I'm not going to be one to ever second-guess a player when a player's in the heat of battle and he has to make a decision that's very much a split-second decision. I would never second-guess anyone.

"I think there's a tendency in our society, to be quite honest with you, to accent the negatives. People sometimes think that's what people want to see and read. My point is very simply that as we point out the negatives I think it's important that you also point out the positives. That's how I feel. I think that's how you should deal with people. I try to always see the glass as half-full, not half-empty.

"I think there's a tendency, and a very natural one, and the job of the media is to accentuate the highs and to accentuate the lows. My point is in trying to write the balance that says when everything's high, I don't think we should get that high. And when it's low, it's probably not as bad as you think it is. I'm trying to create a consistency and a balance. I'm trying to keep the scales balanced so they don't get tipped too heavily in either direction. And I think that's my job as a head football coach.

"At the lowest point in the (1995) season, we were 3-4 and had just been embarrassed at home by Cincinnati on national TV. But even at 3-4, we were still in first place in our division, and there were nine weeks left in the season. What more can you ask ?

"So we had some meetings and changed our outlook. At that time, we started looking at it as a nine-game season and adopted the outlook that the bottle was half-full and not half-empty.

"A lot of players made sacrifices. A lot of unselfish things were done. We made seven changes in our lineup — some due to injury, some to suspension, some due to a lack of consistency.

"You can make all the changes you want, but for it to work, the players have to believe in it. The way we did it was to take one game at a time and not look too far ahead. And, before you knew it, we were still playing in January."

As Cowher was coming off the field at Sun Devil Stadium following the Steelers' disappointing setback by the Dallas Cowboys in Super Bowl XXX, he was met by his family. His wife Kaye comforted him with a hug and kiss and some kind words. Then he kissed his daughters. The oldest, Meagan Lyn, left the biggest impression of all.

"I looked down at my daughter and what she said to me I'll never forget," said Cowher. "She looked up and said, 'Daddy, win or lose, you'll still be my hero.' I remember telling her, 'You win some and you lose some, and the most important thing is that you do your best.' And I can honestly say our football team did that."

COWHER COMMENTS

Here's a sampling of Cowher comments that have applications in any field of endeavor, not just football:

"You can win games with talent, but you win championships with team."

"How can you achieve a goal you haven't set? Your goal has to be the top. If you're satisfied with something less, are you satisfied with second place?"

"There's a distinct advantage to playing at home. There's an energy that you can draw from crowds. There's an energy that you can draw from having people behind you."

Cowher does not like to yank players who drop passes or who fumble the ball. "I don't think that's how you deal with people," he said.

When the Steelers clinched a playoff spot in 1994, Cowher was asked about the significance of qualifying for the playoffs a third straight year: "There is no significance, until we start to do something in them."

"You can talk about it all you want, but until you go out and experience it, until you go out and kind of expect to win, and recognize that in this business a lot of games are going to come down to the fourth quarter — when you go out and find difficult ways to win, as we've done this year, it's a natural feeling that you should start to gain a confidence and an expectation that goes with it."

"Focus and understanding are going to be a very big part of taking it one step at a time."

"The true competitors are out there to be recognized as the best. If you're in it for any other reason, it may be hard to come in here some days."

"We're in this thing to win football games. It's not our offense vs. their defense. We're in this thing as a football team."

"Sometimes it's harder to handle success than it is to handle adversity. I think we've learned through our experiences. I've been pleasantly surprised by how well we've handled some success."

"My belief is that things have to be thoroughly done. I believe the best chance you have for success is that everyone has a true understanding of what's expected of him. If it means spending time until 2 a.m., we will do it. It is not just talent that can get you someplace. If you make a commitment, and you believe in it, you can obtain anything."

Cowher's advice to young football players regarding goals: "Make them realistic and attainable. Nothing worthwhile comes easy. If you reach your goal early, the goal wasn't high enough. Don't dwell on adversity, but learn from it. Use it as a power source. That's how we deal with life. Our players need to set goals and make a commitment to us as a coaching staff. When you accept losing you become a loser. Learn from losing and you improve. That's what we're looking for. There's a lot of teams that hope to win. Winning teams expect to win. That's where we want to be."

"You want to acquire the right kind of players."

"I don't like to play the what-if game."

"No one hates to lose more than I do. If you accept losing, you're a loser. There's an empty feeling after a loss. That's the way life works. It works in a funny way. All you can do is wake up tomorrow and move on. Hopefully, we'll learn from it and come back next week or next year with even more intense desire to get back here."

On picking the last players on the roster: "There are a lot of great guys out there, but if they can't help you win, then you've got to be very careful how many great guys you allow on your football team."

"The worst thing you can do in this business is take things for granted, overlook your opponent and not give them the respect they deserve."

"We have a mindset where we are thinking too much, instead of just going out there and playing and...knocking the other guy in the mouth and knocking them off the ball. Doing the things we have always been able to do. We are not building a rocket engine. We are playing a game of football. Sometimes, I think it gets analyzed too much."

"You can only grow strong through adversity."

"Football is not a real complicated game. You have to execute, you have to be consistent, you have to maintain your focus for 60 minutes."

"Hopefully, you surround yourself with enough people who are going to come out fighting. The most important thing is not to let frustration overcome determination. Because that is the thing that can happen. You become so frustrated that it starts to affect your focus."

"My wife is great. She is a competitor. She has been in professional sports before. She keeps my demeanor. She keeps me even keel because she has got a way — she will be the first one to tell me there have been some dumb plays called. If I tell her I called the play, she'll tell me, 'I still think it was dumb.' She is kind of my rock and my best friend."

Laird and Dorothy Cowher
The coach's proud parents

"He's not Coach Cowher here.
He's just Billy to us."
— Laird Cowher

Listen to Laird Cowher for a couple of minutes and you can hear his son, Bill, talking about the essence of sports competition. Laird's lines have a familiar ring to them, uncanny at times. The son now repeats some of the phrases he heard from his father in his youth. The father of the Steelers coach culled his personal philosophy from the best possible sources, such as Ben Franklin and Abraham Lincoln, The Book of Proverbs, Vince Lombardi and even one-time Pirates pitching ace Vernon Law. Laird Cowher can quote them all, word for word. "There's no 'I' in TEAM." Or, "Winners never quit." Or, "When the going gets tough the tough get going." Or, "Sweat + Sacrifice = Success." Or, "Winning isn't everything, it's the only thing."

Laird laughed at himself as he ran off some of those oft-spoken lines, and he is a man with strong opinions. At the same time, when invited to call in to a Pittsburgh radio sports talk show a year or so earlier to provide some insight into his son, the coach of the Pittsburgh Steelers, Laird Cowher declined the offer by invoking a line from Lincoln: "It's better to keep your mouth closed and let people think you're a fool than to open it and remove all doubt." Or something like that.

Bill, the second of three sons born to Dorothy and Laird Cowher, obviously listened when Laird repeated those famous quotations at various points during his upbringing. Some of them were posted on signs over his dad's desk in the vestibule of their home on Hawthorne Avenue in Crafton, a suburban community situated just southwest of Pittsburgh. Bill makes similar statements when he speaks about the Steelers and his mission at weekly press conferences during the football season. Cowher, the coach, also knew when to keep his mouth closed. I often wondered where some of his demeanor and sage observations came from, and what was the source of his strong single-minded will. Laird left a trail of telling clues as he proudly toured his home.

Look at Laird Cowher and you can see the face and form of Bill Cowher. They have the same long face, lantern-jaw, and vociferous speech pattern, an assuredness and combativeness that keeps you on your heels. He was a long-limbed 6-4, with large hands. His full handle was Laird Gifford Cowher. He was Scotch-German, thrifty and stubborn, true to stereotype. It was Laird who introduced Bill to playing ball — football, baseball, basketball, bowling, golf, you name the game. He was one of his first coaches. "I'm not an outdoorsman, so we didn't go fishing and hunting," he said. He was taller, more involved with his boys' sports activities, and had a bigger bagful of bromides than my father, yet there was something about his manner, his appearance, the way he combed his hair, and the arthritic hands, the white T-shirt showing over the open-collared golf shirt, that reminded me of my own father. It was a good feeling.

"See that alley out there," said Laird, looking over his shoulder out the kitchen window. "That's where I used to catch him. I taught him a change-up. That's the most important pitch. It sets up everything else. Bill used to practice snapping a football back there when he snapped for punts at Carlynton High School. He was always playing or practicing something. He warmed up in the yard in the afternoon for games he was going to play that night. He was a determined kid. He couldn't wait to get to practice. But he could get down on himself, too. I remember telling him once during a baseball game, 'If you're gonna quit, just go home. I don't want anyone here who's gonna quit.' He stayed and played; he was probably mad at me, but he played better. He used to sit in that same seat where you're sitting, and do his homework when he came home from school. Then, when he was done, he'd start bugging me about what time it was, and how soon I'd be driving him to practice. It'd be two hours from the time we had to leave, then an hour, and he'd be hollering up the stairs to me, asking me when we were going to go. I'd holler back at him that we had plenty of time before we had to leave. He was persistent."

Listen to Dorothy Cowher and you learn where the softer side of Bill Cowher comes from. She had a constant smile, a radiant glow about her fair-skinned face, and reminded us of movie actresses of another era, Mary Martin and Claudette Colbert. "Once upon a time, before three sons and the hair going gray, she was often mistaken for Gisele MacKenzie," offered her husband, referring to a singer who made her mark on the old Hit Parade show on TV. Actually, Dorothy's hair was white, and cut in a short, pixie-like style. She was bright-eyed and enthusiastic in her speech. She seemed to have a good sense of humor, and an upbeat mood. She wore an orange jersey and loose-fitting pale blue jeans, and looked quite spry. She was 72, a year younger than her husband, and moved around a lot better during my visit. He moved somewhat stiffly, especially going up and down the stairway of their home, damning his arthritis. She walked four or five miles each day in the streets of their neighborhood. "She gets around pretty good for someone in their '70s," said her husband, who walked with her a few days each week. The Cowhers were good company, easy to feel comfortable with at first meeting. There was no pretense. They were a for-real couple, at peace with themselves. You'd like them.

Dorothy said Bill is different from the fierce competitor who roams the Steelers' sideline when he visited them or when he was at his home in Fox Chapel. "When he walks into his home, he's a different person," his mother said. "He leaves football behind at the stadium when he's home with his family. He gets great support from his wife, Kaye — she played professional basketball and appreciates the demands of his job — and he really enjoys their three daughters. We're all proud of him — his two brothers are as proud of him as you can be — we all know how hard he works."

Listen to his proud parents, and you learn how Bill is so good at keeping things in their proper perspective. "When he comes in this house, he's not Coach Cowher," his dad declared. "He's still Billy to us. He sits in that same chair you're in; that's his seat. He likes to go into the living room and watch TV. He'll lie down on the floor, prop a pillow under his head, have a beer, and just relax."

At mid-season, I had stopped Mr. Cowher when he was passing through the press box before a game, and he offered other comments about Bill coming to their home.

"When he says, 'Is there a beer in the refrigerator?' I know he's in a good mood. Sometimes he comes here and just wants to sit on the porch. I never talked to him much about football, maybe when he was in Pop Warner Football, but in high school and college I quit doing that. I'll ask him, 'How's the car running?' And he'll say, 'Uh huh.' Or I'll say, 'How's the family?' And he'll say, 'Uh huh.' That's when I can tell he's in a mood. He was really hurting last year after they lost to San Diego in the playoffs. This year he's more positive. Last year there were some guys who thought there was an 'I' in team. It's different this year."

During my visit to their home, the Cowhers mentioned that come May of 1997 they would be married 50 years. "Of course, I'll be happy just to survive this year," said Laird, sounding like his son and his one-game-at-a-time approach to the National Football League.

"I know Pittsburgh and Pennsylvania like the back of my hand," he said. "I was always driving to Somerset or Bedford or Altoona to go over someone's books or reports. I was on the road quite a bit, but I never stayed away more than two nights. I wanted to be here to help Dorothy raise our boys.

"I worked hard. No matter what you do there are no gimmies. You have to want to win."

"We still feel real comfortable here."
— Laird Cowher

The Cowhers live in a huge yellow-brick home on Hawthorne Avenue. It's a stately three-story affair. Laird and Dorothy live on the second floor. Laird converted a bedroom into a kitchen, recalling what it was like to tear out a fireplace. Their oldest son, Dale, 46, a CPA who worked out of an office on McKnight Road in the North Hills, lived by

48

Dorothy and Laird Cowher were proud parents at YMCA Scholar-Athlete Dinner on May 23, 1996, when their son, Bill, the head coach of the Pittsburgh Steelers, was honored as Man of the Year.

Photos by Jim O'Brien

Bill Cowher's brothers, Dale and Doug, with Doug's wife, Janet, attended YMCA affair at Hilton Hotel where Bill and the area's top student athletes were presented awards.

himself on the bottom floor. The third floor was closed off. A young couple, an attorney and registered nurse with a newborn baby, rented an extension on the back of the house. There was a big bright-green carpeted porch with a sturdy swing, something new homes usually lack — there's nothing more relaxing than sitting on a porch swing on a summer's day, reading a good book and watching the world go by — and green-and-white aluminum awnings that provide additional shade. They were the same color, and probably the same make, Koolvent awnings, that were still on my boyhood home in Hazelwood at the eastern end of the city. They last forever.

They raised three sons there, Dale, Bill and Doug, 38, who lives in Hankey Farms, out near Pittsburgh International Airport. They had lived in this house since 1962. They previously lived in Beechview, moving to Crafton when Bill was about nine years old. Laird is originally from North Belle Vernon and Dorothy, whose maiden name was Dorothy Case, grew up in Guys Mills, a small town about 12 miles from Meadville in the northwest end of Pennsylvania.

Crafton is a borough on the city's border, just southwest of West End, about four miles from Three Rivers Stadium on the city's North Side. There were many grand homes and even more not-so-grand homes in the community. They were older, high-maintenance homes, with big heating bills. There was an old-fashioned charm about the ones that still looked good, and a sense of neighborhood one seldom found in the newer suburbs. There were kids playing roller-blade hockey in a nearby schoolyard. There were basketball hoops in many driveways. There were lots of kids who liked to play sports when Bill and his brothers were growing up there. "It's a nice neighborhood," allowed Laird. "We still feel real comfortable here."

There are lots of nice touches about the house on Hawthorne Avenue: authentic cut glass panels framing the front door, a vestibule, tall windows, some of them stained glass that were particularly beautiful when the sun came out on this Wednesday. The rooms had 10-foot ceilings and lots of natural light. The guest room had a dark-stained baby crib where the grandchildren once slept during visits when they were smaller. There were pictures of the children and grandchildren atop the mantelpiece.

This was an especially important Wednesday in Pittsburgh, at least for Steelers fans. It was D-Day or O'D-Day, when quarterback Neil O'Donnell had promised to make public his decision as to whether he was staying with the Steelers or signing as a free agent with the New York Jets.

Dorothy and Laird had offered some thoughts about the situation, most of it off-the-record — they were a thoughtful, cautious couple, not wanting to upset their son with any remarks they might make — and were wondering what was going to happen. Dorothy answered the telephone twice, and one of the calls was from Kaye Cowher, their daughter-in-law. In the course of their conversation, Kaye said the Steelers had upped their offer to O'Donnell, but she didn't think it would be enough. As it developed, O'Donnell delayed his decision. The word didn't come out until the next morning that he had opted to take the money and run, to play for the Jets at Meadowlands Stadium in New Jersey, not far from his boyhood home in Madison, where his mother still lived, close to many of his brothers and sisters and their respective families. Laird and Dorothy didn't have to like O'Donnell's decision, but they could appreciate the appeal of coming home to continue one's pro football career. After all, their son had done it. O'Donnell was signing a reported five-year contract worth $20 million, plus a $5 million signing bonus.

There were trophies on display on top of bookcases in the vestibule where Laird Cowher still kept the desk he worked at when he was a casualty insurance auditor, for five years with Ohio Casualty and then 31 years with North American Casualty before retiring in 1985. The trophies were won by all three boys in kid sports leagues of one kind or another, and from high school teams. Most of them belonged to Bill, including one plaque for being named to the WPIAL Coaches All-Star team when he was a senior at Carlynton High School, and several plaques acknowledging North Carolina State's appearances in post-season bowl games in his three varsity seasons, two in the Peach Bowl and one in the Tangerine Bowl, when the Wolfpack defeated Jackie Sherrill's Pitt Panthers, 30-17. They still talk about the impassioned speech team captain Bill Cowher delivered in the dressing room before that Pitt game. There was a plaque presented to him as N.C. State's MVP after his senior season.

Cowher was recruited to N.C. State by Lou Holtz, more recently the head coach at Notre Dame. "I remember him coming to our house," said Laird Cowher. "He came to the top of the steps and said, 'Shall we pray?' He also asked me if I had a 50 cent piece, and he performed a few magic tricks. He's an amateur magician, you know." Holtz was at N.C. State for Bill's freshman season, then left to become coach of the New York Jets. He stayed only one season there, absolutely hated the job, and abandoned it in favor of Arkansas. He also coached at Minnesota before going to Notre Dame.

He was succeeded at N.C. State by Bo Rein. Rein coached Bill for his three varsity seasons. Rein died in an airplane crash when he was on a recruiting trip for LSU a few years later. "He was my friend," said Laird. "I liked him a lot."

Laird said he traveled regularly to N.C. State to see Bill play ball there, and made an occasional road trip, recalling fondly a trip to a game at old Archbold Stadium at Syracuse. "It was like the Coliseum; you sat on stone stairs and there were pillars all around the place. I wanted to see that place before they leveled it. They had some great ballplayers play there through the years.

"I went to most of Billy's games, but I kept track of the Steelers at the same time. We'd go to Raleigh for a game on Saturday afternoon or Saturday night. Then we'd leave at 4 a.m. on Sunday, and everybody knew they'd better be ready or we'd leave without them.

We'd push it pretty good, and hope the highway patrols were looking the other way when we'd pass through. We'd usually get back here in time for the one o'clock kickoff for the Steelers' game on television. We might have to listen to the first quarter on the radio passing through and out of West Virginia. But we got to see most of the game on TV. I've always been a big Steelers' fan.

"I never took that many pictures."
— Laird Cowher

When I asked the Cowhers if I could check out their family album of photographs, they said they had no album. "I never took that many pictures," said Laird. "We were so busy raising them, and I never had a good camera. Someone stole the one I had and I never replaced it."

They showed me some photographs they had of Bill that were taken by other people. Some were in envelopes. Laird pulled a program out of a drawer in the kitchen from a banquet Bill had attended at his high school alma mater.

"Show him that one where Billy had a Don Eagle haircut," said Laird. "He had a strip of hair down the middle of his head, and that was it. I wondered what in the world he was thinking."

Dorothy demurred. "I don't think Billy would want me to show that picture," she said. And she didn't.

Laird's desk downstairs was stuffed full of game programs from the Pittsburgh Hornets and even one from the Pittsburgh Shamrocks, one of the city's early professional hockey franchises. He mentioned some of the more famous Hornets like Gil Mayer, Frank Mather, Bobby Solinger, Willie Marshall. He showed off a game program from when Willie Somerset was playing basketball at Duquesne University in the early '60s. "That's my school," said Laird. He was graduated in 1951 from Duquesne with a degree in business administration.

"Billy played Pop Warner and Mitey-Mite football, Little League baseball and he played basketball for our church team," his father went on. "Dale, Billy and Dougie all played sports. I coached Billy's baseball team. I was probably pretty demanding.

"Billy was determined, very determined. He had a good outlook, and a good work ethic. In his sophomore year, he added to what he was doing for the high school football team by snapping the ball for kicks. I'd go out in the yard and let him snap the ball to me. He'd study everything he could get his hands on about football. We'd go over it together on Saturday afternoons.

"He worked around here. He cut people's grass. He worked for a local landscaper, Inches Nursery. He was a good worker. One year he dressed up and played Santa Claus at the nursery. He got paid the same as he would have if he'd been out digging and trimming shrubs. He thought it was a great deal.

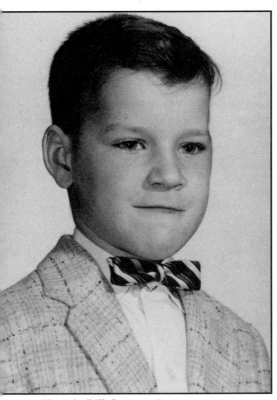

"Bowtie Billy" at age 7

one of North Carolina State's players
ere as enthusiastic as Pittsburgh
port Bill Cowher.

At 16, Bill Cowher was a standout
with Carlynton High School football team.

North Carolina State Sports Information

Year-old Bill Cowher sits in lap of older brother
Dale, aged 7. Does Bill's facial expression look
familiar?

"One summer when he was at N.C. State, he worked with the boilermakers at Duquesne Light Company at Shippingport.

"When Billy started playing in the National Football League, a fellow who grew up just a block away came over to the house to say hello. It was Bucky Pope, who played for the Los Angeles Rams, and was known as "The Catawba Claw" because he was a pass-catcher from little Catawba College (in Salisbury, N.C.). He introduced himself. I said, 'You were some kind of football player.' He said, 'Thank you, I just wanted to say it's nice that we finally got another kid from Crafton in pro football.' That was nice of him to come over.

"Billy just got his feet wet playing ball in Beechview, but he really got involved in sports when we moved here. He competed in the Crafton-Ingram-Thornburg (CIT) Sports Association. We'd go back in the alley here and I'd pitch to him and he'd hit the ball. He was big for his age and he was playing against kids from Pony League, two or more years older than he was. But he handled himself OK. I remember once he didn't go to an all-star baseball game in which he was supposed to play because he wanted to go to football practice instead. He liked football better than any other sport.

"In the summer of 1966, he was bored and complaining that there wasn't anything to do. I told him, 'I can't invent something for you to do. How'd you like to go to a football camp?' So I sent him to Jim Carlen's camp at some place in the wilderness of West Virginia. He went to camps there, then at Virginia Tech in Blacksburg, Virginia, and at Indiana University of Pennsylvania. He got other kids in the neighborhood to go with him. When he was away, his baseball team wasn't the same. Something would be missing; they lost their spark. He was a leader even then, someone who talked it up, and kept his teammates enthused."

Cowher mentioned that his son had a chance to learn from Carlen, Bobby Bowden, Frank Cignetti and Bill Neal, and that he got good reports from all of them, especially Cignetti. "Your son has the legs you dig with; he'll make a great linebacker,' he told me. And I said, 'Thank you very much. Coming from you, that means a lot.'

"I liked Vernon Law a lot, and what he was all about. I clipped this list of his favorite sayings from one of the Pittsburgh newspapers, and showed it to the boys."

I mentioned to Laird that I had reprinted that list in one of my books about the Pirates, called *MAZ And The '60 Bucs*. Some of the thoughts and ideas Law collected through the years included these:

* "True sportsmanship is usually displayed following defeat."
* "There is no pillow as soft as a clear conscience."
* "It is better to be alone than in bad company."
* "A discouraged man is not a strong man."
* "Don't be satisfied with mediocrity."

"Billy used to look at that list when I'd pull it out. He knew all that stuff," continued the elder Cowher.

"I think he'd have been happy as a head coach, wherever he might have been. This was just icing on the cake. He was with Marty Schottenheimer for seven years, in Cleveland and in Kansas City. He was with Sam Rutigliano in Cleveland, and he was a classy fellow. They had a lot of guys coaching there who've been heard from since, like Schottenheimer, Lindy Infante, Rich Kotite, Dick MacPherson, Dave Adolph. He just wanted to coach somewhere.

"When Billy got cut by the Eagles, he went back down to N.C. State to go to school. He got a degree in the school of education, and he was a grad assistant to Bo Rein, coaching the special teams. That's how he got his start in coaching.

"We were at home on a Friday night, and we were preparing to go to see Carlynton play a Section 4 basketball game with Sto-Rox. Bill was out at Stanford in Palo Alto, California. We got a call at our home that Bill had been selected over Dave Wannstedt and Kevin Gilbride as the new coach of the Pittsburgh Steelers. We were thrilled. Carlynton lost that night, but they came back to beat Sto-Rox later on and won the state title that year. They had a banquet to honor that team at Peter's Place in Bridgeville, and Billy was an honored alumni guest at the dinner.

"He enjoys coaching the Steelers; he puts in a lot of time, but he loves his job. He's been involved with football since he was nine years old. This is the ultimate for him."

The Cowhers passed up an opportunity to go to Tempe, Arizona to attend Super Bowl XXX, and be a part of their son's big week at the big dance. "We enjoyed it right here; we didn't want to go," said Dorothy Cowher.

"I wanted to stay here; I'd have more freedom," said Laird. "Let him have the glory. It was his hour. He told me that there'd be a lot of media people who'd want to talk to me if I went out there, but he said the decision was up to us. I wanted to be where I could get up and move around, get a beer from the refrigerator if I wanted one. Andrea Kremer wanted to send an ESPN camera crew to our home and catch our reaction to the game, but I said 'No'. Hey, I didn't want to have to worry about some vulgarity going out over the air. I wanted to be myself. I just wanted to be me, at home with my wife. You won't see me sitting around bragging about my kids; they don't need that."

Dorothy Cowher couldn't help herself. "He was the youngest coach ever to make it to the Super Bowl, and they came very close to winning it all."

Then her husband regained my attention.

"It's nice to have your son coaching the Pittsburgh Steelers, and it's good to see him down there on the sidelines," he said. "You have to be proud. But I go to the games with a different feeling than when he was playing. Now, I don't have to worry about him getting hurt. You know, some of those guys out there are real monsters. Dorothy used to put her hands over her eyes whenever Billy would be in a pile-up.

"Billy worries about us being able to continue to live here, and live the kind of lives we've always lived. He'll ask, 'Do you and Mom still walk around the neighborhood?' I told him we did, and that people honk the horn or wave at us, or stick up a finger that the Steelers are No. 1. Billy laughed about that. He said, 'Yeah, they're like that now. But, if we lose, they'll run over you. Be careful out there.' I think we'll be just fine, as long as we can stay healthy."

Hometown hero Bill Cowher is flanked by his parents, Dorothy and Laird Cowher, and young football aspirants at "Welcome Home" activities held by Carlynton Little Cougars Association.

Thumbs up for Billy, 4, and Doug, almost 3.

Four-year-old Billy Cowher and three-year-old Doug look contented on Santa Claus' lap. Wonder what Billy wanted for Christmas?

Bam Morris
Marie's baby

"Mamas, don't let your sons
grow up to be Cowboys...or Oilers."
— Chuck Noll's rendition of
song by Waylon Jennings

B am Morris asked me if I had received the photos and information his mother was to send me. I nodded affirmatively, and
said, "You know, I liked the stories you told me about your
mother. She sounds like quite a lady."

"She's special, all right," Bam came back.

"I wish all the mothers would send me the kind of stuff she sent
me," I told him. "She's really proud of you. I'd like to know more
about her. Tell me some more stories about your mother."

Morris reached into his dressing stall in the Steelers' clubhouse
and pulled out a mobile telephone. He unfolded it. "If you want to
know more about my mother, you talk to my mother," he said, a mischievous light in his eyes.

So he dialed up his mother in Cooper, Texas — that's pronounced
Cupper, as in supper — and said, "Hey, Mom, Bam. There's a writer
here who's doing a book about the Steelers, and he wants to talk to
you. OK? I'll talk to you afterward. OK? Here he is."

I took the telephone and sat down on a four-legged stool that
belonged to Alvoid Mays, a diminutive defensive back who stored his
stuff in the stall alongside the one that belonged to Morris. Here I
was, in a corner of the Steelers' clubhouse during the midday break
when media are moving throughout the room in search of a responsive
body to comment on the state of the Steelers, and I'm on the telephone
with Marie Morris. Some of my colleagues noted my activity and
wondered what I was doing. It was definitely a first in my journalism
career.

I had seen photos of Marie Morris. She had a stern countenance
and looked like a woman who wouldn't put up with any nonsense. I
could picture her as I spoke to her on the telephone.

After she said hello, and I introduced myself, Marie Morris
opened with a question for me.

"Mr. O'Brien, can I ask you a question?"

"Sure."

"Are there many churches in Pittsburgh?"

My investigative reporter instincts told me where this was going,
so I responded with a question of my own.

"Why do you ask, Mrs. Morris?"

"Well, Bam's been telling me that he can't find a church there to go to, and I was wondering..."

"I know this city better than Bam," I replied. "I'll help him out with that. You can rest assured about that."

Mays emerged from the shower room and tapped me on the shoulder, seeking a return of his stool seat. So Morris reached up over his dressing stall and secured another stool, and sat it down on the carpeted floor for me so I could continue my conversation with his mother in comfort.

"Bam's my baby, you know," Mrs. Morris continued. "He's the youngest of my ten children. He always needed more attention than any of my other children. He needed a lot of lovin'. And I did the best I could to keep him happy."

"He must be getting more comfortable in Pittsburgh, and with the Steelers this season. When he first got there last year, he used to call me three times a day. Now he calls me about once every other day. And he seems to be playing better."

I had to smile. Here's this guy named Byron "Bam" Morris who's standing over me as I am talking to his mother. He's been called Bam since he was in kindergarten and he was beating up on the other kids. He'd been one of the biggest football stars in Texas high school history — Marie Morris had sent me a file of clippings on his high school career that were as complete and compelling as anything the NFL publicity mill turned out — and he had broken records established by Earl Campbell, a Heisman Trophy winner at Texas and a Pro Bowl star with the Houston Oilers when they were one of the chief nemeses of the Pittsburgh Steelers in the AFC in the '70s. Here was this guy named Byron "Bam" Morris who stood 6-feet tall and weighed somewhere between 245 and 255 pounds, and liked to run over and jump over opposing players, and he'd been calling his mother three times a day when he first reported to the Pittsburgh Steelers. So much for his macho behavior...

He had expressed a stout-hearted approach to the game: "I like hittin' folks, runnin' over folks." Even so, like many of the Steelers, Bam Morris was just another mama's boy. It took one to know one. Bam was still somebody's baby.

I remembered how Chuck Noll, the former Steelers coach, used to say, "Strong mothers make for good football players."

"How stupid are these guys?"
— Joe Theismann

I met Marie Morris the morning after Super Bowl XXX, speaking to her at a team breakfast for the Steelers and their families at the Doubletree Inn in Scottsdale, Arizona. Her son had conducted himself in a sterling manner and had outrushed Emmitt Smith, so he could salvage something to be proud of, even though the Steelers had come up short against the Dallas Cowboys. Morris had a game-high 73 yards rushing on 19 attempts (Smith had 49 yards on 18 rushes and two TDs) and Morris had scored the Steelers' last touchdown on a 1-yard burst that put them in position to win the game. They trailed by 20-17 at that point, with 11:16 still to play.

Bam Morris, who first made his mark as a schoolboy in Texas and as one of the nation's leading ground gainers at Texas Tech, had gone up against his home state's favorite pro football team and done himself proud.

I thought about that and about Marie Morris and her family when I heard the bad news about Bam Morris. I was motoring on the Parkway East in Pittsburgh, traveling home after speaking to students at Gateway Middle School in Monroeville about how they could improve their writing and reading skills, and sharing stories about the Steelers, including the one about Bam Morris and his mother, when I heard the word about Bam on the hourly news report on WTAE Radio, the Steelers' home station.

Bam Morris and one of his buddies had been arrested that morning while traveling on Interstate 30, about 15 miles east of Dallas. The police found marijuana and cocaine in his car. Bam Morris was suddenly up to his mischievous dark eyeballs in trouble.

I pounded the steering wheel when I heard this. I had gotten to know and like Bam Morris during his first two seasons with the Steelers, and suddenly his pro career and his personal reputation were in dire jeopardy.

I could only imagine how Marie Morris must have felt when she got the news.

According to the original arrest report, Officer Mark Spears saw Morris weaving through traffic in his 1995 Mercedes-Benz with Pennsylvania license plates and pulled him over.

This report brought to mind how Jonny Gammage, the best friend, cousin and business partner of the Steelers' Ray Seals, had been stopped at night for driving a luxury car in a strange manner in suburban Pittsburgh in October of 1995 and died during a seven-minute altercation with five suburban police officers.

Morris had been luckier than Jonny Gammage.

Officer Spears, of the Northeast Area Drug Interdiction Task Force, cited Morris after he stopped him. They were on a highway notorious for drug trafficking in Texas. Spears said he then asked Morris for permission to search the vehicle, and permission was granted.

That's where many of Morris' friends and acquaintances were dumbfounded. Why did Morris give his permission for a search? Morris was within his civil rights to decline and drive away. If Morris was aware there were drugs in the car, why didn't he refuse?

Spears found a Reebok sports bag in the trunk of the car, and it contained about six pounds of marijuana. Then Morris and his buddy,

Rodney Reynolds, age 26, a friend from Texas who had lived with Morris during part of the 1995 football season, were arrested. Reynolds was a hanger-on; they permeate the pro sports world these days. Every wealthy young athlete should have a caddy to carry his bags.

Both were taken to the Rockwall County Jail, and both posted $25,000 bond and were released that night. There was video tape on TV, and photos in the next day's newspapers, showing Morris wearing orange overalls with ROCKWALL COUNTY JAIL in big black letters across the shoulder blades. If it bothered me and Steelers' fans to see Morris in that situation, handcuffed and in orange jail garb, imagine how Marie Morris must have felt.

Upon further search, the police found 1.5 grams of cocaine under the car's ashtray. Possession of these drugs each carried a sentence of 2-to-20 years and a $10,000 fine. Morris and the Steelers were both in a fix. Morris was later told by Bill Cowher not to come to mini-camp because he thought it would be a distraction. The cocaine charge was dropped in late June.

Morris had been a third round draft pick from Texas Tech in 1994 and he rushed for 826 yards and was named the team's Rookie of the Year by the Pittsburgh pro football writers. Partly because of the promise offered by Morris, the Steelers traded Barry Foster, who had lost his desire to play, to the Carolina Panthers in June of 1995. Morris and Erric Pegram shared the running duties during the 1996 season. Morris had come on strong near the end of the season and was bowling over would-be tacklers.

In the aftermath of the Morris arrest, stories started circulating on the Pittsburgh radio talk shows about him traveling with the wrong people in the wrong places during his two year stay in Pittsburgh. I learned from a former Steeler who was now a successful business executive in Pittsburgh that Morris told him he had been stopped for speeding on six occasions since he signed with the Steelers. One wonders how anyone can retain their driver's license after six speeding offenses. It hardly appeared that the Steelers or professional athletes were still getting special treatment from the police. There was talk on KDKA Radio that he had tested positive for drugs earlier. The NFL does not disclose initial discovery.

Nearly three weeks earlier, Michael Irvin, the all-time leading receiver of the Dallas Cowboys and one of the NFL's most popular players, was indicted on two counts of drug possession resulting from a March 4 drug bust in a motel in Irving, near Texas Stadium.

Commenting on the mess that Morris and Irvin had gotten themselves into, Joe Theismann, the former NFL quarterback who was now an ESPN analyst, asked: "How stupid are these guys? I can't conceive anybody making an excuse for these grown men when they realize what's at stake in being so downright ignorant."

Those were the sentiments of some Steelers' officials as well, even though they were smart enough not to go public with their remarks. It was their policy not to comment on such legal matters.

Irvin came off as cocky and had made some outrageous remarks prior to Super Bowl XXX, doing his best to be as independent and defiant as teammate Deion Sanders, but I also remembered him saying something insightful about the positive influence of his family on his outlook on life. It brought him off his pedestal and down to earth.

On Media Day, Tuesday, January 23, 1996, those who gathered round Irvin on the sideline at Sun Devil Stadium heard him relate where he had gotten his outstanding work ethic.

"My work habits come from my father," he said. "I watched my father work, and I mean really work. I remember my father said, 'Mike, if you don't want to go to school, that's fine, you can come out and work on the roof.' I said, 'OK, I don't want to go to school.' So I went out on the roof for a couple of days. Soon enough, I said, 'Dad, I want to go to school. I want to be a scholar.' That roof took it out of me. It was tough work. And when I went out there to see it was tough work, I noticed how hard it was. I also noticed that my father never complained. He just kept working. And that's my job. Not to complain and keep working."

I wondered how Michael Irvin's family was dealing with his run-in with the law.

Super Bowl XXX wasn't far behind us, and already one of the Steelers' stars and one of the Cowboys' stars were in serious trouble. Nothing super about that.

During the first day of the NFL draft on Saturday, April 20, the Steelers traded some draft picks for former Rams running back Jerome Bettis. The Steelers had no idea how the Bam Morris situation was going to play out, or whether he would be back in uniform for the 1996 season. They were taking no chances. They had wanted to beef up their backfield in the first place, and they were not counting on Bam Morris. Some media were already writing him off. That was too bad, but the Steelers were being prudent, protecting themselves just in case Bam couldn't get out of this jam.

"Boy, you better say your prayer."
— Mrs. Marie Morris

I remembered asking Bam Morris to describe his hometown of Cooper, Texas. "There's nothing there," he said. "Close your eyes driving through and you'll miss it. The town was small; everyone knew you. It was great. I had little kids looking up to me in high school.

"Everyone knew the Morrises. My brother Ron had played ball at SMU, and J.C. had played at TCU. There were six boys in our family before who played high school football. I was the youngest. I had six brothers and three sisters. There were ten kids in our family."

His mother Marie had played basketball and had run on the track team in high school, and later balanced 10 kids and a household

61

and a job. She was a nurse's aide. Both of his parents were hard-working people.

His dad, Herman Morris, had been a custodian and carpenter, and built mobile homes. I asked Bam if he had ever helped his dad with his carpentry work. "I didn't do nothing when I was growing up," Bam came back. "I just got money from my brothers and sisters."

What did he gain from growing up in a big family? "Fighting. You could get in a fight and run home and get your brothers. We were all close, all sticking together. It's good having a big family, because you're close. If something goes down, everybody's together."

That explains why his family and so many people in Cooper came to his defense when stories of his drug-related arrest came to the community. Not their Bam, they told everybody.

Herman and Marie Morris had done their best to bring up their ten children correctly. It wasn't always easy.

Their son, Tommy, nine years Bam's senior, was supposedly the best student and athlete in the family, but he died in an automobile accident at age 15.

"My mom is a strong, black lady," said Bam Morris. "There were ten of us to raise, and my father wasn't much of a sports fan. She always supported us, in everything we did. My mom taught me, 'You got all of these doors put in front of you, you've got to stick with it. Go on through them.'

"My dad did stuff around the community, and everyone knew us. We had strict rules at our house. If you was a minute late you didn't get to eat. There was just food all around the table. You'd say a prayer and go after the food. If you were out of line, Mom would be upside your head. 'Boy, you better say your prayer.' If you came in late, you had to say a prayer by yourself before you started to eat.

"Every Sunday, we'd be in church Sunday morning, Sunday afternoon, Sunday evening, Sunday night. I'd say, 'Man, when I get to be 20, do I have to go to church all the time?'

"Me and my dad were not close when I was growing up. He was there for us when we needed him, but he wasn't into our sports. He had played basketball and track when he was young, but he didn't come out to see us play. But my mom was always there for us.

"My dad started coming when I was a senior in college. On Friday nights, when we were playing our high school games, he'd be half asleep on the couch at home, watching Ric Flair on TV. Wrestling was his big thing. Sometimes you'd like to look up and see him in the stands. He'd come once in a while. Mom, she put in a lot of time. Rain, sleet or snow, she was going to be there. My mom told me I had a lot of talent. Even now she says do what you have to do in order to use your talent to the fullest."

This conversation with Bam Morris came a few days before I spoke to his mother on the telephone. But the same thing was obviously on his mother's mind. It was also months before his run-in with Texas lawmen.

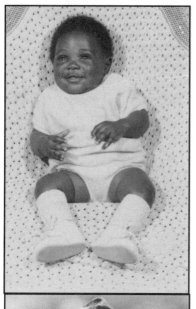

Bam Morris was a big kid, the last of 10 children born to Marie and Herman Morris, as an infant and as a Little Leaguer. "He always needed more attention than my other kids," said his mother.

n Morris won the Doak Walker Award as the nation's outstanding running back in his senior r at Texas Tech. Bam's parents, Marie and Herman Morris, were present, along with Walker, a endary Texas football figure, for the ceremonies.

"I talked to my mom this morning," said Bam. "She was asking me if I found a church up here yet. I said, 'Mom, it's hard to find a church. We play our games on Sunday; we're in a hotel.' She'd say, 'That's no excuse! On Sunday, you should find a place to go to church.'"

I mentioned to Morris that when the Steelers won their four Super Bowls in the '70s that about 20 to 25 of 45 roster players would meet on a weekly basis for Bible study or sessions with priests and ministers to discuss and practice their religion.

"They have religion meetings here; that's still not like church," said Bam. "I'm not really involved."

"Bam had to wait his turn."
— Brian McKamry
Cooper High coach

Originally from Wolfe City, Bam Morris' family moved to Cooper when he was still a baby. There they remained. Morris began playing football in the seventh grade. Back then, he expressed a dream to play college football and some day to play in the National Football League.

Cooper is a town located an hour northeast of Dallas. Cooper claims 2,300 people, a cobblestone town square, one blinking yellow light, and a main drag littered in fall by stray tufts of cotton, once the principal industry. The town, found halfway between Commerce and Paris on Highway 24, is easily bypassed.

But college coaches knew the road because the Morris family had attracted them there through the years, and Bam showed early that he could be the best of them all.

He was big for his age and often bullied other kids. He said he spent nearly every afternoon of junior high school in the principal's office. A paddling one day angered him so much that he ran home, where he found his mother waiting for him.

"She had a switch," he said, smiling, "and she whipped me all the way back to the schoolhouse, where I got some more licks. She said if she hadn't taken me back, there's no telling where I'd be now. I would have thought I could do whatever I wanted and then just go home. That wasn't the life to live."

When Morris was a little kid, he was guilty of beating up on neighborhood kids while he was in the care of his uncle, L.C. Perkins. "He said every time I would beat on them, I would go, 'Bam! Bam!' So they called me Bam Bam, and then they shortened it to Bam."

Bam was the seventh son of Herman and Marie Morris to play football there. Between 1972 and when Bam came on the scene, there had been only one season when there wasn't a Morris on the Cooper varsity.

Bam was, by far, the biggest of the Morris bunch. He was not as fast as his brother, Ron, who went on to play at SMU and as a receiver with the Chicago Bears. Ron had won the state Class 2A championship in the 100 meters in 1982 and still held several Cooper track records.

Morris began his football career in earnest at Cooper High School as a 200-pound tight end, and the team went farther in the playoffs than it had in 17 years. Morris made that possible by running an end-around for a 23-yard touchdown and hauled in a pass for a 73-yard touchdown.

That team had senior backs running behind senior linemen as Cooper High won nine of 11 games and won its first bi-district championship in school history.

In his first varsity start as a tailback the following season, Morris scored five touchdowns on runs of 10, 18, 27, 46 and 52 yards and totaled 251 yards in a 40-28 win over James Bowie. Morris was named the Red River Valley offensive player of the week by *The Paris News* for his efforts.

He was named the offensive player of the year by the same source when he finished his sophomore season with a school-record 2,022 rushing yards. Morris was a positive factor from day one.

"We knew last year that Bam would be our tailback this year," said Bulldogs coach Brian McKamy. "Bam had to wait his turn. He'll be a lot better. He could be awesome."

As a junior, Morris rushed for 1,942 yards on 208 carries, and scored 23 touchdowns. It was no surprise when he was named the Red River Valley's Most Valuable Player. He helped his team to an 11-1 record, claiming a district championship.

"He's a tremendous kid," said Coach McKamy. "He's matured a lot this year. He's also very personable. He gets along well with the other kids. We have a good relationship. He adds a major dimension to our offense. He's strong, he's powerful. Every time he touches the ball he has a chance to break it. He missed the first couple of games this year. If he had been able to play, I think he would have scored four or five more touchdowns."

He had to sit out track season in the spring of his junior year because his grades had slipped. Judy Falls, an English teacher at Cooper High and a big fan of Bam, said he was only an average student. She called him congenial and likeable and, at times, a con artist. She said he had a good sense of right and wrong.

Before Bam's senior season in high school, he received high praise from one of his brothers. "He's a natural," said his brother J.C., who rushed for more than 4,000 yards at Cooper before a modest career ended at TCU in 1982. "He's got good instincts, good vision. A lot of heart. He's the best thing going."

Bam was enjoying all the attention he was getting. He said he recognized that he had become a role model for Cooper children who found him an accessible hero in the town's centrally-located school system.

"All these kids would be hollering my name, and I don't even know them," he said. "Everybody knows me here. People look up to me. People watch me."

His name was mentioned in the same breath as some of the greatest running backs to ever be produced in the state, such as Earl Campbell, Billy Sims, Eric Dickerson, Craig James, Kenneth Hall, David Overstreet, Joe Washington, Greg Pruitt.

Morris idolized Campbell and San Francisco running back Roger Craig.

As a senior, Morris set the single-season rushing record for a Class 2A back with 2,972 yards on 272 carries, and repeated as the Offensive Player of the Year for the third straight time. He returned a kickoff 90 yards for a touchdown against Harmony in the area championship game victory. He finished up with 38 touchdowns. The Bulldogs finished with a 12-1 record, the best in school history.

In three years as a durable, hard-hitting running back, Morris gained 6,970 yards and 89 touchdowns.

"I want people to say, 'He always tried hard. He never quit trying. He went through some tough times, but he never gave up,'" said Morris.

"Texas has a lot of pride in its football. We thought we had the best players in the country. We played our hearts out on Friday night. I was told so often that I wasn't this or that, I thought I was supposed to accept that. I started doing what people expected me to do. Then I started thinking I'd be the best player."

"My mom's been a great help in my life. She's always been there for me."

Morris had to sit out his first season at Texas Tech as a Proposition 48 case. He lost confidence in himself that year, and nearly quit.

"I think the key for us is I never gave up," he said. "I had a lot of problems when I was coming out. I still have problems now. I have overcome problems. I think as it goes I get better. My mom's been a great help in my life because she's always been there for me."

As a senior, he led the nation with a 12.2 ppg scoring average, was second in the nation with 159.3 rushing yards per game, had 10 100-yard rushing games and broke Earl Campbell's Southwest Conference rushing record. With Campbell's record in sight, Morris averaged 223 yards and three touchdowns in the final three weeks of the season, and finished with 1,752 yards and 22 touchdowns.

Morris won the Doak Walker Award as the top running back in college his final year. He was honored at halftime of a Cowboys-Eagles game at Texas Stadium. He stood next to Earl Campbell, Tony Dorsett, John David Crow, Roger Staubach. He won the award over San Diego State's Marshall Faulk.

He discouraged comparisons to Campbell. "There is only one Earl Campbell," he said.

Despite his spectacular numbers and All-American honors, Morris drew mixed reviews from many pro scouts. They didn't file the most convincing reports on Morris. "I don't think a piece of paper can tell the person," he said. "I don't think you can sit back and evaluate a tape and say he can't make it with those moves. How can you make that comment when you never played the sport and you really don't know me as a person?

"People were saying I was lazy and had a bad attitude. I'm the nicest guy in the world. I don't have a problem with people. I get along with everybody. It was a lot of stuff that people were giving me a bad name. People were like, 'We don't want to take a chance with Morris.'

"I'm fine. I'm glad the Steelers picked me up and gave me a chance to come in and learn behind Barry Foster. I'm focused, I'm having fun and I got a lot to prove to everybody."

The Steelers selected him on the third round, the 91st player picked overall. "He had some amazing runs," Donahoe said. "He isn't real smooth and he isn't effortless, but every time you looked up he gained 8, 10, 12, 15 yards. When it was our turn to pick again, he was too good to pass up."

"You'd better find a way to hang onto the ball."
— Bill Cowher

Morris got his first start in the seventh game of the 1994 season against the New York Giants when Barry Foster was sidelined by a sprained knee. Morris lost the ball twice on fumbles that led to two field goals by the Giants.

His second fumble led to an animated conversation with Coach Bill Cowher on the sideline. "We're not going to take you out," Cowher cried into his face. "You're staying in there, so you'd better find a way to hang onto the football."

It was the same speech Cowher gave to Foster after he fumbled three times against the Jets in the second week of the 1992 season. Foster regained his composure, the Steelers bounced back to win the game, and Barry wound up rushing for 1,690 yards that year.

It worked this time as well and Morris came back to help lead the Steelers to a 10-6 victory over the Giants. He set a Steelers' record for a rookie with 146 yards on 29 rushes and one touchdown.

"We're a team," Morris said. "We win as a team, and we lose as a team. But I'll take the blame for the fumbles. I'm not the first one to fumble and I won't be the last."

The Steelers were 6-3 when Foster injured his ankle in 1994 and struggled to a 3-4 the rest of the regular season. Foster went down with a sprained medial collateral ligament in his left knee on the first play of the 14-10 win over Cincinnati. Morris took his place that day and led the team with 82 yards on 21 carries. In his fifth start that season, against Cincinnati again, Morris rushed for 108 yards and had his first two touchdown game.

"I wouldn't compare his style with anybody," said Ron Erhardt, the Steelers' offensive coordinator. "Right now, he's a big kid who can run good, with balance, good vision, and makes people miss. He has Bam's style rather than Earl Campbell's or Franco Harris's."

Morris had a hard time learning the offense. John L. Williams helped him in that regard, as did offensive backfield coach Dick Hoak.

"Coach Hoak's been on me every day. He's a great guy. That's what I need. I think it's going to make me a better player in the long run," said Morris.

As good as he was, the top rookie running back was Marshall Faulk, a franchise player with the Indianapolis Colts. "Seems like I've never gotten the respect I deserve," Morris said at the end of the season. "Must be my style. I have kind of a roughneck style when I'm running.

"I'm not pretty. I've got a lot of Earl in me. I just get the job done. I'm not fast, but I'm carrying 240 pounds. My new motto is, 'It ain't where you start, it's where you end.'"

That was certainly prophetic for the 1995 season. The Steelers and Morris got off to a slow start, and more than one media source laid much of the blame for the team's disappointing 3-4 start at the stomach of Bam Morris.

"When you're on top of the world, you can weigh 600 pounds and nobody cares," said Morris. "Then, when you're 3-4, you become a scapegoat. Everyone kept saying I wasn't ready to play, that I had lost the desire. They were saying I wasn't doing the job and that's why we were losing, and I think I pretty much became the scapegoat for all the team's problems.

"I was never upset with Coach Cowher because, to me, he's a good coach and a good man. I never had a problem with Erric, because we're best friends. But I was upset with what people were saying, because it was all bullshit.

"I had a lot of pressure on me — too much pressure, I think. All the emphasis was on me replacing Barry Foster, and there was all this stuff like, 'If Bam gets 150 yards, we'll win,' and all that.

"The expectations for me were just too high. Hey, this is just my second year in the league. The fans, the media, they blew things out of proportion about my weight. That was never a problem.

"Everybody says I ran better last year. I don't know what they mean. Last year I ran harder and this year I'm not running as hard? How can they tell me that? They're not in my body. As a spectator,

you can say things like that, but get into combat and see how it feels. I have been taking criticism since college; I'm used to people putting the blame on me."

Dick Hoak had this to say about Morris: "I think he has the ability. He has to know and understand what it takes to be in this league. You can't be in this league because you are just physically better than anybody else. Everybody here is as good as you. You have to know what it takes. You have to understand you can't just go out there and be physically better than most of the people you play against, because you're not. You have to work at this, it just doesn't come easy.

"I'm not sure Bam really understands what it takes to be a great player. That's something I think he'll learn; he just has to work at it. Maybe it came a little too easy for him last year."

Fortunately, Morris and the Steelers turned things around. He and Pegram combined to give the Steelers the sort of running game they needed to complement the passing game directed by Neil O'Donnell. When the Steelers defeated the Houston Oilers, 21-7, to win the AFC Central championship, Morris rumbled for 102 yards, wrapping things up with a 30-yard touchdown run with 3:27 left.

"I don't want to be a one-man show," said Morris. "I did that in high school and I don't want that kind of pressure again."

He was charged up when the Steelers went up against the Cowboys in Super Bowl XXX.

"Growing up, I was a Houston fan because I idolized Earl Campbell. Everyone else in my family — parents, brothers, cousins, aunts and uncles — were all Cowboys fans, and I just wanted to be different. I wanted to be a maverick and I never liked all that 'America's Team' stuff, anyway.

"I told my father that if he roots for Dallas, I'm going to disown him."

After the game in which he nearly powered Pittsburgh to a comeback victory, he said, "I'll get some respect when I go back home. Being from Texas, and playing the Cowboys, I had some extra motivation. I had a good time. That's not to say I'm happy with losing the game. But no one gave us a chance. And we had a chance to win.

"My number got called, and I had a good time. Everything worked well with our running game. We just didn't play 60 minutes."

He remembered where he came from, and the source of his strength and power. "If it wasn't for my mom, I wouldn't be where I am today in the NFL. I've had a lot of adversity. She was my mom, but more than that she was my friend."

After his problem with police in Dallas, nobody was quite certain where Bam Morris was in the NFL.

On July 9, 1996, Morris was released by the Steelers. Two days later, he was sentenced in Rockwall, Texas to a six-year probation and fined $7,000. "I let my family down," admitted Morris at the sentencing. "I let my friends down. I made a mistake."

Jerry Olsavsky
The Comeback Kid

"Jerry is a football player,
pure and simple."
— Bill Cowher

Jerry Olsavsky was hardly a happy camper. Olsavsky strode the sideline at St. Vincent College, shouting encouragement to his fellow linebackers, complimenting them on a job well done, exhorting them to shut down Neil O'Donnell or Mike Tomczak and the Steelers' offensive unit. He seemed to be enjoying himself. Olsavsky was masking his true feelings, as best he could. He hated being on the sideline.

He wore his gold jersey with the black numerals — 55 — black shorts over longer skin-tight black Spandex pants, a black ballcap set backwards on his head, and he wore tight-fitting, flared sunglasses, perhaps to hide the disappointed look in his dark eyes as much as to provide relief from the bright sun.

"This sucks," he said after the day's second practice session, expressing himself in his usual no-nonsense manner.

He could not participate in this practice on a sultry Monday afternoon, August 7, 1995, because he had broken a toe in a workout a week earlier. Olsavsky sat out the exhibition opener with the Bills in Buffalo, and it appeared he was going to miss the second pre-season contest with the Green Bay Packers at Three Rivers Stadium the coming Sunday afternoon.

"The toe is something stupid in your life," Olsavsky said, his mood as dark as the whisker growth on his long, well-chiseled chin. "It's not like being out because you've wrecked your knee."

Olsavsky certainly knew of what he spoke, since he had been sidelined most of the two previous seasons by a knee injury that was so severe many thought it would end his career. But Olsavsky showed them, those doubters who had nipped at his heels like his two pet dogs, ever since he started playing football as a kid back home in Youngstown, Ohio.

He was 6-1, 220, about the same size as another linebacker in Steelers' history, Hall of Famer Jack Ham. Olsavsky was familiar with Ham's success. If a Penn Stater from Johnstown could succeed in the NFL jungle, so could a Pitt man from Youngstown, as Olsavsky saw it through rose-colored glasses. He was, by the way, back in the lineup for that pre-season game with Green Bay. Olsavsky never sat well.

Olsavsky suffered his most serious injury on October 23, 1993. Three Cleveland Browns players fell on his exposed left leg. Three ligaments were torn in his knee. "It was pretty ugly," recalled Olsavsky. "The bottom of my leg was off to one side."

Dr. Jim Bradley, the Steelers' orthopedic specialist, will never forget that incident. "We got out on the field to Jerry and all the players were turning away." recalled Dr. Bradley. "They couldn't look at him. I could see right away his knee was dislocated. I told him, 'Jerry, I have to put this thing back in right now.' He cursed and said to do it. I can still hear his scream..."

Dr. Bradley was not sure how Olsavsky's recovery would go. "We just wanted him to be able to walk again. With a dislocation, you can lose your leg. It's bad enough sometimes that you have to amputate."

The knee was surgically repaired with two ligaments from a cadaver; the third ligament was put back together by surgeons. Even his best friends felt his football career was over. Olsavsky disagreed.

"A career-ending injury?" he asked in response to a question. "The draft was supposed to be the career-ending for me."

Dr. Bradley, a Penn State grad, spoke in admiration of the Pitt product. "We fixed it, but it wasn't us," said Dr. Bradley. "This was all Jerry. He just had an unwavering positive attitude. He worked as hard as anyone I've ever seen."

Olsavsky said of his ordeal, "I'm not going to say it was fun, but I took it as a challenge. Before I could rehabilitate my knee for football, I had to rehabilitate my knee to walk again. I couldn't stand up in the shower for eight weeks. I had to learn how to walk all over again."

He returned to the Steelers late in the 1994 season, with a new contract and a spot on the roster, brought back mostly as a practice player. He had been helping out as a volunteer assistant coach to Rich Lackner at Carnegie Mellon University, when he got the call from the Steelers. Now he was a backup, not a starter. He was happy to be back, but Olsavsky was hardly satisfied with his status.

Olsavsky had always been too small, too slow, not strong enough, not athletic enough, you name it. Yet he had persisted. He had overcome all that, and the ugly knee injury two years earlier, to stick with the Steelers. No one ever said he didn't have the head, or the neck, to play the game. You notice his neck right away; it's like a tree trunk. It's been built up to handle collisions.

Now, as Cowher was trying to make decisions about who to keep for the 1995 season, another obstacle had sidelined Olsavsky. Not for long, he promised.

"I just told Greg Lloyd I'd rather be rehabilitating than standing around watching practice," Olsavsky said.

Olsavsky might have viewed his toe as a "stupid thing," but it was a "turf toe" injury that cut short the Hall of Fame career of another Steelers' linebacker out of Ohio, Jack Lambert. No one thought that injury was going to be quite so serious. Olsavsky simply shrugged at the reminder. "I'll be back soon," he said. Who could doubt him?

Certainly not John Marous or Bill Baierl or Bill Hillgrove who also stood on the sideline that same day and watched the proceedings. They had all rooted for him during his days at Pitt (1985-88), and continued to take pride in his efforts as a Steeler linebacker. Barely recruited, he got one of the last scholarships offered by Pitt in 1985, and went on to become one of the school's all-time leading tacklers.

Marous was the former CEO at Westinghouse Electric and the former chairman of the board of trustees at Pitt; Baierl was the owner of Baierl Chevrolet in Wexford, and one of the biggest patrons for the Pitt athletic program; Hillgrove was the "Voice of Pitt" during Olsavsky's collegiate days, and was now calling the action for the Steelers as well on WTAE Radio.

"I remember when he was a freshman at Pitt," recalled Hillgrove. "I remember a fourth down play at Temple when he came up and hit the ballcarrier — wow! — and stopped him cold to save a victory (21-17). And he was just a freshman! I remember this year a big play he made against the Redskins to turn the scrimmage around.

"When they snap the ball, he knows where it's at. You can't coach that. He was born with it."

Everybody talked about Olsavsky's instinctive feel for the game of football, his football smarts, his big heart, his quickness in a limited area, his indomitable spirit, his dogs. Jerry Olsavsky was an old-fashioned football player, a throwback to another era. So was his usual attire.

"He fits right in with the crowd at Steelers' games," added Hillgrove. "There's no pretense there. He doesn't subscribe to Gentleman's Quarterly (GQ). His whole year's clothing budget is less than $100. Olsavsky is a perfect fit for Pittsburgh."

That was why Olsavsky was such a favorite of head coach Bill Cowher. Cowher could never prounounce Olsavsky's name properly, but he loved him like a brother just the same. They were of the same mold. They had the same lantern jaw, the same wild glint in their eyes, the same cat-that-just-ate-the-mouse grin. They had similar roots and a similar story. They were both high-octane linebackers, and special team demons. "Jerry is a football player, pure and simple," said Cowher. "I don't have to worry about him. He's always going to give you his best effort, whether that's rehabilitating himself from an injury, or playing football."

"I want to be on a team that wins the Super Bowl, and I want to be in the Hall of Fame someday."
— Jerry Olsavsky

Olsavsky stopped on his way from the practice field at St. Vincent to the dressing room to discuss his latest dilemma. He was asked if he was concerned about his status on the Steelers, considering he was missing valuable time when decisions were being made about who would stay with the Steelers for the season's opener.

"I just want to get back out there," he said. "I don't think about making the team. I just want to be playing."

Things had been going so well before that damn toe gave way. "It was fun, real fun," said Olsavsky. "It was just great to be out there again. I missed training camp last year. When you're not playing, you miss the whole thing, even the bad stuff."

Having overcome such a serious injury the year before had to help his spirits, knowing he could overcome such setbacks. "I think it's something to hang your hat on, but it's just a small consolation," he said. "You just want to get back."

Rick Burkholder, the assistant trainer for the Steelers who personally oversaw Olsavsky's rehabilitation effort from his knee injury, said, "I can still hear him screaming in the weight room, trying to get his range of motion back."

Burkholder said he tried to establish some goals for Olsavsky, something to motivate him, when Olsavsky was starting what seemed like an impossible comeback mission.

Olsavsky smiled when he was reminded how he rebuked Burkholder, and told him he didn't need any new goals, thank you just the same. "There are only two goals any football player should have," said Olsavsky, recalling what he told Burkholder. "I want to be on a team that wins the Super Bowl and I want to be in the Hall of Fame someday.

"I may not get there, but I'm going to bust my butt to do it. To me, winning the AFC championship doesn't mean anything. It's just a step along the way to a goal. When I was little, growing up in Ohio, I'd go to the Pro Football Hall of Fame. I've always had a feeling for that place.

"It's got an atmosphere; it's like a church. You could feel it. You got to see Dick Butkus in the highlights. You'd see the busts of all the great football players. There's something like only 180 players in there. It's special. Not a lot who got there. I loved it."

Olsavsky sounded like Lambert, who grew up in Mantua, Ohio, and used to visit the Hall of Fame as a youngster. Lambert loved to look at the primitive pads, pants and helmets worn by the pioneers of pro football, the old-timers from places like Latrobe, Jeannette and Pittsburgh, Massillon, Warren and Canton. Now Lambert is a Hall of Famer himself.

Like Lambert, Olsavsky believed it was best to be a bachelor when you were playing ball, that pro football was a demanding mistress in itself, and that it was better to wait till your playing days are over to wed and have a family. Olsavsky was 28 years old at the start of the 1995 season.

So Olsavsky had his sights set on more than just backing up Chad Brown and Levon Kirkland at inside linebacker, and being a member of the special teams.

erry Olsavsky liked to play
all and to cook when he was
kid growing up in
oungstown, Ohio. The fear-
ome foursome, at right,
ncluded his brother Tommy
No. 44), Jerry, Brian and
Iichael Zordich. Michael
ater played with the
hiladelphia Eagles.

"It's a lot of fun being out there," Olsavsky said. "If people think I'm just glad to be out there, they don't know me. I can't ever be satisfied with that."

I had seen Olsavsky during the off-season in the lobby of the Steelers' offices at Three Rivers Stadium. He was standing near the plexiglass case where the team's four Super Bowl trophies are displayed, near the Steelers' own Wall of Fame, where all the team's greats are pictured.

He was accompanied by his two dogs, Fran, a golden retriever, and Max, a pit bull stray he found in his travels.

Olsavsky was definitely his own man. He could be seen steering his bicycle about town, riding from his apartment in Shadyside through the city's streets, his dogs running behind him.

Olsavsky was supposed to be able to read any situation in football, but he was wrong when he said, "They all like my dogs. Max has been on a few desks." There were some Steeler executives who squirmed, and shook their heads, when they saw Olsavsky show up in shorts, barefoot, with his dogs at the door.

That was part of Olsavsky's carefree lifestyle. "I just like to play, on and off the field," he offered. "I'm not a good athlete. I'm not big. I'm not strong. I just like to play. So many people have jobs they don't like. I have a job where I make a lot of money, and I love what I do. I have the best of both worlds.

"I'm lucky to play a sport I love, and I'm lucky to have the ability to play at the highest level of football. I hope I can prove I still belong here. To me, it's no big deal that I'm doing what I'm doing. That's what I do. I'm a football player. This is hard, but it's nothing compared to learning how to walk again."

Olsavsky loves to tell stories about his dogs, like the one where after he fed his dog he came back into the room to find the dog eating Jerry's dinner as well. When he was asked why he had reported early to camp, Olsavsky said simply, "My house is clean, my dogs are taken care of, why not?"

Olsavsky did not make nearly as much money as most of his teammates — he had an opportunity to sign a contract for a fat increase, but chose to hold off, then he got hurt — but he was not complaining. "I have a couple of expenses," he said of his simple lifestyle. "I need food for me, and food for my dogs. I don't even have to pay to play golf. My brother Tom works for Titlelist, and he sets it up for me. Tom used to beat me up when I was little. Now he's trying to make up for all that abuse."

"I just like to play."
— Jerry Olsavsky

Marvin Lewis, the linebacker coach of the Steelers for four seasons (1992-1995) before becoming the defensive coordinator in Baltimore after Super Bowl XXX, was an admirer of Olsavsky even before they teamed up with the Steelers. Lewis first got to know Olsavsky when he was an assistant coach on Paul Hackett's staff at Pitt, and Olsavsky was a frequent visitor to Pitt Stadium.

Lewis grew up in McDonald, Pennsylvania and had long been an admirer of Marty Schottenheimer and Bill Cowher, and liked to see a linebacker with local ties showing the way with the Steelers.

"Through the whole thing, Jerry has just been so great," allowed Lewis. "Jerry is such a fun person and player. He finally got an opportunity to start for the Steelers. He was playing great; we were playing great. He lost the opportunity he had worked so hard to earn. And our play dropped off for a while after we lost him. It's something we all had to go through.

"He wanted to come back before he was really ready. It didn't surprise me that he worked so hard to get back. If he didn't have an obstacle in front of him, he wouldn't be Jerry O. He's always working to overcome something.

"He used to come out to Pitt and speak to our players at a team meeting from time to time. Paul used to have former Pitt players come in to talk to the team. Like Tommy Flynn. Jimbo Covert. Mark May. Emil Boures. Jerry would tell the guys what a great opportunity they had, and not to waste it. He really has a grasp of what you need to be successful in life. He doesn't take his position of being a pro football player lightly. To him, it's a serious commitment. The Pitt kids knew he'd played there, too, and that he knew what it takes to get to the NFL.

"Jerry was on the sidelines at most of our home games at Pitt. He wouldn't miss a home game if he could help it. A year ago, when he didn't have a contract with the Steelers, he worked as a volunteer coach at Carnegie Mellon. At CMU, he was dealing with a different kind of kid; they were there for school first and football second, and there was no question about that. And Jerry found it easy to teach those guys; he takes the game intellectually to a different level.

"He has some physical limitations, but he doesn't waste movement or steps. He makes good reads. Certain guys are like that. You won't fool him twice. If he's seen it before, he'll be in the right place to make the play."

"He'll be lucky if he can walk again."
— Dr. Jim Bradley

Rick Burkholder was a work study student in the sports information office at Pitt in the mid-80s when I served as the assistant athletic director in charge of that office. He was on the soccer team and was also a student trainer at the time. Later, I bumped into Burkholder when he was working as a graduate assistant at the University of Arizona, where he earned his master's degree in athletic training. The Pitt basketball team played a first round game in the NCAA tournament at the McHale Center on the Arizona campus. He came back to Pitt as an assistant trainer for the football team, and after two years was hired by the Steelers in July of 1993.

"When Jerry got hurt at Cleveland, it was kind of like a black cloud hanging over the sideline," recalled Burkholder, taking a break from his chores at summer camp. "When Jerry went down out there, it was like no matter what happened in the game, this was going to be a bad day.

"That day, Dr. Bradley said, 'He'll be lucky if he can walk again. It's a bad, bad injury.' I said, 'If anyone can come back, it'll be Jerry.' Dr. Bradley said, 'Don't get your hopes up.'

"But Jerry is just a different cat. I was working at Pitt during Jerry's freshman and sophomore years. He was a different cat then, too. He was so hard-nosed. He'd go into full contact workouts without pads or gloves."

I interrupted Burkholder to tell him that I had seen Olsavsky playing with the Steelers' basketball team the previous winter, and that Olsavsky was not even wearing any braces on his knees. "He plays with the same reckless abandon he always has," said Tom O'Malley Jr., who coordinates the Steelers' basketball team's activities. "He plays like nothing ever happened."

A footnote: Siulagi Palelei, a Samoan guard from UNLV who was also playing that same night in the gym at Bethel Park High School, blew out his knee playing in a basketball game later in the winter, missed training camp, a good deal of the season, and was released when he recovered.

"When I came back to Pitt after two years at Arizona," said Burkholder, "I'd see Jerry out at the Stadium and in the training room. He liked to hang out at Pitt. He'd be in the locker room and on the sidelines and in the weight room. We became friends, drinking buddies of a sort, and I hung out with him. When I got this job, I was fortunate enough to be reunited with Jerry.

"John Norwig, our head trainer, is responsible for overseeing all rehabilitation activities. John knew I was close with Jerry, so he let me work with Jerry. John and I would sit down and discuss what Jerry was doing, and what he needed to do the next week.

"I did one-on-one stuff with him. It was the funnest rehab, if you can say such a thing, I've ever done. There was no way I wouldn't be successful. Guys like Jerry make a trainer look good. He took my knowledge and put it into his body. Jerry would take my coaching points and take them to an extreme, and get it just right. He'd use the leg press machine so earnestly and exactly. He'd lie flat on his back, and he'd keep an eye on the weights on his right, and if he was supposed to extend his leg to a 45 degree level, that's exactly what he'd do. He's a perfectionist. He would do however number of reps he was supposed to do, and he'd make sure it was perfect.

"He'd always want to know what we could do next. He's so good. I still challenge Jerry with things I don't think he can do. We run together through the city at times. He'll run steps with his dog. Most guys, if I was there, they'd blow it off, but not Jerry. He and I will run five miles, and he always sprints ahead of me at the end. He has to win. I was concerned about how his knee would hold up to two-a-day workouts, but when it didn't swell up after we'd run the five miles, I knew he'd be all right."

Burkholder had a thought during the 1993 season to nominate Olsavsky for John Madden's all-pro team. Madden likes to glorify lesser-known down-in-the-dirt guys like Olsavsky.

"Jerry hurt his little finger in a game early in the season," said Burkholder. "He yelled to Bryan Hinkle to throw him some finger tape. Jerry pushed his finger back into its proper position and started to wrap it. A play started and he simply held the roll of tape in one hand, and went into a pileup. Then he finished taping his finger before the next play, and tossed the roll of tape back to Hinkle on the sideline. He never missed a down. But then he got hurt in the Cleveland game and was out for the season. So I wasn't able to nominate him for Madden's team."

"A lot of guys are rooting for him."
— Dermontti Dawson

Dermontti Dawson, the veteran center, was an Olsavsky supporter. "You'd think that someone who suffered an injury so devastating as Jerry wouldn't want to play again," said Dawson. "It's totally amazing that he came back. But that's just part of his uniqueness. Jerry's always happy. I've never seen him down.

"On the field, he's a player. A lot of guys are rooting for him. I've always liked him since I've been here. He's always defied the odds. And he's done it again. Jerry worked hard. I remember seeing him in the locker room during the off-season. He put in some long hours. Before long, he was practicing without a brace, like it never happened."

Chad Brown, who replaced Olsavsky in the starting lineup, said, "I don't know if I would have been willing to go through what Jerry went through to come back. I admire his spirit."

Jeff Zgonina, one of his pals on the Steelers who went to the Carolina Panthers in the expansion draft, said, "I knew he'd get better. He's a hard worker, the way he goes about things, the way he puts his mind about what he's doing. He defies logic every way you look at him: his dogs, his bikes, his fantasies, his women friends. His injury was a nasty one, that's for sure. His leg was really mangled. We'd kid him when he was rehabilitating himself; we'd tell him he wasn't going to make it. To see him playing again makes all of us feel good. He'd say, 'Everybody's always writing me off. I'll show all of you.'

"When he came to the sideline after he was hurt, he was so stone-faced. 'I'll be back,' he told everyone who came over to check him out. 'I'll be back.'

"He's so smart on the field. He's unbelievable the way he recognizes what's going on when he's out there. He doesn't take unnecessary steps. He's going to be in the right place at the right time. And he's got great tackling form.

"He's a strange bird, don't get me wrong. He never wears socks. He gets in your car and pushes his shoes off and he can stink up a whole car. I've roomed with him on the road and he's a good roomie. He always comes back to the room with a pizza, which is good."

Olsavsky's success story was inspirational for others on the Steelers' squad. It certainly helped Deon Figures, who was working on his own during the 1995 summer camp to come back from a freak off-season setback.

Figures was driving his car through a bad neighborhood in his native Los Angeles in May, 1995, when he took a wild 9-mm bullet to the knee. It was thought he might miss half the season, or possibly never be the same again.

He worked hard under the watchful eye of team trainer John Norwig. "Look at him," Norwig noted one day, as Figures ran short sprints. "He's running twice as fast as I ever did in my life, yet he's probably going about fifty percent."

Figures said he never sat down with Olsavsky and compared their knee rehabilitations. "From what I know, though, his knee problem was real severe," offered Figures. "I look at it this way: if Jerry can go through that and come back, working hard the way he did, then I can, too. That motivates me.

"Jerry is a cool person. To me, I think all the athletes on the team all want to prove other people wrong. He's back on the field, and he's faster and stronger than ever before.

"The Steelers have never dealt with a bullet injury (unless you count Rocky Bleier's comeback from shrapnel wounds suffered in Viet Nam), but I think injuries are something a lot of football players have to deal with. People tend to look at these things negatively. 'He'll never come back. He's through. He's done.' I was temporarily handicapped, that's the way I look at it. At first, I couldn't walk around the house without crutches. Now I'm running pretty good. You want to prove people wrong.

"I can't speak for Jerry, but when I hear people speak about my situation negatively, it fires me up. This helps your self-discipline. You have to dig deeper, you have to strive harder. You know what you're capable of doing. You know your own body. You know your own limits. Some of us keep stretching our limits."

"When the ball is snapped, Jerry knows where it's going."
— Tom Donahoe

Tom Donahoe, the director of football operations for the Steelers, smiled when he spoke about Olsavsky. "He's a different cat, no question about that," he said. "In a lot of ways, he's a special type guy. He's overcome a lot of obstacles. Coming out of college, he was too small, too slow. His knee injury could have been a career-ending injury, but he worked as hard as anyone I've ever seen. He was a pest, too. He wanted to come back before he was ready.

"Eventually, he got mad at me and the whole organization (for delaying his return). He was mad at the world.

"It's good to have him back. There was a huge dropoff in our run defense after he got hurt. Jerry is such an instinctive football player. When the ball is snapped, Jerry knows where it's going.

"He's a throwback. He loves the game. He loves to practice. Unfortunately, you don't get a lot of guys like that today. Whatever they did to repair his knee, they did a great job. Whatever cadaver they used, he must have been a fast one. Jerry is actually faster than he was before. He's very strong from the waist down; he's got great leverage. For ten yards, he's as quick as anyone on the team."

Doug Whaley, a former Pitt defensive back, was working as an intern in the player personnel department at the 1995 summer camp, and learning how to evaluate talent. Whaley was asked how he would be able to recognize Olsavsky's specialness if he were to assess him as a pro prospect.

"He knows his football," said Whaley. "You can't teach some of the things Jerry does. He gives you 110 percent effort. I don't think Jerry ever considers doing anything less than his best. He expected to come back. That's one of the things they taught us at Pitt — to be the best. We weren't always successful, but we thought we were winners."

Bobby April, the Steelers' special teams coach for the 1994 and 1995 seasons, was looking forward to having Olsavsky on his teams again. "He knows how to make the play," said April. "He can't worry about getting hurt again. If the doctors say he's OK to play, then we have to play him. We can't protect him. This is a game where there's great contact. You know that when you get into it. No matter when you start, you know you can get hurt. You know it can happen to you. It's part of the game. There are some people not playing today because they couldn't deal with that factor. When you decide to play this game, you can't excel at it if you have a mind frame of self-preservation.

"Rick Burkholder believed this guy would make it back, and I believed him. So I was more optimistic than a lot of other people around here. It's such a positive development for our team. We plan on using the hell out of him on special teams this year. He has to help our special teams. We have to have him to get better."

Olsavsky said it best. He knows what football is all about. "It's about running into people, and getting run into," he once said.

"You never know where they're going to come from," he added. "I don't want to be one of those guys you meet in a bar, a guy who says, 'I could have played, but the coach didn't like me.' Or, 'I didn't like to practice.' Or, 'I had a knee injury that ended my career.' They're all out there, you know. I don't ever want to have to wonder what I could have done."

Olsavsky returned to practicing with the team two days after he was seen standing on the sideline, and it didn't take long for everyone to know he was back. He got into a fight with LaMonte Coleman, a rookie running back from Slippery Rock University. The rookie lost his helmet and wound up pinned on the ground. There hadn't been many fights or skirmishes at the summer camp. "We haven't had enough fights," complained Cowher with a crooked grin.

Once again, Olsavsky's quick return didn't surprise the coach. "Knowing his pain tolerance," said Cowher, "you knew he wouldn't be out that long."

"My dad would just walk around with the biggest smile on his face." — Jerry Olsavsky

The 1995 season was supposed to be a wonderful one for Olsavsky. The team was winning and, when Chad Brown was sidelined by a bum ankle, Olsavsky was starting at inside linebacker once again, and showed that he was equal to the task. He started in six games altogether, including the playoff wins over Buffalo and Indianapolis, but gave way to a recovered Brown for Super Bowl XXX.

That was a disappointment. But it paled by comparison to something else that happened late in the schedule. His dad died. Don Olsavsky was 66 when he died from a heart attack on December 1.

There were 17 family members, including Jerry's mother, two brothers and a sister, in the stands at Sun Devil Stadium in Tempe, Arizona to see Jerry play in Super Bowl XXX. His brother, Tom, his

Jerry Olsavsky was "almost as big as his ma" in 1979 scene in the Olsavskys' kitchen in Youngstown.

Jerry was "bigger than his dad" in 1991 family snapshot provided by his mother, along with her personal notes.

sister, Mary Jo, and his step-brother, Jack Crish, were all there cheering for him. They were the ones wearing Steelers jerseys with "OLSAVSKY" on the back. But his dad was not there. That hurt more than the knee injury in Cleveland.

"He was Jerry's biggest fan besides me," said Nancy Olsavsky, speaking in the lobby of the Steelers' hotel in Scottsdale. "It's hard to believe he's gone. I keep talking to him, but he doesn't come back."

The son was just as sad about his dad's absence. "It's tough because this game is big," said Jerry. "This is where he always wanted to be. My mom likes to talk a lot. She's not embarrassed to call me her baby or tell people how she thinks I am the best player on the team. But my dad, he would just walk around with the biggest smile in the world. He wouldn't say much, but you knew he was so happy his son was a football player.

"I think about it all the time and I think about him. Before I left home, I went to the cemetery and it was tough. But the hardest thing is that no matter what I do, he's not coming back. That's been the toughest part of this year. People talk about a knee injury? You lose your father and that really gets you. That's what's tough to do.

"It's just weird because they went to so many games together. And now they have a kid playing in the Super Bowl and it's something to be really proud of. But part of her just isn't going to be there because my dad's gone."

When I met and talked to Nancy at a breakfast at the Doubletree Inn where the Steelers were staying in Scottsdale, Arizona, I told her what a nice son she had in Jerry, going back to my days with him at Pitt. She loved it. "He's my baby," she began. "He'll always be my baby." Jerry just blushed, muttered something to get us to stop, and walked away.

Nancy showed me a Super Bowl pin she had bought for her husband. He had always worn pins and medals all over his hats and jackets. "He loved to collect them," noted Nancy. "I thought I'd get him something special."

"This is a dream for me."
— Jerry Olsavsky

Olsavsky was sitting in the Steelers' locker room on a Saturday afternoon, talking and having some fun with his friend and next-door neighbor, Justin Strzelczyk, looking forward to Monday and an airplane trip to Phoenix for Super Bowl XXX.

Once again, he was downplaying what he had done to get to this special moment in his football-playing career.

"I'm just an average guy and I play football," he said.

"If you go to church, try to be a good person and work hard, your dreams might come true. This is a dream for me."

A friend of mine, by the way, tells me he saw Olsavsky attending mass regularly at St. Paul's Cathedral in Oakland.

"If we win the Super Bowl, I'll still hang out in the same places," said Olsavsky. "I'll still be the same, I'll still have the same friends. I'll still shave once a week.

"I do a couple of things. I try to do them well. I don't try to impress people, and I don't want people to try and impress me. I just like good people. I probably got a lot of that from Pitt.

"I met guys from out of town for the first time in my life. In the beginning, you like everyone. After a while, you find someone steals something from you. You learned that you couldn't trust everyone, that everyone was not your friend. Today, I hang out with the same guys I hung out with at Pitt."

I asked him how he was going to take care of his friends and family for the Super Bowl. "I just got 22 tickets and I'm going to try to make everyone happy," he said. "What a headache. Above all, I'm supposed to have a good time on this trip. It's still a week of work for me, but I'm looking forward to it. It hasn't really sunk in yet that we're going to the Super Bowl. I'm not down yet from being excited from the Indianapolis game. I'd much rather play good teams than bad teams. So I love this time of the year.

"I remember going out to Pitt these past few seasons, and I'd talk to those guys. I liked them. But they didn't know how good they were; they were always talking about how good the team was they were about to play. Hell, I never cared who we were playing. Bring 'em on.

"I remember when I was little, before I knew anything, I liked the Dolphins. Then after that, when the Steelers were going good, I really didn't like them. That's because everyone else did. I didn't want to be on the bandwagon. I wanted to be different. I liked Lambert and Ham, but that was about it.

"After I came to Pittsburgh, I met Lambert and Ham and had a beer with them. They said they both liked the way I played. Just by them talking to you meant something to me. If they talk to you they must like you, especially Lambert. If they tell you you're worth some mention it means something to me."

He said he had learned the day before that Chad Brown would be starting in Super Bowl XXX. "I wouldn't say it was a surprise, but, of course, starting in a Super Bowl would have been something you want to do. But starters don't lose their jobs here because of injuries; that's the way it goes. I think I still bring something to the defense. This is still the biggest game of my life. I want to be the MVP in the Super Bowl — that's the way I'm going into it — but I don't think it will happen.

"My dad won't be there, and that's on my mind, too. I remember taking him out to Chiodo's Bar in Homestead, where they have all those lifetime Steelers fans and all that Steelers' stuff hanging from the walls, and what a great time he had with everybody. He fit right in. He and Joe Chiodo hit it off. I'll miss him."

Olsavsky grew up in west Youngstown, and started playing football at St. Brendan's Catholic Grade School and with the Chaney High School Cowboys. His dad and mom were always in the stands rooting for him.

There were three Pelusi brothers — John, Jeff and Jay — who came out of Youngstown to play football at Pitt. Matt Cavanaugh came from Chaney and quarterbacked the 1976 national championship team at Pitt in his junior season.

Youngstown had always sent good football players to Pitt. During my student days, Jim Traficant, Ernie Borghetti and John Holzbach all matriculated to Pitt from Youngstown. Former pro quarterback Frank Sinkwich had similar roots. Nick and Al Bolkovac and John Congemi also came to Pitt from Youngstown to make their mark.

The Pelusis and Cavanaugh turned Olsavsky into a Pitt fan. One of his boyhood and St. Brendan's buddies, Michael Zordich, went on to play for the Philadelphia Eagles. Back then, Olsavsky was hoping he could be good enough to play at Pitt someday. He wanted a football scholarship.

"I was trying to save my parents some money; that's the way I looked at it," Olsavsky said. "I wasn't thinking about the NFL then. With my size, and I'm not real quick or anything, I really never dreamed of pro ball. I was just going to keep playing as hard as I could and, hopefully, good things would happen."

He was given the last scholarship available in 1985. He got a scholarship after somebody else backed out on an offer. He was boosted at Pitt by Sal Sunseri, another undersized but enthusiastic competitor who had come out of nearby Central Catholic High School to become an All-America linebacker at Pitt, and was later drafted by the Steelers. Olsavsky followed in Sunseri's footsteps in many ways. Sunseri was on the Steelers' injured reserve list for two seasons (1982-83), and then became an assistant coach at Pitt.

Olsavsky was at Pitt at the same time as Burt Grossman, Tom Ricketts, Mark Stepnoski, Craig Hayward, Tony Siragusa, and Randy Dixon. "We all went to the same bars and we all worked out hard in the weight room," Olsavsky said. "When you think about it, it's a pretty impressive list." Siragusa and Dixon both lined up for the Indianapolis Colts in the AFC title game at Three Rivers.

"I feel really blessed," Olsavsky said, "but I feel blessed to be an average guy with great football ability. I just enjoy myself and I have so much fun just wandering around doing the little things I do — walk my dogs and play in pick-up basketball games. I think that if I ever started thinking that I was more important than someone else then I would stop enjoying it."

Once at a Coaches Corner luncheon at the Allegheny Club, Olsavsky told the audience, "I had some good tools to work with. My parents are good people."

"Jerry Olsavsky has the heart of a champion."
— Tom Donahoe

During the 1996 NFL draft, Olsavsky signed a new contract with the Steelers as an unrestricted free agent, one of the few in that category to continue with the team. It was reportedly for $1.6 million over three years.

"Now I can fulfill a long-time dream and buy my own bar in Lawrenceville," Olsavsky said.

"Jerry Olsavsky has the heart of a champion," said Tom Donahoe. "He's proven that as a player. He's proven that through his rehabilitation. And it's certainly good to have him back on our team."

Olsavsky had more than a large heart going for him.

In truth, Olavsky was odd-shaped. Equipment manager Tony Parisi pointed out that it was difficult to outfit Olsavsky, one of his locker room favorites. "If his legs were in proportion to his upper trunk, he'd be 6-5 or 6-6," Parisi said of Olsavsky. "And he has long arms for a guy his size."

Parisi told Olsavsky he had ordered some tailor-made pants for him. "I've only been here for eight years," Olsavsky shouted in mock outrage, "It's about time you start taking care of me!"

George Gojkovich

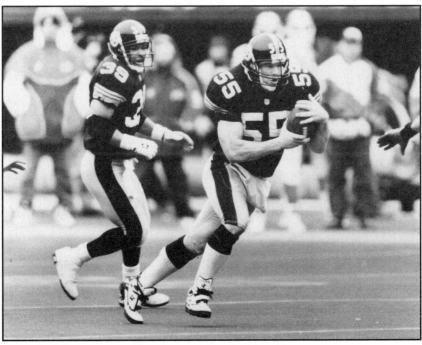

Inside linebacker Jerry Olsavsky runs with interception as teammate Darren Perry looks on in NFL action at Three Rivers Stadium.

Dermontti Dawson
A Kentucky thoroughbred

"Family is No. 1 with me."

The Appalachian Mountains cut a wide swath through Kentucky. There was a line in a 1988 novel called *The Bean Tree* by Barbara Kingsolver that said wherever one looks in Kentucky the view is limited by the hills, so some never look beyond. Others wonder about and dream about what might be on the other side of those hills.

It was more wide open where Dermontti Dawson grew up near Lexington, located in the north central part of Kentucky, in the heart of the bluegrass country. The grass really isn't blue, but in May its flowers give it a bluish tint. Spring water runs through the limestone deposits and feeds the grass and the horses, and is thought to give both its special strength. Horse farms abound there, and thoroughbreds romp in the pastures. As a three-year-old, one of them may even wear the winner's roses in the Kentucky Derby.

Dawson, the starting center for the Steelers in Super Bowl XXX and for the AFC in the Pro Bowl, grew up in Versailles, just west of Lexington along Route 32, on the way to Louisville on the western border. He grew up like few others in his neck of the woods. Dawson developed into a thoroughbred of a different sort.

Dawson's dreams were ambitious ones. He looked beyond those hills and mountain ranges. He wanted to be somebody special. As a young man, he wanted to be an Olympic athlete. He was well-bred by his parents, Robert and Bonnie Dawson, taught old-fashioned values and instilled with a great work ethic. This helped explain why he became one of the best and most cordial and good-humored professional athletes one can ever hope to meet. Dawson was a sportswriter's dream come true.

I had visited Lexington a few times in the '60s, back in my days on the American Basketball Association (ABA) beat when the Kentucky Colonels played a few games there. Lexington was basketball country as much as horse country. I had a chance to meet and interview the revered Adolph Rupp, who had coached the Kentucky Wildcats and established one of the nation's elite college basketball programs.

Dawson played a little basketball in his schoolboy days, and wasn't bad, but he was much better at football and track and field. He was a strongboy shot-put and discus state champion as a high school phenom, then a solid guard for Jerry Claiborne's football team at the nearby University of Kentucky, and he became a Steelers' center who could be mentioned in the same breath as Mike Webster and Ray Mansfield and Bill Walsh.

Pittsburgh was a city that could appreciate a thorougbred from Kentucky. Steelers founder Art Rooney had horse farms in Maryland, and won the money with which he bought an NFL franchise in 1933 on a big day of betting at Saratoga. Former Pirates' owner John Galbreath raised Kentucky Derby winners at his Darby Dan Farm near Columbus.

There were also lots of caves and coal mines in Kentucky and the Steelers scouting department mined a black and gold gem in Dawson, who was voted to his fourth consecutive Pro Bowl for his efforts during the Steelers' splendid 1995 season. Dawson had played in 104 consecutive games with 100 starts over the previous seven seasons. Dawson was the offensive captain and had started at center for the Steelers since the departure of Webster, a nine-time Pro Bowler, and was thought to be of the same substance as the blond farmboy from Tomahawk, Wisconsin. He was even bigger, 6-2, 286 pounds, hard as Kentucky limestone, and just as agile as Webster. He could pull out of the line and lead the end sweep.

Dawson loved Lexington as much as Rick Pitino, whose University of Kentucky basketball team won the 1996 NCAA title. Pitino turned down a long-term offer at $5 million a year to coach the NBA's New Jersey Nets to stay with his Wildcats in Lexington. Dawson built a home in Lexington in 1994 and planned to continue to live there. He came to Pittsburgh each year to play football.

"Football is a job. It pays the bills, and it's the best kind of job," Dawson said, while sitting across a desk from me at an interview room set up by the Steelers' public relations staff at Bonaventure Hall at St. Vincent College in Latrobe on the first day of the 1995 summer training camp. "Family is No. 1 with me. All those surveys point up the problems with families today, so many black families without fathers at home...I know the importance of growing up with an intact family.

"You can't separate the two. The only way to have a successful family is to be a husband and father first, and a football player second. You have to keep those two things totally separate. I don't care how bad a day I've had...I don't let bad practices or bad games affect me when I get home. We don't talk about football. I learn from it, but I don't dwell on it. Some don't know how to vent their anger. You don't want to do it at home."

Checking out his spartan surroundings at St. Vincent, Dawson drew a deep breath and sighed and smiled at the same time. "It's about to start again," he said. "I don't think about football too much when I'm home in the off-season. My attitude changes when I arrive here. Now this is my main business. I like to think of myself as a pro in that respect."

He was making more than $2 million a year, not bad for a center in the NFL or the NBA, because he was believed to be the best in the business. He had just turned 30 and was about to begin his eighth season with the Steelers. He had common sense and maturity beyond his years.

"I know what's expected of me. I have a year's work ahead of me. I'm looking forward to it."

"Everything we got, we had to work for."

Lexington, Kentucky was where it all began for Dermontti Farra Dawson ("I don't know where my mother came up with that one."). His roots run as deep as the underground springs which feed the bluegrass and ultimately those thoroughbreds in his native land. He was the oldest of four boys. His mother must have had a fondness for D-Day as Dermontti's brothers were named Demarcus, Desharon and DeArron.

"Lexington's not a huge town; it's grown through the years," said Dawson, describing his home area. "It's basically a small town, with horse farms, like Calumet and Keeneland. When you get a little older, you get to go to Churchill Downs in Louisville to see those horses race."

Louisville was the biggest city (340,000 population) in Kentucky and Lexington was second (190,000 population). The Dawsons lived in Versailles (pronounced Ver-sails), just 13 miles west of Lexington, like Coraopolis or Oakdale are to Pittsburgh.

In his early teens, Dawson had modest designs for his life. He wanted to be a woodworker.

"I took woodworking classes in junior high and won blue ribbons in state-wide competitions," recalled Dawson. "I made tables and lamps. They were a real source of pride. Four things I did won blue ribbons in one competition.

"My father, his name is Robert, worked at IBM and the Board of Education in Lexington. He went on to work in Versailles at United L-N Glass Company; they make windshields for Toyota vehicles. He heads up his division. My mother, Bonnie, is a nurse, also in Versailles. We've been very blessed. My parents always had jobs.

"I never needed or wanted anything I couldn't get. Maybe sometimes — that's just greed as a kid — not because I didn't have anything I really needed. Everything was provided. When I was young, I worked with my grandfather. He was my maternal grandfather. His name was Manlius Neal. He owned a motel, a hotel and liquor stores. I had an uncle, Porter Neal. I helped him build a liquor store. It was a brick building. I helped out doing anything I could do; I mixed cement and so forth. That's the way it was: if we needed extra money, there were usually jobs to do to get it. Everything we got, we had to work for.

"You were off school for the summer and we each had a chore list. We were expected to clean our rooms, to run the vacuum, to cut grass, to take trash out. We had anything we wanted, but at the same

In third grade

In high school

Dermontti Dawson poses with head coach Jerry Claiborne during Dermontti's freshman season at the University of Kentucky, and, below, with his family: his three brothers (left to right) DeArron, Deshawn and DeMarcus, his parents, Bonnie and Robert, and their foster child, Marc McIntyre.

time we learned that nothing's given to you for free. The times weren't as bad as they are now. Drugs weren't the big thing they are today. There weren't gangs like you have today. There were opportunities to get into trouble, but it wasn't as dangerous as it is today.

"There wasn't random killing or drive-by shootings in my community.

"My parents made the rules. I can hear them now: 'If you're with your friends and they do something wrong, just walk away,' they'd say. To this day, I can see where that sort of advice helps."

It reminded one of those NBA-sponsored TV commercials aimed at giving behavioral tips to young people who run into problems in school hallways or on the neighborhood streets and playgrounds, and featuring Patrick Ewing, Vinnie Baker, Grant Hill, Sean Elliott and David Robinson.

"When I'd see my friends doing something I knew wasn't right, I'd walk away," Dawson said. "It's paid off; it's paid off for me. I just chose not to go along with the gang. I lived on the west side of town. We had projects. Stuff happens. There was lots of stuff to get into. I worked hard at staying out of trouble.

"You have to have a lot of confidence in yourself. If you feel uncomfortable about doing a certain thing, then don't do it. Make your own decisions."

It helped, however, having parents setting strict standards and making sure they were obeyed.

"I don't care how old you get, you're always trying to please your mother," declared Dawson.

Now he was at the Steelers' training camp and he had to please Bill Cowher and his position coach, Kent Stephenson. At his first training camp, back in 1988, he failed to please Chuck Noll and Hal Hunter. Hunter was the offensive line coach and he thought Dawson was trying to get by on his size and strength, and wasn't picking up on the proper technique quickly enough. Hunter was critical of Dawson's approach.

Dawson has not gotten off to a bad start at training camp since then. He had learned his lesson.

"When I come to camp now, I'm totally business, but you also have to make camp fun," Dawson said. "If you don't make camp fun you'll go crazy. Training camp is the best and worst of the football business. There's a bonding that goes on. But you work hard. At my stage of the game, you want to make sure you're not losing a step.

"Besides the football, you're bonding with the guys, 24 hours a day. Once the season comes around, the married guys get back with their wives and kids. Then your responsibility is your wife and kids. You get into a different schedule.

"Training camp is a special time. Your only retreat is your room in the dorms. During the first two or three years, I had roommates. Now I like having my own room. I want things in a certain place. You get fussy as you get older. You don't want to bother anybody, and you don't want anybody bothering you. My room is on the first floor on the far side, the shady side by the cemetery. Seeing all those tombstones on the hill is an eerie sight. It's something you have to get used to. No, it doesn't keep me up at night. After two-a-days, nothing keeps me from sleeping when this head hits the pillow.

"The hardest part about camp is just coming here. After today, it will be camp as usual."

I requested Dawson for starters at the opening of the 1995 summer training camp. Pat Hanlon, the public relations director of the New York Giants, had previously worked in a similar position with the Steelers, and earlier as my assistant in the sports information department at Pitt. Hanlon was a big fan of Dawson. Dawson used to make a lot of public appearances in the community and Hanlon didn't have a more cooperative ambassador or better friend in the playing ranks.

I remembered how Hanlon thought the world of Dawson. He had been singled out to me as a good guy. I thought I'd pace myself before I took on the likes of Greg Lloyd and Kevin Greene, guys who liked giving writers a difficult time.

Dawson still thought he had it made. "There are a lot of people who'd come to work for us for nothing," he said. "Some guys get lucky here and stick with the Steelers. There are no guarantees. I brought along a hodgepodge of things, like a good book, to help pass the free time."

When Dawson made those appearances on behalf of the Steelers, he was often in the company of John Jackson, another offensive lineman. Dawson was a close friend of Jackson.

"We're always unknown, so you learn to live with that as a lineman," said Dawson. "The only true friend you have is another lineman."

Jackson remained one of Dawson's most devoted boosters. "He's the best," Jackson said. "They really worked with him. They really work with offensive linemen here to teach you your craft."

Listen to Tunch Ilkin talk about Dawson. Ilkin, a long-time Steelers' offensive lineman (1980-1992), was working for NBC-TV as an analyst during the 1995 season. He told Ed Bouchette of the *Pittsburgh Post-Gazette* of his high regard for Dawson.

Ilkin said that during the height of his athletic career, the two best centers in the NFL were Mike Webster and Dwight Stephenson of the Miami Dolphins, Webster because of his durability, size and strength and Stephenson because of his athleticism and speed. "Dermontti is a combination of both," said Ilkin. "Before Dermontti is through, I think he is definitely going to make an impact on that position as far as NFL history is concerned — if he stays healthy.

"He's a walking contradiction in a lot of ways," Ilkin said. "Here's this guy who's as big and strong as they come and he doesn't spend a lot of time in the weight room — not like we used to do when

Webby was here. He knocks people over easier than most and he's the first one to help them up; he's just a real nice guy.

"He takes tremendous pride in his work, but he never seems to get nervous or shook up or, if he makes a mistake, it's no big deal. He doesn't seem to get stressed out before games. He is the total antithesis of most offensive linemen.

"He's *such* a nice guy, such a humble guy," Ilkin continued. "He doesn't toot his own horn. He's good for the game, a great guy in the locker room. He's good for the team. He's one of the most likable guys I've met in my association with the Steelers over 16 years."

Endorsements don't come any better than that.

Dawson was the strong silent type, but he didn't need a big mouth to command Coach Bill Cowher's respect.

"I don't want to make a general statement that if you're not jumping up and down then maybe you should get out of the game," cautioned Cowher at one of his weekly press conferences. "Don't misinterpret me on that. Dermontti loves to play the game of football. You may not see it because he's not displaying it like some other people are, but he loves to play the game of football. He was the first guy in here. He loves meetings. He loves being around it. You don't have to display it in a manner that everyone can see it, but when you talk to people you can see it in their eyes. When you talk to people, you know whether or not they love their job. You work with people all the time, and you know whether or not they're coming in just to pick up their paycheck, or whether they're just doing enough to get by."

If you want noise from Dawson you have to catch him far from the football field when he's firing an AK-47, one of 45 or so military-type weapons he owns. He liked to go hunting with some of his teammates when he could get away. He also liked to go golfing. This is a man who walks softly and carries a big stick.

"My mother let us cook a lot."

Early in his pro career, Dawson drew some off-beat feature stories about his fondness for baking chocolate chip cookies. He became almost as famous as Amos for his moonlighting activity in the kitchen.

"It's true," said Dawson. "I do bake. I started at home. First cakes and brownies. But chocolate chip cookies are my specialty. I still bake, almost every night. And if I don't bake, I'll go out and buy them. I've got to stop it, though. I'll eat a dozen at a time.

"Sometimes my parents had to work and they left the cooking up to us. My grandmother, she was a cooker, too. I think I got it off my grandmother.

"Growing up, I was always a sweets lover. My parents bought me a cookbook to make little meals. So I guess that's where it started. My mother let us cook a lot. I just grew up doing it. I was always in home economics in junior high and high school. I was really into it."

He also learned how to sew, something he had in common with Steelers' defensive line coach John Mitchell.

Their parents thought it was important to make them self-reliant. Dawson became known as "The Cookie Monster," which made him shy away from talking too much about his hobby.

He quit bringing in chocolate chip cookies to the clubhouse after several newspaper articles called attention to it.

"I didn't want to be known as 'The Cookie Monster' anymore," he said. "One day I was walking in a shopping mall and a lady and her son came up to me and said, 'Oh, aren't you the football player who bakes cookies?'"

"My dreams were to go
to the Olympics."
— Dermontti Dawson

Dawson played sandlot ball as a kid, and tried football in ninth grade, but didn't get to play much. "I had no interest," he said. "I didn't like it. I wasn't playing. I said, 'This is not for me.' And I walked away from it."

When he was walking the halls at Bryan Station High School in Lexington, a 6-2, 220 pound sophomore, the school's football coach, Steve Parker, spotted him and wondered where he had come from.

"At first, I thought he was an adult visiting the school," recalled Parker. "He had the upper body of a professional wrestler and the legs of a sprinter.

"The first time I saw him it was like, 'Where have you been all my life?' He was walking the halls and I asked him, 'Son, what are you doing? Why aren't you playing football?' He said he was on the track team. I said, 'Why don't you come down and lift weights with us in our winter program?' And he did and the rest is history."

Dawson turned down an invitation to come out for the football team that year. He was happy to be the best discus and shot-put thrower in the state of Kentucky. He had won the county championship in both events as a freshman.

Some friends at school talked Dawson into going out for football in his junior year. Those friends, Cornell Burbage and Dawson's cousin, Marc Logan, all went to the University of Kentucky and played pro ball.

I spoke to Dawson about his high school days during Media Day at Sun Devil Stadium in Tempe, Arizona, just a few days before Super Bowl XXX.

"I didn't care too much about football," he said. "We played at home all the time. We used to play street football. We'd play tackle on the grass. I loved the contact, everything else, but I never did play as far as organized ball was concerned. I was having fun with it, but I didn't want to work at it.

"Track was my first love as far as sports went. I never was into baseball. I played one year of baseball, but it really didn't turn me on. I played basketball in the parks, but track was my very first love. My dreams were to go to the Olympics. I wanted to throw the javelin, too, but they didn't have that event in Kentucky high schools. Schools like Yale and Harvard expressed interest in me for track. I thought that's where my destiny was."

I told Dawson that Terry Bradshaw had been a national champion javelin thrower in high school. His strong right arm later propelled the Steelers to four Super Bowl championships.

"He kicked around at sports and they came easily to him, but he could never get serious about it," said Robert Dawson, his father.

Dermontti didn't give up track; he was a high school All-America in that sport, first in the state in both the discus and shot-put. "If football didn't go my way," Dawson said, "I had a few scholarship offers for track."

As a senior, Dawson placed first in the state in discus (163-3) and shot-put (56-9). He could run the 40 in 4.7 seconds. "I think my speed is my greatest strength," he said.

Whatever he did, Dawson kept smiling through his braces. "He's always smiling," said Parker. "He's just a super person."

Dawson made all-state in football, too, and signed with UK, where he was red-shirted his first season. He held three UK records in weight-lifting: squats (750 pounds), bench press (415), cleans (425) and total lifts (1,590). He was the team's quickest interior lineman (4.7 in 40).

During the pre-Super Bowl XXX interview session, a sportswriter wanted to know why Dawson was perspiring.

"I'm just one of those guys who sweats a lot," he said.

He didn't sweat the small stuff, however. Of his late start in football, Dawson said, "I think that's the reason I love the game so much. It's never been life and death to me. It's a business in a sense, but I also don't get stressed out over it. It's basically a game. But I don't let it consume me."

"Hard work breeds good luck."
— Jerry Claiborne

Dawson played under Jerry Claiborne at Kentucky. "He's from the old school," Dawson said. "If you play football for him, you work hard. Very hard."

Claiborne's message to his football players was a simple one: "Hard work breeds good luck." Dawson wore No. 57 with pride for the Wildcats.

"He's a really nice guy, really easy to talk to," said Jake Hallom, offensive line coach at Kentucky, when the Steelers selected Dawson on the second round in 1988. "He's full of life. Always smiling. Courteous. He's got more personality plusses than any kid I know. You'll love him."

His nickname at UK was Dirty D. How did he come by that nickname? "Sometimes they say I got over-aggressive," said Dawson. In short, he came by it honestly.

He admitted he had a different personality when he was playing football from the one he displayed away from the field.

"I was raised at home to be a good person, but when I'm playing ball I'm like a different person," he said. "I have to be." He sounded like Greg Lloyd when he said that.

"I was taught to say all the right things: 'Yes, sir. No, sir.' I didn't curse. I was a happy-go-lucky guy. Sunshine personality. That was my resume."

He takes a different approach to playing golf, for instance. He learned to play golf from his father. He has broken 80. His kid brother Demarcus won a golf championship at Tennessee State in 1987. He had a lot of fun whenever he played basketball with the Steelers' touring team in the off-season. He was a good athlete. He could dunk a basketball when he was in school. He and first-year teammate Tom Newberry went hunting together during the 1995 season and had a great time.

Going into his senior season at the University of Kentucky, he wasn't sure he could make the pros. He pointed out that only one percent of college football players make it in the pros. He graduated with a degree in kinesiology and health promotions. He had a somewhat erratic college career, so he didn't get a lot of pre-season All-America recognition before his final year. He did get some good notices close to home.

John Clay of the *Lexington Herald-Leader* wrote:

"There's never been a stronger player in the history of Kentucky football."

"Dermontti was taught to respect others and to have good manners."
— Mrs. Bonnie Dawson

His mother, Bonnie Dawson, wrote me a letter about her son:

"Dermontti was the oldest of our four sons. On my side of the family, he was the first grandchild. His dad was one of 13 children and Dermontti was the first grandchild of many grandchildren. Dermontti was born on June 17, 1966 and he weighed 8 lbs. 13 oz.

97

"Throughout his toddler's days, he had to have shoes every three months and his clothes sizes were always two sizes bigger — age wise — than he was.

"He was a spoiled baby. Montti was my baby for four years before his first brother was born. When his brother was born, Montti loved him. He would change his diapers and clothes whenever he could to help me out. They slept together and were good babies throughout. Even now they are good friends.

"When Montti went to elementary school, he was a good child and did his work. He was very shy. He didn't stand out within his class. In middle school (7th to 9th grades) he did play softball and he was a pitcher. His coach wanted him to keep playing, but he played only one year. He played softball because his cousin played. He also played football in middle school one year because one of his buddies encouraged him to try out. The year he played (1979) his team won the district tournament.

"In high school, he was encouraged to come out for wrestling in tenth grade.

"He had two friends (Marc Logan, who was playing for the Washington Redskins and Cornell Burbage, a former Dallas Cowboy) who encouraged him to play football and go out for the track team. Montti excelled in both sports. Mom just thought he was playing sports for the fun of it until the University of Kentucky contacted him for a possible scholarship.

"He was red-shirted his freshman year, when he devoted himself to weightlifting. He excelled in that and broke records in that respect. They used to call him 'Dirty D.'

"While at UK, he played center as a backup and offensive guard. He did well at both positions. He made the all-star team his senior year and played in the Blue-Gray Bowl. Chuck Noll was the coach and Montti played center throughout the whole game. This was the beginning of Montti's association with the Steelers and how he came to be selected by them. Montti was drafted in the 2nd round in 1988 as an offensive guard and center.

"From a mother's perspective, Dermontti was taught in his early years to respect others and to have good manners. Montti has maintained this. He was encouraged to be a good role model for his brothers (Demarcus, 26; Desharon, 20, and DeArron, 19) which he has done. He was taught how to cook, to wash and to clean his room. He had to be encouraged to be a good student. He was also spanked with love as a child.

"Mom believed in discipline, which is lacking in a lot of kids today. I had to be the disciplinary person and believed that kids should be able to take care of themselves because Mom and Dad had to work.

Dermontti Dawson and his wife, Regina, at their in-season home in Gibsonia. Both are graduates of the University of Kentucky, Regina with a marketing degree.

Pro-Bowl center Dermontti Dawson (63) works in tandem with rookie guard Brenden Stai to protect quarterback Neil O'Donnell.

"Education has been stressed in our family and I made sure they went to school. His Dad was a golfer, so he taught Montti how to play. So Montti, Demarcus and Dad have been on golfing outings to Hilton Head and other places. Dad played basketball and football, and he was quite good."

"He has the right attitude to be a great football player."
— Mike Webster

Dermontti Dawson had a difficult time establishing himself in his first year with the Steelers. He was drafted as a guard. The Steelers selected Chuck Lanza of Notre Dame on the third round as a center candidate in the same class.

As a rookie, Dawson made five starts at guard alongside Mike Webster. Dawson got his first start replacing John Rienstra at guard when Rienstra broke his leg in 1988 during a 17-12 loss to the Bengals at Three Rivers Stadium.

The Steelers went through a wretched 5-11 season and Webster went to Kansas City as an assistant coach after the season. Noll did not like what he saw of Lanza and shifted Dawson to play the center position in the wake of Webster's departure.

"I came in one day and they told me they wanted me to start taking snaps and playing center," said Dawson.

Dawson had not played center since his sophomore year in college, except for the Blue-Gray Game. With the Steelers, he never got comfortable or competent at snapping for placement kicks and occasionally — even in the Super Bowl — had problems snapping the ball when the quarterback was in the shotgun formation.

In his first start at center, his first snap in the shotgun formation, he snapped the ball over quarterback Bubby Brister's head.

Playing center, Dawson had a tough act to follow. Webster became eligible for the Hall of Fame in 1996, and his fans were disappointed that he didn't draw enough votes when the writers met at Super Bowl XXX for their annual selection meeting. Neither Webster nor Lynn Swann nor L.C. Greenwood were voted in, a shutout for the Steelers. Someday both Webster and Dawson should be inducted into the Canton showcase.

Both were the best of their respective eras.

At Super Bowl XXX late-night media sessions, seven current players were regarded as virtual locks for eventual Hall of Fame induction: Dan Marino, Jerry Rice, Ronnie Lott, John Elway, Reggie White, Barry Sanders and Bruce Smith. In time, Dawson should draw support to be considered in that same category.

Webster played 15 seasons and 220 games for the Steelers, both team records. He played in nine Pro Bowls, tied for the league record.

He wore four Super Bowl rings and anchored the Steelers' offensive line. He also set the standards for weightlifting and the training regimen for many of the Steelers of the '70s and '80s.

"Those are going to be big shoes to fill," Dawson said when he attempted to replace Webster. "He was All-Pro nine years. He was a player-coach because he knew it so well. He made all the calls. He was a big influence and a big part of the team. I consider him a legend."

Webster shared the job with Ray Mansfield his first two seasons, starting only one game. Mansfield knew that Webster was going to oust him from his job.

Similarly, Webster recognized real early that Dawson would be a strong performer. Webster told Dawson it would take time for him to develop his game. "He gave me some tips to speed up the process," Dawson said. "He left a great impression on me. He showed how perseverance and dedication are the keys to success. He was like a father figure to me his last year."

A center lines up with the nose guard three inches away, about to smash him as soon as his wrist quivers to make the snap. The center is the quarterback of the offensive line, calling out signals along the line. Some observers felt blacks couldn't play center. It was too cerebral a challenge, they thought, the same sort of ignorance that deterred many pro and college coaches from having a black at quarterback.

Until Dwight Stephenson came along with the Dolphins in 1980, there was never a great black center in the NFL. Ray Donaldson of Indianapolis also became a good one. There were still not many black centers. The best athletes among the linemen usually don't play center in college.

Dawson had his critics on the coaching staff of the Steelers. Hunter and Ron Blackledge didn't boost him in the early going.

"Dirt" is what Hal Hunter called him, shortening his nickname. They had their disagreements. Hunter didn't think Dawson had the proper attitude or approach to his assignment.

Webster used to lead the linemen when they were running 350s, around the sideline of the field. Dawson was bringing up the rear; he hated them.

"I didn't think Dermontti worked hard enough on fundamentals when he first came to camp," said Hunter. "He wanted to get by on pure size and strength. Everybody's big and fast and strong in this league."

Blackledge had no one in particular in mind when he said: "You can't replace Mike Webster. It's impossible."

As it turned out, Dawson did replace Webster and the Steelers never missed a beat. Even his most fervent fans have to admit that Webster wasn't at his best at the end of his stay with the Steelers.

"Everybody I talked to said, 'You're replacing a legend, you're replacing a legend.' I know that. But as long as I give it my all, give it my best, that's all I can do," Dawson said in the early going.

"It's scary," he said of following Webster. "It's a case of everybody having high expectations for you."

Noll assessed Dawson this way: "His quickness, his speed and strength, his ability to break down the defense, his ability to strike. He can be a very efficient player with great physical tools." The faint praise was damning to Dawson.

Webster liked what he saw. No one endorsed Dawson as strongly as Webster, which had to be reassuring. "The kid's amazing," Webster said. "He's so big and strong, yet he has quick feet. He has the tools and the right attitude to be a great football player."

Mansfield made 182 consecutive starts, Webster 177 in a row, and Dawson 119 going into the 1996 season. Dawson fit nicely into the Steelers' ranks of ironmen.

After he had settled into a starting position, he talked about the challenge.

"That was a question when I started here — taking over Mike's spot. I had big shoes to fill and everyone was wondering whether I could do that. I think right now I'm starting to come into my own. I can't be another Mike Webster. I can try to be another me. I can try and set the standard for me. Everybody has their own style."

There were plays in the Steelers' playbook that called for Dawson to pull like a guard and lead sweeps. It's an impossibility for most squat centers who don't have Dawson's mobility or versatility.

"Dermontti is low-key, doesn't say much, doesn't seek the spotlight and stays in the background," said Tom Donahoe. "But we do things with him that other teams simply cannot do with their centers."

"Dermontti is the real deal."
— Mike Tomczak

Dawson was well rewarded for his overall excellence. He was making a reported $2 million plus a year through the 1997 season. His contract was negotiated by Ralph Cindrich, an attorney-agent from Mt. Lebanon. Dawson received a $1.885 million signing bonus and a new three-year contract worth $1.84 million annually when his contract was extended. He would have become a free agent in 1995.

"I remember one year Bubby signed for $1.2 million. I ran home and told my wife, 'Wow! Can you believe that? Can you imagine making that much money? Now look at me. Is it any wonder I feel blessed?"

He only had to consider what happened to some of the people who had played alongside him on the Steelers' offensive line. The guards included John Rienstra, Terry Long and Carlton Hasselrig, all celebrated head cases whose careers were cut short simply because they could not handle the demands of the profession. Dawson was a good friend of Hasselrig, who went from being one of the league's great success stories to one of its great tragedies.

Dawson demonstrated in every way that he had what it took to stay the course.

Rick Gosselin of *The Dallas Morning News*, one of the league's most respected reporters, wrote of Dawson: "He's the best center in the game. He's agile enough to get out on the middle linebacker and also can seal the corner on sweeps. In a league where few centers even attempt pulling, Dawson is the best. He can lay his 288 pounds on any member of the Dallas front seven on any given day."

After Dawson was voted to a fourth consecutive Pro Bowl, teammate Newberry noted, "He'll be in the Pro Bowl however many more years he wants to play."

"Dermontti is the real deal," said Mike Tomczak, one of the Steelers' quarterbacks.

Dawson doesn't have a hard time keeping his feet planted firmly on the ground. His wife comes from Lexington, so she knows where they came from. Regina was his high school sweetheart. They had two children, a 4-year-old Brandon Neal and a one-year-old daughter Briana.

"His idea of a fun time is to go home and make chocolate chip cookies and drink iced tea," said offensive line coach Kent Stephenson.

He also liked to drink Pepsi and Mountain Dew and other kick-start sodas. Bring on the caffeine. Bring on new challenges.

During one of our interviews at mid-season, 1995, Dawson spoke about some of his goals.

"The ultimate goal is to get to the Super Bowl," he said. "Some of my friends have Super Bowl rings, so I'd like to be in that number, too. The Pro Bowl was my ultimate goal. A guy can go his whole career and not make the Pro Bowl. And I've been there a few times. But the Super Bowl is my ultimate team goal. That one I can't do by myself. I'm just trying to play one year at a time and trying to play for as long as I can. The more I play this game the more I enjoy it"

Pittsburgh Steelers

Dermontti Dawson (63) discusses line strategy during 1993 season with close friend Carlton Hasselrig (77) and Leon Searcy (72).

Carnell Lake
Midland blood runs deep

"There's a quality of players here.
How are you off the field?"

This is a history lesson for Carnell Lake and his family and fans so they can better appreciate where he comes from and why he was such an attractive success story: Three Rivers Stadium sits on the same site where Exposition Park once stood when Steelers' founder Art Rooney was a boy, and the neighborhood was known as Old Allegheny. It was a city unto itself, separate from Pittsburgh. There is a history here, for sure. This is at the confluence of the Allegheny River and the Monongahela River and the beginning of the Ohio River. They are the reasons there was a Pittsburgh in the first place.

The Ohio River runs northwest for a while and then makes a U-turn and heads south through Ohio and West Virginia. It passes through many milltowns, once hard-working prosperous communities when steel-making and all its associated businesses flourished, when Pittsburgh was honestly known as The Steel City, from whence the Steelers drew their nickname. I grew up two blocks from the Monongahela and learned an early respect for its monstrous power — a military airplane once disappeared in its waters when I was a youngster and was never found — and know firsthand how the rivers run through us.

The Ohio River runs through some milltowns that have produced some of the finest athletes in America. Mention these milltowns and the names of great ballplayers and coaches come quickly to mind. There's Ambridge, Aliquippa, Hopewell, Freedom, Rochester, Monaca. Pistol Pete Maravich and Tony Dorsett were born in the same hospital in Aliquippa, only a few years apart. Then come Beaver Falls, Beaver and Midland. Joe Namath and Joe Walton. Mike Ditka and Babe Parilli. Jim Mutscheller and John Michelosen. Doc Medich and Tito Francona. Mickey and Brad Davis. Dennis Wuycik and Dick DeVenzio. And so many more came from this area. As it heads south through Ohio and spills into West Virginia on its way to the mighty Mississippi, it runs through towns like East Liverpool, Weirton, Steubenville, Tiltonsville, Martins Ferry, Bridgeport and Wheeling. Bill Mazeroski, John Havlicek, Bill Jobko, Alex and Lou Groza, Joe and Phil Niekro were all Ohio Valley boys. One story after another, so many high school, college and pro stars came out of these communities to make their mark. Even Henry Mancini, Dean Martin and Jimmy "The Greek" Snyder grew up in these river towns.

Midland is a magic name, for instance, especially for any sports fans from western Pennsylvania over 45 years of age. The Midland High School basketball team won the 1965 WPIAL boys basketball title, and was one of the best-remembered schoolboy basketball teams in Western Pennsylvania history. Hank Kuzma was the coach, and its star players were Simmie Hill and Norm Van Lier — who both went on to play pro ball — and Ron Brown and Brent Lake.

Before Brent Lake, there were Eugene Lake and Herb Lake. When Midland made its mark as one of the schoolboy basketball powers in Pennsylvania, there always seemed to be a Lake in the lineup.

Eugene Lake was the father of Carnell Lake. Brent and Herb were Carnell's uncles. And those were only the beginning of the links that have tied Carnell Lake to Pittsburgh and Western Pennsylvania and the Steelers and their rich sports tradition.

Gene Lake was graduated from Midland High School in 1960.

"My father enlisted in the Navy, and then he got a scholarship to the University of Utah. After graduation, he moved to Los Angeles. I was seven then, and I used to come back to this area every summer and stay with my grandmother.

"When I was little, my dad used to always tell me about Midland. He used to say that I could catch fish as big as I was if I went fishing down by the Ohio River."

Midland, like so many of the milltowns along the rivers, was a ghost of its old self by the time Lake came back to play pro football. Many of the mills were closed. Many of the businesses were boarded up on its main streets.

"It hurts me to see Midland now," said Lake. "It's not the same. But no matter where you are, the kids shouldn't suffer because the town is."

"You have to consider yourself a Steeler."
— Carnell Lake

Gene Lake also played football at Midland, and he played basketball at the University of Utah, and that is where he met and befriended Roy Jefferson. It is also where Gene met his future wife, Ingrid, who would become Carnell's mother.

Jefferson would go on to become an outstanding receiver for the Pittsburgh Steelers. He was probably the best player on the team when Chuck Noll became its coach in 1969, but he was constantly challenging Noll's authority, undermining his rule with the rest of the players. So Noll got rid of Jefferson, dealing him to the Washington Redskins where he starred.

When Carnell Lake was baptized at the Trinity Baptist Church in Los Angeles, his godfather was Roy Jefferson. Later on, it was

Jefferson who first introduced the young Lake to Joe Greene when he was the greatest player on the Pittsburgh Steelers' roster. Lake even had boyhood links with Lynn Swann, the Steelers' great receiver of the '70s. Lake lived in the same California community as Swann. "There are so many things like that," said Lake. "When I look back on it, I don't want to say I was destined to become a Steeler, but there were some strong early signs."

From his father, Lake drew the Midland blood that runs deep in his well-muscled body, one of the most striking figures since another defensive back named Mel Blount rode one of his horses off into the sunset. From his maternal grandmother, who was Italian, he drew his light brown complexion and his middle name — Carnell Augustino Lake — and from his mother, a school teacher, he drew his class and discipline and refinement. He may have been the classiest occupant of the Steelers' locker room during the 1994 and 1995 seasons. As disruptive as his godfather was in the Steelers ranks — I had interviewed Jefferson a few times from 1965-69, and he was both charming and a challenge — Lake is looked upon as a positive leader, one of the most respected and stabilizing influences in the organization. In 1995, Lake was also the best paid player on the team — making $3.7 million, including his signing bonus. That was more than the entire starting offensive or defensive units made during the '70s when the Steelers were acknowledged as the NFL's Team of the Decade.

He demonstrated what a team player he was when he agreed to switch from strong safety, where he had been a Pro Bowl performer, to cornerback when a desperate need developed there early in the 1995 season. He still made the Pro Bowl, and he was picked by Bob Labriola of *Steelers Digest* as the team's most valuable player.

Being a Steeler meant something special to Lake. He had grown up with a healthy respect for the Steelers — his father's family have always been big fans — and the mix of his heritage helped him appreciate his good fortune.

"Pittsburgh is a town that's used to having good football teams," said Lake. "These fans have tasted the Super Bowl before. Anything short of the Super Bowl is a good season (in their view), not a great season."

Club owner Dan Rooney grew up with the Steelers, and inherited an outlook and perception for the business and its people from his father, the team's legendary leader. He believed the Steelers were somehow special, that they were different from most teams in the NFL in the way they went about things, and Lake went along with the program. Asked what it meant to be a Steeler, Lake put it this way:

"You're a hard worker and you're not going to embarrass the organization or the city. Your mindset is to excel at football and not just to be compensated. There's more than performance. There's a certain quality of the players here. How are you off the field?

"In order to be considered a Steeler, there has to be an investment of time. There's an attitude that goes along with it: a hard,

106

grid and Charles Fields

With father, Eugene Lake, at high school graduation.

In UCLA days

Monica and Carnell Lake in dating days.

Stepfather Charles Fields and Carnell's mother flank him on UCLA graduation day.

gutsy, hustling player who'll always give it his all. There's not a lot of flash in Pittsburgh. It's definitely not a Hollywood town. It's always been a blue collar town but it's been changing toward a white collar town. You have to be able to fit in and communicate with both constituents.

"It has to get into your blood first. You have to consider yourself a Steeler."

"I'd never been near anybody as big as Joe Greene in my life."
— Carnell Lake

Carnell Lake can trace his earliest interest in sports to the Steelers. "I watched the Steelers from the beginning," he recalled, "because my godfather, Roy Jefferson, played for them. My dad and he went to college together at the University of Utah. My dad played basketball there. They both had families when they were in college, and they'd get together with their wives and kids."

As a baby, Carnell made an immediate impression on Jefferson. "He called me 'Screamin' Sam.' I'm told I'd just holler all day," said Lake. "My family moved from Salt Lake City in 1974 to the Los Angeles area.

"In 1975, Roy drove out to L.A. and picked up my brother and me. We were going to Virginia, where he was living at the time, outside of Washington D.C. He drove through Texas. He said, 'I have to stop at my friend's home.' I remember he rang the door bell, and he had me open the door...I was eight at the time. The man who opened the door was Mean Joe Greene.

"My dad is 6-3, but I'd never been near anybody as big as Joe Greene in my life. But he was a nice guy."

Jefferson and Greene had been teammates with the Steelers in 1969, Greene's rookie season and Jefferson's fifth and final season with the Steelers.

"The next time I saw Mean Joe was at the scouting combine in Indianapolis during my senior year at UCLA," Carnell continued. "He was a coach with the Steelers at the time. I said to him, 'I don't know if you remember me or not, but Roy Jefferson brought me over to your home in Texas when I was a little kid.' He said he remembered."

Through the years, Lake said Jefferson kept in touch. "He would call every now and then," said Lake. "I was too young for some things. He had a football camp and he'd send for my brother. My brother Desmond was six years older. He'd go to the camp in northern California.

"I played Pop Warner football. My first number was 88 — Lynn Swann's number. Later on, I was No. 12. That was Terry Bradshaw's number. We wore black jerseys, black helmets and gold pants with a black stripe. I knew a lot about the Steelers. Little kids are very aware of that stuff.

"If you go to elementary schools, and ask first, second and third graders, 'Who's your favorite player?' they will surprise you by how many of the guys they know on our team, and who they like the best.

"I was not old enough to get caught up in Steelers fever when they were winning Super Bowls. I was just old enough to know how good they were. I was lucky enough to be around with two of them and then my father being from here."

As a youngster, Lake was taken by his father from his home in Inglewood, just outside of Los Angeles, to western Pennsylvania during the summer to visit family in Midland, about 40 miles west of Pittsburgh. As a child, he stayed at his grandmother's home in Midland. He also remembered visiting relatives in Slippery Rock.

His parents divorced and his mother remarried and the family moved to Culver City, the home of MGM Studios and Larimar Television, just minutes on bicycle from the Pacific Ocean. Lake went to high school in Culver City. It wasn't Hollywood, either, but Lake liked the glitz and flash he found there.

"My mother remarried when I was 12 years old and in sixth grade. Everyone thought my step-father, Charles Fields, was Lynn Swann's father. He looked like Lynn Swann.

"My real father lived in California to make sure we had a father figure. We had a close relationship with our dad."

Carnell's brother, Desmond, played football at the University of Utah, his parents' alma mater. Carnell would end up at UCLA, where he was an honorable mention All-America.

He remembered the first time he saw Lynn Swann, one of the Steelers' Super Bowl heroes. Swann had played his college ball at USC, one of UCLA's biggest rivals. "Lynn's parents lived in Foster City; he lived in the same complex as we did," Lake recalled.

Lake had an opportunity to meet and become friends of Swann when he came to Pittsburgh to play for the Steelers. Swann still resided in Sewickley, a suburb to the north of Pittsburgh, and had an office in Downtown Pittsburgh. He visited the Steelers' complex on occasion.

Lake was a second round draft choice of the Steelers in 1989. They had two first round selections that year, and they took running back Tim Worley and offensive lineman Tom Ricketts. Both proved to be bad picks. Lake was a starter from the first game and was named the team's outstanding rookie.

"When I came here there was not a lot of fanfare for me, not a whole lot of pressure," said Lake. "From the start, I liked being here. All the pictures on the walls and the memorabilia made sense to me because it was all so familiar. I would just walk around and marvel at the trophies."

"You can tell in a minute
what a classy guy he is."
— Bill Priatko

Carnell Lake was the last veteran to report to camp for the Steelers in the summer of 1995. He had been a holdout for a big contract. On his first day in camp, August 16, 1995, he looked in better shape than just about anybody who had been there.

He was walking from the dormitory to the dining hall following his first practice when he spotted me talking to Myrd Milowicki, a woman from nearby Greensburg who had been coming to the team's daily practices for the past 25 years.

Players like Lake knew Myrd well and liked her a great deal. She was a special fan. She was old enough to be their mother and found the camp a delightful break from her housekeeping. She had a warm relationship with many of the team's players, had them to her home for dinner and picnics. Rocky Bleier once lent her money to go to the Super Bowl. She attended Lynn Swann's wedding in California.

Myrd called out to Carnell and he looked up our way on the nearby slope. When he saw me, he said, 'Jim, I haven't forgotten you. I know you wanted to talk to me, and I said I would. But I didn't want to do anything until I got my contract straightened away. We can do something soon. I just didn't want you to think I'd forgotten you."

Lake was thoughtful like that. That's what I liked about Lake. He was always easy to approach and talk to, and he was a man of his word. There was always a gleam about his bright eyes and bald head, and he looked people in the eye when he spoke to them .

Two special friends of mine, Bill Priatko and his neighbor, Rudy Celigoi, both high school athletic directors and former football players from North Braddock, were with me that day at the Steelers' training camp. They had accompanied me to the Pro Football Hall of Fame induction ceremonies the previous summer when Tony Dorsett was among the honorees.

I introduced Lake to Priatko, who had played at Pitt and for a year with the Steelers, Browns and Packers and was an active member of the NFL Alumni, and Celigoi, who had played college ball at Rutgers. Lake could not have been nicer. He talked to them in an enthusiastic and genuine manner. When he left, Lake had made a most positive impression on both of them. Lake is like that. He was the Steelers' best goodwill ambassador. "You can tell in a minute what a classy guy he is," said Priatko.

I wondered how Lake felt that day. How did he feel about the new contract he had signed? I could not comprehend how he could deal with his newfound wealth.

He would be the best paid player on the team that season. The $3.7 million for the year, including bonus, compared to Rod Woodson's

As first grader

Carnell Lake at age 9

Pop Warner days in 1976

As middle school student

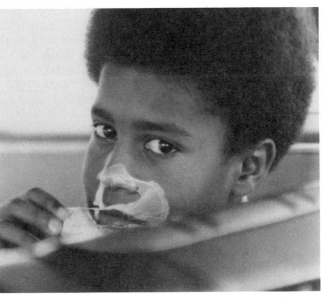
Blowing bubbles can be sticky situation for 9-year-old.

$3.1 million and Neil O'Donnell's $ 2.4 million. His contract, calling for $9.2 million over a four-year period, would average $2.3 million. "He was the third highest paid safety in pro football. He received a $2 million signing bonus, the second-highest in team history after Woodson's $2.8 million roster bonus in 1993. Lake would earn annual salaries of $1.7 million, $ 1.9 million, $ 1.9 million and $1.7 million. What do you do with that kind of money? The Steelers had designated him as their franchise player and did not want to lose him.

"I really wanted to stay here," he said. "I feel I've invested a lot of time and energy into this team. This shows their commitment to keep the team at a high level. And it shows their belief in me. The No. 1 goal would be to finish my career as a Steeler."

"He's very committed."
— Ingrid Fields,
Lake's mother

Lake liked to talk to school kids, and made frequent visits to Pittsburgh area schools. "He's very committed," said his mother, a school teacher. "He came and talked to my class when he was home for a visit and his message was 'Preparation Is The Key.' I think he keeps that thought in the back of his mind."

He was raised in a one-parent home for a spell, but he was quick to add that his father remained involved in his upbringing. Gene Lake worked for Delta Airlines at LA International Airport. No one was happier when the Steelers selected him in the 1989 college draft. "I think my father almost jumped through the roof when he heard I had been drafted by the Steelers," said Lake.

His mother remembered that Carnell had difficulties with his academic responsibilities when he first enrolled at UCLA. The lessons he learned from that experience make him even more effective when talking to youngsters because he can appreciate how there are other attractions, or distractions, competing for their attention.

Early on, Lake nearly dropped out of UCLA because of bad grades. He moved back home with his mother and stepfather, Ingrid and Charles Fields, because the dormitories had become too noisy, so he could study properly. He changed his attitude and his approach — school became more important than football — and he finished up as an Academic All-America. He was in the same class at UCLA as Troy Aikman, and Lake liked sacking him in practice, blitzing from his linebacker position.

Lake was a standup guy in many ways. He represented his team in the Steelers Caring Program.

He was involved with school visits and in helping people with special health insurance needs through a matching contribution effort in partnership with Blue Cross and Blue Shield.

"There are a lot of people not as fortunate as I am," he said, "and if I can help, it just makes me feel a lot better."

The Steelers' publicity office pointed out that Lake established a scholarship ($1,500 annually) at his high school.

Lake went back to UCLA in the off-season while he was playing pro ball to get a degree in political science. He took a class at UCLA in jurisprudence and this piqued an interest in going to law school someday.

Lake has often talked about going to law school, following in the footseps of Dwayne Woodruff, a defensive back for the Steelers during Lake's first two seasons with the team. Woodruff went to Duquesne University's Law School and has been working at a Pittsburgh law firm since he retired from the Steelers.

"Dwayne is an inspiration," said Lake. "I didn't know he was a lawyer when I got here. So I know it can be done. It's something I think I can do."

"He'll sacrifice anything for the team."
— Rod Woodson

Carnell Lake was five years old when Franco Harris made the "Immaculate Reception." That helps put things in their proper perspective. Lake had been in Pittsburgh long enough, however, to know and appreciate the team's history and the expectations of the long-time fans.

"Now that I'm in this league and know how hard it is to be at your best for so long, it's amazing how much talent they had on those Super Bowl teams," allowed Lake. "Those guys set the standards here and gave the fans high expectations every year. I'm still respectful when those guys come around the locker room, or when I am involved with them at banquets or promotional programs. Every time I get a chance to talk to them, I'm always asking them questions."

I shared some stories with Lake about Mel Blount, the Hall of Fame cornerback of the Steelers, who was one of my personal favorites when I was covering the team on a daily basis for *The Pittsburgh Press* from 1979 to 1983.

"We still talk about him," said Lake. "We say, 'How could he have been a cornerback?' He looks like an outside linebacker to this day. He'd still be the prototype cornerback."

Then again, some of Lake's coaches can't get over him, either, and what a big contribution he has made to the team's success ever since Bill Cowher succeeded Chuck Noll as the head coach.

When Lake was playing strong safety at the outset of the 1995 season, Cowher said of him: "Carnell is such a valuable player on our football team. He plays like a safety on first and second down and can come up and play bump coverage (like a corner) on third down. He just never comes off the field."

That knowledge might have prompted Cowher to consider switching Lake from safety to corner when the need arose.

Rod Woodson, who got hurt in the season opener and was not able to return until the Super Bowl, was a big booster: "Carnell is such a great athlete," Woodson said. "I was a little surprised the coaches took so long to move him to corner. Carnell could have said no. He would have said he wasn't comfortable at corner and no one would've blinked. But that's not him. He'll sacrifice anything for the team."

A sportswriter from Phoenix suggested at Super Bowl XXX that Lake at least deserved a volunteer-of-the-year award.

Dick LeBeau, the defensive coordinator of the Steelers during the 1995 season, had been responsible for the defensive backs during Cowher's first three seasons on the job.

"Nothing that Carnell Lake does athletically would surprise me," said LeBeau, an outstanding defensive back for the Detroit Lions in the 1960s when they had one of the best teams in the National Football League. "He and Woodson are two of the finest athletic backs I've seen. We knew that Carnell could cover, and we knew athletically he could do it. But he'd always been in the middle. And even when we played him in the extra-back situations, with Rod in one slot and Carnell in the other, he was still in the middle of the field. Until he did it, you had to be guardedly optimistic. But I knew he had the athletic ability.

"I really believe Carnell would line up with any group of athletes, any all-star team you would like to select, and play well and hold his own. He runs like a defensive back and supports like a linebacker. He's a 200-pound man with the speed of a 170-pound man, which is a rare combination.

"I'm sure he's the first guy who ever, ever played linebacker in college that went on to play cornerback. And not just half a game...and play it well."

After cornerbacks Rod Woodson and Deon Figures were lost to injury, and Alvoid Mays wasn't always up to the task, Tim Lewis, the Steelers' first-year defensive secondary coach, asked Lake to consider moving from safety to corner, a position that demands far greater coverage skills, with a much higher risk factor of being burned by a big play.

On January 12, 1996, before the Steelers' AFC title game with the Indianapolis Colts, Lake talked about his initial reaction to a change of position in the Steelers' secondary.

"I said I would do it if it helped the team," said Lake. "Coach Lewis said, 'Hold on, let me get Coach Cowher on the phone.' It only took about five minutes. The following day, I came in early to get a jump on the transition.

"I didn't think they were serious at first. It was difficult, at first, and it was always a challenge, but I think it will be a benefit to me in the long run. It was the biggest growing year of my career. I learned so much this year. If I don't get hurt, doing this will add to my career."

Carnell Lake and wife Monica with their daughter, Sienna.

Carnell Lake calls out assignments while playing both cornerback and strong safety during 1994 and 1995 seasons.

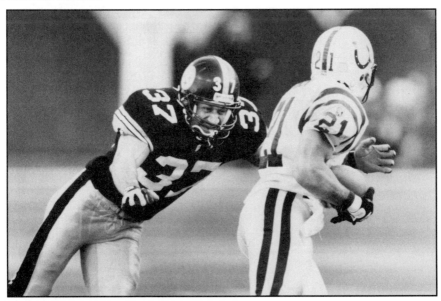

Lake had been critical of some of the Steelers after the Steelers got off to a 3-4 start. "I'm worried about our focus; I'm worried about our desire," Lake said back in October. "When you start losing some games you should win, it makes you wonder where our head is, because right now the only thing that's stopping us is us, and it's all in our head. When we change our mental attitude, that's when we'll start changing outcomes."

Pittsburgh won 10 of 11 games, including two playoff contests, after that setback to Cincinnati. Lake was burned by the Bengals early — he was easy pickin's for Cincy's Carl Pickens — but survived to get more comfortable at that position. Lake and the Steelers bounced back from that embarrassment by the Bengals.

Lake had an explanation for the difficulty of his new assignment.

"Safeties tend to take a more aggressive approach to their game because they can afford to," he said. "They're usually tied in to the run more than the corner is, and depending on the coverage, if a safety rotates closer to the line of scrimmage, he can make a mistake with his eyes. Meaning on a play fake, he still may be able to get back into coverage. A corner can't do that.

"To go out there on an island at cornerback is a little different. Out there, you don't have much room for error. If you do make a mistake, it can be crucial to the game."

His size helped him in defending against big receivers. He did not have the same problems as super pests like Willie Williams and Alvoid Mays, both 5-9, between 175 and 185 pounds. Even so, opposing passers picked on him because of his lack of experience at the position.

He thought the team's attitude turned more positive and productive after its bum start (3-4 record). Lake believed the players turned themselves around.

"As a player, you hate to say the coach has to crack the whip because when you have to crack the whip, it's too late. Players should want to do things, they should want to improve and all those things. Cracking the whip just implies that in order to get these guys to be productive, you have to threaten them, and I don't think this team is at that point. I think we just need to start looking at ourselves and holding ourselves accountable."

"I do believe that we can achieve Dr. King's dream of a better world. I can see a world where children do not learn hatred in their homes. I see a world where mothers and fathers have the last and most important word."
— Rosa Parks,
Mother of civil rights movement

Mike Tomczak
A tough survivor

"I was only 23 years old then,
a kid from Chicago
living a boyhood dream."

Mike Tomczak once threw a pass that broke my heart. And I didn't realize it until I returned to Sun Devil Stadium at Arizona State University in Tempe, Arizona with the Pittsburgh Steelers for Super Bowl XXX.

I was walking around the stadium on Tuesday, January 23, 1996, checking out the facility, from top to bottom, taking in a scene that was special and unique to the Super Bowl. This was the eighth Super Bowl I would be covering, but it had been 13 years since my last one, and I wanted to enjoy this one for all it was worth. I found myself stepping back and watching what was going on instead of simply plunging into the crowd down below.

This was Media Day when the Pittsburgh Steelers and Dallas Cowboys both appeared in game uniforms at morning and afternoon interview and photo sessions on the stadium turf, and over 3,000 media types descended on the scene for sound bites, taped interviews, photos and stuff, or simply to soak up the sun and rub shoulders with some of the greats of the game. It was exciting, for me at least, to see some of the sportswriters from around the country I knew from my days on the daily beat. Some of my boyhood heroes — Furman Bisher, Jim Murray, Jerry Izenberg, Edwin Pope — were still at it.

I bumped into Bullet Bill Dudley and his beautiful wife, Libba, and the one-time Steelers' star was still as big a fan and follower of his former team as ever. He was still rooting for the Rooneys. Such reunions get more special as time goes on.

This was the second time in my life that I had been in Sun Devil Stadium. Seeing an old friend, Joe Gilmartin, the sports columnist of *The Phoenix Gazette*, helped bring the first visit back into focus.

I had accompanied the University of Pittsburgh football team to Tempe for a Fiesta Bowl battle with The Ohio State University during the Christmas season of December, 1983. I had changed roles and was in my first year as assistant athletic director and sports information director at my alma mater. It was much easier to be a writer and be waited on than it was to be a publicist and be waiting on the writers and sportscasters. But there was pleasure and satisfaction in both roles.

It had been a terrific season. Pitt came into the game with an 8-2-1 record, the tie (24-24) coming in the final regular season game against Penn State. There had been victories at Tennessee and Notre

Dame, and over Florida State and Syracuse, and losses that shouldn't have been at Maryland and West Virginia. Foge Fazio was in his second season as head coach of the Panthers.

My family was with me for 12 days in the Tempe area, and it was the best vacation we ever enjoyed together. Kathie and I had our own suite at a five-star resort hotel, The Pointe, and our daughters, Sarah, then 10, and Rebecca, 7, had a suite next door. They loved having their own space; they were having such a great time. This was going to be a great job.

It came up cold for the Fiesta Bowl on January 2, 1984, but things heated up in a hurry as Pitt and Ohio State waged a terrific football game. It was a pass-happy, back-and-forth affair, and the outcome was always in doubt.

It was John Congemi's greatest game as a quarterback at Pitt. He completed a school-record 31 passes for 341 yards, but a late Ohio State pass spoiled Congemi's and Pitt's afternoon.

Ohio State took a 7-0 lead, but Pitt came back to tie the score. Ohio State took a 14-7 lead, but Pitt came back to tie the game early in the fourth quarter. Ohio State's Keith Byars scored his second touchdown by returning the ensuing kickoff 90 yards. Congemi, a handsome, gritty kid out of Youngstown, Ohio, completed six of six passes on the next touchdown drive, culminating with an 11-yard touchdown pass to Dwight Collins. Pitt went for a two-point conversion pass, but it failed, so the Panthers trailed, 21-20.

Congemi directed the Panthers on a 17-play drive late in the fourth quarter that led to Snuffy Everett's 37-yard field goal which put the Panthers on top, 23-21.

Ohio State got the ball for one last drive. The Buckeyes began at their own 11-yard line. Time was running out. I stood at the other end of the field, along with many media people, in the right corner of the end zone as Ohio State was looking at it. Tomczak threw a third-and-long pass right into the hands of Pitt linebacker Troy Benson, but Benson dropped the ball. It would prove fatal. Tomczak hit John Frank, a tight end from the Pittsburgh suburb of Mt. Lebanon, with a fourth-down strike, just making the sticks.

There was a heat wave across the middle of the field, like in those desert movies. Here they come, I thought. Ohio State started advancing the ball toward us, and I started expressing anxious thoughts. Gilmartin and Kay Kessler, a sports columnist from Columbus, Ohio, couldn't understand my anxiety. Ohio State was so far away, and time was quickly running out. They thought Pitt had the game in the bag.

But I had seen victories get away before, and I knew an impending disaster when I saw one.

The memory of that day kept swirling through my mind as I toured Sun Devil Stadium on this Tuesday before Super Bowl XXX.

Ohio State scored the game-winning touchdown on a 39-yard pass from Mike Tomczak to Thad Jemison with 39 seconds showing on

118

the clock, and the Buckeyes added the extra point to beat Pitt, 28-23, in a real thriller.

I had thought afterward that I should have shouted at Jemison as he looked up to catch the ball as he came through the center of the end zone. I thought I should have hollered, "Look out for the wall!" Anything to distract him and make him miss the ball. I had thought of Chuck Noll's incessant pep talk line: "Whatever it takes." It might have worked. There was a wall right behind the end line.

I was not writing about that game that day. So I didn't take notes, and the names on the Ohio State team meant nothing to me. I was there to assist the media who were covering the contest. I was there to provide service.

When the game was over, it was my job to get Fazio and some of the Pitt players and bring them to the media tent for post-game interviews. The coaches and players didn't want to see their family and friends after a loss like that, let alone the media. So it wasn't a pleasant task. The vacation was over.

So I didn't recall, at least 12 years later, that it had been Tomczak who threw that pass. That it had been Byars, who went on to become one of the best running backs and pass-catching backs in the NFL, who had scored two touchdowns for the Buckeyes that day in Tempe. Byars nearly became a Steeler during the off-season in 1996. Frankly, it didn't matter that day who threw the pass. It just ruined my day, as well as everyone else's day who was pulling for Pitt.

I had thought about that pass a year before, when I stood in the end zone at Three Rivers Stadium, in the same end of the field, but at the other corner of the end zone, and had that same sinking feeling as Tony Martin of the San Diego Chargers got behind Steelers' defensive back Tim McKyer and caught a 43-yard touchdown pass on a third-and-14 pitch by Stan Humphries to beat the Steelers in the AFC championship game. Bye, bye, Super Bowl XXIX in Miami. Talk about *deja vu*.

Tomczak was thinking about that day at the Fiesta Bowl, too, as he surveyed the scene at Sun Devil Stadium five days before Super Bowl XXX.

"It was pretty exciting, and the great victory capped off a great week," Tomczak said of that Fiesta Bowl.

He thought it was ironic that it was a team from Pittsburgh that he and his team had beaten that day.

I thought it was ironic that Tomczak had stolen the hero's role away from Congemi. It was one of those near-misses that would haunt Fazio, and eventually cost him his job after four seasons as head coach at his alma mater.

During those four seasons, there was another near-win at Ohio State, a disheartening setback by SMU in the Cotton Bowl, two games that should have been won against West Virginia, and games against Boston College and Maryland that should have been wins. Fazio loved being the coach at Pitt, and Pitt was looking for a coach that would stay the long haul like Joe Paterno at Penn State. It could have been great.

People like Tomczak tossed that dream into a garbage can.

It was ironic, as I saw it, because Tomczak could not have been a nicer guy or more cooperative when I first came calling in the clubhouse of the Steelers at Three Rivers Stadium, eager to get started on this book. Tomczak and I had never talked before, but he was instantly warm and helpful. He became an ambassador for me with other Steelers when I started doing the interviews and research for this book. He talked to reluctant Steelers on my behalf, selling them on the idea of being open and cooperative with me.

"Have you talked to C.J. yet?" Tomczak would ask me. "Have you gotten an interview with Greg Lloyd? Let me know."

Tomczak experienced some highs and lows as a fill-in quarterback behind Neil O'Donnell during the 1994 and 1995 seasons. He handled the highs and lows with the same class. Tomczak was a throwback to a more innocent era when more professional athletes treated the media with a modicum of dignity.

Tomczak treated people the way they ought to be treated. He was the sort of guy I wanted to see succeed, much the way I felt about Fazio and Congemi when I worked at Pitt.

"Coach Ditka helped me fulfill a dream."
— Mike Tomczak

Tomczak had been to the Super Bowl before, and he shared some insights with Coach Bill Cowher and his teammates, helping them get ready for the biggest test of their lives. He had helped O'Donnell with his demeanor right from the start, and he tutored the two young would-be quarterbacks, Jim Miller and Kordell Stewart. He shared his knowledge with all. He had a generous spirit.

He had made the Chicago Bears team as a free agent out of Ohio State in 1985. That team, coached by Mike Ditka, had beaten the New England Patriots, 46-10, in Super Bowl XX.

"Coach Ditka helped me fulfill a dream by keeping three quarterbacks that season," said Tomczak. "Then we win the Super Bowl. We felt we were starting a dynasty, that we'd be back. Little did we know. But I was only 23 then, a kid from Chicago living his boyhood dream with the Bears.

"We just celebrated our team's 10th anniversary of that season in October (1995), and it was a fun gathering."

Tomczak also shared a story about how he had managed to get himself into that Super Bowl game even though he was his team's No. 3 quarterback.

Mike Tomczak was classy competitor as backup for QB Neil O'Donnell.

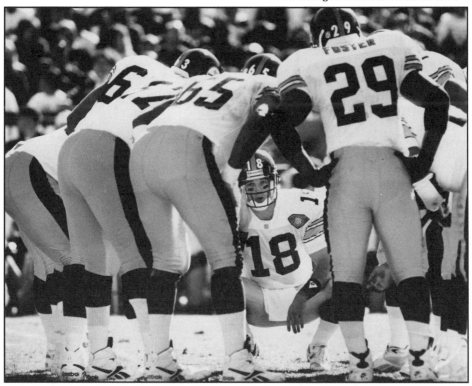

"I went in on special teams for a punt, and I tackled Irving Fryar," said Tomczak. "Actually, I grabbed his face mask and threw him down. I was running scared. As a kid, all coaches tell you to tackle the guy with the ball. I just closed my eyes and stuck my hand out. It's probably the toughest hit Fryar ever suffered.

"It's like going into a basketball game and committing a foul so you can be in the box score. There's one thing no player wants to see and that's DNP (did not play) after his name. I've had a few of those this year. I didn't get to throw a pass, but I did throw a great party after the game."

Tomczak also threw a great party after Super Bowl XXX, despite the disappointing setback. Three weeks later (February 17), he married Michelle Macek, a schoolteacher he met when he came to play in Pittsburgh.

Because he was the most prominent of the three Steelers who had been to a Super Bowl before — reserves Alvoid Mays and James Parrish also wore Super Bowl rings though Parrish had not even dressed for the game during a brief stint with the Dallas Cowboys — and because he expressed himself well, and was a media favorite, Tomczak was a natural to provide diary reports for newspapers in Pittsburgh and Phoenix the week before Super Bowl XXX.

He shared some interesting insights:

"Super Bowl media exposure is twice what it was ten years ago. It's unbelievable. Even as exciting as the Bears were ten years ago, everything is magnified ten times greater because of the exposure. Ten years ago, I wasn't carrying a camcorder around on media day. Ten years ago, all the media people probably didn't have tape recorders.

"This is exciting for me. I'm a lot more mature, hopefully. And I can appreciate it more. This is the greatest event in sports today. Not too many guys get the opportunity to be a part of it once, much less twice.

"We haven't see anything this week as enlightening as Jim McMahon mooning a helicopter ten years ago in New Orleans. We have a few personalities on this team, but not as many as the Cowboys.

"I've come full cycle, no doubt. I've played in a lot of games and started enough to satisfy my ego. Something like this recharges your battery, though. I've been very blessed to stay healthy. I don't enjoy getting hit. I try to get rid of the ball before that happens.

"I think I've helped Neil O'Donnell out, helping him keep his demeanor. I've experienced every amount of stress one can experience through my NFL travels. I have a lot of pride in my conditioning. I spend a lot of time in the weight room and the film room. They are the two places where you make your game better.

"I'm happy for the organization and Mr. Rooney. This is something he's waited for a long time, because ever since his father passed away he's never had a chance to say, 'I've been to a Super Bowl with my team.' This is his team.

122

"Some fans are more intelligent than others, and I think the fans in Pittsburgh know this game pretty darn well. They know the X's and O's of football, and we kind of educated them a little further this year with our five wide-receiver package. And Kordell Stewart educated them a little more on athleticism."

In another installment of his Super Bowl diary, Tomczak touched on some things I felt myself about coming back to this special scene which I might have taken for granted once upon a time. Tomczak offered the following thoughts in a diary that appeared in the *Pittsburgh Post-Gazette*:

"Coach Cowher wanted to talk with me about what the Super Bowl was like, since I'd been there before, and I was only too happy to do so.

"We talked about football, about primary preparation, but mostly we talked about the importance of the experience. The week comes and goes so fast...it took me ten years to get back there. I want to enjoy everything, remember everything.

"I'm more mature about things this time, more appreciative of the opportunity. I realized now that so many great players never get to this game. I didn't realize that the first time. Only later did I resolve that if I got there again that I would share as much as I could with teammates there for the first time.

"There is nothing like it. Winning the Super Bowl is the ultimate. Just playing in it doesn't mean nearly as much. One thing players always say to me is, 'Let me see your ring.' They didn't know who the loser is, they don't know who we played against. They just want to see the ring. Winning is what it's all about."

Tomczak provided different diary installments for *The Phoenix Gazette* and *The Arizona Republic*:

"I grew up in Chicago, but it wasn't a highly-recruited area by Ohio State, so I figured I would go to either Michigan or Notre Dame. But prior to my junior year, OSU came into the area and started recruiting heavily. It turned out I knew in my heart Ohio State was the best place for me. That's how I wound up in Columbus.

"My dad was my high school coach, and he and I kind of filtered through all the offers. We just knew somewhere in the Big Ten would be the best place for me, and it was OSU. Bob Tucker and Coach (Earl) Bruce were the men who sold me.

"My biggest moments at Ohio State were obviously our victories over Michigan. We beat them three out of four years. I remember our one trip to the Rose Bowl, where we lost to USC. I think it was 20-17, after we got down 17-3. We just ran out of time."

And, of course, he remembered throwing the touchdown pass to beat Pitt in the Fiesta Bowl. But enough of that.

"I've played enough to satisfy my ego."
— Mike Tomczak

Tomczak was a thoughtful study in the Steelers' clubhouse. He was the perfect backup quarterback. He didn't make Neil O'Donnell nervous. Bubby Brister bristled when Neil got the nod to start at quarterback, and said things that unnerved Neil and made him feel uncomfortable. Tomczak knew better than to cause trouble. Deep down, he wanted to start as much as O'Donnell, or Stewart or Miller or Brister. But he had learned how to play the role.

In his first season with the Steelers in 1994, Tomczak started twice and directed his team to victories over Miami and Oakland in late November. Given the chance, Tomczak had shown he was equal to the task. There were also times when he was not, but the same was true of O'Donnell.

He took over when O'Donnell got hurt in the 1995 opener with the Detroit Lions and missed a few games. Tomczak was flattened early in the fourth quarter in a scary collision — he lay flat on the field for five minutes before moving — but he came back to rally the Steelers to victory when some worried whether he'd ever walk again. Tomczak performed well in other outings and not so well in others, but surrendered the starting position to O'Donnell as soon as O'Donnell was healthy enough to return. I kept a close eye on Tomczak that week, and I could tell he was brooding about having to give up the job, but, to his credit, he kept his disappointment to himself. He had learned how to handle such setbacks.

"I've been to the top," he said when I spoke to him about his status as a second-string signal-caller before Super Bowl XXX. "I played on a world championship team. I know what it takes to get to the Super Bowl. And that was my rookie year. When you experience success at such a period in your life, you want to get back there.

"By now, I've played in 160 some games, and I've backed up a lot more than I've started. I try to keep an even keel. I'm at peace with myself. I've played enough to satisfy my ego.

"There are a lot less fortunate people than myself. I came into the league with an opportunity. I wasn't drafted. I signed as a free agent with my hometown team and I made the final cut.

"To me, everyone looks for an opportunity. In life, you only get so many opportunities. However many you get you want to respond to them. I think I've done a good job of responding to them.

"This clubhouse here has loosened up tremendously this year, more so than my first season here. A lot of it has had to do with winning and success."

Tomczak had played six seasons with the Bears, and one each with the Green Bay Packers and the Cleveland Browns. I asked Tomczak if he were comfortable in the Steelers' clubhouse?

"I know how to communicate with the majority of guys," he said. "I'm the player rep, so I have to keep in touch with everybody. One of the unique things about sports...it's a vicious cycle. You have players from all walks of life. All of us are just mere acquaintances. If you can carry one or two friendships out of it for a lifetime you're doing well. How many best friends do I have? There's a space factor....you allow some teammates into your private space...but there's not many I'll tell personal things."

Tomczak's mother died when he was two years old. His father Tom, who taught him how to play football and other games, remarried. His father was a constant in his life, much more so than most of his teammates could say.

Kordell Stewart's mother had died when he was 12 years old, and Stewart had had an opportunity to spend more time with his mother than Mike had. But Stewart said, "I'm definitely a daddy's boy." The same could be said for Tomczak.

"I'm very blessed," said Tomczak. "The older I get the more I realize the values my dad instilled in me at a young age. In today's society, discipline is often overlooked — in the household and in school. How disciplined can you be if discipline hasn' t been a part of your upbringing? You have to adapt to things. You should always have some sense of discipline.

"When you tell a child 'no,' you have to explain what you mean, and what you expect. 'No' doesn't have to be a negative word."

Tomczak talks about such ideas when he goes out to represent the Steelers or Blue Cross of Western Pennsylvania at school assemblies.

"I talk about heroes," he said. "A lot of my heroes are people outside the sports world. I define a hero as someone who's made the world a better place to live.

"They have had plenty of heroes to look up to with the Steelers. They've been looking at Joe Greene, L.C. Greenwood, Rocky Bleier, Mel Blount, Franco Harris, people like that. This is truly the City of Champions. I love the people here. I'm attracted to it. But I want to put some seeds in their minds as to where else they might look for heroes, hopefully, in their own homes or neighborhoods or schools.

"I do some work for Blue Cross. The main issue I talk about is the power of choice. We have the ability to choose our friends, or whether or not to do something right or wrong. I spoke to over 10,000 kids in the last month and a half.

"Howard Cosell said Jackie Robinson was his hero. Everyone has an opinion in that regard. He was a true sports hero.

"I truly believe that society as a whole spends too much time sensationalizing over negative things. Let's talk about some positive things. News anchors come on and say, 'Good evening.' That's a nice thing to say. And then they tell you about all the bad things that happened locally, nationally and throughout the world that day. There's so much negativism. It's no wonder so many people have so many problems. Everyone gets such an influx of negativism.

125

"Parents, peers and media are the main influences in society. If the media changed the format and said, 'good evening' and then told you all the positive things that happened that day it would be better. Give us some good news so we can have a good evening. Why don't we try it? What we've been doing isn't working. I'd love to see a column in the newspaper that was just good news items.

"I have a friend, Robert Shook, who writes books about successful people, about real heroes."

Who was Mike Tomczak's personal hero?

"My dad is first and foremost. And it took me time to realize that. Robert Shook has helped out so many individuals. In that respect he has accomplished a great deal on his walk through life, inspiring them, encouraging them. He makes good points. If you tell a kid he's a bad kid enough times he'll believe you. If you boost them you'll get a better kid.

"I worked with Walter Payton of the Chicago Bears with the Better Boys Foundation and the Mackey Awards in Chicago. They honor the best kids at a banquet every year. I have worked with handicapped people, worked in a warehouse for Opportunity, Inc. Everyone does labor, intensive work. You were able to make a lot of things better for people."

As he talked, a tear formed in the corner of Tomczak's right eye. Thinking about some of the kids he worked with obviously tugged at his heart.

"Regardless of whether you want to be a role model or not, if you're a professional athlete that role is placed on your shoulders," said Tomczak. "I take exception to what Charles Barkley said about not being anybody's hero."

Tomczak shared my feeling that many of today's pro athletes don't appreciate how good they have got it, and how they are obligated to give something back to society.

"If you brought back a lot of guys who've played different games in earlier years, and you brought them back and had them talk to the players, I guarantee you they'd humble these superstars. There's a big difference in their outlooks.

"The reason? Those guys from different eras...they played the game because they loved it. I sincerely love it. Some of the guys complain about coming in here to work out. They could be working for a living, you know, a real job. You should be thankful for what you have. You should do your best to accommodate people who seek your attention or want to talk to you about what you do.

"Whether we like it or not, soon enough we'll all be part of the past. We should enjoy the present and prepare for the future. A lot of these guys are afraid to step up to the plate. Is it because they're shy and timid or not happy with themselves? We only do this for a short time. What's the big deal about talking to someone?

"I was touched by what Howard Cosell did as a sports journalist and broadcaster. He came onto the scene during a difficult time:

Mike Tomczak, at left in these three photos, first as a two-year-old with sister Susan, five months, brother Ronnie, three-year-old; bare-chested with Ronnie, and the three of them at a school assembly.

civil rights and protests of the war on college campuses — Ali and Kent State, stuff like that. How about Ali? There's a guy who was truly a hero.

"I lost my mother when I was two years old. No one wanted to talk about it. I was just supposed to accept it. Just accept it and go on. My father remarried. Those were the cards I was dealt. That was it.

"My grandparents grew up in these parts, in Butler and in Greenville. Now they live outside of Chicago. I grew up with Forbes Field and all that stuff.

"One of my best friends grew up in Squirrel Hill. Stan Glick. He died of colon cancer in 1992. He was a good friend. He asked me to look after things for him. So, again, it's great that I'm here.

"Stan died just as I was finishing my last season in Cleveland. Then I came here. It was like Stan had been talking to Art Rooney up in heaven. So much good has come from me coming here.

"I met a girl here. That alone made my coming here a great thing. There's something special about being in Pittsburgh. I always had a lot of success against Pittsburgh. Now I'm enjoying doing a good job here."

Mike has overcome a lot of adversity."
— Steve Tomczak

There were clanging sounds in the background. It sounded like barbells banging around. It sounded like a gym. I didn't know the telephone number Mike Tomczak had given me for his father was at a family-owned health club, the Sports Club Fitness Center in suburban Chicago.

Steve, the 25-year-old stepbrother of Mike, was looking after the place. Their sister, Jennifer, was looking after little children in a nursery area. The sounds of children could be heard in the background as well. Ron, Mike and Sue were the children of Ron Tomczak's first marriage, and Jennifer, Steve and Gina were the children of his second marriage. They regarded themselves as one family.

Ron was a personal fitness trainer elsewhere in Chicago, and had just picked up a teaching degree and was hoping to get a teaching/coaching position. In addition to running the gym with his father, Steve was a coach at Lincoln Way High School.

"I learned the value and rewards of hard work from our father," said Steve. "All six of us benefited from growing up in a strong Catholic family. There were so many things going on with my father when we were growing up. He was a full-time teacher and coach and he was a running a health club on the side.

"He'd get up at six and go to church every day first thing in the morning. Then he'd get to school (Thornton Fractional North in Calumet, Illinois) where he taught physical education. He'd be done at 2:30, and then he'd be at football practice till 6. Then he'd go to the health club and be there until 12 or 12:30 at night.

"Yet he still had time for his wife and kids. He was still there to throw a football with you, or to work with the girls on their volleyball. We'd all be playing four sports a year. My mom, whose name is JoAnn, was also very involved in all our activities. She was always taking us everywhere for our games and different school events."

I suggested that so much sports activity assured that none of the kids could get into any trouble.

"You wouldn't dare get into trouble," said Steve. "Another thing, you didn't have the time to get into trouble.

"I admire Mike a lot. He fought through a lot of adversity. Between faith and hard work, he's managed to make his way through it. I think he's very happy now."

Steve played quarterback in high school and at the College of St. Francis in Joliet, Illinois, while his brother Ron was a tight end and a strong safety at Western Illinois University in Macomb, the same school that sent Mike Wagner to the Steelers.

"Woody Hayes was inspirational."
— Mike Tomczak

Mike Tomczak talked to us about his days at Ohio State. He spoke in positive terms of his experience there.

"I remember my very first day on the campus at Ohio State," said Tomczak. "I was getting ready for rookie camp. I was walking with Jim Lachey. This man was walking our way. Jim said, 'That's Woody Hayes coming this way.' He stopped as he neared us. He said 'You're Mike Tomczak. You're from Calumet City, Illinois. Your parents are Ron and JoAnn. You're Jim Lachey. You're from St. Henry, Ohio. Your parents are Ken and Joanne.' Can I buy you guys a cup of coffee and a donut? He took us to Buckeye Donuts. He didn't discuss football at all. All he talked about was education. I knew then it was a special place. He didn't recruit me. He helped recruit Jim.

"I had another special meeting with Coach Hayes. I broke my leg, very severely, before my senior year. The doctors told me I could never play again. That was 1983. I was sitting in my room in our apartment. I was in a cast from my hip to my ankles. There was a knock at the door. It was Woody Hayes rapping at the door. It was half open. I said, 'Come on in, Coach Hayes?' Jim came out of his bedroom. Coach Hayes said, 'Have you guys had lunch yet? Would you like to go out for lunch at Bob Evans?' His wife, Ann, had dropped him off and he didn't have a car. 'Ann will be back in an hour and a half to get me.' I couldn't drive, but Jim could. Coach Hayes was in his office at ROTC in those days. I roomed with Jim for four years. He's still playing pro ball; he's with the Washington Redskins.

"Woody is asking me all kinds of questions, none of them about football. 'What do you want to do with your life? What are you majoring in? Communications. You should start making some contacts with alumni. Have you considered law school?' He was inspirational."

I met Woody Hayes in the press box when Pitt played at Ohio State when I was working at Pitt. I also heard Hayes speak once at a Football Foundation Hall of Fame dinner at the Waldorf-Astoria in New York City. He received a standing ovation when he finished his talk.

I mentioned to Tomczak that Woody Hayes' image slipped considerably in his last seasons at Ohio State. He was portrayed as a tyrant, as an out-of-control bully.

"That's not my impression of Woody Hayes," said Tomczak. "That's unfortunate. There are probably millions of millions of people who think of him as man of high moral principles. He was an inspirational man to so many. He visited kids in hospitals and in their homes unannounced. But he had some problems and did some things that gained him a negative image as far as those who only knew him from TV were concerned. But that was not the real Woody Hayes."

Mike Tomczak and his dad, Ron, during Ohio State days.

Deon Figures
Getting away from L.A.

"I wasn't no angel."

Sometimes it's better to just stand back and watch. The Steelers' dressing room gives up some ghosts under quiet observation. Deon Figures did not feel right or good about himself most of the 1995 season, and that was apparent by his somber presence in the dressing room. He did not hide his feelings well. He did not feel like he was still a part of the Pittsburgh Steelers. It was obvious by his behavior. So often, he was seen sitting on his folding chair, facing into his dressing stall. His back was to the rest of the room. Like he was hiding.

Sometimes he would be eating his lunch like that, other times he was just sitting there in silence, his chin on his chest. He was an unhappy camper, and few could console him. There was so much on his mind.

Once in a while, he would catch himself, be aware of what he was doing, brooding, and push himself away to visit with his closest friends on the team, talk to them a little, try to get going again. At times, Figures was his old self.

Before long, he would be back sitting on his chair, staring into his dressing stall. It was, understandably, a difficult and frustrating year for Figures, who turned 26 a few weeks before Super Bowl XXX.

Figures was flanked by two former University of Colorado classmates and teammates, C.J. Johnson and Chad Brown, and both did their best on occasion to lift his spirits. Both of them ended up with injuries and their own moody times. Johnson, who had known difficult days in his troubled youth, would joke with Figures from time to time, trying to get a smile on his face. Johnson somehow was able to smile and laugh through the most difficult of times.

Occasionally, Johnson would succeed in his merry-making efforts and the frown on Figures' face would give way to a great big grin. Like he couldn't help himself. Then he would scold Johnson and plead with him, half-jokingly, half-serious, to leave him alone. Kordell Stewart, who dressed nearby, in a corner on the other side of Willie Williams, was also a Colorado alumnus. Sometimes they would be comparing gold chain necklaces or something frivolous like that, laughing in each other's faces. Other times, they would all be sitting silently, tending to their own business. They were no longer in college, but they had not yet entered the real world, either. Professional sports provided a limbo of sorts.

Their old college coach, Bill McCartney, a born-again Christian who founded a national religious movement for men called "Promisekeepers," could have boosted their spirits had he been there to counsel them, as he had done at Colorado.

131

It is no wonder Figures felt disenfranchised. He had gone through a most difficult nine months. It was hell on earth. On May 13, 1995, he was shot in the knee while driving through Los Angeles near his hometown of Compton. He required surgery to repair the ligament damage in his knee.

No one knew how long it would take him to return to form from that kind of injury. He came to training camp with the Steelers, but worked out on his own, under the watchful eye of trainer John Norwig. He did not participate in any team drills or workouts at St. Vincent College. At first, everybody was impressed with his rapid progress. He went about his rehabilitation quietly, but with great enthusiasm.

To the surprise of most people, Figures got back in time to play a little in the last pre-season game against the Philadelphia Eagles. At first, it was felt he would not be able to return until five or six games into the regular season. In retrospect, he may have come back before he was really ready. He played sparingly early in the season as a backup in the defensive secondary. He was not his old self and he was put on the inactive list for the ninth and tenth games of the season, against the Chicago Bears and Cleveland Browns. Figures felt like he was being left behind, like he was missing out on the fun.

That seemed like the low point of the season. "That was rock bottom right there," said Figures. "I was the lowest of the low. There wasn't any place to go but up. I just lifted my head to the sky and said, 'I've got to get back, whatever it takes.'"

But his surgically-repaired knee was not up to the physical strain. He simply was not sound enough. He had lost a step and his job.

Then his mother died. In the space of nine months, he had been shot in the knee, was unable to practice with his team at training camp, surrendered a starting job, found himself out of uniform for two of the team's biggest wins of the season, and then he lost his mother, Mrs. Hermeon Figures.

During that same span, and here is where it's difficult for an outsider to comprehend what had been happening in his life, six of his friends were shot and killed in separate incidents back home in his old neighborhood near Los Angeles.

That has to be too much for anybody to absorb. He wore a black bandana on his close-shaven head, large gold hoop earrings on both ears, a black T-shirt with the sleeves cut off just above the biceps and a disgruntled mask. He looked like a gypsy in grief.

He must not have had the greatest self-esteem in the first place. When I asked him to get me some photos from his childhood for this book, he told me he didn't have any. When I pressed him about it during later conversations, he said, "I burnt them."

"Why?" I asked. I had heard about photos and other personal possessions being lost in a house fire, and I always cringed at the thought. It happened with Willie Williams, his teammate, and in recent months to Dick Groat, a former Pirates MVP. But what happened here?

"I didn't like the way I looked in them," offered Figures in the way of an explanation for why he had destroyed the photographs. "I don't think there are any pictures."

He left the locker room one day during the lunch break and sat and talked with me in a conference room down the hall.

Just the two of us. Deon Juniel Figures opened up and discussed what was bothering him. He could not have been more honest.

He talked about growing up in Compton, California, and what he faced in his daily existence there in his youth, and what he faced whenever he returned home to visit family and friends.

"Growing up in L.A., it was the bad gang capital of the world," he began. "Then when I got here, I realized there are gangs here, too. But it's not nearly as bad here as it was there.

"Where I grew up, it's Bloods and Crips. I did not belong to any gangs myself. I had friends who were in a gang. We lived in a Crip neighborhood. There's guilt by association. They're your friends. They'd go gang-banging, challenging people from different neighborhoods. I'd be walking with them, before or after school, but I was not a member. There was a lot of tension. It's even worse now.

"When you're walking down the street with your friends, you get dirty looks from guys from other places. If you've got something nice, they want it. They want good things quickly; they don't realize you have to work for it."

How did he manage to walk that fine line, to stay away from joining the gang in his neighborhood?

"I had a strong family background," offered Figures. "My mother and father were both at home. That really helped. My father got me and my brother involved in sports, and we always had a busy schedule. I started playing football at eight. My first love was baseball, but I also liked basketball."

When I asked Figures about boyhood heroes, he said his father, Willie Figures, was his best model. "He's been a strong positive force in my life," said Figures. "He's always backing me up. I couldn't pick a better hero."

His dad, Willie, was a maintenance engineer at a chain of grocery stores in California. He maintained and fixed machines as they broke down. Willie was there for Deon, a brother named Juniel and a sister named Renel.

A lot of Figures' friends were not similarly blessed. Most of them lived with their mothers, grandmothers and aunts. "I have to give guys credit who've done it, and have made out OK," he said. "They went through some difficult times."

Some of them, he said, drew support from people outside their home who lived in the same neighborhood.

According to a 1995 Census Bureau report, 65 percent of American black families were headed by single parents. Among whites, the figure was 25 percent.

"I had the best of both worlds," said Figures. "My neighborhood's kind of close. A lot of my friends liked my parents. They were nice to all of them. Where I live it's crowded with family members. My uncle lives next door. I have another uncle around the corner. My brother is two houses away."

In a sense, the Steelers' locker room was something like that. There were familiar faces there when he first arrived, players he had known when he was at Colorado. Brown, Johnson, Stewart and Ariel Solomon all resided in the same corner of the locker room, the farthest one from the entrance.

"I call it 'the Colorado corner' of the locker room. Coming to the Steelers was a good thing for me. I had some problems at Colorado, but things worked out at the end. I was drafted on the first round; I was the 23rd pick. There were some other guys from Colorado who were here when I first got here."

They were Ariel Solomon, a reserve offensive lineman, and Joel Steed, a starting nose tackle. Holdovers from the 1992 team were Solomon Wilcots, a safety from Colorado, and Garry Howe, another nose tackle, but they didn't remain on the roster for his first season. Chad Brown came in with him from Colorado, and Johnson and Stewart showed up in successive seasons.

"I came in and started four games in my first year," recalled Figures. "I was a starter in my second year. I started to get into the flow. I was coming into my own as a starter. Then I get shot in the knee."

"People out there who still have their mother don't know how lucky they are."
— Deon Figures

Figures took me on a journey with him back to Compton. It was a world different from any I had ever personally experienced.

"From November on, over a period of four months (from 1994 into 1995), I had six friends killed," he said, without blinking one of his dark eyes. "One was shot and killed around Thanksgiving. Two were killed the day before Christmas, on Christmas Eve; they were killed in the same incident. Two more were killed in January and February.

"One of them was supposed to sign a record deal last Saturday. He got killed on Friday. That was done by the Bloods. He was on his porch, just sitting on the porch. It was a drive-by shooting; no sense at all."

As he spoke about his family, something didn't make sense. He explained that it was actually his step-mother who had died, that his real mother was living in Las Vegas, and had come to California for the funeral. "I called her my mother because she's the one who actually raised me," he said of the deceased. "During my senior year in college, I found out my mother (step-mother) had cancer. She tried to hide it from me. She had an operation and they had to take out half of her lungs."

As Deon saw it, she was his mother because she treated him like a son. He spoke of the special quality that a mother can bring to her children's life. "She worries about you, she lets you know you weren't someone who got in the way when she wanted to be with her husband," he explained. "She loves you no matter what. And her love is unconditional. She'll back you up. People out there who still have their mother don't know how lucky they are."

To illustrate the special love he felt for the woman he called his mother, Figures tugged at his T-shirt and rolled it up toward his neck, revealing a tattoo he had gotten soon after she died. Above his left breast, there was a broken heart with an arrow splitting the middle of it. Within the heart there was a written message: *Rest In Peace*. I felt strange to have Figures reveal and share this personal tribute to his mother the way he did. It had taken me a year to gain his trust, and sometimes he would still be difficult, or resist my entreaties to talk again. I thought he needed someone to talk with him.

"I talked to my mother for an hour and a half on the telephone on a Sunday," he recalled of their last communication. "She got sick on Monday, and my dad took her to the hospital on Tuesday. She died on Wednesday (August 23, 1995), the day before the Eagles' game. She was feeling real good when I talked to her. I kept her on the phone longer than usual. She sounded good; she sometimes had trouble breathing.

"When my mom died, I talked to Coach Cowher and told him what happened. I also told him I wanted to play the next night. He understood. I played in that game on Thursday; I dedicated it to her. I told Coach Cowher I didn't want any of the guys to know. He told them after I left the following day. When I got back, they offered sympathy and gave me hugs and talked to me about my loss (They also dedicated the next game — the opener with the Detroit Lions — in her memory).

"Rod (Woodson) took me aside. He said he knew what I was going through. He lost his father; by him losing a father, he knew what I was going through. Some others took me aside, but no one said quite what Rod said to me. Rod knew. It was real helpful that he did that. If you have been though it, you know there's nothing you can say that can really ease the pain. But it's good to know the guys are there for you. You feel less alone. Life goes on. I knew my mother wouldn't want me to be sulking. She's in a better place. Sometimes I'm sitting in the locker room, or at my place, and I just drift off and think about it. I get down.

"But I didn't want to discuss it with too many people. I don't want to disrupt the focus of our football team. I keep to myself. I'm a private person. Sometimes I like being on my own. It's no big deal. When I'm around friends, I'm real sociable....definitely, even when me and Chad get together."

"What was he doing out so late? He must have been up to no good."

Figures doesn't have to look far to find someone who has suffered losses, or had difficult times. Right next to him in the Steelers' locker room is C.J. Johnson. "Twenty-four hours a day, he has a smile on his face," Figures said of Johnson. "He has the mark of a strong person. His childhood was rough. Being homeless is not easy. His mom had all those problems..."

Johnson was also raised in California, so he could relate to what Figures referred to when telling stories about the mean streets. Johnson knew Figures wasn't lying when he gave the details of the off-season shooting incident that disrupted his pro career. Johnson's mother was a reformed crack cocaine addict. She had often left him to fend for himself in the streets, and took money from him to support her drug habit. Johnson had overcome that to succeed in school and in sports and, best of all, in life. He was a shining beacon in the club-house. He knew that Figures came from a different world than the one most familiar to most Steelers' fans.

"If I was from L.A. and heard it I'd believe it," said Figures. "But if you're from Pittsburgh, if you hear a story like that one about me, you'd say, 'Yeah, right, he's out at three o'clock in the morning. What was he doing out so late? He must have been up to no good. He shouldn't have been out at 3.' It's an unbelievable story, at least for people who don't know L.A. I put myself in their shoes. I'd say, 'That's probably not true. He was doing something else.' People have to let the facts come out before they know what was true. Hey, I'm 25 years old. I could have been at my friend's home. Times have changed. Parties start late. I'm always cautious, but I couldn't prevent this from happening."

Al Martinez, a newspaper columnist in Los Angeles, wrote a book called *City of Angles* (copyright March, 1996), in which he shed some light on what Figures was referring to. Martinez mentioned in the introduction that it could no longer be called the City of Angels:

"Murder runs wild in the new L.A. County, contrary to the national trend. More people — 1,554 — were shot to death in the county in one year (1994) than died in traffic accidents, despite our five hundred miles of freeway. Another 6,500 were treated in local hospitals for gunshot wounds. The total of 8,000 is 13 times the number of American military personnel killed and wounded in the Gulf War, and we're just getting started."

Pittsburgh Steelers/Michael F. Fabus

Jim O'Brien

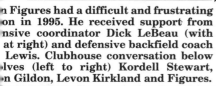
n Figures had a difficult and frustrating
on in 1995. He received support from
nsive coordinator Dick LeBeau (with
at right) and defensive backfield coach
Lewis. Clubhouse conversation below
lves (left to right) Kordell Stewart,
n Gildon, Levon Kirkland and Figures.

Figures was shot at 3:10 a.m. on Broadway, north of Florence Avenue, in the South Central section of Los Angeles. That was the hot spot during the L.A. riots, where whole blocks were reduced to charred ruins in burn, baby, burn outbursts. He was driving a rented Mustang home to Culver City, heading toward the Harbor Freeway after dropping off two friends, when a detour on the road took him out of his way. A bullet hit him in the left knee after piercing the metal of his car door. A 9 mm bullet was removed from his knee at Kaiser Permanente Hospital. He listed his occupation on the police report as "clothing designer." No suspect was found. The LAPD confirmed his story.

"I grew up in Compton and I've been shot at before," said Figures. "I've been lucky. This is the first time I'd been hit."

"It's not uncommon to get shot in that section of the city," reported an LAPD officer.

William Baird, watch commander of the Newton Division of the Los Angeles Police Department, said, "It apparently was a random act of violence while he was trying to get back to the freeway."

Figures underwent followup surgery at St. Margaret Memorial Hospital in Aspinwall after he returned to Pittsburgh to repair a separated patella (kneecap) tendon sustained in the shooting.

Sometimes when Figures would attempt to talk to me, usually about serious stuff, Johnson would start needling him, forcing him to smile. Mimicking him.

"C.J. is following me everywhere I go," Figures said "He's from California and he followed me here to Pittsburgh. When he got here he needed a place to stay. He stayed at my place. Now I'm in Brighton Heights. I bought a townhouse. Now he did the same thing. He's on the same street. Sometimes we just sit and talk to each other."

They used to work out together at Colorado, Figures covering Johnson when he was going out for passes. They were a great test for each other.

"We went one on one a lot at Colorado," said Figures. "We helped each other get better. He's tough, real tough. It was a California thing. Now it's a Pittsburgh thing."

"I could feel the heat coming out of the room."

Figures had an up and down rookie season, too, and managed to get into Bill Cowher's doghouse on more than one occasion, just as he had gotten into Bill McCartney's doghouse at Colorado. McCartney kept Figures sidelined for his entire sophomore season because he did not care for his attitude after he had a fine freshman season. Figures thought about transferring to another school.

"I was taking a lot for granted. There are a lot of guys who would have liked to be in my position, and there I was messing it up," offered Figures. "It helped me get my priorities straight. I was more focused on school, got ahead, and it helped me graduate. That year really did help me out. It helped me get where I'm at now."

There have been some bumps on the road, however. When Figures missed a team meeting before the Steelers' Monday Night Football game at Houston during the 1994 season, he was called on the carpet by Cowher. He went to see Cowher in his hotel room. "He opened the door and I could feel the heat coming out of the room, so I knew. I think I lost about five pounds talking to him. It was something else." Cowher suspended Figures for one game.

Figures was playing a position, cornerback, that former Oakland Raiders coach and Fox network analyst John Madden called "the most difficult in pro football."

As a rookie in 1994, Figures replaced D.J. Johnston at corner when Johnston signed as an unrestricted free agent with the Atlanta Falcons.

Defensive coordinator Dick LeBeau was one of Deon's biggest boosters. "He's a 200 pound man, which is big for the secondary, with real fine balance and athletic ability," allowed LeBeau. "And he has great ball skills."

Figures relished the challenge of performing on the hot corner in the Steelers' defensive secondary. "That's why I chose it, because it is a challenge," said Figures. "Linemen, the fans don't see when they mess up. But in the secondary, you're the last line of defense. Everyone sees you. If you get beat for a touchdown, they see it, even though it may not have been your man. It's a real challenge.

"Playing on the other side of Rod, who's a great cornerback, you're going to catch the heat most of the time. You have to be a man and deal with it and handle the challenges that are thrown at you.

"If you are a quarterback and you saw me on one side and Rod on the other, it's only obvious that you're going to come to my side. That's a good position. I have a lot of confidence in myself and that's an opportunity to make big plays.

"Rod's paid his dues. He's been in the league, a five-time Pro Bowler. So you can't compare a lot of people with Rod."

Figures watched Woodson in action, and on tape, and tried to pick up things that would help him get better. He also studied his own movements on tape.

"I let other people watch my highlights," he said. "I like to watch the lowlights because you learn from it, see what you did wrong and try to correct it. I'm overlooking the little things, trying to make big plays and not taking care of the small things, as far as jams, keeping my head in the backfield too long, taking my eyes off the receivers.

"I've been dealing with adversity throughout my life. This is just another obstacle in the way. I'm sure I'll get a grasp on it."

Deon learned about working through pain from his father, Willie Figures. He had chronic swelling of the joints in his hands and wrists. "But he went to work every day, whether he was feeling good or not," said his son. Deon did the same thing during his troubled second season.

The Steelers had spoken at length to Coach Bill McCartney at Colorado before they drafted Deon.

"Deon was good enough to start here as a freshman," said McCartney. "It was the next year that we held him out, but he went on during his career here and won the Thorpe Award as the nation's top defensive back. He became a guy who was a complete player, from the standpoint that he played on special teams and just was a gifted and unselfish athlete."

McCartney suspended Figures simply because he had gotten carried away with himself. McCartney told the Steelers that Figures had gotten a big head over his early success at Colorado. McCartney said Figures wasn't doing some things he was supposed to do to go along with the program.

Sitting out a season gave Figures an opportunity to mature in more ways than one.

On Draft Day, 1994, Tom Donahoe, the director of football operations for the Steelers, explained why the Steelers selected Figures with the team's first round draft pick. He mentioned how he had checked him out with McCartney.

"He said Figures played at 172 as a freshman and came back, after sitting out a year, at 190 pounds," said Donahoe. "Coach McCartney said he went in as a boy and came out as a man."

Figures also had a DUI (driving under the influence of alcohol) suspension before his senior season at Colorado, and had to sit out the opening game as a punishment. He had been involved in two disturbances in Boulder drinking spots.

Was there any question about this guy's character? Didn't his rap sheet send up some sort of red flag?

"Yes, but we check out those things," Donahoe said. "Somebody from Blesto once described him and said 'He's not a choir boy,' but we found out in his biography that he was once in a boy's choir in high school. So much for that.

"He's an aggressive corner," continued Donahoe. "He's tall. He's about 190 pounds. He has long arms, he has big hands, he's strong, and he plays the game physically."

He was regarded as an outstanding athlete. He was the best runner and a jumper on his high school track team at Serra High in Compton, California. He had been recruited by UNLV to play basketball. He was a terrific power forward in high school, averaging about 20 points a game. He was a slick-fielding infielder on the school baseball team.

At Colorado, he was a sociology major in the School of Arts and Sciences. He also studied criminology. He could have been an interesting subject for a senior term paper by a sociology or criminology major. One pre-season magazine said of him prior to his senior season: "He's a great talent who can't seem to stay out of trouble."

Figures came to his own defense. "I'm a good guy, easy to get along with," he told a sportswriter in Denver during Colorado's early-fall camp. "I'm a quiet person, laid-back. I don't give anyone trouble."

Figures felt he brought something special to his assignment. One thing he didn't lack was self-confidence.

"I'm a competitor," Figures said going into his senior season at Colorado. "Some DBs, if they give up a touchdown, are lost. They can't function. But you have to be able to bounce back."

He learned some lessons about life during his days at Colorado that helped him grow up, and count his blessings.

He had a teammate, quarterback Sal Aunese, stricken with stomach and lung cancer, die early in the season — the one he sat out — that helped Figures put his life into perspective. "'Look what he's going through, and this is just a single semester that's been taken away from me.' I thought to myself," recalled Figures. "The way Sal dealt with his life-threatening illness helped me to keep my head up.'"

"You want them confident and competent."
— Tim Lewis

Steelers' defensive backfield coach Tim Lewis liked Figures' competitive zeal. Figures wanted to be challenged. He wanted opposing quarterbacks to test him.

"That's what you play this game for," said Lewis, whose own career as an NFL cornerback was shortened by a spine injury he suffered while playing for the Green Bay Packers.

"Rod Woodson will go down as one of the great cornerbacks ever and he gets challenged. So you know they're going to go after Deon. These guys want that. 'OK, come at me, baby, come on.' You don't want guys who say, 'Oh, no, he's throwing my way.' Those guys don't last too long. You want them confident and competent."

I asked Figures how he felt about LeBeau, his boss and the Steelers' defensive coordinator.

"He was my coach my rookie and second season. He's a lot like one of my college coaches, Gary Brown, who's now with the Raiders," said Figures. "Same philosophy, same style, laidback, get to the point. LeBeau can sit in the locker room and have as much fun as we do. He's the type of coach I like. He told us, 'I didn't like being shouted at or sworn at, so I'm not going to coach that way, either.' He'll compare football to life.

"That's true enough. This is your job, but you don't want to hear football all the time, every time you run into the coach. He can talk about other things."

Figures' secondary coach his last two years at Colorado was Greg Brown, who coached three years with the Tampa Bay Buccaneers and two with the Denver Gold of the USFL.

"He doesn't have any wasted motion on his change of direction," said Brown. "He's real smooth. He's the kind of guy who you could put a cup of coffee on his head when he's running, and he isn't going to spill it."

At Colorado, everyone knew Figures could run backwards without a hitch, but he could also travel across the width of the field on his hands — yes, on his hands — and he could do a backflip in full pads.

Figures was thought to look a little like Eddie Murphy, which made him popular with the women at Colorado, and it also helped him to amuse others with his shenanigans.

"I've had some tough times and, fortunately, my family has been very supportive of me. They've helped me make it."

He thought about transferring after getting into trouble.

"I wasn't adjusting to the culture shock," he said. "It seemed like I was having the hardest time adjusting of all the guys I came in with. I kept asking myself, 'Why me?'"

"I heard that little voice from my parents. It was always there."

Figures was wearing the black bandana, a black jersey, and two gold hoop earrings when we talked at length on November 1, 1995. His black jersey was one of Ray Seals' "60-Minute Men" specials, the sleeves cut off just above the biceps.

Kordell Stewart and C.J. Johnson were flanking him, animated and laughing a lot. Nearby, Eric Ravotti, Ariel Solomon and Kendall Gammon were talking to each other.

Brentson Buckner walked by, wearing a No. 96 Penguins jersey. He might have helped the Penguins at the defensive end of the ice.

Darren Perry was limping badly after splitting his big toe open when he stubbed his foot on a bed post.

Someone had left a loaf of fresh-baked bread in every dressing stall that day. Food to nourish the needy, no doubt.

Figures was talking about how he was drawn to sports as a youngster, and how it all came so easy to him.

"My favorite sport was baseball, but I liked basketball, too," he said. "For a while, I thought it was going to be basketball for me. By the time I really started attracting some attention for basketball, I'd already gotten letters from colleges for football. The coach told me people were looking at me. I didn't always take basketball seriously, but I wanted to win, and I turned some heads, I'm told.

"I was forced to run track. The football coach forced us to go out for track. I played baseball for a little while in the spring and ran track, too. Sports came easy to me, a gift from God. I've always been an athletic person. I didn't need sports to fit in. Sports was a vehicle to get me to higher education."

C. J. Johnson was eavesdropping. "I liked the way you used that word — vehicle — the way you said it, just like a college professor," interjected Johnson. Then he smiled, it started out as a smile anyhow. Then he just cracked up.

Figures got back at Johnson by saying that C.J. didn't do his homework at Colorado, that he had girls do it for him. C.J. broke up, curled up, holding his sides.

Figures was asked if his sports activity helped keep him out of trouble in his school days.

"You could have played sports and still gotten in trouble," he said. "There was time after practice or after the games, if that's what you wanted to do. I had friends who were better than me or as good as me, but after sports they still had time to run with gangs. It can be done.

"You have to stay focused on what's really important to you. It all starts with parents. I had strong family values. They were there, every step of the way. Once I sprouted wings and was on my own, I still had my conscience, like a little voice, to make the right or wrong decision. You'd think, 'My parents wouldn't like that.' We all did devious things. But everything I did I heard that little voice from my parents; it was always there. We're not perfect. I wasn't no angel. We all make mistakes"

"I could be dead.
I could be paralyzed."
— Deon Figures

Was he still haunted by what happened to him that morning in L.A., how it could have been much worse?

"It still does," he conceded. "After I left the hospital, I thought about it. I could have gotten shot somewhere else, in the head, in the heart. I could be dead. I still think about it. I'm blessed. I'm out here, having a chance to play football. I could have been paralyzed. No, it won't go away."

Figures said he saw the guy who did it. He saw the man pointing the gun. But he was puzzled. Why was the man — someone he didn't know — pointing the gun at him?

"I didn't know what it was. I was just the victim."

The tendon had been ripped from the muscles surrounding it when a bullet pierced the driver's door of Figures' car and struck the left knee.

When he realized he'd been shot, which wasn't for four or five minutes, his first thought was, " 'What hospital am I going to?' When I felt I was bleeding, I thought I was just grazed. But when I reached down there and felt my leg again, I could feel the bullet. The bullet was so big it was like a lump on my leg."

He had friends who had been shot, and he felt he could get himself to the hospital. "I had full control over everything," he said. "I wriggled my foot all the way to the hospital to make sure it was all right."

Once there, he said he had to wait 40 minutes at the hospital before he was seen by a doctor.

"You're talking about L.A., the gang capital of the world, and on weekends, they are short-staffed?" said Figures, a quizzical look on his face.

"I guess everything happens for a reason, so I am going to try to turn this negative into a positive. It's just another obstacle I have to overcome. I'm going to do what the doctor told me to do and get back as soon as possible."

Growing up in L.A., he resisted the temptation to join a gang, even though many of his friends were members. Sports provided an option to staying out of trouble. Being a part of a team appealed to him more than being a member of a gang.

"A lot of guys were better than me in sports," said Figures, though that's difficult to accept. "They chose to do what they are doing, but my main goal was getting to college and getting my education paid for. Peddling drugs can provide a quick payoff. Yeah, it's easy money, quick cash. You have teenage friends, driving cars that you know their parents can't afford. But there's no long-term goal in it. For me, the drug world was self-destructive. It was the difference between right and wrong."

Did he feel safer in Pittsburgh?

"L.A. is labeled to be this bad place. But Pittsburgh can be bad, too. At least, in L.A. I know where to go and where not to go, or at least I thought I did. Pittsburgh is proof that you can run, but you can't hide."

That sounded a lot like what heavyweight boxing champion Joe Louis said after he disposed of Billy Conn — "The Pittsburgh Kid" — after the first of their two title fights.

"I know L.A. That's where I grew up," said Figures. "That's what I know. I know some of the things police did. You've got good cops and you've got bad cops. Two bad cops can spoil it for the rest. They can bring down the entire police force, as far as the people in the streets are concerned. Look at what happened here with Ray Seals' cousin."

Was he ever tempted to join a gang? Did it have an attraction for him?

"It was real attractive," said Figures. "A lot of my friends were in it, so in a sense I was, too. I was guilty by association. When I went to school, I went with my friends. If another gang saw us, they figured I was in a gang. You're damned if you do, damned if you don't. If you try to distance yourself from them, what about the rival gang? Who was going to help you?

"I separated myself by being in sports. I wasn't no angel. I did things. Sports kept me out of the gangs. I knew, and I told myself there wasn't no future in this. You can't do this all your life. I started focusing on sports. If it weren't for sports, I might've slipped and gotten into real trouble.

"My friends who were in gangs even helped me out to keep me clean. I'll tell you a story about that. When I was at Colorado, I got suspended my second year, and wasn't permitted to play. When I came home, all the fellows in the neighborhood were mad at me. They said, 'You could have messed up at home. What are you doing, messing up at school? You're the one who made it out; we were proud of you. We could see you on TV playing ball, and be proud of you.' When they did certain things they knew could be trouble, they wouldn't let me go with them.

"I can still stop and see the guys in my old neighborhood. They'll recognize me when I'm driving by. I'll stop and talk to them. Most of them are glad to see me; you have the jealous few."

"I messed up. We all messed up."

After the AFC title game loss to San Diego at the outset of 1995, Figures was one of the few Steelers who stood up to be counted when the media entered the locker room. He was a standup guy.

"A lot of guys didn't want to talk to the media and were feeling bad," Figures later told Jerry DiPaola of the *Tribune-Review*. "I mean, I was feeling bad, too. But when they came to me, and asked me what happened, it was sort of a relief. Instead of running and throwing helmets and jumping up and down, I spoke to the media.

"I messed up. We all messed up. It wasn't just Tim McKyer who gave up the game-winning touchdown. It takes a man to admit his mistakes. All I can do is learn from that and, hopefully, it won't happen again.

"It took me a couple of months to get over it. It's still not out of my system. But you just have to look forward and leave things in the past. As long as you can learn from them

> *"Tis grace has brought me safe this far*
> *And grace will lead me home."*
> —From the hymn,
> Amazing Grace, How Sweet Thou Art

A Clinic with Bill Cowher
Remembering his roots

"Wouldn't you like to play for this guy?"
— Johnny Majors

Bill Cowher came to the campus of the University of Pittsburgh on a Friday evening, March 22, 1996, to be the featured speaker at the Pitt Football Coaches Clinic. The head coach of the Pittsburgh Steelers was less than two months away from Super Bowl XXX and his popularity was at a peak.

He was to address high school coaches from the tri-state area in a lecture hall of the School of Pharmacy in Salk Hall, just across Sutherland Drive from Gate 3 at Pitt Stadium. Cowher would be speaking in an area of the building where Dr. Jonas Salk conducted experiments in the mid-1950s that led to his discovery of the anti-polio vaccine, one of the major breakthroughs in medical history. Sutherland Drive was named after Jock Sutherland, a Hall of Fame coach at Pitt (1924-1938), another reminder of the school's rich history.

As a youngster, Cowher had trekked up that hill a few times with his father, Laird Cowher, coming in from Crafton to catch a Pitt or Steelers football game at Pitt Stadium. But he had been a stranger on the Pitt campus since then, and required directions to get there. He had been away too long.

The room was full of coaches, all with notebooks at the ready on their student desks.

Pitt's head coach, Johnny Majors, credited the appearance of Cowher for the increased attendance at the clinic, a jump from a registration of 95 coaches the previous year to over 150. It was the first time Cowher had come to speak to these coaches in his four years as the Steelers' coach. He said he was happy there were no conflicts on his schedule this time, so that he was able to accept Majors' invitation.

It was the first week of spring, according to the calendar, but it was snowing and it was 20 degrees, hardly spring-like weather. It had been a difficult day for Cowher and Majors, and the frigid weather didn't help.

There was an alarming news break on Pittsburgh TV and radio stations that afternoon that gave Cowher great concern. His star running back, indeed, one of the team's brightest lights in the loss to the Dallas Cowboys in Super Bowl XXX, had been arrested earlier in the day in Texas.

Bam Morris and a buddy had been stopped by police when Morris was driving too fast and weaving in and out of traffic in his black Mercedes-Benz. Morris gave the police permission to search the car — which he was not required to do — and the police said they found seven pounds of marijuana in a bag in the trunk of the automobile. Morris was jailed for several hours before he posted bail. If found guilty of drug possession Morris would face a jail sentence and fine. Later, the police would come up with a small amount of cocaine under the ashtray as well.

No matter what the outcome, it looked bad for the Pittsburgh Steelers who had already had more than their share of off-the-field incidents that cast a bad light on the team. The worst incident was when Jonny Gammage, the cousin and best friend of defensive tackle Ray Seals, died from an altercation with Pittsburgh suburban police officers after he was stopped while driving an expensive auto owned by Seals.

Cowher was visibly upset at the Steelers' offices that day. He did his best to put on a happy face for the clinic and he succeeded in a big way.

Before Cowher spoke to the coaches at the clinic, he declined an interview request from Andrew Stockey, a sportscaster from WTAE-TV, who came with a cameraman to Salk Hall and wanted to ask Cowher some questions about Morris.

Majors was scheduled to introduce Cowher at the clinic, but could not be there because he was across the street at Presbyterian-University Hospital looking after one of his players who had been critically injured that afternoon.

Demale Stanley, a redshirt freshman receiver from Belle Glades, Florida, broke his neck during the team's fourth session of spring practice. He was injured during a workout at Pitt's indoor practice facility, the Cost Center, when he lost his balance and fell into a padded wall while trying to catch a pass. His father, Wayne Stanley, had played football at Iowa State and was an assistant coach at Ohio State from 1979 to 1983. If it hadn't been so cold, Pitt would have practiced outdoors and this might never have happened...

Majors didn't make it to the clinic until Cowher had completed his remarks. He had remained with Stanley, and was greatly concerned about his condition, understandably enough. Majors already knew from the doctors that Stanley had suffered a fractured vertebrae, and there was reason to fear that Stanley had suffered spinal cord damage. Pitt neurosurgeon Dr. Donald Marion would perform emergency surgery later that evening.

No one knew it that night, but Stanley would end up a quadriplegic from the injury. Everyone knew it was a grave situation, though, so everyone was grim.

It is not easy to be a football coach in the best of circumstances, and that was hardly the case on this particular day. Cowher and Majors were both on edge, Majors was downright ashen-faced when he first entered the room, but they managed to put on a happy face for the coaches who had come to learn from them. Coaches are always preaching about the need to fight through adversity.

"You may or may not agree with me."
— Bill Cowher

Cowher got comfortable in a hurry when he arrived at Salk Hall. He was there about 25 minutes early for a scheduled 7:15 p.m. speaking appearance. He discovered two of his football coaches from his days at Carlynton High School in the back of the room and took a seat next to them and talked to them at length. Bill Yost had been his ninth grade coach, and then Chuck Saunders had him for three years with the varsity.

While he was talking to Yost and Saunders, another coach sitting in the row ahead of them turned around and introduced himself. It was John Haught, a silver-haired veteran of 20 seasons as the head coach at Chartiers-Houston High School in Washington County.

Haught knew Cowher was a close friend of Marty Schottenheimer, and had been an assistant coach on Schottenheimer's staff for seven years at Cleveland and Kansas City. "Marty and I were classmates at Fort Cherry High," said Haught. "I was the quarterback of our team. Marty was quite an athlete."

Cowher smiled in response to that remark, and made a few lighthearted comments. So Cowher had connections with this crowd. He felt at home, and he felt good about being the head coach of the Steelers in his hometown. He would have felt even better if Bam Morris had not been arrested in Texas that day.

Cowher was introduced by Jim Earle, assistant director of football operations at Pitt, who pointed out that Cowher had never coached with a losing team in his 11 years in the National Football League, and that he was with 10 teams that made it to the playoffs in that same span. Cowher, of course, had coached the Steelers to the playoffs all four years he had been the head coach, and had taken them to the AFC title game and the Super Bowl before losing the last two seasons.

The Steelers' coach looked good. Cowher, at 38, appeared in great shape as he strode back and forth on a raised platform, demonstrating defensive secondary techniques.

He wore a red windbreaker with dark blue trim over a white turtleneck jersey, dark blue sweatpants, and brand new white sneakers. He spoke with great enthusiasm, moved about smartly, swiftly, showing proper hip rotation moves, proper form necessary for defensive backs to stay with pass-receivers, techniques for linebackers to shed blockers to get to ballcarriers or passers, slick and assured as can be. He went through the motions, step by step, like an instructor at an Arthur Murray Dance Studio.

He was humble enough, conceding that he didn't have as much experience as some of the coaches who crowded the room, that he had learned these things from all the coaches he had met along the way, confessing that he wasn't a very good pro athlete, much self-deprecat-

Bill Cowher chats with Johnny Majors at Pitt football clinic.

Cowher enjoys reunion with two of his boyhood coaches, Bill Yost, his 9th grade tutor, and Chuck Saunders, the head coach at Carlynton High School during his days with the Cougars.

ing stuff. "You may or may not agree with me...," he said more than once before introducing his ideas about some aspect of playing football.

He invited a young coach to come up on the platform with him so he could demonstrate some methods to strip the ball from passers and runners. Cowher kept chopping on the young man's arms, and he did so with great fervor. There's a good chance that the young man awoke the next morning with red welts on his forearms. Cowher apologized to the young man when he completed that segment, saying he hoped he hadn't hurt him.

More than anything else, it showcased Cowher's intensity as a coach, and the great enthusiasm he brings to his task. That had to leave an impression on all the coaches.

"Those were some of the most wonderful days I had in football."
— Bill Cowher

Cowher was politically-correct in everything he said to the coaches. "Coming back to Western Pennsylvania, and the people who are most important to developing our game and our kids, is still a thrill for me," he said. "It goes back to the grass roots, to high school, even to Pop Warner days."

Unwittingly, Cowher had called upon the name of another Pitt football legend. Pop Warner coached several national championship teams at Pitt during his tenure (1915-1923).

"Some of the coaching I've gotten, even back in those Pop Warner days," continued Cowher, "I still remember very, very vividly. Those were some of the most wonderful days I had in football, because it was all in fun."

He told the coaches that getting a chance to talk to them about football — just football — would be a welcome break for him from talking about salary caps and "everything else that's been happening lately. It's great to get away from of the things I've had to deal with, and just talk about football, pure and simple."

He told them he thought that he would discuss defensive secondary techniques and practice drills that might be useful to them in preparing their teams. He had been a linebacker as a player and a special teams coach and then defensive coordinator as a pro coach before coming back to Pittsburgh. That was his area of expertise.

To set the tone, Cowher showed them a recently-released four minute highlight tape put together for team use only by NFL Films. It had some great moments from NFL action in the past season, including looks at Danny Marino and Marty Schottenheimer, two of Pitt's finest, and finished up with the Steelers and Cowboys at Super Bowl XXX. It had the usual exciting visuals, vibrant colors, heart-pounding music, sportscasters shrieking to describe great catches or touchdown scores, hard-hitting stuff. Cowher had a cameo appearance, addressing his team in the locker room before the game. It ended with the Cowboys celebrating their triumph in Tempe.

At its conclusion, Cowher said, "I was going to cut out that last part before I showed it to you." That drew a laugh from the coaches, as did the one joke Cowher told later on to lighten up things.

He told them the sort of inside stuff football coaches and fans love to hear at such gatherings. He mentioned some of the early-season problems experienced by Willie Williams and Carnell Lake in playing the cornerback positions. He talked about learning how to read the offense, the discipline and practice needed to make it second nature.

"When Willie first came in, he could run with anybody, but his biggest thing was playing the ball," said Cowher. "He's small (5-8, 180 pounds), and I'm sure that was part of it. He kinda panicked when he saw the ball coming toward the receiver he was covering.

"You only have to cover the receiver when the ball gets there. We tell our defensive backs, 'Don't panic.' Most quarterbacks will allow you time to recover, to move on the receiver as the ball is being released. You don't have to be on the receiver all the way. You can get back to where they are.

"You've got to practice this. Some coaches are afraid to get their guys banged up at practice, but the defensive backs have to learn how to play the ball. You have to do it in practice. I used to think it was just something that came naturally, or was instinctive, knowing when to leap and go for the ball. But it's like anything else, I'm now convinced, the more you do it the better you get at it. But you can teach it and it can be learned. We do it every so often after the season starts. Yes, you can get hurt. But I don't think you can do it enough. You learn the timing.

"The biggest thing about playing the corner is up here," said Cowher, tapping his head with an extended finger. "The best cornerbacks have short memories.

"We had a tough time in our opener with Detroit, even though we won the game. Willie had a tough time against Detroit. It turned out, though, that he took on a wide receiver (Herman Moore) who gave a lot of people similar trouble all year long.

"We got to Miami two weeks later, and Willie started making plays. There was a big difference. We had told him at practice to play the ball. To go for it at the same time the receiver was going for it.

"We played a game at midseason against Cincinnati, and Jeff Blake was throwing rainbows and they were beating us to the ball. Carnell Lake couldn't do anything right. We had moved him up from safety to play the corner, and he was having a difficult day. I talked to him on the bench and I asked him, 'Carnell, how do you like playing corner?' He said, 'I hate it coach.' I said, 'Keep making them make perfect throws.' If you're beat up here (Cowher pointed to his head again), you're a defeated man. That position, more than any other, is played up here in your head."

Then he posed a question for his audience: "What's the single most important key to defensive success?"

No one in the audience volunteered an answer. "Coach Yost?" Cowher called out to his ninth grade football coach.

Yost blushed in the back of the room. "Thanks, Bill," he said for openers.

Just as Cowher continued to talk, Yost yelled out, "Tackling."

"No question," Cowher came back.

Yost smiled like a student who had pulled the right answer out of the bag at the last second.

"Tackling is such an important aspect of football, but none of us teach it enough. We tend to take it for granted, and so do most of the players. Many of them are doing things that have been ingrained in them since they were ten. Tackling is one thing that we don't do well. 'See what you hit.' That's one thing we've got to get across. The guy who puts his head down gets hurt 90 percent of the time. You've got to keep your head up. It's OK to close your eyes when you hit. The biggest thing in tackling is running through the guy. Put the hit on him, not the other way around.

"Use these arms (he extended his arms full length from his side). You've got a bigger margin for success if your arms and hands are outstretched than you do if you try to knock people down with a rolling block, or by propelling yourself at them like a missile. You've got to create the angle and wrap those arms around the ballcarrier."

When he spoke about stripping the ball from quarterbacks and ballcarriers, Cowher pointed out proudly that the Steelers had led the league in takeaways the previous few years.

Then he said something that, honestly, I'd never heard expressed.

"The No. 1 order for the defense is to get the ball back," he said. "It's not to hold them on third down, or to force a field goal try on fourth down. You want to hit the quarterback's arm before he releases the ball, you want to go for the ball when a ballcarrier exposes it. You want to make sure you tackle him, first, of course, but you can use your other arm to strip the ball and force a fumble."

Cowher talked for about an hour and a half, and went into the time scheduled for his former special teams coach, Bobby April, who had surprisingly left the Steelers soon after Super Bowl XXX to join Jim Mora on the staff of the New Orleans Saints in his home state.

"I'm on your time," Cowher commented when he spotted April appearing at the back of the room, "but to hell with you. You're with the Saints!" Cowher got the laugh he was looking for, and came back with a complimentary remark about April. "You're going to learn a lot from this guy; he's a wonderful special teams coach. And we're going to miss him."

Then Cowher complimented his audience, and all the people who work in similar capacities.

152

"People ask me what coaching is," he said. "To me, it's about you guys. You guys are so important to this whole process. You guys don't get enough credit. You guys don't get to go to Super Bowls; you don't get playoff money; you don't get big salaries.

"But you might be the most instrumental people in the lives of young players. You set them in the right direction. I remember the group of guys I played with in high school and even before that. I remember it more so than college, maybe because football was just fun back then. You guys have an ability to truly create the proper environment for young people, and help keep them off the streets, and out of trouble.

"I know the kinds of sacrifices these guys have to make to practice with your teams. During summer camp it's hot and some of their friends are at the swimming pool, and they have to be at practice. It requires a real commitment, and a lot of hard work. You guys promote that stuff: team, sacrifice, hard work. Those are the most important qualities they can learn at that point in their lives. You give them direction, you create camaraderie, an option from the gangs and life on the streets. I can't thank you enough for what you do for young people. Coaching is a consuming business, but it's so satisfying at the same time.

"I wouldn't do anything else in the world. You can go to the Super Bowl, but you never forget where you came from. I know there are guys back there (at the rear of the room) who were so important to me and my development. I wouldn't be where I am today if I didn't have them on my side at the start. We've got a great game; I truly believe it is our best game. We can make our society better."

With that, Cowher came down off the stage, and started signing autographs for anybody who approached him, and answered some more questions. When April approached the podium and started sorting through a loose-leaf binder, Cowher cried out, "If that's the Steelers playbook, you better leave it right here!"

Cowher cracked an ear-to-ear grin; it was all in good fun. And April responded with a smile of his own.

Majors showed up about that time, and took the microphone. He apologized for not being there earlier, explained the situation about the serious injury to one of his players, then praised Cowher.

"Wouldn't you like to play for this guy?" he asked all in attendance. "I'm not that familiar with the Steelers' organization and how they do things, but I talk to Marty Schottenheimer, and Marty swears by Bill Cowher. Wouldn't you like to play for a guy who is so emotionally involved in the game?"

Then Majors made a confession to the crowd. Majors was in his first coaching stay at Pitt when Cowher was playing ball at Carlynton High School. Cowher was graduated in 1975. Had he gone to Pitt he would have been a sophomore when the Panthers won the national championship.

"We didn't do a very good recruiting job," Majors admitted in hindsight. "We didn't get this guy."

153

Chad Brown
Cut from a different cloth

"I don't like football, but it pays well."

C had Brown was a different breed of football player. Physically and mentally, he moved to the beat of a different drummer. Don't get the wrong idea, though. He was not different, in the sense of a Dennis Rodman or Deion Sanders, just different. Not disruptive, not a tap dancer, he did not wear out his welcome.

Brown boasted that he had always been different, from his earliest days in Pop Warner leagues in Altadena, California. He moonlighted in the snake and reptile business, for beginners. He was interested in Black History studies and Eastern religions. He had often questioned his participation in the rugged sport in which he had long excelled, yet he hated it when he was hurt and unable to play or perform to his immense ability. He was tough to keep on the sideline. He said things that left you wondering.

"He's different all right," said fellow linebacker Levon Kirkland. "But so are Jerry Olsavsky, Greg Lloyd and Kevin Greene, and I love playing with those guys."

"Just don't let Chad talk you into buying a male and female python or boa constrictor and getting into the snake breeding business," said Olsavsky with a laugh. "That could cost you."

Brown should have been there to witness that locker room exchange. He would have laughed, too.

He even took exception to the layout of the locker room, believing it to be an antiquated setup, and wondered why they didn't have a locker that was more like a modern day office, with lots of cubicles or space partitions, desks, computers, room to read and to relax or to write, with a little more privacy. He questioned the behavior of some of his teammates on the field, on the sideline, in the locker room and, especially, in the shower room, and away from the office, so to speak, yet he was no prude or party pooper.

Sometimes he appeared to be aloof, stony and indifferent to the media moving about the locker room, but he was easy to talk to once you got past the petrified mask. He smiled a great deal, and made sense even if some of his ideas were out of left field, as far as football players were concerned. He was at his best when he was in the company of his wife, Kristin, whom he met during their student days at the University of Colorado. She was a petite, dark-haired, dark-eyed beauty who had done some modeling, been involved with Chad in several charity-related fund-raising projects on behalf of the Steelers and carried herself well. They were a handsome couple. They lived in a

George Gojkovich

Chad Brown is ready to strike.

Lynn Johnson

Snake-charmer

Pittsburgh Steelers

Chad and Kristin Brown

Pittsburgh Steelers/Michael F. Fabus

Equipment manager Tony Parisi adjusts helmet for Brown in his rookie season.

Chad accompanies Kristin down walkway at fashion show to raise funds for cancer research for women. Kristin and Nicki Woodson were co-chairpersons for the annual event in 1995.

Pittsburgh Steelers

comfortable home near North Park, which was an easy commute for both of them to the city.

Chadwick Everett Brown was different in another respect. He came from an interracial marriage. His mother was white and his father was black. It was something he had in common with Rod Woodson, whose locker was only two away from Brown's, with Deion Figures and Charles Johnson separating them. Yet Brown said he had never discussed this natural bond with Woodson, or compared notes with him on his personal experiences in that regard.

"From what I've read, Rod had some bad experiences because of it," said Brown. "I've read up on it, but I didn't think it was my place to bring up the subject. Where I grew up in Altadena, it seemed like a quarter of the children came from interracial marriages. My mother, her name is Marcia, liked the surroundings. So it was never a big deal for us. My father, James, is an auto mechanic or technician with an associate arts degree. My mother is the head teacher and a supervisor at our local school. I learned people skills from my mother."

Chad Brown had his wife's name — KRISTIN — tattooed over his heart, and I have to admit that when I first saw it the thought that crossed my mind was that he had better stay married to this woman, otherwise the next woman in his life might have a problem with the signage on his body. In that respect, apparently, I was as boorish as some of his teammates on the Steelers.

"I was a little surprised by the reaction of some of the guys on the team," said Brown. "When I first got it, I walked into the showers one day, and a few guys got on me about it. 'You must really love her,' they said. Stuff like that. As if that were a bad thing. Like it was bad to love your wife.

"We both come from stable families, and we're most serious about our relationship. My wife has a little tattoo of her own, with my name on it, only hers is not as visible as mine. It's just something we wanted to do. Some people come to marriage and don't view this as an agreement that you're going to stay together. That's the only way we approached it. That bothers me...that some guys think the way they do. To me, there's nothing frivolous about being married to Kristin."

"He's a very proud individual."
— Coach Bill Cowher

Brown was big and fast, at 6-2, 240 pounds, and played the inside linebacker position. He missed the last five games of the regular season in 1995, with a sprained ankle and did not start in either playoff game, but was restored to his starting position for Super Bowl XXX. Brown went to the coaches the week before the game and requested that he be returned to his starting position for the prestigious assignment in Super Bowl XXX.

The Steelers were 6-1 in the won-lost column with Jerry Olsavsky starting at the same inside linebacker position, but Brown had been the starter at the outset of the schedule, and starters were not supposed to lose their positions because of injuries once they were rolling again at 100 per cent of their ability and skill level, as Brown reminded the coaches.

Brown had been leading the league with 5 1/2 sacks after five games. Brown sprained his ankle on October 19 when Cincinnati's Harold Greene blocked him below his knees. Brown rushed back to play the next three games, but wasn't right. Along the way, he reinjured his ankle on October 29 in a game against the Jacksonville Jaguars. He had to sit out the last five games of the regular season schedule. He alternated with Olsavsky in the two playoff games, and believed he was playing to form again and wanted to start the championship game.

While he regarded Olsavsky as a superior technician, who read the offense better because of his experience and natural instinct for the ball, Brown wanted back in the limelight. He was thought to be bigger, stronger, swifter and more versatile by most observers, though Olsavsky was a local favorite and had his own fan club. So it was a touchy situation.

"That's the most frustrated I've ever been," Brown had said when he tried to play before his ankle was completely healed. He wasn't nearly as effective. It stripped him of quickness and explosiveness.

"I've seen what I can do when I'm in my complete zone. I reached a really high level in college," he continued. "Now, I want to get back up to a really high level here. I won't be satisfied until I reach that level again."

Steelers coach Bill Cowher offered this comment on Brown: "He's his own worst critic, and that's a great quality to have. He's a very proud individual."

In just three seasons with the Steelers, Brown had made a big impact on people throughout the league. He was a rising star when he was, first, slowed by the ankle injury and, then, sidelined by it for five games. People had been talking about Brown as a Pro Bowl candidate before he got hurt.

"I always had the fire."
— Chad Brown

When Chad Brown goes back to the beginning, he has to smile to consider the success he has enjoyed at every level of football competition. His mother remembered him poring over the Sears catalog when he was a young child, looking for pictures of the Cowboys, his favorite team, in the sporting goods section.

"All the neighborhood kids played football," he said during a break in practice on January 1, 1996. "We'd get Sears football uniforms for Christmas. We played in our front yard. I had a Dallas Cowboys uniform. One of my best friends, Joel Bryant, who was two years older than me, wore a Steelers uniform. He wore Lynn Swann's number — 88 — and I wore number 34. I don't think anybody on the Cowboys wore that number back then. Everyone wanted number 33 or number 12, but I didn't want to be Tony Dorsett or Roger Staubach. I just wanted to be Chad Brown. And I still feel that way... see, even then I was different.

"My entire neighborhood was sports crazy in Altadena. There were maybe 10 or 15 Division I scholarship holders that came out of my neighborhood; most of those guys were older than me. Playing with older kids helped me. I always had the fire. I was a true competitor. I had seven brothers and sisters, but not too many of them were interested in sports."

His father was his first coach for the YMCA flag football teams. In California, a candidate must be seven or eight to play tackle football in the Pop Warner League. His mother remembered that, in middle school, he even played with a broken thumb against her wishes.

His mother recalled his good fortune on January 15, 1996, just two weeks away from Super Bowl XXX. She said, "He's been very lucky with the teams in his life. They seem to run on the winning side. My husband, Jim, has a theory that it is the third year cycle championship. His third year of Pop Warner, they won the championship; his third year of high school they won the CIF championship; his third year of college they won the 1990 Orange Bowl and the national championship. So stay tuned for the Super Bowl 1996."

Well, Brown and his teammates certainly had a chance to keep James Brown's theory intact, but they came up short in Super Bowl XXX.

Marcia Brown also remembered when she first realized that her son, Chad, had a certain gift and that others recognized this and were willing to work with him to make sure he realized his potential.

"In high school, they were coached by Jim Brownfield, a man dedicated to the team, the school, the game, but especially to the players," wrote Mrs. Brown. "When Chad was first on the varsity, Coach Brownfield invited my husband and me to meet him at a local coffee shop. He sat and told us what he saw as the potential of our son in football and wanted us to support the school and the player. He stated then that if Chad were interested, he could help him get a scholarship to college, but Chad would have to do the academic work and he asked us to support him in that. One of the things for which we were grateful to Coach Brownfield was that not only did he instill the game techniques in Chad and his players, but also a real confidence in self and a determination to attain whatever you dare to dream."

Chad recalled that he devoted a great deal of time to preparing himself to play football. "My parents let me focus on football," he said. "It's all I had to do. We spent 50 weeks a year working out, sometimes on our own. We practiced at 7 o'clock at night. There was not much time off.

"I was thinking about this, and all my life I have been on a scholarship to play football. It's always been a job instead of a dream to attain. In high school, my parents said I didn't have to have a job if I played football. I still had to do my chores, but no outside job. If there was a Saturday night game, Chad was out in the yard with Dad doing the yardwork. But my parents completely supported me. They came to all my games. They picked me up and took me everywhere I had to go."

The regimen was not for everybody. "I have a younger brother, Van, who's 14, and we're just two different people. He's still trying to figure out what the differences are.

"It bothers him to live in my shadow. It really upsets him. He just wants to be Van, but people won't let him. When he played Pop Warner, he had the same coach I had, so the comparisons were inevitable.

"Van needs a better sense of self-worth, a sense of confidence. Somewhere along the way, I just had supreme confidence. Throughout all my life I have believed in myself. I have not always believed in football, or whether or not I belonged, but it wasn't because I was down on myself."

Brown believed that football also gave him a challenge that occupied much of his time during his days at Muir High School, and helped keep him out of trouble.

"I went to a high school where I was the only player who went to college. Our quarterback was in and out of jail. I never felt peer pressure to get into trouble. If you used crack you were looked down upon. People who were into crack were called the cluckers. I never felt any pressure to do that. There was peer pressure to drink, but I've never been much of a drinker, even during my wild days in college. I just always played football. I always had my focus. What happens with some kids is that they lose focus. At college, I'd see my friends around me making mistakes, but I knew better because of what my parents had pointed out to me."

There was a point, however, when Brown had his fill of football and its demands and wanted out. Midway through his career at Colorado, Chad called his father James and wanted to leave school and come home. "My dad had told me every year that if you don't want to do this you don't have to," said Brown, "but he talked me out of leaving when I said I wanted to. I had been playing since I was six, and I was just tired of it." Brown admitted there were a few times he just wanted to hang it up.

"It ceased to be fun," he said. "I just wanted to be a regular student. Some guys on this team didn't play till they were seniors in high school. It had gotten to be a routine. I wanted to be a regular person.

I was struggling with my identity. I wanted to be more than a football player. All my life I always had a perspective that there was a lot more to learn outside the classroom. I learned a lot in my travels. I didn't want to be at spring practice. I wanted to be in Costa Rica.

"At Colorado, we had to stay in the dorms with the rest of the students for the first two years. I had a chance to see how the other students lived. To see the regular students come back to the dorm and take a nap when we were headed for practice always gave you pause for thought.

"Being of interracial parents, I'm able to slide in and out of groups. It was something I picked up in high school. My roommate was a black guy. Both of his parents were black. He was much darker than me. He couldn't blend in as easily. I could see that most of the white students were more comfortable with me. I can mix easily with white guys and with black guys. To me, I'm both. But I'm smart enough to know that they may not all see it that way. In college, black students want to be blacker. They're trying to establish their identities. It's a pride thing. My parents just always made me feel comfortable wherever I went. I've always been comfortable with who I am. From the books I've read, and talk shows I've listened to, I know a lot of interracial kids have problems. From what I've read, Rod Woodson had a hard time. I just never felt it."

He was glad he stayed at Colorado. Bill McCartney was a good coach and he ran a great program. McCartney espoused moral values and founded Promisekeepers, a national organization for Christian men. The Steelers certainly thought highly of Colorado football because they had drafted so many of its players. "That says something about the program at Colorado," said Brown. "McCartney speaks about the will to win. 'It's in the heart of a man,' he'd say. It got a little old after four years. He'd say, 'Everyone wants to win, but do you have the will to win?' He worked on the mental aspects as well as the physical aspects of the game. He wanted you to be excited about being out there. And I am. I still talk a lot out there."

In his last Orange Bowl appearance, Brown made ten tackles and had two pass deflections and forced a key fumble that led to the game-winning touchdown in a 10-9 win over Notre Dame when Colorado won its first national championship.

He was graduated with a degree in marketing and did some graduate work in physiology in his fifth year at Colorado.

"He reminded us a great deal of Jack Ham."
— Tom Donahoe

The Steelers selected two Colorado players with their first two picks in the 1991 draft, defensive back Deon Figures and linebacker Chad Brown.

Big catch for young fisherman

Chad Brown was center of attention at John Muir High School Baccalaureate in June, 1988, with father James, kid brother Van, 7, and mother, Maria.

At graduation with sister Angela on June 28, 1988.

Before his first haircut in winter of 1972.

Brown men include dad, James, and brothers Darryl, Chad, Van and Jimmy.

Chad at two months with his mom

Tom Donahoe, the director of football operations for the Steelers, offered this comment about Brown on draft day: "When the guy worked out he reminded us a great deal of Jack Ham, only he's bigger. He's just that kind of athlete."

Brown signed a three-year $1.2 million contract with the Steelers. He was making $316,500 in base salary during the 1995 season.

While he appreciated the Steelers' rich tradition, Brown was eager for the Bill Cowher-coached edition he was playing for to make its own mark. Keep in mind that he wasn't a Steelers fan in his youth, and actually preferred college ball to pro ball when he was in high school. "I never idolized any of the old Steelers," he said. "My athletic hero was Muhammad Ali."

Even so, Brown confessed that he quickly recognized that the standards for the Steelers were quite high. "It didn't take too long at all," he said. "The whole organization and the whole city is about winning. I had instant respect for that because I'm about winning."

He was voted Steelers rookie of the year in 1993. He quickly followed the Steelers' tradition for getting involved in community service. His wife, Kristin, who majored in kinesiology at Colorado, joined him in that activity. Her family had a history of cancer, so she teamed up with Nicki Woodson as coordinators for the Steelers' annual fashion show, which benefited cancer research for women.

Brown also was the Steelers' representative for a summer football camp for the Western Pennsylvania School for the Deaf. "They wanted the biggest name player they could find," said Brown. "They were talking to Joe Gordon and Ron Miller of our public relations and community relations department, and they told them Chad Brown's a great guy, right? Well, they recommended me, anyhow, and I went along with it. Kristin has contributed her time and efforts as well, so it's something we're able to do together."

Brown believed it was important to appear in public, and to help where he could in the community, to make connections, to look to a future without football.

"I wouldn't say I'm rare that way, but I don't think as many players think about it as they should," said Brown. "This is a temporary job at best. If you play nine years, you've more than doubled the average.

"I think people appreciate it. If they see you see the need to lend yourself to a project, to doing extra things."

"It's an unusual environment, the locker room. It's not the real world."
— Chad Brown

Chad Brown begs not to be misunderstood. While he has some questions about playing pro football for a living, it is not something he does with a half-hearted effort.

162

"I have great pride," he said. "I don't want the other guy to beat me. I don't like a lot of things about football. It pays well, I have pride in my performance, and there's nothing else I can do where the rewards are as great.

"I've been playing football since I was six. Sometimes I wonder if that's all there is. Sometimes I get tired of hitting people. It sounds kind of funny. It hurts. But it's not a bad job. You get six months off. But you do get sore. Sometimes you'll be coming back from a west coast trip, and you're hurting all over, and you say to yourself, 'There's got to be an easier way to make a living.' But there's no other way that compares with the way I make my living.

"Most guys are happy on Monday. It's fun to pick up the paycheck. Some are sore. Our college coaches would say that everyone wants to play on Saturday. 'Do you have the will to prepare to win on Monday, Tuesday and Wednesday? To be a champion, that's what you have to do.' "

Brown was not planning any early retirement.

"Football is what I've chosen to do," he said. "I'm going to do it as hard and as best I can. Every time I'm out there, I have a lot of pride in my performance. It's not important if I like it. If I choose it, I'm going to do it to the hilt."

Brown looks about the locker room, and is asked to assess what he sees. He is not a noisy occupant of this place. More often than not, he appears to be an observer. He smiles a thin smile at some of the things he sees and hears. He is amused by this arena.

"The locker room is loaded with characters. Guys are joking, having a good time. When you walk away from the game, this is probably the part you will miss the most.

"But there are some aspects I won't miss. The whole thing is kinda crazy, if you think about it. I'm amazed sometimes. I'm disgusted. There's something I just don't get. I'll tell my wife. I'll tell the players, 'Sometimes I don't understand you guys.' There will be a scene like 20 naked men, hovering together in a corner of the shower room as one of the guys is spraying cold water from a hose on us. We're jumping and screaming and trying to hide behind somebody else. What kind of picture is that? It's like kids at a summer camp. Are you understanding me, or is this just an old hang-up?

"At the same time, one of the good things is just being around the group. Everyone is a character. Everyone has a story to tell."

My sentiments, exactly.

"I like to check people out," Chad continued. "I read stories that are written about some of these guys. I read it, if it's there. Some people are intriguing. Some of them have a public persona, but that's not really them. Why are they like this? They're definitely not that way outside of this room. It's an unusual environment, the locker room. It's not the real world."

"You don't take it for granted."
— Greg Lloyd

Brown's comments brought Greg Lloyd to mind. Like Brown, Lloyd is a linebacker with the Steelers. Lloyd is disliked by most of the media because he makes their job difficult. He was never warm to them, but early in the 1995 season, he stopped talking to the local media altogether. Some people I know and trust tell me that Lloyd was a different person when he appeared in public, when he spoke at a sports banquet, or when he was with the kids at Children's Hospital. They say he's warm and good-hearted and a real ambassador for the Steelers. Then again, Art Rooney once remarked, "I never had a player I didn't like." Other people I know and trust despise Lloyd. They think he is a hypocrite, a fraud. I think the truth is somewhere in between. To hear Brown talk, he can appreciate why Lloyd confused a lot of people.

"My first exposure to Greg Lloyd was in a workout in Barcelona before a pre-season game there," recalled Brown. "I had been a 10-day holdout as a rookie before signing my contract. And now I'm in Barcelona, which was a strange way to get started in the NFL. I wasn't sure whether to go full-speed or what."

He was playing on the same side of the line as Lloyd, yet in one sequence he wasn't sure whose side he was on. Lloyd bolted him and leveled him.

"He put me flat on my back. I realized this is for real. You don't take practices off."

When Lloyd was asked about the introduction he offered Brown to the world of the NFL, he said, "The standard is when you come out here, you are ready to play. You strap on that helmet and somebody's coming at you 100 miles per hour. You don't take it for granted. Even though we are practicing against our own teammates, it's like they are our enemies."

Brown might take exception to such strong talk, but he allowed that Lloyd backed up his bold talk with bold play.

"I'm impressed by Greg Lloyd," conceded Chad. "I get a kick out of his approach to this. His intensity and his fierce pride and determination on the field are incredible. Sometimes it gets misunderstood. Sometimes he's hollering at us, or at me, and I'll say, 'Hey, I'm doing the best I can. Don't yell at me, What is it you want me to do? Just tell me.' I don't like some of his carrying on when we're on the sideline, but I'm sure he doesn't mean it on a personal level. I'm out there and I'm doing my best, too.

"I admire his fire. People's perception is that he's always walking around with an evil glare. I see Greg in a relaxed mode, too. And I've seen him when he doesn't want to practice. He wouldn't admit that, though. But he's always intense on the field for the games.

"He'll start hollering at us, some of us swear it starts happening when the cameras get close, and we don't need that. It gets tiresome. I don't like him or anyone else throwing his helmet."

There was an incident when Rod Woodson hurled his helmet onto the turf in disgust the year before, and it bounced up and struck Brown in the face. He took five stitches under his eye for that outburst, so it was understandable he thought the players would be better off exercising some self-control, or taking it out on opponents only.

Brown doesn't play follow-the-leader with Lloyd, but he did manage to get fined $12,000 for a helmet to helmet hit on San Diego quarterback Stan Humphries in the fifth game of the 1995 season, after Lloyd had been hit with the same fine for a similar hit on Bret Favre of the Green Bay Packers in a pre-season game at Three Rivers Stadium. "It was a bigger fine for me," said Brown, "because Greg makes a lot more money than I do."

"I've never been anything but a starter."
— Chad Brown

Chad Brown and Jerry Olsavsky were competing for the same job. Olsavsky said toward the end of the 1995 season that he was not sure he would be back with the team for the following season. This was even before Brown was returned to the starting lineup for Super Bowl XXX. "They're going with Brown; the job's his. That's pretty obvious," Olsavsky said. As things turned out, Olsavsky was wrong. The Steelers still wanted him.

When Hardy Nickerson signed as a free agent with the Tampa Bay Buccaneers before the 1993 season, Olsavsky moved into the starting position at inside linebacker, alongside Levon Kirkland.

Olsavsky started the first seven games of the 1993 season until he tore three knee ligaments in Cleveland in a sickening collision. It was thought to be a career-ending injury.

When Olsavsky was brought to the sideline, Brown figured he would be going in to take his place. Bill Cowher and linebacker coach Marvin Lewis looked instead to another rookie, a free agent named Reggie Barnes. Getting snubbed in favor of a free agent woke up Brown.

"I was upset, but I wasn't ready," Brown said. "Reggie was hungrier than I was. I was a second-round pick. Reggie was a free agent. He came in with fire that I didn't have."

There was a bye week, and then Brown got his first start against the Cincinnati Bengals on November 7, 1993. Brown forced a fumble and had two sacks in his first start.He started nine games, plus the playoff game at Kansas City.

Olsavsky is a popular individual in the Steelers' locker room, with the players, equipment guys, and certainly with the press. Even

Lloyd liked him. "He says I'm his favorite white player," Olsavsky said with a broad smile on more than one occasion.

Brown respected Olsavsky, but still felt he was the superior performer and deserved to start.

"Jerry O's experience in coming back from such a serious injury has taught us all a lesson," said Brown. "You just gotta do it. He doesn't look pretty, and sometimes he doesn't do the proper technique, but he sure is a football player. It's a good feeling to see somebody come back from something as devastating as that. I can't say I would have come back, but it's a testament to his competitiveness."

Brown believed the competition for the starting job didn't have to get personal, though that was sometimes difficult because of the pride factor.

"That's a coach's job, to determine who is going to play," said Brown. "Just get me out there and let me play. I know what I'm capable of. When Jerry went down in the Cleveland game, I thought I'd go in. But the coaches played Reggie Barnes. I was devastated. I told Marv Lewis, 'I'm a player. Put me on the field. I've done this all my life. You have no reason to doubt me.' That was true. I've never been anything but a starter, always.

"At Colorado, I was red-shirted my freshman year, but I understood that was the way it worked. I have a starter's mentality. I don't have a backup's mentality. Reggie had been a free agent. I felt as if it would all come to me. My time would just come. In my mind, I was ready. 'Yeah, it's my turn.' I have extremely high expectations for myself. I didn't come close to practicing the way I was capable of playing."

When he hurt his ankle midway through the 1995 schedule, he could appreciate how Olsavsky felt when he lost his job because of an injury. Brown was reluctant to sit, and tried to play even though he was limited in his mobility.

"I'll be better than I was before," he said as the playoffs approached. "My ankle was bothering me and it was limiting my performance. I was half the player I was before my injury. They told me it was for the good of the team that I take some time off. I wanted to stay in there to help the team. When you're sidelined, you don't feel as much a part of the team.

"They'd go out to practice and I'd go to rehabilitate. They'd travel on Saturday and I stayed home. It's tough. It's definitely most disappointing. It's the toughest time I've had to deal with.

"This is something I have done since I was six years old. It's how I support my family. You get a sense of vulnerability. When things are going well, you think of yourself as invulnerable. You can't even do what you've been doing. As a player, you deny to yourself the extent of the injury. I came home on crutches one day. And I said, 'It's not that bad. I'll be all right.' I started walking around without my crutches. My wife got after me. 'What are you doing?' She studied the body and all its functions at Colorado, she was more critical of me than the average wife might have been."

166

His neighbors in the clubhouse, Figures and Woodson, had both been sidelined by injuries during the 1995 schedule, and could appreciate his plight.

"I'm sure Rod and Deon understand the impact of it," he said. "You don't realize what it's like until you've had to deal with it. I'm not capable of doing the same things. When the reality of that sets in, it scares you. The pressure is self-induced. The coaches yell at me and swear at me when I'm at my best or at my worst. But the pressure has always come from within. The desire to be the best I'm able to be....You see a guy like Yancey this year. You are able to find the top of your game and maintain it, and that's a special thing. I was just getting to the top of my game. Then I got injured. That hurts in more ways than people might realize."

"Life is so interesting with these animals."
—Marcia Brown

Chad Brown can be seen wearing jerseys that read NO FEAR above his heart. That's a line of men's sports clothes he endorsed. It was also fitting for his sideline of breeding and selling snakes and reptiles. He even put out a calendar in 1995 featuring him and other Steelers playing with snakes and reptiles, scary stuff for most people.

I consulted Kristin, his wife, to find out what she thought about her husband's moonlighting business.

"I think it's fantastic as long as they're not in my house," said Kristin.

It sounded like something his mother had told me earlier. "I just don't want to find them in my clothes basket," she said.

Chad's parents bought him a tarantula when he was a teenager and had asked for it as a birthday gift. He assured them it would not get out of the tank and that its bite was not life-threatening. Chad bought his first snake his freshman year in college. Chad used to keep them in aquariums around the house, but they frequently got out. His family would find them in a pile of clothes or outside on a tree. "Life is so interesting with these animals," said his mother.

"When I was young, I always wanted to have a pet snake and my mother wouldn't let me," said Brown. "When I got to college, I decided that since she wasn't around, I would get one. Then I got two and the next thing I knew I had ten."

Naturally, pets were not permitted in dorm rooms, but Brown kept boas, pythons and king snakes in his room, usually hiding them in the closet during room inspections.

He was fascinated by animals, and was in constant search of snakes for his collection. He drove the backroads of Texas in search of them. He went on a snake collecting trip to Costa Rica. At Colorado, he was nicknamed "Snake Charmer."

167

He suffered minor nerve damage to his left hand once when a nine-foot boa clamped down on his hand while he was dangling a live rat over its cage at feeding time. That was a mistake. "It was my fault," said Brown. As a result, he has no feeling in the pinkie on his left hand.

While he was playing for the Steelers, he bred and sold snakes from a warehouse in Boulder, Colorado, not far from the campus.

"I don't know what it's like not to win." — Chad Brown

Brown was boiling before the AFC title game, following a playoff victory over the Cleveland Browns at the end of the 1994 season and before the Steelers hosted the San Diego Chargers. There had been a cover story in *Sports Illustrated* strongly suggesting that the real Super Bowl was being played in the NFC title game between the Dallas Cowboys and the San Francisco 49ers.

"It kind of ticks me off, the whole AFC thing — getting no respect — almost like we don't matter, almost as if we're the Canadian Football League," said Brown.

"Seems like there is a lack of respect, just as there was before we played the Browns."

Brown had been with winning teams before, and he felt the Steelers were capable of the kind of success he had previously enjoyed on every level in which he had ever competed.

"I've always been on winning teams," he said in January of 1995. "I was talking to Rod Woodson the other day in the shower, and he said it's the first time he's been this far. That was not my personal experience.

"My last five or six years of Pop Warner we lost maybe five or six games. We won 28 games in a row in high school, and won two championships in a row. We were 14-0 in my junior year, winning the CIF championship, and 9-1 my senior year. At Colorado, we won three Big Eight titles and one national championship. I don't know what it's like not to win.

"When I was making my choice for a college, I was looking for a team that was on the rise....when the draft was coming up, I was saying, 'Please don't let me go to Tampa Bay or Cincinnati.' I don't know how I'd react to that. I wanted to be with a team that would be a winner."

Brown called the defensive signals for the Steelers, taking his cue from the coaches in the box upstairs.

He was a more versatile athlete than many who played his position. He played inside linebacker in their base, 3-4 defense, then slid to the right outside rush position in their dime package. Not many can do that.

"You have to be more conscious of technique on the inside because you have things coming at you both ways," explained Brown. "If you mess up it affects the defense in a much bigger way than it does from the outside. At outside linebacker, plays only come from one way and you have more time to think. You can freelance more, whereas at inside you have to be more technique-conscious, more physical and be aware of what's going on around you.

"I'm just trying to be the best football player I could be. I'm not really happy unless I play well. Yes, if the team wins that's always good. That makes it much easier. But unless I feel like I've played a great game, I don't walk out of the locker room happy."

Pittsburgh Steelers

Chad Brown with Joe Greene Award as 1993 Rookie of the Year for Steelers.

Jamain Stephens
The biggest Steeler of them all

"Money's never excited me.
I never had it."

The new kid on the block was so big that there was hardly any room on the block for anybody else. His name was Jamain Stephens, and make sure you spell that first name J-a-m-a-i-n.

It bugged him when people spelled his name wrong. He was the biggest player ever drafted by the Pittsburgh Steelers, and no one wanted to bug him.

When he stood in front of the dressing stall he was sharing with Brenden Stai in the team's clubhouse at Three Rivers Stadium it would have been difficult to slip some fan mail past him.

He stood 6-5 1/2 — make sure you include that 1/2 — and weighed between 335 and 340 pounds. Hardly any of it appeared to be fat. "I was checked out at the NFL combine," he said, "and they said I had 15 percent body fat." Whatever, Stephens looked pretty solid, and was mostly muscle and grit.

Veteran reporters who had been around the Steelers scene for a long time, like Bob Smizik of the *Post-Gazette*, Norm Vargo of *The Daily News* in McKeesport and this author, stood in the locker room on the opening day of mini-camp, April 26, 1996, and just gawked at Jamain Stephens as he strode across the room.

I had spent a lot of time in locker rooms with basketball players and boxers and Stephens was still an impressive specimen.

"How big are they gonna get?" said Smizik in a stage whisper. "Once upon a time it was rare to have anyone 300 pounds. Now they're common across the line on the good college teams. When are they going to have 400 pounders?"

"I remember when they made a big fuss about Les Bingaman of the Detroit Lions weighing 305 pounds," noted Vargo.

"God, is he big!" said Sam Nover, another media member with more than 25 years on the Steelers scene. "He looks in great shape for someone who weighs that much."

Stephens wasn't sure what all the fuss was about. After all, he'd always been big. "I weighed 300 pounds when I was in tenth grade," he said.

Stephens didn't smile much as he answered all the questions about his size and skills and expectations, but he was thoughtful, well-mannered, pleasant and had time for all.

When someone asked him about the prospects of signing a contract that would make him an instant millionaire, Stephens didn't seem impressed. "Money's never excited me," he said. "I never had it. I love the game. I'm not worried about money."

No. 1 pick Jamain Stephens was a show-stopper at Steelers' mini-camp in May, 1996. Line coach Kent Stephenson started to show the ropes to the rookie from North Carolina A&T.

Pittsburgh Steelers/Michael F. Fabus

Not at the moment perhaps, but his agent would soon change his mind about that. Plus, he wanted to help his family back in Lumberton, North Carolina. There were relatives and friends who could use a little help as well, so money would become more important as Jamain Stephens went along.

He spoke with pride about his parents, especially his mother, and thanked God more than once in his remarks about his situation. He seemed like such a nice young man. How long would that last?

"It depends on whether he models himself after Dermontti Dawson or Greg Lloyd," allowed one wag.

Stephens seemed a little innocent and naive, perhaps because he was the product of a small college, North Carolina A&T, or officially North Carolina Agricultural & Technical State University, located at 1601 East Market Street in Greensboro. The Blue & Gold, the Aggies, are better known for their basketball teams than their football teams. It's not really that small of a school since the enrollment is nearly 6,000 students. Nearly all the students are black.

Its teams compete in the MEAC, the Mid-Eastern Athletic Conference, Division I-AA in football and Division I-A in basketball. The basketball team has qualified a few times for the NCAA basketball tournament.

"I was never really challenged," said Stephens. "I never felt real taxed. I never had a game where I thought I'd have a problem with an opponent. I saw a big difference when I went to the bowl games. There was a difference in tempo. The Division I guys were definitely a step up in ability.

"I'm just like everybody else. I just want to show what I can do."

"He's going to have a great future in the NFL."
— Bill Nunn Jr.

A sportscaster representing a black radio network asked Stephens several questions along the same story line:

"Do you think there are other players at the black colleges who should have been drafted?"

Stephens said, "I suppose so. I didn't see many, myself, but I'm sure they're out there."

"A lot of people don't think the coaches are as good at the small schools as they are at the big schools. What do you think?"

Stephens said he thought they were, but I wondered how in the world he was supposed to know the answer to that question. What comparison could he make based on his own personal experience? And who doesn't think the coaches are as good?

Who are those people?

The Steelers always had a high respect for players and coaches from the so-called black colleges. They built some of their best ball-teams by judiciously scouting all college football teams.

They had an edge in this respect because they had Bill Nunn Jr. on their side. Nunn had followed his father into the newspaper business and was the sports editor of the *Pittsburgh Courier*, a nationally-respected and distributed weekly about news in the black community. For years, back in the '60s, Nunn went around the country covering the black college sports competition and picked an annual All-America team. Pro teams took players in the draft based on Nunn's observations.

Nunn started out working part-time for the Steelers and then became a full-time member of their scouting and personnel department, and had been involved with them in one role or another for nearly 30 years. He helped forge the teams that won four Super Bowl championships in the '70s.

Great players like Mel Blount, L.C. Greenwood, Donnie Shell, John Stallworth and Sam Davis came from black college programs, and came highly recommended by Nunn and other Steelers scouts.

Nunn was now retired, but still did some bird-dogging for the Steelers in a consultant capacity. He was well aware of Jamain Stephens.

Nunn noted that Stephens had quick feet. Scouts like to talk about things that escape the attention of the average reporter. Nunn offered some of these observations in an interview with Vargo, an old friend on the beat.

"He's pretty agile for a man his size," said Nunn, as nice a man as you will ever meet in pro sports, or anywhere else, for that matter. "And he's got great body control.

"I can't compare him to anybody we've had. I feel he's unique in himself. He's a raw talent. Once the rough edges are smoothed, he's going to have a great future in the NFL."

"I'm going to give you everything you ever dreamed of."
— Jamain Stephens, to his mother

Stephens said he was going to work hard and bide his time, learn the Steelers' system, and be patient. The coaches would know when he was ready. Some reporters were telling him how the Steelers had selected Leon Searcy of Miami as their No. 1 draft choice in 1992, and how Searcy had to wait a year before he became a starter. Searcy didn't start in any of the 15 regular season games in which he played in 1992, but started in all 16 his second season.

Maybe the media should have told Stephens about Stai, who was stretching on the floor right alongside where Stephens was sitting. Stai, a third round choice in 1995, became a starter on the offensive line midway through his rookie season. After all, they were sharing a locker because there are more players than there are dressing stalls at the outset of each season, and last year's rookies have to make room in their stalls for the newcomers. It's just the way things are done, and it doesn't matter whether you are Stai or Kordell Stewart. You share your locker. It lets you know where you stand.

"I can't jump out there and start if I don't know what I'm doing," said Stephens.

"I just want to contribute in any way possible. The first thing is to learn the system. I'm just like everybody else coming here for the first time. I just want to show what I can do.

"From what they tell me, everybody will be real patient. I've only played the offensive line for two years; I used to play on the defensive line. Coach Cowher and the offensive line coach have told me they're not expecting me to start right away.

"I know what's important, the keys to what I'm doing. My family is important to me. God comes first; they're second. It was a real struggle coming up. We never had much. My mom took care of us as best she could. My mom always instilled in me the difference between right and wrong. Without her, I think I'd have lost my focus."

His father, Joseph, was on disability because of an auto accident back in 1985. Joseph and a friend were driving a van in West Palm Beach, Florida, and the vehicle flipped over a guard rail. Joseph was hospitalized for a year, with a ruptured kidney and two crushed knees. He had to be kept on a rotating bed for six months to keep his blood flowing properly. He could get around a little better in 1996, even though he could not bend his knees. He slid sideways to get in and out of chairs.

Jamain's mother was out of work as well. She had been laid off the previous July from her job as an inspector for Converse, the sneaker shoe company that turns out Chuck Taylors.

"My mom was laid off half the time, same deal with my dad," Stephens said. "Moving place to place...home wasn't that great...leaky ceilings and all that...some people don't realize what you have to go through."

Stephens seemed surprised when I told him I had been to Lumberton, North Carolina.

I went there in 1987 to visit the parents of Lee McRae, a sprinter at the University of Pittsburgh who was pointing toward the Olympic Games in 1988 in Seoul, Korea. McRae came from Lumberton. I was visiting relatives in Raleigh and was curious to see what Lumberton looked like.

I remember McRae's father telling me that blacks were the "second minority" in Lumberton, as many American Indians lived in the area. McRae's father picked me up in his car, a beat-up old Volkswagen bug, and took me on a tour of the town.

174

There were a lot of fields with single room shacks on them where tenant farmers had once resided. The McRae home was a humble one, and so were most of the others in the immediate neighborhood. I remember there was a Bible on a reading stand in the center of the family room.

It didn't appear that there was a lot of money floating around in Lumberton.

Stephens said he remembered Lee McRae, and how he was one of the community's more famous athletes. "Everyone knew who Lee was," said Stephens.

But McRae was on the small side. So Stephens was certainly the biggest athlete of note to come out of Lumberton.

Stephens was a cousin of Tim Worley, a running back who also grew up in Lumberton and was the Steelers' No. 1 draft pick in 1989. Worley turned out to be a drug addict and was a flop with the Steelers and Chicago Bears. "I know what you're thinking," said Stephens, "but you don't have to worry about that."

His mother, Dollie Stephens, drove the family car around Lumberton after she had learned of her son's selection by the Steelers in the NFL draft. She was honking the horn to celebrate the occasion and to alert her neighbors to the good news.

Jamain's money would go a long way toward lifting the Stephens' status in the community. "That's all I am concerned about, the well-being of my family," said Stephens.

"He used to always say to me, 'I'm going to have mine,'" Dollie Stephens said in an interview with Gerry Dulac of the *Pittsburgh Post-Gazette*. "He would say, 'I'm going to give you everything you ever dreamed of.'"

Stephens had hoped he would go higher in the draft and he thought some other teams had expressed a great deal more interest in him than had the Steelers. But there was great joy in Jamain's home when he was selected by the Steelers. Jamain was the third of four children in the Stephens' house, and his oldest brother, Joe, was " the Steelers' No. 1 fan," according to Jamain. "He's been a Steelers' fan from Day One," Jamain told me. Jamain had two brothers and a sister, and they were all with him when he heard the good news from the Steelers. They had quite a party at their home.

"We all thought it was a great place to go," said Stephens. "We knew they'd been to the Super Bowl. You'd have to search pretty good to come up with a better place and an opportunity for me. I grew up aggressive and rough. My lifestyle, it explains everything. I'm not a criminal or anything like that, but I had it hard all my life.

"One day, not knowing whether or not I would have a place to lay my head, and the next day everything was OK. But it was a constant struggle for my family."

This was a big family, if not in number, certainly in size. Joe Jr. was 6-3, 280, Cameron was 6-5, 285 and sister Deborah said she was 5-8, 220. "I'm big," Deborah said of Jamain, "but he's BIG!"

Jamain Stephens was so big that he was as tall as his mom, 5-6, when he went to first grade. He weighed 270 as a high school freshman, 300 as a tenth grader, 330 as a college freshman.

He was recruited by Miami, Florida State, Clemson and South Carolina, but he didn't have the grades or SAT scores to get into those schools. He didn't want to go to a junior college. So he went to a state school in a Division II program and sat out the first season because he was not academically eligible there, either, and was a Proposition 48 case.

"She wanted to make sure I knew the difference between right and wrong."
— Jamain Stephens, on his mother

I asked Jamain to detail his mother's influence on him, and he was happy to oblige. Players, for the most part, love to talk about their mothers the way their mothers love to talk about them. "She wanted to make sure I knew the difference between right and wrong," said Stephens. "She told me what to do and what not to do. Every so often, she'd sit me down and say, 'This is what you do.' When I was young, I was spanked. When I did something right, I might not get praised, but I knew I was on her good side. Everything I've achieved is all because of her.

"She'd say, 'If there's something you believe in, you can't hope it will happen, you have to make it happen. You have to go after it.' We were always taught to put God first in our life. We didn't go to church every Sunday, but we had morals in our house. We had the Bible, and I was always taught that there's a higher power than myself. I was taught to believe in the right things."

Author Richard Wright (*Native Son*) said he never knew a black person who didn't read the Bible.

Dollie Stephens told Dulac that she had always lived in Lumberton, and that her husband, Joseph, had come there from Hoboken, New Jersey, where he had been a spot welder at Bethlehem Steel before his accident. They were married in Brooklyn and lived there in 1975. When Jamain was just a year old, they moved to Lumberton for good.

"It was tough, but I always had them and that was my goal right there — survival for them," said Dollie. "No matter how rough it was, it never got to the breaking point. It was hard, but it was never that it got too hard.

"Our house was always clean, livable. They were always clean and fed. That was the most important thing. As long as I could keep them in school, I thrived on keeping them in school. I never had a problem with any of them staying in school."

s Aggies' standout

Jamain dances with his mother, Dollie, in driveway of their home during Christmas break, 1995.

As 8th grader

As 9th grader

His father Joseph is disabled.

As 11th grader

I asked Jamain what his mother had to say when she heard about pro ballplayers getting into trouble, like Bam Morris of the Steelers and Michael Irvin of the Dallas Cowboys did with drug possession charges leveled against them in separate incidents in Texas shortly after Super Bowl XXX.

"She told me that you're going to get a lot of attention as a professional athlete, and that you had to be careful not to get careless," recalled Jamain. "Once you get a name for yourself, people are going to be watching you more closely. If you get in trouble, everyone will know about it."

Stephens said his mother was not the only one who talked to him like that. His grandparents and his aunts and uncles all urged him to stay squeaky clean and to stay clear of trouble. At his size, everybody would know who he was.

"They all did their part to keep me out of trouble," he said.

"But my mother did it the most. She always knew how to preach. And I never had to worry about whether or not there'd be something to eat."

Jamain didn't miss many meals, that's quite obvious. If first impressions mean anything, Joe and Dollie did a good job of raising this young man.

"He blocks out the sun."
— Kent Stephenson

The Steelers were sure happy to have Jamain Stephens on their side on NFL Draft Day. The Steelers picked 29th out of 30 teams because of their runner-up finish to the Cowboys in Super Bowl XXX.

They traded for a big running back in Jerome Bettis of the St. Louis Rams, and then they drafted a big lineman to eventually fill the void left by Leon Searcy, who had signed as an unrestricted free agent with the Jacksonville Jaguars soon after the Super Bowl.

"He blocks out the sun," said Steelers' offensive line coach Kent Stephenson in reference to Stephens.

"He's a man," said chief college scout Tom Modrak.

Asked what he liked best about the Steelers' No. 1 choice, Stephenson said, "I'd say his character. I think this is a very sincere kid. He has his priorities. He's a good person, and he's a very competitive kid. Put all those in a 6-5, 337-pound frame, and that helps."

Bill Cowher couldn't say enough about his enthusiasm for having someone like Stephens in a Steelers' uniform.

"Jamain Stephens has everything we're looking for," commented Cowher when he discussed his draft picks with the press at Steelers' headquarters within minutes of making the top pick. "The guy has size. He's powerful. He has a great mental approach to the game. He's a very physical player.

"Overall, from a technique standpoint, we think it's an ideal situation. We're not asking him to come in and start right away. The upside to this player is very big. We feel very fortunate that we were able to come away with him. These types of guys are hard to find. It's hard to get guys who have this kind of potential. This is an ideal situation for him to come in here."

Tom Donahoe, the director of football operations for the Steelers, concurred with Cowher's comments.

"He is raw; there's no question about that," said Donahoe. "He's only been an offensive lineman for two years. But he's a big, powerful, aggressive football player.

"We signed a couple veteran offensive linemen to give us some experience on the line. It's a good learning situation for Jamain to be able to come in here. He likes to eat, but he's fine. He carries his weight very well."

Phil Kreidler, a 30-year-old college scout in his fifth season with the Steelers, recalled meeting Jamain's high school coach the summer before at the team's training camp in Latrobe.

Russ Stone was in training camp, doing some scouting for the Shreveport franchise of the Canadian Football League. "He's a great guy; he's in Winston-Salem now. He had played for Charley Bailey's college coach, Bill Hayes. He was bragging about this big kid at North Carolina A&T. I took a bunch of notes on him. I later scouted him during their two-a-day workouts, and Modrak and Charley went in during the season. Tom Donahoe saw him in the spring. We checked him out pretty thoroughly. Coach Stephenson watched him. We belong to Blesto, so two Blesto people scouted him, and four of our people filed reports on him. So we had seven different opinions on him.

"His competition wasn't top-notch, but you can see the defensive mentality on the offensive side of the ball, and the best ones are like that. He liked physical contact, we know that."

When that same Bill Hayes wanted Stephens to switch from the defensive line to the offensive line before his junior season at North Carolina A&T, the move was met with some resistance. Stephens didn't know if it was to his benefit to change positions midway through college.

"He explained to me that it would help the team and it would help me," recalled Stephens.

"I felt I could go either way, but I just didn't want to cause any confusion or upset Coach in any way. I just wanted to remain coachable and get my shot.

"He broke it down for me and said if I were to move to offense that all my dreams would come true."

Stephens signed a contract on July 17, the day the Steelers opened training camp. It was a five-year deal that would pay him $4.66 million, including a signing bonus of $1,225,000. "I'm going to build my mom a home," he said, "a home of her own, a place where she can call home. We've been renting all our lives."

Ray Seals
Still standing tall

*"I opened doors for
a lot of famous people."*

It would have been a treat to have seen Ray Seals in action as a doorman at the Hotel Syracuse. It was a shame there was not any video tape showing him doing his thing back home in upstate New York. "There was none better," he boasted. "I hustled."

You can bet he was good at it. Seals commanded respect by his sheer size, but he was always a friendly fellow, and brought a special enthusiasm to all his tasks. He had a gleam in his dark eyes, a positive shine to his handsome face, a gift for gab and a glad hand. Seals always had a good sense of humor, and hustled to keep his customers happy and to make more money.

Service was Ray Seals' middle name. He knew the best way to make a buck. Take care of your customers. Don't keep 'em waiting. Keep 'em movin'. Keep 'em smilin'.

He met a lot of famous visitors, pointed out where they could park their cars, favored big tippers, and knew, in his big heart, that someday he wanted to be on the other side of the meeting and greeting gig. He wanted to be pulling up to the big hotel in his hometown in a huge car with a huge grin and be on the receiving end of the V.I.P. treatment.

He had known trouble as a teenager. He spent a night in jail at age 17, thanks to his father, a policeman in Syracuse, who wanted to teach his son a lesson. Seals had gotten mixed up with the wrong crowd. Seals never wanted that to happen again. He started being more selective about the company he kept.

He had not worked as hard as he should have in high school, and did not attract the sort of scholarship offers a young man of his immense size and athletic skills might have otherwise merited. Plus, his mother moved at a critical time in his life, before he had completed his senior year of high school, to look after her mother in Florida, and that didn't help. He got lost in the shuffle, somehow. But he was determined to turn his life in a positive direction, to make things happen in his favor. He was looking for a door to open to get him to the big time. He obtained a diploma at a vocational school in Orlando. It was tough getting started.

He had worked at several low-wage-jobs — a cook at Taco Bell, an appliance salesman at Sears, in addition to his doorman duties — played sandlot football, charmed the young ladies, and was waiting for something good to happen so he could realize his dream to play pro football and make some big money. Buy a big car. Buy a big house.

Ray Seals relaxes in Steelers dressing room.

Jim O'Brien

Help his mother and father enjoy a finer lifestyle. His parents were apart, but they were still together when it came to caring about him.

He had shared his dreams with his cousin and best friend, Jonny E. Gammage. They were an interesting duo, as different as could be, except when it came to promoting and marketing themselves and making an extra buck. Gammage was a graduate of the University of Buffalo, while Seals had never gone to college.

Jonny was just 5-6, 165 pounds, about the same size as sportscaster Myron Cope, while Ray was 6-3, and well over 300 pounds. They were the Odd Couple, but they got along better than most brothers. Jonny took care of a lot of things for Ray. "He was my main man," said Seals. In truth, he was Sancho Panza to Don Quixote on their quest for "The Impossible Dream."

They were going to the top together, working as a team to realize their ambitions. No one was going to stop them. Ray, who also worked as a bouncer at several Syracuse night clubs, would look after his little cousin, and he knew he could trust Jonny to look after his best interests.

Seals, a starting defensive end for the Pittsburgh Steelers in Super Bowl XXX, was one of the great rags-to-riches success stories in the National Football League. At that time, he was one of only two players in the NFL who had not gone to college (Eric Swann of the Arizona Cardinals was the other).

Thanks to his strong showing on and off the field on behalf of the Steelers, Seals was one of the finalists for Pittsburgh's Man of the Year in Sports honor at the annual Dapper Dan Club awards banquet.

Along the way, Gammage became one of the great tragedies associated with today's challenging sports world.

It all started back in Syracuse.

I knew that scene. I was familiar with the Hotel Syracuse. I had stayed there with the Pitt football team in 1961 when I was a sophomore and had just been named the sports editor of *The Pitt News*. I stayed there later on when I was working at *The New York Post* and I was covering the New York Knicks, who were playing a preseason NBA game in Syracuse, which had been one of the regular stops in the league's pioneer days. Once upon a time, there was an NBA team called the Syracuse Nats (Dolph Schayes, Johnny Kerr, Larry Costello, Hal Greer, George Yardley, Earl Lloyd, Red Rocha), and most visiting teams stayed at the Hotel Syracuse.

But that was before Ray Seals was hired as the doorman there. Seals was one of the most delightful and compelling figures to be found in the Steelers' clubhouse during the 1994 and 1995 seasons — he always addressed me as "Book Man" and was consistently cordial and helpful — and it doesn't require much imagination to picture Seals standing out in front of the Hotel Syracuse, charming those who came and went.

"I worked in a sharp black suit, but I wouldn't wear the tall round hat they had for the doorman," said Seals at one of several interview sessions. "I didn't like it. I hustled. I was good. I hustled parking space in front of the hotel. There was a one-way street that had five or six good car spaces. They were premium parking spaces...

"Somebody would pull up and plead with me, 'I was looking for parkin', can you help me?' And I'd say, 'You can go up to your room and I'll take care of your car if you take care of me.' I'd almost sing it. They bought it. I averaged $100 a day in tips. I made more than the bellman.

"I opened doors for a lot of famous people. I met movie stars, the Globetrotters, famous politicians, Oliver North, you name it. I loved the job. I enjoyed it."

Seals was not the only former doorman who became a big star. Nicholas Turturro went from being a doorman in New York to being a detective, James Martinez, on ABC's TV hit "NYPD Blue."

"I used to be this crazy little charismatic doorman," said Turturro. "I'd see the world go by me. But all of a sudden, it's 'Mr. Turturro, can I have your autograph?'"

Ray Seals could appreciate that turnaround.

"I always had dreams of being somebody special."
— Ray Seals

Seals was easily the most enterprising and industrious of the Steelers when it came to promoting and marketing himself and his sports-wear. He was a good guy to begin with, but he also worked hard at developing a positive and generous reputation. He got into community service sponsored by the Steelers, and then developed some of his own ambassadorial efforts. He and Jonny Gammage organized and coordinated Christmas gift-giving events along with other Steelers at shopping malls throughout western Pennsylvania, and they looked after disadvantaged kids in Pittsburgh and Syracuse. They came up with the "60-Minute Men" T-shirts and ballcaps and posters. Between practice sessions at Three Rivers Stadium, Seals could be seen hustling through the hallways, hauling boxes of his latest creations, getting media attention, getting his stuff out to all the appropriate stores. Myron Cope was racing through the same hallways with his latest supply of Terrible Towels, and there was always the chance that Seals and Cope would crash into each other and go down in one big heap.

Naturally, Cope fell in love with Seals. Cope could relate to his creativity and entrepreneurial spirit. He was a lot of fun. He was a character. And Cope loved characters. So Cope and the media called attention to Seals and his promotional efforts. For a while, it was a joy ride for one and all. "Christmas Seals" was the real deal.

"I always had dreams of being somebody special," said Seals. "I always felt I would be, but didn't know how I was going to do it."

Back at the Hotel Syracuse, Seals sometimes drove nice cars that belonged to other people. He wanted to have cars like that of his own.

He said the minimum salary when he first broke into the NFL in 1988 with the Tampa Bay Buccaneers was about $60,000. He was on the practice squad half the season — "I was a project kind of thing," he recalled — and made about $30,000. "I thought I was rich. Actually, I was. I went out and bought a GTA Trans Am car that cost me about $30,000. I figured I'd be staying with the team and I wouldn't have any trouble making the car payments. It would give me some incentive."

When I suggested that was a bit foolhardy, Seals smiled and said, "I was just crazy. I just wanted to take advantage of the opportunity while it was there. Young and crazy. That was me: young and crazy. I still am. It gave me a chance to put things in line. 'I've got to play for this,' I reminded myself.

"It was just myself and people who had high expectations, for me and for themselves. There was this girl I dated. Her name was Julie Aimes. She was going to Syracuse University, and she always told me, 'I'm thinking I'm in love. But, if you don't make $100,000 by the time I finish school, I can't marry you.' I was working at a bar back then, as a doorman and bouncer, a place called Sutters Mills, after that place in California where they had the Gold Rush. She was a sharp lady. She pushed me. She's the reason I'm where I'm at today.

"She didn't end up with me, though, and now I'm making $1.2 million a year. We joke about it now. We didn't end up together, but we're friends."

He had come a long way in the interim, but the trip had been so fast and furious that he didn't have time to completely appreciate what he had achieved. "It hasn't hit me yet," he said.

"He has shown a lot of class."
— Debbie McManus

Raymond Bernard Seals and Jonny E. Gammage grew up together in Syracuse. They were nearly a year apart in age, Gammage the older of the two. Their mothers were sisters.

On the evening of October 11, 1995, Gammage, who was living in Coraopolis at the time, took Seals' car, a dark blue Jaguar with Florida license plates, out for a drive. Gammage had his own set of keys for the car.

Gammage was driving north on Route 51 when he was stopped by police at about 1:30 a.m. on October 12, 1995 in Overbrook, a suburban community just south of the Liberty Tunnels. According to the police report, Gammage was driving the car in a strange herky-jerky manner, which prompted police to pull him over.

There was a scuffle involving Gammage, a black man, and five suburban police officers. All were white. Gammage was combative, according to the police reports. They contended that Gammage had gotten out of control. Pressure was applied to his upper back to subdue him as he lay flat on his stomach on the ground. Too much pressure, as it turned out. He was subdued and handcuffed. Leg irons were also placed on his ankles. Whatever happened, and there were varying stories, something went terribly wrong. Something got out of hand. Gammage didn't move. Blood and oxygen could not flow to his brain because of the pressure to his chest and neck, it was later determined. He was not drunk or high, lab tests disclosed, though police did find a small amount of old marijuana in the car. But Jonny Gammage was dead. An autopsy indicated he died from "compression of the neck and upper chest." Tests revealed he had a few beers, but nothing that would have affected his judgment or made him go on a rampage. Many in the Pittsburgh community were outraged by what happened, especially the NAACP and other black organization leaders. To them, it was another case of police brutality to a black citizen.

It became a controversial case which captured national attention, gaining more notoriety because of Gammage's relationship with Seals. Coincidentally enough, Rodney King was involved in a court case in nearby New Castle on a drunken driving charge while visiting relatives there. King had first come to the public's attention after he was beaten by police in Los Angeles, an incident that was captured on video tape and repeatedly shown to TV audiences around the world. There were natural parallels.

Understandably, Seals was both distraught and angry when he learned of his cousin's death. It was a senseless killing, as he saw it.

Even so, Seals showed a lot of personal restraint and discipline in how he dealt with this setback. He wanted justice, but he did not want any rioting or further misbehavior on anybody's part.

Seals drew community-wide praise for the calm he brought to the controversy. Gammage's family came to Pittsburgh and they, too, showed a lot of class in how they refused to be drawn into the media circus or to say anything inflammatory.

"Everybody ought to just be calm," Seals said to a packed news conference which followed his cousin's death. "To me, it was never meant to be a racial situation. This could happen to anybody."

He had said at one point that if the police were not punished for their action, there was no way he could continue to stay and play in Pittsburgh. I had gotten friendly enough with Seals to caution him about his remarks. I thought he had won the respect of a lot of Pittsburghers, and that he had to be careful not to condemn Pittsburgh or Pittsburghers for what happened to his cousin. It was a terrible thing, no doubt about it, but everybody was not to blame. He realized that.

At a later press conference, Seals said, "I know how important this is. I know if I were to go 'boo,' a lot of people might go crazy in this town. It just seems like a lot of bad stuff is going on between blacks and whites right now.

"But if I started screaming, 'They killed Jonny. Let's kill them,' what good would it do? Who would pay the price then? I'll tell you who. A lot of innocent people who had nothing to do with the situation.

"I just think we all need to work together to prevent this kind of crazy stuff from happening. It's not just the black community that feels that way. It's the white community, too. People don't want that happening here. They shouldn't have to be afraid to go into any neighborhood. This isn't a racial thing, it's a human thing."

Debbie McManus, an advocacy manager for the Allegheny County Center for Victims, saw Seals on TV and praised his efforts.

"He has shown a lot of class, a lot of dignity," said Ms. McManus. "Because he has gone through a lot himself. He's tried to do things within the system, which is hard. He's trying to hold the community together. I think he's a great spokesman for victims, for his cousin, for the community."

Seals dedicated the 1995 season to his cousin. Gammage died on a Thursday and was buried the following Wednesday. Seals attended his funeral and played the next night against the Cincinnati Bengals at Three Rivers.

"I'm just going to go out and play hard and try to win for Jon," said Seals. He wore a "60-Minute Men" T-shirt which he and his cousin had created.

When Seals signed as a free agent to play for the Tampa Bay Buccaneers, Gammage accompanied his cousin to Tampa. When Seals signed with the Steelers as an unrestricted free agent in 1994, Gammage joined him in Pittsburgh.

They made an impact in Pittsburgh, doing lots of community work. They formed Athletic Promotions, Inc., to market the "60-Minute Men" line of apparel and other business deals.

The previous Thanksgiving, Seals collected money from his teammates and he and Gammage bought food and distributed it to needy organizations. Gammage organized Steeler autograph sessions at district malls to earn money to buy toys that they gave to needy children at Christmas.

Gammage helped Seals organize the busload of Syracuse kids that he brought to Steelers' exhibitions in 1994 and 1995. Seals brought them back for a playoff game in 1995. Seals distributed gifts again during the Christmas season of 1995, and cited his cousin's contribution. "He put so much time and effort into this," said Seals, "that it would be a shame to let it go to waste."

Seals and several of his Steelers teammates signed autographs and "60-Minute Men" T-shirts to raise $5,000 worth of Christmas presents for about 20 underprivileged families. He was joined by Leon

Searcy, Greg Lloyd, Levon Kirkland, Darren Perry and Willie Williams, among others.

During a visit to Allegheny Center on the North Side on Christmas Eve, 1995, Seals said, "This is the kind of stuff we should be doing. We're in a position to help. I've been so blessed that it's not hard to give something back. I beat the odds, beat adversity. I didn't allow myself to get caught up in the things that would have kept me from being here.

"Somebody helped me. Ray Perkins took a big chance on me at Tampa Bay. I wasn't a college football player. I was just a big, vain kid, but he gave me an opportunity. I really have been blessed. I couldn't live with myself if I didn't try to help people."

Seals spoke about his cousin to remind people of his specialness, and to continue the demand for a legal resolution of the case. "I want to find justice, try to find out what really happened, somehow," said Seals. "I knew that reflected on a lot of people. I wanted to make sure I didn't say the wrong thing. Justice in this case will do a lot of healing, even if it doesn't bring Jonny back. I have to keep making this case known nationally. I know if it would have been me, my cousin wouldn't rest until everybody knew the truth.

"Jonny was just a real smart business guy, a guy who could get things done. That's why we joined forces together. I thought we had the perfect thing with me playing football and him being able to get things done. Everything I've done since I've been here the last two years is actually what my cousin has done. I just pointed him in the direction and he went out and coordinated everything.

"Jonny was basically the creator of the '60-Minute Men' shirts, hats. It was weird because as soon as I walked out of the coroner's office, after seeing him and feeling real bad, I walk out the door and here comes a guy down the street with a '60-Minute Men' shirt on and it just crushed me because I knew what it meant to him."

Attorney Robert G. Del Greco, representing the Gammage family, said, "Deep down, Ray feels these pangs of potential responsibility because he brought Jonny to the town where Jonny died."

"I'm still tight with my dad. Without my mother, I'm nothing."

Seals grew up in Syracuse. He was the second of three children. His father was a police officer there and also worked in security at Syracuse University, where his son met some of the football and basketball players for the Orangemen.

In junior high, Seals was encouraged in reading lab by Maxine Sistrunk. She told him stories about her husband's cousin, a fellow who made the NFL without the benefit of college — the Oakland Raiders' Otis Sistrunk. The seed was planted, perhaps.

The young Seals was a football stud at Henninger High School in Syracuse when he stumbled in with the wrong crowd. He was involved in a burglary and he wound up in jail. His father left him there. "A lesson of a lifetime," Seals called it. He played on a pretty good basketball team at Henninger. He wasn't much of a student, however, and was sort of laid back in his approach to life.

During his senior season, Seals heard from Penn State, Alabama and Iowa, but didn't have the academic credentials to get serious consideration. Some questioned his desire, too. He moved to Florida with his mother, and worked at Taco Bell and Sears while there. He later came back to Syracuse and played semi-pro football for the Syracuse Express.

His father, Tom Seals, had been a member of the Syracuse police force for 31 years. His mother, Blonirene, or "Blondie," had worked 22 years at AT&T.

"My parents are separated, but I'm still tight with my dad," said Seals. "And, without my mother, I'm nothing. My mother raised us in church. We went to church twice on Sunday, and on Tuesday and Thursday for Bible study. If there was a revival going on, it was every night that week. We were Pentecostal, and church was very important to our family. We were church people. We learned very early the difference between right and wrong. My parents expected us to respect people, to stay in the church, to keep a Godly mind, not to take things for granted. My mother takes a good look at everybody, she wants to get to know you. I'm blessed. When I finished up high school, my grandmother was sick, so we moved down to Florida. I was 18 at the time. I was 21 when I returned to Syracuse. That's when I got a job as a doorman at the Hotel Syracuse.

"I played in a two-hand touch league while I was working at the hotel, trying to support myself. A lot of people have that football desire, but it's hard to work and stay in shape. Somehow I was able to pull it off."

Then he started playing semi-pro football in a traveling league. The Syracuse Express played at Albany and Utica and Watertown. He played tight end and outside linebacker. I asked him if he was paid to play, and that drew a smile. He wagged his head sideways.

"Most I ever got from those games was a hamburger and a bag of chips," he said.

"I was paid nothing. I was working at the time. I was working at Rib's Inn as a cook. At least I was working. A lot of guys I knew weren't working, or they were lazy. At least I went to work; I had a job. You've gotta get some kind of job, something to start out. You have to believe in your dreams. I've always worked to do more.

"You have to utilize your gift. I feel I'm where I am now because this was my gift. I can remember as a kid, playing junior high football. I was known for having quick feet. Today, I still have the quick feet, and it's one of the things that sets me apart from the pack.

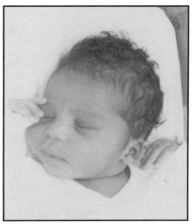
Baby Ray on birth day

Ray, as teenager, and his father flank relatives at family reunion in Syracuse.

racuse police officer Tom Seals receives award wife Blonirene and son Ray flash proud smiles.

Ray is the middle guy with the bowtie, beside brother Mark and in front of father, Ray, at church gathering.

"Once I started playing football again, I started thinking about the NFL. That's what it was — a dream — for most guys....wish and hope to get a chance to try out....not ever thinking it would really happen."

He was invited to try out for the Buccaneers by Ray Perkins in Tampa Bay. Perkins had been interested in recruiting Seals when he was at Alabama.

Four years after high school, Seals signed to play with Tampa Bay. He was released by the Bucs. Then he was signed and released by the Indianapolis Colts. Then he went back to the Bucs. Back then, he had a history of getting hurt.

"When I first got with Tampa, I'd go home to Syracuse and I'd ride the city bus. I'd park the car and ride the city bus, and see all the same people I used to see on the bus. The same people were still riding it. It reinforced the feeling that I had been so fortunate."

Seals broke into Tampa Bay's starting lineup in 1991 and had 14 sacks and 151 tackles. That's when he gained the nickname "Big Play Ray" Seals.

"I'd like to think I'm a giving person."
— Ray Seals

Seals sponsored a bus-load of kids from a kids' football league in Syracuse to come to Pittsburgh twice during the 1995 season. Many of them were in the clubhouse after the Steelers beat the Buffalo Bills, 40-21. "My father was president of the football organization when I was a kid in Syracuse, and I participated in it," said Seals, explaining their presence. "This is my way of paying back. Kids get to come down and see some players close-up. When I was a kid, the only pros I ever saw were on Monday Night Football on TV."

There were 46 kids who came down in a bus. Mike Fabus, the official photographer of the Steelers, was shooting photos of the kids in the clubhouse as a favor to Seals.

"The way I was raised, in the church, with strong family values," said Seals, "we didn't have a lot of serious role models, especially male models. I was the only one to come out of my city at the time to play pro football. I do what I do because I feel that kids need more positive role models. There are so many negatives out there right now. And it's not trying to be a role model; I'm trying to give them an opportunity to meet many role models. That's why I involve the other players.

"I'd like to think I'm a giving person. I'd like to think I'm generous with my friends, somebody looking for some money, some help."

After the Steelers defeated the Indianapolis Colts, 20-16, in the AFC championship game the following week, Seals drew quite a crowd to his dressing stall. The out-of-town media wanted to know more about how he was dealing with the death of his cousin, and how he could manage to continue to play so well with that on his mind.

"It feels good, but it hurts. I just wish my cousin were here. Jonny and I used to talk about this, getting to the Super Bowl. I know he's smiling right now."

Seals was still perspiring, and a rivulet was running down the right temple.

"For me, personally, not having played college ball, this is like something I dreamed. The guys come in here talking about how their college teams did that weekend; I don't say nothing. So the Steelers are the only team I'm rooting for. We offer this up to the Pittsburgh fans. They have been great. From the littlest kids to the oldest people, they have come up to me to let me know they're thinking of me, and that they're behind me.

"For a minute there, it looked like we were going to walk away without a win again. When they (the offensive unit) pulled out the big play to Ernie (Mills), I'm falling all over the place. Then they (the Colts) nearly scored on that last pass into the end zone. That was scary stuff."

Seals started fingering a gold crucifix he wore around his neck. He started talking about how Cowher didn't panic after a bad start, or get down on them after they were 3-4. "He didn't punish us, or run us to death," said Seals. "He just stayed with it. I've been in places like Tampa Bay, with Sam Wyche, and he'd would have had you run all day on Monday. It all starts with the leader.

"It's a different atmosphere here. I was a kid in Syracuse when the Steelers were winning all those Super Bowls. Jonny and I talked all season long about going to Arizona and about going to the Pro Bowl. After I didn't get picked for the Pro Bowl, I really wanted to go to the Super Bowl.

"It's been a tough road. He was my main man. But at the same time, I'm accomplishing some things that we were all about. I was trying to get to the Pro Bowl. That was one of our goals. The next was to get to the Super Bowl. We talked about it last summer in Orlando."

The out-of-town media asked Seals to speak about the police action that resulted in his cousin's horrifying death. He mentioned to them that his father had been a police officer for more than 30 years.

"I know there's bad ones, and there's good ones," said Seals. "I can't say I hate all cops, because I don't. But there are bad cops. It just so happens that night he ran across four or five cops who were just out of control."

During the 1995 season, Seals had missed practice from time to time to attend court inquests into the death of his cousin.

"You can only imagine what I think about," he said. "I have to live it. I have to live with the reality. All I can do is keep going and make the best of it."

Seals kept his cool. Noble is a word that comes to mind to describe his behavior during difficult times. He said he didn't want to drag the team down with his personal problems. "I don't want them to carry that burden," he said. "They're professionals, and this is their job. This is my problem."

Seals spoke about looking up to the stadium box where his family sat during the game, and how his thoughts drifted back to Jonny Gammage.

"I looked up there, I saw my mom and my pop, but I didn't see him. Once we won it, damn, I was thinking about how he would love this. He'd be blown away."

Looking ahead to Super Bowl XXX, Seals said, "This game will be in his honor, I'm playing the Super Bowl like it's a requiem for a dead man. A dead man I couldn't have loved more if he was my brother."

"It gives you inspiration."
— Brentson Buckner

Seals gained increased respect from his teammates for the way he managed to balance his grief and the demands of playing for a football team that needed him to play at his absolute best.

"Ray handled it a lot better than I would," said Steelers tackle Leon Searcy, a close friend who lived in Orlando. "If a situation occurred where a family member of mine was unjustly murdered by police, I would've reacted in a totally different manner.

"When we first heard about it, it was in the midst of the Million Man March. Ray got on TV and said it wasn't a racial issue; he didn't try to incite the people. If there was an award to be given out for the way Ray handled it, he should get it."

Carnell Lake said, "More than anything, you just have an open ear for him so there's someone he can feel comfortable talking with."

"A lot of people would have folded their tent," said Brentson Buckner, who lined up at the opposite end on the Steelers' defensive line. "When you see a person go through something like that and doing all that, it gives you inspiration. It's been a 24-hour battle for him. I'd say it's made him a stronger person. Any other person could have cracked."

Tom Donahoe, the Steelers' director of operations, said, "When you think about it, how many people under the same circumstances would react the way he has and still play his best football? He's been able to deal with it, and he has dealt with it rationally and sensibly."

Seals' measured words provided quite a contrast to statements he had uttered the year before, just prior to the AFC championship game with the San Diego Chargers. Seals spoke with great confidence, and said that he thought the Steelers could shut down San Diego's offense if the Steelers played their regular game. It came off stronger than it was said by Seals when it showed up in newspaper reports.

Before that game with the Chargers in the 1994 playoffs, Cowher called Seals into his office and told him to think before he made inflammatory statements before the Steelers played anyone. It wasn't the first time Seals had ever been called to the principal's office for disciplinary measures.

Seals felt at home in Pittsburgh and with the Steelers despite the personal hell he was experiencing concerning his cousin's death. He didn't regret coming to Pittsburgh.

"I was an unrestricted free agent and I could go to any team in the league," said Seals. "I thought at the time, 'Here's a team that can go to the Super Bowl.' I looked at this team as a team that can go all the way. And I was right. I came to Pittsburgh first. Once I met Coach Cowher, I was so impressed. It was important that he was impressed with me."

Seals was Cowher's kind of ballplayer as an over-achiever, a highly-motivated individual who wanted to be part of a winning team. He signed a three-year $2.8 million contract as an unrestricted free agent with the Steelers

Asked where he got the idea for the "60-Minute Men" promotion, Seals said, "From listening to Coach Cowher; he kept saying you've got to be a 60-minute man. You can ask my wife and she'll tell you I'm no 60-minute man.

"He impressed the hell outta me," Seals said of Cowher. "You're allowed to be yourself here as long as you perform on Sunday and take care of business.

"In Tampa Bay, they had an ideal player in mind. They required you to wear suits on planes. Don't smile during the game.

"If you give your all, Coach Cowher doesn't bother you with a lot of nonsense. It shows you the reality of life, of having to be a man and going out to work and supporting yourself. I told Coach Cowher he's going to have a true blue collar worker."

Upon signing with the Steelers, Seals said, "I"m as good as Michael Dean Perry. I think it's all in the surroundings. Now, I'm with a team that has a lot of great athletes and I can shine."

He also mentioned his own name in the same conversation as Reggie White and Bruce Smith, two superstar defensive ends.

"Anything's reachable," said Seals. "I'm here. Is there a more successful story than being here without going to college? A lot of guys are Pro Bowlers, but not many of them can say, 'Damn, I'll just walk on and do it.'

"I'm the man — write it down."

When Seals was in training camp in Latrobe, and he'd hear players complain about the heat, he would remember that it felt a lot hotter working in that Taco Bell kitchen in Tampa Bay. "Latrobe gets hot, and I'd be out there on the practice field and I'd say, 'What am I doing here?' Then I'd think about what it had been like working in the kitchen. I worked in three or four restaurants. The hottest was frying the shells at Taco Bell. One mistake could cost you a hand. That grease was so hot. That grease was sizzling. It gets in your skin. It keeps you continuously sweating. Believe me, pro football is a breeze by comparison. I could be back sweating in the kitchen, grilling ribs forever."

Pittsburgh Steelers

Ray Seals celebrates a sack.

"Our idols are us, the reflections of the American Dream itself."
— Robert Lypsite and Pete Levine, *Idols of the Game*

Kevin Greene
The gung-ho soldier

"I play football like a dadgum war."

Kevin Greene would have been a great poster boy for a U.S. Army recruiting campaign. Put him in combat fatigues, an M-16 rifle slung over his shoulder, charcoal smudges under his shining ice-blue eyes, and have his bare arms protruding from an unbuttoned flak jacket. Cut his blond hair to a more military-like length. If it were a TV spot, have Greene glare sternly into the camera and cry, "Be all that you can be!"

No one could say it with more gusto than Greene, a fiercely-determined and gung-ho outside linebacker with the Steelers for three seasons (1993-1995). Greene grew up in a military family — his father, Therman, and older brother, Keith, were both career officers who were decorated for heroism in combat action in the U.S. Army — and Kevin wore combat fatigues for his Halloween costume as a child. He carried a wooden tommy-gun, screamed rat-tat-tat and played the part with great enthusiasm.

Greene is a guy who went from being a high school athlete who didn't draw attention from any major colleges to being a walk-on starter at Auburn University and an NFL standout with both the Los Angeles Rams and Pittsburgh Steelers.

He built himself up through weight-lifting and a demanding training regimen to be big enough and strong enough to play with the big boys on all levels of competition.

He was in ROTC during his college days, and in the U.S. Army Reserve for many years during his pro career before it became impossible to keep his military training commitments. So he was a good soldier.

No one drew more attention than Greene in pre-game interview sessions at Super Bowl XXX. Only the Dallas Cowboys' Deion Sanders outspoke and outsparkled the Steelers' blond bomber as a prime time entertainer in Tempe, Arizona. He carried on like a blown-up version of Nicholas Cage, mockingly menacing everyone with those wild eyes of his.

He was an unrestricted free agent at season's end and, in early May, 1996, he signed a two-year contract at $950,000 per year, plus incentives, with the Carolina Panthers. He would be reunited with Dom Capers, the head coach of the Panthers who had been the defensive coordinator and mastermind of the Steelers' "Blitzburg" defensive scheme in Greene's first two seasons in Pittsburgh. The Steelers did not attempt to sign Greene, much to his chagrin. He would soon turn

34 and they decided they wanted to go with younger players at lower prices. At the announcement of his signing in Carolina, Greene got in a few parting shots at the Steelers, suggesting he got bad vibes in his final season that he was no longer wanted. Welcome to the world of free agency, Kevin. Yes, loyalty has been lost, but the Rams might have some theories about that, too. It's a two-way street.

"We have to find out about some of our young players," said Tom Donahoe, the Steelers' director of football operations. "We think they can play, but we have to get them on the field and see what they can do. They can't get better standing next to Coach Cowher.

"Kevin was great. We appreciate everything he did for us. He's been a big part of our success here the past three years. It worked out well for him and it worked out well for us."

Greene's story should be an inspiration to lightly-regarded high school players, and confound all those fellows who provide scouting reports for college and pro coaches. This was a guy who upset all the rating charts.

He was the 113th player chosen in the NFL draft in 1984, on the fifth round by the Rams, and played for them for eight seasons. Playing outside linebacker, he led the NFL in 1988 with 16 1/2 sacks. In 1989, he recorded 16 1/2 sacks to finish fourth in the NFL and earned his first selection to the All-Pro Team, the Pro Bowl, and the All-Madden Team.

The Steelers signed him as an unrestricted free agent in 1993. He led their team in quarterback sacks for three seasons, indeed, was the NFL sack king in 1994. Asked to pinpoint the source of his success, Greene looked deep into the eyes of the interviewer and said, "Just drive and determination. I've seen people come into the league who are bigger and stronger and faster than me, but I've outdriven them."

That is how he made the All-Madden team. The recognition he drew from NFL TV analyst John Madden as an old-fashioned football player who played the game with great passion meant as much to him as his Pro Bowl selections.

"Get the dream.
Hold onto it."
— Kevin Greene

Greene lived in Destin, Florida during the off-season, and was part owner of a Gold's Gym in Anniston, Alabama, near Oxford, where his parents grew up, and where they have lived since his days at Auburn. He has had a home there as well.

A month after Super Bowl XXX, I talked to him over the telephone, still seeking the real Kevin Greene. After spending the previous two seasons on the Steelers' scene, I still wasn't sure about him.

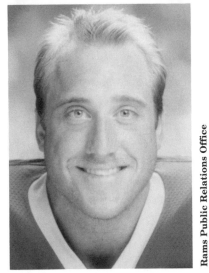

In clean-cut days with Rams

Greene grew his hair long as he pointed toward Super Bowl.

Kevin's wife, Tara, talks to him before she sang National Anthem at one of the Steelers' games at Three Rivers Stadium.

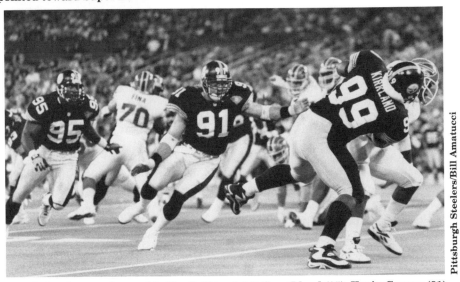

1-2-3 defensive punch provided by (left to right) Greg Lloyd (95), Kevin Greene (91) and Levon Kirkland (99).

I'd seen a hard side and a soft side. He was so popular with the fans, so reviled by many in the media. Which was the real Kevin Greene? Were there two Kevin Greenes?

"All these guys are pretty good," offered Tony Parisi, the Steelers' equipment manager for 32 years and the warden of the locker room. "They'll do anything I ask them to do. They never turn me down. Some of them just don't like dealing with the media. They're funny that way."

Suffice to say that Greene did not show his best face to those employed to portray him to the public.

Kevin Greene did not feel that there were two Kevin Greenes, or that any of his antics constituted an act. He often reminded one of Rambo, Ric Flair, Hulk Hogan and Jack Lambert all rolled into one. "He's just himself," his father insisted. "He's just a good ole southern boy." Kevin's own wife, Tara, said she did not really know the guy who went through all the theatrics out on the football field. "So who is the real Kevin Greene?" I asked. "That's a deep question." said Kevin Greene. He made no attempt to answer it.

This was early April, 1996, three weeks before the NFL draft, and Greene was also living in limbo. His three-year contract with the Steelers was up. He was an unrestricted free agent once again, but it appeared there was not a great deal of demand for his services. Not yet, anyhow. Even though he had cleared out his locker right after Super Bowl XXX, he wished he could return to the Steelers. He felt that would only happen, however, if he were willing to take a severe cut in compensation from what he had enjoyed. He would be 34 by the next training camp, and making the kind of money he was making, the Steelers would have problems keeping him and staying under the salary cap. He thought he was still playing the game with great gusto.

"I try to play the game of football with the passion and a zeal that a kid growing up dreaming about playing football in the National Football League would have," he said.

"I try to play it for the game, rather than for the money. I enjoy the accolades that come with it, from being in the NFL."

When his family came to Pittsburgh, Greene liked to give them a grand tour. He took them to Point State Park, to Station Square, to the usual tourist sites. "I'm a Pittsburgher now," he said. He did not shy away from appearing in public, though he was one of the most recognizable and most popular players. "I do get a lot of attention wherever I go," he said, "At times, I'll slow down and sign autographs on anything they hand me. I try to be as accommodating as possible. I stand around the outside of the stadium and sign autographs. I sign a lot of autographs at training camp."

With that in mind, it had to be especially upsetting to Greene to find himself in a much-publicized controversy during the summer of 1995 for refusing to sign one youngster's football after practice at St. Vincent College.

"That was very disheartening," said Greene, "because I go the distance with the fans, and I know I give them a lot of time. Most people are pretty good about the way they approach athletes for autographs. But some are not very considerate. I don't like it when people demand something, or when they get pushy. I don't like it when I am with my wife in a restaurant and we're eating dinner and somebody comes over and waves something under my face to sign. I don't want to be asked for an autograph, for instance, when I'm eating pizza and I've got cheese dripping down my chin. Maybe I'm out shopping for a Christmas gift for my wife, and I'm in a store and I really don't want to do autographs in that setting. I have to have time to be normal as well."

After Greene got slammed for not signing the kid's football, I thought Greene worked overtime at St. Vincent trying to restore his good-guy image among the fans. He extended himself in signing autographs after practice, and played to the crowd on his way to the locker room.

It had been obvious by his behavior throughout his career that he wanted to share himself with the fans. When Greene played his last game with the Rams at Anaheim, for instance, he ran around the rim of the field and slapped hands with fans in a goodbye gesture. After the AFC title game at Three Rivers, he once again went to the sidelines and into the end zone and waved to the fans, holding the AFC championship trophy overhead for all to see. "I took the championship trophy from Coach Cowher and tried to reach out to the fans so that they could be part of the celebration," recalled Greene. "In case it was my last game with the Steelers, I wanted to say goodbye properly."

Those fans might not have recognized Greene a few months later when he altered his appearance. On March 19, 1996, Greene finally had his long blond locks clipped by his wife, Tara. "She got out the scissors and the shears and went to work," he said.

Greene had long hair when he played midget football and high school football, but he never let it grow as long as he did during the 1995 season.

"Just dream what it is you want to do."
— Kevin Greene

Greene was not big enough or good enough to draw a Division I football scholarship when he came out of high school. He built himself up through a demanding three-year bodybuilding program and made the Auburn University football team in his fourth year in school. There were whispers that he had used body-enhancing steroids, but he insisted his growth came the natural way, and he never had a problem with drug-testing along those lines in his college or pro playing career. He was starting by mid-season of his second year on the team

199

at Auburn. That's almost unheard of in today's highly-competitive college sports scene.

When Greene spoke to kids at sports banquets and luncheons, he had a personal message to inspire them, based on his own climb to the top, which he related:

"You have to believe in yourself. You can do anything that you want to do. Just dream what it is you want to do. Get the dream. Hold onto it. Go after it whatever the cost. You'll always hear from people who'll tell you you're not big enough, fast enough, strong enough. You'll get that, no matter what you want to do. You have to go for it. It won't come to you."

When Kevin was a kid, he and his older brother, Keith, played on the same football team, and their father was always their coach, and they were constantly moving from one military base to another every two years. He and his brother became a traveling dog-and-pony show. Kevin's uniform number then was 19, the reverse of what it would be when he played for the Steelers.

"When my dad was trying to show the kids on the team how they needed to be intense in their play, he would always have Keith and I go at each other to demonstrate his points," said Greene. "He wanted us to show the other kids about being physical and intense. We set the pace. It was tough on us. We were the stars of the team, and we'd be pitted against each other, banging into each other, blocking or tackling. We'd just hammer each other into oblivion. It was difficult."

It sounded like a scene out of Pat Conroy's book, *The Great Santini*, when a Marine officer/fighterpilot named Bull Meecham, played by Robert Duvall in the movie version, pushed his son beyond reasonable expectations to be a fiercely-competitive athlete.

Greene said it wasn't like that in his case or in Keith's case. "My dad was demanding, but he was always fair," said Greene. "He's still that way. He genuinely cared about us, and we benefited from his personal interest and involvement. We are closer to our father because we spent so much time with him."

Kevin had two sisters, and their names also began with the letter K. Karen wanted to be a nurse and Kristin wanted to be a teacher. Karen realized her dream and Kristin was still in college pursuing hers during the 1995 season. Two of Keith's children, and two of Karen's three children were part of the large Kevin Greene contingent in attendance at Super Bowl XXX.

"Sometimes we make judgments about kids with long hair."
— Therman Greene

While Retired Colonel Therman Greene looked like a military man, with close-cropped strawberry blond hair, he sounded reasonable enough, certainly not like any bully or tyrant. He could not have been more thoughtful, kinder or cooperative than he was in our conversations and communications. Greene's father was on the telephone with a report on Kevin. It was March 11, 1996, a day after a big event in the Greene household. "Kevin got his hair cut yesterday," said his father. "His mother didn't want him to do it, but his wife, Tara, cut his hair. He kept all the locks; I'm not sure what he's going to do with them."

I asked Ret. Col. Greene how he had felt, as a retired full bird colonel in the U.S. Army, about his son's long locks. After all, at age 60 and retired since 1986, he still had his hair cut in a military fashion, and his other son, Keith, still had his hair cut short, and was a major and a pilot of one of those Blackhawk helicopters in the U.S. Army's 101st Airborne Division, winning a medal for service during the Mideast Crisis and operations "Desert Shield" and "Operation Desert Storm." Maj. Keith Greene saved the lives of two American servicemen stranded in the Iraqi desert. For that, he won a Bronze Star.

"It was OK with me," said Col. Greene, who won two bronze medals of his own for meritorious action in combat. "The boys always had a buzz-cut most of the time when they were kids, but when we were stationed in Granite City, Illinois, and they were both going to high school, they begged me to let them wear their hair long like their friends. So we relented. Sometimes we make judgments about kids with long hair and different looks like that, but they've always been good kids. A lot of those kids are still good kids.

"Kevin did his military training at Fort Knox, Kentucky, and he loved riding in those tanks. If he hadn't become a pro football player, I think he'd have made a career of the military service.

"There was no racism or prejudice in my family."
— Kevin Greene

I talked to Kevin Greene in the Steelers' locker room on October 12, 1995. It came at a lowpoint on the Steelers' schedule. The team had gotten off to a 3-4 start, and was reeling.

Greene was grateful to talk about his family rather than football. His family had been at the Houston Astrodome for the second game of the season when he recorded his 100th career sack. He met with them briefly after the ballgame in the parking lot outside. It was good to see them, as always.

I asked Greene what he learned from his father. "Discipline and regimentation," began Greene. "He always expected honesty. He taught us to respect elders. He taught us politeness, dedication and commitment to succeed.

"Dad got Keith and I involved in Boy Scouts. He wanted to keep us busy. Dad was an Eagle Scout, my brother and I became Eagle Scouts; that's as high as you can go.

"We grew up in a military environment. It's not like we got up and made our beds and put our footlocker in gear and ran five miles before breakfast, but my mother and father didn't believe in sparing the rod and they didn't. They believed in discipline. They didn't abuse us; there's a difference. But we were definitely disciplined. He instilled that discipline so that Keith and I could be successful. I'm a firm believer that kids need discipline to keep them from getting out of line."

Kevin said his mother, Pat, came from Anniston, Alabama, and that his father grew up nearby on a farm in Choccolocco, Alabama. "She had a certain role," said Greene. "My dad was a career military man, and she knew her role, making sure the kids were fed and got off to school. She chauffeured us to and from practice. She looked after our home. She managed everything. She was always there for us, and I think that's critical for people to grow up in a wholesome environment. They taught us to be respectful of things."

Greene said something about learning politeness. As he said it, he spit some more tobacco juice into a cup he held between our noses as we spoke. Somehow there was a conflict in what he was saying and what he was doing. And that's what always confused me about Kevin Greene.

They lived in some places like Schenectady, New York, and in Fort Leonard Wood, Kansas; Bryn Mawr, Virginia; Mannheim and Munich, among several cities in Germany where they stayed; Granite City, Illinois.

"We'd move every two or three years," said Greene. "I wouldn't trade it for anything. I saw a lot of things, did more things than most kids. But there were adjustments to be made at each stop.

"At those military outposts, we had to get along with all colors, races and creeds, and we learned that we're all just people. There was no racism or prejudice in my family. My best friend in the world is Isaac Russell, who happens to be black. I met him during my first year at Auburn. We've had a great relationship for 15 years. He's my partner in Gold's Gym, which we opened in 1990. I don't keep up with too many people I met along the way, but Isaac and I are close.

"My dad was in Vietnam in 1969. He was in ordnance and munitions, flying helicopters. My dad wasn't in the bush, but he was in the line of fire. My dad would tape messages and send home cassettes. He'd tell us how much he missed us. In the background, you could hear the sound of artillery fire. You could hear my dad, in a hurry, saying, 'I've got to run, the Viet Cong are shelling again. I've got to get to the bunker. Goodbye.' We never understood the stress my mother was under, raising four kids. He was in a combat zone; not being able to see and talk to each other had to be difficult for them. We'd make a tape and we'd tell him how we were doing in school and sports. At the end, we'd all shout, 'I love you, Daddy.'

vin and Keith flank father in 1978 after earning
gle Scout honors.

Keith, 15, and Kevin, 13, wore long
hair when family was living in
Worms, Germany.

herman with two-year-old Keith
nd five-month-old Kevin in 1962.

Therman and Pat Greene were great Steelers' fans.

Therman Greene commissions his sons as officers in the U.S. Army in 1982.

"We were too young to realize how dangerous his situation was. I thought war was a game. I'd always dress up in an Army uniform at Halloween. And at Christmas, I'd ask them to get me a military police outfit and tommy gun.

"I'm closer to my father than my mother, seeing him as a buddy; and loving and respecting my mother. My dad and Keith and I did a lot of bonding on camping trips when we were all in Boy Scouts."

"I like to make things happen."
— Kevin Greene

None of the Steelers played to the press or TV cameras more than Greene at Super Bowl XXX. He charmed the media with his animated stories. He enjoyed being on a bigger stage, and wasn't in a hurry like he always seemed to be in the Steelers' locker room when the Pittsburgh media sought his attention.

It was a carryover from the way he conducted himself during a football game. He was always noticeable on the sideline, shouting, taunting, pointing at people, hollering: "I want you! I want you!" Like a professional wrestler. Like Jack Lambert, only lifting it to another level.

Greene said it was all in fun, to have a good time.

"I consider myself an impact type of guy," he said. "I like to make things happen, dramatic things."

He was asked to explain how the Steelers had rallied from a poor start to win eight of their last nine regular season games, as well as their two playoff games to get to the Super Bowl. He credited the coach, Bill Cowher, for keeping the team together and turning it around.

"We had just swallowed two bad losses, one against an expansion team, the Jacksonville Jaguars, and one against Cincinnati," said Greene. "We got our heads handed to us in Cincinnati on a Thursday night nationally-televised game. The Cincinnati game had kinda broken our spirit, but Coach Cowher said, 'Hey, this is not the Steelers.' At that point it became the consensus, 'Hey, we are better than this, and we can turn this thing around.' And with Coach Cowher's motivation, we did turn it around."

At 38, Cowher was one of the youngest coaches in the league. Greene was asked if Cowher's youth helped him communicate better with the ballplayers, some of whom, like Greene, were not much younger.

"It's not just being a young coach," said Greene. "He's a players' coach. He has been an NFL linebacker himself, and he knows how players feel about everything in pro football, from training camp to injuries to the stress involved."

Speaking of stress, Greene was asked about the exciting finish to the AFC championship game, in which the Steelers escaped with a 20-16 victory over the Indianapolis Colts.

He spoke about the Hail Mary pass by Colts' quarterback Jim Harbaugh, heaving the ball from midfield into the end zone on the last play of the game. The ball landed in Aaron Bailey's lap in the end zone, but Bailey couldn't hold it.

"I saw it come down and fall into the belly of an Indianapolis Colt who was lying on his back," said Greene. "The pile fell on him and I lost (sight of) the football. The next thing I saw was the referee patting the ground and saying it hit the turf. But during that one second, I thought, 'No, no, it can't happen again.' The season before, the Steelers lost to the Chargers and that also came down to the last play, a failed three-yard pass from Neil O'Donnell to Barry Foster.

"He has an exceptional work ethic."
— Tara Greene

In June, 1993, Kevin Greene married Tara Turner of Coldwater, Alabama, whom he met at the Gold's Gym he co-owns in his hometown of Oxford. Tara was a former Miss Jacksonville State University. Greene called her "an Alabama country girl." It was his second marriage. His first wife, Peggy Greene; was from Muscle Shoals, Alabama. He had another serious relationship in between.

Tara sang the National Anthem before a Monday Night Football game with Houston at Three Rivers during the 1994 season. She enjoyed sharing the spotlight with her husband.

"I majored in music, got my B.S. degree and was working on my master's," said Tara. "Then Kevin came and swept me away."

She helped get Kevin ready to play. They said they would say a prayer together, then Tara pounded on Kevin's shoulder pads, screaming, 'Rack 'em, sack 'em, crack 'em, frack 'em.' She ended the ritual with a peck on the cheek.

"I'm not sure what 'frack 'em' means, but she yells it," said Kevin. "She's been doing it for four years. She's as motivated as I am."

Tara was one of his biggest boosters. "He has an exceptional work ethic," she said. "He studies film, he stays late. He knows if they look a certain way, it means something. He knows his opponent."

I saw Tara and Kevin mingling with fans in the parking lot outside Three Rivers Stadium on several occasions. They gave of themselves and seemed to draw strength from the fans. Kevin loved the fans and the fans loved him.

"Kevin is a normal man like any man," said Tara. "The person on the field who is ready to kill a quarterback? I don't really know that person very well. It only comes out on the field."

For whatever reason, Kevin is more considerate of the fans than he is of the media. During the season, in dealing with the regular beat guys, he was almost always in a hurry when people were trying to talk to him, always checking his watch, always cutting them off quickly. He was expansive when it suited him, curt more often.

"I know, maybe sometimes people get the wrong idea about me," he said, "but when it comes to football I have to be single-minded. When I'm focused, I can't be bothered. That's the way I've always been. I respect discipline. I believe in it."

What was he saying? How did that explain away his often rude manner? He had been known to jump on the media, and berate an individual, when anyone approached him after a loss. It's the fierce competitor in him; he doesn't deal well with defeat, that's the way he sees it.

"Americans are born winners," he said. "Americans hate to lose, no matter what it is. My family, especially, my brother, my dad. Whenever we get together and play ping-pong, horseshoes, cards — it's all out!"

No one should take him too seriously, he said, in the make-believe world of professional sports.

"I'm living a dream life," he said. "The money I'm making, it's a dream. It's not real. What's real is getting up at oh-five hundred and working on tank engines, freezing your fingers off to get a tank in combat condition. That's real money, hard-earned money. Those guys are working for a living. All we're doing here is playing a game.

"I'm intense in every endeavor, whether it's football or horse-shoes or croquet. I mean, I play intense croquet. I'm an emotional person. I just let it flow. I'm not one to hold back what I feel. I don't know moderation. Hey, this is pro football. Heck, this baby gets ugly. Only animals play this game, anyway. A linebacker is ugly, slobbering and drooling. Hey, I'm him. I'm intense, but I guess that's part of the linebacker mentality."

Greene said he couldn't reveal the secret of his pass-rushing success. "Top secret," he said with a smile. "I could tell you, but I'd have to kill you." More seriously, he said, "Pass rushing is more desire. It's more a hunger than anything. I'm not really a mental giant, so just point me to the guy with the football."

He led the Steelers all three seasons in sacks, and that was his calling card. What's the big deal about sacks?

"It's just a big play, a show-stopper," he said. "If you can sack the quarterback in this league, you can go a long way. And they'll treat you right financially. It's been a blessing for me.

"I've hit some quarterbacks and they've flat out cried on me, trying to get a flag. I hate quarterbacks that do that. I respect quarterbacks who, well, hang in there, take a shot and say, 'Hey, let's play.' I have flat out knocked the crap out of Phil Simms, Joe Montana and John Elway. And they've gotten up smiling, saying, 'Keep coming, Kevin.' I love it. I've been a fan of guys like Simms, Elway and Montana, guys who make things happen and take their shots. They're big-time quarterbacks."

What's important to him?

"God. Family. Friends. Health. It's that simple. I think you have to put your priorities in order. I play football like it is a dadgum war. I probably tick off a lot of people."

"Kevin Greene is your ultimate pro."
— Coach Bill Cowher

On December 18, 1988, in a nationally-televised Sunday night game, Greene sacked Joe Montana four times in the first quarter in a 38-16 victory by the Rams over the 49ers. It was the last game of the season, and Greene completed the year with 16 1/2 sacks. That was second behind Reggie White of the Eagles, but Greene did not get picked for the Pro Bowl. Other highlights in his career included sacking Dan Marino four times in a game, intercepting a pass by Warren Moon and returning it for a touchdown, a safety against the Raiders and getting to Super Bowl XXX.

"I was just a working guy trying to get the job done," said Greene. "I'm enjoying the publicity. It's fun seeing my name and picture in the papers."

During his Rams days, he drove a red Porsche around with a California license plate that read SO BAAAD. With the Steelers, he drove a Mercedes-Benz, a Viper, several classic Plymouths — he was a collector — and a minivan.

When he played for the Rams, he listened to old war tunes before games, had his captain's bars on the inside of one thigh pad, his paratrooper wings on the other pad.

He signed a three-year $5.3 million contract with the Steelers, $1.5 million up front, which was money well spent by the Steelers. It worked out to an average salary of $1.75 million. It got the Steelers off to a great start in the new free agency setup.

"I want to have fun," he said upon coming to Pittsburgh. "Oh, sure, the money is great. But honestly, the most important thing to me is to be able to have some fun.

"Bill Cowher played the biggest role in my decision to come here. We had dinner together, and I had a chance to talk to him on a number of occasions. He kept telling me this is what I've been looking for. You've got a coach going down the dark alleys with you. It's fun having a coach who bleeds with you, and he does bleed with you. I wanted a team that would let me play."

Greene was put at left outside linebacker. Greg Lloyd was at the right outside linebacker spot. Together, they put a lot of pressure and pain on opposing backs. He and Lloyd were often difficult and distant with the daily media, but they mixed well with the fans. So most fans saw them in a different light than the literati.

Greene was credited with 12 1/2 sacks his first season, the most for a Steeler since 1984. He replaced Gerald Williams, who had been a teammate at Auburn, who signed as a free agent with San Diego and ended up with the Kansas City Chiefs.

Greene was chosen first team All-Pro by Associated Press in 1994 when he led the league in sacks with 14.

"It's a blessing that it worked out the way it did," said Greene. "I hope the Steelers think they got a pretty good deal. They're paying me to put the quarterback down. I'm just a working class guy busting his butt. I'm having a great time here. This is a real blue-collar team, and I feel good in those colors, playing for a franchise with a great tradition. There is a commitment here."

His bosses were quite happy with him during his three season stay with the Steelers.

"Kevin Greene is your ultimate pro and what we do fits his style," commented Bill Cowher. "He can blitz, he gives you that element of toughness, and he's also a very smart football player."

"You've got to love the guy," said Tom Donahoe. "He comes to work."

Greene and Lloyd had similar backgrounds, hailing from the deep South, being Boy Scouts, starting college in ROTC, training at Fort Knox, Kentucky. Lloyd was a weapons man, Greene was into tanks.

Dom Capers, the defensive coordinator of the Steelers during the 1993 season, loved players like Lloyd and Greene, Rod Woodson and Carnell Lake. Capers called them "difference makers. They make a difference by making big plays."

Lloyd didn't praise many players, but he conceded of Greene: "His determination is what impresses me. I tease him about being lucky, but he just knows how to get to the quarterback."

He and Lloyd have a gameplan: " 'Let's meet at the quarterback'; that's what Greg and I always say to each other."

At training camp and during the season, Greene loved to strut around in his black and yellow striped spandex pants. He wore white socks up to his knees. He usually wore a black ballcap backward on his head. His blond hair flowed down to his shoulder bones. Sometimes he wore sun glasses. Sometimes he was scowling. Sometimes he was screaming, or spitting chew tobacco. He was always a sideshow.

It was fun to watch Greene and Lloyd strutting around, flexing their muscles, posturing to the crowd, seeking attention. Greene doesn't see it that way. He said, "I see myself as a country bumpkin."

"He's proved money isn't everything."
— Pat Greene,
Kevin's mother

His parents grew up in Oxford, the family lived there when Kevin's father was in Vietnam, and they returned there for his father's last military assignment. "I grew up outside of Oxford. My mother and father were Auburn fans. We moved to Granite City, Illinois. I was always Auburn. I followed Terry Beasley and Pat Sullivan when they were playing."

He went to Auburn because he loved the school as a child and because his brother Keith was there. "Everybody in the state wanted to play at Alabama or Auburn because they had great programs," said Pitt athletic director Oval Jaynes, who once was an associate athletic director at Auburn.

Oxford is a town of about 10,000. Kevin and his wife Tara had a house across the street from his sister Karen and near their parents. The parents' home on Robin Hood Drive resembled a museum dedicated to Kevin. There was a picture of Kevin shaking hands with former Alabama governor George Wallace. There were photos, programs, guides, pennants and memorabilia.

There is a lot of good in Kevin Greene, his parents point out. They like to tell of his goodwill gestures.

Greene has gone back, for example, to his high school in Granite City regularly to speak at sports banquets.

"I really enjoy coming back and telling the kids they've got to have a game plan," said Greene. "If they want a bright future, they've got to go to college."

In Pittsburgh, he went to schools for anti-drug talks. He once bought 100 hamburgers to feed Steelers fans waiting in line for play-off tickets. He hung around after home games, sometimes for hours, to sign autographs. He donated football uniforms to Granite City South. He and Tara handed out meals to the homeless at the Light of Light Mission on Pittsburgh's North Side as part of a team community outreach project.

"He's proved money isn't everything," his mother said. "It's the way you live your life. How you touch people."

Another Auburn ballplayer, All-NBAer Charles Barkley, has often proclaimed that he was no role model, and said kids should not look up to professional athletes.

"Regardless of what Charles says, he is a role model," said Greene. "If you're an athlete, or in Hollywood, or the president, or on television, you're in a position desired by millions of kids, and they want to be you, look like you. You are a role model, regardless of what you do. Michael Jordan, Charles Barkley and other professional athletes are role models whether they want to accept it or not.

"I try to handle it the best way I can. I understand I am a role model, and when kids look up to me I try to be a good one. I try to say the right things. Say your prayers and stay in school and study hard, and say 'no' to drugs.

"Professional athletes need to be grateful and realize how rare it is to be involved in such a profession. They need to understand that they are blessed.

"Playing football has been one of the best experiences of my life," Greene said during his days at Auburn. "I have a lot of friends on the football team and it is fun to be fighting together for a common goal. I like the oneness of football and the feeling of complete team togetherness."

"He loved the regimentation of the Army."
— Therman Greene

Keith, the oldest son, was born in Fort Campbell, Kentucky. Next was Kevin, who was born in Schenectady, New York. Karen was born in Fort Knox, Kentucky, and Kristin, the baby of the family, was born in Munich, Germany. This happened all in the span of eight years.

For Col. Greene, his 28 years in the Army included two combat tours — one in Korea and one in Vietnam.

In 1970, when Kevin was eight and his dad was in Vietnam, the family lived in Anniston, Alabama.

"It's easy to look back on it now and see that our parents gave us a good home environment to grow up in," said Keith from his home in Fort Dix, New Jersey. Keith followed his father's footsteps into the military and was a major. "They are the ones who gave us the attitude that we can achieve anything."

Physically, Therman and his wife Pat were both skinny, so Kevin had quite a contrasting physique. He was much bigger than Keith.

Therman said he always made sure his sons went to practice for local kids football teams. "If you're going to take the time to try something you're interested in," he said, "you should take the time to dedicate yourself to it."

Both girls played softball and basketball. Karen also played volleyball and was a cheerleader. Therman played ball in senior leagues.

Kevin attended different schools throughout the United States and Germany. He was graduated in 1980 from Granite City South High School. That was the ninth of ten stops on the military tour for Kevin.

He earned honorable mention all-conference as a 185-pound outside linebacker. He also played basketball and high jumped. He was into motorcycle riding as well. He listed his brother Keith as the athlete he admired the most in a yearbook dossier. He also participated in various scouting activities. He earned the rank of Eagle Scout in 1978.

Kevin, at his brother's urging, actually joined the National Guard while he was in high school to get him one step ahead of the game. In 1979, Kevin served with National Guard units in Missouri and Alabama.

"He was going to follow his brother's footsteps and mine," said his father. "He wanted to be an aviator. He loved the regimentation of the Army. He loved the traveling."

He was an Army Reserve captain during his early days in the NFL. He had driven, loaded and fired tanks, over the rolling hills of Fort Knox, Kentucky. "I'm a tanker," he loved to tell people.

"I believe in America," said Greene, sounding like one of his boyhood heroes, General George S. Patton. "I believe in the flag. I believe a strong national defense is the only way to deter foreign military aggression."

Greene family portrait (from left to right) includes Karen, Kristin, Pat, Keith, Therman and Kevin.

As 8th grade running back at age 13 in Worms, Germany in 1975

More recent family portrait includes (from left to right) Kevin, Pat, Kristin, Keith, Karen and Therman.

He was once asked why he was still active in the reserves when he was making a six-figure salary in pro football. "I'm here being all that I can be," he said with a straight face.

"You win with confidence."
— Pat Dye, Auburn coach

After Granite City, the family came home to the Anniston Army Depot near Oxford. The summer after his senior year in high school was spent at basic training and advanced training (military police) at Fort McClellan, Alabama. Then it was on to Auburn. He received his airborne wings at Fort Benning, Georgia in 1981.

He received his commission as a second lieutenant from the Reserve Officer's Training Course (ROTC) at Auburn University in 1982, and later became a captain in armor in the Individual Ready Reserve Program. He was graduated from Auburn with a b.s. degree in criminal justice in 1985.

He tried out for the football team at Auburn about a week into his freshman year (1980) and felt he was not physically up to the challenge. He took a beating. So he quit. Then he dedicated himself to three years of concentrated body-building.

"If I do a sport, I do it to win," said Greene. "It was the same with body-building. That's just my determination. I'm always going to do the best I can."

Kevin hit the weights with great zeal. He ran and he went on a fairly strict diet, all in the interest of gaining weight and muscle mass. He went from 185 to 240 in college. He consumed mass quantities of protein supplements, potatoes, eggs. It resulted in 50 added pounds of heft in three years.

"I remember very well how dedicated he became to making the team," recalled Karen. "I remember him drinking those nasty shakes with raw eggs in them."

He was a demon during the same span in Auburn's intramural football league. Some of the guys in that league urged him to go out for the varsity; they didn't want to have to go up against him.

He returned for a second try before his senior year. He was going out for a major college team three years after graduating from high school. Some thought he was crazy. "My friends knew different," said Greene. "They knew how determined I was."

He made it back on "internal desire," he said.

This time he was 6-3, 240 pounds. Auburn coach Pat Dye liked what he saw and Kevin was kept on the team. He had another year of eligiblity, so he returned to school for a fifth year. "I would not accept the fact that I was a wimp," he said. "I watched the game in college and felt those guys weren't any more physical than I was. Once, I got the chance to be on the team, I told myself there was no way I should be sitting on the bench."

He became a maniacal devotee to the weight room. He was the first player in Auburn history to bench press 500 pounds. Greene did not gain immediate acceptance in Auburn's locker room as a walk-on. He was referred to by the scholarship players as "the musclehead from the downtown gym."

Incredibly enough, Kevin Greene started only five games in his college career at Auburn.

Pat Dye was the head coach when Greene was given a second chance. "I still remember the things he said to the team," recalled Greene. "He said, 'How do you win? You win with confidence. You win with motivation. You win with technique. You win being downright meaner than the other team. You win by playing physical football.' That has carried over to professional football. It's worked out well."

Greene helped Auburn win the 1983 Sugar Bowl against Michigan. In his final season, Greene led the SEC in quarterback sacks with 11 even though he didn't become a starter until mid-season. Playing defensive end, he was voted Defensive Player of the Year in 1984. He did not get invited to any post-season all-star games, where he might have gained more attention from the pro scouts.

"It's been a lot of hard work," he said. "I was determined and I never lost faith in myself. The coaches contributed a lot to my development, too."

Dye remembered the determined kid. "He was a long way from being a finished football player, but as far as raw talent he had as much as anybody on our team besides Bo Jackson," said Dye.

"He's the sweetest guy in the world. He's got that ole long, shaggy-looking hair and you think he's some kind of outlaw. But he's the farthest thing in the world from an outlaw. He comes from a great family, he's community-oriented, and he stands for the right things."

Kevin Greene grew up a lot in his years at Auburn. It remains a special place. He said he would like to be a football coach someday. "Ultimately," he said, "I'd love to go back to Auburn."

George Gojkovich

Kevin Greene exhorts his teammates to get crazy.

Brentson Buckner
A Steeler from the start

"My father was a big Steelers fan.
This is more of a dream
come true for him."

Brentson Buckner was born and bred to be a Pittsburgh Steeler. His father had photographs of Brentson as a baby, then at 4, 6, 8, 10 and 12 years of age, delightful photographs he liked to show people in which his son was wearing something with "Pittsburgh" or "Steelers" emblazoned across his hefty chest.

Here was this bright-eyed, determined-looking toddler in Columbus, Georgia, of all places, wearing snug-fitting yellow pajamas with "Pittsburgh Steelers" on them, wearing all kinds of black and gold sweatshirts through the years.

He was always a chunky kid, and he was still a chunky kid, having celebrated his 24th birthday at the start of the 1995 season. In his second season with the Steelers, he had become a celebrated defensive lineman, 6-2 and about 310 pounds, for his boyhood favorites. He had the same bemused look as the little kid in the photos and this made him popular as a bubbly, fun-loving resident of the Steelers' locker room.

Buckner was born on September 30, 1971, the same year the Steelers drafted the likes of Frank Lewis of Grambling, Jack Ham of Penn State, Steve Davis of Delaware State, Gerry "Moon" Mullins of Southern California, Dwight White of East Texas State, Ernie Holmes of Texas Southern, Mike Wagner of Western Illinois. That was quite a draft class.

The Steelers were putting together the final pieces for the squad that would be recognized as the "team of the '70s."

The following year, they would draft Franco Harris of Penn State, Gordon Gravelle of Brigham Young, Steve Furness of Rhode Island and Joe Gilliam of Tennessee State. They would get to the playoffs for the first time under Chuck Noll at the end of the 1972 season — Franco would come up with "The Immaculate Reception" in an unbelievable AFC playoff victory over the Oakland Raiders — and in 1974 they would win the first of four Super Bowls in a six-year span. They captured many hearts with their hard-working, hard-hitting style.

The Dallas Cowboys became known as "America's Team" during that same period, and they were the much-celebrated darlings of network TV, but the Pittsburgh Steelers also picked up a lot of fans around the country. Their defensive unit was known as "The Steel Curtain," and it found a big fan in Brentson Buckner's father down in Georgia.

214

"Back in those times," explained Brentson Buckner, during an interview in mid-January, 1996, just two weeks before the Steelers would meet the Dallas Cowboys in Super Bowl XXX, "the Steelers were more of a middle class team for America. They weren't as glitzy as the Cowboys. People like my family and friends could relate to the Steelers better."

Brentson's father, Richmond Pitts, loved the Steelers. His boy was a big kid, maybe the biggest kid his age in Columbus, and Richmond reared him to succeed White, Holmes, Joe Greene and L.C. Greenwood as a defensive lineman for the Steelers some day in the future.

"My father was a big fan of the Steelers," recalled Buckner, who goes by the maiden name of his mother, Thelma, because his parents separated. "He was constantly talking all about them. From the first time I played ball, he said 'It'd be good if you could play defensive line for the Steelers.' This is more like a dream come true for him.

"I always wore Steelers jerseys. If kids were playing in the street, I'd always be a Steeler. I never cared for the Dallas Cowboys. In those days they were high and mighty, the Hollywood style. We couldn't relate to that. I liked L.C. Greenwood and I liked Lester Hayes of the Oakland Raiders. Everyone was a Joe Greene fan.

"On Sundays, my dad and I always watched the game together. We'd go to church, and come home, and watch the game until it was time to eat dinner."

Family was still important to him; even though his parents had split up they remained supportive of their children. Buckner lived in Columbus during the off-season. During his first season with the Steelers, he married Denise Deavin, whom he met at Clemson. She was from Columbia, South Carolina. During the football season, they shared an apartment in the North Hills of Pittsburgh.

"There was always someone in my corner."
— Brentson Buckner

How did his father feel now that his son, Brentson Buckner, was about to play in the National Football League's championship game before a television audience that would number over 130 million fans?

"Like most parents are, he's proud," said Buckner. "He's also proud because he knows what I had to endure to play. He remembers when I wasn't able to play as a kid."

Buckner was too big to play with the squirt and peewee teams in his hometown. He was well over the maximum weight permitted in his age group. Whereas Tony Dorsett said he put stones in his pockets so he'd weigh enough to qualify for a kids' football team in his hometown of Hopewell, Buckner had the opposite problem.

"When I first found out I couldn't play with the other kids, my father went out and bought me all the equipment," said Buckner. "I'd put on my own uniform and we'd go out every weekend together. We'd catch and we'd tackle each other a little bit. I was playing ball with my father in the backyard.

"I hung out at the Boys Club. We had a lot of family outings. Everyone was close-knit. I was supported well. No matter what I did, there was always somebody there for me. A lot of guys didn't. No matter whether I won or lost, I always knew I had fans in my family. No matter what I did, I was still their favorite player.

"I did all right in school. I was a pretty good student. I was advanced for my age. I was moved ahead in grade school in fourth grade."

What did his father say to keep up his spirits?

"He never did say anything in particular, like a saying," said Buckner, "but he was just instilling the right stuff in me. If my father wasn't there, my mother was there. And my brothers and sisters. There was always someone in my corner.

"Organized football was new to me in junior high, and I didn't know how to handle it. But when I got to high school (George Washington Carver), I knew I was better than a lot of the kids, and I got impatient. It took a while for me to establish myself. I wanted to play. I was frustrated; my father helped me get through that, too.

"My mom and dad were separated. I spent time going back and forth, between my mom and my dad," said Buckner. "I'd go to school, do my homework and play ball, and then enjoy time with my friends."

Was it a setback when his father and mother separated?

"In my neighborhood, it was normal," said Buckner. "I still saw my dad. He was still involved in my life. I took turns staying with my parents from one year to the next. Even though my mom and dad were separated, I was raised by both of them.

"It was difficult. Because I had to grow up fast. I was the baby-sitter. I had to make sure they had something to eat, and that they did their homework. I had to do some housework to help my mom. She'd be tired when she came home from work. It was an odd way of learning responsibility. I didn't want her working in the mill. I wanted to get my degree, to play pro football, to be able to help her.

"My mother worked hard. She taught me responsibility. She'd be tired and I'd have to help my two younger sisters get ready for school. She wasn't there all the time to watch them. My mom would often tell me, 'You've got to be the man of the house.' She'd say, 'You know the dos and don'ts and what your sisters should be doing, and what they shouldn't be doing. Who they should be with, and who they shouldn't be with. I always knew that I had to have that discipline. I knew she wouldn't always be there to look after things. I had to take what my mom and dad taught me and put it into practice. I had a cousin, five years older than I was; she'd come over and watch over us."

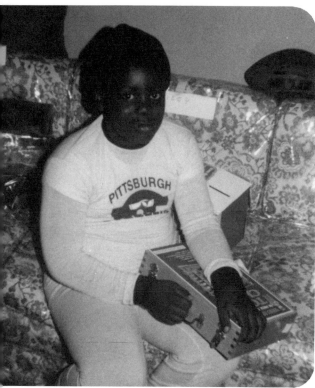

Brentson in black and gold pajamas

Brentson in Steelers uniform

At high school graduation

In uniform his father bought him

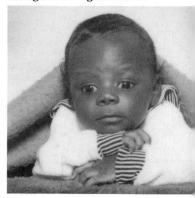

As an infant in Columbus, Ga.

Asked what his younger sisters were doing, he said Lanana was a sophomore at Columbus (Ga.) College, and Shanise was a sophomore in high school. He said Shanise wanted to go to the Naval Academy.

His mother worked in the textile mill along the Chattahoochee River that runs through Columbus. It was the Fieldcrest Textile Mill, where they made towels, bed sheets and linen. In Brentson's younger days, his mother worked from 11 at night until 7 in the morning. His dad worked the same shift. Which means, quite often, there was not an adult at home when Brentson and his brothers and sisters were sleeping. Later, his mother worked three till 11. "She'd come in, with lint from the mill on her, looking tired," Buckner said. "It took its toll on her, standing on her feet all day.

"She was worried about me. She didn't want me to get into trouble. We didn't have gangs as such, but kids from one neighborhood didn't like the kids from other neighborhoods. She didn't want me getting involved in any of that stuff. She wanted me to keep busy, with school and sports.

"In the summer, I had an uncle who was a tile installer, and I helped him do it. I definitely didn't want to do that. It made me more aware of what my mother was going through. My mom worked so hard. One day I wanted to make it so she didn't have to work, or that she could work at her discretion.

"I never worked in the textile mill. I didn't want to go in there. The Fieldcrest Textile Mill was unbelievable. It's so hot; it has to stay hot. If you go down there it's like a prison. There's no windows. That's another reason I wanted to succeed in sports. I didn't want anybody to work that hard. Too many of my friends worked too hard. All that time and they were working for peanuts.

"Now that I'm making good money, I'm able to do some things for my mom. She doesn't have to work now, but she still works because she wants to work. She has a lot of pride. She has a condo, and I'm planning on getting her a house in the future.

"My dad was a computer operator on the Army base in Columbus. He had been in the Army, and he liked the environment.

"He came to everything. He and my high school football coach — Wallace Davis — became good friends. A lot of guys whose fathers were at home didn't see their dad as much as I did. It was a big problem for some of my friends. You need to have parents in your life. If you don't have somebody there to tell you right from wrong, who you gonna listen to?

"I'm appreciative that my mom and dad were there. My mother would tell me, 'It's hard working out there. You have a chance to do something. You better do it.'

"My dad was more of a talker. He didn't want me hanging out in the streets. He'd take me to neighborhoods and point out people who had ability as ballplayers, but didn't do anything with it. There was this one guy who'd been a high school All-America about four years ahead of me. He thought that hanging out in the streets was the thing to do. He was at a party and somebody slipped something into his drink. It was a friend who was jealous of the attention he was getting. That was his introduction to drugs and it got him started. It was his downfall. He never overcame his problem.

"There were a lot of people who didn't want you to succeed. You've got to get away from people who want to pull you down. It's the old crab effect."

What's that?

"If you ever cook crabs...you get a big pot and bring the water to a boil and drop in the crabs. They all try to get out. If one is getting out one of the others will reach up and pull them back down."

"I was too big to play Pop Warner football."
— Brentson Buckner

Brentson Buckner was the eighth of 10 children. He had seven sisters and two brothers. Buckner said Columbus was the second-biggest city in Georgia, but that it had a small-town atmosphere. "Everybody knows everybody, everybody clinging together," Buckner said of his neighborhood.

His favorite relative was his maternal grandmother. "My grand-ma passed when I was in seventh grade," he said. "She was my mother's mother, Grandma Madeane Buckner. I used to visit her. She gave me my name 'Bam-Bam.' She was cool. Telling me stories about my mother and my aunts. As a kid you look at her and love and respect her. I'd like to be able to go back as an adult and see her; I missed out on that.

"She was my only grandparent. My father's mother and father both died before I was born. And my mother's father had passed. But my Grandma Buckner took me to the candy store. She'd take me to all the fast-food places, Burger King and McDonald's, every place my mom didn't want me going."

When it came time to get involved in sports, his father took him around to see what they could line up.

"I was too big to play Pop Warner football. It hurt. Here you are eight or nine years old and the rest of your friends are playing, and you're told you can't," said Buckner.

"I was big for my age. The only way I could play was to play with older guys, and my mom and dad didn't want me to do that. I had to wait until it was my turn.

"Even when I couldn't play, my dad went out and threw me a football. We'd catch and kick. He'd show me how to do things. He played in high school and in the Army. His name was Richmond Pitts.

"I'll never forget what he said one day when I found out I couldn't play. He said, 'One day people will wish they let him play football.'

"Coach Wallace Davis from our high school saw me walking home that day. I was real sad, and he stopped the car and asked me what he could do to help. I later played high school ball under him. He helped me get a scholarship to Clemson."

What was Clemson like? How did it compare with what he experienced in Pittsburgh during the playoffs that followed his first season?

"Clemson...they call it Death Valley. We have 80,000 for our home games there, and its reputation is that it's tough to win there. But I never heard noise there like I did here. For Pittsburgh only to hold 60,000....and be that loud...it felt like the stadium was moving."

I was with other members of the media standing behind the end zone at Three Rivers Stadium as the Steelers were putting the finishing touches on a 17-7 playoff victory against the rival Cleveland Browns back in December of 1994. The Steelers had an insurmountable lead, and Buckner was obviously enjoying himself. He was among the Steelers jumping up and down and celebrating every time they put the hurt on Vinny Testaverde or one of the Browns' backs who were pinned at their own goal line. He and Greg Lloyd were banging helmets like rams.

"It was fun," recalled Buckner. "Once you know the game is not at stake, you just pin your ears back and go after the quarterback. You're not worrying; it's fun. We just came strong. Everybody gets a chance to rush the passer. Felt like we were finally getting respect."

As for bumping heads with Lloyd, he regretted that. "I wasn't expecting that part," said Buckner. "He got caught up in the excitement. I hate doing that in the cold. It brings you back to reality in a hurry. I tried to stay away from him after that."

Going into the San Diego game in the AFC title game the following week, Buckner was upbeat. "My confidence level is real high," he said. "We can play against anybody. I'll be fired up. There's no stopping us now. If we're on top of our game, no team can stop us.

"Everything is ahead of me. It was a dream rookie year. I'm starting on defense for a team that has a chance to go to the Super Bowl." He would have to wait a year to realize that dream...

"College helped me grow as a person."
— Brentson Buckner

In high school, Buckner won four letters in football, three in track and field (shot put and discus), three in basketball, two in baseball where he was a third baseman. He won the state shot put title with a heave of 58'- 3 1/2". He gained *Street & Smith's* All-America attention for his football play in high school. And he accepted a scholarship to Clemson University in Clemson, South Carolina.

They still talk about how strong he was during his school days at Clemson. He set a school record with a 1,120-pound lift on a leg sled.

As a senior, he was named first-team all-ACC. He graduated with a degree in English.

He was the only member of the 1994-95 Steelers teams who could claim a college degree in English. He said he majored in English to be different. "All the other athletes were majoring in criminal justice or stuff like that," said Buckner. "I wanted to do something no one else did."

He passed up an opportunity to apply for the NFL draft after his junior year because he wanted to get his degree. He said one of his favorite subjects was Shakespeare.

"The thing I like about Shakespeare is that what you see at first glance is not always the true meaning. The surface is just the surface, but underneath there are many different levels of meaning. I like to think of myself like that. On the outside, I look like a big, tough guy, but inside there's a lot more there."

Shakespeare sounded a lot like Dwight White, I thought.

"I played baseball when I was young. I played with Frank Thomas of the White Sox and Cary Ingram, second baseman with the Dodgers, when they were kids. I played first base. Baseball was a big thing. Frank was hitting 25 home runs in Babe Ruth League. He was always beating everybody all by himself. Everybody wanted to play on his team, to play with Big Frank.

"In Columbus, I hung out mostly with blacks. At Clemson, you hung out with everybody. You learned there were people from all kinds of places and backgrounds. It was part of growing up, and learning there was a better side to life. You had to learn to look after yourself. You had no mom or dad to wake you up and get you to school. You had to be self-motivated.

"I'm self-motivated. A lot of people don't understand why I do what I do.

"Football comes so easy to me. I get bored. I have to make it more challenging. I want to be in the Pro Bowl. I have a great opportunity. If push comes to shove, I'll be the best player I want to be."

I asked Buckner if he realized he made more money than Joe Greene and Jack Lambert combined throughout their careers.

"I don't look at the money part," said Buckner with a straight face. "I look at the rings they got. The money's nice, but if you don't have that world championship ring on your hand you're wasting your time.

"Speaking of money, a lot of people were trying to talk me into turning pro early," said Buckner. "A lot of agents — that's their job — wanted me to declare myself eligible for the draft. I had done some research. It was a weak year for defensive linemen. I might have gone just as high as I eventually did. But it goes back to my mom and dad. They wanted me to get a degree."

He was the first in his family to do so. "I'm glad I stayed," he said. "College helped me grow as a person."

"I do believe I can be a dominant player."
— Buckner on Draft Day, 1994

Buckner said some things the day he was drafted by the Steelers that showed he didn't lack confidence when he first came to Pittsburgh.

What did he know about the Steelers when they selected him?

"You have a lot of great players, great defensive players who've been here," he said. "I'm familiar with them because I've played with Levon Kirkland for three years in college, and I know about the tradition they had with the Steel Curtain, the great defensive line. Coach Cowher's just a great coach. Levon told me that and I can see the way the players respond to him."

Some scouts had compared the collegiate Buckner to Michael Dean Perry of the Browns. Was that a good comparison?

"It's a good comparison in some ways, because he came from the same school and played under the same coach and we have similar styles," Buckner replied. "I believe I'm a little bit bigger than Michael Dean and that makes me a little bit more powerful than him, and more durable than him. Otherwise, I think it's a great comparison."

Buckner was asked if he thought he could become a better pass rusher than Perry?

"I believe I am," Buckner came back, not a hint of hesitation in his soft voice. "If everything goes right and I play to my potential, I can be, one day, just as dominating as Reggie White.

"I do believe I can be a dominant player, because I have the speed, size and ability to go against anybody. Surrounded by great players and a great coaching staff that cares about me, put me in the right spot and I could be the dominant lineman in the draft."

Buckner has often had a problem with his weight. It was thought that he was too big to play for the Steelers when he reported to his first training camp at St. Vincent, and again the following May when he showed up for a mini-camp at Three Rivers Stadium. There was nothing *mini* about Buckner on either occasion, as he weighed between 340 and 350 pounds. He had been the Steelers' second round draft choice out of Clemson in 1994, and the Steelers had high hopes for him. He got off to a slow start, however, and found himself relegated to an early spot in a corner of Bill Cowher's doghouse. But he had overcome earlier disappointments, and could not be deterred or "dee-teared," as Cowher would say.

It took a while, but he felt that Cowher was in his corner. "His voice like grabs your attention. He's always straight to the point," said Buckner, doing his best to portray his relationship with his strong-willed coach.

"He came to work me out at Clemson. He told me he was the coach who'd get me to play to my level of ability. He said, 'I can make you use that ability. I can make you the player you want to be. I'm going to stay on you so that you're going to show me your true potential.'

"Cowher was watching me closely at camp. It was like a personal challenge. He talks about tenacity, and the hustle that sets the team apart from the pack. He talks about the way football is played here, that we're a blue collar team. In the fourth quarter, we're going to find a way to win."

When did he feel that Cowher was coming around to his side in that first season?

"The week before we played Indianapolis," said Buckner. "Ray Seals got hurt and I was in his spot. I practiced pretty well that week. He came to me on Thursday that week, and said, 'That's the Brentson Buckner I've been looking for. That's the way you gotta be every day.' I felt I had reached the point that I was the player they drafted."

What did Brentson learn from his own boyhood experience that affected his behavior or outlook since he joined the Steelers?

"Things won't always go the way you'd like," he said. "You need other people to keep you up. Nobody lives forever. If you know a person is hurting, you should try to help them. Pats on the back or a friendly comment can help them. You have your real family, but you also have a family on the team. You have two families.

"As a team, we have experienced some lows. But great teams overcome that. People start saying we're not the Steelers they knew. But we can control our own destiny. If you're in this league, you're a professional. You have to play and just take advantage of the opportunity."

He mentioned how he moved over to play nose tackle when Joel Steed was suspended for four games at midseason of 1995. "I could have said, 'The only thing I can play is end; I don't want to move,'" he said. "But I did it for the team. They're paying me a lot of money, so I owe them something. It was a challenge for me.

"I've always considered myself a versatile player. I had a chance to prove it. I know so much about the defense. I understand where defensive backs fit in. I'm not where I want to be. I just keep trying to be better and better. I don't want to take any steps backward. My best football is in front of me."

"I started to question myself."
— Brentson Buckner

Buckner signed a $1.72 million three-year contract, plus an option year, as a second round draft choice out of Clemson University. It called for a $400,000 signing bonus, a salary his first season of $235,000, $297,350 in 1995, $352,500 in 1996 and $387,750 in his option year. That's about three times as much as Joe Greene ever made in a season.

The Steelers had loved what they saw of Buckner in game film and from his workout numbers, relating to his size, speed, strength and agility.

He got off to a slow start with the Steelers, to put it mildly. Ed Bouchette, the beat writer for the *Pittsburgh Post-Gazette*, referred to Buckner's "training camp from hell."

Buckner reported late, overweight, out of shape, and low on energy and enthusiasm. The Steelers had drafted so many prospects for the defensive line in past years who failed, for one reason or another. The list included the likes of Darryl Sims, Kenny Davidson, Keith Gary, Willie Fry, John Goodman, Aaron Jones and Gabe Rivera. So Buckner was regarded prematurely as another in that category. Many unkind comments were offered about him, and not all of them behind his broad back. There were a lot of people down on him at his first training camp at St. Vincent.

"I never did think it was right, what happened to me then," he said. "Bad thoughts creep in: 'Maybe I'm not as good as I think I am. Maybe I don't work as hard.' I had myself in a real predicament. Every time I picked up a newspaper, I started to question myself."

Why was it so difficult for him to find his way at his first training camp at St. Vincent?

"What hurt me," he said, "was I didn't know the speed at which professional football was played. I was pretty much redoing my whole approach."

Was there anyone in particular who came to his rescue, who tried to help him through those difficult days?

"Levon Kirkland. He always kept on me. He'd say, 'You know you're good. I know you can play.' He kept my head up. He told me things would get better. Levon is like a good friend. He knows what I can do. Everybody wanted me to be so good so soon, right from the start. I was surprised how long it took me, longer than I expected to get situated."

Another Buckner booster was John Mitchell, who had come over from the Cleveland Browns to look after the Steelers' defensive line, and was himself feeling his way around the training camp.

"Once he realized he could play at this level," said Mitchell, "he got his weight down and started doing the things we saw him do at Clemson. Down the road, this guy is going to be an All-Pro, if he continues to improve.

"I haven't been around anybody who's more intelligent than he is. You could put the guy at linebacker right now and not have to teach him a thing. He might be one of the brightest guys on the team.

"When I went with Coach Cowher to work out Buckner, I can remember it was a rainy, drizzly day. He was 305, maybe 310 pounds at the time, and he ran a 4.9. Then when you looked at him on film, you saw that he had quick hands and quick feet, but you never had a chance to see him accelerate to the ball. You could see that when he cut it loose that he had the athletic ability to play in this league."

There were some good times that first season that perked up Buckner's spirits.

"I feel every play I'm out there is a big play," said Buckner after he made two tackles and his first NFL sack against the Bengals in October of his first season.

Buckner got more playing time when Seals broke his thumb. Buckner got to play a little against Seattle in the fourth regular season game of the 1994 schedule. "I got my little taste of action, and it's driving me to get better," he said at mid-season. "That fueled me on and each week it has gotten better and better."

Buckner was taken off the inactive list to fill Seals' spot, and he played in the next eight games. He started the final five after Gerald Williams tore a triceps muscle. So promising was his play that the Steelers allowed Williams to go to the expansion Carolina Cougars in the off-season without a fuss.

"The most important thing to me personally about playing football is the challenge," said Buckner. "Knowing that if you're in the NFL, you're one out of, say, 100,000 to make it. Then if you're a starter, those odds are even greater. Then out on the field, you're an entertainer, just like actors in movies. On Sundays, that's your stage, your scene, your time. It's a way for me to entertain people."

He tried to put a positive spin on some of the criticism that was heaped on him at the start.

"If a coach is constantly getting on you, then he knows you're a player and he has expectations for you," said Buckner. "He knows you can play better than what you're doing. Once you find a coach that doesn't say anything to you and doesn't really care, you know you're in trouble.

"My father instilled in me, going back to when I used to get punished, that there was a reason for how people treat you. Why did he punish me? I needed discipline; I got that from my father. If he didn't discipline me, he wouldn't have cared. I just switched that over to football. I look at it as another way of people telling me I can't do something, and that just charges me up.

"I have to credit the guys who've been here, like Levon Kirkland. They told me, 'You know what you can do. You're a player. Just learn and let your ability take over.' That's pretty much what has happened.

"Ever since I was drafted by Pittsburgh, Levon Kirkland has been like an older brother to me, telling me what to expect, just laying down the law," Buckner said. "He was ahead of me at Clemson, and he helped me there as well. I've been lucky to have him on my side in college and in the pros. When times get hard, it's good for me to have somebody to talk to and he can help me get through it."

"It's like a big boys' club in here."
— Brentson Buckner

Flashback to the early fall of 1995: Brentson "Bam-Bam" Buckner was playing dominos with his buddy, Myron "Boo" Bell, in the recreation room, just off the locker room, where the Steelers retreated to play games, eat their meals, watch TV — the noon KDKA-TV newscast was on the overhead screen — and just to get away from the media. It was usually off limits to the media. No such room existed when I was covering the Steelers of the '70s as the beat writer for *The Pittsburgh Press*.

Most of the Steelers had gone home, and so Buckner and Bell allowed me to join them at the table. This was at the outset of the 1995 season. Imagine two tough guys named "Bam-Bam" and "Boo" playing dominos in the Steelers' inner sanctum.

Buckner was bare-chested except for a gleaming gold chain; his chest was thick with dark hair, and he had an ample stomach that sagged between his legs. He had a Buddha-like ebony body. But Buckner proudly announced that he had already dropped 20 pounds, going from 344 to 324 pounds in just over two weeks of training at Three Rivers Stadium. He had a homemade tattoo on his right bicep, with his nickname "Bam-Bam" imprinted there. Bell, a second-year defensive back from Michigan State, also had a tattoo on his arm. After Byron "Bam" Morris saw Buckner's tattoo, he went and had "Bam" tattooed on his own right bicep. Just like little kids...

"During high school," said Buckner in explaining how he came by his nickname. "I was kind of young and I was just as strong as the guys that were seniors and juniors, so all the players said that I reminded them of Bam-Bam on the Flintstones, to be so young and have the strength of several of them. It just carried through high school and college."

Buckner had lively dark eyes that gleamed and danced as he entertained a visitor with his observations. He was having fun, until he lost badly to Bell. Then he frowned.

"That's what's wrong with him," said Gary "Roc" Brown, an offensive tackle from Georgia Tech, when Buckner looked upset over losing, and started sneering. Like most athletes, Buckner hated to lose any kind of competition.

Buckner believed that athletes should be free to express themselves, and mentioned Muhammad Ali and Dennis Rodman as people he admired for their individuality. He felt that Cowher and his teammates allowed him to be himself. He and Erric Pegram, in particular, prided themselves on their stylish attire, and had the kind of dress-off competition on occasion that once featured John "Frenchy" Fuqua and L.C. "Hollywood Bags" Greenwood back in the '70s. Buckner beat out Pegram in the contest, but Pegram protested later that he got a bad deal from the judges. It was all in good fun.

"The nature of these guys is just to be themselves and enjoy the camaraderie," Buckner said. "There's a good feeling on this team. Everyone's treated me fine. It's like a big boys club in here, like the gang you hung around when you were a kid. There's loud guys, quiet guys, jokesters, pranksters."

Asked to expand on why Muhammad Ali and Dennis Rodman were attractive to him, Buckner first spoke of one of his boyhood heroes.

"I looked up to Ali, and what my dad told me about him. He knew he was good and he didn't mind telling you. He was a strong person who stuck by his beliefs. He was willing to take some unpopular stands. Now he's starting to get respect and some credit for what he did. I always admired him."

What about Dennis Rodman, the NBA's best rebounder and most outrageous character, with the hair dyed different colors from one month to the next, all the body tattoos?

"Dennis sticks up for himself," said Buckner. "People get mad. He has an image problem. People forget you have your own life outside of sports. They're scared to let people bring their own personality into the game. Dennis is one of the players who bring their own personalities into the game. There's not another player in the league who rebounds as well as he does. Yeah, he has tattoos all over him, but put him on the court and he's all business. You see the things he does, but you can be yourself and still be successful. He's been criticized for not going into the huddles. Charles Barkley and Michael Jordan don't go into the huddles, either. They listen from a distance. Any little thing...it's magnified when it comes to Dennis Rodman.

"When I first got here, I'd come in the locker room and people would be so serious. I was dancing around my dressing stall and I think I offended a few people. They didn't think I was serious enough. I could tell by the way they looked at me. People have to realize that the outside personality has nothing necessarily to do with your game performance. Once I leave the stadium, I'm a regular citizen. You have to have a life outside the stadium."

There was a down-home, slow-talking Southern drawl manner about Buckner, and a boyish mischievousness that belied the fact that his coaches regarded him as one of the brightest players on the team. This is nothing new. Back in the '70s, the Steelers had a defensive end named Dwight White who was nicknamed "Mad Dog" and was always cutting up in the dressing room, and getting into fights, or into people's faces, on the field because of his fierce never-take-a-step-backward approach to the game and a good argument, and no one gave him credit at the time for being one of the smartest of the Steelers. He has since shown his other side as a sharp investment executive.

> *"I tell young people all the time: Disappointment and failure are part of life.*
> *The only thing you want to do with them is examine them, see what you did wrong —*
> *not what somebody did to you that caused them — and learn from that. Then bundle it all up, wrap it up and throw it away."*
> — My American Journey,
> a memoir by
> Ret. Gen. Colin Powell

"Everybody has that dream of being a hero."
— Brentson Buckner

And now here he was...just two weeks away from Super Bowl XXX. "It hasn't set in with me," said Buckner. "I know it's going to be something spectacular."

He had his work cut out for him. He would be matched most of the time against the Cowboys' right tackle, Erik Williams, even bigger than him at 6-6, 324 pounds. "You got to be man enough to say he's physical and you got to be physical with him," Buckner said.

"I dream about big plays all the time. I dream about the game coming down to me making a big play. Doing something that helps us get a victory, especially in the Super Bowl. I see all kinds of scenes. Everybody has that dream of being a hero."

Does he ever have a hard time telling the difference between a dream and reality? Between real gold and fool's gold?

"I woke up plenty of times during my dreams," he said. "I'd say to myself, 'Did that really happen?' Sometimes I dream it and it actually happens. I'll think, 'Haven't I done this before?' After the game, you realize that you had thought of doing it during a dream."

How were his family — he was one of ten children — and friends back in Columbus treating him now that he was making such a big splash on the pro football scene, especially after he appeared on the cover of *Sports Illustrated* in his rookie season? "A lot of them are complimenting me on making it," he said. "I'm going home this weekend. Guys that never talked to you are suddenly your best friends. They'll be hanging around, like we've been friends for life."

Buckner made a funny remark without meaning to, when I asked him what he did when he went back home. "I don't drive around in any limousine, trying to look big," he said. No, but how many guys in Columbus were cruising around in a burgundy Mercedes-Benz with a gleaming gold grille and gold strips over the wheels that sells for about $97,000? "I bought the sports car with my playoff money. I traded my Toyota Land Cruiser in on the Mercedes," he said. "Got to think of my image. I got it to be different."

When Buckner's comment was relayed to Levon Kirkland, the Steelers' linebacker said, "No way you're going to slip in and out of town in that one and not get noticed. Buck is big time. Don't let him fool you."

Buckner, by the way, traded in the burgundy Mercedes CE300 for another top-of-the-line pearl white Mercedes 600SV12 after Super Bowl XXX. It was another show-stopper. It had his name and number — 96 — stitched into the leather seats. There weren't many limousines that looked any more impressive. It cost about $125,000. "It was just time to move up," he said.

Buckner smiled a big smile and shook his head when I questioned him about his choice of automobiles. He had his hair tied in knots, with black shoots sticking up here and there. He seemed happy with himself. "I hope to play up to my car," he said.

"People always tell me I have a baby face. I try to act mad most of the time so people won't say that. I guess I still look like a baby, but at least I look like a mean baby. I'm basically just a friendly type of fellow. I try to cover up sometimes. I can live up to that tough image, but usually the real me comes out.

"Football is fun, like a big party. Just because I'm big and physical doesn't mean I don't have fun. I'm usually laughing out there on the field. I love to win. I love the competition.

"This is a once-in-a-lifetime opportunity," he said. "You can enjoy yourself. This is the dream of a lifetime."

Pittsburgh Steelers/Michael F. Fabus

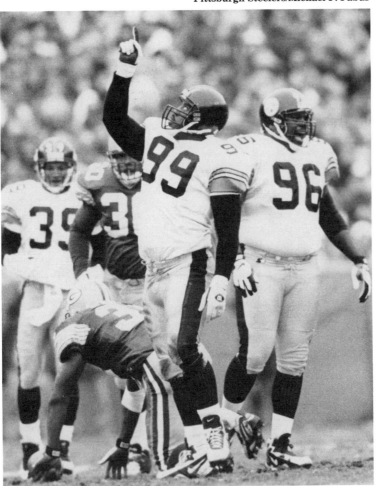

Levon Kirkland (99) and Brentson Buckner (96) celebrate a big stop against the Green Bay Packers.

DREAMS —
"A Kid's Tears Turn to Gold"

The original version of this essay was hand-printed by Richmond Pitts, the proud father of Brentson Buckner. It was written in August of 1981 on a yellow legal pad, which he has kept as a prized possession.

Every child born into this world wants to be like Mom or Dad, especially little boys. They want to play football or baseball like Dad. They dream dreams. Some come true. Most of them don't, for reasons beyond their control.

There was a young boy who had a dream and high hopes. He and his father went to every location where they were signing up boys for Little League football, and was told that the boy was too big and couldn't sign up. His father pleaded to each of them to allow his son to run and exercise with them, even though he wouldn't be able to play, just so he could get the exposure, and give him the feel of organized ball. But the answer was still no.

With a broken heart and crushed dreams, this kid and his father returned home to seek what direction they would go.

As they traveled slowly home, this young man with all of his hopes of playing football going down the drain, began crying out of control.

His concerned father called upon all of his knowledge and resources in trying to reassure his son that this was not the end, just the beginning, assuring him that with faith in God, he would win out over all, telling him that life was full of stumbling blocks and the only way to get anything out of life was to put something in it. He went about trying to reinstill his son with faith in life, and to reassure him that his Daddy believed in him, and that he would always stand by him no matter what the situation might be.

As they slowly neared their home, they were approached by Coach Wallace Davis, who was in the area taking care of some personal business. As a parent and instructor with concern for the welfare of all kids, Coach Wallace noticed the tears still running down this kid's face, and wanted to know what was wrong, was there anything he could to to help.

The father explained to him how his son had been turned down by all of the Little League teams because of his size. At the time, he was nine years old and weighed 190 pounds. And his heart was broken.

Coach Davis took time to reassure this kid so he could hold his head up and told him that all was not lost. He gave this kid a good pep talk, telling him he was blessed to have a father that would stand by him no matter what comes up. He told the son that he had known his father all his life. At that time, the father told Coach Davis that Georgia had Herschel Walker, and that Columbus had Brentson Buckner and that he would train him himself, with that point in mind, that someday he could be just as good at football as Herschel Walker.

The father went to Neil's Sports Shop and bought a complete football uniform for his son. Then they returned home and started on a physical program in which the son would run sprints, do sit-ups, push-ups, swinging a sledge hammer from both the right side and the left side. After the exercises, the father would throw him a football hundreds of time, from every angle. Together, they were going to prove that the people who had turned him down had made a big mistake.

Even with this reassurance from his father, there was still that hurt and scars left within from being flat turned away at a time when his hopes had been high as the sky, scars that would carry over to junior high where he first was given a slim chance only because he was such a large seventh grader, but not much playing time for the Rothschild's Falcons. They were at that time the junior high all-sports champions in Columbus.

After two years at Rothschild, he moved on to Carver Senior High. As fate would have it, the same coach — Wallace Davis, who had given him that pep talk and assured him that all was not lost that Saturday afternoon when the Little League team had turned him away — was there to greet him that August morning when players reported and signed up to play football.

Although he had a father who had stood by him and labored to train him on his own, and a coach that had given him assurance on the facts of life, doubts still lingered inside of him. He had never gotten over being turned down. Following the first morning practice, he said he was quitting because he didn't want to play anymore. He didn't feel he'd ever get the chance to play, and revealed to his father that he felt the same thing would happen all over again.

But he stayed and, with renewed confidence, he excelled for four years at Carver High School, even helping them defeat Valdosta High in the state playoff, breaking Valdosta's 27-game winning streak. As he winds down his college activities at Clemson, which he and his family dearly love, his tears have truly turned to gold.

Brentson Buckner fires out of line.

Baby Joseph
He belonged to all of us

"I was writing about where the Steelers came from, and now I was going back to my own roots."

A nun was on the telephone talking to my mother, a note of urgency in her voice. "Mrs. O'Brien, we'd like you to come down to school. We need to talk to you about your Jimmy!"

"What's wrong?" my mother asked. "I don't understand. What could Jimmy have done wrong? My Jimmy is my most affectionate child. He brings me flowers on the way home from school."

"We know, Mrs. O'Brien, that's what we want to talk to you about," replied one of the so-called Sisters of Charity.

A certain Mrs. Roscoe, it seems, wasn't too thrilled about the idea of me picking flowers from her front yard. Her home was located midway between our home and St. Stephen's Grade School in Hazelwood, a milltown along the Monongahela River at the southeastern end of Pittsburgh.

I thought of that incident on a Thursday afternoon, April 11, 1996, on a bright, warm spring day, as I stood across the street from where Mrs. Roscoe once resided, and studied the scene. Now there were no flowers, no front yard, really.

Her house, on the corner of Mansion Street and Gate Lodge Way, had been abandoned and boarded up for some time. It was once one of the nicest and neatest houses in our neighborhood. This was in Glenwood, which borders Hazelwood, and was often referred to in news reports as Hazelwood.

I remember when Mrs. Roscoe had new siding and new awnings put on the house. Now the siding had a permanent dust coating on it and the awnings were faded to the bare metal, and falling apart, some slats swinging in the wind. Pigeons flitted about the rooftop, and their droppings stained the sun-bleached green shingles. She would have died if she had seen it, as they say, but then she had already died years ago.

This was a block away from my boyhood home, from the block where I had lived the first 24 years of my life. There was a sign in the third-floor window at the house across Gate Lodge Way from Mrs. Roscoe's house that read "LET'S GO, STEELERS!" It was a sign left over from happier times.

I was in the midst of writing this book about the Steelers when I felt compelled to return to my hometown. I had been writing about where the Steelers had come from, the kinds of communities that had spawned them, and now I was going back to my own roots, where I always feel like I'm still 14.

232

On Easter Weekend, 1996, someone had abandoned a newborn baby boy in a narrow walkway between Mrs. Roscoe's house and St. Paul's Lutheran Church. One of my best friends, Marty Wendell, went to that church when we were kids. I went to St. Paul's to attend meetings for Cub Scouts and Boy Scouts. My Grandma O'Brien lived two doors away. My sister once owned a beauty shop on the corner of the same intersection there at Second Avenue and Mansion Street. My mother worked as a secretary for several years at an office in that same block.

As I stood there, I saw yellow buses bringing children home from school, and a crossing guard was escorting students across a busy intersection, smiling and talking to them as they passed in front of her outstretched arms. Soon, they would be going out to play. It was a beautiful day for kids to play.

I had to go there when I heard about the baby. It was left out in the cold, lying nude, next to a pink towel, on a cement walkway, and it died from exposure. It had been bitter cold that weekend, only the week before my visit. A woman walking to Easter Sunday services at St. Paul's discovered the body. Easter Sunday is supposed to be a day that offers hope, a day of resurrection and renewal, and this was a downer for the entire community. Everybody was embarrassed and angry and felt a sense of shame that such a senseless death had occurred at their collective doorstep. They called him "Baby Joseph," after the husband of Mary, the mother of Jesus, and they had community prayer services and gave the baby a proper burial. It pulled the town together, at least for that week.

Only a year earlier, a woman was shot in the head and killed execution-style on the street where I lived and played as a youngster because she was going to testify at a criminal court hearing. She lay dead on a spot where I had often drawn roads in the dirt with my fingers and played with my miniature plastic automobiles as a five- and six-year-old. A few weeks later, two children were taken into custody by police for playing with and firing a loaded gun. My wife and I saw my boyhood home in the background on the news at 11 that night. What was going on in my old neighborhood?

During my post-Easter visit, I jumped up on the wall in Mrs. Roscoe's front yard, an act that would have gotten me in trouble as a student at St. Stephen's, and walked back on that narrow walkway.

The spot where the baby boy had been left to die was marked with a memorial of sorts. There were several kinds of artificial flowers, stuffed animals, bears and bunnies, a cross fashioned by two foot-long wooden rulers with the names of children hand-printed on it, along with some hand-drawn hearts. There were several candles in glass tubes. One of them had fallen over, perhaps blown by the wind, and the glass tube had broken.

"I have a dream."
— Dr. Martin Luther King, Jr.

"Who was telling the kids
about colleges now?"

It squeezed your heart. It was a sad scene. As I stood there, I could see the back of my grandmother's house. She lived there with my Uncle Phil and Aunt Martha and Cousin Patsy when I was a little boy. I was about eight when Grandma O'Brien died. I liked to visit their home. They always had cake or cookies for me.

I saw a building where Doc Irwin had his dentist office. His claim to fame was that he had been a reserve quarterback on one of Jock Sutherland's teams at Pitt. He lettered in 1924 and 1925.

His office was over a bar once owned by a man named Elmer Trapp. Later, it was called Marie's. When I turned 21 my father took me there and bought me a beer, sort of a rite of becoming a man. I remember that there were 17 other men at the bar, and I was the only one who didn't have a shot of whiskey — or a "shooter" — beside my glass of beer. It was still a bar. Many of the bars from my boyhood had survived. They just had different names. There was a sign posted at the door of this one warning customers not to bring drugs inside. It was a sign of the times. Bars and funeral homes are the last businesses to disappear from a community. People still drink and they still die, no matter how bad the economy gets.

There were homes missing from the neighborhood I knew in my youth. There were entire blocks missing. There was much debris in those empty lots, old sofas, all sort of garbage strewn along the sides of the roads, blocking what were once walkways. It seemed to me that there was paint and pride missing as well.

I could go to some of those homes as a child and enter without knocking on the door or ringing a doorbell. I might be offered something to eat; I could sit and watch TV, go to the bathroom. There were people who looked after me and the other kids.

I knew everyone in the neighborhood. It was my paper route, where I delivered the *Post-Gazette* in the morning. It had been my brother Dan's paper route before I took it over. Somehow the neighborhood made more sense then.

I could see the Pittsburgh Railways Company where my Grandfather O'Brien worked as a streetcar motorman. I could see the Baltimore & Ohio Rail Road, where my Grandfather Burns was the yardmaster, where my father went to work at age 15.

There were mills and jobs in the community then and people could walk to work, or take a streetcar to the mills along the Monongahela River. There were stores on Second Avenue, a mini-mart in every block, barbers, dentists, bars, bowling alleys, shoe repair shops, beer distributors, movie theaters, pharmacies or drug stores, furniture stores, five and dime stores, social clubs, restaurants, fruit and vegetable stands. They were all gone. So were all the professional people.

The doctors and dentists and pharmacists and attorneys told the kids about the colleges they had attended, and pointed the way to Pitt and Duquesne. Who was telling the kids about colleges now? Now the kids call Hazelwood and Glenwood by the name Plywood. That's because all the storefronts were boarded up. Hazelwood and Glenwood, regarded collectively as Hazelwood, was known as a tough town when I was growing up there, and the citizens took a certain pride in its reputation. But you had to go looking for trouble; it didn't come looking for you. Now it was becoming a ghost town. There were still good people there, but many of them were confused, afraid and felt abandoned.

I saw mothers walking little children and dogs. I didn't recognize any of them. One woman sat on the steps of St. Paul's Lutheran Church, cuddling her young child and keeping an eye on a little boy nearby. I wondered how those mothers felt about Baby Joseph, what they were thinking as they caressed their own kids. No matter where we live, that baby belonged to us, too.

That baby was a black male. Only the week before, I had written an article about a boyhood hero of mine, a gentleman named Herb Douglas who grew up about a mile away, at 160 Hazelwood Avenue, just down the street from Gladstone Junior High, which had since become a high school. Herb Douglas won the bronze medal in the long jump in the 1948 Olympic Games in London, England, and had been a track and field and football standout at the University of Pittsburgh. He was the second black, behind only Jimmy Joe Robinson, to play football at Pitt in the late '40s. He became a corporate executive in New York City and created one of the most prestigious international athletic awards in honor of his boyhood hero, Jesse Owens.

To my knowledge, Douglas was the only Pittsburgh-born and bred male ever to win a medal in the Olympic Games. Suzie McConnell-Serio, a more contemporary basketball star out of Brookline, was the only woman who could make that claim.

Just across the street from Douglas' boyhood home, around the corner on Sylvan Avenue, there was a vacant lot where a home once stood. As a teenager, August Wilson often visited a teacher there and frequented the nearby Carnegie Library branch. Wilson lived a block away on Flowers Avenue. He won the Pulitzer Prize twice in the early 1990s as a playwright. He and Edward Albee were regarded as America's greatest living playwrights. He drew upon that neighborhood as well as the Hill District, where he lived on Bedford Avenue most of his youth, for material for his plays about black life during various periods in Pittsburgh.

I had told the stories of Herb Douglas and August Wilson when I spoke to students at schools in Pittsburgh and Western Pennsylvania. I wanted to inspire youngsters with their success stories. If these black men could come out of an inner-city community that had fallen on hard times then others might realize that they, too, could accomplish great things in their lives.

As a grade school student, I had often stood in front of the boyhood home of Herb Douglas on the way to wood shop and metal shop classes at Gladstone Junior High. We went there one afternoon a week from St. Stephen's Grade School to get some manual education experience. They were called "released time" classes. I was fascinated by knowing that someone had once lived in that house who had gone on to win an Olympic medal. I was lucky to get to know and become friends with Douglas as an adult. I have cherished our relationship. I would have lunch with him within two weeks. He lived outside of Philadelphia, but he had heard about the baby that had been left to die in his hometown of Hazelwood. He would shake his head when I filled him in on the details over lunch at the Holiday Inn on the Pitt campus.

Now I was standing on Mansion Street, across from Mrs. Roscoe's old home. I was standing in front of what had once been a sign painting store owned by Carl Downey. I used to stray into his workshop on occasion and look over his shoulder as he painted letters, admiring his handiwork.

Next door was the home of Bud and Gracie Forden. They owned a confectionary store downstairs on the street level, where we used to play pin ball machines. The Fordens didn't have any children of their own and were quite generous, always giving us money for good grades in school and to help us buy uniforms for our sports teams. They were also the "numbers writers" in our neighborhood. That was supposedly illegal, but there were no better people in our community. I had half a scholarship as I was about to enter Pitt, and my mother hit the "number" at Forden's two weeks before school started to get the other half of my tuition. A numbers runner named "Slim" had brought her the money, and kept his hand extended for a "tip" for handling the exchange.

When I played for midget football teams I was good at soliciting money from local merchants to pay for our uniforms. I would take a booster card around and sell space on it. Bud Forden was one of my first stops; he was always generous as a patron of local sports teams. The spaces paid for by the local bookies always read simply "From a Friend." They didn't advertise their business by name.

The home of Rege and Doris McLaughlin was missing. They had about seven kids, I can't remember for sure, and the youngest, Petey, was killed in the Vietnam War. I know it was never officially called a War by our government officials, but tell that to the McLaughlin family. Rege was a streetcar motorman and only had to walk across the street to get to work. Their home was like a community house in our neighborhood. Anyone in the neighborhood could go into their home or ride the swing on their porch without an invitation. There was a fruit and vegetable store, Heckman's, on the first floor of the building. I once saw a rat as big as a cat come out from under that building before someone crushed it with an empty fruit crate.

Now the building was gone, and so was the one next to it, and a garage where we used to wrestle on old mattresses. But the memories remain. Carole Jean McLaughlin, who was in my room at St. Stephen's, taught me how to smoke when I was about nine years old. I was caught soon after and punished when I got home. My father removed the belt from his slacks, swatted me two or three times on my backside, and it stung like hell. I never wanted to get swatted with that belt again. I stopped smoking that same day, and never tried it again. Lucky me.

Carole Jean's brother, Jimmy "Horsey" McLaughlin, organized and coached the first kids' football team I was ever involved with, the Golden Eagles. That team became the Hazelwood Steelers and we played our home games at the top of Mansion Street at Burgwin Field. Jimmy's kid brother, Johnny "Doughboy" McLaughlin, played on those teams. A younger sister, Regina McLaughlin, was one of my first girl friends.

I kissed a girl for the first time at the front door of that house. Her name was Mary Elaine Brain. Within a few days, I was in bed with the mumps. I always blamed Miss Brain for that.

Two boyhood friends and former teammates of mine went on to play pro football in the Canadian Football League.

John Sklopan grew up on Gertrude Street, just a block from where the baby was abandoned. His sister still lived there. He went on to star at South High School, Mississippi Southern University and with the Edmonton Eskimos.

Dave "Rooster" Fleming, who grew up at the top of Mansion Street, played on the first football team at Gladstone High School in the late '50s and early '60s. He didn't go to college, but nearly stuck with the Steelers when he got a tryout at the age of 20. He ended up playing ten years with the Hamilton Tiger-Cats of the CFL. Hamilton was known as "The Pittsburgh of Canada," so Fleming felt at home there.

Sklopan, Fleming and I all played for the Hazelwood Steelers. Rick Reagan, our quarterback, lived nextdoor to my Grandma's house. Dave's uncle, Bill Fleming, who worked at the B&O, was our coach.

I wrote stories about the games we played, and that's how I became the sports editor of *The Hazelwood Envoy*. That's how I got started. It would lead to writing about the Steelers and the Pirates and the Penguins and Pitt, and sports teams across the country. It was the beginning of a wonderful journey in the world of fun and games.

Jack Fitzhenry followed me as a guard on the St. Stephen's CYO basketball team. He grew up on Gertrude Street, across the street from Sklopan's house, and he grew up to be 6-6. He played basketball at St. Francis of Loretto and Duquesne University and later with a team that toured with the Harlem Globetrotters.

Back in the early '50s, the Steelers' best running back, Jerry Nuzum, lived nearby on Winston Street. That was a big deal in Hazelwood, having a Steelers' star living there.

Forbes Field and Pitt Stadium were about five miles away, but we had a Steeler living among us.

"The first time you see your parents' faces you are looking at yourself. They are in you."
— From eulogy for Art McKennan

I was almost killed in an automobile accident on the Glenwood Bridge before my third birthday. But doctors at Mercy Hospital saved my life, and gave me a chance to grow up.

It's a shame someone couldn't have given that baby boy that was abandoned on Easter Sunday a similar shot at life. Who knows what that baby might have become?

I got my start in Hazelwood and it led to wonderful things. In my second year at Pitt, I had an opportunity to travel with the football and basketball teams to places like Miami, Seattle, Syracuse, Waco, Notre Dame, Los Angeles and West Lafayette, Indiana.

It was more of the same when I worked for daily newspapers in Miami and New York and later back home in Pittsburgh.

I had been to Europe, and walked the streets of Paris, Madrid and London. I lived for nearly a year in both Kansas City and Alaska when I was in the U.S. Army.

But wherever I went Hazelwood went with me. This was my beginning. I had so many memories of this place. As a writer, I remembered so much stuff, faces and events, things that were said, my triumphs and failures, times I was elated, times I was scared.

I remembered a line from my favorite writer, Ernest Hemingway, offered to one of his friends in 1950: "If you are lucky enough to have lived in Paris as a young man, then wherever you go for the rest of your life, it stays with you, for Paris is a moveable feast."

And wherever I went, Hazelwood went with me. Now I returned mostly for funerals.

I wondered what the people sitting on their porches were thinking as they checked me out. This was my neighborhood, not theirs, yet I felt like an intruder and I'm sure I was viewed in that respect. They probably thought I was a detective, looking for clues about "Baby Joseph" and trying to solve the case. Who did this baby belong to?

I saw a fellow named Jack Ianacio strolling by. He had a mustache and wore his brown hair in a ponytail. I recognized him by his walk as much as anything. He had this certain swagger, which he had mastered as a teenager. Jack always had a certain style about him that separated him from the pack. Now he was in his mid-50s, and he walked with the same swagger.

When I was playing midget football, the highlight of my career was when I intercepted a pass against the Allentown A.C. at Burgwin Field and returned it 44 yards down the left sideline for a touchdown. Jack Ianacio and one of his buddies, Mussy Lougene, both threw critical blocks for me. I needed all the help I could get. I wasn't too swift. I was tackled from behind and fell forward, just crossing the goal line.

238

The memory of that majestic run on a dimly-lit field was so vivid in my mind. So many memories are so deeply etched in my mind like that. Things that happened in grade school and high school seem to have happened only yesterday.

A part of me would always call Hazelwood home.

A few days later, I attended a funeral service at the Freyvogel Funeral Home in Shadyside for a friend from the sports world. Art McKennan, who had been the public address announcer at Forbes Field, Pitt Stadium and Three Rivers Stadium, had died at age 89. McKennan had so many memories of Pittsburgh's sports history. He had witnessed so much.

I thought of an observation by Alex Haley, the author of *Roots,* the saga of an American family: "Every time an old person dies it is like a library being burned down."

A minister presiding at the funeral service for McKennan said, "The first time you see your parents' faces you are looking at yourself. They are in you."

That line will stay with me as well. Hometowns and parents are what this book is all about.

Author seen in football and baseball (Pirates) uniforms in backyard of boyhood home in Hazelwood, about five miles from Forbes Field where the Steelers and Pirates played in 1950.

Greg Lloyd
An intense leader

"I'm just out there playing football.
And football is a tough game."

The O.J. Simpson verdict — not guilty — had been announced only moments before my unscheduled one-on-one meeting with Greg Lloyd on Tuesday, October 3, 1995.

I was coming away from the clubhouse of the Steelers, walking down the hallway alongside Rod Woodson. Woodson had been the only player in the clubhouse. The players had Tuesday off after a Sunday game during the regular season. Woodson was wearing a black-encased walking cast on his right leg, and was walking with the aid of aluminum canes. Woodson had torn the anterior cruciate ligament in his right knee while tackling Detroit Lions running back Barry Sanders in the season opener, and was expected to be out the remainder of the season. He refused to accept that verdict, however, and he came in every day to work on his rehabilitation. He thought the Steelers could get to the Super Bowl, and he thought he could be ready to play by then.

Lloyd came around the corner and was walking our way. He smiled and said hello to Woodson, and asked him how he was doing. Lloyd didn't say anything to me. It was like I wasn't there. He passed most writers without a word; he wasn't picking on me. I thought of Ralph Ellison's book, *Invisible Man.*

This was just over two weeks after Lloyd had leveled Danny Marino in a Monday Night NFL game in Miami. Marino was hurt, with a bruised sternum, and had to leave the game. This appeared to be the realization of a pre-game threat by Lloyd to "knock him into next week," which Lloyd vehemently denied ever saying. Lloyd had not been very cooperative with the media before that game, and now he had declared he wouldn't talk to the Pittsburgh media anymore. That game left him in a bad mood, anyhow, because Miami had won, 23-10. The Steelers had defeated the San Diego Chargers, 31-16, two days earlier at the stadium, so I was hoping Lloyd might be looking at the world through rose-colored glasses.

Undaunted, or daffy, I decided to double back to the locker room and introduce myself once again to Lloyd and tell him about my book project. When I got there, he was on the telephone, standing in the doorway of equipment manager Tony Parisi's office. I just stood in the clubhouse and waited for him. Admittedly, it was an uneasy wait. Lloyd looked at me as if I were waiting for the telephone.

Finally, Lloyd came out. I approached him, putting on my best game face, and extended my right hand. Lloyd took it and held onto it with a firm handshake. He held my hand for an extended period as I explained what I was after. He told me he had come in on a day off for the players to do some Taekwondo work. He had earned a 2nd degree black belt earlier in the year. It was good for any sane sportswriter to keep his martial arts credentials in mind.

Lloyd told me that he had never mentioned Marino by name in a post-game interview three weeks earlier in Houston. I think he talked to me because there was no one else in the clubhouse to witness the event.

"I was talking about the NFL and their rules regarding quarterbacks after the game at Houston," he said. "I've always been after the quarterback in every game I play. I was talking about quarterbacks at large.

"Now where the hell do you get me saying 'I'm going to knock Danny Marino into next week' out of that? Those words never came out of these lips. Believe me, I've said some other things and I never backed down from what I said. That's not my style."

It was a shame Lloyd was not letting the media get his side of the story. He has strong feelings about everything he does, has a powerful voice, and certainly a compelling presence. Lloyd demands your attention when he wants it, his baleful eyes seizing yours and never letting go, like his initial handshake.

"I was talking about the rules...and about Darren Perry's hit, and how I felt about it," he insisted. "I didn't mention Marino."

When he dropped Marino, I was watching the game on TV. Marino reached up and clutched the front of Lloyd's jersey. Marino looked hurt and angry and he shouted something to Lloyd, apparently in protest. It was a poignant picture. Lloyd refused to discuss the incident after the game. He didn't want to talk to anyone about anything.

"What did Marino say to you?" I asked Lloyd.

"He was talking some trash to me," allowed Lloyd. "I didn't say anything to anybody about it because it's none of their business. That's between him and me, something that was said in the heat of battle."

Neither Marino nor Coach Don Shula said anything critical of Lloyd after the game. Shula said the official was right on top of the play and didn't throw a flag. Marino said, "That's part of the game. He hit me hard and clean."

Of course, Lloyd believes that's the way he sacks all quarterbacks. Talking about Marino, who grew up in Pittsburgh and was an All-American at Pitt, Lloyd said, "He said he could've come back in the game. Then why didn't he?"

Lloyd let that line hang a while before he continued.

"I wasn't out to hurt him," said Lloyd. "I'm just out there playing football. And football is a tough game. I'm against the NFL rules. I know why they're doing it. They want to keep the quarterbacks out there. But they can't have different rules for them than everybody else. There's no 'I' in team. One person can't be more important than everyone else. I'm going to hit everybody as hard as I can hit them. I expect them to do the same to me.

"I know what they're thinking. Marino is marketable. That's why Marino makes $5 million dollars a year. That's why he does the McDonald's ad and the Isotoner ads, and he can be held up as someone pure and good and someone the kids should want to grow up and be like. I understand that. It's the same way with Aikman.

"But they can't make rules to put them above my law. They don't put any money in my pockets. I'm just out there doing my job."

Lloyd sounded a lot like Jack Lambert with those lines. Lambert had once suggested the NFL rules-makers put skirts on quarterbacks to protect them.

"That (the Marino stuff) was the pre-game hype," said Lloyd. "They're looking for inflammatory stuff like that. They're looking for some excitement. It makes for a good headline.

"No one asked me if I said it. It was certainly a controversial line and no one else heard it, but no one asked me if I'd said it. I'm not going to talk to those guys."

Gene Atkins, a safety for the Dolphins, responded angrily in a story in *The Miami Herald*, and attacked Lloyd for the remarks about Marino that were attributed to Lloyd. "The guy doesn't have any character or class," said Atkins. "A Lawrence Taylor, a Rickey Jackson or any other great outside linebacker would never say anything like that. It makes me think he is a thug or criminal. You can tell him I said that."

Marino would not get drawn into the controversy, "I think it's just about playing hard," Marino said. "I wouldn't expect him or the Steelers to play any other way, which is 100 miles per hour."

The newspapers and radio sports talk shows all bristled with comments about Lloyd's alleged comment that week. There was a real furor in Miami over it.

"I'm friendly with Bryan Cox (then an equally stormy and controversial Dolphins linebacker)," Lloyd told us. "He had me on his radio show the week before the game. I talked to him from my house here. He told me to clear up the stuff down there; he said everyone down there was upset with what I said. I told him off the air that I didn't say that, and he said he knew that. But I wouldn't apologize on the air. And I wouldn't call Marino and apologize for something I didn't say.

"I'm not kissing anybody's ass. I know what people want me to do, but that's not me. I tell people what's on my mind, not what they want to hear.

"I had some chances early on to take out Danny Marino if that's what I wanted to do. I could have went for his knees. He's got bad knees. If the NFL doesn't want us hitting the quarterbacks in the head maybe we can go for their knees. I could have went for his knees. That would put him out for sure. I don't know any NFL quarterback who wants you to go for his knees instead of hitting him high."

Greg Lloyd

George Gojkovich

George Gojkovich

George Gojkovich

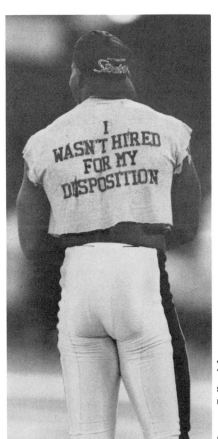

George Gojkovich

Pittsburgh Steelers

g and his wife Rhonda with local kids in United
TV ad shooting

Maybe Lloyd was protesting too much. One suburban reporter insisted he heard Lloyd say he was going to knock Marino into next week. Lloyd denied it. But in a taped interview which was aired on WTAE-TV before that game, Lloyd did say this when asked about Marino:

"I think everybody on our team, you know, respects the heck out of him, but we're still going to come after him. We can hit him, we can hit him, we can get him out of the game, and that's a bonus for us."

And what did that mean? Wasn't he saying the same thing?

Lloyd looked toward some family photographs he had displayed on the shelf at the top of his dressing stall. There were pictures of his wife, Rhonda, and his three young children, the two boys, Gregory Lenard II and Jhames Isaac, and his daughter, Tiana Cassandra.

"I'm not so bad," he said. "I love my children. I care about my family. I love my wife. That's my first priority.

"Man don't scare me. I quit letting people scare me, or boogie me. I quit doing that since I was 12 years old."

Lloyd loved to return home to Georgia where he had built a beautiful home. "I like to be there with my family. I like to go golfing and fishing, and forget about football for a while."

"His actions speak a lot louder than his words."
— Bill Cowher

In a pre-season game with Green Bay in August of 1995, he stepped on Kevin Greene's hand and broke it.

"When you're out there, you're not worried about whether you're stepping on anyone or not. That's part of the game. But if I did, I'm not going to apologize to him. If I stepped on it, I stepped on it. It's not the first time someone got their hand stepped on playing football."

Ouch! Where's the love, man?

In the same game, he dealt a hard blow to the head of Green Bay quarterback Bret Favre. No flag was thrown at the time, but the league later fined Lloyd $12,000 for what they felt was an illegal hit.

He delivered this hit with his right shoulder, forearm and the top of his helmet. It was borderline dirty, according to Green Bay coach Mike Holmgren. I remember saying in the press box that if one of the Packers had leveled Neil O'Donnell like that the whole stadium would be in an uproar. Steelers' announcer Bill Hillgrove told me he thought it was a simply a good hit.

Lloyd had spoken about his approach to playing football on several occasions during his stay with the Steelers. He was unrelenting in every respect. He exhausted everyone. All of his teammates respected his enormous skills and his great enthusiasm for the game, but they grew tired of his histrionics, his hollering at them, and the offensive unit certainly didn't like it whenever he would rant and rave in a them-and-us posture.

"If you're not fired up," said Rod Woodson, "he'll fire you up or tick you off, one of the two."

Several of his teammates can tell you about how they were injured, bloodied or had bones broken, by Lloyd coming late into a pileup. Most of them think there were times when Lloyd ought to have lightened up.

"When you play football for 60 minutes the way I do, you don't have to answer to anybody," said Lloyd with a sneer.

"If I have to scream, if I have to shout, if I have to get a 15-yard penalty, if I have to curse one of my coaches out — if it constitutes winning, then that's the ultimate thing. And, if you don't like it, the hell with you. The shirt (he was wearing) says it all — I didn't get hired for my disposition."

I have stopped young fans to ask them why they were wearing Lloyd's No. 95 jersey, and one middle school student said, "Because he's the meanest man in the NFL."

Lloyd liked to keep everyone on edge. He had arrived at the 1994 training camp wearing a T-shirt that read: "Real Men Are Black." That, of course, also caused a controversy. It went well with his other T-shirt, "I Didn't Get Hired For My Disposition."

Fellow linebacker Jerry Olsavsky only smiled when he saw Lloyd's latest T-shirt. "He's OK with me," Olsavsky said. "He told me I'm his favorite white player on the team. He used to say that me and (Bryan) Hinkle were the only white friends he had."

When Lloyd went to the Pro Bowl, he invited his fellow linebackers to join him in Hawaii as his guests.

There was mixed reaction to Lloyd's T-shirt, the majority viewing it as a racist statement, the minority defending Lloyd's freedom to express himself, some mixed, wondering why he felt compelled to stir the stew pot that way. It drew some thoughtful essays from both sides in the op-ed pages of the city's newspapers. Some also thought it was much ado about nothing.

Steeler fans loved the way Lloyd played football; there was no controversy about that.

"You just go out and prepare and get ready to play football, get ready for war," was one of Lloyd's stock lines.

When writers would come to Lloyd before a big game, say one with the Cleveland Browns, and told him what somebody on the Browns had said about the Steelers, Lloyd would recognize the story line, and cut the conversation short. This happened during the playoffs at the end of the 1994 season. I was among the writers who were leaning in on Lloyd's words of wisdom, filling up a notebook.

"It's more hype, that's all," Lloyd said. "One person said this, another person said that...I'm not concerned about what happened the last time we played them. It doesn't matter.

"On game day, our intensity is going to be higher because we're playing the Browns and because it's a playoff. It's a love-hate thing between us, mainly because we're in the same division. Houston and Cincinnati are the same way."

Lloyd simply wouldn't buy into the standard story lines. "Let everybody else make the comparisons," he said on more than one occasion. "You can't get caught up in those things. You don't play into that.

"Playoffs present a very simple situation. It's now or never. There's no other way to view it. We have to play our game. We can't control what they're saying; we can control what we're saying. Let's go out and play our style of football."

Staring sternly into the eyes of the assembled sportswriters and radio and TV reporters, Lloyd straightened them out: "You guys can't come out and play. You don't put on the pads. You can't have anything to do with the outcome."

After the Steelers beat the Browns, 29-9, the Steelers were somewhat subdued in the dressing room, as they looked ahead to the AFC championship contest, which would pit them against the San Diego Chargers.

To the Cleveland media corps, Lloyd said, "Get on that plane ride back to Cleveland. We couldn't beat the Browns three times in one season, right? You guaranteed yourself a spot in the Super Bowl.

"You don't see anybody celebrating here. We did a little, but now we've got our senses back. That's only one game; we've got another one to play. They'll hype this one, too. They'll call it The Game."

OK, Greg, but don't you feel a teeny bit good about beating the Browns again?

"It feels good," he said, begrudgingly. "I can't say that about this old body of mine. I feel like a guy 60 years old. You won't get me saying, 'I'm going to beat anyone.' Even if you know you're better, you don't tell them.

"They (the Browns) said they hadn't played two good games against us. Now they haven't played three. They tried to hype this up, but it didn't work.

"We may not have gotten a lot of sacks, but an incomplete pass, a hurried pass, is just as good in our book as a sack. We certainly put pressure on their passing game. They kept guys in to block. That plays into our hands."

Lloyd allowed that the Steelers' offense did its part, and then some. "It was their day," he said. "The offense took care of business. We just had to go out and hold the fort."

Lloyd was asked about the Steelers' tradition, and whether the signs of the Steelers' success that are evident everywhere one looks in the lobby and the hallways leading away from the reception desk were still of value. Team owner Dan Rooney had thought about removing the Lombardi Trophy collection and associated memorabilia for fear it had become an albatross around the necks of more recent squads.

"I don't come in the front door," said Lloyd. "I come in through the back door. I go up front to get my check, and that's it."

Once again, Lloyd sounded a lot like Lambert with those lines.

"Even if the team wins and goes to the Super Bowl and wins," asked Lloyd, "do you think we'll be compared to those teams? If you're coming in to work for an organization like this, it's best to learn your history. But these fans are hard to satisfy.

"They won the Super Bowl. That's all you're going to hear about."

Reflecting on how good Lloyd could be when he talked to the media it only reminded one of what everybody was missing during the 1995 season.

"When you mess up, you miss out."
— Greg Lloyd

On his day off in early December 1995, Greg Lloyd paid a visit to Peabody High School in the east end of Pittsburgh. It's an inner-city school familiar with violence in the streets rather than the sort Lloyd is identified with in the football world.

Less than a year earlier, 16-year-old junior Dorion Reid, a star running back and linebacker on the school's 1994 City League championship team, was shot and killed in an early morning incident at a Shadyside fastfood restaurant. This was only a few weeks before the team would be honored at a banquet. Reid had been named to the All-City League team, and the best was yet to come.

There were about 350 students at the assembly to hear Lloyd speak. He had been brought to the school by former teammate Chuck Sanders and Schneider's Dairy as part of a series of inspirational messages at city high schools.

It was a test for Lloyd in several ways. Talking to school assemblies is a tough assignment in any part of town, but it's doubly difficult on the inner-city circuit. Lloyd lost his patience with a few students who spoke throughout his talk, and ordered them out of the auditorium.

"That's what happens when you mess up," Lloyd told his audience. "You miss out."

During his talk, Lloyd occasionally singled out a student or two, and asked them to be quiet while he was talking.

The students who were out of line were lucky Lloyd let them off so lightly. One can only wonder what they're like in a regular classroom, when a staff teacher is instructing them, if they won't give proper attention to Lloyd, one of the most popular and most-feared players in the National Football League.

He had twice been named the MVP of the Steelers, in 1991 and 1994, had been a first-team All-Pro three straight seasons, had made five straight Pro Bowl appearances and had been the recipient of the 1994 Pittsburgh Man of the Year Award. In the 1995 season, Lloyd had led the team with 117 tackles to go with 6 1/2 sacks, three interceptions and had a team-high six forced fumbles.

When Lloyd was finished with his address, students were rewarded with prizes for paying attention. Imagine that.

Lloyd was there to pass along some messages to help them navigate some mean streets. He had it rough when he was a kid, and with some help from the right people, he managed to be successful. He was raised by an aunt after being abandoned first by his father, then by his mother. He was born in Miami, but raised in Georgia.

"Nobody's going to hand you anything because of what your mama did or what your daddy did or the color of your skin," Lloyd told his young listeners.

"I want you to join up with people who care about your future."

He urged them to care about one another and to respect their parents, teachers, administrators and fellow students.

"If you don't respect that person sitting next to you, how are you going to respect your peers and teachers and mother and father?"

Lloyd told them he got upset when he heard about youngsters fighting over colors and neighborhood turf wars. He urged the students to set goals for themselves and to stay focused on their education. He told them that when he was a student at Fort Valley State he signed up for summer courses so that he could earn his bachelor's degree in electrical engineering. It was something he dearly wanted.

"That's what you have to do, but it's so tough because you can't see the light at the end of the tunnel," he said. "It's all up to the individual."

When Lloyd asked his audience how many of them attended church, less than ten out of the 350 raised their hands. He shook his head at the response. This, he recognized, was a tough audience.

He told them of Biblical passages about the need to love God and to love each other.

Lloyd had always been a hard hitter. Lloyd was proud of the fact that he graduated 28th in a class of 250 at Peach County (Georgia) High School. He made quite an impact on the football team there, too. His teammates called him "Hit Hard Lloyd."

"I know I haven't played a good game unless my hand has been stepped on or if somebody isn't bleeding," he has said.

"It isn't football unless your shoulders are numb after the first quarter."

Football provided a supervised area for young people to flex their muscles and give vent to their aggressive tendencies. Watching the way players like Lloyd play the game, always trying to wipe out opposing players, it has struck me that the NFL has become legalized gang warfare.

Greg Lloyd with Rod Woodson

Lloyd at 1994 team MVP press conference

When Lloyd spoke to students a year earlier, he explained his mission to sportswriter Steve Hubbard for a profile for the August, 1995 issue of *Inside Sports*:

"When a kid sees a Michael Jordan or Magic Johnson, they don't realize the hard work that went into that, the education that goes along with that," Lloyd said. "They think they can skip school and just shoot hoops and some agent is going to drive by and say, 'Hey, kid.' Somebody has to be there to tell them life isn't like that. Maybe you can do something to help their lives. You're trying to get a kid to think with his head and not with a gun.

"You try to let them know there are no shortcuts in life. You have to work hard, you have to bust your butt and it's not going to come easy. There are going to be days when you think the end of the world is coming, but you have to get up and dust yourself off and keep going.

"Hey, you have to hang in there, you gotta stick to it. It's how you deal with problems, it's how you deal with adversity that makes you a better person."

"His mother must not have given him enough love when he was young."
— Nate Newton, Dallas Cowboys
prior to Super Bowl XXX

Early in the 1995 season, I said hello to Greg Lloyd for five days in a row without any kind of response. On the sixth day, I said hello a little louder. He mumbled something in that deep voice of his, something I couldn't quite make out in the way of a response on that sixth day. I was beginning to wonder how long he might go without saying hello. And I guess I was putting him to a test.

It was once said of a famous difficult athlete that he did not learn how to say hello until it was time to say goodbye. Lloyd looked like he was headed in that direction.

Lloyd liked to hold his head high and walk by and through people, especially anyone associated with the media. What was so difficult about saying hello, about acknowledging the presence of another person?

I had heard and read all sorts of stories about how he visited the patients at Children's Hospital on a frequent basis, and what a big hit he was with the kids, and how popular and warm he was when he did autograph signings at area shopping malls. So why did he come off differently in the dressing room of the Steelers? Why did he seem to have a large chip on his shoulder?

Just before Super Bowl XXX, one of the largest members of the Dallas Cowboys made a comment that may have been, unwittingly, right on the mark in helping to explain Greg Lloyd.

"His mother must not have given him enough love when he was young," noted Nate Newton, a 320 pound offensive lineman. Newton's Theory may be most insightful. Lloyd's mother abandoned him and his brothers and sisters, at least the way Lloyd looks at it, when he was only two years old.

Maybe it's what motivated Lloyd to visit Children's Hospital on occasion, and to talk to children with life-threatening illnesses or injuries and try to lift their spirits.

"We complain that we have to play with pain every day," said Lloyd, "but it does not compare with what these kids are going through at the age they are going through it. You can't even imagine the pain.

"They say, 'I have cystic fibrosis.' Or, 'I just had an appendix taken out,' or, 'I just had a liver transplant.' Your pain is under three layers of soil compared to these kids' pain."

Lloyd was the youngest of nine children. He was born in Miami and dropped off at his aunt's house in Fort Valley, Georgia, when he was two. Lloyd said it took him a long time to deal with the pain of growing up without parents.

Lloyd related the details of his difficult childhood to Steve Hubbard for a magazine report.

His aunt, Bertha Mae, raised Lloyd and four brothers and four sisters. "The complete family, the mom and dad, the milk and cookies? No, I got a taste of reality real fast," Lloyd said in the 1995 interview.

"I missed my father early in my life. I don't, anymore. I missed him at Little League football games. I was one of the best players out there and people would slap me on the back and tell me how good I played. But it don't mean shit if it didn't come from someone who put food in your mouth and clothes on your back. After the game, kids would go with their father to the Dairy Queen or whatever. I had to bum a ride home."

He said one of his sisters told him the story of what it was like the night all nine of them were dropped off at their aunt's home by their mother. "She tells me we just sat on the floor at our aunt's and everybody wondered, 'OK, what now?'" At two, Lloyd was too young to think about anything.

"My Aunt Bertha Mae, she taught us discipline," continued Lloyd. "We had to go home when the street lights came on. The worst thing you could do was lie to her. She was direct and honest and I learned that from her. I studied hard in school. I was in the church. I was a Boy Scout, imagine that, me a Boy Scout.

"When I was nine or ten, I was playing in the front yard one day and someone just drove up and said, 'Hello, I'm your mother.' How do you drop off a two-year-old and then just show up years later? My dad, I have never met him. In both situations, I have had to overcome the bitterness, and I'm still working on that.

"I love my aunt more than she will ever know even though I have told her that. But the love from your mom, your own parents, is something that, really, you can't replace."

Like several other great defensive players of the past, such as L.C. Greenwood, Dwight White and Mel Blount, among others, Lloyd worked in the fields during the summer, picking peaches in rural Georgia. "It was slave labor, 35 cents a basket," Lloyd recalled.

Lloyd learned something about working hard as a youth, however. "When you get a job, you get there on time and you do it right."

Lloyd may have looked at his young life through different eyes than some of his siblings. His brother, Darell, of Tamarac, Florida, wrote a letter in response to the piece about Greg's upbringing that appeared in a later issue of *Inside Sports*.

"I would like to set the record straight concerning what my brother, Greg Lloyd, has said about my family in your magazine. First of all, Greg was too young to know anything. He had to go by what my Aunt Bertha Mae told him.

"The truth is that my mother, Nettie, did call my aunt to inform her we were coming, and my mother has the evidence to prove it. The story about (my mother) going to the store and never coming back is a plot to destroy my mother.

"My mother had a good reason for what she did. She wanted us to have a better life. She couldn't support us financially and did everything she could to keep shelter over our heads. My father — I love him dearly, but he wasn't there for my mother at the time. They used to fight 365 days a year. I would stay up with my mother and cry with her late at night because she was so hurt.

"That's when she made her decision to call my Aunt Bertha Mae and tell her to keep us until she got back on her feet. When my mother came back for us, my aunt told my mother the kids were all in school and doing fine, so let them stay. My aunt always taught us to be against our mother and father, and if we mentioned or said anything about them we would be whipped. That's a fact.

"I can't see how my brother has the nerve to say these things about my mother. She is a very strong, supportive woman, and she knows how to treat people and do what she has to do to survive. She never asks anybody for anything unless she has to. When my uncle died, my sister called Greg to help my mother bury him. He did, but he demanded that his money be paid back. But he can go and buy houses and cars for other people. You say he has a softer side. I don't think so.

"My mother knows she has the support of some of her children, if not all, and many other people know the truth behind our family's story. We don't need Greg's money, heroism or pride. All we ask is for him to stop trying to hurt our family with these fictional stories that he is assuming. If he reads Proverbs 1:31 and Matthew 1:28, maybe he will be a stronger and more knowledgeable man than he is."

"Greg plays like I always thought you were supposed to play."
— Jack Lambert

Lloyd gained two admirers from two former Steelers linebackers, Jack Lambert and Jack Ham, stars of the '70s who are both properly enshrined in the Pro Football Hall of Fame. Andy Russell, an outstanding linebacker who helped show Lambert and Ham how to play when they first appeared on the scene, was also a Lloyd fan.

"Greg is one of the select few to whom football is more than just a game," Lambert told Ron Cook in the *Pittsburgh Post-Gazette* in early December, 1995. "He absolutely hates to lose. It's confusing to many people, myself included, why so few players conduct themselves that way. Greg plays like I always thought you were supposed to play.

"I think Greg realizes the tradition of being a Steelers linebacker. He takes great pride in that. He should. He isn't just maintaining it. He's adding to it.

"I saw him at the stadium a few weeks ago. I told him, 'Doggone it, your legs are almost as skinny as mine.' He has a big upper body, but his legs aren't much to look at. He told me, 'You don't have to be big to play this game.' I said, 'Greg, you're right. Only certain parts of you have to be big — like your heart. That will never be a problem with you.'"

Ham, a network radio NFL analyst who gets around the league and checks out the other teams, had this to say about Lloyd: "I don't know who people are pushing for Defensive Player of the Year, but Lloyd deserves consideration.

"I know Bryce Paup has a lot of sacks in Buffalo and Neil Smith is playing well in Kansas City, but I don't think anybody is making the big plays like Lloyd is.

"Lloyd is just so relentless. He keeps coming and coming and coming. He refuses to be blocked. I've seen some superstars take a play off when it's away from them. Not Lloyd. He hustles every play.

"You can see he's a great leader on that defense," said Russell, who has maintained that today's Steelers teams could whip the teams of the '70s, insisting that today's players are bigger, stronger and faster.

"You do it by playing. Your teammates don't miss that. They see the second effort, the third effort, the extraordinary effort. Big-play guys are all the same. They take risks. They aren't afraid to make mistakes. They let it all hang out.

"Greg has had that look in his eye since I first met him. It must have been his first year and he was rehabilitating a knee injury. He just had that look that said, 'Russell, I'm going to be somebody.' He was right."

At a press conference at the scene of Super Bowl XXX, Lloyd was asked how he felt about the respect he had gained.

"The respect thing is something that you earn, it's not one of those things that you just go out and you play and you run around, you're there," said Lloyd. "It's called consistency and year in and year out, you gotta be consistent. That's something I try to do and it's hard every year, trying to do something better and have a better season than you had the year before. I guess that's the difference between the average players and the players in the elite group. Every year you gotta go out and prove yourself and do something different than you did the past year. That's all I try to do. There's no secret to it or anything like that, but that's what I try to do.

"You can either stand in front of a camera or in front of a reporter and say what you want to say. But on Sunday, you gotta start out there and you gotta play. That's what we're going to do. We're not concerned about what somebody says or doesn't say about us. We're going to line up and we're going to play for 60 minutes and it's going to be smash-mouth football. You want to say it's your house, then you come out there and prove it, but understand we're all for all that talking stuff, but when that whistle blows, it's over with. You can't talk about this game anymore, you gotta play it. If we have to bite, we'll bite. If we have to spit, we'll spit. If we have to scratch, we'll do that. You have to do that."

Following the difficult defeat to the Dallas Cowboys, Lloyd appeared in the press tent, but was in no mood for post-game analysis. "This game's over," he said. "There's nothing you can do about it."

How true. Asked whether the Steelers drew some satisfaction from making it a true contest, something rare in Super Bowl history, he said. "You're never proud of losing. I'm proud of the way our team — especially our defense — hung in there after all the stuff (that was in the newspapers). You guys wrote all week that they were 300-some pounds, these guys were going to blow us off the ball...it would be a blowout by the fourth quarter. We don't have to go out there and.. 'well, this is not going to happen.' We knew within our hearts."

Then Lloyd left.

"Just because you know No. 95, you don't know Greg Lloyd."

"You think Greg Lloyd's a tough guy," said Ray Seals. "But you get him working with a needy child, he melts like butter. He loves to work with charities. Some people don't even know about that because that's the way he wants it."

Lloyd gave his time to visiting kids in hospitals and people in need at shelters, and such, but didn't want TV cameras there during his visits. "That's not what it's all about," he said.

Like some other recalcitrant ballplayers, Lloyd does not understand why he doesn't have a better image. He's unkind and inconsiderate to the image-makers; that might help explain it. Maybe if he were more cooperative with the message-bearers, people might be more aware of his good side.

Then, too, he might be better off simply being consistent in his approach to people at large.

"At every function or whatever I go to, it's always the same thing," said Lloyd. "Someone will say, 'Man, I can't believe he's that nice a guy.' I even have relatives, people that know my brothers and cousins, and when they finally meet you, they're like, 'Man, you're nothing like that guy on TV!'

"I tell them I don't have a uniform on right now and you're not standing in my way when I'm trying to win a game. If the situation was different, you'd see the other side. Just because you know No. 95, you don't know Greg Lloyd."

Lloyd was a sixth round draft choice of the Steelers in 1987 out of Fort Valley (Georgia) State, a Division II program.

Lloyd spent the first seven weeks of his rookie season on injured reserve after suffering a knee injury in a game against the Philadelphia Eagles, and had to undergo arthroscopic surgery. By the end of the season, he started four games.

"From the time I came into the league, I think I have surprised myself. Not just coming from a small school, but overcoming one serious knee injury, and another that kept me out for half a year, overcoming that and becoming a starter, being, I think, an impact player, making a difference. I have exceeded what I expected of myself at this point. But now I have gotten to a point where my expectations are higher.

"I don't like being mediocre. I don't like to be the one at the back of the line. When I came out of Fort Valley, some scouts thought I was undersized for a linebacker.

"A lot of people said, 'You're too small, and if you played at the University of Georgia, you'd be third team.' That sticks in the back of your mind. Every time you step on the field, it's 'in your face.' It feels good to come from a small school that most people never heard of to be considered one of the top players in the league."

Just before the 1996 college draft, Lloyd's agent, Dick Bell, issued a declaration to the Steelers that if they wanted to keep Lloyd beyond the 1996 season, the last on his contract, they would have to make him the highest paid linebacker in the NFL. San Diego's Junior Seau ranked No. 1 in salary in the NFL at outside linebacker with just over $4 million a year. Lloyd was earning an average of $1.787 million annually on a contract he signed in 1993. Lloyd, 31, was scheduled to become an unrestricted free agent at the end of the 1996 season, but the Steelers were actively trying to sign a contract extension as the team held its minicamp in early June.

Lloyd was quite proud of his achievements, and he was quite demanding of the men on his team. "He likes to scream and holler," said Rod Woodson. "He's not the fastest guy — he's got two flat feet — but he's done a lot for us."

Lloyd laughs at his own image. "It's not something somebody gave me," he said. "I think it's more my personality than anything else. I'm the kind of guy if things are going well, I'm still going to fuss. And if things are not going well, I'm going to get in your face. It's not done to demean a guy. It's done to get better as a team.

"The leadership thing is not something somebody gives to you; it's more of a personality game. Some guys are quiet out there, never say anything, they just play. Sometimes when things aren't going well, that can be a negative. Everybody checks everybody on this defense. It's not done in a demeaning way. It's just, 'Hey, that play was for you. You've got to make it.' Some guys, I try to make sure they don't become complacent because of what they've read in the newspaper."

Seals isn't the only one who speaks in support of Lloyd, even though he's been chewed out by Lloyd on the field and on the sideline.

Marv Lewis, who was the coach of the linebackers during the 1994 and 1995 seasons, said, "No matter what Greg does, he wants to be the very best at it."

Bill Cowher, his coach, had no complaints. "Greg Lloyd plays the game the way I wish a lot of players on this team would play the game," commented Cowher during the 1995 season. "He has a great passion for it, and people around the league respect him for that. Sometimes he doesn't say things diplomatically. He says them emotionally, and sometimes it gets misconstrued. I'm very serious about that. There's not a guy that has a bigger heart and a greater passion for the game than Greg Lloyd. Greg Lloyd plays this game hard."

Did Cowher ever caution Lloyd to lighten up, or to tone down what he said, and to leave the game on the field?

"I think he does a good job of taking care of himself," said Cowher. Cowher had also come to Lloyd's defense after he was fined $12,000 for the hit on Green Bay's Bret Favre in a pre-season game. The coach called it "a good hit."

Tom Donahoe, the director of football operations for the Steelers, said, "You have to respect that and appreciate people for what they are. On and off the field, you know you're getting someone that's very genuine and very intense about what he's doing. That's something you admire. He plays football the way it was intended to be played."

> *"Another form of running away is substituting a white father for the unreachable or unknowable or unacceptable black one."*
> — John Wideman,
> From *Fatherless*

"Talk is cheap.
You have to line up and play."

Lloyd was allowing himself to be interviewed on January 5, 1995, a few days before a playoff game with the Cleveland Browns. Paul Zimmerman of *Sports Illustrated*, a former colleague when we were both at *The New York Post*, was spearheading the effort involving other out-of-town writers.

Lloyd looked like an old-time newspaperman in that he had a pencil sticking from behind his right ear. He was wearing a black and gold stocking cap, a gray sweatshirt, black and white zebra-like spandex pants. He was signing photos and cards that had been sent to him by fans with a black magic marker. He was looking after his equipment, tidying up his dressing stall as well, hanging up his Gucci bag. He was doing several things at once, so as not to give his full attention to the roving reporters.

"You can't talk it," he said of the upcoming battle with the Browns. "The game has to be played."

Zimmerman asked him if he was pretty good about answering his fan mail. "You gotta," he said. "We were taught that in grade school."

Barry Foster came by at that moment, and brushed away some inquiring reporters. "I don't have anything to say," Foster told them. He hesitated and spoke only to Norm Vargo, the veteran Steelers writer and sports editor of *The Daily News* in McKeesport. "People are saying you're the Man of the Hour," Vargo said to Foster. "This is your kind of game."

Foster wasn't biting, and kept walking, so Vargo leaned into the crowd around Lloyd.

"If you don't believe you can win when you step on the field, then you're in trouble," Lloyd continued his litany of football, according to Greg Lloyd.

"We believe we have to fall apart in order to lose this game."

Lloyd was asked about Vinny Testaverde, the quarterback of the Browns, as he slid some photos and cards into envelopes that were self-addressed and had a stamp on them.

"I'm going to be going after him," said Lloyd. "If I happen to get the ball, that's a bonus.

"All we know is we're in for a fight, we're in for a dogfight...it's going to be a physical game. After losing two games, it's still in their head that we're not that good. That's disrespectful. Talk is cheap. You have to line up and play. If things are going well, they're going to write good things about you and if you play bad, well...I'm probably more critical of myself than most. Some are satisfied with being mediocre. Not me. I never want to be mediocre.

"I can understand where Cleveland is coming from. It's just confidence on their part and trying to build up confidence. That's what happens. They have to deal with the disappointment of losing two games to us. They had higher expectations. We're not gonna lay down for anybody, that's for certain."

As he continued to sign playing cards that were sent to him in the mail, someone asked him if he responds regularly to his fan mail. "I sign them and and leave them up there (front desk) for them to mail it. I open them...I can't say I read them all.... cut through all the bullshit....get to what they want....they want you to sign their card.....I think it's important (to answer his mail). Some people hire someone to sign them. That's not right. That's not fair. They're writing to me, not some secretary. But I'm not going out and send them for 32 cents, either. If they send me a self-addressed stamped envelope I will do my best to get them back to them. I'm a good guy, right?"

George Gojkovich

Greg Lloyd may smile more often after signing a three-year contract extension worth $11.2 million in early June, 1996. Lloyd, a five-time Pro Bowl pick, received a $2.7 million signing bonus. The three-year extension averaged $3.15 million.

"I don't have to be what you want me to be. I'm free to be who I want."
— Muhammad Ali

Justin Strzelczyk
A biker from Buffalo

"I've always done crazy things."

In another age, Justin Strzelczyk might have been an explorer. Strzelczyk had a grand sense of adventure and liked to go where others dared not go. He looked the part. He had unruly shoulder-length dark brown hair and a full beard, a mountain man if you ever saw one. Strzelczyk (pronounced STREL-zik) had a special zest for life, and he lived it in the fast lane. He was happiest riding on his Harley-Davidson, driving his motorcyle through the challenging streets of Pittsburgh or the mountain roads of Pennsylvania, or sitting in the backyard of his home in the North Hills with his lovely wife, Keana, bouncing their baby Justin Jr. on his large lap.

At the core, Strzelczyk was a good-hearted guy. There was a sweet innocence about him, and you had to like him. Teammates called him "Jug" or "Jughead," like the character in the "Archie" cartoon series, a nickname he first picked up in college when he was clean-shaven and had close-cropped hair.

Strzelczyk surprises once in a while when he says something like "I just want to win the championship and go visit President Clinton at the White House. I'm not worried about the money or the ring. I just want to go to the White House."

Equipment man Tony Parisi said, "He fools you. He's smart. His parents are both educators."

Yet Strzelczyk always seemed to be pushing the pedal to the metal when he was away from the Steelers' scene. Keana was concerned about some of his recreational pursuits, but was unsuccessful in getting him to change his ways. It looked instead that she was going to join Justin in his wild ways.

He was a man of great contradictions. He was so big, 6-6, 295 pounds, and, at age 27, looking forward to his seventh season with the Steelers in 1996, but there was still a lot of little boy in him. "You still trying to figure me out?" he'd ask, straining a cup of chicken noodle soup through that thick beard at lunchtime. "I am what I am. I'm a good, fun-loving guy."

The 1995 season had been his first as a full-time starting right guard on the team's offensive line, and he was maturing as a football player. But under all that hair beat the heart of the little boy who played baseball, basketball and football back in Seneca, New York, just outside of Buffalo. He had been a Bills' and Cowboys' fan in his youth. There weren't many NFL players who had come out of the University of Maine. No, Justin Conrad Strzelczyk was his own man.

He can afford to be. In July, 1996, he signed a new four-year contract for between $6 to $7 million, including a $1.5 million signing bonus. Keana told him he could buy a different motorcycle for each day of the week if he wanted to.

Justin and Keana didn't keep many secrets from each other. There shouldn't have been any surprises. As burly as he was, she was petite and pretty as can be, 5-5, 130 pounds. They had first met at a nightclub in Downtown Pittsburgh. For Justin, it was love at first sight. "We met through a friend at a club downtown," said Strzelczyk. "We went out and we got along great." Keana Capone came from Altoona so she knew something about football.

Keana could have fun at her own expense. She appeared on Radio B-94 (WBZZ) in Pittsburgh the week before Super Bowl XXX and told some light-hearted and revealing stories about her relationship with Justin. She was such a big hit that the deejays — John, Dave, Bubba and Shelley — had Keana come on their early morning show from time to time afterward. Keana and Justin just moved to the beat of a different drummer. Keana threw off some sparks with her spicy stories.

"She talks about very personal stuff on the radio," Strzelczyk scolded her, raising his voice playfully, when I was talking to her at their home in O'Hara Township in early June, 1996. "She was telling people about my Sesame Street undershorts this morning. Nothing is sacred."

Prior to the Super Bowl, she told the B-94 audience that she and Justin had sex before every Steelers' game and that this was the secret to his success.

"I guess I say some crazy things," Keana confessed.

"I like to have fun and I guess sometimes I have it at Justin's expense. I'm a fun-loving person, happy-go-lucky, and I'm easy to get along with. Justin and I get along great."

She explained how she met Justin. "One of his teammates at Maine was getting married to a friend of mine. His name is John Lapiana, and he's the chiropractor for the Penguins. Justin and I were supposed to be in their wedding party. I was going to be the maid of honor and Justin was going to be an usher. But they eloped. So we missed out on the opportunity to meet at the wedding.

"These friends had pointed out Justin to me in a Steelers' squad photo and said we'd be perfect for each other. I saw Justin one night at a club Downtown and went over and introduced myself. We went out for pizza and three months later we got married. We really do get along well. We're just perfect for each other."

When we first met, in Scottsdale, Arizona when the Steelers were there for Super Bowl XXX, Keana said she didn't like Justin riding his bike so much. I asked her five months later if she still felt that way.

"I'm not crazy about it," she said. "I don't like the drinking and driving. But I can't get him to quit doing something he likes to do. Now I'm thinking of getting one myself. Maybe I wouldn't be as critical. It would be something we could do together. Ariel Solomon bought his wife a Harley. I have a horse up in North Park. I may

Justin Strzelczyk

Strzelczyk provides protection for Neil O'Donnell on pass play.

Justin on Harley at Three Rivers

Keana, Justin and "Little Juggy" relax at neighborhood bowling establishment.

trade it in for an iron horse. Justin just had his bike re-painted and he had my name and our baby's name painted on the rear fender. It says 'Keana and Little Juggy.' He calls the baby 'Little Juggy.' He rides him up and down our street on his bike sometimes."

Justin and Keana became parents of "Little Juggy" on January 21, 1995, just six days after the Steelers lost the AFC championship game with the San Diego Chargers, quite a consolation prize. Justin said that their son's birth had settled them both down, and it helped assuage his disappointment over the Steelers' setback.

I told her that Justin said he didn't have any tattoos, but that he said she had three. "Yes, I do, and I have a pierced belly button, too," she said, laughing. "And I'm pregnant again. I'm expecting around Super Bowl time again."

Strzelczyk was the resident biker in the Steelers' dressing room, like a character out of that former HBO series *First And Ten*, an inside look at pro football that featured O.J. Simpson. Anyone acquainted with Strzelczyk would not think that Hollywood depiction of pro football was such a far reach. Strzelczyk liked to wear black leather jackets with chains hanging here and there, and he liked hanging out with some bikers at a bar named Smitty's in Turtle Creek, a milltown just east of Pittsburgh. One day in the dressing room, he called for my attention and proudly modeled a pair of jeans with torn-out knees with decorative patches appearing under the holes that he thought were really sharp.

Strzelczyk wore his best biker's attire when he accompanied Keana down the walkway at the Steelers' annual fashion show to raise funds for cancer research. They were a stunning couple. Lee Marvin and Marlon Brando (who starred in an early '50s movie, *The Wild One*, about a motorcycle gang that terrorized California) would have loved them.

Strzelczyk was always coaxing me to take a ride with him on his Harley, and go out and choke back a few beers with the boys at Smitty's. I begged off. I was tempted to take a ride, to see what it was like, to better appreciate Justin's joy of the open road for this story. The literati call it "immersion journalism." But I remembered a boyhood promise to my mother that I'd never get on a motorbike. A kid named Butchie Buffo, who lived across the street from my boyhood home, had a motorbike and had frequently offered me a ride. It was one of the rules I had obeyed, and I thought I'd like to keep my streak going. Why blow it at age 53?

Then I heard how Strzelczyk had taken Tom Pratt, a cameraman at Channel 4, on such a bike ride, and scared the hell out of Pratt when he hit speeds of 80 miles per hour. "I like Tom; he's a good man," Strzelczyk said, when I mentioned the incident to him .

"Don't be a wuss!" Strzelczyk scolded me. "Live a little! You must have been the well-behaved kid in your neighborhood. Break out!"

Jerry Olsavsky, the linebacker from Pitt, was Strzelczyk's next-door neighbor in the Steelers' dressing room and a good friend.

Olsavsky was single and rode a regular bicycle — the kind you pedal — to and from Three Rivers Stadium and his apartment in the Shadyside section of the city. Olsavsky was a biker of a different sort. His wheels were safer, but he was reckless in his own way. He went skiing and played basketball without a knee brace in his first year back from a career-threatening knee injury. Olsavsky showed up barefooted a few times at the Steelers' offices. And Olsavsky thought Strzelczyk did some scary things... They were soul brothers in a sense. Olsavsky got a kick out of listening to Strzelczyk's stories about his wild antics, his backyard barbecues, his wife, Keana, his infant son, Justin Jr., and his biker buddies in Turtle Creek. Olsavsky shook his head and smiled a lot while listening to Strzelczyk's stories.

"I wear some pretty ratty stuff," said Olsavsky, "but I don't go around bragging about my clothes. Jugs thinks he looks good."

"There's no pretense with the guy."
— Robert Smith

I had spent about an hour at a bar in Scottsdale, Arizona with Strzelczyk's friends from Turtle Creek, and that was a challenging evening. A few nights before Super Bowl XXX, I was out looking for Steelers' fans near the hotel where I was staying in Scottsdale. I visited Old Town, a tourist attraction there, and was walking down a street that housed about fifty or sixty art galleries. One was devoted exclusively to work by artist LeRoy Neiman, an old friend from my days in New York. I bumped into Neiman the next day at media headquarters for Super Bowl XXX and we had a brief reunion. I didn't spot any Steelers' fans in those toney galleries in Old Town, so I checked out the only bar on the street. That's where I came upon Strzelczyk's friends.

There were five of them at the end of the bar in Minglers, all in black and gold: black outfits with gold chains. They included Robert Smith, 47, the auburn-bearded owner of Smitty's Bar, and his kid brother, Gary "Fireplug" Smith, 43, also bearded and pink-cheeked, Doug "Tarzan" Sellman, 35, Bob Wentroble, 50, and Carl Kosko, whatever. Smitty had left a sign on the door of his Monroeville Road bar that read simply: "CLOSED FOR THE SUPER BOWL."

Gary got his nickname after he lost a leg in a biking accident in 1982. He was short and squat and had an artificial limb. He was also called "Plug" for short and was a twin, a scary thought. Sellman kept showing everyone who passed him at the bar the tattoo that covered his entire back. He'd pull his black jersey up to his pony-tailed blond head to make their night. Sellman once caused a stir at the Steelers' training camp at St. Vincent College when he came there on a loud motorcycle searching for Strzelczyk. He looked like something out of Hell's Angels. He was into body-building and bikes. It helped that he smiled a lot. He and Justin first met when they were working out at a gym in Turtle Creek.

Justin's buddies stole kisses from every woman who walked by us, nuzzling necks and ears — they were just being sociable — and given another half hour, they might have cleared the bar out without even starting a fight. I had grown up sidestepping these sort of characters in my hometown, and recognized them for what they were: fun for a half hour, trouble in the long run. Going to jail at evening's end was always a possibility. They could be smiling one minute and volatile the next minute. I bumped into them the morning after Super Bowl XXX and they were telling stories about how they had been evicted from Sun Devil Stadium after the first quarter when fans around them complained of their behavior. Real smart, I thought. Go to all that expense to purchase airplane tickets and a hotel room and tickets for the Steelers' showdown with the Cowboys, and then get tossed out of the game.

I had lectured Strzelczyk about keeping company with these guys. So had Keana. Those guys liked Keana. "She's a great kid," one of them said.

His biker buddies were disappointed the Steelers had lost, but Strzelczyk was still their hero, and would be welcome to belly up to their bar back in Turtle Creek.

"We have a ma and pa bar," said Smitty. "We get all kinds, bikers with tattoos, grandparents, professionals and regular people from the neighborhood. Justin gets along with everybody there. There's no pretense with the guy. If he likes you, he'll tell you. He can be himself there, a little wild."

Someone I know told me he went there once and found a couple of guys trying to break open a parking meter on one of the dining tables. Someone there must have come up short on coins when they wanted to call home.

When Justin's biker buddies first mentioned Turtle Creek, I responded by bringing up the name of Leon Hart. It was like a Pavlovian response. Leon Hart was the biggest sports hero ever to come out of Turtle Creek. He was an All-American end and a Heisman Trophy winner on a national championship team in 1949 at Notre Dame and went on to star for the NFL's Detroit Lions in the '50s.

Wentroble, a Notre Dame diehard, said sternly, "Leon Hart was the only lineman ever to win the Heisman Trophy!"

I leaned backward, taking my chin out of striking distance, and calmly corrected this man, the best-behaved of the bunch, with a well-measured tone. "No, Larry Kelly was the first lineman to win the Heisman Trophy."

"No, he wasn't!!! You're WRONG!!!"

I felt a dragon's breath and knew a challenge when I heard one. I backed up a little more and in my most soft-spoken voice, I continued, "Yes, he was. He was an end at Yale, and it was in the early years of the award."

"An end? Hell, that's a trick answer! Yale? You gotta be kiddin'."

End of discussion...

I could see Strzelczyk sitting with these guys and having a good time. Strzelczyk reminded me in some ways of Wendell Ladner, a reckless strongboy forward for the Dr. J-led New York Nets when they had the ABA's best team in the early '70s. Ladner came out of Necaisse Crossing, Mississippi, and made his mark as a hell-raising combatant in the ABA. He got into more than his share of on-the-court and off-the-court scrapes.

His coach, Babe McCarthy, once said of Ladner, "He doesn't know the meaning of the word 'fear' — as well as a few other words." Ladner was killed in a commercial airplane crash while coming into Kennedy Airport at the height of his playing career.

Ed Bouchette, the Steelers' beat writer at the *Pittsburgh Post-Gazette*, suggested to Strzelczyk that he was a free spirit. "I don't know," said Strzelczyk. "I like to enjoy myself. Free spirit? Sometimes when I'm out partying and having fun I get a little crazy. But then again, I'm under control. But a free spirit? What's the definition of a free spirit?

"I wouldn't say I'm a free spirit. I'm a very laid-back person when sometimes it looks like I don't care. But I'm more of a relaxed person. I don't let things get to me. I think life should be an enjoyable experience where a laugh is the best medicine ."

"He's a safe driver."
— Kent Stephenson

"He definitely lives on the edge."
— Tom O'Malley, Jr.

Kent Stephenson, the offensive line coach of the Steelers, was coming down the hallway after an early-morning workout during the Steelers' five-day mini-camp in June of 1996. The Steelers had received their AFC championship rings a few days earlier. They were hoping to get back to the Super Bowl. They were counting on Strzelczyk as a starting lineman, especially after guard Tom Newberry had officially announced that he was retiring after one season with the Steelers and ten in the NFL. The Steelers had also lost Leon Searcy, their starting right tackle, who had signed as an unrestricted free agent with the Jacksonville Jaguars during the off-season.

I asked Stephenson if he slept well knowing that Strzelczyk might be out riding his motorcycle on any given day.

"He's a safe driver," Stephenson assured me. "I don't like it, and I wish he wouldn't be riding his bike, but I believe he's careful. The guys who drive those bikes and aren't careful are called 'donors' at the hospitals."

If Stephenson thought Strzelczyk was a safe driver, Justin must not have shared his story about his evening run to ski country near Johnstown in February of 1995 to play with the Steelers' off-season basketball team.

Tom O'Malley, Jr., who succeeded Baldy Regan in running the Steelers' basketball team, had booked a game at Shade High School near Johnstown. It was 95 miles from Pittsburgh, the farthest the Steelers' basketball team would travel that winter. The players make about $300 a game to go up against a rag-tag team of teachers or policemen or local celebrities, or a mix of same, for some good cause. It was all in good fun. Strzelczyk and Olsavsky were two of O'Malley's most reliable recruits. They liked to play and they liked the pay. O'Malley was the son of Tom O'Malley, a former advertising executive at *The Pittsburgh Press* and the mayor of Castle Shannon, and an associate of former Pirates pitcher Bob Purkey who had owned an insurance agency in Bethel Park for many years. O'Malley knew a "high risk" client when he saw one, but he had to smile at the mention of Strzelczyk's name. "He's a good guy and a lot of fun," said O'Malley, "but he definitely lives on the edge."

Strzelczyk started out that memorable day, February 25, 1995, at Smitty's Bar in Turtle Creek. "I was drinking away with my buddies," he said. "It was about 50 degrees during the day. I went home and told my wife I was going to drive to the game on my bike. She'd grown up in that area of Pennsylvania and she knew how bad it could get in the mountains. My wife said, 'You're crazy. It's snowing.' I knew it was far, but not that far. It turned out it was the farthest trip on our schedule. I had a buzz on, I was feeling very spontaneous that day."

O'Malley had given him directions: take the Pennsylvania Turnpike East to the Somerset exit, then north on Rt. 281. The school was about 20 miles off the turnpike. The rest of the team were going up in cars.

"It started to snow when I was up there in the mountains," recalled Strzelczyk. "I had a windshield and a mask to protect my face. I saw some ice on some of the parking lots at the roadstops along the way. The high school gym turned out to be about 100 miles from my house in the North Hills. It was a long, cold trip.

"After the game was over, there was a trace of snow on my bike. I was worried that I would hit an ice patch. But I got home OK. It was a relief to go through my door."

When I suggested the trip might have been foolhardy, Strzelczyk simply shrugged it off. "It was just one of those things," he said. "Maybe next time I won't go. When I got home, sitting in front of the fire warming my toes with my wife and kid, I felt glad I'd gotten through the night. If I had to do it again, maybe I'd think twice. But you get a few drinks in you and you're liable to do anything. Being young and pig-headed sometimes, I don't know. I've always done crazy things; I'm borderline stupid. You can't be timid. You're trying to be the best driver."

Strzelczyk was an 11th round draft choice out of the University of Maine in 1990. He made the team as a long shot when Chuck Noll was the head coach. Ron Blackledge was his line coach. "I don't think he thought I was that good," said Strzelczyk. He made the team as a rookie and was one of only five 11th round draft choices to make an NFL roster that year.

He filled in originally for Tunch Ilkin after Tunch ruined his elbow. The Steelers selected Leon Searcy, an offensive tackle, as their No. 1 draft choice, and Strzelczyk was bummed out when they did that. But the Steelers still had plans for Strzelczyk.

"We like Justin's versatility," said Tom Donahoe, the Steelers' director of football operations. "He's worked hard. He's been a good soldier. He's just kept working at it here."

Stephenson, the line coach, appreciated Strzelczyk's versatility, too, and his willingness to switch to suit the Steelers' needs. "You know how those things go," said Stephenson. "How many times have you heard someone say, 'Well, boy, this is the deepest we've ever been there,' and then in two plays you're down to one? So I don't think you can have enough good offensive linemen around. And it helps when you can plug them into different holes.

"He's a pretty good athlete," Stephenson said of Strzelczyk. "He's like a fat man who can polka well. He plays on the basketball team the players have in the off-season and they tell me he's very good."

In 1992, Strzelczyk started three games at left tackle and four games at right tackle. In 1993, he made a career-high 12 starts at right guard, and played in all 16 games. He filled in for Carlton Haselrig. It took him four years to become a starter. In addition to playing right guard in 1995, he also started four games at left tackle when John Jackson was sidelined by a knee injury.

"I'm just happy to be where I am, to be part of a good team," said Strzelczyk.

He said he didn't have to be on a Harley to get high.

"You can get thrills playing football — like when you run it down their throat. It's a dominating feeling. Scoring. Winning. Then watching the fans go crazy.

"I'm a battler. I'm a scrapper. I seem to get the job done. I don't have too many plays where I'm outright terrible. As far as my lifestyle, I'm a little different. I think I'm more open-minded.

"When it comes to playing football, when I step onto the football field, I'm all business and the coaches know that."

> *"Sports teams should be concerned about their image. Like it or not, players are role models. Maybe that shouldn't be, but they're looked up to by kids and fans. They — all of us — have to be responsible for our actions."*
> — Tom Donahoe

"You always know where he's at."
— Bill Cowher

Strzelczyk loved to ride his 1,340 cc Harley Davidson. "My motor-cycle is my hobby and my way of relaxing," he said. "Riding is one of the ways I celebrate after a win. I don't like to do crazy, stupid things, but I like to feel alive.

"I'm not a true biker. I don't live in a clubhouse or ride with gangs all the time, especially since I'm married. I spend more time with my wife now, so I don't have as much time to go out riding."

None of the Steelers made more noise than Strzelczyk at train-ing camp. He could be heard roaring back to the dorm at St. Vincent College room at 10:55 p.m. to beat the 11 o'clock curfew. He didn't exactly slip in discreetly. "The one thing about him is you always know where he's at," said Bill Cowher.

Strzelczyk talked about his beginnings as a biker.

"I just knew some guys with Harleys and they kind of showed me the ropes. It's just fun. You go on runs with guys, 15 to 50 guys, with Harleys, on the road. It's a great feeling. It's kind of like a parade.

"I'm like any thrill-seeker. Some people like sky-diving or bungee-jumping or extreme skiing. It's like riding a roller coaster. It's a rush, man. I love the feeeling of riding a bike, though. You go around sharp bends, with your floor boards scraping and the sparks flying. That's exciting. You make it out of that turn, you're like 'Whew! That was fun!' So's football."

There was a time when he wore a World War II German military helmet while riding his bike, but caught some flak for doing so on the side streets of Squirrel Hill, a predominantly Jewish community.

"I didn't mean to offend anyone; I wasn't thinking," he said. "So I quit wearing the helmet. I didn't want to keep on wearing it because of the skinheads and racism."

He had his Harley custom-painted black with yellow and orange flames. It was a sight to see.

He recalled an incident during the 1991 season, when Chuck Noll was still coaching the Steelers. "I was coming home from a friend's house after drinking at a party, and I was riding down the road. I avoided a lady going into her driveway by dropping my bike. I hurt myself. I had a big bruise on my thigh; I had a real charley horse. I was trying to hide my limp when I came to the stadium that week. Luckily, I didn't get in the next game at Indianapolis.

"It could have been worse. I guess I've been lucky, too. Luck happens to good people."

I asked him to characterize himself. "You can say he's a man who has a really good side to him — like I love my baby; I think I was more choked up when he was born than my wife was. You can say he has a temper and a selfish side here and there. He's one who is kind of humble. I'm a pessimist, though. I look for the worst. I'm not too optimistic.

Early in the 1995 season, I asked him about his goals or dreams. "If I had a dream in life, it would be to go to the Super Bowl, and to play at least ten years in the league," he said. "I'd like to be in the league a decade.

"Money isn't really it, either. It will come. I can be cheap. I'm generous, when it comes to partying and drinking, but I didn't go out and buy the biggest house. We live in a normal neighborhood. I could live there right along. We have great neighbors. I love my neighbors. They help me out.

"We're into having a beer and barbecues in the backyard. Playing for the Steelers, you can't go to the bars where you live; it's just not a healthy thing to do. So you just get a keg and do your drinking in the backyard with your wife."

Did Strzelczyk think Bill Cowher and the Steelers' coaches worried about his motorcycling and such?

"If I was Neil O'Donnell or somebody more important to the team, I think they'd say something," he replied. "If I were Rod Woodson or a franchise player, they'd be concerned. I also like to ski. They don't tell me not to ride my bike or to ski. If they did, they'd take something away from me."

Strzelczyk said he thought assistant coach Kent Stephenson liked him a lot more than his original line coach, Ron Blackledge.

"I'm a tough guy, physical. I play hard. They love that. Like the old Steelers. It takes a whole camp for me to impress anybody. They know what they're getting from me.

"I have a coach who likes me. I don't think Blackledge thought much of me as a player when I first got here.

"When Cowher came in, at first he seemed so hard. He seemed like he was always coming out blazin'. He was like a drill sergeant. Now I think the world of him. I can't think of a better replacement for Chuck Noll. He's broken up the routine. Noll had the same regimen every day. Cowher will talk to you more. You never wonder what he's thinking. Cowher tells you what he's thinking."

How did he fare when Joe Walton was the offensive coordinator for two years under Noll?

"I thought Joe Walton's offense was different, but I didn't think it was that difficult," he said. "He blamed Bubby (Brister) for complaining so much. That's just Bubby.

"That's why they like me. I don't bitch about anything. They know I'm a good guy. They know I can get along with everybody. We got rid of some bad attitude guys and we've got a better chemistry. You don't have to love everybody, but you need to have a common goal. You can't be worried about what you're making, bonuses and incentives. You have to want to win. You can't be out there for the money.

"Olsavsky is one of my favorites. We've been buddies from the beginning. We went to Jimmy Tsang's together out in Shadyside where he lives. It was the first time I had been in a Chinese restaurant in Pittsburgh. I admire Jerry for what he did. It was great for him to come back from injury. Jerry is more laidback than me, but we get along fine.

"I don't know why I hated the Steelers."
— Justin Strzelczyk

Strzelczyk was raised two miles from Rich Stadium (as was former Steelers' offensive lineman Craig Wolfley) in the Buffalo suburb of West Seneca, New York.

He attended Bills games as a boy with his father, and watched them on TV when he was in junior high and senior high school. He went from being a defensive back in high school to being a tight end and then a defensive tackle in college to becoming a versatile offensive lineman in the NFL.

"I wanted to be a baseball player and then a basketball player," he said. "I was all-Western New York in football and basketball. I got a football scholarship to go to Maine. I was an undersized tight end at Maine and grew into a defensive lineman.

"I grew up a Dallas Cowboys fan as well as a Bills fan. I don't know why I hated the Steelers so much. Even when I played at Maine, I hated the Steelers. I look back now and I think maybe I should have liked the Steelers. They were my kind of team.

"I wear my hair long, I let my beard grow, I'll wear the same shirt during camp for a couple of days in a row and my clothes are kind of rough looking. I like black T-shirts. They don't stain, you know? I mean they stain, but you don't notice."

He had a Bohemian personality, and wasn't impressed with appearances. He paid $800 for a 1977 blue and white Ford pick-up track in 1990. The truck had 130,000 miles on it, and it looked out of place among the Mercedes, BMWs and 300Zs in the Steelers' parking lot.

"I like to enjoy myself and try new things and experience life. But I'm not trying to impress people with my life style.

"My mother and father don't live together. They're separated, not divorced, but both of them were always there for us. My dad lived in the next town. He didn't move across the country, thinking of only himself. He still thinks about his family first. That's the good thing. I always felt I was lucky. If they would have stuck together and fought all the time, it would probably be worse."

His parents' breakup may have contributed to his feelings of

With sister Melissa at Maine

At age 12 in hockey gear

As 11-year-old trombone player

With mom at age 2 1/2

On "Hot Wheels" at 4

Flanked by mom and dad at Maine

insecurity, though Strzelczyk wasn't sure about that.

"My goal is just to survive," he said. "I'm not a great player or a star. I'm a second-level, sometime starter. I'm not a great player. I was always worried about getting cut. It's a short fall from the penthouse to the outhouse. One day you're starting, the next day you're cut. It's happened before. No job is 100 percent secure. I guess I'm a pessimist. I don't take compliments too well."

He told someone in college that if he didn't make it in the NFL he'd probably wind up pumping gas. After four seasons with the Steelers, he still felt insecure.

"I don't know what I'd be doing if it wasn't for this," he said in an interview back then. "You get spoiled, you know? Four years of college, you've got your scholarship. Now I'm in my fourth year of this, making good money. It's like you didn't know what it's like to make an honest living.

"Football is a job, but I have fun like it's a hobby. No one enjoys camp. It's grueling. There are always certain parts of a job you don't like. It's rare when someone enjoys all aspects of their job. Dealing with injuries, stuff like that. There's a lot of pressure in making the team every year. They spend the first two years of getting you built up and then they start looking for someone to replace you.

"If I have a bad day, it's not as bad as when I was young and they have questions about you. It takes a lot of pressure off you. That's the biggest thing — the pressure to perform."

"I'm very fortunate to be where I am today."

"Football wasn't a big deal at Maine. Hockey was the No. 1 sport. Football was second or third to baseball. We were getting better. We went to playoffs two years in a row, but football was my thing there," said Strzelczyk.

"When I was at Maine, I didn't know where I was going with my life. I skipped class; I was more into the social scene, hanging out with my buddies.

"I'm very fortunate to be where I am today. I went to college and goofed around. I didn't apply myself and prepare for life after football."

The Steelers projected him as an offensive tackle when they considered him for the draft. "Offensive tackle sounded like it was my opportunity — others had told me that when I was playing defensive line at Maine — so I figured I'd better jump at it," he said.

"I was an all-around athlete, even back in high school, but to play offensive line you don't necessarily have to be a good athlete. You have to have good feet to be an offensive lineman and fairly good hands.

"And just the will to want to learn how to use the right technique, that's what it's all about. It's all about thinking, learning technique and footwork. If you've got the size and strength you can make it. The more aggressive you are, the better it is for you. That catches coaches' eyes. When you see a big man who's quick and aggressive, that's where No. 1 picks like Leon come from.

"I didn't know what the future held for me as far as pro football or anything else was concerned. It was late in the draft, and I hadn't heard from anyone.

"I'm getting bummed out. I'm thinking, 'Hey, this is my last ticket. I'm not going to graduate. What am I going to do?' I was a little scared.

"Then the Steelers called and asked me some questions. They said, 'Can you play offensive tackle? We're looking at you as an offensive tackle.'

"I said, 'Sure, I just want to play. If I can get drafted, I'll play anywhere.' I just wanted to play in the NFL.

"So I asked them, 'Does this mean I'm drafted?' They said, 'Well, no, not yet.' I'm like thinking 'What?' I thought this was THE call and they said, 'Well, hold on.' And then I'm on hold. Then I hear, 'Congratulations, you're a Pittsburgh Steeler.'

"It's like they did it all right there. Like, if I would have said I wouldn't play offensive tackle, they would probably have just said, 'Well, we were thinking of drafting you, but...' And that would have been it. I wouldn't have been drafted. I guess I gave them the right answer when I said, 'Yes.'"

"Justin was a big, happy baby."
— Strzelczyk's mother

Justin's mother, Mary Joyce Strzelczyk, wrote me a letter on February 12, 1996:

"Where did Justin come from? A broken home, but really more fractured than broken as his father and I have been legally separated for 20 years, living apart, but both very much involved in our three children's lives.

"Justin is the middle child, with a sister, Melissa, 16 months older, and a brother John, 2 1/2 years younger. His father is Conrad 'Connie' Strzelczyk, of Polish ancestry, whose size and athletic ability and persistence won him a basketball scholarship to Montana State, and then an experience on the fringes of semi-pro baseball.

"He became a phys ed teacher in grammar school, P.S. 28 in Buffalo, which is where we met. I taught second grade at the same school. He was later a high school teacher and coach. He continued as an adult to be involved in sports himself while encouraging and becoming involved with his children and their participation in sports. Justin was the only one who persisted in these interests past the preteen years.

"My side of the family contributes some interesting blood (full Irish on one side and mixed Irish, Scotch, Welsh, English on the other). My maternal grandfather, Robert Summers, was a Buffalo

273

City Court Judge and John J. Joyce, my dad's dad, was one of the original founders and officials in the Long Shoreman's Union. He was a strapping auburn-haired giant of a man, and Justin is said to have taken after him.

"Justin was a big, happy baby — 9 pounds, 12 ounces at birth — and I was happy, too, as it was the easiest delivery of the three, just one bad pain! He was a little slower to crawl than his sister had been. By a year, he was up to speed, taking his first step and emitting with much excitement his first real word, 'Baw! Baw!' What else? He was saying ball, ball.

"With his father's encouragement, Justin took part in just about everything involving sports: soccer, baseball and hockey. He did not play organized football until junior high school. He was being scouted by several colleges late in his junior year. Le Moyne wanted him for baseball, and Kent State and Maine for football. It may be hard for you to imagine this, but Justin could dunk a basketball back then. He was 125 pounds lighter and could soar with the best of them.

"Justin's academic record did not measure up to the Jesuit standards at LeMoyne, thus narrowing the field to the football opportunities. He loved Maine after he made his visit. He did well there, and Maine's football team got some attention from *Sports Illustrated*.

"Let me tell you a few qualities of Justin. He is an observant, tenacious person. At 7 or 8 years old, he insisted on recounting every detail of any movie that really impressed him.

"He had a tendency for concentration and immersion into anything that seized his attention. I can remember him staying up late, working over blueprints for his mechanical drawing class, just for the sheer enjoyment of it, long after the work itself was completed.

"Just this past year, with instruction books, tapes and help from some musician friends, but mostly from his own concentrated effort and practice, he has become a pretty decent guitar player, who has recently added harmonica and banjo playing to his repertoire.

"He is a person who will do what has to be done. When Justin was about 11 or 12 and looked 15, some tough guys who were about 15 and looking for a challenge to boost their egos came calling at our home. He didn't want to fight, but they kept coming around the house, yelling taunts. So, finally, he gave them what they wanted and went out and beat them up. He wasn't bothered anymore.

"He is a kind and thoughtful person. One of my favorite memories of Justin was on stage at his high school graduation. Diploma in one hand, he stopped halfway across the stage, opened up his blue academic gown and spread it wide to reveal the oversized message his sister, Melissa, had helped him tape inside just hours before. It read: HAPPY BIRTHDAY, DAD! He was always a good, light-hearted soul."

"Strong mothers make for good football players."
— Chuck Noll,
Pittsburgh Steelers Hall of Fame coach

John Mitchell
One of Bear Bryant's prize pupils

*"When I had an opportunity to come
here, I had tears in my eyes."*

A warm and fascinating figure, John Mitchell might have had the most inspirational success story of any of those associated with the Pittsburgh Steelers during the 1994 and 1995 football seasons. As a young boy growing up in Mobile, Alabama, he fostered more than his share of dreams, and he had done his best in his 44 years to pursue them with an unrelenting passion and purpose.

Mitchell did not come in for much mention by the more than 3,200 members of the media who were present at Super Bowl XXX, but it was their loss. His name was seldom seen in stories about the team's daily doings, even in Pittsburgh, though it was quite obvious he had made a positive impact.

The Steelers' defensive line coach was not one to seek the spotlight. He went about his work with great enthusiasm, but in a quiet, efficient manner that often escaped notice. Four assistant coaches left the staff soon after the Super Bowl — two were let go, two decided they would be better off with other opportunities — but Mitchell was among those who remained.

He is a strong, silent type who wears eyeglasses and could be mistaken for a college professor, but, make no mistake about it, Mitchell is a football man with a mission, a man with great depth and determination, and a heritage as far as family and football are concerned that would be difficult for any of his colleagues to match. He was so fortunate in that regard, he is the first to acknowledge, indeed, blessed. He was instilled with old-fashioned values. There is a genuine goodness, a compassionate, caring attitude that is so appealing.

"He's such a nice man," said Mary Regan, a Steelers' staff member who was the late Art Rooney's personal secretary.

Mitchell spoke with such pride about his parents, John Sr. and Alice, both deceased, his wife, his brother and sisters, and two college coaches — Paul "Bear" Bryant and Lou Holtz — who helped shape him and his philosophies about football and life. He was the first black to play for Bryant at Alabama, and gained All-America mention as a senior in 1972 as a defensive end. Wilbur Jackson, a running back who later played in the NFL with the San Francisco 49ers, was recruited the year before Mitchell and was the first black player to actually sign at Alabama, but didn't see action as quickly. Mitchell later served as an assistant at his alma mater for Bryant (1973-76) and then for Holtz at Arkansas (1977-82).

He went to the pros, the Birmingham Stallions of the United States Football League, working for three years (1983-85) for Rollie Dotsch, a former assistant to Chuck Noll when the Steelers were winning their third and fourth Super Bowls in the late '70s. It was Dotsch and some of his former co-workers on Noll's staff who would visit and swap stories about their Pittsburgh days who originally sparked a desire by Mitchell to someday work for the Steelers.

"They talked about Mr. Rooney and the tradition and the way the fans and the city embraced the ballclub," recalled Mitchell, "and I thought that if I ever get a chance to get to the NFL that would be the team I'd like to be with. The tales they would tell would be great. When I had an opportunity to come here, I had tears in my eyes."

Mitchell returned to the college ranks for one year (1986) with Temple, and then worked with linebackers for four seasons (1987-90) at Louisiana State University. Then he joined the Cleveland Browns in 1991.

He had been with Bill Cowher for two seasons, coming over from Cleveland, and he had made a huge contribution to the development of a defensive line that was the base for the team's much-heralded defensive unit.

The Steelers were hosting their annual blood drive — tabbed the "Drive For Five" to reaffirm the team's continuing search for a fifth Lombardi Trophy and Super Bowl rings for their jewelry collection. Part of the lure was for fans to get a look inside the team's locker room, where the blood units were taken. Visitors might have noticed that the nameplate over Neil O'Donnell's dressing stall had already been removed, just a week after he had departed Pittsburgh, where he had been voted the team's MVP for the 1995 season, to return home to quarterback the New York Jets.

In a way, no one gave more of themselves at the Steelers' offices that day than John Mitchell. He was open and honest, and willing to share feelings many men might mask in some false sense of manliness. His willingness to share his heartfelt feelings and sensitive side remain rare in the coaching ranks. His blood runs deep and it's Crimson all the way. At 44, he stood 6-3 and weighed 235 pounds, five less than when he was playing at Alabama, and had a commanding presence.

Talking to Mitchell for more than two hours on a rainy day in early March of 1996 was a distinct pleasure. It removed the chill from the morning. This is a special man, a product of a special family. Mitchell has so many good stories, and he knows how to tell them.

He delivered renditions of speeches he had heard by Bear Bryant at Alabama and Lou Holtz at Arkansas, and said he thought he knew all their talks off by heart. He read books during the so-called off-season — there really is no such thing in pro sports these days — and offered a Winston Churchill story as well from a book he had recently read.

Paul "Bear" Bryant with John Mitchell, who went from playing for Bryant to coaching on his staff at Alabama.

Mitchell as All-American at Alabama

John Mitchell is flanked by father and mother as family and football coaches witness his signing a letter-of-intent to attend Alabama on a football scholarship, only the second black to do so.

Mitchell is a man of great pride, soul, strength, insights and he had a sharing spirit. He has so much to offer young people, all the wisdom he has culled from coaches and players and his parents. As good as he had been as a coach in the National Football League, Mitchell seemed better suited to be a college coach or a teacher.

"Coach Bryant didn't want me to go to the pros," admitted Mitchell in one of the many references he made to the legendary Alabama coach. At the conclusion of our session, I posed this question: "What would be your dream job?"

Mitchell, expectedly, did not hesitate in his reply.

"I want to go back to Alabama someday and be the head football coach."

"Do you think you can?"

"Yes, I think I can," said Mitchell. "Some people might have to stand up and say, 'He's our man,' but I think they know I'm here, and how I'm doing. Yes, I think I can."

"Then you'd know that you were really one of the boys."
— John Mitchell

When Mitchell was playing football at Alabama, Bear Bryant used to stand atop a tower on the sideline and oversee the workouts. The Bear cut a very impressive figure from his tower. Jackie Sherrill, who also played for Bryant at Alabama, did the same, overseeing practice from a sideline tower, when he became the head coach at the University of Pittsburgh. So the sight of Bryant observing practice from on high obviously had a lasting impression on many of his former players.

Mitchell remembered some of Bryant's best former players showing up from time to time at practice, Alabama greats like Joe Willie Namath and Ken Stabler, Dennis Homan and Paul Crane, Ray Perkins and Johnny Musso, and that they were invited by Coach Bryant to join him in his tower to watch practice.

"He only invited special people to come to his tower," said Mitchell. "I used to think that maybe one day when I'd come back to Alabama that he'd invite me to come to his tower. Then you'd know that you were really one of the boys."

Mitchell was an assistant coach at Arkansas in 1980 when the Razorbacks went to Birmingham to play there in the Hall of Fame Bowl. Upon arrival, Mitchell called Bear Bryant on the telephone in nearby Tuscaloosa, the main campus of the University of Alabama. Bryant was preparing his Alabama team to go to the Cotton Bowl in Dallas.

Bryant invited Mitchell to come and see him. After they had talked in Bryant's office for a while, Mitchell was invited to stay for practice. "So I walked with him out on the football field," recalled Mitchell. "He's walking toward the tower. I'm wondering what's going to happen. He turned to me and said, 'Come on, I want you up in the tower with me.' It was a feeling I can't express. I still get chills thinking about that moment. Not just anybody watched from up there. I thought about Joe Willie and Kenny Stabler and Dennis Homan and Paul Crane. Going up there in that tower with Coach Bryant was a special thrill, a real acknowledgment of what I had accomplished. It was probably the highlight of my life."

"Know who you are and where you come from."
— Mitchell's Parents

John Lee Mitchell, Jr., was born on October 15, 1951 in Mobile. He was a superior student in grade school and in high school, in a community where all the students were black. He grew up during a period when civil rights marches and Dr. Martin Luther King Jr. and his peace crusades were grabbing the headlines, and Mobile was a hot spot on the national news scene. But he wanted to go to the University of Alabama when he grew up, and this was before Alabama had any black athletes on its teams. "Where I grew up, you either wanted to go to Auburn or Alabama," he explained. "Those were the two major schools in the state. They say in Alabama that when a baby is born it's either going to be a War Eagle or a Roll, Tide."

When asked to summarize his story, Mitchell said, "It's the story of a young black male growing up in the South, coming from a blue-collar family with good principles, learning from good people along the way, and making the most of opportunities that presented themselves. "We were a close-knit family, with strict discipline. Good manners came before money. 'You have good manners and you'll make good money.' We were told that. 'Know who you are and where you come from.' My parents were always making points with us."

According to an article by Barbara F. Meltz that appeared in *The Boston Globe* in March of 1996, teaching good manners to the young instills sterling values. "In an age of rudeness, this is no easy task," Meltz wrote.

"Teaching manners sets the stage for the development of a more deeply rooted value system," said Frank Vitro, chairman of the psychology department at Texas Woman's University in Denton.

> *"My mother did not want me coming home, complaining about being black. Her motto was 'If a white boy can do it, you can do it, too. And you better do it better.'"*
> — Gordon Parks,
> Photographer-Writer

So Mitchell's parents did him a favor when they taught him to say "please" and "thank you" and to address adults as "Mr." and "Mrs."

His father died in 1978. "He was 61 when he passed," offered Mitchell. His mother died in 1985. "She was 58 when she passed. I think about them daily, and a day doesn't go by that I don't miss them dearly."

His father went as far as seventh grade in his formal education, and his mother went as far as eighth grade. His father's father was from Mobile, and his mother's father was from Shreveport, Louisiana.

John Jr. was the third of five children. "I had two older sisters, then a sister and then a brother after me," he said. "My brother was killed in an automobile accident four years ago."

The standards were set high in the Mitchell home by his parents. "They expected us to give our best. We had two parents in our home; there was always leadership and guidance. We showed love to one another. I hugged my mom and kissed her. When I'd spend some time talking to my father, at the end I'd say, 'Dad, I love you.' And he'd say, 'Son, I love you, too.' He didn't try to hide his feelings. He laughed loud, and I saw him cry, too. He didn't think it was soft. When we visited friends and relatives, we hugged and kissed. We'd say, 'We're happy that you're here.' Or, 'We missed you.' There was open affection in our house. I always felt loved and wanted."

"When your friends came to your home," I asked him, "were they ever surprised or stunned by what they saw in that regard?"

"Both," said Mitchell. "They might have been a little envious. In our family, with my sisters and me and my brother, we never wanted to do anything to bring shame to our parents. We never wanted to put our parents in a fix.

"Where we went to school, the teachers would physically spank you if you did something wrong. If word got home about that, you got another beating. If you were disrespectful to any adult, you were going to get a beating. Or they might withhold your allowance that week.

"We were taught that whenever we were addressed by adults, whatever their color, to say, 'Yes, sir.' Or, 'No, sir.' Our father talked to us boys about proper manners. He told us that when we were walking on the sidewalk with girls, we should always walk on the outside. He told us to hold doors open for girls, to defer to them and let them go first. Today, that's thought to be out of fashion, or politically incorrect, but I still do it."

He had said that Bear Bryant wanted his players to behave in a certain manner, and stressed proper etiquette, too. He taught them how to behave in a restaurant, how to order from a menu, how to use a napkin, you name it. I told him a story I had heard about Bear Bryant. After a Sugar Bowl game at the Louisiana Superdome, Bryant was asked by a sports announcer why he wasn't wearing his signature porkpie hat as he stood on the sideline.

"Son, let me tell you something," Bryant came back, "My Pappy told me that you remove your hat when you go indoors."

Mitchell smiled in recognition. Yes, he had also heard that story. "The Superdome was inside, the way Coach Bryant saw it, so he wasn't about to wear his hat."

"My father struck me as a very smart man."
— John Mitchell

"My father was a cook in the military service. He was in the military all over Europe for 20 years. One of our chores was to take turns, for a week at a time, and get up and fix breakfast for everybody else in the house. Our father would help you: how to do the cooking for everybody, how to keep everything hot. You had to plan the menu, and make up a shopping list for what you needed. It didn't matter whether it was pancakes, grits, cream of wheat, biscuits, my dad would show you how to do it. But you had to do it, and you had to stay and clean up the kitchen afterward, before you went to school.

"Sunday was special. We went to our Baptist church. You wore your Sunday best, something you didn't wear to school unless it was some special occasion. We'd keep our Sunday clothes on when we came home. We'd have an early meal. My father always cooked on Sunday, and he was a great cook. He'd always prepare something out of the ordinary, and he'd always make some kind of dessert: pie, cakes, you name it. Everyone in the family was expected to be there, to eat together. We'd say grace and then eat. Afterward, you had to stay at the table, and we'd take turns talking about what happened to us that week. They wanted to know how things were going at school. Everyone had to report on their activities."

I suggested to Mitchell that many people feel our society has lost its spirit of civility, that good manners simply were not stressed by parents these days. That some of the behavior he had spoken about had become outdated.

"My mother told us that good manners don't change, they don't come and go, that she didn't care if you'd go into the 23rd Century that they would still be appreciated

"My father would always refer to us as a young man. He'd say. 'Young man, you're next in line to take care of your mother and your sisters.' For a guy who just had a seventh grade education, my father struck me as a very smart man. Being a military man, there were certain rules and regulations he had to live by. He had a lot of common sense. My mother used to say, 'I'm going to educate your hands; you're going to school to educate your mind.' She taught me how to sew a button on my shirt. If a hem on my pants came apart I knew how to stitch it back together again. When I went to college, the guys were amazed by what I could do on my own. If there was a hole in my pants, I could stitch it up. I can do those things the rest of my life.

"My father used to like to cut my hair and my brother's hair on Saturday night, so we'd look good at church the next day. I hated that. It took him about an hour. I went first because I was the oldest. My dad would put a bowl on top of our heads and cut around it. It was awful. My mother wouldn't go for an Afro or anything fancy. I couldn't have one. My mother thought that to be respected you have to respect yourself. You were going to be neat and clean. We were told we had to be especially good about this because we were black. 'They'll judge you on your outside appearance,' my mother would often tell us.

"A lot of black families today don't have a father in the home. There are mothers only. It's tough on boys and girls; it's tough on everybody. When I was growing up, all my friends in my neighborhood had a mom and dad at home. I'd walk through the neighborhood and see the parents on their porches. I'd say, 'Hi, Mrs. Jones,' and chat with them for a while. Everyone looked out for one another. I didn't have any friends that didn't have a mom or dad."

The way Mitchell remembered it, blacks were held up to a higher standard by their parents. "Integration was really big, and we were told you have to carry yourself better than anybody else. Some white kids might be able to get away with certain things we couldn't, they'd say. My parents didn't want us doing anything just because our friends wanted to do it. 'Be a leader, don't be a follower,' they'd say.

"As a kid growing up, my mom and dad both smoked, but told us not to. They never drank. As I became 13 or 14, she said you have to make some decisions about what choices you'll make about things like smoking and drinking. 'We'll help you,' she said, 'We'll show you what your options are.' When we had those Sunday dinners, and we each had five to ten minutes to account for yourself, we probably told more than we should have about our friends, and what we were doing, so our parents always knew what was going on. I might say I was with Jim, and he was trying to get me to smoke. My father would say, 'You make the decision and be man enough to live with it. If you make a decision and it's the wrong decision, then shame on you. If you make a bad decision, what did you learn from it?' My dad would never make my decision for me. 'You make the decision,' he'd say. A lot of kids are short-changed when it comes to having someone teach them in that regard."

I asked Mitchell how his brother and sisters had fared.

"My brother Wilson had a master's degree in business from Tuskeegee (Ala.) Institute. He was killed in an auto accident, on August 31, four years ago. He and his wife had driven over to Biloxi, Mississippi to do a little gambling at the riverboat casinos there. On the way back, he got hit from the rear by a guy who was intoxicated. His car flipped over and he was killed instantly. His wife, Ramona, was hospitalized for nearly a year. She returned to her hometown of New Orleans and obtained a doctorate degree at Southern University in Baton Rouge.

"My older sisters, Vivian and Shirley, both received their education at Alabama State and both are teachers. My younger sister, Jacqueline, has a master's degree from Tuskeegee Institute."

I asked him how he dealt with his brother's senseless death. "We did everything together," said Mitchell. "We had spent two weeks together and he took me to the airport when it was time for me to leave. We shook hands and hugged each other. I told him I loved him. Then, in less than a month, he was gone. It still hurts. I think of him often."

All of the Mitchells excelled in school, and it was particularly a challenge for John. His sisters and brothers all attended predominantly black colleges. "At Alabama," recalled John, "I never had a class with another black student. What motivated me? If I had to stay up till 3 a.m. to go over my classroom work or reading, I would do it. I wasn't going to go to class and have some professor call on me and have to tell him or her that I wasn't prepared. I didn't want them thinking I was just another dumb jock, or worse yet, a dumb black jock. I wouldn't give them that satisfaction. I always thought I was going to get my degree, and I'm going to know the damn answer."

"She believes she's doing something worthwhile."
— Mitchell on wife Joyce

He had been married for 17 years to Joyce, a social worker who was a director of a program at the Child Welfare Center in Akron. "They look after about 120 kids, mostly abused kids, and she's the director of planning for a six-county region," said Mitchell. I mentioned that I had been in Ohio a few days earlier to attend a "Dad's Weekend" at Ohio University, where my younger daughter, Rebecca, was a freshman, and that I had read a horrifying story on the front page of the *Akron Beacon-Journal* about a child abuse case. A couple who were not married, but living together in a mobile home, had bound the feet of their three-year-old son, and then the father had smacked the child in the head with a blow severe enough to kill the child. I had clipped the story to show to my wife, who is a social worker at Allegheny General Hospital, when I got home. John Mitchell just shook his head sorrowfully. "My wife might have been aware of the child," he said. "She comes across some bad stuff on a regular basis. But she likes her job because she believes she's doing something worthwhile to help young people and their families."

That helps explain why Joyce decided to remain in Ohio when John left the Browns to join Bill Cowher's coaching staff in Pittsburgh. "She used to commute from Cleveland to Akron," said John. "We talked this out, and she wanted to keep her job. So we bought a home in Akron, where she lives, and I'm in an apartment at Allegheny Center. It's not easy. Our time is precious when we do get together. When we get together we really enjoy the time. My wife is a professional person also. If we make a decision, we want to know how it's going to affect both of us."

They met when they were students at Alabama. "I was a senior and she had just finished graduate school when we first met," he recalled. "I tell people, kiddingly, that I married an older woman. She had just accepted a job at the University of Georgia. She'd come back to Alabama as often as possible and watch us play. We dated for a while, and then we dated others; the distance made it difficult for us to maintain the right relationship. I went to Arkansas to work, and I'd bump into mutual friends from time to time and ask about Joyce. I came to New Orleans on a recruiting trip, and I invited Joyce to join me there — 'Come and we'll have a good time. No strings attached.' — and she agreed, and that's how we got back together again. We dated, on and off, for six years before we got married." They had no children, but Mitchell mentioned that they had plenty of nieces and nephews with whom they were involved.

"You're not a regular student."
— Bear Bryant

As a child who went to schools that had all black students, Mitchell's desire was to some day go to the University of Alabama. "You knew about Alabama football," he said. "It was always my dream to go to Alabama, to see if I could measure up to their standards.

"When I graduated from high school in Mobile in 1969, they weren't recruiting any black players. And, in truth, at that time I wasn't good enough to get recruited by a school like Alabama.

"I did very well as a student in high school. Four of my schoolmates and I did a science project and entered it in a state science fair in Alabama. We won a state-wide award. I think they were surprised to see five black kids with such an ambitious science project. They offered us all scholarships to different schools in Alabama, at Auburn and Alabama. I knew I was bright enough to go there and be a regular student. But I wanted to play football.

"There was a young man in my high school who was going out to Eastern Arizona College. I had never heard of it. But he told me we could go to school there and play football. I was under the impression we'd have scholarships to play football. But I learned upon getting there that we had to go through a tryout, and then the coach would determine what level of aid we would get. The coach, his name was Ladd Mullenaux, looked just like John Wayne. After the workouts, he put up a list of who was being offered aid and how much. I was so relieved to see I was getting a full scholarship. Otherwise, I would have had to go back home to Mobile because we couldn't afford to pay tuition."

Ladd Mullenaux, the John Wayne lookalike, later became the athletic director at Eastern Arizona College. The school is located in Thatcher, Arizona, the school colors are purple and gold, and the nickname of the teams as well as the school band is Gila Monsters. They compete in the Arizona Community College Athletic Association.

"It was a Mormon school — that was another shock — but I made good grades there," Mitchell continued. "My coaches recommended me to coaches from the University of Southern California. I went there for a visit and my hosts were Charles Young and Sam Cunningham. That was the first time I ever met O.J. Simpson. He was there, visiting his old coach, John McKay. I signed to go to USC. What I didn't know at the time was that John McKay and Bear Bryant were good friends. McKay told Bryant he was recruiting a young man out of Mobile. Within hours of their conversation, I was later to learn, I had three coaches from Alabama in my living room. Coach Bryant got after these coaches, I was told, and gave them some heat about missing me somehow when they were rating prospects. Pat Dye was one of the coaches who came to my home. Hayden Riley and Clem Gryska also came to my home. Wilbur Jackson was the first black to be offered a football scholarship at Alabama. Wendell Hudson came in that same year for basketball.

"I remember we visited the Alabama campus. Keep in mind that my mother didn't know anything about football. We're sitting in this big office, and my mom was on one side of me, and my dad was on the other side. My dad was a quiet man. My mom was listening to Bear Bryant's spiel and, at one point, she leaned forward in her chair, and said, 'Tell me your name again.' I nearly sunk into the floor when she said that. He said, 'My name is Paul Bryant.' And we all smiled. We laughed about that incident later on. When I accepted their scholarship offer, my mother never missed a game in two years.

"Bear Bryant is one of the best things that ever happened to me. I had two good parents I miss daily. I'll be driving my car and I'll say, 'I miss you, Dad,' or 'I love you, Mom.' But if I didn't have a father, Bear Bryant would have been my father.

"Coach Bryant taught his players how to be men. He told us up front, 'We won't have any Afros here; our white players won't wear their hair long, either. There will be no beards or mustaches. If you can't live with that, you should go elsewhere. You can't wear hats in classes.' He told us how to dress. We all wore crimson-colored blazers wherever we traveled (a lot of schools provided similar sportscoats to their athletes in those days, but it has since been deemed illegal by the powers-that-be of the NCAA). He wanted everyone on the team to look the same. He said, 'When you talk to people, look them in the eye.' He had the sports information people film our interviews so that they could improve our posture or our speaking, and taught us how to be more comfortable. He was a man for details. He was a stickler about some things. He wanted us to be prepared, for our classes as much as for football games.

"He often compared getting ready for a football game to getting ready for a math test. You have to read your notes, and review all your material, otherwise you won't have the confidence when you go into the class to take the test. It was the same way with football. You'll be confident that you have properly prepared, and you'll persevere and you'll win.

"He was larger than life. There are no Bear Bryants in football anymore. There are no long-time established coaches like Bo Schembechler, Woody Hayes, Dan Devine, Frank Broyles. Bear Bryant taught me how to be a man. He'd say, 'We expect things of you because you're here. These are the things an Alabama player does. Don't fool yourself; you're not a regular student. More is expected of you, and you will be under greater scrutiny.' "

In truth, you still have a Joe Paterno at Penn State and a Hayden Fry at Iowa, but there are fewer coaches who remain at one school for over 30 years, and Mitchell still makes a good point.

I mentioned to Mitchell that I would bet he had committed Bryant's talks to memory. "I can give all his talks from when I was a player, and when I was a coach. I remember one Wednesday night when he got up when we were getting ready to play Tennessee. I was an assistant coach at the time. You have to understand how big the rivalry is between Alabama and Tennessee. It was 7:45 p.m., I remember it well, when Coach Bryant began to talk. 'I want to tell you what it meant to be a football player at Alabama,' he started to say. 'It meant something to wear that crimson jersey. My parents would come over from Arkansas to see me play. When we lost to Tennessee, I couldn't hug my mother or my father. I felt like I had let them down. When I put on my crimson jersey, I thought about all the great players who had worn those same colors. Whether you win or lose, the sun will come up tomorrow. You don't have to beat Tennessee. Tennessee has to beat you because you're from Alabama.' "

It sounded like something I can remember a Virginian saying in the Civil War movie "Gettysburg," and Mitchell is moved by it every time he retells the story.

"Coach Bryant had tears in his eyes, and we had tears in our eyes. I was 24 or 25 years old, and I thought I had heard all the talks. It was 1975, and we played them and we beat them, 35-0.

"Coach Bryant invited me back to be an assistant coach at Alabama in 1981, but I told him I couldn't afford to do it. The assistants never made much at Alabama. Coach Bryant didn't make much when he was an assistant there, and he didn't think anybody else needed a lot of money, either. He thought you should be there because you loved Alabama.

"In 1983, I went back to Alabama as an assistant coach with the Birmingham Stallions of the USFL. When I got to Birmingham, the first person I called was Coach Bryant. We were playing phone tag.

286

We missed each other three times that day. I didn't get to talk to him. That was a Monday. He died that Wednesday. And we never connected. Yes, I went to his funeral. It was one of the saddest days of my life."

It couldn't have been easy for Mitchell to have been a trailblazer at Alabama. Ret. Col. Therman Greene of Oxford, Alabama, the father of Steelers' linebacker Kevin Greene, who went to Auburn, remembers when Mitchell was the first black to play football at Alabama on TV. "There were a lot of jokes about that," said Col. Greene. "It had to be hard for him."

When I told Col. Greene that Mitchell admired Bear Bryant, he responded, "Everyone did. Even if you were an Auburn fan, you loved Bear Bryant. But you hated Alabama. I remember when I was stationed in Germany, we got up at 2 a.m. to see Notre Dame play at Alabama. Ara Parseghian came down there twice and beat Alabama. We were so upset because state pride was still involved."

"He was the smartest football guy I've ever been around."
— Mitchell on Lou Holtz

"I was 25 when I went to Arkansas. Coach Bryant thought I should go elsewhere and learn from somebody else. He recommended me. I went to Arkansas in 1977 and stayed there until 1983. I often asked myself why Coach Bryant and why Coach Holtz were so successful. Coach Bryant taught us timing was the most important thing. With Holtz, he wanted to cover all the bases. He had a checklist to make sure we touched all areas in our coaches' meetings. He didn't take anything for granted. With Lou, oversights were inexcusable.

"I was with Lou before he became the big after-dinner speaker. He was the smartest football guy I've ever been around. He can get the ball into the end zone against anyone — even against the Green Bay Packers. He could look at film and he'd find a weakness. He'd come into our defensive meeting each week and he would say, 'Tell me how many points I need to score to win.' We'd get a kick out of it. He always said, '...I need to score.' But he was serious. He wanted to know how many points we thought we could hold them to, and then he'd do what he had to do to get more points than that. He'd work and work, and he was demanding of his staff, sometimes working through intimidation. He wasn't much of an athlete when he was at Kent State, but he sure learned his football to become a great coach."

What had he learned during his two seasons with the Steelers that gave him some clue to Cowher's success?

"He's a very intense person," said Mitchell. "He doesn't leave anything to chance. When he has a staff meeting he is always ready. He knows what he wants. He gives everyone his long-range plans.

287

You can make your own plans. You can schedule your life. I know what I'm going to be doing or what is expected of me on Wednesday. He's a guy that you know where you stand with him. He'll tell you. He'll let you know if you're doing well, and he'll let you know if he thinks you're performing below his expectations."

"It's difficult for these guys to make the adjustment."
— John Mitchell

I asked Mitchell if he was able to impart some of the wisdom he had gained from his family and football coaches like Bryant and Holtz to the players he was responsible for with the Steelers.

"In two years' time, I have seen a tremendous improvement in them as players and as people," said Mitchell. "Kevin Henry is a good example. He hadn't played a lot, and he wasn't sure he could play on this level. He'd do anything to stay and play now. He's gotten stronger, he talks more. He wouldn't put his face in my door unless I asked him to come and see me. I think he's matured as a person. I see a difference in him. He's happy to be here, and now he feels like he belongs here.

"It's difficult for these guys to make the adjustment. Many of them come from backgrounds where they haven't had much, and all of a sudden they have a lot of money. You put them in a foreign city, with high visibility, making a huge amount of money...it's a lot to ask of a guy who's 23 or 24 or 25 years old.

"You take Brentson Buckner. You're talking about a guy who came to camp overweight. He thought he was going to take the NFL by storm. His first year he learned in a hurry he wasn't going to take the NFL by storm. He has to work at it, and he has worked at it. He learns real fast; he's very intelligent. He might be the smartest guy on the football team.

"He really studies the game of football. He knows every position. He could play defensive back; he might get beat, but he knows where he's supposed to be, and his responsibilities. Quite often, I let him give the scouting report on the other team. He can tell you what each guy does well, what his weaknesses are. He knows everything about them. He's really a sharp guy.

"Ray Seals was a guy who'd been in a losing situation before he came here from Tampa. He wanted to win, but he didn't know how to. He thought he could do it by himself. He didn't know how hard he'd have to work. We had to convince him there's a right way and a wrong way. He's very intelligent for a guy who's never been to college. He'll have more success doing it by the system, not his way.

"Joel Steed...I knew him from my days at Cleveland. He's what I call a great pro player. He knows what he has to do. He gives you an honest day's work. He'll work hard every day. He was very embarassed by the incident when he was suspended for four games for steroid use. When he came back, he apologized to me first. He said, 'I know the Steelers are going to cut me. I'll clear out my locker.' I told him to hold on. 'You made a bad decision, and you paid for it. I hope you learned from it.' He's a good person. He has a great wife, a beautiful woman, and they're both good people. He's very sensitive, and I have to be careful what I say to him in front of others. Everyone is different."

Mitchell believes that certain tenets and basics work for everyone.

"I read this book about Winston Churchill. When he was very old, and not getting around too well, he spoke at a commencement exercise at some college in Canada. He was introduced to speak, and it took him a while to get up out of his chair, and make his way to the microphone. When he got there, in a real raspy voice, he said, 'Never give up, never give up, never, never, never...' And then he sat down. He received a standing ovation."

Pittsburgh Steelers/Michael F. Fabus

●elers assistant coach John Mitchell adjusts ●ace for prize pupil, Brentson Buckner.

University of Arkansas Sports Information

Mitchell served as an assistant to Lou Holtz at the University of Arkansas in 1980.

Marty Schottenheimer
Bill Cowher's mentor

"When I come to Pittsburgh,
I am coming home."

Marty Schottenheimer was one of the most successful coaches in the history of the National Football League. What he had done as the head man in Cleveland and Kansas City was incredible, and a few more years of similar success would assure him of someday being enshrined in Pro Football's Hall of Fame.

He had been criticized for coming up short in the playoffs, and for not coming away with any post-season championships — "he can't win the big ones," his critics cried — but Schottenheimer still had one of the outstanding career coaching records. He must have been doing something right.

Schottenheimer was sitting across a table from me, over breakfast in a bright, airy dining room at the Hilton Hotel at the Point in Pittsburgh, and I was thinking about how far he had come since we were students at the University of Pittsburgh in the early '60s, how far he had come from his hometown of McDonald, Pennsylvania, how confident he appeared, how assured he sounded no matter what the topic, how he smiled when we shared war stories.

We had much in common. We both had roots in western Pennsylvania, and were both English majors at Pitt in the early '60s. I was a year ahead of him, but we had some classes together. I was the sports editor of *The Pitt News* when he was playing for the Panthers. He remembered that I had not endeared myself to some of his teammates at Pitt, but he and I never had a problem. He was making a lot more money than I was, so I didn't balk when he grabbed the check.

When I was covering the Pittsburgh Steelers for *The Pittsburgh Press* (1979-1983), whenever I would enter the Browns' clubhouse in Cleveland, head coach Sam Rutigliano would always call Schottenheimer out from the next room to say hello to me. "Here's your Pitt buddy," Rutigliano would say. Bill Cowher was in that same clubhouse, as a reserve player for the Browns (1980-82), but I never had occasion to speak to him. I didn't know him then. Cowher later coached in Cleveland and in Kansas City on Schottenheimer's staff and they would become the closest of friends. They became confidants.

Schottenheimer was in Pittsburgh to introduce Cowher at the Dapper Dan Sports Dinner that March evening, 1995. He did not know at the time that Cowher would be named Pittsburgh's Man of the Year in Sports for the second time in three years. The announce-

Bill Cowher was honored as Man of the Year by Pittsburgh YMCA with mentor Marty Schottenheimer speaking on his behalf. Schottenheimer, of McDonald, Pa., was hugely successful as head coach of the Kansas City Chiefs.

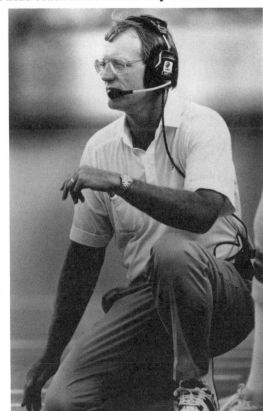

ment would come at the dinner. Marty and Bill were going golfing that morning at the Pittsburgh Field Club in Fox Chapel.

Schottenheimer could speak from an insider's standpoint about several people of interest to Pittsburgh sports fans: coaches like Rutigliano and Cowher, John Michelosen, Steve Petro, Chuck Noll, Richie McCabe and Paul Hackett, and players like Joe Montana and Dan Marino. We shared a passion for Pitt, Pittsburgh, the Pirates and Steelers. He could talk about Roberto Clemente and Bill Mazeroski and Bobby Layne and Jerry Shipkey with some authority and conviction.

When I mentioned McCabe to Schottenheimer, he seemed stunned for a few seconds. Tears welled in his eyes, especially his right eye, and those tears gleamed through his eyeglasses. He paused to collect himself, before he said anything. So the tears stayed in his eyes, and never streamed down his cheeks, but he was obviously moved. I had pressed a magic button. Suddenly, Schottenheimer seemed more human, like a teenager away from home, and hearing some bad news in a letter, or over the telephone.

He was wearing a burgundy sweater over an open-collared beige shirt, but he was no longer as casual as he had been at our breakfast meeting.

Schottenheimer had been sharing his thoughts about a lot of famous football and baseball people, from near and far, some of the greats of the game, some particularly special to Pittsburghers, but none tugged at his heart as much as Richie McCabe.

Schottenheimer had overcome setbacks in his career to become one of the most successful coaches in the professional football ranks, but he didn't do it alone, he was the first to admit as much, and McCabe was among those who contributed to his climb to the top.

Schottenheimer played for the Buffalo Bills from 1965 through 1968, and that was when he first became involved with McCabe. Schottenheimer was a linebacker and McCabe was the defensive coordinator for the last three of those years.

"I came to love the guy," said Schottenheimer. "He took over when Joe Collier left. I've never been around a more knowledgeable football guy, including Noll and Collier. Richie and I used to have some shouting matches, about what to do, how to do it, stuff like that. We'd argue about things. Oh, God, was he a competitor. Nothing in his life meant much to him other than his family, his religion and football."

McCabe died on January 4, 1983 at age 48 of colon cancer when he was an assistant coach with the Denver Broncos. He had grown up on Pittsburgh's North Side, played in the same backfield as Dan Rooney at North Catholic High School, and later played at Pitt. Along the way, he was a waterboy for the Steelers. He was skinny and wore eyeglasses, and hardly looked like a football player, but he had the heart of a lion and he surprised his best friends by playing at Pitt and then with the Buffalo Bills in the early days of the American Football League. He was one of Art Rooney's all-time favorites.

I wrote an article about McCabe when he died that appeared in *The Pittsburgh Press*. This prompted one of McCabe's former teammates at Pitt and with the Steelers, Bill Priatko, to pen a complimentary letter to John Troan, the paper's editor. Troan passed the letter along to me. I called Priatko to personally thank him for his kind words and it was the beginning of a beautiful relationship. Priatko, who also put in a year with the Cleveland Browns and Green Bay Packers back in the late '50s and has served in an administrative capacity with college and high school athletic programs, has become a surrogate brother in my life. He was a big fan of McCabe, of Chuck Noll, of Art and Dan Rooney, and he was a man in the same special mold, a man of great faith and substance. Like Schottenheimer, I am in Richie McCabe's debt, for the legacy he left me.

"When I finally got a chance to coach, I was broke," said Schottenheimer, explaining how McCabe came to his rescue when he was trying to get established as a pro football coach.

Following his retirement from the National Football League, Schottenheimer hooked up with the Portland Storm of the World Football League in 1974. He started the season as a player, but a shoulder injury ended his playing career. He continued as a tutor of the linebackers. He said the last eight checks he received from the Storm all bounced high at the bank.

"I wanted to go to the Senior Bowl in Mobile, Alabama, but I only had a few dollars to my name," said Schottenheimer. "This was in January of 1975. Richie let me share his room at a hotel in Mobile. I slept on the floor of his room. In my eyes, he was truly a great football coach. And he was a great friend to a guy trying to get started in the business."

Schottenheimer was scratching for money, and he was asked by the New York Giants to file a report on the personnel in the World Football League, which was folding. He thought he was going to be paid $1,000 for it, and it turned out that he was paid $100. That was a real shocker. There had been a misunderstanding. But Bill Arnsparger was so impressed with Schottenheimer's scouting report that he hired him on his staff for the 1975 season. Being an English major at Pitt was finally paying some dividends.

Schottenheimer coached the linebackers for the Giants for 1975 and 1976 and was named the team's defensive coordinator for the 1977 season. Then he spent two seasons looking after the linebackers for the Lions in Detroit, and then caught on with the Cleveland Browns in 1980, working as a defensive coordinator for Sam Rutigliano.

He replaced Rutigliano as head coach after eight games during the 1984 season. The Browns were 1-7 under Rutigliano, but finished 4-4 under Schottenheimer, losing three of those games by the margin of a field goal.

His record in 4 1/2 seasons at Cleveland was 44-28, and he won three AFC Central titles there. He ran afoul of owner Art Modell, however, when he refused to hire an offensive coordinator to call the plays. Schottenheimer was stubborn and insisted on making the calls himself in his last season.

He was hired by the Kansas City Chiefs and they should send Modell a "thank you" card on occasion. They couldn't be happier, unless, that is, the Chiefs could win an AFC or NFL championship or two.

"He is, without a doubt, the fiercest competitor I have ever met," said Chiefs' president and general manager Carl Peterson. "His record clearly speaks for itself."

"He understands that nothing comes easy."
— Marty Schottenheimer on Bill Cowher

Following our meeting in late March of 1995, Schottenheimer entered a white Cadillac Seville awaiting him outside the Hilton. He was on his way for his golf outing with Cowher. There was a time when he was so poor that he didn't have a dime with which to mark his ball, and now he was going to be a guest at Pittsburgh's posh Field Club.

Schottenheimer had been Cowher's mentor at Cleveland and Kansas City, and one of Bill's biggest boosters. They talked to each other on a weekly basis and exchanged football information, and shared their thoughts on sundry subjects. Those who have covered both clubs say they conduct themselves similarly.

Both have great relationships with the national media, especially network TV and NFL Films, because they open their locker rooms to their camera crews and comply with most of their requests. Both can be difficult and distant, hard to get close to, with the local beat people. If looks could kill...

Though he had great success in other cities as an NFL coach, often at the expense of the Steelers, Schottenheimer remained "a Pittsburgh guy," as Art Rooney would have called him. "When I come to Pittsburgh for something like the Dapper Dan Dinner," said Schottenheimer, "I am coming home."

He and his wife, Pat, lived in Overland Park, a suburb of Kansas City, but he continued to call Pittsburgh home.

Schottenheimer had to have mixed feelings about Cowher and the Steelers competing in Super Bowl XXX. It was supposed to be the year the Kansas City Chiefs went all the way. It was supposed to be Schottenheimer's season. His Chiefs had the best regular season record in the National Football League at 13-3.

They would have had the home field edge in every playoff game. But they stumbled and were upset by the Indianapolis Colts, 10-7. Had the Chiefs won that game, the Steelers would have had to play the Chiefs at Kansas City for the AFC title. The Chiefs would have been heavy favorites. I wondered how this was all sitting with

Schottenheimer. Could it hurt his relationship with Cowher? Had Cowher come too far too fast? Had he stolen Schottenheimer's show?

Even Cowher cracked a line one day late in the season at one of his weekly press conferences when he mentioned about talking to Schottenheimer and questioned whether Schottenheimer was giving him the best information. After all, they were now both chasing after the same Lombardi Trophy. But they continued to talk and confide in one another right up to Super Bowl XXX.

"Our relationship is a product of us working together for quite some time," said Schottenheimer at our breakfast meeting in March, 1995. "Bill is like you and me. He understands that nothing comes easy. You have to work for everything you get.

"It's important how you communicate ideas to people. Working hard is part of the ethic of western Pennsylvania. There's nobody around who'll give you something for nothing. There's no free lunch. You learn all this stuff early in life, and then you pass it on.

"I've been impressed with Bill for a long time. The thing that's enabled him to be successful is that he's such a great competitor. He has very strong beliefs about some things. Yet he's willing to listen."

This had not been my experience. I shared a story with Schottenheimer about how I had asked Cowher during his first season with the Steelers if he was open to a suggestion. He said he was. No sooner had I offered my advice when I could see that Cowher had misled me. No sportswriter could change Cowher. I liked Cowher and was looking to help him. I learned a lessson that day to keep my advice to myself. When I told Schottenheimer about Cowher getting hot with me, getting red in the face, and flaring up in my face, Schottenheimer couldn't contain a smile. "I can see Bill's face like you're talking about, definitely," he said.

His players swear by Cowher, and many refer to his great communication skills. Better to communicate with the ballplayers than with the media if you want to win.

"I hear he's a players' coach or one of the guys," said Schottenheimer. "Today, you have to listen to people. He's a hard worker, demanding. But no one's harder on themself than he is."

I asked Schottenheimer if he had any interest in coaching the Steelers when Noll decided to retire after the 1991 season, or at any point in his career. Schottenheimer had been mentioned in media speculation about possible successors because of his Pittsburgh background. It came down to Bill Cowher and Dave Wannstedt, who grew up in Baldwin, played at Pitt and had been the defensive coordinator of the Dallas Cowboys.

"Chuck was a fixture here for so long," said Schottenheimer. "So in my mind, I never gave it any consideration. There was no opportunity here. When there was an opportunity, I was ecstatically happy where I was. But I'm still a Steelers fan, and a Pirates fan, and a Pitt fan. I root for the Steelers except when they're playing our team."

He had great respect for the Rooney family and the Steelers' tradition, however, and thought Cowher was fortunate to be in the right position at the right time to land the job. He recommended him highly.

"The Steelers job is one of the three or four best jobs in the NFL, because of Dan Rooney," said Schottenheimer. "In our business today, the owner is the most important thing. And the next most important thing is the owner. That's why I think I've got the best job in the NFL. There's no better owner than Lamar Hunt. He has made sure we have all the support we need to win. We have a great complex, a fantastic football-only stadium, the finest stadium in pro football, in my mind. He gives us the opportunity at every turn to be first class. He went from artificial surface to grass. He is an excellent businessman and promoter. He's like you and me in the sense that he's a fan."

How did he get to know Dan Rooney?

"I competed against the Steelers twice a year when I was in Cleveland," said Schottenheimer, "and I'd see him at league meetings. Dan Rooney is not given to pontification, so when he says something people listen. He gets a tremendous amount of respect from everyone in the National Football League.

"Dan made the right choice when he picked Bill. An important thing about Bill...he was 34 when he became the coach of the Steelers. He succeeded Chuck Noll. There had to be a temptation to try and do some things like Chuck. But Bill never did that. He knew he had to be himself. He never tried to be someone he wasn't. A lot of people do that, and the players can spot it in a minute. I see the Steelers play from time to time on TV and I can see the job Bill has done here. When we have a bye in our schedule, I sit down and watch all the games. I'm a fan.

"Bill was not my first choice as a defensive coordinator. Bill Arnsparger and Joe Collier were, but I couldn't get them. Bill kept telling me he was equal to the task, and he was right about that. So I got lucky.

"The thing about Bill that made me realize he was going to be a great coach was his competitiveness, and his ability to communicate. I've always said he got more out of his ability than any player I'd ever seen. But he didn't have much ability, so that wasn't that hard."

Schottenheimer laughed at his own joke. "After I introduced Bill at the Dapper Dan Dinner two years ago, Joe Theismann came to the microphone a little later and wanted to know why Bill had me introduce him since I said so many bad things about him. But it was all in good fun."

What is it like to play golf with Bill Cowher? Was that good fun?

"It's great competition," he said. "The last time we played, we were in a foursome, and we happened to be teammates. We had a little deal with two other guys. We were down significantly after the front nine, and we came on to prevail. We were grinding. We absolutely had the competitive juices going. You should've seen us."

"My mother was very enterprising."
— Marty Schottenheimer

Marty Schottenheimer was born on September 23, 1943 in Canonsburg. His father, Martin, was a salesman in the food business. "He was a very hard-working guy," said his namesake. "He always put in a full day's work. He never really fostered our interest in sports, because it wasn't that important to him. He could've gone to Duquesne University on a football scholarship, but none of his buddies were going to school, so he didn't go." His father passed away in 1976.

His mother was Catherine, but most everyone called her "Tass," except her kids. They called her "The Rock." She celebrated her 80th birthday on June 1, 1996. The family lived in McDonald, out in Washington County.

"My dad never made a lot of money, but we never lacked for anything. My mother was very enterprising," said Schottenheimer.

He had two brothers. Bill was living in Pittsburgh and worked in a mill. Kurt, six years younger than Marty, was working as an assistant coach on the Chiefs' staff. They had a sister Lisa. Her husband was a lieutenant colonel in the military and they were living in Maryland.

When asked to describe what it was like growing up in McDonald, Schottenheimer said, "It was great. I enjoyed McDonald High School. We used to walk to school every day and come home for lunch. After my sophomore year, we went into a jointure, Fort Cherry, which required us to take a bus. There were something like 3,000 people in McDonald. When I was a youngster, it sticks in my mind, they had a banner that they hung across the main street in McDonald. It was red and white, the school colors, and it simply said FOOTBALL TONIGHT. 8 P.M. WEST END PARK. That's the end of town where I lived. It didn't say who was playing, just a game tonight.

"Football and basketball were the two sports I played. One of the guys involved in my development was our basketball coach Ed Hepe, who now lives in Butler, Pa. He left McDonald the year after we won the WPIAL Class B basketball title in 1961. We beat Wampum in the finals at the Pitt Field House.

"Wampum was a big favorite. Don Hennon's dad, L. Butler Hennon, was coaching their team. Richie Allen had finished, but his brother, Ronnie Allen, was on the team. They wore vertical striped socks. They had some guys who could dunk. Hepe took us up early for our warm-up, but he took us back downstairs to the dressing room before Wampum took the floor. He didn't want us to see them warm up. He told us 'We have nothing to lose, because nobody thinks we have a chance.'

"Jim Garry was the other coach in our high school who helped lay the foundation for my athletic success. He has had one of the longest tenures in high school coaching. He's been the football coach at Ft. Cherry since its inception in 1959. He's been working in McDonald for 36 years, all at Fort Cherry High School."

Schottenheimer was successful in every respect at Fort Cherry High School. He was an honor student and a football and basketball standout. He was an all-WPIAL linebacker and the center on the state championship basketball team.

"I thought Pitt was an ideal environment for me."
— Marty Schottenheimer

As Scottenheimer and I shared stories of our experiences as Pitt students in the '60s, we learned something that bonded us in another way. We learned that we were both walking in the same block, just below the Cathedral of Learning, when we heard that President Kennedy had been shot in Dallas on a Friday afternoon, November 23, 1963.

"I was walking across from the Cathedral of Learning to the Student Union," said Schottenheimer. "I went inside and just stood there and watched the news on TV. I went to class afterward and the professor let us out early."

I had been walking past the University Shop, a campus clothing store under the dorms on Forbes Avenue, when a clerk came out and told me the President had been shot. I went to the Student Union and watched the television coverage there. Schottenheimer and I might have been in the same room.

There were members of the Penn State *Daily Collegian* on the campus that day. We were supposed to play our annual touch-football game with the respective staffs of the rival student newspapers. But we called it off. The next day's football game between Pitt and Penn State was also postponed. The NFL played its Sunday schedule and it was a source of criticism for Commissioner Pete Rozelle and the club owners.

Pitt would finish with a 9-1 record that year, but that postponement would cost the team an invitation to a major bowl game, and the squad ended up going nowhere on New Year's Day. Imagine a college team finishing with a 9-1 record, losing only to Roger Staubach and Navy on the road, and not being picked for a major bowl game.

In truth, it wasn't thought to be a big deal in those days. Most of the players of that era thought they were at Pitt principally to get an education and, hopefully, a degree. Football was a bonus, a great way to get a free education.

Those were definitely different days.

"I thought Pitt was an ideal environment for me," said Schottenheimer. "It was far enough away from home to develop my own responsibility as a person, and close enough if I had a need I could get home and back in a few hours.

"I wasn't a fraternity guy, but I mixed socially and met a lot of different people on the campus. It was the cornerstone of my development socially. McDonald was such a small town. I had to adapt to the social environment at Pitt. It was very important in my overall development. I remember a teacher like Dr. Lawrence Lee in English. He was so flamboyant and spirited. The way he dressed, the way he talked."

I also had Dr. Lee, so I knew of what Schottenheimer spoke. Dr. Lee had wavy white hair, a pronounced Southern accent, and always wore a silk pocket handkerchief. He had flair, style, and I loved to hear him read excerpts from stories we were studying.

"I spent a lot of time with the average Pitt people," said Schottenheimer. "I liked Al Grigaliunas, the captain of the 1963 team. He came up the hard way. He had spent time with his mother in a detention camp in Lithuania as a little kid. He grew up in Cleveland. He was a very positive guy, a real role model. I had a great deal of respect for him. He got a degree in engineering and became a real success in the business world. I was surrounded by guys like that. That 1963 team had a lot of special achievers on it, guys who graduated and have been so successful in life.

"I have a great deal of respect for guys who compete. Grigaliunas was one of those guys who did that. I had a lot of respect for Brian Generalovich, He played basketball for four years and he didn't come out for football until his fifth year, when he was in Dental School. I liked Bob Sorochak, a good friend and a good grass roots kind of person. There were very few guys who were pretentious and aloof. It was a solid group of people.

"I was a junior on that '63 team. The record of that '63 bunch...I think it's remarkable. I don't know that it's been duplicated anywhere. So many dentists and doctors and professional people. Unreal.

"I was keeping good company. After I got out, I realized how special it was. I wasn't aware of it while I was there. I have a great deal of pride in that team; I often talk about it.

"Billy Kaliden and Steve Petro were two of my coaches, and I thought they were really good people. Like everybody, I loved Steve Petro. He was like a surrogate father for so many of us."

He said he loved to see certain guys at the Dapper Dan Dinner, like former teammate Jim Dodaro. Pirates people like Steve Blass and Jim Leyland. "They're good guys, too. Bill was really pleased when he won the big award. It's nice to be honored in your hometown. There were a lot of other people who had a major hand in his success. I thought Theismann and Joe Walton were very good. Lanny Frattare and Chuck Tanner. The pride of New Castle. All good guys.

"I still get a kick out of Myron Cope. He's a good example of what makes Pittsburgh special. Maybe every city has these kind of guys. There's a Damon Runyon character if there ever was one. There are so many of them who are a part of the Pittsburgh landscape."

He had gone out to Pitt the previous night on his own. He said he always goes out to the O — the Original Hot Dog Shop — whenever he returns to Pittsburgh.

"When you used to study, someone would make a run to the O, and come back with hot dogs and subs," he recalled. "I remember one time that Sal Sunseri, when he was coaching at Pitt, sent me a half dozen hot dogs from the Dirty O, as it was affectionately called, to me in Cleveland. He had the hot dogs packed in dry ice."

Being back at Pitt the night before refreshed his memory about what that scene was like in the '60s. I was lucky enough to get to Pitt a year before Schottenheimer in September of 1960. A month later, the Pirates were playing the mighty New York Yankees in the World Series right on our campus, just a block away from the Student Union.

Schottenheimer said he remembered the view from the top floor of the Student Union, what once was the Schenley Hotel, and how you could see the one side of the field, the first baseman and second baseman, the center fielder and right fielder. "For me, that meant Dick Stuart, most of the time, at first, and Billy Mazeroski at second, Bill Virdon in center and, of course, Roberto Clemente in right field," said Schottenheimer.

"Oakland and the Pitt campus were like another world to me from what I had known in McDonald. The thing I remember is what I generally would do after a football game. When the game ended, I would go home and I'd be down with my family and stay for awhile. And then I'd come back to school on Saturday night, or I might sleep over and come back to school on Sunday morning.

"I remember when I'd come back and I'd come off the Parkway and come up the Boulevard of the Allies a ways, and then onto Forbes Avenue. As you were coming up the hill you could see the Cathedral of Learning looming over everything. It was like a beacon in the night, a lighthouse."

We mentioned all the little people we loved in the athletic department, the equipment guys, the trainers, the ticket sales staff, all the support people.

"I worked for the University during the summer on the buildings and grounds crew," said Schottenheimer. "I worked for Matt Long, he was my foreman, and then for Dominic Sciulli. Bruno Sammartino was one of his buddies.

"We got paid on Fridays. I'd go to the bank, and then I'd go to the Clock Restaurant and have lunch. It was catty-corner from the Original Hot Dog Shop. For a 20-year-old kid, it was something special, eating there with the men on the crew. I enjoyed those summers. I was making something like $3.25 an hour. That was a lot of money in those days for a kid working in the summer. Those were unique people."

Oakland was the center for all cultural and sports entertainment in those days, and Schottenheimer had fond memories of that special experience.

"Of all the idols I've had, I recall Clemente as a special one. He was the most significant of all the ones I watched when I was young. Sitting up in Schenley Hotel and seeing him out there. In baseball, it was Clemente and Mazeroski.

"Before I even got to Pitt, I paid attention to the Pirates and the Steelers from the '50s on. I can remember when I first got into paying attention to football. I remember Joe Geri was one of their backs. Jerry Shipkey was a linebacker. I remember when Lowell Perry got hurt. Jack McClairen, Jim Finks, Dale Dodril, John Nisby, John Henry Johnson. Ernie Stautner...he was probably my favorite. Frank Varrichione and Elbie Nickel.

"When I was at Pitt, I played in a basketball game once with some Steelers, some kind of benefit event. John Henry Johnson was playing. We were one down or tied at the end of the game. John Henry throws up the ball from about 45 feet away and it went in and he never stopped running. He went right under the hoop and onto the dressing room. I'll never forget it.

"When I come back to the Dapper Dan, I'm always coming home. It's a little bit unusual, but I still refer to them as 'our Steelers.' With the exception of when we play them, they're still my team."

He was a fine linebacker at the University of Pittsburgh, but — contrary to information found in his biographical sketch in the Chiefs' media guide — he was neither an All-American nor a member of Pitt's all-time football team. There is not an official all-time Pitt football team. For the record, he was good enough to be named All-East, and he played in the Senior Bowl and the College All-Star Game. In the latter, he played alongside Dick Butkus, Fred Biletnikoff, Roger Staubach, Bob Hayes and Bill Curry. He was a fourth round draft pick of the NFL's Baltimore Colts and a seventh round draft choice of the AFL's Buffalo Bills.

He played pro ball in Buffalo and Boston, and had a brief stint under Chuck Noll in Marty's last NFL summer training camp.

He played for the Boston Patriots in 1969-70 before they traded him to the Steelers in 1971. I visited with him and Jim Nance, a fullback from Indiana, Pa., in a shabby dressing room next to a hockey rink at Boston U. when the Patriots were playing their home games at the BU campus.

After a training camp stint under Chuck Noll in 1971, Pittsburgh traded him to the Colts, who had originally drafted him when he came out of Pitt. He retired three weeks later when Baltimore released him. Then he worked in real estate in Denver before resurfacing with the WFL.

"Order and stability follow this man wherever he goes."
— Paul Zimmerman, SI

In 1977, Schottenheimer was promoted to defensive coordinator of the Cleveland Browns. He was 34 at the time. Bill Cowher would later become the head coach of the Steelers at the same age. At age 41, he replaced Sam Rutigliano as head coach midway through the 1984 season.

Nine of his ten teams since then had 10-win seasons. At the end of the 1995 season, his overall record in regular season competition was 116-66-1. His playoff record as coach was a forgettable 5-9. Schottenheimer's regular season winning percentage (.637) during the span was the league's third best, behind only George Seifert (.760) of the San Francisco 49ers and Don Shula (.677) of the Miami Dolphins. Hard to believe the kind of criticism Shula was subjected to in his final year.

Then again, Schottenheimer got shoved out in Cleveland though he had great success there. He lost a power struggle to owner Art Modell, and was gone after the 1988 season.

Paul Zimmerman, the pro football guru of *Sports Illustrated,* has said of Schottenheimer: "Order and stability follow this man wherever he goes. He had the Browns in it every year, while overcoming some insurmountable obstacles."

During our breakfast meeting at the Pittsburgh Hilton, Schottenheimer was approached by a man in a gray suit who stopped by the table and extended a hand, which Schottenheimer shook heartily. "I'm from Kansas City," the man interjected, "and I like your Chiefs."

It was no wonder. In Schottenheimer's seven campaigns, Kansas City had averaged ten wins and advanced to the playoffs six consecutive seasons. That was quite a contrast to what the Chiefs accomplished before Schottenheimer showed up.

In the 17 years before Scottenheimer became the head coach, the Chiefs averaged six wins a season and made the playoffs once.

The Chiefs were a once-proud franchise. They had been, indeed, a great team in the AFL under Hank Stram when I was in the military service in 1965, and served as a spotter on my days off for Charlie Jones and Paul Christman for AFL telecasts.

I remain a Chiefs' fan because of that personal involvement in my days at the U.S. Army Hometown News Center at 601 Hardesty Avenue in Kansas City. Lenny Dawson was the quarterback then. They had great players like Johnny Robinson, Bobby Bell, Buck Buchanan, Otis Taylor, Jim Tyrer. I covered the 1970 Super Bowl in New Orleans when Dawson directed the Chiefs to a victory over the Minnesota Vikings.

I root for Schottenheimer's Chiefs the way I root for Dan Marino's Dolphins unless they are playing the Steelers. I root for the New York Jets and the New York Giants because I lived and worked in New York for nine years. This way there's a good chance I will be feeling good about some of the results each weekend in the NFL.

The Chiefs' owner, Lamar Hunt, was one of the founders of the American Football League. He has been inducted into the Pro Football Hall of Fame. He has always been a class act.

I asked Schottenheimer to comment on some people with whom he had been associated during his distinguished football career:

* **Joe Montana** — "Why the magic? I always go back to the environment in which we were raised. Why is Montana so great? Because he's such a competitor. Competitors are a special breed. Winning is important in everything they do. I think people who are raised in this area are special competitors. You learn lessons growing up here, I believe. People here respond to hard work. And doing extra things. That you never get anything for nothing. Then again, Joe credits Iron City Beer for the reason so many great quarterbacks have come out of western Pennsylvania.

"I'm glad I had a chance to coach him at the end of his career. I had said, somewhat with tongue in cheek, that while he's had great success with the 49ers we're anxious for him to be like that in Kansas City. But it never quite happened. Maybe it was too late for him. His ability as a quarterback is based upon two things: he has a tremendous ability to know where everybody is. I'm not so sure he doesn't see everybody on the field. He has the ability to make a play. He can get himself out of trouble, avert tacklers. He is gifted in many ways.

"We played Pittsburgh in the post-season a year ago (January 8, 1994). It came down to a fourth down play. I'm talking to Paul (Hackett) and Joe at the same time. Paul gave me a play and I gave it to Joe. Paul said, 'What does he think of it?' Joe said, 'It's a good play.' Paul had another idea. I gave it to Joe. 'What do you think of that?' I asked Joe. 'That's fine,' he said. In short, he didn't care. What he was saying was 'Just give me a play and I'll go and do it.' When a play is over, it's over, and you go on to the next one.

"In San Diego, we came back late to beat them. There was a series of four plays. On the first three downs, Joe threw as bad of throws as you could make. But on fourth and ten, he threw a perfect pass. It was such a difficult pass to complete. He put it right on the money. He was oblivious to the fact that he had just made three lousy passes."

How about the AFC playoff game with Miami at the end of the 1994 season? Marino outplayed Montana and Miami advanced, 27-17.

"It was something, boy. In the final analysis, we just didn't hold up defensively. It was a real shoot-out at the OK Corral. Those two guys were both humming. You know, the really great ones like Michael Jordan, if they're hot you can't do anything about it. When the great ones are in the groove you can only sit back and admire it. We ran three safety blitzes against Marino, and they had no one to block the guy, but Dan got it off, and hit his man all three times."

* **Chuck Noll** — "I learned a lot during a short stay with the Steelers in (1971) training camp. I learned a tremendous amount of football. I was there about five weeks. He was a great, great teacher. He had a unique ability to communicate and instruct. He got me one day when he gave a lecture — and that's the only way you could properly label it, a lecture — on tackling. He was the linebacker coach at the time, too. He gave a lecture on tackling. I wish I had a tape of it. It was concise, well-organized and it was right on. I remember thinking, 'Yes, that's what it's all about.'

"Jack Ham was a rookie that year. Henry Davis started in the middle. And Andy Russell was there. And Jerry Hillebrand. I came in and I was so excited about playing at home, and I stunk the joint out. So he traded me."

* **Sam Rutigliano** — "One of the things I learned from Sam was that the best way to establish a position of excellence in the NFL is to expect it. He's a really bright guy. He always had a lot of one-liners and sayings. I remember him saying, 'If you ever have an opportunity to say nothing take advantage of it.' Do you know the story about his daughter's death?"

I nodded that I did. When Rutigliano was an assistant coach with the New England Patriots, he was driving down a highway, and he was tired from not getting enough sleep. He fell asleep and went off the road and his daughter shot through the rear window, and died from her injuries.

"I think that's the framework from which he put football in its proper perspective," said Schottenheimer. "He still has a home in Cleveland and a condo in Lynchburg, where he's coaching at Liberty University. I learned from him that you have opportunities to do something special and you better make the most of the moment.

"One night I was sitting with him and his wife, Barbara, at Stouffer's in Cleveland. He said, 'Marty, when you lose nobody hurts like the head coach.' I said. 'That's crazy. I hurt as much as you do.' When I became a head coach, I found out what Sam was talking about. He was right.

"He had a great ability to put things in perspective. He put things behind him and moved ahead."

* **John Michelosen** — "I really liked him. He was our head coach when I was at Pitt, and I had a great deal of respect for him. Thought he was a real good football coach. His personality was such, he wasn't that close to any of us. He was unpretentious. He was outstanding at teaching fundamental football. That's why he was a good coach. Don't remember that he had the greatest schemes.

"He had coached the single-wing when he was an assistant to Jock Sutherland, and when he succeeded Sutherland with the Steelers (1948-51). Pitt played the wing-T when I was on the team.

304

"Jack Wiley recruited me and he was one of the reasons I went there. Then he left before I became a varsity player. Since I've been with the Chiefs, Jack Wiley came to our training camp in River Falls, Wisconsin, about 15 miles east of Minneapolis-St. Paul, and it was great to see him again. Frank Lauterbur came in and coached the defensive team when I was there. Phil Dahar was our captain my last year. We had some great guys, but we didn't have a great season in 1964."

* **Paul Hackett** — "He's good. He is, in my opinion, the best fundamental quarterback coach-teacher that I've been around. It may not have worked out for him as a head coach at Pitt, but Bill Walsh raves about his work as the offensive coordinator with the 49ers. And Joe Montana swore by him. There are some strategists and theory and scheme guys. Some are nuts and bolts guys. He's both. He's a great teacher. He can teach the mechanics of quarterback. He's excellent in that regard. He calls the plays."

Schottenheimer said he had no regrets. He enjoys calling the shots for the Chiefs, and hopes to continue in that capacity. He doesn't second-guess himself too much.

"My father told me, 'Sometimes you have a decision to make, and you might make the wrong decision. Now you have an opportunity to make another one.' I always try to keep my father's words in mind."

Marty Schottenheimer as coach of the Cleveland Browns

Richie McCabe as assistant coach with the Denver Broncos

305

Jonathan Hayes
Still a poster boy

*"He's a good example
to the younger guys."*
— Tom Donahoe

Sometimes it really is a small world. I learned just how small the more familiar I became with Jonathan Hayes and his story. He signed with the Steelers as a free agent before the 1994 season after playing nine seasons with the Kansas City Chiefs, and was a steadying influence on the Pittsburgh football team during the 1994 and 1995 seasons.

They signed him as insurance when Eric Green was a holdout in 1994. Hayes was the starting tight end for the Steelers at the outset of the 1995 season, after Green had gone to the Miami Dolphins as a free agent, then Hayes shared the position with his prize pupil, Mark Bruener, the team's No. 1 draft choice that year. Hayes was an impressive person in so many respects, a dynamite sports success story, and we had some common ties that made him even more appealing.

Hayes was born and bred in Bridgeville, once a booming railroad and coal mining town about 15 miles south of Pittsburgh, a neighboring community to Upper St. Clair, where I had lived the previous 16 years. One of his neighbors was John Metro, one of my best boyhood friends. Metro lived six doors away from me on Sunnyside Street in Hazelwood for over 20 years. He was a month younger and we had gone to school together for ten years and played sports together for about fifteen years. He was in my wedding party as an usher.

When Hayes went to South Fayette High School, Metro was a physical education instructor there, the baseball coach and assistant football coach, and he drove Hayes to school each day. "Jon has always been an exceptional individual, a real class act," Metro said when we talked. "I've watched him and his brothers grow up, and I'm proud of all of them."

Hayes had quite a story to share with others, and he often did so to help those who needed a boost and some direction and goals in their lives. He had overcome the constant peril of diabetes to succeed as a professional athlete. He came from a special family, remembered his roots and the values he learned from his parents. There was a real substance to this man. He had never been a spectacular pro pass catcher, but he had always been a solid contributor, catching a clutch pass here and there, blocking better than most who play his position, and bringing a positive influence to his team's locker room. He was a leader by example.

"Maybe his biggest strength is he's such a high-character, quality guy," said Steelers Director of Football Operations Tom Donahoe. "He's a good example to the younger guys."

One did not often hear Hayes in the locker room. He went about his business in a quiet, most professional manner.

He was a solid citizen in every respect. He did his best to help Eric Green grow as a pro, but found a more willing protege in his second season with the Steelers in Bruener, a tight end from the University of Washington who had a similar background and shared similar values. Bruener wanted to be the best, and had an eager ear for what Hayes had to say and show him. Bruener moved into Green's old dressing stall, right next to Hayes, and they became a model mentor-pupil pair in pro sports.

They came in early each morning to lift weights together, and stayed late after practice to watch film. They were at the stadium before and after most of their teammates.

"My job is to do what I can to contribute to this football team," said Hayes, "and to do *whatever it takes* to make Mark better. I give him advice when he asks for it. But I help them all. And if I can help them in any way, in running a route properly, blocking, taking the proper step, or seeing a defense, I'm going to help them.

"It's not about me trying to keep everything I know to myself. Knowledge is to give to other people so that it will help everyone, especially our team. I want to give Mark as much knowledge as I can so we can get farther along to taking a shot at a championship. When I first broke into pro football, I found some older players who'd steer you wrong on purpose to protect their own turf."

Hayes could have viewed Bruener as an over-paid prospect out to get his job, but he did not have a selfish bone in his body. Veterans teaching newcomers had always been a strength in the Steelers' organization. In mid-August, prior to the start of the 1995 season, Hayes said, "There's a reality to the situation. Mark was brought in, paid a certain amount of money, and eventually they're going to have to give him an opportunity to start. That's what he's here for. But I'm not going to hand him the job."

I came home one evening after spending the day at the Steelers' complex at Three Rivers Stadium, and was sharing stories with my wife, Kathie, talking excitedly about Jonathan Hayes. She did not make the connection right away, but eventually she said, "I know his family; his father was one of my patients. I heard them talking about him and I met him."

Kathie was in her fourth year as a social worker in the oncology unit at Allegheny General Hospital, located on East North Avenue on Pittsburgh's North Side, about a mile from Three Rivers Stadium. She worked with cancer patients and their families, trying to help them with their challenge. Jewett Hayes had been a patient at AGH in 1993. His wife told me he had Hodgkins Disease, prostate cancer and had suffered a stroke when he was hospitalized.

"His dad was in bad shape when we had him," continued Kathie. "I'm glad to hear he's doing well. He was a real nice man. His family was always in his room with him. They were such pleasant and positive people, easy to work with. They had a lot of class."

The word "class" is often invoked by those who talk about Hayes and his family. One day I was in the Steelers' locker room, talking to Jerry Olsavsky and Justin Strzelczyk. Olsavsky was flanked by Strzelczyk and Hayes. I was trying to get them to urge their parents to send me the photographs and information I had requested in letters I sent to them. "You should see the great stuff I got from Brentson Buckner's father," I said. Buckner's dressing stall was also nearby.

Hayes smiled, something he often does, and interjected, "You're going to be getting a package from my mother real soon. And I'll bet you it will be the best one you'll ever get. My mother is the most organized person in the world. Wait till you see what she sends you."

Within a week, I found a large package in my post office box. It contained a bright red booklet, a three-ring affair, that Mrs. Florence Joy Hayes had assembled with a mother's loving touch that chronicled the career of her son. It was easy to see she had been a school teacher as well as a proud mother. There were sheets of information, copies of press clippings, magazine stories, book excerpts, photographs, you name it, covering the career of Jonathan Michael Hayes from his days at South Fayette High School to the University of Iowa to the Kansas City Chiefs and, back home at last, to the Pittsburgh Steelers. All in plastic sleeves, so neat. Every time his name appeared it was highlighted with a yellow Magic Marker.

It reminded me of a similar booklet that I had seen in doing an earlier book about the Steelers. That one was about John Bruno, who had played briefly for the Steelers during the strike-shortened 1982 season. Bruno had been a punter at Upper St. Clair High School and Penn State University. He died at age 27 of melanoma, a skin cancer, in April of 1992. His parents, John and Alfrieda Bruno, shared their pride and grief with me on several visits to their home, and had remained special friends. Mrs.Bruno had also highlighted her son's name with a yellow Magic Marker in every list in which it appeared in the scrapbooks she shared with me.

The Bruno and Hayes families were both close-knit, shored up by strong religious beliefs and regular church attendance, and it was not surprising that they spawned children of substance.

Jonathan Hayes gave of his time to help others. He was active with the Allegheny County chapter of the American Diabetes Association, United Way and American Cancer Association. Hayes was honored on June 4, 1996 as Man of the Year for his tireless promotional efforts by the local chapter of the Diabetes Association at a fund-raising premiere of *Jitney*, a play by Pulitzer Prize-winning Pittsburgher August Wilson. Hayes had a charity called "Hayes Huddle" in Kansas City where he worked with disadvantaged youngsters to help them find their way in life.

eelers tight end Jonathan Hayes

Tri-state connection at the University of Iowa included (left to right front) Jonathan Hayes (Bridgeville), head coach Barry Alvarez (Burgettstown), Michael Stoops (Youngstown); and (rear left to right) Bill Glass (Portage), Mark Vlasic (Monaca) and George Little (Duquesne).

At South Fayette High School

Hayes family portrait (left to right) Jewett, Jeffrey, Florence, Jonathan and Jay.

Jonathan Hayes is flanked by father, Jewett, and mother, Florence in Arizona before Super Bowl XXX.

He was single and had a farm near Kansas City where he raised and rode cutting horses. Like another former Steeler stalwart, Hall of Famer Mel Blount, he loved to ride horses and entered competitions with them.

He majored in sociology with a minor in criminology in college, graduating a year ahead of schedule, and had thought about going to law school. He worked during the off-season with the Cass County (Missouri) Sheriff Department as a posse member. He was the lone ranger, at times, but he never wore a mask. He wanted people to know who he was, where he came from, what he was all about, and helped wherever he could.

"As a family, we pulled together to give him any support he needs."
— Florence Joy Hayes

Jonathan Hayes had written a book — *Necessary Toughness* — about his ordeal with diabetes, and had been featured on billboards throughout western Pennsylvania that were aimed at heightening awareness of diabetes and the mission of the Allegheny County chapter of the American Diabetes Association.

Even the strongest-looking Steeler could have diabetes, that was the message. In most cases, it could be controlled with proper diet and medicine, and one could lead a relatively normal life.

Hayes had a passion for volunteerism because of the health problems he and his family had experienced. He learned after the last game of his senior season at the University of Iowa that he had Type I (insulin dependent) diabetes.

"I draw blood four times a day for tight control of my diabetes," he said. No matter one's age, that routine has to be a real bummer. He administered his own insulin shots.

His mother, Florence Joy Hayes, wrote me a letter: "When Jonathan was diagnosed with diabetes, I personally was devastated. Jonathan was away at college and had to deal with this phase of his life and then his own health problems."

His mother read up on diabetes and became an expert on the subject, as did her son.

"As a family we have pulled together to give him any support he needs," his mother related. "He wrote the book, *Necessary Toughness*, to help others who are suffering and trying to deal with this problem."

There was still no cure for diabetes as Hayes talked about his concerns. When he was at Kansas City, he and Walt Arnold, the team's other tight end, both had diabetes. Both learned they had diabetes in the spring of 1984. What were the odds of that double coincidence? They helped each other.

There had to be constant vigilance. There were dietary restrictions, daily shots. They had to be fastidious about what they ate and how much exercise they got. It can be a real hazard during physical workouts, practices and football games, as if those efforts were not challenging enough in their own right.

Two Hall of Fame athletes who battled diabetes were baseball pitcher Jim "Catfish" Hunter of the Kansas City and Oakland A's, and Bobby Clarke, a hockey center for the Philadelphia Flyers. They also were spokesmen for the disease in national awareness campaigns.

Diabetes is a condition in which a person has excess sugar in his blood. It is characterized by an inadequate secretion or utilization of insulin and excessive amounts of sugar in the blood and urine and, at times, by thirst, hunger and loss of weight.

Untreated, diabetes causes the sugar in your blood to build up in your body. This buildup of sugar can cause you to go blind, suffer a heart attack, lose your feet or legs to amputations, stop your kidneys from working, and even kill you. Insulin is taken to lower the sugar level. I am familiar with diabetes. My sister, her late husband and her children were all diabetics. My father-in-law and his late father had diabetes. His father lost a leg to diabetes. There are all kinds of complications. It's serious stuff.

The diet for a diabetic is high carbohydrate, low-protein, low-fat, lots of breads, pastas, noodles.

"My body gives me signs when my sugar level is too low," said Hayes. "If I start to feel it in the middle of the game, I'll drink more Gatorade or eat a couple more oranges. If the level is a little too high, a good hard workout at practice will lower it. I like to come into a game with my sugar level a little on the high side so as not to bottom out during the game."

The source of his strength was always the same.

"Life in my home was disciplined," he said. "I learned self-control and an ordered lifestyle. I developed an inner strength from a healthy family upbringing that left me a step ahead when confronted with the lifestyle changes required to properly manage diabetes."

In his book, *Necessary Toughness*, Hayes related his thoughts about his dilemma.

"For me, the stakes are high. First of all, my livelihood depends on my physical health. Keep my body strong, I keep my job. Let my body slip below top condition, I lose my job. I like to feel good. I don't like feeling tired all the time. I don't like to feel pressure build up behind my eyes. I don't like for my hands and feet to tingle and go numb. I know that if I let up on managing my diabetes, not only will I lose my job and the advantages of feeling good. I'll be in danger of losing my eyesight, losing my kidneys, losing a foot to amputation....

"We are challenged every day of our life. You get out of bed, you are challenged. Whether it is for your company, or personally, in a relationship, something like that. This is just one of those things that is also part of my life."

Anyone who sized up Hayes, all 6-5, 248 well-muscled pounds, would find it difficult to realize this was a man coping with such a challenging disease. What he learned from this, however, he believed had far-reaching implications.

"Sure, the book is about my story and my dealing with diabetes," he said. "But I think it is also a story that anyone can relate to, whether they have the disease or not. All of us have to overcome things at various times in our lives. Nobody walks through this thing without having to fight somewhere along the line for something they felt was important. That's so much easier to do when you have a strong family behind you. I am where I am today because of my parents."

"Athletes, like everyone else, are just people."
— Jonathan Hayes

There was always the family. His father was a supervisor for the State Parole Board in western Pennsylvania. His mother was a school teacher for 36 years, retiring in 1993 after a long stint as a second grade teacher in the East Allegheny School District. Hayes has the stuff that makes for good role models in the sports world, where it has become increasingly more difficult to find same, but when he was growing up he did not look far for standard-setters worthy of emulation.

"My true role models are my mother and father," said Hayes. "If it wasn't for them, I wouldn't be playing professional football. Kids need to find someone who is constantly an influence — not just during a sports season. And even though some come from broken families, there's always someone who can reach out to them. Athletes, like everyone else, are just people; they have their failures and the media will capitalize on them. Kids need to find someone in their daily lives, like a teacher or parent, to truly make a difference. They should always have at least one person who will reach out to them and, I hope, keep putting positive reinforcement in their minds.

"My grandparents lived next to a church and people would stop by thinking it was the pastor's house and ask for a meal or help. They couldn't tell them no, so they always gave to strangers. My mom is a teacher and is an incredibly giving person. Dad came from a large family and knows what it's like to share and give to others. It comes from my family. I've always been taught to give back to the community. It is really my family's attitude and commitment to helping others that keeps me involved."

Jonathan was the youngest of three boys in the Hayes family. His older brothers were Jeffrey and Jay. Their father, Jewett, introduced them all to sports. His brother Jay played for the Lions, the

312

Redskins and three years in the USFL and coached at Notre Dame and Wisconsin.

"Athletics ran in our family," said Jonathan. "Dad just felt that athletics was the way to keep us off the streets and out of trouble."

His dad played football, baseball and basketball. His mom was involved in track and field as a schoolgirl. The boys all took dance and piano lessons. One brother studied clarinet. They were encouraged to participate in extracurricular activities at school and in the community.

All three boys played football, baseball and basketball in high school. Jonathan was the captain of all three teams as a senior at South Fayette High School. He was president of the Monogram Club, secretary and treasurer of Key Club, and vice president of Student Council.

When he was growing up, Jonathan was a good friend of Ron Sams of Bridgeville, who played football at Pitt and in the NFL with the Green Bay Packers, Minnesota Vikings and New York Jets, and with Doug Kotar of Muse, who played football at the University of Kentucky and with the New York Giants, and died tragically of a brain tumor while with the Giants.

Jerry Zeman was the coach at South Fayette from 1977 until 1980. The team, led by Hayes, won the West Hills Conference and qualified for the playoffs with an 8-1-1 record in 1980. "He had the best work ethic in high school," said Zeman. "He worked in the pre-season and off-season with weights and running. His work ethic is great, but he does have a lot of good abilities, too."

In the high school yearbook, there were some bits and pieces that drew a picture of Hayes. His nicknames were Jewett and Jon. His sayings were: "This is true." And "Don't do it!" He had a dog named Champ. He listed his favorite teams, incredibly enough, as the Steelers and Chiefs.

He said he loved his family.....and among the "likes" he listed were making a good play, considerate people, steak, ice cream, the football parties. His dislikes were people who think they know it all, pushy people, navy beans, lima beans, cold food.

He dreamed about being a pro athlete:

"As an athlete in high school it's always in the back of your head," Hayes said. "I played baseball, basketball and football and I enjoyed them all. But you never know what's going to happen because there's so much time between then and now; you can never tell. I thought my future might be in baseball."

From South Fayette, he matriculated to the University of Iowa. He played linebacker his first two seasons at Iowa and then switched positions. He played offense and defense in the same game while at Iowa. He was a favorite target of All-American quarterback Chuck Long and was a first team Gannett All-American after catching 39 passes his senior season.

Barry Alvarez, originally from Burgettstown in southwestern Pennsylvania, was his linebacker coach at Iowa. Jonathan's brother Jay joined Alvarez as an assistant when Alvarez became the head coach at Wisconsin.

Hayes was the first tight end taken in the 1985 draft, a second round selection and the 42nd choice overall, by the Kansas City Chiefs. He played for John Mackovic, then Frank Gansz and, finally, Marty Schottenheimer at K.C. He started 96 of 136 regular season games while with the Chiefs. He was primarily a blocking tight end, and thought to be just a fair pass-catcher. Hayes has always felt that had he been used differently he would have had a better reputation as a receiver.

"It's a fine line between being a good tight end and a great tight end," said Hayes. "A great tight end is one who persists and prepares better than anyone else. Great tight ends are utilized in the passing game."

The Chiefs wanted to keep him, and were willing to resign him, but he jumped at the opportunity to play in Pittsburgh. The Steelers offered him a three-year $1.2 million deal, and the Chiefs offered to match it. He said he wanted to be closer to his parents. Yet he continues to reside in the off-season at his ranch just south of Kansas City.

"I have five horses, all quarter horses, five dogs, cats, and the geese that land on the lake," he said.

He trained his horses for cutting competition. A cutting horse is trained to maneuver through a herd of cattle and pick out a steer. He rides horses in competition.

When he was at Kansas City. he worked with the Chiefs Academic Corps. He worked with youngsters in K.C.'s inner-city schools, emphasizing the benefits of working hard in high school and trying to achieve success in school that will lead to success later in life. He spoke at all sorts of school assemblies, speaking out against illegal drugs.

"It's so easy to turn your head, but there's always someone out there that needs help," he said.

He also formed his own kids' group, called "Hayes Huddle." These were mainly high school sophomores. "We talk to them about achievement, setting goals, self respect," he said. "We talk to them about how they have to take pride in themselves before other people will respect them. We need to help them. I'm not talking about a handout, but an opportunity to stand on common ground with everyone else and to do their best.

"We try to make them understand that sometimes the easy way out is not the best way. That sitting back and getting marginal grades, cutting up and being the class clown is not the way to achieve their goals. That it's important that they work hard, buckle down, get their lessons, do the extra things in school."

He was nominated by the Chiefs as NFL Man of the Year. That award goes each year to the NFL player whose dedication to community service as well as on-the-field performance shows an outstanding balance for civic and professional responsibilities.

"Marty didn't want Bill taking me away."
— Jonathan Hayes

As a youngster, Hayes used to travel with his brothers and friends to see the Steelers practice at St. Vincent College. He can remember sitting on the hillside at the campus in Latrobe. When he was in college, he got to know a few of the Steelers who worked out together, Tunch Ilkin, Ted Petersen and Craig Wolfley.

When he was with the Chiefs, one of Schottenheimer's assistants was Bill Cowher. The Chiefs quarterbacks were Joe Montana and Steve Bono. Montana was from Monongahela, Pennsylvania, and Bono had played for the Steelers, so there was plenty of conversation of topics familiar to Hayes.

Hayes hauled in two passes in the Chiefs' 27-24 overtime victory over the Steelers in a 1993 wildcard playoff game.

He signed with the Steelers in July of 1994. "I had worked with Bill and he knew me and was comfortable with me," said Hayes. "Marty and he are good friends, and Marty didn't want Bill taking me away."

His older brother Jay was at St. Vincent that same summer, working with the Steelers on an NFL internship for minority college coaches. Hayes had been a childhood friend of Marvin Lewis, the linebackers coach of the Steelers from McDonald.

When he had come to the Steelers' camp as a high school student, Hayes went home with quite a few signatures one year. He was disappointed that he didn't get the signature of center Mike Webster.

Webster was a player and coach with the Chiefs when Hayes was playing there. Hayes told Webster the story of how he once turned him down for an autograph at the Steelers' camp. When Hayes went to his locker later in the day, there was a signed photo of Webster waiting for him.

"It was probably a zillion degrees out (that day in the '70s)," recalled Hayes, "and Mike said, 'I'll catch you later.' Well, I got it later, 15 years later. That was fine. It still worked out."

Asked to characterize Cowher, he said, "I see Bill is the same straightshooter that he's always been. He's going to tell you like it is. If he doesn't like what you're doing, he'll tell you. And if he's happy with how you're performing, he'll tell you that, too. I think that's all you can ask from a coach.

315

"I have a lot of respect for him. He's a man of his word and that's all you can ask for as a player.

"He's always been a very enthusiastic person; he gets after it. I have a lot of respect for a guy that young becoming a head coach in the NFL. I think he's done a great job. He allows his players to express themselves, but not to the point of wondering who's running the asylum. We do have a bunch of characters on this team."

At 33, following a decade in the pros, Hayes said the music, clothes, hairstyles and attitudes had all changed since he came out of college. "I can barely relate," he said. "And the way they dress; the players are more flamboyant.

"Back when I broke in, players played first and worried about getting paid second. I don't know now. I don't think it's affected the way the game is played, but there's a different approach to the game. I guess you just have to keep adjusting to it, or you'll get left behind. You have to be a professional and remember why you're here. We don't get paid to play; we get paid to win.

"There's so much money in the game now. Some guys don't think they have to pay their dues. Some guys try to get the paycheck without doing the work. I was taught to do an honest day's work. When I broke in, older guys would bust their butts in practice. They said, 'Hey, we set the standards here.' There's no limitations to how hard you can work.

"A lot of people like being professional football players, but they don't want to be professional. They're doing it in a fashion.

"You should always be on time. You should know your assignments. My dad and mom never missed a day of work. I remember talking to Joe Greene about this. He talked about the importance of treating the equipment people and the trainers with respect. You should be a man and do what's right, and be courteous to others."

"He is one of those very rare people who is dedicated to giving back to society."
— David Donahue

The Pittsburgh regional chapter of the American Diabetes Association chose Hayes as the first volunteer worker they wanted to recognize at what they said would be an annual reception, Tribute for Distinguished Service to the Cause of Diabetes.

He was honored at the Pittsburgh Public Theatre on June 4, 1996. The event was tied in with the premiere performance of the play "Jitney" by Pulitzer Prize-winning playwright August Wilson. Wilson spent his formative years in The Hill District and my hometown of Hazelwood. He's written about his teen years when he recalls traveling from Hazelwood to Pitt Stadium and Forbes Field to see his favorite ballplayer, Jim Brown, perform for the Cleveland Browns against the Pittsburgh Steelers. He lives in Seattle, but most of his subject material is drawn from his days in Pittsburgh.

Explaining his group's choice, David Donahue, Regional Director for ADA, offered this tribute to Hayes: "He works six days a week from early morning until late at night and he spends his only day off helping people with diabetes. If he's not talking to children and their families at Children's Hospital, posing for photo shoots for our ads, signing books at Barnes & Noble, or talking to the media about diabetes, then he's off sharing his time, treasures and talents to help in some other way."

Hayes had an easy explanation for his zealot approach to the cause. He liked to help where help was needed. He felt grateful to those who helped him along the way.

"I don't think diabetes should stop you from doing anything," he said. "We're all dealt a hand in life and I think it's the people who can adjust, who cope and understand what they've been dealt — they are the ones who are going to succeed. The failures are the ones who can't get past it and they feel that someone owes them something now that life's a little harder....

"No one says life is going to be easy; that it's just going to be a walk in the park and you're not going to have any problems. If that was the case, then everyone could do it and there wouldn't be any problems in the world.

"You have to realize, 'I'm going to have some setbacks, but I'm not going to let them set me back; I'm still going to go on and reach my goal.' I think everyone has to feel that way.

"I just think if you have a goal, you shouldn't let anything stop you from attaining it."

Jewett, Jay with daughter, Florence and Jonathan Hayes at Steelers' training camp at St. Vincent in Latrobe. Jay was there in 1994 on NFL internship for minority college coaches.

Erric Pegram
In the footsteps of Tony Dorsett

"Not everything is going to go perfect in life."

As a youngster playing pickup football games in the projects of West Dallas, Texas, Erric Pegram pretended to be Tony Dorsett, the great running back of the Dallas Cowboys.

Erric Demont Pegram prematurely suited up for a kids' team at age 5 after his father agreed to take out an insurance policy on him when Erric was given a chance to play before he was old enough to qualify. He was playing with and against kids seven and eight years old, but he scored a touchdown the first time he touched the ball in a real game, and he had been running for paydirt ever since.

Football fields and playgrounds were usually the easiest and safest places for Pegram to operate back then. His neighborhood was not on the right side of the railroad tracks. Every time Pegram left his home there was an opportunity to get into trouble. Life in the project in West Dallas was a constant challenge.

"I was surrounded by alcohol and drugs," said Pegram. "The project was my life; I was surrounded by drug dealers. They were the big guys in the neighborhood; everybody knew them."

Pegram knew the difference between Dorsett and Duney and Snoop, some of the neighborhood street guys who got into trouble with the law routinely, and he was smart enough and athletic enough to walk the tightwire between right and wrong. Duney and Snoop sound like rap stars, but they were strictly bad news. Pegram picked his heroes carefully, and became one himself, with heroic action in a neighborhood crisis and more often for what he did on the local football fields.

His parents were helpful to him in that regard, and his coaches recognized something special in him before he even entered grade school, so sports provided a solid support system.

Imagine how Pegram must have felt, shortly after turning 27, to be playing for the Pittsburgh Steelers against the Dallas Cowboys in Super Bowl XXX.

"I was a Cowboy fan and Tony Dorsett was my idol," Pegram recalled of his childhood. "I was aware they had a rivalry with Pittsburgh, and I used to hate the Steelers."

Strangely enough, Pegram was pictured at seven different points in his early days in football in photos provided by his father, and he was seen wearing seven different uniform numbers, but none of them was Dorsett's No. 33.

Dorsett, of course, had won the Heisman Trophy in leading the University of Pittsburgh to a national title in 1976, and had gone on to be named to both the college and pro football Hall of Fame in the same year — 1994.

Erric's wife, Sonja, his high school sweetheart, gave birth on January 14, 1996, to their second daughter, Taylor, to go with five-year-old Alexandra, and Pegram promised to provide the same sort of solid and disciplined home that helped him get off to a good start. The baby was born during the Steelers' AFC championship game victory over the Indianapolis Colts, and Pegram rushed from Three Rivers Stadium to join his family at Sewickley Valley Hospital.

Pegram became a popular player in his first season with the Steelers, and the picture of him holding his newborn baby beside his wife at the hospital only added to his appeal. Pittsburgh provided Pegram with an opportunity to restore the shine to his pro career after he had lost his starting position with the Atlanta Falcons to Craig "Ironhead" Heyward, another former Pitt running back.

Pegram signed with the Steelers as an unrestricted free agent, picking them over the Cleveland Browns because he thought they had a better chance of contending for a championship, and it was another great move on Pegram's part. He was a positive, upbeat, team-oriented guy who got along great with the media because he was always approachable and quotable. He had taken over the dressing stall once occupied by Barry Foster, who refused to talk to the media most of the time. Foster had an official-looking sign posted at his dressing stall that said **"Positively No Visitors,"** so Pegram was quite a contrast in that regard.

He not only replaced Barry Foster, but also "Frenchy" Fuqua, in a sense. When Fuqua was a running back with the Steelers in the mid-70s, he used to have competitions with L.C. Greenwood in the locker room to determine who was the best-dressed Steeler. Pegram competed with Brentson Buckner in similar "dress-off" competitions. In short, he quickly got into the spirit of things with his teammates.

Most of the time, anyhow. Pegram teamed with Bam Morris to give the Steelers a 1-2 running punch that nicely balanced the air attack in a highly sophisticated offense orchestrated by quarterback Neil O'Donnell during the 1995 season.

Pegram had his ups and downs with the Steelers, as did Morris, but he had learned that this was what life was all about a long time ago. Unlike Morris, he was fortunate enough not to get into any trouble with the law relating to drugs. Pegram had learned as a child that alcohol and drugs did not mix well with athletics and career success. Some have managed to pull it off, but more have stumbled and fallen and never realized their potential because of off-the-field problems.

"Life is full of highs and lows, so I try not to get too high or too low," explained Pegram. "Not everything is going to go perfect in life. You've got to go with the flow."

In an interview in the Steelers' locker room on November 29, 1995, Pegram talked to us about his early life.

He was born in a West Dallas housing project, and took pride in his ability to resist the temptations of the streets. He was described as "a hungry kid." He wanted nice things, like the drug peddlers had, but he didn't want to come by them in the same way. At age 25, he was driving a huge black 1971 Cadillac because "it was good enough for Sidney Poitier and Bill Cosby." As a youngster, Pegram saw a movie called "Uptown Saturday Night" in which Cosby and Poitier drove a 1971 Cadillac, and he was captivated by their choice of wheels. He still had that Cadillac in 1996.

"Everybody knew I was Tony Dorsett."
— Erric Pegram

Billy Ray Pegram pulled a power play to get his son, Erric, an early entree into organized football. Erric was too young, at age 5, to be eligible, but his father told the coach that if Erric couldn't play, then he wouldn't permit two of his older brothers, Vic and Chris, to play, either. The coach relented, telling the father he'd have to take out a special insurance policy on his son since the league's policy would not cover him. That was no problem for Billy Ray Pegram.

"I was the youngest on the team," recalled Erric. "They gave me a uniform; I hardly did anything. I worked out every day, but I seldom got to play in the games. The first time I did carry the ball I ran for a touchdown. My daughter is that age now, and I can't imagine playing football at five."

He thought he was about seven when he first came to know Tony Dorsett. He wanted to run the ball like No. 33.

"Any time I'd play, as a kid, as soon as the game was done on TV, we'd run out in the street and play football. Everybody knew I was Tony Dorsett. Someone else would be Drew Pearson or Tony Hill. Someone would shout, 'I'm Golden Richards.' But I was always Tony. I loved his style. Tony D. was my man. A friend of mine, Benny Singleton, was always Robert Newhouse."

The real hero in his life back then, though he didn't know it at the time, was Billy Ray Pegram.

"My friends had fathers, but they weren't at their homes," said Erric Pegram. "They had broken homes. No one had a mother and a father together. As a kid, you take some things for granted.

"My father didn't want me getting involved with alcohol or drugs. My father really stressed that. My mom never thought I'd do it. I didn't have my first drink until I got to college. I was 18 when I had my first drink. It never appealed to me. I don't know how people drink. My father was always questioning me. 'You don't drink, do you? Drinking and drugs ain't nothing. You don't need that,' my father would say."

rric Pegram, at age 10, shows off ish catch at South Padre Island, ff coast of Texas.

Billy Ray Pegram, in tuxedo, is flanked by his four sons, left to right, Erric, Victor, Derric and Chris.

rric, at age 7, in Pop Warner football uniform

As 11th grader at Hillcrest High School

And Erric managed to avoid those pitfalls. Single-mindedness helped Pegram stay clean, but his father's strong hand often kept him from even considering trouble.

"The one person I could always depend on, and who was there to talk to was my father," said Erric.

"I knew he'd make me proud," said Billy Ray Pegram, who lived in Denton, 35 miles north of Dallas, and was among the Pegram contingent at Super Bowl XXX. "But he's made me doubly proud. Erric was born to play football. I never had any doubt. When he was sitting on the bench, I would tell him eventually they're going to let you play and they'll see your talent."

In addition to Vic and Chris, Erric also had a twin brother named Derric.

"My dad was always there to spend time with us." said Erric. "He would take us fishing or whatever. But he was tough."

His mother, Marian Pegram, worked in a government office, dealing with food stamps.

"She wouldn't let me play when I had bad grades," said Pegram. "If parents want to keep athletes in line all they have to do is not let them play if they are not doing well in school."

The threat of keeping him from football worked best as far as discipline was concerned. If Erric wasn't doing what was expected of him in school, he was warned that he would not be permitted to play football. It brought to mind that a former Steelers running back, Warren Williams of the University of Miami, often spoke about how his mother wouldn't let him suit up for a playoff game in high school because of a sub-par report card, and how he became a more serious student from that day on. Williams credited his mother with his graduating with a degree from Miami, a real point of pride with him.

"To take football away from him would be like taking candy from a baby," said Pegram's father. "He had the right attitude."

It was difficult to keep Erric Pegram from playing. There was the time at Hillcrest High School in Dallas that he played with a broken arm (removing his cast without his father's knowledge and clumsily rewrapping the break). He scored three touchdowns , running the last one in backward.

Pegram wanted to win a college scholarship, and no one was going to stop him.

"My advice to kids is to stay focused on what you want to do. For me, it was football. Focus on what you want and nothing can stop you.

"I met my wife when she was 15 years old. She already had plans for her life. I knew that if I was going to keep her I needed to have plans for my life."

Pegram was urged to reflect on those days in the West Dallas project. I asked him to recall some vivid memories of life in his neighborhood when he was a kid.

"You always knew who was who," he said. "It was just a big grapevine; one big world going by itself. You knew where the drug houses were, where 'the candy lady' lived. I wasn't ever in that mode. But some of my friends were. They were buying or selling it for them. It was all about money.

"One of my best friends, Steve, had a brother who was involved in drugs. Steve never was. He was always the good brother. Steve's brother was in and out of jail; he was in all kinds of trouble. Steve and I were about 17 at the time..."

"I remember this time when I saw Steve's brother and he'd just gotten out of the pen. He did eight years. He had just gotten out, mind you. And he was pistol-whipping somebody in the street. Steve's brother's name was Snoop and he was cool. He was whipping this guy named Duney. He said he whipped him for taking his jam box. Duney was 50 or 60 or something, and Snoop was about 30. I got so scared; I thought Snoop was going to kill him. I hollered, 'Snoop, maybe he didn't do it!' And Snoop snapped at me. 'You don't know me, do you?' He scared me to death. He was waving a gun in the air, and I knew I was going to die right on the spot. He looked like he was ready to rip into me.

"Later, during that same day, after everything calmed down, I saw Snoop again, and this time he had a girl on the hood of the car and he was trying to rape her. Right there in the street.

"The whole world was one big obstacle for him. I think he was trying to get back in the can. He was trying to get sex. The police came and got him. He went back to the pen.

"There was another thing that happened that was profound in my youth. I was riding with my mom in her car. She was taking me to school. We saw a house on fire. 'Do you think anyone knows the house is on fire?' I asked her. She said, 'I don't know.' And I said, 'Mom, wait!' She stopped the car and I got out and went and pounded on the door. I heard screaming inside. I busted down the door. There was a Mexican family in there. This guy grabs me as I go into the house. He hollers, 'Help me get my family out of here.' I saw a rat that big — nearly a foot long — jump out of the fire. I'm grabbing kids. Passing them out. I never thought that much about it. There were birds and stuff, all kinds of stuff in that house. There were at least four kids, small children, a baby. It was this Mexican man and his kids; it was weird. We took them to our house. I got some ink in the paper over that."

Living in a project was all that Pegram knew, and he was not complaining. He had good parents and he enjoyed his friends and the games they played in the project playground. He was also grateful for his coaches when he was just getting started, Larry Oliver and Kenneth Sparks.

"Later on, you realize you're in a poor environment, but you didn't need much anyhow. We had food and friends and play. I don't want anybody being in the projects using it as an excuse for not being successful in life.

"I always felt I was going to accomplish something special in sports. I've been saying since I was a kid that I'd be playing pro football. Later, I said, 'If I ever get the opportunity I'm going to make it.' As a grownup, you realize that such a small percentage of players get picked to play in the NFL."

Pegram did point out that Dennis Rodman, the controversial badboy-rebounder supreme of the NBA, came from a nearby neighborhood.

Pegram felt his parents provided a framework for him and his brothers to keep them busy and out of trouble.

"I am a strong believer in household discipline," said Pegram. "That's the way I am. I don't want my daughters acting up or misbehaving. I just give Alexandra a look and she knows to settle down.

"Just being a kid, you want to do things your own way. I can't sit here and tell you I was any different. When I was young, I didn't like rules. You want to go and come as you please.

"I'm going to raise my daughters with discipline. It's going to be my way. It's not going to be my way or the highway, but they'll have to respect me for having rules for them. I can't stand to see kids out of line. Some parents don't discipline their children. Nowadays, everyone is reading books about how to raise children. Old-fashioned discipline should also be used."

"Don't quit until the whistle blows."
— Erric Pegram

Pegram's best game in his first season with the Steelers may have been a nationally-televised Sunday evening game with the Bears at Chicago Stadium. He scored three touchdowns for the first time in his pro career. He rushed for two of them, which was a career best, and caught a seven-yard pass from Neil O'Donnell for another. That was the first TD pass he had ever caught and it came after he had, first, tossed a block and was face down on the field. He got off the ground, slipped into the end zone and waved to O'Donnell. It was a great second effort on Pegram's part to get up and get back into the play. Pegram provided O'Donnell with an unexpected option. Pegram had gotten up off the field after throwing a block and had thrown a second block in a sequence earlier in the same contest. The Steelers won a thriller, 37-34. It was one of the big games that helped the team turn things around at midseason.

I asked Pegram about those second-effort plays, one of which resulted in a big touchdown.

"I just think you should get back up and keep going," he explained. "When I got up, Neil was scrambling, he saw me and tossed me the ball. It's an example of the old stuff of 'never quit, don't stop until the whistle blows.'"

I asked him where he learned that. He said a lot of coaches had told him that, but it really hit home, he said, when Jerry Rice, the great receiver for the San Francisco 49ers, came to the North Texas State University campus to shoot a movie when Pegram was still playing there.

"I hadn't even seen an NFL game in person at that point in my life, but I knew Jerry Rice to see. I approached him and asked him for some tips. He told me several things. 'When you feel that you have done enough, you haven't.' 'When you think that you're in the best possible shape, you're not.' He practices and works so hard at his game, other players talk about that.

"I saw him and Herschel Walker and Dick Butkus and Tony Dorsett. They were all there for this movie shoot. My favorite was Tony D, so I had to say something to Tony D — I think he knew he was my idol. Being from down south, I never paid much attention to college football in other parts of the country. So I never knew Tony Dorsett until he got to Dallas. That was the first time I saw him in person. The movie was called 'Necessary Roughness' and those guys all had cameo roles."

North Texas State was Joe Greene's old school, located in Denton. Pegram said a No. 78 jersey that had belonged to Joe was displayed in a big trophy case on the campus filled with memorabilia just of Joe Greene.

During his days at North Texas State, Pegram put up great numbers, to little acclaim off campus. He led the Mean Green with 957 yards and 56 receptions, while ranking second in the Southland Conference in both rushing and receiving. He had been recruited out of high school by both Nebraska and Oklahoma, but chose to stay close to home.

He didn't know for sure whether he would be selected in the NFL's college draft, so he went fishing on the day of the draft with his backfield coach at North Texas State — former Steeler receiver Ron Shanklin.

"I thought I might get a shot as a free agent. I had played only one full year in college, so I didn't know how good my chances would be. But I knew that if I got a shot, I would make it," said Pegram.

Shanklin had lined up with Franco Harris and Walter Payton of the Bears during his own NFL career, and he thought Pegram could play with the best of them. He once said that Pegram would be mentioned in the same breath as those ballplayers some day.

"His center of gravity is so deceptive," said Shanklin to pro scouts who came to check out the talent. "He also has superior body strength, a lot like Walter Payton."

Shanklin taught Pegram a valuable lesson: "Be ready to play when the opportunity comes."

Pegram points to Shanklin as a real positive influence in his life. "He got me mentally ready for the pros," said Pegram. "He told me what to expect. He always makes me feel better. He told me how to approach it. He made me a smart player."

Pegram was picked in the sixth round of the 1991 draft by the Atlanta Falcons. He was third in the Atlanta pecking order at running back, behind Steve Broussard and Mike Rozier. He started seven regular season games and two playoff games that year.

Pegram managed 349 yards on 101 carries that rookie season. He didn't see much action in his second year, carrying the ball only 21 times for 89 yards.

The Falcons had brought in older running backs like Eric Dickerson and Mike Rozier, and they had first round picks like Broussard and Tony Smith. "I knew I was better than those guys who were being used ahead of me," said Pegram.

In his third season, Pegram broke out and rushed for 1,185 yards and averaged 4.1 yards per carry in 1993. During that big year, he had four games over 100 yards, including a 192-yard performance against the San Francisco 49ers, the best one game rushing performance ever against the 49ers.

The thing Pegram was proudest of was that he earned everything the hard way. "I wasn't like Steve Broussard or Eric Dickerson and Tony Smith — guys who got big money up front and who kept getting second and third chances," said Pegram.

When Jerry Glanville got fired following that 1993 season, however, new coach June Jones decided to go with a bigger back in a run-and-shoot, and Pegram was replaced by Craig "Ironhead" Heyward. Jones said Pegram didn't fit into his plans.

"Glanville gave me a chance to start," said Pegram, "and I was grateful for that. A lot of people say bad things about Jerry, but he gave me my opportunity to make my first 1,000-yard season. In fact, Glanville gave me the chance to play pro ball; everybody was trying to cut me and send me off, but Jerry said 'no.'"

Pegram does not even have any hard feelings toward Heyward.

"He had some athletic ability, and I'm proud of him for the things he's done," said Pegram. "Craig is doing great. He's straightened out his life. God's looking after him now. They gave him my job. It all ended up well. Craig is with a better team and he has a better life. It's given him a chance to turn his life around."

Was Pegram a pretty good guy or what? He was pretty positive about a lot of his former teammates. During the week before Super Bowl XXX, many members of the media asked Pegram what his former Falcons' teammate "Neon Deion" Sanders was really like.

Pegram played three years (1991-93) with Deion in Atlanta, and they used to hang out together quite a lot.

Most fans either really like Sanders or they really dislike him, and much of the division is along age lines. The kids get a kick out of Sanders' shenanigans and the oldsters are often turned off.

"Deion's quite a guy," said Pegram. "That's what a lot of people don't know. The 'Neon' stuff is public persona. He's a different kind of guy in front of the camera than he is personally. He's soft-spoken. He's really a nice guy and that's what a lot of people just don't know about him."

Erric Pegram was proud figure in Steelers' clubhouse.

Pegram shares exciting moment with teammate Yancey Thigpen.

Sanders spent a season with the San Francisco 49ers, helping them win the Super Bowl, and then signed with the Cowboys for six seasons for $35 million, $13 million in upfront bonus. Many of his critics said Sanders shied away from tackling ballcarriers. They conceded that he could cover receivers with the best of them, but that he didn't want to risk his body by too much contact work.

"He's a hell of a practice player," pointed out Pegram. "He isn't just out there going through the motions. I know he doesn't hit, but he claims he's paid to cover. He has the capability to hit. He just doesn't do it."

"This offense is a running back's dream."
— Erric Pegram

Pegram signed as an unrestricted free agent with the Steelers on April 27, 1995. Once the Steelers had him it freed them to dump Barry Foster, whom they thought had a bad attitude and had lost his desire to play. They shopped Foster around the league and finally unloaded him on the Carolina Panthers. He was cut by the Panthers for the same reasons that the Steelers wanted to get rid of him. He later signed with the Cincinnati Bengals, but quit after the first workout because he was badly out of shape and lacked the spirit to continue.

Pegram was eager to play for anyone, and especially for the Steelers. "I knew I was coming here as soon as they asked," he said. At the outset of the season, he said, "This offense is a running back's dream.

"You don't walk into everybody's offices and there's four Super Bowl trophies. You just know you're going to win."

After an early scrimmage, Pegram said, "I gave them what they wanted — speed, versatility and dependability. That's what they wanted to see and that's what I wanted to show them. I don't plan to sit on anybody's bench and I do mean that."

Pegram was pitted against Bam Morris, a second-year running back, to see who would start. They ended up splitting time in most games. It depended on who was hot and who was not. "As far as Bam and me," said Pegram, "there's no sense quarreling; we don't make the decisions."

Pegram's place in the locker room was Foster's old dressing stall, next to Woodson, just outside of Tony Parisi's workshop. "We've never had a running back with Pegram's speed," Woodson said. He was, indeed, the Steelers' fastest runner and a rock hard 5-10, 185 pounds. He could cut to the outside and elude tacklers. Morris was more of a power runner.

Pegram signed a three-year contract with Steelers. It included a $125,000 signing bonus and annual salaries of $550,000, $625,000 and $725,000. His cap value for 1995 was $592,000.

The 1995 season was a rebirth for Pegram. He rushed for a team-high 813 yards and five touchdowns, his best since 1993 with the Falcons. He was in and out with Morris. He missed the season finale with Green Bay because of sore ribs he picked up in the New England game the week before.

Morris was the leading rusher the first four games until Pegram took over as the starter with a 95-yard effort in a win over San Diego. Pegram was confident he could help the Steelers as a pass catcher coming out of the backfield as well. "If the ball is in my vicinity I'm going to catch it," he said. He was willing to sacrifice his body for the good of the team.

"Everybody wants to run the ball, but if you're going to be a complete back, you have to block, too," he said. "I want to be the workhorse. I want them to use me in every way possible."

"If you watch him block on film," said teammate Jonathan Hayes, "you'll see he's not afraid to bloody somebody's nose. He's so shifty, but he's really strong for a little guy."

Bill Cowher was patient with Morris and Pegram when they fumbled the ball. Cowher sent Pegram back in after he fumbled against Oakland. "I told him to keep his head up after the fumble, and that nobody's lost confidence in him," said Bill Cowher. And Cowher's vote of confidence meant a lot to Pegram.

Pegram wore a Pirates cap backwards on the sideline. He tried to put his football helmet on over top of it in his excitement at one game. "I felt a little foolish," he said.

He chose to play in the AFC championship game even though his wife was due to have a baby that day at a nearby hospital. He had her blessings. "At half time, a ballboy told me my wife had a baby," said Pegram. "I couldn't go to the hospital with a loss. I thought I'd had a heart attack on that final play of the game until I knew for sure that the Colts hadn't come up with the ball in the end zone. When it was quiet, my heart probably jumped out of my body. Then there was this big roar and I knew he had missed the ball and the ref made the signal and I think I went berserk."

After the game with Indianapolis, Pegram went to Sewickley Valley Hospital where his wife, Sonja, had given birth to their second daughter, Taylor. He got to the hospital in a hurry and held the baby for everyone with a camera who came calling from the local media outlets.

"I had asked Sonja if I should play and she said, 'Of course, you should play.' I wanted to play, but I wanted to do what was right at the same time. She told me to go play the game and win it for her."

Cowher told me the decision was up to me. "He asked me if I wanted to miss the game and I said 'no,'" said Pegram. "I just think it was good of him to give me that option because it shows that he has some concern for my family and my well-being as well. It was great; I got a Super Bowl berth and a little girl as well."

Pegram said he was thinking positive thoughts when the Steelers got the ball for the final time against the Colts. "One thing I kept saying was, 'We've got to believe.' We were moving the ball on these guys, we just weren't getting in the endzone. So we got in there and the rest is history."

"All he's ever wanted was an opportunity."
— Bill Cowher

Pegram expressed his outlook on life in detail in an interview with Bob Labriola of *Steelers Digest:* "If I say I want the fame, I want the money, of course, everybody wants that, but that also comes with the territory. But what does that guy feel inside? How does he feel about his peers? His teammates? The difference between confidence and cockiness is respect for the players around you.

"Cockiness is all about 'me.' I want this. I want that. I,I,I. When you're confident, you tend to have respect for the players around you, and you realize it's going to take a team effort to get these things done. It's not just you. You do your part , Greg Lloyd does his part, Neil O'Donnell does his part, and so on and so on."

In several outings up to that point in the season, Pegram would pile up most of the rushing yardage and Morris would go in to punch it in from the two or one yard line. Pegram said he could live with that. "As a running back, if you ask me if I could have scored those touchdowns, I will say, 'of course.' But it's also good coaching to put the big guy in and let him bang it in there. It just makes sense. Besides that, it gives Bam a chance to play and get a feel for the game. We have to have that unified feeling at all times. It can never be, 'I want to do it all myself.' It has to be a unified effort."

Any observer of the Steelers scene would know that Pegram was the first to high-five Morris when he was coming off the field following one of those short-yardage TD dives.

Cowher appreciated Pegram's contribution, for certain: "This guy has come in here since Day One, and all he's ever wanted was an opportunity. This young man has made the most of every opportunity he has been given. I have a lot of respect for him, and I think he gave this team a lift that was needed at the right time."

Pegram pointed out, though, that any running back believes he needs more work to be at his best. "If you give me the ball enough I am going to make it happen," he said. "No back in the league can do well if he doesn't carry the ball 20 or more times. That goes for Barry Sanders or Emmitt Smith. Sometimes you carry the ball three or four or even five times and nothing will happen. I've got to carry the ball 25 or 26 times a game to be at my best."

Otherwise, he said his goals were simple: "I want success on the field, camaraderie in the locker room and, most importantly, plenty of time with my family."

Kordell Stewart
They call him "Slash"

"I want to be a quarterback.
That's why I'm here."

Bill Cowher gave him a chance to play and a nickname that will serve him in good stead for the rest of his life. But Kordell Stewart wanted more. Everyone associated with the Steelers recognized that Stewart was a superb athlete, but he was still the No. 4 quarterback and had not played a down when Cowher called upon him in several roles to help salvage the 1995 season that was fast going down the tubes after a disappointing 3-4 start.

Stewart was pressed into service as a spare receiver for the scout team at practice when Johnnie Barnes injured his knee in a September 13 game at Miami. Stewart was so good at catching passes, while posing as an opposing receiver in workouts, that Cowher and his assistants, Ron Erhardt and Chan Gailey, thought he was too good to remain on the sideline for the real stuff.

At first, Stewart was simply catching passes at practice. But he was too good to keep under wraps. "Nobody could cover him," said Tom Donahoe, director of football operations for the Steelers.

So Stewart became a multi-purpose offensive weapon, someone who could line up just about anywhere and work some magic. He could play quarterback — as he did with distinction the year before at Colorado — running back, wide receiver and he could even punt. Cowher would employ him for a third down quick kick in one contest and Kordell came through with flying colors. He was an exciting throwback to another era.

It was fun for the fans, wondering what he would do next, and fun for the coaches, coming up with different schemes to surprise the enemy with Kordell as the key to five-receiver formations and all sorts of mischief.

Kordell kept reminding everyone that eventually he wanted to be the quarterback of the Steelers, the No. 1 quarterback that is, and he wanted the job even if Neil O'Donnell decided he wanted to stay with the Steelers for the rest of his pro career.

This was strictly a temporary job. Yes, he could type, but he wanted to be a writer, not a secretary.

When Donahoe talked to Stewart at the scouting combine in Indianapolis prior to the 1995 college draft, he asked him if he would like to play any other position. "Absolutely not," Stewart told him. "I want to play quarterback."

Kordell was confident he could do the job. This kid believed in himself and then some.

At his weekly press conference, Cowher kept getting asked about Stewart's status. "He's still a quarterback slash receiver," Cowher kept saying. That was later shortened to "Slash" and, as these things go, the rookie's odyssey took on a life of its own.

He became "Slash" Stewart. He smiled for the TV cameras, kept opposing coaches up late at night, linebackers and defensive backs back on their heels, and the fans jumping up and down in the stands, screaming for more "Slash" Stewart shenanigans.

As a quarterback/wide receiver, "Slash" Stewart took the NFL by storm, and started showing up regularly on national highlight shows. Myron Cope loved this kid and went crazy coming up with new adjectives to describe his heroics. "Slash" was becoming a star.

It was a great nickname. It might not have the staying power or punch of "Bullet Bill" Dudley, a triple-threat back of an earlier era in Steelers' history who made it to the Pro Football Hall of Fame, Dick "Night Train" Lane, "Bronko" Nagurski or Charlie "Choo-Choo" Justice, but it will hold its own against some early Steelers backs like Johnny "Zero" Clement, Johnny "Blood" McNally or Jim "Cannonball" Butler.

It started against the Jacksonville Jaguars at Three Rivers Stadium in the eighth game of the season.

The Steelers whipped the first-year expansion team 24-7, beating a team that had upset them earlier in the season in Florida, and O'Donnell was delighted afterward to discuss the "new gimmicks" the Steelers started employing to put some spark in their attack.

The most interesting gimmick of all was Cowher's use of Stewart on a third-and-2 from the Steelers 28. O'Donnell moved to wide receiver, and Stewart lined up in the shotgun and ran up the middle for 16 yards.

"I went up there like I had been there all day, and just took off," said Stewart. "I don't think too many people expected me to go up the middle."

As Jerry DiPaola wisely predicted in the *Pittsburgh Tribune-Review*, "The play did not lead to a touchdown, but it will keep defenses guessing the rest of the season."

It did that and more. Stewart added some dash and splash to the Steelers' offensive package, and helped spark the team to eight straight wins. There was some intrigue each time out as to how Stewart would be used. He was liable to line up just about anywhere, and no one — not even his coaches — knew what he would end up doing.

In the tenth game of the schedule, Stewart sparkled in a 20-3 victory over the Cleveland Browns on November 13, 1995, at Three Rivers Stadium. In the second quarter of a scoreless battle with their most bitter rival, the Steelers had a first down at the 2, but two running plays went nowhere.

George Gojkovich

George Gojkovich

Kordell "Slash" Stewart was named winner of the Joe Greene Award as Steelers' Rookie of the Year in 1995 after starring in several roles as an exciting triple-threat back.

George Gojkovich

Ron Erhardt, the offensive coordinator of the Steelers, oversees huddle with 1995's top two draft choices, quarterback Kordell Stewart, left, and tight end Mark Bruener. Erhardt was bitter about the way he was cut loose by Bill Cowher. "I just know you don't treat people that way," he said. "I think we did a tremendous job for him. We put him in four straight playoffs."

Cowher called a timeout and when the Steelers returned to the field, Stewart went into the shotgun at quarterback and O'Donnell split out wide left.

Stewart took the snap and rolled out to his right. He was looking for an open receiver, but couldn't find one. He ran about as far as he could go to the right side and ran out of room, so he reversed his field and went the other way. His receivers went with the flow. O'Donnell flashed open, but Stewart instead passed to Ernie Mills in the left corner of the end zone. The touchdown gave the Steelers the lead and the crowd went crazy.

It would have even been better had Stewart tossed the two-yard touchdown pass to O'Donnell. Stewart also ran an option play ten yards for a first down, ran three yards on a quarterback sneak for a first down and caught two passes for 21 yards and another first down.

"Obviously, Kordell played a big part in the offense and will continue to do so," said Cowher.

Stewart was succinct in expressing his feelings: "It feels good to be able to go out and contribute."

Stewart became a bonafide hero in Game 11 when, rallying from an 18-point deficit in the second half, O'Donnell passed to Stewart down the middle. The 23-year-old caught the ball, twisted away from a couple of would-be tacklers, and raced 71 yards to put the Steelers ahead for good, 35-31, on their way to a 49-31 triumph. It was the longest TD strike of the year for O'Donnell.

Dave Ailes, a veteran observer of the Steelers' scene and the sports editor of the *Pittsburgh Tribune-Review*, offered these thoughts in his column:

"Stewart is Pittsburgh's Santa Claus, a bearer of precious gifts for the streaking Steelers, the hottest story in the National Football League. There hasn't been so much enthusiasm, so much speculation, about a Steeler since Art Rooney Sr.'s people won a coin flip with George Halas's people for the right to draft Terry Bradshaw out of Louisiana Tech in 1970. All eyes train on No. 10 when he enters the huddle."

Ailes fell in love with Stewart. He said the Steelers could use him the way the Boston Celtics once used John Havlicek, coming off the bench to provide a boost.

Stewart flashed more of the same in ensuing games.

Defenders were unsure what he was out there for. In a 20-16 win over the Indianapolis Colts for the AFC title, Stewart's leaping catch of a 5-yard TD pass from O'Donnell put the Steelers ahead, 10-6 in the second quarter.

Stewart was not a factor in Super Bowl XXX, however, and dropped a critical pass midway through the third quarter that would have given the Steelers a first down. O'Donnell was intercepted on the next pass, and it was one of the turnovers that doomed the Steelers to defeat by the Dallas Cowboys. It led to a short touchdown run by Emmitt Smith and put the Cowboys ahead, 20-7.

Stewart didn't throw or catch any passes and ran the ball four times for 15 yards, the longest for seven yards. Some suspected Stewart was no longer a surprise and that the Cowboys had seen enough film of him to know how to properly defense him. That remained to be seen.

"Keep Kordell right where he is."
— Neil O'Donnell

During the off-season, I spoke to Neil O'Donnell over the telephone from the New York Jets minicamp on Long Island, and we got into a conversation about what the Steelers might do with their quarterback situation. He had some thoughts on the subject.

I passed along O'Donnell's remarks to Gailey, who had been promoted to offensive coordinator when Cowher chose not to keep Erhardt in that role. "I talked to Neil O'Donnell yesterday," I told Gailey. "He sends his regards. He said to keep Kordell right where he is."

Gailey grinned. "Neil is on a team that wants to beat us now," he said. "How do we know he's giving us his best advice?"

Gailey was going to have a tough time trying to decide whether to go with veteran Mike Tomczak, third-year candidate Jim Miller or Stewart at quarterback. He knew Stewart had the stuff to succeed somewhere, but wasn't sure where he could be most effective. Used the way he had been used as a rookie, "Slash" Stewart was something else, something few teams could claim.

Stewart wanted to call signals and be the man. He and Miller spent much of the so-called off-season with Gailey, going over the playbook, watching film and tossing passes in Three Rivers Stadium with anyone they could talk into running routes for them.

When he started gaining national stature as a pro, something he had also enjoyed at Colorado, Stewart spoke eagerly to the national news media.

"It's just a name Coach Cowher gave me," said 'Slash' himself. "It pretty much has gone not nationwide, but worldwide. I've just kept everything in perspective."

Stewart said he would like to have a sneaker line of his own someday. He was getting into the spirit of things, what pro athletes were most caught up with these days. His dark eyes sparkled when he considered his chances of someday demanding the kind of attention afforded to the likes of "Neon Deion" Sanders of the Cowboys, or Shaq and Michael in the NBA.

Stewart had shown enough to capture the fancy of a lot of folks. He had fans in the stands and fans in the broadcast booth, rival sidelines and his own clubhouse. Stewart became a hot item. Suddenly,

Steelers fans were showing up at the stadium wearing his No. 10 jersey. And "Slash" became a household word in the 'burgh, right up there with an "Iron" as a pause that refreshes.

"You never know where he's going to pop up," said ESPN analyst Joe Theismann.

"He's liable to do anything," said Jeff Fisher, Houston Oilers' head coach.

"He gave us a spark," said Dermontti Dawson, the Steelers' Pro Bowl center.

"You haven't even seen Kordell yet," said C.J. Johnson, Stewart's friend and former teammate at Colorado. "You see him doing different stuff, but he can make all those great plays as a quarterback. He just needs the ball in his hands."

Stewart beat out Mark Bruener, who started 11 games at tight end, and Brenden Stai who became a starting guard in the eighth game of the season.

Stewart wasn't surprised by what he achieved. This was no shy kid. "They're just letting me be me," he said. "I'm confident, relaxed. When I was in college I was relaxed and being myself."

He admitted he wasn't thrilled by his early season status. He didn't even suit up in the first five games of the season.

"I was on the down side," he said. "I've been fortunate to be called upon. I'm taking advantage of this opportunity."

Some suggested he might be foolhardy to risk his health as a wide receiver. Mark Malone, a former Steelers quarterback who had become an analyst for ESPN, questioned the wisdom. Malone had suffered a knee injury when he played wide receiver briefly with the Steelers early in his pro career.

Doug Williams, who once directed the Washington Redskins to a Super Bowl victory, said he wouldn't have taken the risk, during a network TV interview.

Cowboys offensive lineman Nate Newton said: "I really admire what he's doing. He's the most unselfish player on that team, I think. A lot of guys, especially black quarterbacks, they don't want to get labeled as anything else. Believe me, he's going through something."

Stewart didn't second-guess his decision. "It's just chances you take sometimes," said Stewart. "I know I'm taking a chance by being a receiver. I'm trying to make the most of it. When you're 3-4, you can't say nothing. What we were doing earlier wasn't working. So you have to do something else"

Two quarterbacks who were impressed with his ability were Troy Aikman of the Cowboys and O'Donnell, who talked about him at pre-Super Bowl XXX press meetings.

"I think he's extremely talented," said Aikman, "and he's a guy who obviously can do a lot of different things, a lot like Deion from that standpoint."

O'Donnell offered the following comment: "When Kordell came in here, everyone knew he could run. The thing that surprised me the most is how soft his hands are. He catches the ball extremely well and he finds a way to get open. Not many people are coaching him. They are just letting him go out there and find a way to get open. He's been a big benefit to our offense.

"They know Kordell's out there. It's just that we use him doing so many different things, it's hard to gang up on one play."

The comment that meant the most to him, however, was offered by Deion Sanders: "Kordell Stewart is a great individual...a great athlete...and he brings a lot of things to this game. I hope I don't get caught up watching him because he's a great player.

"I think the league has gotten a little boring in the last few years, and I think we need more players like Kordell," continued Sanders. "We need exciting guys — guys who can make the normal, everyday guy sit and fantasize — like a Kordell Stewart. That's what the league truly needs: a little more versatility and a little more freedom."

Stewart told newsmen that Sanders was a role model. So it had to be the highlight of the week for Stewart when he and Sanders met on a street in Scottsdale.

"When I spotted him, I was shocked to see him," said Stewart. "I wound up shaking his hand. I just wanted to have an opportunity to meet him."

"I was my Daddy's kid."
— Kordell Stewart

Stewart was born October 16, 1972 in New Orleans, one of America's most storied cities, the city of Mardi Gras, Super Bowls, Sugar Bowls, Tennessee Williams, Al Hirt and Pete Fountain and even Pete Maravich. Make that "Pistol Pete" Maravich, talk about great nicknames. New Orleans — "The Big Easy" — has always been a city of intrigue, interesting characters, a streetcar named Desire and saints come marchin' in. Mel Ott came out of nearby Gretna. Stewart starred at John Ehret High School in suburban Marrero, and was named New Orleans Player of the Year and Louisiana MVP in his senior year.

Stewart started young and he had his sights set on being a quarterback, right from the beginning.

"I started playing ball when I was a baby," he said during an interview at his station in the Steelers' clubhouse, in the deepest corner of the room. "I started playing basketball, football, running track, you name it, as a little kid. I was always out playing some kind of game. I was brought up like that. I was more of a Chicago Bear fan, a Walter Payton fan, when I was growing up.

"New Orleans, Louisiana is a big city, and I grew up close to the Mississippi River. It was a rough place, but you were OK as long as you knew everybody. People from outside sometimes posed a problem.

"My dad, his name is Robert, is a barber and a painter. My Mom is deceased. I was 11 years old when she died. From what I remember, I was sad because I didn't have a mom. I had a dad. I was my Daddy's kid, no doubt about it. He was there the whole time. He was a strict father. He gave me what I needed. He had me understand that if I wanted things I had to work for them. He never pushed me. He never let me get too down about anything, especially after my Mom died. He told me things happen for a reason. I have a brother, Robin, and a little sister, Felicia; she's the baby."

"I have my own style."
— Kordell Stewart

Kordell Stewart was a star at Colorado as well, but took a back seat to Tommy Frazier of Nebraska in national regard. He was best remembered for coming through with one of the most miraculous game-winning touchdown throws in college history at the end of the 1994 season. He threw a "Hail Mary" pass to Michael Westbrook in the endzone on the final play of the Michigan game. His 64-yard scoring strike gave Colorado a 27-26 win over Michigan with six seconds left in the nationally-televised game. The ball traveled about 73 yards in the air.

The play was called Rocket Left. It was one of the most dramatic finishes in college football history.

So Stewart knew what it was like to be in the national limelight before he suited up for the Steelers for Super Bowl XXX. He was a big hit in mass interviews on January 23-24 in Arizona.

"I feel I'm more valuable as a quarterback than just a receiver," he said. "It's just a matter of time when I have the opportunity to get out and run the offense. In due time, I'll be able to get out there and have as much fun (at quarterback) as I'm having at receiver."

On comparisons with Cowboys' Deion Sanders, he said: "He and I, I guess you could say, are multi-talented players. It kind of goes together a little bit, but he has his own quality and I have my own style. I play quarterback; he doesn't play quarterback. I think I have the edge."

Asked if he had any previous experience as a pass-catcher, he said, "Just messing around with my brother. I never actually did it in a game. No...never."

It was just a stepping stone in his career, as he saw it. He wanted to be a quarterback.

"That's something I want to do. You may be a successful sportswriter, but you may have something else that you may love. That something else may be in the future that you want to do. That's my situation. I'm just part of what's going on right now.

"I was just sitting back and waiting for my time. It was a hard time for me. I tried to handle it the best way possible, which I think I did. After coming from Colorado and having such a great career there, it was a transition for me. I wouldn't say I was getting impatient. I'm not a down person, but I just wanted to go out and do something. I felt that as a young kid coming up I did a lot of things — basketball, track, baseball, football and things like that — and I felt like I was capable of doing whatever was being asked of me except playing defensive line, linebacker and offensive line. If they would have asked me to do anything like they are doing right now, I would have said yes. And by me saying yes, I have the opportunity to play in the big one.

"It just gives me the opportunity to let my talents go. It gives the opportunity to go one-on-one with a man and do all I can, just use my ability, do what I was brought up doing, which was being an all-around player."

Did he ever think this would happen? Was it something of a fantasy?

"I won't say it's a fantasy. I'm not trying to be cocky, but I feel when people work real hard, you get the best things. I feel I personally worked hard and so did this team. After being 3-4, we could have easily laid down and said, 'Hey, the season is over. We might as well go ahead and work for next season.' But every person on this team knew that we were capable of doing whatever we wanted to do. In mini-camp and training camp, we all said we wanted to take it to the big one.

"I feel every player here is a blessed player, in my opinion. Not too many guys get this opportunity to be an entertainer, that's what you can call us, or have the opportunity to make it to something nice like this — the Super Bowl."

Sanders had suggested that the league needed more players like "Neon Deion" and "Slash" Stewart to keep up with some other pro sports as far as imagination and marketing were concerned. Stewart drew great satisfaction from bringing some life to the league. He liked all the attention.

"You guys like to have a little fun in doing your jobs, and I like to have fun in doing my job," said Stewart. "I try to have a good time doing it, and do have a good time doing it. I've been blessed all my life. This isn't the first time I've been in the spotlight. I've been that way since I was seven years old."

After the game, a disappointing setback, Stewart showed just as much poise in the press tent.

"We went out there and played our hearts out," he said, "but when you make turnovers, you pretty much don't give yourself a chance at all."

Asked about the critical interceptions thrown by O'Donnell, he said, "Things happen. You know, you can't blame Neil for that. You've got to know that things happen and we came up short."

"I felt like a rat out of a cage."
— Kordell Stewart

Stewart knew what a difficult job O'Donnell had. Stewart had been disappointed and critical of himself in his training camp and pre-season outings as a quarterback.

He looked bad in a scrimmage in late July at Edinboro University. He was sacked seven times. He had said in a diary that appeared in the *Pittsburgh Post-Gazette* during training camp that he wouldn't consider playing any other position.

Any chances he'd change his mind? "Zilch," he said.

"It takes time to understand the system," he said. "I'm the type who wants to go out and do well right away, but maybe that was unrealistic...for me and the fans.

"I wanted to do whatever I could to help us get going. I try to go out and do what's asked of me.

"The coaches were patient. They want you to feel comfortable with it before they toss you in the fire. But they know I want to be a quarterback; that's why I'm here. The team's been winning, so I couldn't complain."

Prior to the AFC championship contest with the Colts, I spoke to Stewart about his ambitions. I reminded him of the statement he had made at training camp that he had vehemently declared he had no interest in playing anywhere but quarterback.

"When I said that, I was still in the running at quarterback," he said "Once I saw I wasn't going to play, I changed my mind. I wasn't catching on as a quarterback as fast as I thought I would. So I guess I bit my tongue a little bit. When we're 3-4, I'm not going to say, 'No, I'm not going to do that.' I think I made a good decision.

"It's not in my best interest now to speculate about my status next season. I still want to be the quarterback. It's just a matter of me sticking to my guns. I know I'm a good quarterback. I know my ability. I know I'll be there. It's a matter of me having the right tutoring. Right now, I'm doing what I do best, helping us to win.

"This year was not a good year for me as far as being a quarterback. I was disappointed in the way I performed at camp. I didn't think I played as well as someone should who was drafted in the second round."

Even so, he was disillusioned by the camp experience.

"I was lost. I felt like a rat out of a cage," he recalled. "I just had so much going on in my head. I wanted to be the complete football player. So I was down on myself. When you know you can do better, it gnaws at you. I was disgusted at times. But I couldn't control it; I was just not ready.

"A lot of fans have been talking me up, but I hope they don't think I'm a god or something because I'm not. I'm human. And I make mistakes, just like Bradshaw did when he first came in. I just ask the

Kordell "Slash" Stewart shares a fun moment with his coach, Bill Cowher, during practice session at Three Rivers Stadium.

fans to stick with me, be patient until I get over this. This is a process every quarterback has to go through.

"A lot of the coaches and other players came up to me, and they were talking to me, saying stuff like 'Don't be upset with yourself; we've all been through it.' They were all behind me, they know I'm a quarterback. They know it takes time. I wanted to play; that's why I did what I did. I'd rather do this than sit on the bench until I'm ready.

"Before I went out and played receiver on the scout team, they told me, 'Don't worry, you'll be a quarterback.' I say to myself, 'I'm not worried. I will be a quarterback.'"

"I've been having fun."

During the regular season, Stewart caught 14 passes for 235 yards, including a 71-yard touchdown reception against Cincinnati November 19. He completed five of seven passes for 60 yards and a touchdown and carried the ball 15 times for 86 yards and a touchdown.

He sparked the Steelers. He changed them from a stodgy, run-oriented offense to an almost-anything-goes game.

During the course of the season, it seemed there wasn't anything he couldn't do.

Stewart smiled and confessed he had his limits.

"I'm scared of hammers. And skiing. I don't mess with that. I try not to do things I can't do. Football is something I've always been able to do."

"I'm not worried about money."
— Kordell Stewart

Stewart and Tomczak had to be taken aback by the big numbers the Steelers had on a contract they extended to Miller, the third man in the quarterback equation, during mini-camp in June, 1996. Miller was going to make $96,000 a year in 1996 under the terms of his original contract, but the Steelers tore that up and gave him a four-year contract that would pay him between $6.2 and $11.7 million, depending on whether he was a backup or a starting quarterback. Tomczak thought it was a lot of money to give to somebody who had so little playing accomplishments on their resume.

It figured to make for an interesting year. After all, Stewart had some big incentives in his contract if he could become the starting quarterback. The quarterback competition was a continuing saga at the Steelers' 1996 summer training camp. Stewart showed he had learned a lot in a year with the Steelers.

In an interview during the 1995 season, Stewart had said, "I'm not worried about money. I've never had any until now. It's not about money, it's all about how you play. I'm a businessman now and a wealthy man, and I can concentrate on football."

According to the terms of the contract he signed as the Steelers' No. 2 draft choice coming out of Colorado, if he was a starter for the 1997 season, he would receive a $900,000 bonus. If he was a starter in 1998, the bonus would go up to $1 million.

If he were a starter in 1999, his bonus would total $1.4 million. That could be a problem.

Bet that when Miller signed his contract in June of 1996 that Stewart was looking to do the same. He was represented by Leigh Steinberg, the same agent who had represented O'Donnell and Tomczak.

Stewart received a signing bonus of $350,000 to go with a first-year contract worth $372,500. He was to get $432,500 in 1996, $492,500 in 1997 and $552,500 in 1998.

When he was drafted, he said, "The arm strength — that's just something I've been gifted with," said Stewart. "My running ability — that's something also I've been gifted with. I feel I have the all-around package as far as being able to throw, and when I get in trouble, being able to run fast enough to get where I need to get and slide."

He was confident he would get a fair break from Cowher.

"He's a players' coach," said Stewart. "He's a guy who's very inspirational toward his players because he wants you to win. He's young also and when you're fired up, he's that much more fired-up. He has more energy than we do because we take all our energy out on the field every day. He has that extra energy that we don't have, to try to get us fired up again. He just wants the best when we play, regardless of what you go in as, and who you are. You're here to do a job. You get paid well to do it. He just wants you to come out and have fun and enjoy yourself and not let the business side of this whole thing take over. 'Go out there and do what you know how to do best and have fun.' That's what we've been doing and here we are.

"Quarterback was my thing, though, and that's what I'm after. A lot of teams wanted me to try out for another position, but I told them no. I didn't think anything of it. Then at the same time, when I was sitting on the bench, I felt like I could contribute in some kind of way. When Coach Cowher came up to me and asked me to play some wide receiver, I asked him, 'Will quarterback be my thing in the future?' He said, 'Yes.' I'm trusting him on his word. He's a good man, anyway. It's just a matter of me being patient and accepting my slash role.

"I'm doing this more for the team, because we need it. But quarterback is my No. 1 position."

> *"Most of the truly important moments of our lives go by unnoticed. We recognize them only in retrospect after we have chosen one road or another and have seen where it has taken us."*
> — August Wilson,
> Pulitzer Prize-winning playwright

Brenden Stai
A California dreamer

"I always reach for the stars."

Brenden Stai should have been a contented young man. He had so much to be thankful for. So many positive things had happened in his life in just over a year's span that he had to pinch himself to make sure he was not just having one of those dreams he had as a youngster — when he prayed that good things would happen for him and his family.

This was for real, though. He was a rookie starter with the Pittsburgh Steelers, so unusual for an offensive lineman in the National Football League, especially with a legitimate championship contender. Even Leon Searcy, then the Steelers' premier offensive lineman and the team's No. 1 draft choice out of the University of Miami in 1992, had to wait until his second season to gain a starting position. Stai had been the Steelers' No. 3 draft choice from Nebraska the previous spring, taken after they had already selected tight end Mark Bruener of Washington and quarterback/receiver Kordell Stewart of Colorado. Stai did not get to start at Nebraska until his junior season, his fourth year at the Lincoln campus.

And Stai, a 6-4, 305-pound blocker, was a week away from starting at right guard for the Steelers against the Dallas Cowboys in Super Bowl XXX. He had been a starter since the eighth game of the season when he moved into the right guard spot after Justin Strzelczyk was shifted to left tackle in place of the injured John Jackson. When Jackson returned to the lineup, Stai stayed at guard. The Steelers won eight of their final nine regular season games, and two playoff games with Stai as a starter. Nebraska lost only one game with Stai in the starting lineup. He was a handsome, able fellow who was becoming quite popular with the Pittsburgh football fans. It appeared that the best was yet to come.

"Can you believe this? I'm going to be starting in the Super Bowl," said Stai. "My wife looks at it and says, 'It's been rough for you, and you deserve it.' It's a beautiful feeling."

He was going back to Phoenix, where he was born 23 years earlier, where he said most of his relatives still resided, where ghosts of a surprising not-so-pleasant past might be revisited. There were people in Phoenix familiar with the skeletons in the family's closet, even though his parents moved to Southern California when he and his brother were quite young. Some had been critical of him and his mother when he went to Nebraska rather than Arizona State University. If he had gone to ASU, Brenden would have played at Sun Devil Stadium a lot sooner. So he had mixed emotions about his homecoming.

What could possibly bother Brenden Stai besides the monstrous, highly-regarded defensive linemen he would be facing at Super Bowl XXX? What demons from his childhood still danced in his handsome, suavely-bearded head?

On the surface it seemed that all was right in the world of Brenden Stai, considering his early success with the Steelers. A year earlier he concluded an All-American (Walter Camp and Football Writers Association) career at Nebraska by helping the Huskers defeat Miami in the Orange Bowl to win the national championship. It was a redemption for Nebraska and its coach, Tom Osborne, after a series of post-season failures. Stai was so proud of his national championship ring. And now he was going to play in the Super Bowl. The Steelers had already won the AFC championship, so one way or another, he would be getting a second championship ring. In between that time frame, he had been drafted by the Steelers, married his high school sweetheart, bought his first automobile and a house in the suburbs north of Pittsburgh, became a starter for the Steelers and became the father of a baby, Christina, just before Christmas. "My child makes it so special," said Stai. "It's been quite a story."

He had grown up in Anaheim, near Disneyland. Stai's rags-to-riches story would have appealed to Walt Disney.

I saw Jennifer Stai pushing their baby in a stroller on a holiday season shopping tour at Ross Park Mall, near their home, only a few days before Christmas. She looked pale, perhaps drained by the experience of giving birth only a few days earlier. Jennifer was in the company of her newfound friend, Keana Strzelczyk, the wife of the Steelers' offensive lineman. Keana was pushing their 11-month-old son, Justin Jr., in a stroller. "They get along so well," Stai said. "And Justin and I share a passion for motorcycles and the open road and playing the guitar."

"I had it tough when I was growing up."
— Brenden Stai

During the playoffs, Brenden's father, Chris Stai, was a visitor for a few days at his son's suburban home. Chris Stai had graduated from Cal State-Fullerton with a degree in liberal studies when Brenden was seven and his brother Heath was ten, and had worked in recent years as a manager/bartender at a fine Italian restaurant in La Habra, California. Brenden was happy to have his dad around at such an important period in his life, to share the scene, and Brenden had let go of some long-held hangups about his upbringing. Brenden's parents had divorced when he was 11 years old. His father remarried, but that marriage also ended in divorce. His mother remarried, but that marriage ended in divorce as well, after just 11 months.

345

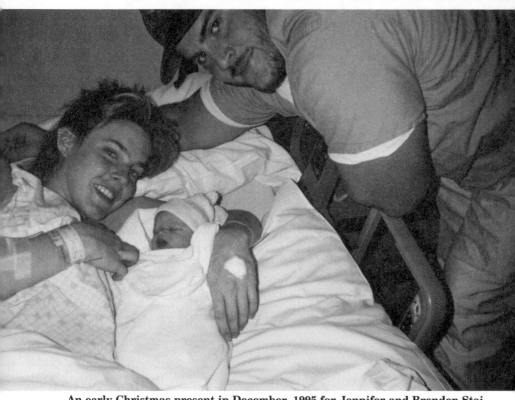

An early Christmas present in December, 1995 for Jennifer and Brenden Stai came in the person of their first child, Christina.

It didn't take long for Christina to wear her dad's number.

Brenden Stai is still "a baby" to his mother, Sharon Kell

His mother, Sharon Kelly, had worked at several medical-related jobs through the years, as a nurse at St. Jude Hospital, at a physical therapy office. She had worked in the medical field since she was 14. Yet her own health had been poor for as long as Brenden could remember. She had cancer, had undergone several back surgeries, was often in pain, and came close to dying. Hers had been a difficult life. "My medical problems led me to go back to school," said Ms. Kelly, "to re-educate myself to keep up with current trends in medicine and insure that I could always provide for my sons. During their high school years, we would often all be in the kitchen studying together."

Brenden Stai can still remember those nights in the kitchen. "I had it tough when I was growing up," said Stai. "My parents didn't have a lot of money. We didn't go on vacation. When I was real young, my parents loved each other a great deal. Then my dad decided to call it quits. And he left. That was when I was 11, a critical age.

"It wasn't easy. Things were so tough after my dad left. Growing up, it was tough. The lowest point was when my dad left. My mom was very strong, and she did her best to hold things together for our family, but we missed our dad.

"I still see my father from time to time. We have a strange relationship. I have forgiven him, and I try to move on. When he left, he tried to show us he didn't leave us because he didn't love us. I think he really tried his best in that regard. We talked. My dad tried. He didn't stay away, he stayed in touch with us. He made an effort to make it a family.

"But we hated what he did to our mother. She needed him. She came close to dying from cancer. Some times we were almost out in the streets. That's how bad it got. My brother, Heath, was really upset when my parents split up. He was three years older than me. He took it hard. My mom got mad at him. My brother ran off. He came back, but he was bitter about the whole episode. If I'd been older, I might have done the same thing. My brother was really torn up by all this. He had a lot of anger toward my father.

"Then my mother met another man and she got married again. Things got better for a while. We lived in something like a condo. It was nice. The man my mother married the second time was well-off. I was in 10th grade and I thought things would be good for us again. Then there were arguments. It was quite a life. Then they got divorced. My father got remarried. The woman he was with made it difficult for my mom and us. His wife gave my mother a tough time. My mother opened her home to her, but my dad's wife was a real problem.

"Then my mother's back went bad. She'd hurt her back in a bad car wreck, and re-injured it in another car accident. When my mother had the back surgery the first time, I was in college. She had back surgery three times. She has had tumors in her legs. She is star-crossed; I think her life's been difficult.

"Thank God, my mom had some great friends. She borrowed money from them and eventually she paid it back. They helped out. I worried a lot about my mom. I still do. Now she's still struggling, as far as her health is concerned. I remember what she did for me. At least now I can help her.

"My dad wanted it to work. My dad was there for me. He'd send me $100 every so often when I was away at college. But what he did really hurt us. His leaving her was his biggest mistake. They had a lot of problems, but I think they could have worked it out. I was always a proud kid. I was never ashamed of my family.

"My brother went to a technical school. He's very successful. He's an architectural engineer. And things have worked out well for me. I've forgiven my father for what he did. We're trying to move on; I want him to be involved with my own family. He's my dad and I love him."

Sharon Kelly — she reclaimed her maiden name after her divorce — recalled that Brenden's college career was exciting for both her and Heath. "We were his biggest fans," she said. "Heath has played an important part in Brenden's career. He had to grow up fast and he took on the role of father, brother and best friend to Brenden. I think that he challenged Brenden a great deal, as brothers will often do, just because they were brothers, but also because he felt responsible for Brenden. Heath became an old man fast.

"Brenden earned a starting position at right guard during his junior year, played till late October and had his right ankle broken in the Missouri game. I happened to be there to see him play for the first time that year. It was awful. Brenden was so upset that his career chances appeared to be gone.

"Then, as Brenden has always done, he turned it around in his head, made it a challenge to get well and returned to play in the national championship game against Florida State. Nebraska lost, but not without a battle. Brenden had told me during his healing period that 'I can feel my leg healing.' I have never forgotten those words and often use them myself to help me overcome my pain.

"My son's story is one of hard work, determination, luck and God's good graces. All of us are challenged in this life. It is unfortunate that not all of us realize that challenge and do something with it. Brenden and Heath have done just that and I am very proud of both of them."

> *"She was always there. With me.*
> *If she had disappeared,*
> *no there would exist."*
> — John Wideman,
> On his mother in
> *Fatherless*

"When a team does as well as Nebraska, people want to tear you down."
— Brenden Stai

Nebraska snapped a seven-game losing streak in bowl games when it defeated Miami in the Orange Bowl at the outset of 1995. The team had a choker's label in the big games going into Stai's last game, so it was a face-saving victory.

The Huskers' coach, Tom Osborne, showed how much he respected Stai's ability by switching Stai from right guard to left guard to battle Miami defensive tackle Warren Sapp, an All-American who had personally destroyed many of his opponents and would become a first round draft pick of the Tampa Bay Buccaneers. Stai held his own, even though Sapp was hardly shut down.

Stai, an especially strong run-blocker, helped the Cornhuskers win the national rushing title (340 yards per game) and limited opponents to only five sacks.

"It was unbelievable," recalled Stai. "I'd never won a championship at any level in any team sport, so it was a chance to realize a dream. To help Tom Osborne win that championship and then to finish school and have my degree (criminal justice, with a minor in business), it was the climax of my college career."

Osborne and Stai formed a mutual admiration society. Stai was eager to explain what his coach was all about, being a bit defensive because Osborne and his Nebraska program had been under a great deal of scrutiny and criticism because of the off-the-field shenanigans — outright crimes in a few cases — of some of the players, plus the fact that the Huskers had such a consistently successful team.

"Osborne is a very simple man," said Stai. "He expects a lot out of you. What you see is what you get. With some people, you see one person one day and a different person the next day. He's not like that. He's very religious. He believes in God; he stresses that. He believes God's a very important part of your life. Coach Osborne is there to support you. He is not only a coach who wants good athletes, but a coach who wants good people."

That might sound like Stai was spewing a Nebraska recruiting pitch, but he seemed earnest enough in his defense of Osborne and his football program. He was, if nothing else, loyal to his Lincoln roots.

One of the most celebrated situations at Nebraska involved the way Osborne dealt with his star running back, Lawrence Phillips, who began the 1995 season as a strong contender for the Heisman Trophy. That was before Phillips was convicted of a misdemeanor and placed on a year's probation for beating up his girlfriend. Osborne suspended him for several games, but permitted Phillips to return to the Nebraska team. A group of women faculty at Nebraska protested the decision, saying Osborne's response was a weak one.

Another Nebraska ballplayer, cornerback Tyrone Williams, was hit with a felony weapons charge. Wide receiver Riley Washington was charged with second-degree murder. There were several other Nebraska ballplayers who suffered legal problems the previous season.

"I feel for the whole team," said Stai. "It takes a few people who've done things to put a black mark on the entire team. When a team does as well as Nebraska, people want to drag you down. It's sick. He made the right decisions the way he disciplined those who got in trouble. If he had kicked Lawrence Phillips off the team for good, I don't think it would have been a wise thing. Phillips lost the Heisman because of the suspension. He'd have won the Heisman if he had played the entire schedule. I don't fault Coach Osborne for bringing him back."

Stai stuck up for Osborne the way Myron Bell and Jim Miller were steadfast in their support of George Perles, their coach at Michigan State who had been accused by some of his former players of grade-fixing and other nefarious activities to keep his players eligible.

Bill Conlin, a Philadelphia sports columnist and a regular panelist on ESPN's *Sports Reporters*, labeled Osborne "the Father Flanagan of a Boys Town from Hell."

Even so, Stai seemed like a solid citizen. And he insisted most of the guys in the program were just as clean-cut. "College is a growing-up experience, and different people handle it different ways," said Stai.

"They have a great academic support program at Nebraska, for instance. There's a real commitment to it. They're always after you, helping you. It's a big thing that Coach Osborne stressed. He always said it was great to be an athlete, but it's even greater to leave with a degree. I graduated the year before we won the national championship, and was able to begin some graduate level classes.

"In all honesty, a lot of people don't take advantage of tutors. They are available 24 hours a day at Nebraska. They are always on call.

"We had a great place to study. It's called Hewett Center. It's monitored to make sure people aren't there just socializing. It's an environment that allows you to study. There are 30 to 40 computers, all you need. They have an outside linebacker now with a 4.0 grade point average.

"You learn to budget your time. When I first got there, I had a 3.8 (out of 4.0) my first term. I kind of got off track my second semester. I worked my way back up. I had a 3.25 GPA over five years. I received some recognition from Nebraska's athletic department for my academic achievement. Some people had questioned my academic ability when I first came out of high school, but I benefited from the structure and support I had at Nebraska."

thers Heath and Brenden Stai have weath-
d some stormy days together, but have
ded and prospered as adults.

nden Stai (No. 66) was a member of a beefy
proud offensive line on national champion-
p team for 1994 season at Nebraska.

Brenden and his mother when he
received his degree at University of
Nebraska commencement.

Stai assumes pass-blocking stance to give Nebraska's All-American quarterback Tommy Frazier time to fire the ball.

Stai played in a losing effort only once in his last two seasons at Nebraska. That was in the national championship contest at the end of the 1993 season. Given a chance to redeem themselves after the 1994 season, Nebraska came through.

"When we won the Orange Bowl, we went out with a bang," said Stai. "I did it the way I wanted to do it. I accomplished just about everything I had in mind when I went to Nebraska in the first place. I wanted to take guitar in college; that's the only thing I didn't do."

But his buddy Justin Strzelczyk had taken up the guitar, getting tutoring from teammate Steve Avery, so Stai had an opportunity to make up for the one thing lacking from his college experience.

"Nebraska more than lived up to its billing," said Stai. "It was such a showcase of team talent. Tommy Frazier was a great quarterback, but the talent was great and deep at every position. We were three lines deep with hearty red-blooded Americans. None of them were fat, either. There is a sports nutritionist on staff. A lot of thought goes into preparing meals for the athletes at Nebraska."

The Steelers' college scouting director, Tom Modrak, raved about Nebraska's set-up. "It's something to see," he said. "Their players lift weights in a large area that has glass walls. So you can watch them work out, and a lot of people do just that. Their players are well-conditioned."

Stai said Nebraska believed it would be the better-conditioned team in the fourth quarter when many games are decided. It's all pretty basic stuff, as Stai sees it. "Let's bang into a wall 100 times and see who gets tired first," Stai once said during his schooldays.

"More colleges are kinda doing what Nebraska has done for the past ten years. They emphasize proper conditioning and preparation. They're very into running, stretching, lifting. They take pride in their program in that respect."

Stai smiled when I mentioned Modrak's comment about players lifting weights in a fishbowl environment.

"It's kinda like a museum," said Stai. "I didn't like the fact that people stood there and watched while we were lifting. I felt like an animal, it was like they were coming to the zoo to watch the animals perform."

Even though he left Arizona before his second birthday, Stai said that throughout his days at Esperanza High School in Anaheim he thought he wanted to go to Arizona State University. When it came time to choose a college, though, it came down to Arizona State, UCLA, San Diego State, Washington and Oregon.

"Then Nebraska came and asked me to visit and everything changed," said Stai. "When I got there, Coach Osborne walked across the campus with me. Here was this legendary coach, and I was walking with him. It hardly mattered that there was snow covering the campus. It was snowing hard and I saw a guy walking to school in the snow. He seemed to be dealing with it. They showed me a good time, I liked Osborne from the beginning, and it wasn't a hard choice to make.

"I rode motorcycles in high school, and I got hurt right before I went to Nebraska. It happened in California, on the same day UCLA and Arizona State coaches came to my house to talk. I was going to my wife's basketball game; she was my girlfriend then. She was good. But I never made it. A lady turned left in front of me; I smacked into the side of her car. I did flips over her car. I had glasses on, and they got all messed up. I was lucky there was a witness; they confirmed my story."

His scrape didn't scare Stai enough to keep him off a motorcycle. He liked to ride Strzelczyk's Harley-Davidson and wanted to get a bike of his own. "We like to pal around, him and me, his wife and my wife.

"It's fun; it's one of the best feelings in the world. Riding through the wind. The engine under you. All that power. And, sure, the temptation of danger. I'm definitely a motorcycle fan. I collect motorcycle cards."

As exciting as riding a motorcycle seemed to be for Stai, it paled by comparison to the excitement he felt on game day at Nebraska.

"During the five years I was at Nebraska, things got better every year. I was red-shirted as a freshman, and got acclimated. When Nebraska is playing, the stadium itself is the third largest city in the state. There are over 76,000 in the stadium. That ranks behind only Omaha and Lincoln. It's really a sight to see. Everyone is wearing red; it's just a sea of red.

"For someone like Frazier or Phillips, a star on the team, there's a lot of pressure. Everyone wants the athletes around. Then there are people who are always looking to challenge the players, put them in their place, that sort of thinking. So some of the guys are always getting into fights and into trouble. Most of it is no big deal. Some people say, 'Why do they have all those animals at Nebraska?' But it's a bad rap."

Stai's mention of Frazier brought a thought to mind. One of the keys to the Steelers' success was the triple-threat play of another rookie, Kordell Stewart, selected just ahead of Stai in the 1995 college draft. How would Stai compare Stewart and Frazier?

"Tommy is stronger than Kordell at running the ball, but he doesn't have as strong an arm. Tommy is not as fast as Kordell. He has a lot of heart and a lot of confidence. He'll let you know it." When I suggested to Stai that Stewart would do the same, he said, "That's what makes him Kordell. Great athletes are usually quite confident individuals."

> *"My philosophy is: I will play on whatever part of the field you let me play on, and I will do the best I can. I can only play in this corner? Fine. I'll take that for now. I will still beat you. So you'd better be ready."*
> — *My American Journey,*
> a memoir by
> Ret. Gen. Colin Powell

"I know where I came from."
— Brenden Stai

Stai seemed satisfied with the way things were going in his life, and he was especially proud of his wife and newborn child, Christina. "I'm a father for the first time," he said, "and my wife is the best thing that ever happened to me."

He and Jennifer were married on July 2, 1995. "We've been dating since 11th grade," said Stai. "We've had some ups and downs; it was difficult for us when I was away at school. Long-distance relationships are hard to maintain. She didn't go to Nebraska. It was sometimes rocky; things didn't work out for awhile. But I'm glad we stayed together.

"She was my high school sweetheart. I took her to the prom," said Stai. "We've been through a lot together. We get along so well. We're made for each other.

"She truly appreciates the fact that I have family values. I learned early in my life that marriage isn't easy. It's easy to leave it; it's hard to be committed to it.

"When I think of all the things that have happened to us this past year, it's a dream come true. But I try to keep things in perspective. I know where I came from. I'm very thankful. I'm very conservative when it comes to spending money. My parents didn't plan for the future. I was lucky I got a scholarship to go to college; otherwise I wouldn't have been able to continue my education."

"He's a winner."
— Kent Stephenson

Scouts liked what they saw of Stai at Nebraska. The Steelers gave some consideration to selecting Stai on the second round of the draft, but decided to take Stewart instead.

Stai's strength and experience was mostly at run-blocking in an option offense. The Steelers felt they could improve his pass-blocking ability. He had the size and strength and all the elements — dedication, work ethic, commitment — coaches look for in an offensive lineman.

"Nebraska is one of college football's foremost smashmouth offensive teams," wrote Rick Gosselin of *The Dallas Morning News*. "The Cornhuskers run the ball down everyone's throat — game after game, year after year, decade after decade. Stai's proficiency as a drive-blocker made him an All-America and helped Nebraska win a national championship."

After the Steelers drafted Stai, the team's college personnel coordinator, Tom Modrak, offered this observation: "This guy has real good physical ability. He's probably the strongest guy on Nebraska's team. He's a physical player and a tough guy."

Kent Stephenson, the Steelers' offensive line coach, always refers to Stai as "a winner."

Stephenson said, "He's improved, basically because he wants to. He has a burning desire to be real good and he works at it. He's a winner. He's a real competitor. He has a great future."

Stai says the kinds of things that put a smile on Stephenson's face.

"Pro ball has always been a dream of mine. I want to be relentless on every play. Like Coach Cowher said, 'It comes down to what you have to offer the team, not what the team has to offer you.' I was upset I didn't go higher. I thought I was better than some of the guys who were taken ahead of me. But I'm glad I went to a team like the Steelers. I'm glad I didn't go to the Jets, for example.

"I liked coming here. There is a lot of tradition.There are a lot of high expectations, and that's good. All the success they've had. The tradition of hard-nosed football. It's like Nebraska in that respect. It's something I like to be around. I like being around people who like to win. Losing is not acceptable. It makes you want to become a part of that tradition.

"It was an ideal situation for me, coming from Nebraska to a team that runs the ball like Pittsburgh. I'm always up for running the ball. We take pride in our ability to run the ball. We like to run the ball, wear them down and keep our defense off the field. We believe the offensive line sets the tempo in a game.

"My desire to play in the pros has come true. I didn't think I'd be starting so soon. I always reach for the stars. It's really lofty. I'm definitely surprised. I think the coaches were impressed with our attitude and hard work, in the weight room and in meeting rooms and on the field. I am always trying to outdo somebody.

"I do all my weights in the afternoon. I can't do it in the morning. I have to have food in me. I have to have my blood sugar level up. Just ask anybody on the team. They'll see me in the weight room after every practice. You've got to work on a lot of things. You've got to be willing to dedicate the time and your body to getting better all the time.

"Football strength is all about legs and leverage. If you're not able to apply leverage, it doesn't matter how much you can bench-press. You don't bench-press during games.

"That's why our weight program here, under Chet Fuhrman, is slanted more toward football strength. Because everyone is strong at this level. Being strong isn't enough.

"The game has definitely changed. Back when you couldn't use your hands, they (defensive linemen) could head slap you, and the demands on both sides were a little different. Today there's more speed and technique.

"You have to realize you're getting paid and it's your job to go out and practice."

He said he discussed the ups and downs of the daily regimen with Steelers' center Dermontti Dawson, who resides in the dressing stall next door, and plays alongside him on the front line.

"Some days I'm so disgusted," said Stai. "I get out on the field, and something goes wrong and I'm so disgusted. Dermontti seems to be able to keep an even keel. I never met anybody who is as nice to everybody as he is. He's always going to greet you. He'll talk. And he's such a great athlete, and he sets a perfect tone for the other guys. I feel so lucky. I thank the heavens I'm here.

"The guys had open arms. The veterans have been helping me every step of the way. They talk to you, and teach you things. This is fun."

"My dream started back in the third grade."
— Brenden Stai

Having fun. For a fellow who remembers his mom going through so much difficulty, who missed his dad during his challenging adolescent days, things have really turned around for Brenden Stai.

"It's like a dream, that's all," said Stai when I spoke to him at another time, just before the Steelers' first playoff game in early January, 1996, against the Buffalo Bills. "My dream started in third grade, back when I first played football. The Marlins were my first Pop Warner team. I was playing the line, I was always a lineman. Guys were one and two years older than I was, but I fit right in. Derrick Brown, who plays for the New Orleans Saints, went to Nebraska, too, and we talk about how things have worked out for us. My dad was a big Minnesota Vikings fan; he's from Minnesota. He had the boob tube on all the time, and I liked watching the games with my dad. I liked the whole idea.

"I never had a car in my life until I came to Pittsburgh. I bought a brand new car. I have a chance to go to the Super Bowl. It's been quite a story.

"There's a sense of an even more competitive atmosphere. This is the first time I've been in the playoffs as a pro. This will probably be the biggest game of my life. As far as what's at stake, it's like winning another national championship.

"Every kid who ever plays football dreams of this. This is to make dreams come true. This is the first step to winning the Super Bowl."

"I'm not a brave person. I had two boys and I just did what I had to do."
— Sharon Kelly

Sharon Kelly came across loud and clear from Auburn, California. She was enthusiastic in her speech, she sounded upbeat, positive, self-deprecating, so honest, and had a good sense of humor. She had been to hell and back, in a sense, and she sounded so much better, during an extended long-distance telephone call, than I had anticipated based on her son Brenden Stai's stories about her problems. Yes, her life had been more difficult than she would have liked, but laughter was a good antidote. She was proud of her two boys, Heath and Brenden, and forgiving and understanding of her first husband, Chris. She said they were still friends, and doing their best to maintain a relationship that worked for everyone's interests. "Isn't she something?" Stai asked me after I told him that I had heard from his mother.

Brenden Stai's mother was a fighter, a survivor, and she boasted that "I'm a hundred percent Irish." She added, "They say Sharon Kelly has the Irish blessing of constantly stepping into brown stuff and coming out smelling like a rose."

In short, she tried to do the best with the hand that had been dealt to her, and believed that some good comes out of every bad experience, at least some learning.

"Let me tell you what a gutsy kid Brenden was," she said, just when I was about to say goodbye.

"When I was in the hospital having my second back surgery, Brenden was at home. This was in the spring of his sophomore year in high school. He was cooking some taquitos, one of his favorite foods. He'd taken them out of the freezer and he was cooking them in hot oil in a frying pan with a lid on it. He was called away by a telephone call, and he didn't turn off the flame on the stove. He was gone for a while.

"When he came back to the kitchen, the pan was on fire. All he could think to do was to get it out of the house. He picked up the lid, and the whole thing blew up in his hands. It sprayed him with hot oil; it took out two rugs and some wallpaper. Both of his hands were severely burned.

"When I woke up from surgery at the hospital, he was sitting in a wheelchair next to my bed. His hands and arms were all wrapped in bandages. From that point, Brenden went to therapy every day. The doctors said he would probably have to have some skingrafts. Brenden didn't want to do that because there would be some webbing on his hands.

"Brenden kept taking the dead skin off his hands by himself, and treated it himself. It hurt him terribly; there was a lot of pain he had to endure. He went out for football that fall, and he had to wear garden gloves with the fingers cut off. The skin on his hands was so new and thin it would cut and bleed easily. He always had blood in his gloves, but he wouldn't give up playing football.

"If you look closely at his knuckles, he still has some scarring there. That happened in April of 1989, but he was back playing that summer. That's the kind of guts he has. He always had his own mind. He's a taskmaster and he won't let me get down about my physical problems, either. He gets after me pretty good."

Brenden Stai had seen some gritty behavior by his own mother, which served her in good stead during challenging times. "What a mother does might seem heroic to her children, but to me it wasn't," said Stai's mother. "I had two boys to look after, and I just did what I had to do.

"I had a rough marriage. I don't like to beat up on my husband, Chris, but we weren't right for each other. I don't want to take his dad down with my stories. It's not that his dad was a bad guy and the rest of us were good. We never should have been married in the first place. We stuck it out, thinking it was best for the boys. But Daddy had problems and he took it out on us. We all learned from it. We're friends; at least the boys have that.

"Over the past six years, I have had four back surgeries, and two times I've had cancerous tumors taken out of my leg. So Brenden appreciates that his mother has had to keep coming up from the bottom of the pile.

"My boys are more than sons to me. We've been a team; we've been good friends. Brenden is not much of a talker; his brother Heath is more vocal. Brenden knows how to focus; he just goes for it. He did things on his own because he had to.

"I was married to an alcoholic. The relationship, for a long time, was abusive. My older son, Heath, took the heat from that for quite a while. Brenden was younger and was the apple of his daddy's eye.

"Heath was in his first day in high school when the whole thing blew up in our face, that their father was leaving. My husband had a girlfriend, we learned, and he was leaving, all in one swoop. Brenden was 11 and in middle school. So they had to grow up real fast; divorce does that to kids.

"There was a lot of anger for quite a while. But, eventually, we all came to terms with it. It was the best thing that happened. We're all OK now. Their dad has healed. We're all good friends. Their dad and I are still good friends and it works better that way. Out of everything bad should come some good. We didn't let it defeat us. I was a single mother and Brenden didn't have much when he was at Nebraska. He got along on about $100 a month. He rode a motorbike for five years. But he didn't complain. He knew why he was at Nebraska, and he made the best of it.

"Heath went to school and got an associate arts degree. He does architectural drafting for Louisiana Pacific. He's got a good job, and he's done just fine.

The Stai family (left to right) included Heath, dad Chris, Brenden and mother Sharon.

Brenden and his boxer, Miss Mugs

As young soccer prospect

As Little Leaguer

Jennifer and Brenden at first formal dance back in high school.

"Both of my boys are very different. Brenden was quiet. He could stay in his room and entertain himself. He was the original pack rat. He never gets rid of anything. He has a collection of Rubik's cubes, 13 different ones. He has all kinds of treasures. He can go to his box of memories, and tell about his earliest experiences with them. He loves music; he sings really well, I don't know if you know that. As a baby, he was a real cutey pie; he was my John John. Oh, he's going to kill me for telling you all this stuff. He could get into mischief. He could blow bubble gum when he was so young. He was always interested in playing athletic games. He and his brother, both.

"I worked as a nurse, but I ended up being the eternal patient. I suffered a slipped disc in an auto accident. Then Heath and I got hit in our car by a drunk driver. I've had back problems ever since. I had surgery for the removal of a bone tumor in my tibia. It came back a year later and I had to have surgery again. It was tough on the family. But three months afterward, I walked down the aisle at Brenden's wedding. A month and a half ago, I had to undergo surgery again on my back. The boys get fearful about my condition. I'm glued together. I've got two metal bars and eight bolts in my back. Other than that, I'm as healthy as a horse.

"I had to raise two boys. I didn't have a choice. I'm not brave. Even when my husband was at home, he worked nights, and he was not involved in the children's lives. I went to all the games with them."

I asked her how she felt about attending Super Bowl XXX. "That was quite an experience, and I had a hard time with it. I had a lot of family still living there, and to see them, and so many other people who came out of the woodwork. Now they were all behind Brenden. I didn't enjoy the crowd or the scene. There was something repulsive about it. There were relatives who had once given me a rough time about Brenden going to Nebraska instead of Arizona State University, where they thought he should have gone. They kind of blackballed his mother because he didn't go there. We thought Nebraska was best for what he wanted. So they weren't always nice to his mother. Brenden doesn't forget. Until a friend came to my rescue when I was in financial trouble — I couldn't work because of my back — and helped us out, we came close to living in a shelter. I was able to get back on my feet and pay back the man who helped us. We took a count a couple of times, but we never stayed down."

> *"When I tried to talk to my father I realized that, though ties of blood made us kin, though I see a shadow of my face in his face, though there was an echo of my voice in his voice, we were forever strangers, speaking a different language, living in vastly different places of reality."*
> — Richard Wright,
> Excerpt from *Black Boy*

Myron "Boo" Bell
At home in the ghetto

*"I'm trying to make a name for myself,
and I want it to be a good name."*

Myron "Boo" Bell lived in the same dismal housing project in Toledo, Ohio, from the time he was born until he completed eighth grade. His father's name was Ted McVay, which throws up a red flag right away. McVay never married Myron's mother, who was Retha Denise Bell back then. Byron had a sister, Cherise Bell, who was 22 in 1995, his second season with the Steelers. In time, his mother married Tom Martin. Myron had a step-brother, Antoine, who was 7.

"I didn't really have a father when I was growing up," said Myron Bell. "My father stopped coming around when I was about seven. Before that, he'd show up here and there. My mother and my grandmother helped me grow up. My father did nothing. My step-father, Tom Martin, has been good for all of us. We now have a close-knit family."

When it was time for Myron to enter high school, his mother moved the family to a better neighborhood. She wanted a better life, a better opportunity for her children. Frankly, she was scared. There was trouble at the doorstep of their home, and she wanted to get away from it.

Bell was a defensive back and special teams demon for the Steelers during the 1994 and 1995 seasons, his first two in the National Football League. His timing in coming to the Steelers was fortuitous, to say the least. It couldn't have been better. His old neighborhood was something less.

"It was a fairly bad neighborhood," Myron recalled. "My mom decided to move. She felt it was her job to put me in a better environment. I went back to it, because the kids there were my friends.

"I never felt threatened by the old neighborhood. After all, it's all I knew growing up. My mother...she raised me well. She taught us what's good to do and what's not good to do. I'm sure I was bad sometimes, but I kept out of serious trouble.

"I made the best of it. I didn't want to make new friends. I went back there, I suppose, just because I was happy with them. As far as what they did themselves, that was out of my hands.

"At a young age, my mother scared me into staying out of trouble. Whenever something came up, and I had to make a decision, I'd ask myself, 'What would my mother think?'"

His mother also started calling him "Boo" when he was a baby. I told Myron that we had done the same thing with our younger daughter, Rebecca, calling her "Boo" or "Becca Boo" when she was a baby. Who knows why? It just stuck.

"It's a name my mom gave me when I was a baby. He's little Boo, I guess. It's kind of stuck with me," said Bell.

"We're human beings, too. We do make mistakes."
— Myron Bell

Bell got himself into a jam on May 27, 1995, when Pittsburgh police stopped him at 4:15 a.m. for blocking traffic with his 1995 Lexus. Officers said they found an unlicensed semiautomatic pistol in his pants pocket. A judge ordered Bell to stand trial on a firearms violation. In August, he was slapped on the wrists for this breach of the law. Bell was embarrassed by the publicity. It looked bad because of other off-the-field problems experienced by some of the Steelers. It was bad for the public perception of the team. There seemed to be a trend. Couldn't the Steelers stay out of trouble?

"Back home we had gangs, guys selling drugs and stealing car radios and breaking into houses, stuff like that," said Bell, while reflecting on his two years with the Steelers in late December of 1995. "I heard about gang stuff like that here in Pittsburgh. I had something stolen. Some of the guys on the team had stuff stolen from their cars. I had a gun to protect myself. I saw what happened to Deon (Figures) when he got shot by accident back home in L.A. Deon and I are pretty close, and that spooked me. I guess I didn't think that through too well."

What did his mother think when she heard about his run-in with the police?

"That was the thing that really ate me up," Bell replied. "It didn't look good in the paper. But people who knew me...they knew what kind of person I am. I made a mistake, and I guess I didn't realize the seriousness of what I had done. We're human beings, too. We do make mistakes.

"My first concern was my mother. The second was my job. I was worried about that. How will they think about me now? Dan Rooney and Bill Cowher talked to me once about it. They believed me. They knew I wasn't into anything bad. They were very helpful. I appreciated the way they went about it.

"I'm trying to make a name for myself, and I want it to be a good name."

> *"So many names from the past. Isn't it odd how infectious the past is? Yours, mine ... it all somehow becomes cross-pollinated and interwoven, so that we willy-nilly inherit parts of each other's history — and live them out as if they were our own story."*
> — *Missing,*
> A Harry Stoner Novel,
> Jonathan Valin

Myron "Boo" Bell   Jim O'Brien

Myron Bell is flanked by two teammates, future NBAer Jimmy Jackson, left, and Donnie Dobbs, when they led Toledo's Macomber-Whitney High School to state basketball championship in 1989.

"You have to have a passport to get in here."
— Tony Parisi

Even today, Myron Bell is still more at home in the ghetto than in the nicer neighborhoods, as evidenced by where he chooses to store his clothes in the Steelers clubhouse at Three Rivers Stadium.

The Steelers clubhouse was extended around 1990 to handle an expanded team roster, with the addition of a so-called practice squad for each NFL team. The wing holds 14 dressing stalls, seven on each side in a narrow rectangular hallway. They are the same size as the dressing stalls in the clubhouse proper, about seven feet high, 40 inches wide and 40 inches deep.

No one with claustrophobia would want to be a tenant, for this was an extremely tight group.

During the 1995 season, all 14 occupants happened to be black. This wing was referred to by the players themselves as "The Ghetto." Media types were warned not to enter the room. When a brave outsider ventured into "The Ghetto" he might be greeted with general mayhem, or the lights might suddenly go out. And it gets noisy in there. Former Steeler Tim McKyer strayed into there one day, and they tied him up, bound his arms and legs, and left him rolling around on the floor. Scary stuff. Fun stuff.

Most of the players who reside there never know whether or not they will be asked to suit up for the next game, or if they will be jettisoned from the Steelers' squad whenever the team has an opportunity to sign a new player.

When a player's playing status improves and there's a vacancy in the main room, he is asked by Tony Parisi or Rodgers Freyvogel, who look after the clubhouse, if he wants to move up in class.

Myron Bell has chosen to stay in "The Ghetto." His locker was the sixth of seven on the left-hand side. Johnnie Barnes had the last locker, the one nearest the white concrete block wall, on that side of the room. Some of the other occupants of "The Ghetto" were Lethon Flowers, Randy Fuller, Corey Holliday, Bill Johnson and Damon Mays.

"They have a lot of laughs in here," said Parisi, acting as if he had wandered into a haunted house, on a day when none of the players were present. "You have to have a passport to get in here. Every time somebody comes out of here they get cut, so they don't want to leave."

Freyvogel said they were a superstitious lot. "They see what happened to Tim Simpson, for instance," offered Freyvogel. "He was back here for three years. He got cocky and moved out. He changed his number, too. He got the locker just inside the door of the clubhouse, the one next to Levon Kirkland. I told him he was too close to the main door, and his next move was going to be out the door. Sure enough, soon after, he was gone. The other guys see that. So they want to stay here."

Steelers' dressing room extension is known as "The Ghetto" and is home mostly to reserve squad members.

The men who look after the equipment and clubhouse at Steelers' complex are Rodgers Freyvogel, left, and Tony Parisi. In 1995, Parisi was in his 31st season with the Steelers, Freyvogel his 16th.

Parisi told Bell to move his stuff into the main room at the outset of the 1995 season, but Bell declined the offer. "I didn't want to do that," he said, giving me permission to step into the inner sanctum of the Steelers scrubs. "Myself and the guys on the practice squad...we're all trying to make it. I still look at myself as trying to make it. I have a lot of things to do.

"I like being in 'The Ghetto.' There's a lot of joking going on around here. The guys are happy to be here. They want to do what they need to do to make the next step. I don't plan on living back here forever. If they move me, I'll still come back and visit. I'm closer to these guys. Bill Johnson's back here, for instance, and we both went to the same school, Michigan State.

"But I have good friends outside 'The Ghetto,' too. Jason Gildon, Deon Figures and Brentson Buckner are all good friends. One of my closest friends is Deon. I feel like I can talk to him like I talk to my mother. I feel like he can come to me. Sometimes we boost each other.

"Rod Woodson's nearly ten years older than me. He's still helping me. He's like a coach; he can help you. I'm still learning."

Woodson couldn't help Bell or McKyer when they got into trouble in the late going of the AFC championship game at the end of the 1994 season, and the memory still haunted Bell. With just over five minutes remaining, on a third-and-14 call, San Diego quarterback Stan Humphries hit Tony Martin deep behind McKyer for a 44-yard touchdown that established the final score, 17-13, in favor of the Chargers. It's a play the Steelers and their fans won't soon forget. I was with the Pittsburgh media in the end zone where Martin scored and had a close-up view of it. So did Bell.

"I can still visualize that play," said Bell. "I could have helped Tim McKyer. I was coached to do something else, but I could have come over. Everyone played a part in it, not just Tim McKyer."

I asked Bell if he saw McKyer collapse onto the turf at game's end, and how McKyer had to be helped off the field because he was so distraught. It was strange behavior, but his grief was that great. It was the beginning of the end of Tim McKyer as a Steeler. He went to Carolina in the expansion draft when the Steelers left him unprotected.

"I didn't see any of that," said Bell. "I felt badly enough. It takes a lot of luck, too, but he's a good one."

Bell blames himself for not coming to the rescue, even though it was not his responsibility.

"I'm my worst critic," said Bell. "I don't want to disappoint myself. You're constantly being challenged at defensive back. People know when you blow a pass coverage. It usually shows up on the scoreboard. You can go from the penthouse to the outhouse in a hurry."

"George Perles was good for his word."
— Myron Bell

Bell has the best memories of his days at Michigan State. Like teammate Jim Miller, he thought the world of his college coach, George Perles. Other players from that same era had leveled serious charges against Perles, who was the defensive line coach and defensive coordinator under Chuck Noll during the Steelers' glory days of the '70s.

"He's just a real sincere guy; I respect him a great deal," said Bell. "I remember him visiting our home, and sitting in our family room with me and my mother. He promised me three things: he said I'd leave with a degree — I only have three classes to go to get my degree; I plan to do it — and that I'd be more mature as a man — I think that happened in my five years at State — and he said I'd have a shot to play in the NFL — and that has come true. George Perles was good for his word."

Perles was impressed by Bell's ability and his attitude and speed.

"The first thing you want to see is flat out speed," said Perles. "If he can't run it's tough for him to play in the Big Ten. The next question is toughness. The game is won by tough guys."

That's what appeals to Bill Cowher about Bell. He's a tough guy.

"This all started out with my dreaming about it," said Bell, standing before his dressing stall. "In high school or college, when I'd have a big game coming up, I'd visualize playing a great game, making big plays. I'd dream of playing great against Michigan. I'd dream about the biggest games. That's how players are made. I dreamed of playing in the NFL someday."

He almost went to the University of Tennessee when Johnny Majors was the coach of the Volunteers. "I had a great time there during my visit," he recalled. "Two guys I'd played with in high school were there, and my best friend said he wanted to go there. Me and my mom were so close, though; it was just too far from home. In the end, that was the deciding factor. When we visited Michigan State, my mother just fell in love with the place.

"I was real comfortable with Coach Perles and Dino Folino, the defensive backfield coach."

I was also familiar with Folino. I worked with him at Pitt in the mid-'80s. He came out of Greenfield and played at Central Catholic High School. He was an assistant at Pitt under Foge Fazio. He was a good man, a good family man.

"He seemed like a real sincere guy, too," said Bell. "He came across real well. He said I was one of the top recruits. As I learned later, he got along well with the players. He was a great guy. I learned a lot from Coach Folino. We talked a lot. I had a great relationship with him. It was second only to my relationship with George Perles."

"Football coaches are always looking for guys who will hit you."
— Dick LeBeau

Bell was a big fan of Deion Sanders, the Prime Time $35 million defensive back of the Dallas Cowboys. "I get a kick out of him," said Bell. "I've never been a guy who talked a lot of trash. I have confidence in myself, but I don't talk it. When I do it now, it's all in good fun. I want to take the receiver's mind off what he's supposed to be doing. But Deion takes playing the game, and talking the game, well, he takes it to a whole different level. When I have a chance to see him play, I keep a close eye on him. He knows what he's doing. He's one in a million. I enjoy watching him play. He looks like a guy who enjoys what he's doing.

"Some athletes just get caught up in the money part. Nobody makes more money than Deion, but I believe he truly loves to play the game."

Asked if there were any other players he particularly admired, Bell said, "I grew up a Steeler fan. I looked up to Mel Blount and Donnie Shell, Jack Ham and Jack Lambert. Blount comes around the locker room from time to time. It's funny to see him; I didn't realize he was so big.

"The Steelers were my team. Those guys accomplished a great deal. But we're not them. We need to be ourselves. There's a lot of tradition around here, and I like that. They're sort of old-fashioned in their approach."

Bell was comfortable with his coaches with the Steelers as well, starting with Bill Cowher, the head coach, and Dick LeBeau, the defensive coordinator, and Tim Lewis, the defensive backfield coach.

"I couldn't have come to a better situation," said Bell. "Lucky to come to an organization and have somebody like Dick LeBeau as my coach. He should be in the Hall of Fame. He had 62 career interceptions. It's great to have Tim Lewis. He's a technician. That's why he was a first round choice."

Bell appreciates their approach to coaching as well. They don't swear at their charges.

"It's something that I think about," said Bell. "Dick said when he was playing, he told his coaches, 'I'm not the type of guy you have to cuss out.' And he treats his players the same way. So does Tim. They sit down and talk to you like a man. If you keep screwing up, they'll put their foot down.

"I contributed last year (1994). I grew a little more. One of the good things is that I'm learning in a real good situation. One thing I realize, from Deon's experience — when he got shot — is that it can be taken away from you so fast. I don't stay shut up in my house, but I think a lot more about where I go and who I'm with. I've learned from the older guys about where to go and where not to go."

Before LeBeau, Dom Capers was the defensive coordinator of the Steelers. That was in Bell's rookie season. Capers liked what he saw of Bell. He included him in a list of players on the team he called "impact players." Besides Bell, the list had Greg Lloyd, Rod Woodson, Carnell Lake, Levon Kirkland and Kevin Greene. Capers also said of Bell, "He's a playmaker."

LeBeau liked Bell just as much. "Football coaches are always looking for guys who will hit you, and Bell is one of them."

Bell was happy he struck the Steelers' brass that way. "I just try to get there and give it everything I've got," he said of his playing style. "I try to explode into the guy. Luckily, the guys cough up the ball."

"I want to help our youth out."
— Myron Bell

He and his neighborhood buddies in Toledo started their own league. "We had our street football teams," recalled Bell. "I lived in Oakwood, and our team's name was the Oakwood Raiders. We used to play other neighborhood teams. That's how I started playing football."

This was December 27, 1995, when Bell said that, right before the playoffs, and Bell was looking back on his beginnings. "My first exposure to organized team sports came in the eighth grade, when I played both football and basketball," he said.

He did the same at Macomber-Whitney High School. In football, he was the City League's Player of the Year in Toledo, and Co-Player of the Year in Ohio. He also excelled on the track team where he was named to the city's 4 x 100 relay team.

He played point guard for the Macomber-Whitney basketball team, and was a defensive stopper on a team that went 27-1 and earned a state championship and a No. 5 national ranking. The star of that team was a certain swingman named Jimmy Jackson, who would later be an All-American at Ohio State and the No. 1 draft choice of the Dallas Mavericks.

"Jimmy and I are real close," said Bell. "We've known each other since 8th grade. I talk to him about twice a month."

Bell took pride in stopping opposing scorers in basketball and in football. He had his comeuppance, however, when he went up against New York Archbishop Malloy's Kenny Anderson. He recalled that Anderson lit him up for 35 points in a prep tournament in South Carolina.

"I felt bad about that," Bell said. "But after seeing Kenny do so well in college and the pros, I don't feel so bad anymore."

When Bell was a student at Michigan State, he was interviewed about his prospects, and he offered some revealing insights.

"I wanted to go to college and major in something that will help me work with kids in the future," he said. "I guess I want to help our youth out — the problem children. I can see myself being a probation officer or a guidance counselor for troubled youth."

He wanted to do for others what his mother, Retha, and his grandmother, Barbara, did for him and his family.

"The chance is there for me. There's a chance to make good money and help my mother and grandmother," he said of his opportunities.

"It's everything to me. If I don't get it done, I'll feel like a total failure. I like putting pressure on myself to do well. There's enough pressure in going to school, getting the grades, and being an athlete. But I'm ready for more pressure. I can take it."

Some nights, he confessed, it was difficult for him to get to sleep in his dorm room.

"When I finally do get to sleep, I dream about playing in the NFL and making a big hit against Michigan. I jump, kick around and bite in my sleep. It seems so real.

"I think about football every night. And then my mother and grandmother. It always goes back to those two. My grandmother has been having some problems with the bills. I don't have one of the sad stories about not eating at night. I grew up in some bad neighborhoods, but I always had clothes on my back and three meals a day."

He had great confidence as a cornerback in his senior season at Michigan State.

"Whoever lines up against me, I feel like I own that person," he told a student sportswriter on the East Lansing campus. "When I'm running with a guy I can go as fast as he can go. I guess it's complete instinct. I've always been that way. You're not always successful. Every so often, you're going to get buried. It happens in this game. You have to refuse to be beaten."

"Life is about the choices you make."
— Retha Martin,
Myron Bell's mother

Retha Martin sounded like a mother who had always had genuine concern for her children. Myron "Boo" Bell may be a hard-hitting defensive back for the Pittsburgh Steelers, but he will always be Retha Martin's baby. "He is, and he always will be," she said with more than a hint of pride over the telephone from her home in Toledo, Ohio.

She provided some insights into her son's demeanor and drive, her continuing concern about his welfare, whether it was the challenges he faced on the football field or the ones that, as a young high-profile professional athlete with a fat wallet, he faced off the football

Myron at age 11 in 6th grade

At age 17 as 12th grader

Myron, sister Cherise, and their mom, Denise Retha Bell.

As a grade school football player

field. Good mothers never stop worrying. She talked about the love beween her mother, Barbara Bell, and her grandson, and the special bond they shared.

"Myron was always high-spirited, and more determined than most kids," she recalled. "I didn't have to discipline him much. You'd hurt his feelings if you said anything critical of him. He always wanted to be liked. If you ever see a kid who liked everything, he was like that. He was always a peace-maker. If there was something he could do for you, he'd go the extra mile to do it. He aimed to please.

"If he was getting a 'C' in some subject, and you told him you thought he could get a 'B' if he worked a little harder, he would do it. He'd always do what you told him."

Myron had said his mother moved the family to get them into a better environment when they were young, but that he often returned to his old neighborhood to be with friends.

"Our original neighborhood was quickly becoming a drug-infested neighborhood," said Myron's mother. "There was a corner store where all the kids had to pass, and it was a meeting spot for a lot of drug dealers. I didn't want my kids involved in that. I didn't want that at my front door. I never told him he wasn't allowed to go back there, though."

Myron had gotten himself into a mess early in the 1995 season when he was stopped by police and found to have a gun in his possession without having a permit to carry it. That drew negative publicity in Pittsburgh. His biggest concern was how his mother would react when she learned what had happened.

"Myron knows I have always been opposed to guns," said his mother. "He had told me what trouble some of the players had had about being robbed — how Yancey Thigpen and Ernie Mills both had encountered problems like that, how Deon Figures, one of his best friends on the team, had been shot in the leg back home in Los Angeles. I told him if anyone held him up to just give them what they wanted. I told him, 'You can always buy what they take, but you can't replace your life.' When you start carrying a gun it only worsens the problem. He clearly knows my objections."

Mrs. Martin is more familiar than most mothers with the dangers of the streets, not only because of the Toledo neighborhood where they lived, but also because she worked in a staff support position in an alcohol and drug rehabilitation facility in Toledo for 13 years.

"I've seen it all," she said. "It doesn't matter where you come from, or where you are in life, you are at risk when it comes to alcohol and drug addiction and all its associated problems.

"Life is all about the choices you make, and Myron has heard me talk about that since he was a little kid. You have to pay the consequences, good or bad, for the choices you make. When it comes to alcohol and drugs, you have three outs. You either quit, or you go to jail, or you end up dead.

"I asked Myron one day what kept him out of that life. He had friends who did get into trouble in that respect. He said, 'You always told me the three outs. And I didn't like any of them. If you don't buy it, you don't have it.' "

Retha Martin raised Myron and his sister, Cherise, by herself before eventually marrying Joe Martin. "I raised the two of them, for the most part, as a single parent," she said. "I have since had another son, Antoine."

She mentioned that Myron was the Player of the Year two years running on his high school football team, a member of a state basketball championship team, and a silver medalist in the state track and field championship.

She thought Myron made a good choice when he decided to accept a football scholarship from Michigan State. She remembered George Perles, the head coach, coming to their home to talk to them. Prior to returning to his alma mater, Perles had been with the Pittsburgh Steelers when they won four Super Bowls in the '70s, and he proudly wore one of his NFL championship rings.

"Coach Perles has my utmost respect," she said. "Everything he promised to do for Myron he made good on his word. He said they would keep after him to keep his grades up, and that it wasn't going to be all football for him at Michigan State. Everything he said he would do he did."

How did Myron get his nickname of Boo? "When he was a baby, you could tickle him so bad, and say, 'Boo-Boo,' and he just giggled. He was 'Boo-Boo' for a long time. Then one of the 'Boos' got dropped."

She mentioned that one of Myron's boyhood friends and high school teammates was Jim Jackson, who was playing for the NBA's Dallas Mavericks.

"They were best friends," said Mrs. Martin. "They still are. Jim still calls here."

She hoped Myron would continue to make good choices when it came to friends and activities. "He knows you have to deal with the consequences of your choices; that's been drummed into him," she said.

"He had responsibility when he was young. I had to work, and he had to look after his sister. He had to make sure she was fed and that they both did their homework. He was good about that.

"I enjoyed him playing all the sports he did. That kept him busy, too. There was a time when he was a better basketball player. He also knew that if his grades weren't where they should be that the first thing to go was going to be sports. He knew what it took to stay eligible."

"Myron is his own person."
— Retha Martin

A few weeks later, Myron's mother sent me a letter in which she expressed some reflections on raising her son:

"As I look back at Myron's childhood and my parenting, I find myself feeling pretty lucky. Myron has always had a willingness to try and be the best at whatever the challenge was. Myron was never afraid to dream. A dream of what you want is the beginning of what helps motivate you. Myron's desires and expectations (of self) to be the best were his motivation.

"Myron was taught that you always have a choice and that you live with the consequences of your choice. If I had to describe Myron in a sentence, it would read: 'Myron is his own person.'

"I can remember the first time he tried out for his school's basketball team and was not selected. Myron came home that day angry, hurt and determined he would never try out again for anything else because he had been treated unfairly by being cut from the team.

"Myron was told that everything won't always be fair, but to say you won't try again is to say you have given up. Once you stop believing in yourself, no one else will believe in you, either. Needless to say, Myron did play that year for two different teams outside of school, and he was voted MVP and his team won both divisions. The following year the coach at his high school asked him if he would play with his basketball team.

"Myron's football started pretty much the same way. Myron's sense of responsibility and values were impressed upon him at an early age by my mother and myself. Myron was given gifts for birthdays and holidays. All other extras were earned by getting good grades, his paper route or following whatever guidelines that were set for him.

"Myron has often told me that I am his inspiration, because I could always find something positive to say about the worst situations for him, and how I would never give up even when things seemed like they couldn't get any worse.

"Children, like parents, don't come with a manual of 'how to.' I gave Myron love, support and the best directions I had to offer. Again, I must repeat myself by saying I feel pretty lucky to have a son like Myron.

"If I had a message to give to today's kids it would be to love, respect and trust your parents and yourself. Set attainable goals for yourself and don't depend on someone else to accomplish them for you. Lastly, never be afraid to dream.

"I don't know if Myron ever dreamed of being a professional football player, but I do know he always wanted to be successful and knew it would depend on him. There was nothing magical about his success. He worked hard at making something of himself and football was on that path.

"I can remember once telling Myron that he was not going to attend a school because of the reputation the school had. Myron's response to me was 'it doesn't matter what may be going on in the school. If you want to learn, you will learn.' Myron was allowed to attend the school and did very well.

"I have learned and have watched my children learn how anything is possible if you want it and are willing to work toward obtaining it."

Antoine and Cherise with their mother, Denise Retha, and, below, she and her husband, Tom Martin.

Norm Johnson
Still kicking strong

"They're getting a big bang for their buck."

K ickers keep to themselves on the pro football scene. Their daily demands and responsibilities are simply different from the rest of the pack. *They* are different from the rest of the pack, a breed unto themselves, often with mischievous minds of their own. Some of them have been real flakes. They are not involved in the wham-bam of contact work, or the tedious walk-throughs and run-throughs of the practice routine, and they do not spend as much time in the weight room as their teammates. They do not have to study or memorize the playbook.

They are outsiders in most clubhouse exchanges, wallflowers in the daily frivolity. They usually look like students from some stuffy prep school who got lost on the way to a worship service.

They kick when they can, do their best to appear busy, and not just bemused by the proceedings. They try to stay out of harm's way, lest one of the big guys run over them when they are standing on the sidelines. It's happened. They are often targets for put-downs. When things get particularly steamy at the summer workouts at St. Vincent College, or nasty and cold on a gray December day at Three Rivers Stadium, the other Steelers, sweating or chilled, may resent the kickers' penthouse existence. And Bill Cowher can get hot in a hurry, too, and get in their faces over their failures.

When they are called upon to perform their magic, however, there isn't any question theirs is a high-pressure job.

Their placement misses or misplaced punts remain on the minds of most of their colleagues and the fans, especially letter-to-the-editor writing fans or sports talk show-calling fans, long after their successes have been forgotten.

Some of them, like Gary Anderson, were foreign-born. Alex Karras, the former defensive lineman of the Detroit Lions, once suggested that such foreign-born kickers should be deported. Norm Van Brocklin, a fiery coach and quarterback, said the U.S. government should tighten the immigration laws.

Kickers have their own fraternity in the National Football League. Kickers come and go in some places, stay forever in other places, and often spot one another passing through the revolving doors of their often under-appreciated and precarious profession. When things go badly, they are the pariahs of the pro game. Absolute lepers. Even when things go well, some sports columnist, searching for an angle on Wednesday, is apt to call for the abolishment of field

Pittsburgh Steelers

Steelers' placekicker Norm Johnson

Pittsburgh Steelers/Bill Amatucci

goals and extra points in the scoring system. The game's rule-makers are no kinder, constantly tinkering with their life's work, shortening the kicking tees, lengthening the kickoff distance, moving or downsizing the goal posts, making it more difficult for them to contribute in a positive way and earn their keep in their favorite pastime. It is no wonder they look out for each other, tend to talk a defensive game, and require exceptionally loyal and supportive wives and families.

Former Steelers coach Chuck Noll played for the Cleveland Browns when Lou Groza was a Pro Bowl tackle in addition to handling the place-kicking duties better than anybody else in the league, and Horace Gillom was a terrific end in addition to handling the punting chores. Specialists were alien to Noll's nature. He liked his players to be versatile, to get dirty and earn their paychecks.

Norm Johnson and Rohn Stark were both newcomers to the Steelers' locker room for the 1995 season, four years after Noll had given way to Cowher as head coach. Until the playoffs came around, Johnson and Stark were seldom sought after for their thoughts on the Steelers' state of affairs. By that time, everyone realized that Johnson had enjoyed a super season, and merited more attention and praise. Stark was having a so-so season, but he suddenly drew attention before the Steelers tangled with his former team, the Indianapolis Colts, in the American Football Conference championship game. Stark could offer interesting comparisons between Cowher and his former coach, Ted Marchibroda, and keen insights into some of his former teammates. Plus, he was pleasant and more approachable and talkative than, say, Greg Lloyd.

Stark and Johnson were stored away in the corner of the clubhouse in adjoining dressing stalls. They were in the first two dressing stalls to the right as one enters the Steelers' off-the-field domain. They were easily bypassed. Those same slots in the Steelers locker room were occupied the previous season by Gary Anderson and Mark Royals. Johnson, occupying the second slot, was much bigger and sturdier-looking, at 6-2, 202 pounds, than Anderson, a baby-faced 5-9, 175. Whereas Anderson had wandered unwittingly into pro football from the soccer fields of South Africa and Downingtown, Pennsylvania, Johnson had been at least a four-sport star on the southern California scholastic scene. Stark was a decathlete at Florida State University, and qualified for the U.S. Olympic Trials in 1980, but he passed on them rather than delay the start of his pro football career. Stark had to be one of the best athletes in the Steelers' clubhouse. Johnson and Stark certainly looked more like genuine athletes than their predecessors, for whatever that was worth.

Matt Bahr and David Trout, two of the more recent place-kickers, were both little guys, real runts. They and Anderson looked more like acolytes or altar boys than football players. Johnson and Stark were both handsome fellows, their leading-man faces providing quite a contrast, say, to the wizened masks of veteran kickers Roy Gerela and Bobby Walden of the Steelers' Super Bowl winners of the mid-'70s. Certainly, Stark was more reliable and sure-footed than John Goodson, a spaced-out, bare-footed punter from the University of Texas the Steelers experimented with in 1982. Talk about flakes and free spirits...Goodson was good fun. One of the biggest mistakes the Steelers ever made was in letting Bahr go in favor of Trout in 1981. They were lucky to come up with Anderson a year later, as he was one of the best in the business over the next 13 seasons (1982-94). The same could be said of Bahr and Johnson, who rank among the all-time leaders. Bahr, a Penn State grad, kept his home in Pittsburgh's Mt. Lebanon community.

After Anderson and the Steelers managed to wage a war of the wills that left both sides looking bad — a loss-loss situation in contract negotiations if there ever was one — the Steelers' place-kicking situation looked to be a source of genuine concern as the 1995 season loomed ahead. With Anderson, it had always been a source of strength.

I heard Anderson speak to a Christian men's breakfast at the St. Clair Country Club late in his contract dispute, and he told the assembly, "I'm putting my contract problems in the hands of The Lord." I told him afterward that if he did that, and no irreverence intended, he would surely be kicking in some other city come 1995. I suggested he go directly to Dan Rooney and get a deal done. Anderson was more concerned about his agent's feelings than his own welfare.

When Anderson's agent failed to accept the Steelers' last offer, the team turned to the Indianapolis Colts to come up with a place-kicker in Dean Biasucci, as well as a punter in Stark. But Biasucci was a disaster in the pre-season schedule, got hurt and suffered poorly from constant critical comparisons to Anderson, a long-time favorite in Pittsburgh, and the Steelers resumed searching for a proficient place-kicker. They were fortunate to find Johnson, a free-agent who had been left out in the cold by the Atlanta Falcons, similarly to how he had been left out in the cold a few years earlier after nine mostly solid seasons with the Seattle Seahawks.

Johnson was released by the Falcons before training camp in 1995 despite making 52 of 57 field goals the previous two seasons. The Falcons simply fell over themselves when the opportunity to get Morten Andersen came up. The Steelers, at the 11th hour, got the steal of the year, as Johnson pointed out to everybody with a pen, notepad or tape-recorder the rest of the season. Johnson signed with the Steelers for $400,000 a year, about half of what the Steelers had offered Anderson at one point.

"They're getting a big bang for their buck," Johnson said late in a season in which he was a legitimate candidate for the team's most valuable player award won by quarterback Neil O'Donnell. He came up just short of grumbling about being compensated below market value.

"We were fortunate that things worked out," said Tom Donahoe, director of football operations for the Steelers. Fortunate, indeed.

Johnson won over the fans fast. In the season opener at Three Rivers Stadium, the Steelers defeated the Detroit Lions, 23-20, on Johnson's 31-yard field goal with no time left on the clock. Johnson kicked three field goals altogether, also hitting from 39 and 47 yards in the first half, and missed one from 45. Suddenly, Steelers' fans were grunting, "Gary who?" How soon they forget.

Johnson came through for the Steelers again and again with his soccer-style swipes at the ball, and the fans had great faith in his foot. In the final minutes of Super Bowl XXX, before O'Donnell had dumped off his second killer interception, most of the Black and Gold faithful felt confident that if the Steelers could just get within reasonable range that Johnson surely could kick a game-tying field goal to send the game into overtime. That is, if O'Donnell couldn't deliver a game-winning touchdown pass, or Bam Morris couldn't score on a breakaway run. But the fans believed with all their hearts that Johnson would not disappoint them.

It was no wonder. Johnson set Steeler team records by kicking 34 field goals, within one of the NFL's season record, and won the league's scoring championship with 141 points. His field goal percentage (.829, 34-for-41) was second best in team history. At one point in the season, Johnson connected on 25 consecutive field goals inside the 40-yard line. His kickoffs were stronger and longer than Anderson's and the Steelers' kickoff coverage improved dramatically, vaulting the team from 23rd in the league to first, limiting their opponents to an average kickoff return of 17.5 yards.

At 35, with 15 NFL seasons behind him, Johnson felt he was as good as ever. "I'm more proud of what I've done the last five years than anything else in my pro career," Johnson said. "I'm excited that I'm going to the Pro Bowl. I'm real proud of what I've done here."

"I think I'll be OK."
— Norm Johnson

Johnson sat in a soft black leather chair in a small room just outside Dan Rooney's office in the Steelers' complex at Three Rivers Stadium on Wednesday, January 3, 1996, just three days before the team's first playoff game with the Buffalo Bills, and talked about his career during an hour-long interview.

Johnson squirmed in his seat, and was not comfortable. His back was bothering him. He kept getting up out of his seat to stretch or bend over, to try to work out the kinks. At times, he just grimaced. His midriff was wrapped tight, and he held a large ice bag to his ribs. He looked to be in great discomfort. He admitted he was hurting, but he felt he would be fine by game time. "I think I'll be OK by Saturday," he said. This guy is going to kick off and kick field goals against the Bills in three days, I thought to myself. No way. If I were a betting man, I'd have gone out and bet the house against the Steelers. I said nothing about Johnson's physical problems to anyone, not wanting to draw any attention to his dilemma or to cause him any additional difficulty since he had been kind enough to submit to a lengthy interview when he really did not feel so hot.

So what happened? Johnson kicked four field goals in as many attempts to tie a Steelers' post-season record, hitting from 45, 38, 34 and 39 yards, as the Steelers beat the Bills, 40-21, at Three Rivers Stadium. So much for inside information, as the late Jimmy "The Greek" Snyder used to say. A week later, against Indianapolis, Johnson was successful twice from 34 yards out, and was wide right from 40 yards out, in a 20-16 victory over the Colts.

Johnson spoke about his earliest days in sports, and the people who helped him along the way, especially his family, and his journey from being an all-sports standout as a kid in California to coming to the Steelers for the 1995 season.

"My dad was a great athlete who won a lot of awards," Johnson said. "He got into coaching soon after he came out of the military service. My dad did a lot of sports, and I'm sure I was introduced to sports earlier than some kids as a result. I didn't know much about his background in sports. I still don't. I don't know how good he was; he doesn't want to talk about it much. He has clippings and championship awards he has put away somewhere. Now I'm old enough, and I want to find out. I know it's there. My dad is going to be in town. He'll be here for a while. You can ask him some questions. He'd enjoy talking to you because you know the people he's talking about better than I do.

"He must have been pretty good. He's in the sports Hall of Fame at Cal-Santa Barbara."

What were Norm's earliest memories of his parents promoting sports involvement?

"I remember him and my mom...they didn't push me. I want to do that as a parent. I'm sure I was encouraged, but I was never pushed into anything. That's the way to do it.

"I must have been pretty good and I enjoyed it. He was always there to play catch. I played Pop Warner, and he was there every game. I played about three or four sports most of the time and my parents were always there. My dad worked hard through the early years to support the family. He was a school teacher. So was my mom. My dad also worked as a deputy sheriff. They'd call him whenever they wanted him. He loved the midnight shift because it was peaceful, driving the countryside when the roads were clear. He worked so many days a week. Growing up, I didn't think about it. It's just the way it was.

"Now I can appreciate that it was pretty tough, doing what he was doing and still spending time with his kids. It was a good neighborhood. My wife, Lori, tells me it was a 'Leave It To Beaver' neighborhood. Everyone played ball in Little League. It was just normal.

"This was around 1970. I was born in 1960 and grew up in the '60s and '70s in Southern California. Every summer we went up north to Seattle and Alaska. We all had three months off and spent the time up there. My mom was born in Ketchikan, Alaska, which is located on the panhandle south of Juneau, and about 500 miles north of Seattle. We'd pack up a station wagon and drive up there. We had a boat and some property; it was a great getaway place.

"My dad taught phys ed, math and driver's ed. My mom, Charlotte, was nicknamed Bunnie. She taught fourth and fifth graders in elementary school. So we were expected to do well in school academically as well as athletically.

"I was a pretty decent football and soccer player, and I played basketball. I thought I was a pretty good baseball player and I often wonder what would have happened had I pursued baseball. That's what my dad wanted me to do. My main position was pitcher. I was a pretty good hitter, but not a power hitter. I pitched and played third base. I thought I was a good player; I won quite a few awards.

"I dislocated my shoulder playing football. I was seeing a doctor, and my dad was with me. When the doctor learned I was also a kicker, he told us about Ben Agajanian. I didn't know him at all (Agajanian had been a pro football kicker with the New York Giants, among other teams, in the early '50s). He had a kicking camp. I decided to go to it. He must have thought I had some talent, and he worked with me quite a bit. He helped me a lot. He used me to demonstrate what he was teaching the other kids. I give him a lot of credit for my early instruction and development.

"Curiously enough, Agajanian had the toes on his kicking foot cut off in an elevator accident, and he was a straight-on kicker. He wore a special customized football shoe, with a squared-off toe. I went there questioning the whole operation as a result of that. I asked him, 'Weren't you a straight-on kicker? What do you know about soccer-style kicking?' But he had worked with the Dallas Cowboys and he knew all there was to know about kicking, whatever the style. He knew his stuff, every aspect of it."

"He'd call me in and chew out my butt. "
— Norm Johnson on Chuck Knox

Johnson, at 31, was waived by the Seattle Seahawks at the outset of the 1991 season in favor of a rookie draftee, former University of Georgia kicker John Kasay.

"The thing that hurt me is playing with them for so long and giving them my all, and then they said there was this competition thing at camp,' Johnson said. "I was having a great camp and, at one point,

Norm Johnson as 12-year-old in 1972

As 11-year-old baseball player

Norm, at right, visits with his brother Mitch and pet dog Kimba in May, 1996.

they said they were going to take me, but that wasn't their decision at all. They held onto me and dangled me around the league for a trade so they could get something for me.

"They couldn't work that out, so the next thing I know, I'm cut and given an apple and a road map and that's it after nine years of good service to the team and the community."

Johnson and his wife were very involved in community service during his stint with the Seahawks. He and Lori first met when both were volunteering at a Special Olympics event. In 1988, Johnson was the Seahawks' nominee for the NFL Man of the Year for his community service. Anderson was similarly involved in the community during his long stay with the Steelers.

It was generally thought that Johnson fell out of favor with the Seahawks coach, Chuck Knox, after missing two potential game-winning field goals in Denver. Johnson missed one at the end of regulation time and one in overtime against the Broncos.

I mentioned to Johnson that I knew Knox and had toured his hometown of Sewickley with him once when he was in Pittsburgh to play in a celebrity golf outing at the Pittsburgh Field Club. Knox grew up living over a saloon in Sewickley, and took great pride in his blue collar roots. His mother was a cleaning lady in homes in the better section of Sewickley. Knox took me to The Glass Bar in Coraopolis and introduced me to some of his boyhood buddies. His parents weren't among the moneyed people of Sewickley; they both worked hard.

"We heard many Sewickley stories: coal-mining stories, put-on-your-hard-hat and bring-your-lunch stories, from Chuck Knox," Johnson said. "He still says he had nothing to do with drafting John Kasay and letting me go. I think it probably was more Tom Flores, the GM. We had a change in ownership and things kinda were going downhill at that time.

"I wouldn't say Chuck and I had a falling out. I always thought he was a good coach. Things had·changed in the front office set-up and he was losing control. And he finally had enough of it. I don't know if that's the way to say it. But he was friendly with me, even when he was with the Rams. I learned a lot from Chuck.

"But him being a throwback to another era in football, and me being a kicker, well, we'd bang heads about special teams philosophy. He'd call me in and chew out my butt if I missed kicks. Some people in pro ball really stress special teams, and some are indifferent about it. Cowher's background helps in that regard because he coached special teams in Cleveland and in Kansas City.

"Chuck didn't have that. I remember Chuck every so often saying, 'Groza never cared where the laces were...just put the ball down and kick it.'"

It's no wonder Chuck Knox and Chuck Noll were often confused with one another. That comment sure sounded familiar to anyone who spent time around Noll. Remember Gary Anderson screaming for a long-snapper specialist in his latter years with the team?

"Gary is gone.
Life goes on."
— Norm Johnson

The Pittsburgh Tribune-Review ran a box every week of the season showing how Johnson had fared in comparison to Anderson, who signed with the Philadelphia Eagles. So he knew how he was doing. But he hated that chart.

"It's ridiculous," Johnson said late in the season, protesting to the press. "Get over it, will you? Gary is gone. Life goes on."

Johnson felt particularly uncomfortable with the comparison because he knew Anderson well, considered him a good friend, and had socialized with him on several occasions.

"I don't think much of the Gary Anderson thing," he insisted during an interview with several writers earlier in the season. "I don't think I had anything to do with that. Gary made a choice to go out on the market and nobody can control that.

"I didn't watch him kick. I can't make any comments on that. You guys can do all the comparative stats and film work. That's your job. I am just trying to do what I can do to help the team. Let's move on. There are two options to this scenario. Either Gary outshines me or I outshine him, but it's nothing personal." Eyeing the writers who surrounded his dressing stall, he asked, "Why do you want me to rag on the guy, you know? You shouldn't badmouth me or him."

Bobby April, who coached the special teams and oversaw considerable improvement in all areas in his two seasons with the Steelers, would agree. April didn't want to compare the kickers, either.

"Gary was a tremendous field goal kicker and had a tremendous career here," April said. "You are not talking about a guy who is just a guy. Gary at his position was like a lot of great players who played here at theirs."

He thought Johnson had stood up well in a pressure situation. "Whether he is better, worse or whatever, if you are talking about them in almost the same vein in terms of their ability to kick field goals, you are talking about two great kickers," said April, who worked with Johnson in Atlanta. "He is the greatest kicker who ever kicked for the Falcons. The guy is a good kicker — like there is a revelation there. We were one of the best, if not the best, kickoff coverage teams in the league when we were at Atlanta."

In 1993, Johnson enjoyed a streak of 26 consecutive field goals, the second best streak ever in NFL history, while kicking for the Falcons. He kicked 21 straight at the start of the season, to break a record set by Mark Mosely and Morten Andersen, and he had kicked five in a row at the end of the 1992 season to start the streak.

Johnson recognized that he was lucky to come to the Steelers after Biasucci and not immediately after Anderson.

"Biasucci was the fall guy," Johnson said. "He acted as a buffer. That was unfair. He didn't get much of a chance before they let him go. He's a great kicker and he's a friend of mine. I have nothing but good things to say about him. It would have been the same way if I followed Anderson here. I'd have said, 'Thank you, Gary, good luck.' I have no hangups about that."

Johnson seemed like the strong, silent type, but his detachment may have hurt him in regard to publicity or national attention. He recalled how upset his wife, Lori, was when he hardly was mentioned on TV or in the newspapers after he kicked five of five field goals when the Steelers beat the Oakland Raiders, 29-10, on December 10, 1995.

"Morten Andersen made four of four that same Sunday, and it was big news," pointed out Johnson. "Gary Anderson made four of four and it was big news. But I made five of five on a bad field and it was hardly mentioned. My wife was so mad about that when I came home. I still haven't received much good national publicity.

"You need good publicity. The only publicity I received early was negative. The Falcons said a lot of bad things about me. It was so bad, I thought about suing them."

He did admit, however, that he had disappeared from the dressing room after that game in Oakland before anybody could interview him. "I didn't want to hang around," he said. So Johnson had only himself to blame perhaps if he came up short in newsprint the next day. Kickers have something else in common: a propensity to whine and wives who echo their sentiments.

The Falcons had signed Morten Andersen as a free agent after the New Orleans Saints had trouble keeping him under their salary cap.

Johnson signed with the Steelers at the 11th hour. He might have spent the winter at home watching games on TV if the Steelers had not signed him, though the New Orleans Saints were also seeking his services. He came with good credentials. He was named to the Pro Bowl with Seattle in 1984 and with Atlanta in 1993. He had proven his worth over a long period.

"They got a pretty good deal here; let's just leave it at that," Johnson said, alluding to his $400,000 salary, low for a kicker of his accredited stature.

Since this author covered the Steelers when they won their fourth Super Bowl in 1980 and Terry Bradshaw, their best player, still wasn't making more than $200,000 a season, it remained difficult to feel sympathetic to Steelers who complained about their pay these days. James Parrish, a journeyman offensive lineman who was cut by four NFL teams and seldom played anywhere, thought he was underpaid at $190,000 a year. And the bleat goes on.

"I'm very modest," Johnson insisted. "My wife has been bothered by it a lot more than I have. She doesn't feel I've gotten my proper due."

In that respect, Lori Johnson had a lot in common with Carol Anderson.

"One writer (in a national weekly football publication) called us flakes and whores," said Johnson. "My wife went through the roof. She actually wrote a letter back. I thought it was out of line for a guy to call us that."

"I started feeling more and more a Steeler."
— Norm Johnson

Johnson said it took a while, but that he felt quite comfortable in the clubhouse of the Steelers.

"I feel confident if my team and the coaches respect me," he said. "I feel good about what I do. That first game with Detroit sure helped me get established here. The acceptance I felt afterward...and the euphoria I felt afterward, I started feeling more and more a Steeler from then on."

He brought up an often overlooked aspect of the kicking game that made him feel good about being with the Steelers, and that was having long-snapper specialist Kendall Gammon getting the ball to Rohn Stark for placement. Johnson felt the three of them made for a great placement kicking team, and that most fans and sports critics don't recognize the importance of all the elements that go into a successful kick.

"What's good about Rohn...he's a tested veteran. He knows what he's doing," Johnson said. "Rohn is one of the best holders in the National Football League. I've been real fortunate to have good holders. But Rohn's probably No. 1; he's a tremendous holder. It's the last thing in the world I have to worry about. Rohn is a great guy; he's easy to get along with. There are some guys who aren't; I've heard some guys are real pains. And Kendall Gammon is so good and true and consistent with his snaps. I don't have to worry about that, either. If you have the ability to kick a ball, you couldn't ask for better help. If they're not the best, I don't know who is."

He moved his family to the suburbs just north of Pittsburgh during the 1995 season, but he was still more at home on the West Coast.

Johnson had established a trading card business, All-Pro Trading Cards, and originally had two stores in Washington, and one in California. But the trading card business hit a downturn, and when he came to the Steelers, he had just one store in Bellevue, not far from his home in Woodinville, Washington.

"I'm very proud of him."
— Howard Johnson

Norm's football hero was Howard Johnson. His dad was a teacher and coached football and baseball at Morningside High School in Inglewood and later Corona del Mar High School in Newport Beach. He was retired after 35 years in the education field.

His dad was one of five high school coaches who viewed game films to evaluate talent for the Chargers before they moved from Los Angeles to San Diego. Chuck Noll was the linebackers coach for the Chargers at the time.

Howard Johnson enjoyed listing his older son's accomplishments. As a sophomore in high school, Norm was moved up to varsity in 1975 as kicker and punter, and ended up starting as a tight end as well. Norm's leg was strengthened by years of soccer and he benefited by the guidance of kicking specialist Ben Agajanian. Johnson kicked a 49-yarder as a senior in high school. He could catch a football and block, too.

Johnson's father recalled when his son kicked two field goals, intercepted a pass and scored a touchdown in one game.

"As a football player, Norm did more than just kick," said his father, who visited the Steelers' offices during the playoffs at the end of the 1995 season. "He played tight end and outside linebacker and he did them all well.

"Usually people think of kickers as a separate breed of person, who normally is a loner. But not Norm. He didn't have that kind of persona. He had leadership qualities that very few high school players ever have."

As if playing his position wasn't enough, Johnson also played baseball, basketball and soccer and, as his father pointed out, Johnson was good in them all.

Johnson thought about Colorado and Oregon before UCLA called his Garden Grove home.

"UCLA was the biggest school that recruited me," Johnson said. "It was also close to home, had a great football tradition and my dad went there."

Terry Donahoe was the coach at UCLA when Johnson was there, and Johnson doesn't think he set the world on fire as a kicker there. "We didn't kick much," Johnson said. "I went 10 for 14 in my junior year, and 14 for 20 in my senior year. My first two years I didn't kick field goals. I kicked off for the first two years. Effren Herrera was kicking extra points and field goals for UCLA at that time. As far as I'm concerned, I just had two mediocre seasons at UCLA."

Charlotte and Howard Johnson are embraced by son, Norm, 1 1/2 years old, in 1961.

Steelers' placekicker Norm Johnson with his family at Doubletree Inn Resort in Scottsdale for Super Bowl XXX, wife Lori, and sons Jarrett and Jordan.

A check of his records revealed that Johnson was successful on all 34 point-after-touchdown conversion kicks as a senior at UCLA, and was 32 of 33 as a junior. So his kicking performance for the Bruins could hardly be termed mediocre. He signed with Seattle as a free agent in 1982.

It was intriguing to interview Howard Johnson. This one didn't make ice cream or own any hotels, but he had a great deal to do with the development of the Steelers' star kicker. And he couldn't have been more excited. His son had already been named to the Pro Bowl and the Steelers had a good shot at the Super Bowl.

"Oh, I love it," the elder Johnson said. "It's great. It's an outstanding feeling; I'm very very proud of him.

"My wife and I were in Atlanta visiting when Norm was up for grabs, and New Orleans was really after him. It came down to New Orleans and Pittsburgh. He knew it would be Pittsburgh. New Orleans can't compare as far as a place to bring up a family. He has two boys. He's extremely happy here.

"I think it's great. It's a great opportunity for him. He works hard at it. He's very dedicated. He's very humble. He takes success in stride. If something bad happens, he takes that in stride, too. He's very gifted."

I mentioned to Howard Johnson that his son said he had not told him a great deal about his own competitive days or his personal background.

"That's my style," said Norm's father. "You don't toot your own horn. My dream in high school was to be a major league baseball player. I didn't plan on playing football. I was a great Yankee fan; I looked up to Joe DiMaggio and then Mickey Mantle when I was growing up. I was born in 1929. I came close to signing with them in the '40s.

"He (Norm) was 17 when he graduated. I was 16 when I was finished my senior year. I was all LA County as a tackle. I weighed 210, and I was the only 200 pounder in the lineup in 1945. I went into the Marines for two years at the end of World War II. Then I went to college. I attended UCLA in 1948 and 1949, and graduated from UC-Santa Barbara in 1952. I got a commission as a first lieutenant; I went to Korea in 1952 and 1953. I was an infantry platoon leader in Korea for 19 months. When the war ended, July 27, 1953, I spent my time guarding a prison facility. I was discharged after three years in the service in 1955.

"I tried out for the Cleveland Browns that year. They had taken me in the draft in 1952. They kept five tackles. I was No. 7. They kept Mike McCormack, Lou Groza, Bob Gain, Dan Kissell and John Sandusky. You had to play offense and defense in those days because it was the days of the 33-man squad. It was the second year for Chuck Noll; he played linebacker and center behind Gatsky.

"Paul Brown was the owner and coach and the Browns trained in Hiram, Ohio. That was 1955; that was the year Otto Graham retired and they went to camp with George Ratterman and Bobby Freeman as their quarterbacks. Graham came back and they beat the Rams that year in the Coliseum; I went to all the Rams games, so I was there.

"My wife, Charlotte, whose nickname is 'Bunnie,' graduated from Western Washington University in Bellingham. She was the Northwest Blossom Queen in 1956; she and Norm served as the grand marshals for that parade when he was playing for the Seahawks.

"I wanted Norm to play baseball. He took to soccer at a young age. His first competitive sport was swimming when he was five. He played basketball as a freshman in high school. Norm had the proper equipment: the body, strong legs, strong body, strong mind, extremely smart, extremely intelligent.

"His high school football coach had been an old tackle and linebacker for the Steelers (1955-56). His name was Art Michalik, and he played for the Steelers and Eagles. He came over to our home and asked permission to move Norm up to varsity as a tenth grader, and that was on a championship team. He played tight end on the championship team. He kicked a 44-yard field goal in a game that year. He was an all-league tight end.

"I kicked in college, but with no success at all. I kicked off, not very far. I taught for 35 years, subjects like physical education, driver training and math. I started him in high school with an emphasis on math and science, in case he wanted to be a doctor or dentist. He was a scholar-athlete in high school, with a 3.8 GPA.

"They had a big banquet in Orange County for all the scholar athletes. Norm was going to UCLA. There was a fellow with a 4.0 GPA who was at the same banquet who ended up rooming with Norm. They took calculus together. Norm held his own.

"Norm's younger brother, Mitch, followed Norm to UCLA and played center there. He's 6-5, 250 now. He snapped the ball to Troy Aikman. He played with Carnell Lake, Ken Norton, Duval Love and Frank Kornish. He had a shoulder problem, a series of dislocations. He could have been a good center if he could have stayed healthy. He played soccer and tossed the discus and shot put in high school. He's a Costa Mesa police officer now.

"Norm spent every summer with our family in Alaska. He was eight years old when he went there for the first time. That's what we did; it was idyllic. I had the summer off; I refused to work. We just went up there and enjoyed it.

"He was as good an athlete as there was in the California Interscholastic Federation. He was 8-0 as a pitcher; he was a terrifically gifted athlete. He played basketball, which is great for whatever other sport you might play. He simply could do it all."

> "We don't care about being America's team. We're Pittsburgh's team."
>
> — Dan Rooney,
> Steelers owner

John Jackson
The Cincinnati Kid

"I remember as a child,
watching the game on TV,
and dreaming of someday
playing in the Super Bowl."

John Jackson was just sitting there, all by himself, able to survey the strange scene in Sun Devil Stadium in Tempe, Arizona, site of Super Bowl XXX. Nobody was blocking his view. This was Tuesday, January 23, 1996, designated Media/Photo Day. This was five days before the National Football League championship contest between the Pittsburgh Steelers and the heavily-favored Dallas Cowboys.

The Steelers' most celebrated ballplayers were standing before microphones up on platforms on the sideline of the football field, right below where Jackson was sitting. Many media members — reporters, photographers, radio and TV broadcasters and camera crews — were already crowded around the likes of Neil O'Donnell, Carnell Lake and Kevin Greene. The majority of Steelers were spread throughout the stands on the press box side of the stadium, their name on a sign affixed to a pole like the ones seen at a political convention.

The NFL had distributed over 3,000 media credentials to journalists from around the world. There was a crush at some of the interview stations. There was even a crowd gathered around an area in the stands not far from Jackson waiting for Greg Lloyd, the Steelers' outstanding and outspoken linebacker who made a habit of keeping the media waiting for him in Arizona. Greene, in particular, loved all the attention and addressed his audience with the zeal and gestures normally associated with a TV evangelist or a professional wrestler.

When I approached Jackson and called his attention to his surroundings, specifically to Greene's animated delivery, Jackson smiled and shook his head. "That's not me," he said. He had turned 31 earlier that month and was one of the more mature personalities in the Steelers' ranks.

Jackson was sitting in the stands, the backside of his gold pants creased by the top of the back of a bench, his white Reebok sneakers resting on the seat. A gentle giant, the 6-6, 295-pound Jackson sat there, stoically, his chin resting on his white-taped right fist, not a bad imitation of Rodin's "The Thinker." For ten or more minutes, no one had approached him.

I wondered what he was thinking. No one was near him. How did he feel about being virtually ignored in this showcase situation? He had toiled long and hard to get here, and now no one wanted to know his thoughts about the upcoming battle.

Jackson was a distinguished and veteran member of the Steelers' offensive line. He was one game away from finishing his eighth season with the Steelers. He had been chosen as an alternate in the Pro Bowl as recently as the 1994 season. He played the critical left tackle position where he was mostly responsible for keeping pass rushers away from O'Donnell's blind side. As a right-handed passer, O'Donnell was more apt to be looking to his right or down the middle of the field and, even when he was looking to the left sideline, his back was still exposed and vulnerable to the rush from his left side.

Jackson did not know whether or not he would be going up against Charles Haley, the Cowboys' badass premier pass rusher who was trying to come back from injuries that had sidelined him. The situation was similar to what Jackson had experienced a month earlier when he did not know until gametime whether or not Bruce Smith, the Pro Bowl defensive end for the Buffalo Bills, would be able to suit up or not across the line from him. As it turned out, Smith stayed back in Buffalo with a high fever from the flu. Jackson would not be so lucky with Haley, and Haley had embarrassed him in the opener at Three Rivers Stadium the year before. "You can't live like that, hoping someone won't line up against you," Jackson said. "You can't change your game plan. Everyone I'm going to face is good. They put their best pass rusher on that side. No matter who it is, you've got to get inside their mind."

This had already been a difficult season for Jackson. He had his streak of playing in 97 consecutive games broken when he did not play against the Minnesota Vikings on September 24 because of a knee injury. He missed four games after having arthroscopic surgery on his right knee. Some members of the media had been questioning the level of his performance, and that heated up when his coach, Bill Cowher, chose to continue with Justin Strzelczyk at left tackle even after Jackson was pronounced fit to return to action. Jackson was upset later on when Cowher benched him in the second quarter of a game against the Oakland Raiders, right after he had been beaten by defensive end Pat Swilling. Jackson's pride was hurt. It had been that kind of season. He did not need the challenge of fending off Haley, no matter what he might say publicly.

I had approached Jackson in the dressing room immediately after the win over the Indianapolis Colts in the American Football Conference Championship at Three Rivers Stadium. He seemed sober and distant, brushing off congratulatory greetings from passersby. He shook hands, but with no enthusiasm. He seemed upset about something. There had not been much of a celebration by most of the Steelers after that emotionally-draining last-second victory — they realized there were still bigger fish to fry — but Jackson seemed downright upset. As it turned out, he said he was not happy with the way he had played. He had gotten hurt again. It was tough enough to play to the high standards set for him, to begin with, but it was much more difficult when you were hurting. "I was not happy, you're right," he said when I asked him about his odd post-game behavior. "I had reinjured the leg; it was frustrating. How many opportunities do you get to go to the playoffs?"

Normally, no one in the Steelers' locker room looked as regal as John Jackson. There was something about him, the way he held his head high, his proud carriage, the way he walked about the room, that demanded respect. He was quiet and reserved, and usually offered a soft-spoken, thoughtful interview. In that respect, he was a lot like Larry Brown, who toiled at tackle for the great Steelers' teams of the '70s. He also reminded me of Willis Reed, the proud warrior who played the pivot for the New York Knicks' championship teams of the early '70s. They demanded respect by their mere presence. They didn't have to shout to get anyone's attention.

"There's always some feelings of fear."
— John Jackson

Some young people from a Christian TV station identified themselves to Jackson, knowing he prided himself on his Christian approach to his life beyond the football field. "If you walk with the Lord, it makes a big difference," Jackson told them. "They'll play the game with or without you, but you'll be all right as long as God is with you."

Later, when I asked him how his faith figured into the equation for something like Super Bowl XXX, he said, "This game is bigger than all of us, but God is bigger than everything. It's a big game, but it's not the top of the world. It's probably the biggest game of my career. You have to put things in their proper perspective. This year has been a frustrating year for me. I had lots of things pulling at me, the setback of the surgery, stuff like that. But I never swerved in my faith. He gave me a body for this game; I honor Him. I want Him to be with me wherever I am. I don't pray to ask for a win or anything like that. I have my life in order. The bottom line is what's in The Word. If you have a great day, leave it alone. Just leave it as a great day. Don't try to put any more importance in it beyond that. I live one day at a time. I believe He is with me. It's a big comfort."

A week earlier, several Steelers and a couple of the Cowboys had credited God for their victories during post-game interviews, and one had to wonder whose side God would be on, if anyone's, when the Steelers locked horns with the Cowboys.

Those who say such things seem sincere enough in their beliefs, but it makes one wonder whether God gives such personal attention to athletic events. Jackson was smart enough to recognize that God does not get involved with the outcome of sports contests — and here's a possibly heretical statement for us to make — even if Notre Dame is playing.

I mentioned to Jackson that, years earlier, I had covered Muhammad Ali in several of his heavyweight championship boxing outings. I ventured that Ali was often panicky as fights approached, and some of his crazy behavior and shenanigans could be traced to his fear, as much as anything.

In all honesty, did Jackson approach Super Bowl XXX with any fear in his heart?

"Sure, there's always some feelings of fear for a football player, or any athlete," he admitted. "There's a fear of going out and not giving your best effort. That's only being human."

"It's my job to make sure I do things right."
— John Jackson

Approached by a few other writers, interested in focusing on the more secular aspects of the Super Bowl, Jackson switched gears and spoke about the importance of proper execution as the key to the Steelers' chances against the Cowboys. "If you don't execute in the game," he said, "you lose. You can't panic when something bad happens. You have to stick to proper technique, not your personal emotions."

When someone mentioned how the Steelers had overcome a disappointing 3-4 record at the start of the season, Jackson said, "When adversity happens it makes guys draw closer together. But that's in the past. We're a different team now."

As far as preparing to play against the hostile likes of Charles Haley, he said, "He can cause havoc, but it's my job to stop him. It's my job to make sure I do things right, and to play within myself. We'll be up for the challenge."

It was not the stuff that media people seeking red-hot quotations were likely to get excited about, but it was vintage John Jackson. He was an honorable fellow who played football for a living, well enough to get paid more than $1.5 million per season, and the only time he ever said anything that was apt to find its way into a newspaper or radio or TV sound bites was when he was upset about something. But he was not one to publicly gripe on a regular basis, either. He picked his openings.

"We're pretty typical of Pittsburgh," he told a writer who happened by and made it clear he was there to cover the Dallas Cowboys, and wanted to know how the Steelers compared to the Cowboys. "We like to work hard. We know how to work."

I grew up in the heart of Pittsburgh, and take great pride in being a Pittsburgher. I have gone away to work elsewhere — in Miami for a year, then New York for nine years — and had spent time in the Army in Louisville, Kansas City and some godforsaken outpost in Alaska. Yet I had no idea if Pittsburgh was still truly a blue-collar town, if people in Pittsburgh had a better work ethic than those in Dallas, or Denver, Miami or Minneapolis-St. Paul, if people in Pittsburgh were truly friendlier than the folks in New York, Chicago and LA. Whether that was true or not, we like to think we are. So Steelers like John Jackson and Coach Cowher keep spreading the gospel of Pittsburgh as told by Art Rooney, the late owner of the Steelers.

"I'm still in awe of all of this," Jackson said of the scene at Sun Devil Stadium on a sunny, but uncomfortably cool morning. "It makes it that much more different. You can just sit back and watch. I remember as a child, watching the Super Bowl on TV, and saying, 'One day I want to play in the Super Bowl.' So I am truly glad to be here."

How did Jackson feel about the Steelers being so lowly regarded, about some of the stinging comments made about them by some of the Cowboys? How Michael Irvin, their star receiver, had strongly hinted that the Super Bowl belonged to the Cowboys, that they were "at home" in the Super Bowl?

"That doesn't bother me. You have to be above that," Jackson said. "You don't want to get into a war of words, and set yourself up for any embarrassment. As it is, you can get humbled in a hurry in a game like this. I remember when Jackie Smith of the Cowboys dropped a sure touchdown pass in the end zone against the Steelers. I was just sitting there, watching the game, and I remember wondering, 'How would I feel if that was me?' In a couple of days I'll know. I'll be out there in the uniform of the Pittsburgh Steelers. You always see this on TV. To experience it yourself is quite overwhelming. You have to step back and ask yourself, 'Why am I here?' I think I know the answer."

Asked to explain his public outburst about being misunderstood and possibly unappreciated by the Pittsburgh media two months earlier, when he lectured them in the locker room, Jackson said, "It got to the point where you can only take so much. I had to take a stand. Enough is enough. Hey, if you want to know something affecting John Jackson, just ask him. Don't try to be a psychic or God. Ask me. It was something where I did what I thought I had to do."

Jackson was no different from most Steelers, or any other athlete, in that he was never enamored when his play came under critical scrutiny. Offensive linemen often complain that they never get any attention until they make a mistake, or blow an assignment, or get beaten by their man.

He knew his own history. He knew, for instance, that Haley had four sacks to his credit when the Cowboys beat the Steelers in the season-opener in 1994. So he was sensitive to questions about Haley. "Everybody has bad games, bad days," he said of that last match-up. Asked again if he thought Haley would play, he said, somewhat testily, "I don't know; we went through this a few weeks ago with Bruce Smith. He didn't show up. They didn't stop the game, did they?"

Jackson was upset, on the one hand, that Cowher decided not to automatically return him to the starting lineup when he was fit to do so, yet he was unhappy with how his play was scrutinized and judged in that return game and in subsequent games. He admitted he was rusty after missing four games following knee surgery. That was exactly why Cowher was hesitant to change his starting lineup, I thought at the time. The Steelers had won four straight in Jackson's absence and Cowher wanted to work Jackson back into the lineup gradually. "If it ain't broke, don't fix it," said Justin Strzelczyk, who had replaced Jackson in the starting lineup. There had always been an understanding with the Steelers that starters would not lose their jobs due to injuries. Cowher insisted that nothing had changed in that respect. "All my decisions," Cowher commented at his weekly press conference back then, "are based on what is in the best interest of this football team. What gives us the best chance to win? That's what I must concern myself with; sometimes it's not easy."

I was not present for Jackson's outburst, but I had said something to him when he returned to the lineup, letting him know after a game that it was good to see him back again. "I don't know if that's true; I'm not sure about that," he said, miffed that he had not started and had been used only sparingly in his first game back after being sidelined by an injury.

Talking more about the media than in reference to Cowher or anyone in the organization, Jackson said, "They expected me to come back after sitting out four weeks, and be the same. To throw myself back out there would be unfair to the team, and unfair to me. But they wrote stuff like, 'Jackson's not going to get his job back; he's lost his job.' I didn't think that was fair. It took me three or four weeks to shake the rust. Meanwhile, I heard rumors that I might be traded or cut. They were false rumors."

Weren't his own complaints, in the aftermath of some sub-par performances, a bit contradictory? Was he personally offended by the criticism, or the questioning of his ability to come back and reclaim his starting position?

"You have to be," he answered. "I take this game quite seriously. When you respond to those stories by saying something to that effect you look like a bad guy. Or that you're arrogant. 'What's wrong with him?' people might ask."

Jackson looked around the stadium, eager to switch the subject. He had other concerns about his situation, and his status in the high-pressure world of professional sports.

"My sons (Josh, 7, and Jordan, 3 1/2) are coming out. It means a great deal to me for them to be aware of all this. I want my sons to see me here, and be part of the experience. It's been exciting for me. It'll be exciting for me to go home to Cincinnati after this."

"I want to create more awareness around the
community for the need of athletics.
Without them, you take
away a lot of dreams for a lot of kids."

While Jackson takes great pride in playing in Pittsburgh, and partic-
ipates in many local fund-raising and charity-related activity, he has
not forgotten where he came from. While he was born to a military
family at Camp Kwe, Okinawa, he grew up and continued to live in
Cincinnati. He had resided in Pittsburgh for a period, but decided to
have a year-round residence in his hometown. NFL players were
making so much money in the '90s they could now afford to have
homes in several cities.

During the 1995 season, Jackson donated $10,000 to be used to
help fund the athletic program at his alma mater, Woodward High
School in Cincinnati. It would enable the financially-strapped varsity
sports programs to continue through the winter and spring seasons as
the Cincinnati public school system awaited passage of a tax levy to
fund such activities. "I want to create more awareness around the
community for the need of athletics," Jackson said. "Without them,
you take away a lot of dreams for a lot of kids."

Putting together such a distinguished career with the Steelers
was a real success story for Jackson. He was a 10th round draft choice
out of Eastern Kentucky University in 1988.

He was the 252nd player drafted overall. The Steelers spotted
him when they were checking out a defensive end named Aaron
Jones. They took Jones on the first round, and he was a total bust.
Jackson played in all 16 games as a rookie mostly on special teams.
In his second season, he played in 14 games, the last 12 as a starter.
He started at left tackle in all 16 games the following two seasons. He
and Dermontti Dawson often traveled around town together, and were
great goodwill ambassadors for the team. They were both class acts.

They ran into financial problems midway through their pro
careers and they accused their former agent, Joe Senkovich, of
defrauding them of $400,000.

Being with the Steelers had been special. Jackson appreciated
the team's rich tradition, and the high standards that had been established by the four-time Super Bowl winners of the '70s. "Win or lose,
though, the world will go on," he said.

Jackson had the normal laidback demeanor of an offensive lineman, though his dark eyes often revealed an inner fire. "An offensive
lineman has to be under control," he said. "If you're a defensive lineman, you can let it all hang out."

He didn't mind that he was not more of a media draw at Sun
Devil Stadium. "That's not me," he said. "I like a low profile. I enjoy
my privacy."

n Jackson sets to block.

Eastern Kentucky University

John Jackson enjoys lunch in clubhouse during May, 1996 minicamp session.

lementary school

John and Joan Jackson pose with sons Jordan, 3, and Josh, 7.

"Where's the crowd?"
— James Lofton,
Former NFL receiver

James Lofton, a former foe and a friend at the same time, came walking toward Jackson after Jackson had been abandoned once again by most of the media at Sun Devil Stadium. Lofton had been a great receiver with the Green Bay Packers, Los Angeles Raiders and Buffalo Bills over a 15-year span and was working at Super Bowl XXX for the Fox Network.

"Where's the crowd?" asked Lofton as he shook hands with Jackson, who just shook his head and smiled.

"You have one of the biggest match-ups in this game," allowed Lofton.

"I'm just a low-key guy," Jackson said, explaining away the lack of media-types about him in the stands.

"I'm shocked," said Lofton.

After they exchanged a few pleasantries, speaking about their families and so forth, Lofton said, "You guys were a running team and then you had to pass. Now you're a passing team. Unless you play the game or coach it, you don't know how that affects your offensive linemen and your approach to a game."

Jackson just nodded in agreement. When more media joined Jackson at his spot in the stands, I had a chance to talk to Lofton alone, and mentioned to him that his name had come up in a conversation in the lobby of the Steelers' headquarters during the season. I related the story, involving Carnell Lake and Mel Blount, to Lofton.

Lake had left his strong safety position during the season, where he had been a Pro Bowl performer, to play the left corner position formerly occupied by Rod Woodson. In a game against Cincinnati, Lake had given up several touchdown passes.

Mel Blount paid a visit to the Steelers' offices and came across Lake in the lobby the following week. He went over and patted Lake on the back, and tried to console him for his difficulty in the previous game. "Hey, brother, if you're out there on the corner long enough, you're going to get burnt. Don't let it get you down; it happened to the best of us. I remember how I got burnt for three touchdown passes by James Lofton in a game at Green Bay."

Tim Lewis, the Steelers' first-year defensive backfield coach, was standing nearby and he picked up on the story. "I was there!" allowed Lewis, looking directly at Blount. "That was my rookie year as a defensive back in Green Bay, and you were one of my idols from my days at Pitt. I couldn't believe anybody could beat Mel Blount for three touchdowns!"

That was the 1983 season, Blount's last in pro football. When I relayed this tale to Lofton, he said, "That's true," he said. "I had a good day, but we still lost (24-21).

"I had a TV show in Green Bay back then," Lofton continued. "I remember I had four guys from their team on my show, and they'll all end up in the Hall of Fame. I interviewed Franco Harris, Terry Bradshaw, Jack Lambert and Mike Webster. They were dynamite. To me, they were the greatest.

"It would be great to play for a team like that; we had a great tradition in Green Bay as well. When you choose a college, you choose it for its education and usually its sports history. You have to be lucky to end up with that kind of tradition in a pro setting. You remember the past, but you don't live in it."

I asked Lofton if the Steelers enjoyed an edge in those days because they were feared by many of their opponents. "They had an edge," he said, "because they were the best."

"He's a driven individual."
— Tom Donahoe

John Jackson had seen the Steelers blow a big chance to get to the Super Bowl the year before, losing to a lesser team, the San Diego Chargers, in the AFC championship at Three Rivers Stadium. It left the team and the city in a depression for a long period .

"There were a lot of distractions," Jackson said. "That was the first time a lot of us had a chance to play in a championship game. Maybe we didn't know how to go about it.

"This year we know how to act. We've been there. We know how to act because we lost. We have a different kind of discipline this year. We sent away some disgruntled people to other teams. This year people are getting banged up, but they're still doing their best to be out there on the field. There's more personal accountability.

"We still have our fun. When you've been around a while, you know how to relax and you know how to turn things up a notch. They've added some guys here who are working out well. The chemistry is pretty good. You have to watch out for practical jokers on the team. You never know when you're going to be the butt of somebody's joke.

"The team values are pretty good. We seem to have more of a commitment to each other. A year makes a big difference. Our attitude has changed. This year they set the goals higher. We bounced back from a bad start. We've accomplished a lot. The thing that everybody has to understand is that the more you win the better you play.

"It's very important. A lot of guys I know have never had a chance to think about the Super Bowl, let alone get to it. Things have changed because of the free agent market. Everybody wants the almighty dollar. But you don't know what kind of a team you're going to. It may not be as satisfying."

401

By helping out his former high school, Jackson had shown that he remembered where he came from. I wanted to know more about his boyhood.

"I come from a humble background," Jackson said. "My parents were separated. It taught me to be more independent. I grew up in a predominantly black area. I knew how to work. I wasn't afraid to work. And I think that is what most high school kids are afraid of, but just like anything else in life, you have to work hard...you have to pay your dues.

"When I was playing football my senior year in high school, I talked to a lot of people, and I thought it was my best way to make my own way, to earn something. I was more interested in playing golf. I had worked at the Losantiville Country Club. I caddied a lot. I really started to enjoy golf when I got a chance to learn how to play it. During the summer, I got to play golf about seven days a week. I'd be out on the course 14 hours a day. I really got caught up with it. I went back to that same country club during the off-season last year, and I saw some of the same members playing there. They couldn't believe how big I'd gotten. They were flabbergasted. There was an attorney there named Richard Katz. I caddied for him as a kid. I told him, 'You better be nice to those caddies. You never know what will become of them.'

"So I was really into golf and baseball and wrestling before I ever concentrated on football But I was fairly big when I was about 16. I was 6-3 and weighed over 200 pounds. Some of the teachers thought I ought to give football a try. 'As big as you are, some schools might take a chance on you.' So I went out. I give a lot of credit to a line coach I had, Coach Roger Perkins, who really worked with me during my senior year in high school. He had played 13 years in the Canadian Football League, so I was lucky to get someone who really knew what they were talking about. I started out as a defensive lineman, and it was a funny thing how I ended up as an offensive lineman. We didn't have many offensive lineman, and I didn't know any better, so when they asked for volunteers to switch to the other side, I raised my hand. By the time I was a senior, I was 6-5, 230 pounds and a lot of people thought I had the size and speed to go to college. Tom Sharp was our head coach and he was a good man.

"It worked out well for me. I think I heard from 43 schools in one way or another. Even an Ivy League school, Cornell, called me. I wasn't used to such attention. I took a couple of trips. It distracted me as far as my performance as a wrestler on the school team. I was very much into that as well. I wrestled for two years."

As a junior, Jackson finished third in his weight class in the regional tournament.

"I visited two schools, the University of Kentucky and Eastern Kentucky. After I visited Eastern Kentucky, I figured there was no way I was going to a big school. Eastern had won national championships on their level, and I felt comfortable there. I still wanted a

402

safe haven. I thought I could do a lot of things on and off the field, and I felt I could get a degree, and come out of it with something."

The school had a good football tradition. They had won a national football championship in 1982. Jackson was a three-year starter at Eastern Kentucky and was the team co-captain as a senior. He graduated in 1991 with a degree in police administration, minoring in physical education.

Had he gone to Kentucky he would have played with Dermontti Dawson, who ended up being his best buddy on the Steelers. The Wildcats would have had a formidable front line with those two giants in the middle.

"The first year I was here I realized the value of my degree," Jackson said. "I knew that football was just a temporary job, not a lifetime job. A lot of guys get into trouble because they have nothing to fall back on. The last three years I was a spokesperson for Blue Cross, going out to schools to speak to the students in a Drug and Alcohol Awareness Program. I have started doing some broadcasting on a local cable network, and I'd like to learn more about that."

As a Cincinnati kid, Jackson was a big fan of the Reds baseball team. He first got interested in them when they had "The Big Red Machine," and they were one of the best teams in baseball. "Football was never as big as baseball in Cincinnati," Jackson said. "I played baseball in Little League, and liked it a lot." He said he had an opportunity to meet several of the team's stars, Pete Rose, Tony Perez, Joe Morgan, Johnny Bench. "All great guys," he said. "They had a chemistry that was unbelievable. That was the biggest thing I saw. They trusted each other. That's what we have here now."

He grew up with future major leaguers Barry Larkin and Darryl Boston in the same Cincinnati neighborhood.

"My mother was always there for me. Whatever I wanted to do, she supported me. She didn't like me playing football. And now I'm doing what she didn't want me to do. She can tell when I'm hurt even when the coaches and trainers can't tell. It's still difficult for her. You don't want to see your son get hurt.

"In my first year here, we went 5-and-11. We knew that wasn't acceptable to the fans. They let you know how bad you are. In Cincinnati, they wouldn't have shown up. Here, they showed up to let you know how they felt about you. I was a rookie and that wasn't easy to take. People were letting you know they thought you stunk. It gave me motivation to work harder in the off-season.

"Tunch Ilkin took me under his wing. He taught me how tackles played. He taught me a lot. A couple of years ago, he said, 'I can see you making a couple of million dollars a year.' I thought he didn't know who he was talking to. And it's all come true."

Jackson signed a four-year deal to play tackle for the Steelers through 1997. It called for a $1.05 million signing bonus, a $595,000 roster bonus and salaries of $1.4 million in 1995 and $1.75 million annually in each of the final two years.

"Tunch taught me that you had to play through the injuries; it was something expected in this game. There have been times when I have been limited by injuries, but it's something I'd never use as an excuse. I just knew I could play better when I was feeling better, and able to move better.

"I face pretty much the best pass rushers every week. I just have to make sure our quarterback walks off that field in one piece. It's just my responsibility.

"I think you're wrong if you play for individual honors. Your first obligation is to the team because without the team you are nothing. If I had my choice of making the Pro Bowl or the Super Bowl, I'd take the Super Bowl every time.

"I feel really proud. I'm proud of what I have accomplished, and I'm proud of my family, my wife and our two sons. My wife, Joan, is a graduate of the University of Cincinnati. Of all the people I know, they've supported me the most. They're the people I really care about."

He came to a mini-camp in June of 1996. The team had worked out on the grass field at the University of Pittsburgh that morning. Now the players were back at Three Rivers Stadium, enjoying lunch and lounging about the dressing room. Jackson was now one of the established elders. Many of the rookies were running around the room. Jackson was lying on the floor. He would have liked to take a nap. He was an old bull among young bulls. "The off-season was too short," he said. "I've spent a great deal of time rehabbing my leg. It feels stronger. I just have to stay healthy. That's the key. I'm looking forward to a big year."

Jackson shed some light on his roots when the Steelers traveled to Tokyo, Japan a month later to play the San Diego Chargers in the opening pre-season game. Jackson turned a lot of heads because the people there were not used to seeing a black man who stands 6 feet 6 and weighs 300 pounds walking the streets of Tokyo.

What they didn't know was that Jackson shared a common heritage. He was born in Okinawa, the son of a U.S. serviceman and his Japanese wife. Hardly any of his teammates or coaches knew that. "That's my personal life and I like to keep it personal," he said.

Jackson, however, did disclose to sportswriter Ed Bouchette that his mother, Mitsue, was born in the Philippines and that her father died there during World War II, but he didn't care to explain how or why. His mom stood just 4 feet 9 (his dad was 6-1) and he learned only a few Japanese words growing up in Cincinnati.

"I know when somebody's cussing you out; I can tell you that," Jackson said. He said his mother hadn't been to Japan in 30 years and he had never been there before. She gave him no advice about where to go or what to do in Japan.

"She told me a few things not to do," Jackson said.

Jim Miller

A tough kid

> *"He's the man of the hour."*
> — Dan Rooney

T here was no doubt in Jim Miller's mind that he had the right stuff to be the starting quarterback for the Pittsburgh Steelers, starting with the 1996 season.

He was sitting on a stool in front of his cubicle on a Tuesday afternoon, April 9, 1996, the only player in the Steelers' locker room. Kordell Stewart had been there earlier. Both young QB candidates were cramming for the big exam, eager to get a headstart on their homework so they would be as prepared as possible for the team's mini-camp and summer training camp and, most of all, the coming season.

This was vacation time for most of the players, but Ernie Mills was coming in each day for rehabilitation for a knee injury he suffered in Super Bowl XXX, and Erric Pegram was working out, eager to stake a claim to being the prime running back for the Steelers since the status of Bam Morris — arrested a few weeks earlier in Texas for possession of drugs — was unclear at the time.

All of the Steelers pro and college scouts were in the complex because they were making final preparations for the college draft to be conducted on the weekend of April 20-21.

Miller and Stewart were in on their own volition. Players who attend workouts and meetings during the off-season were all paid $240 per week, which was in addition to their regular contracts. They were studying film, going over the playbook with Chan Gailey, who had been promoted from receivers coach to offensive coordinator after head coach Bill Cowher chose not to rehire Ron Erhardt, freeing him and tight ends coach Pat Hodgson to join the New York Jets.

Those two would be reunited there with Neil O'Donnell, who would, in turn, depart Pittsburgh in favor of one of his hometown teams and a four-year contract worth $25 million.

O'Donnell's departure provided an opportunity for Miller and Stewart, as well as veteran Mike Tomczak, to be the No. 1 quarterback for the Steelers. Miller and Stewart were also working on the weights, and throwing the ball to anybody they could beg to come out on the new turf at Three Rivers Stadium. It was not easy to find volunteers to play pitch-and-catch because it was cold and still snowing in Pittsburgh, even though the Pirates had begun their season.

O'Donnell's dressing stall was empty. Tomczak's stall was next to it, and next to Miller's. The stall on the other side of Miller was also empty. It had belonged to John L. Williams, a veteran running back and receiver the Steelers had opted not to sign to a new contract. The Steelers' lineup would definitely have a new look for 1996. Free agency had created constant flux in pro football.

"Williams was a rare player," said Miller. "He'd mess up in practice and drop passes and look bad. But in the game he grabbed everything thrown his way. He was the exception to the rule. He came to bat every week. We'll miss him."

Former Steelers linebacker Bryan Hinkle, a frequent visitor to the locker room, came by and mentioned to Miller that Kevin Greene's locker was empty as well. "He cleared it out right after the Super Bowl," said Miller. "I guess he figured he wasn't coming back."

"Was he ticked off?" asked Hinkle.

"I suppose so," said Miller. "Who knows?"

What Miller did know was that the Steelers would have new personnel for the coming season. The new coaches were already at work, getting ready for the NFL draft less than two weeks away. There would be a group of newcomers coming to camp. Greene's status was not the only uncertain one.

Miller did know that he was eager to show his stuff. Dan Rooney, the president of the Steelers, came walking through the locker room. He smiled when he spotted Miller talking to this writer. "He's the man," Rooney remarked in the way of greeting Miller. "He's the man of the hour."

Miller smiled. "We'll see," he said to the Steelers' boss. "Yeah, we'll see."

He appreciated the acknowledgment from the man who signed his paycheck, just as the Steelers of earlier years always felt special whenever Dan's dad, Steelers' founder Art Rooney, would pass through the locker room and stop and say something to each of the players.

"Everything you hear about the Rooneys and the Steelers' organization is true," remarked Miller. "It's rich with tradition. It's all football and they treat you right.

"When the Steelers got fined during Super Bowl week, Mr. Rooney told me that hurt because he was trying to save some money so he'd be able to sign me the next time around. It makes you feel good when the owner can kid you like that."

After O'Donnell decided to accept the Jets' offer rather than the Steelers' offer, there was much media talk that the Steelers would seek an established quarterback to fill the void, to sign someone like Jeff Hostetler of the Oakland Raiders. The theory was that the Steelers' defensive unit was still intact and that the team was good enough to get back to the Super Bowl, but needed a short term solution to its quarterback needs. Tomczak was thought to be a backup quarterback at best, and Miller and Stewart lacked the experience to lead a team to the Super Bowl. It was thought they might be another year or two away.

Jim Miller moved up in class with departure of Neil O'Donnell.

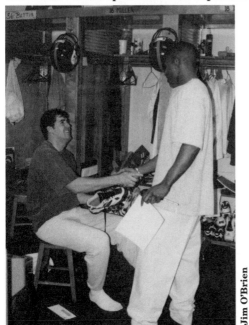

Jim Miller is congratulated on new contract by Andre Hastings, one of his receivers, at Steelers minicamp in May, 1996.

Miller takes off in Michigan State days.

The Steelers ended up deciding they would find the right man among Tomczak, Miller and Stewart. They had to meet the test.

"I want that opportunity," said Miller. "If the Steelers had gone out and gotten somebody else I couldn't care less. If they had gone out and gotten Joe Montana I couldn't care less.

"If Neil had come back, I would have asked to be traded. There's no sense in sitting for another four years behind him. It wouldn't have been any good for Kordell, either. Neil was the No. 1 guy, he was established, and we'd have all been competing for the No. 2 spot. You can't get better standing on the sideline. I'm eager to play and show that I can be a starting quarterback in the NFL.

"There are only 30 people in the world who can say they're the starting quarterback for an NFL team, and I want to be one of them. I've always had to run the extra sprint, and throw the ball a few more times than the next guy. I'll go the extra mile to do what it takes to be the starting quarterback. I'm not competing with anybody else. I'm competing with myself."

It was refreshing to meet Miller. I'll admit I had not spoken to him during the two years he had been on the team except to say hello or to nod if we passed in the hallway. He had been the No. 3 or No. 4 quarterback on the ballclub before O'Donnell's departure, but now he was a more important person in the Steelers' picture. I had missed out on something. After talking to him a couple of times, I was convinced he had the proper attitude for the challenge that awaited him.

James Donald Miller was a gentleman of true grit, a bright individual who had done well athletically and academically in high school and college. He had a great attitude. He looked and talked the part. He welcomed an opportunity to present his case. It was a pleasant departure to talk to a player who enjoyed the exchange.

Later that day, Miller and James Parrish, a reserve offensive lineman who had played as sparingly as Miller in 1995, represented the Steelers at a social function in the team's offices that was hosted by Pat Rooney, the wife of the Steelers' owner.

Mrs. Rooney was chairing an upcoming fund-raiser for the Pittsburgh Chapter of the American Diabetes Association. Two of their nine children, Jim and Duffy, had diabetes. Jonathan Hayes, a tight end with the Steelers, had diabetes and was going to be honored at a tribute in May for all his volunteer efforts to promote greater awareness of the disease and its managed treatment. This was a preliminary get-together to get the ball rolling for the major event.

Miller and Parrish didn't know they were going to speak. Parrish was a huge, fun-loving person who enjoyed a rare opportunity to be in the limelight and to enjoy a classy buffet. He did a little song and dance and amused everyone.

Miller told a story about a former classmate who discovered he had diabetes after a drastic weight loss, and his anecdote was perfectly appropriate to the spirit of the evening.

Miller was outstanding as an impromptu speaker. He made good eye contact, spoke clearly and, like Parrish, made a positive impression on the crowd. Parrish provided some insight into Miller while mixing with those in attendance.

"Of all the four quarterbacks we had last year, he had the best presence in the huddle," pointed out Parrish, who had previously played on teams with Dan Marino, Troy Aikman, Steve Young and Stan Humphries and should know a good quarterback when he sees one. "He's so cool. And he really knows what he wants to do out there."

"The people are nuts here about pro football."
— Jim Miller

Miller was a sixth round draft choice of the Steelers in 1994 after a distinguished career with a mostly mediocre team at Michigan State University. His coach at MSU was George Perles, who had served as the defensive coordinator and defensive line coach on Chuck Noll's staff when the Steelers won four Super Bowls in the '70s. He learned a lot from Perles about playing football, and he especially learned about what it was like to play in Pittsburgh when the Steelers had the best team in the National Football League.

"Playing for George Perles for five years, that's all I heard about," admitted Miller. "So I'm inspired when I see the Lombardi Trophies in the lobby here, and pictures of all the Steelers who played on those teams who are now in the Pro Football Hall of Fame. I'd seen the Rocky Bleier movie before I got to Michigan State, and I'd hear all these stories Coach Perles told, and like a lot of guys, my eyes would roll and I'd say under my breath, 'What's he talking about?' But that all came to life for me when I got here. The people are nuts here about pro football. The standards are so high.

"Coach Perles probably had a little to do with my being here. I'm sure he recommended me to the Steelers. I remember when Coach Perles came to my home to recruit me. I was scheduled to go to Notre Dame, Stanford and Michigan, and thought I had picked some good schools.

"Coach Perles ate a whole apple pie my mother had made when he came to our house. When he left, my parents said, 'That's the place you ought to go.' My parents were completely taken by Coach Perles. My brother Rich and my sister Sue had gone to Michigan, and that's where they wanted me to go. But Coach Perles changed all that. He's the reason I went there. My parents wanted me to play for Coach Perles.

"I owe a great deal to him and to Morris Watts, who was the offensive coordinator at Michigan State. Myron Bell was in my class.

We both feel that Coach Perles made good on all he promised us as far as what to expect at Michigan State."

Miller had been an All-America quarterback at Kettering High in Waterford, Michigan. He was selected the state's Player of the Year. He lettered in baseball and basketball. He was twice drafted as a pitching prospect by the Kansas City Royals, giving him something in common with Pittsburgh's Dan Marino. He was a bright kid, a member of the National Honor Society with a 3.75 grade point average.

A three-year starter at Michigan State, he graduated with a degree in financial administration, and earned athletic-academic honors with a 3.25 GPA. He was second team All-Big Ten and a first-team All-Big Ten Academic choice.

Perles and his staff had succeeded in drafting two other all-world prep quarterbacks, but both transferred to other schools when Miller moved to the forefront.

"I think Coach Perles got the short end of the stick at Michigan State. He deserved better. I think things started to go bad for him at Michigan State when there was talk three years in a row that he was again going to the Jets, then the Colts, then the Packers. For three years in a row he was supposedly going other places, and it killed him recruiting-wise.

Kids didn't want to come to Michigan State if he was leaving to go back to the pros.

"We went 3-8 my senior year when we should've gone 7-4. He was the A.D. (athletic director) and they said he couldn't do both. That wasn't the case. He did a good job as A.D., too, and brought about a lot of positive changes. He just didn't have the talent to get it done in football.

"You'll never hear a player who played for him and really knew him who didn't love and respect him (well, there was that one unhappy kid who talked about killing him). He's one of the best things that ever happened to me in my career.

"We had an 'S' on one side of our helmet, just like the Steelers had a logo on just one side of their helmets. We always heard about how they had done it here. All we heard about was Mean Joe Greene and Rocky Bleier. He wanted you to be tough. He seemed more concerned about us being tough than winning. Before we'd leave the locker room, he'd shout, 'Screw the x's and o's and go out and beat the hell out of someone.' It was enjoyable to play for him. He sent me a copy of his book recently with a special inscription in it."

It brought back memories of his days at Michigan State, and how he got started in sports in the first place.

"My parents wanted me to play sports," said Miller. "I played T-ball in baseball at age 5. I started playing football at 8. I always played basketball. I had a brother and three sisters and they all played sports. I'm the youngest. My parents didn't have to raise me. I just followed my brother and sisters.

"I was bigger than most of the other kids, so I started out at guard in football. Then I became a tailback, and then a receiver. I was always the third string quarterback. My brother, Rich, was a quarterback in high school. He was the second oldest in our family. That's what got me into playing quarterback. He was seven years older than me, and I just wanted to be like him. When he was 16 and 17, I was just getting started and I really looked up to him.

"I'd go watch him play. He was a good football player. I had to give up sports for two years because they voted down a tax increase and we didn't have sports teams in seventh and eighth grades because of a fiscal cutback.

"I was growing so fast I had pains in my knees and ankles, so I might have had problems playing then, anyhow. I resumed playing in ninth grade, and I developed into a pretty good quarterback. I was strong and I could throw the ball.

"I watched Jim Zorn and I watched Terry Bradshaw and John Elway and Roger Staubach and Dan Marino and Joe Montana. They were all my favorite quarterbacks. As a little kid, you want to play and say you're someone. I didn't say I was one of those guys because I wanted to blend their abilities. I wanted to have an arm like Elway and Bradshaw, and be able to scramble like Staubach, release the ball like Marino, see the whole field and make decisions like Montana. I wanted to be a super quarterback.

"Our high school was 10th, 11th and 12th grades, and I started on the varsity as a sophomore. I was named the Gatorade Player of the Year in Michigan my senior year. We were usually about 6-3 in football, and our baseball team was usually in the district or state playoffs.

"Kirk Gibson went to the same high school and college as I did and he was one of the people who played key roles in my development. He played for the Tigers, the Dodgers and even the Pirates for a while (1992). His dad taught me in high school. When I went to Michigan State, Gibson called me and offered me a job to work on his farm. He worked my fanny off, and he didn't pay me much, but he sure got me into the proper mental state to compete in college. I'm not sure I'd have been ready if it hadn't been for Gibson getting after me."

His mental state would be critical in his competing for the top spot with the Steelers. "I have always felt that competition brought out the best in everybody," he said. "I want to take advantage of a great opportunity here.

"Look at my situation in training camp last year. Everybody thought I was going to get cut. I just want a fair shot. If I don't succeed, I won't cry or sulk."

411

"You always have to plan for the future."
— Tom Donahoe

Miller had a difficult time showing his stuff to the Steelers. In a year's time, he broke his right thumb, tore the ligaments in it, broke his left index finger, and broke his right wrist.

He mangled his thumb two days before the first exhibition game in his rookie season, and missed most of training camp.

He was asssigned to the Frankfurt (Germany) Galaxy of the NFL's World League. He started in three games before a pass rusher smashed into him and broke his left index finger. He shrugged that off and stayed in the game. On the next series, two rushers knocked him to the ground. He put out his right hand to break his fall and he broke his wrist. That was in April. Six weeks later, he was throwing the ball again. This is one tough kid. He had played in only three quarters of regular season action in his first two years with the Steelers, yet he was sure he could be their No. 1 guy.

Going into his third summer camp, he was hoping he would stay healthy, as he had done in college, so he would have a chance to demonstrate his real ability. He felt the Steelers had a receiver in the same category, namely C.J. Johnson. "C.J. is the next in a line of great Steeler receivers: Stallworth, Swann, Lipps, all of them," he said.

He remembered how the year before that so many people just assumed that he would not survive the cut when the Steelers had four quarterbacks at the start of camp.

"They never told me they weren't going to keep four, even though everybody assumed I was the odd man out," recalled Miller. "I didn't worry about it. I just went out and played. I went through the same thing at Michigan State. Every day, I've got to tell myself to be a better quarterback today than I was yesterday."

Tom Donahoe, the director of football operations for the Steelers, explained the Steelers' decision to keep four quarterbacks this way: "You can't just look at this one year at a time. You always have to plan for the future."

"Things were expected in our house."
— Jim Miller

Like O'Donnell, Miller comes from a solid family where everyone worked hard to accomplish lofty goals. His father was a computer programmer for 35 years in Oakland County, Michigan. His mother was an accountant for New Horizons from about the time Jim first entered grade school. They were now retired in Florida.

His sister Kim was a nurse in Colorado, his brother Rich an attorney in California, his sister Jane was in the Air Force in Georgia, and his sister Sue was an architect back home in Michigan.

"Our parents molded us to go out and do well; they taught us we could compete with anybody," said Miller. "Things were expected in our house.

"It was expected in our home that you got good grades, that you stayed out of trouble. The fear of getting caught was a great deterrent. If I screwed up, my father was going to come down hard on me."

His sister, Sue, sent me a letter along with some photographs of Jim from her home in Waterford, Michigan. "I'm sure Jim spoke of his home environment," she wrote. "He can attribute some of his success to encouraging parents who were very much involved in shaping our lives with good values, social skills, culture and education opportunities. Jim created his own success as well, using his ability and, through discipline and determination, accomplished tremendous goals."

Miller regards toughness as one of his top qualities. "A quarterback's psyche is a very fragile thing," he explained. "You're in such a visible position. All eyes are on you when your team has the ball. People are quick to boo you if things go wrong. It's the toughest position to play, no doubt about it.

"That's why everyone wants to play it. That's why Bradshaw played the position. I read his book, that's how I know that. It's the toughest position, but it's also the most rewarding position when the team has success. Some guys have great instincts for it. I was very impressed with the way Jim Harbaugh performed for Indianapolis last year. It took him a long time to develop and find himself. The same was true of Steve Bono in Kansas City. They hung in there and they proved they could play and start in the NFL.

"Neil O'Donnell is a very good quarterback. I couldn't believe he didn't get better support here."

Just then, Tony Parisi, pointing toward his 32nd year as the Steelers' equipment man, walked by, picking up stuff from the floor in the locker room. "Tony tells me they booed Bradshaw here; he said they even booed Jack Ham here. They're tough.

"Bradshaw was a good quarterback, so they have high standards for the position in this city. I'd like to think it's tougher here for a quarterback to measure up to the fans' expectations.

"One thing that helped Neil O'Donnell was Mike Tomczak. Mike tested Neil mentally all the time, making sure he was psychologically and mentally prepared. Mike has helped me a great deal, too, with the mental part of the game. Neil helped me more with the physical part of the game, the way you work out, the way you throw and work with your receivers in practice.

"I'll always be in Neil's corner. He broke his finger on his throwing hand early last year, yet he came back as fast as he could, with a curled finger that will always be that way, and he helped turn us around. Neil's tough. He's a tough sonuvagun. He'd play hurt.

"It's hard to blame him for going to New York. He'll make $8.5 million his first year. That will set him up for life, obviously.

I couldn't believe how critical this town was of him, even during the good times.

"I always thought he was a little insecure here. I like Neil, but he could be funny in some ways. Like he didn't show up for Mike Tomczak's wedding, and he had three months advance notice on it. After all that Mike did for him, how loyal he was to him and how much he helped him, I just thought Neil should have been there for him on such a big day in Mike's life.

"I don't know if he was truly happy here, he might have had the feeling of not being wanted. I think there were several factors that worked in favor of New York. When Ron Erhardt and Pat Hodgson went there, that gave him a real comfort zone. Erhardt's system is a proven winner. Erhardt is good at knowing what players can and cannot do. I enjoyed playing under Ron Erhardt. He taught me a lot. Neil knew that Erhardt knew him well and that they could work together. He wouldn't have to learn a new system. He was going back home and there was bigger money, like $7 million more.

"I don't think he should have questioned what the Steelers were doing. But he could see that the Jets were making moves to get him better offensive linemen and better receivers, and that they were putting the elements together to help themselves be more successful.

"I think Neil is underrated. He's a good quarterback. I knew he was good when I first got drafted. Maybe it hurt him because he didn't talk to the media enough. That should make New York an interesting test for him. I'm looking at it now as a great opportunity for me."

"Don't mess with your sister when she is on skates."
— Jim Miller

Miller is a handsome young man. He has dark hair and a pale face. He's got a sizable scar on the left side of his chin that contributes to a tough-guy look. When I asked him about the divot in his chin, he smiled. "I'd like to tell you it was from some heroic act," he said, "but that was hardly the case.

"I was ice skating one day on a lake near our home. My sister was on skates and she was clearing the ice with a snow shovel. I kept skating by and sticking my hockey stick under her legs and cutting her down. It was my sister Sue, and she was a year older than me; she was ten and I was nine. She went down one too many times and she picked up the shovel and swung it at me. She caught me right in the chin. I was a bloody mess and I needed to get a few (48) stitches. The moral of that story is don't mess with your sister when she's on ice skates, and has a weapon in her hands."

He was hoping he'd have some smoother skating in his future.

414

Jim Miller's family (left to right) mother, sister Sue with her son Brandon, sister Jane and dad join him at Liberty Bowl in Memphis on Dec. 29, 1993.

Jim at age 14

Jim at age 3 1/2

Miller thought he was a lucky man to be along for the ride when the Steelers got to the AFC title game in his first year and the Super Bowl in his second year. "Some older guys around the league have said, 'Hey, Miller, you don't realize how good you've got it. I've never been that far.' So I've been spoiled. I know where I want to go. I want to go to another Super Bowl and quarterback the team to a championship."

He had a chance during his second season to see some real combat action. The highlight of the season — "if you can have a highlight in a loss," he was quick to add — was a nationally-televised Monday night game at Miami's Joe Robbie Stadium.

Tomczak got off to a bad start in that game, and had two passes intercepted. The Steelers didn't seem to be getting anywhere and, in a desperate attempt to turn things around, Cowher called upon Miller to play quarterback. That was the game when Greg Lloyd leveled Dan Marino and sidelined him with an injury. Marino's passing line for that game was 16 of 27 for 183 yards and one touchdown. Miller's line, in relief, was 18 of 29 for 210 yards. "I can always say I outthrew Dan Marino in a head-to-head meeting," said Miller, more in jest than anything else. "They had the No. 1 defense in football going into that game. Of their 22 starters, 19 of them were No. 1 draft choices, so they had quite a team. They came into the game with a 2-0 record. I did some good things and some bad things in that game. I just knew I could play; I just knew I had to get into a game. So it was great to get out there, and against Minnesota the following week at home. I was busting my butt to do my best.

"Getting hit hard the first time made me realize I had what it takes. I said to myself, 'Like yeah,' when I finally got hit. It was a great scene; there's something special about a night game; there always has been on every level. It's like everything slows down somehow.

"Tim Bowens hit me, and told me, 'Stay down!' And I said to him, 'Keep on bringing it. I'll be here.' I trusted that my guys could give me time to throw. Bryan Cox hit me and said a few choice words. I just looked at him. He could see in my face what I was thinking. 'If that's the best you've got, I'll be here for a while.'"

Miller got enough playing time to know he wanted more. That's what pushed him to work so hard in the so-called off-season. "I'm working out every day," he said. "I'm meeting with the coaches, going over our offense, reading defensive coverages, everything I can do to better prepare myself."

Stewart wanted the job as well. He had incentive clauses in his contract that would reward him if he became the starting quarterback. Stewart had super confidence, too. Could they co-exist without their relationship suffering?

"We were roommates for the last six games of the season," said Miller. "He knows I want to play and I know he wants to play. Mike feels that way, too. Kordell is a good person. We can get along. Neil often said he didn't get along with Bubby Brister. But he got along great with Mike. Mike was more supportive. Mike helped me and Kordell, too. He was not afraid to share his knowledge. I'm supportive of Kordell and Mike. Whatever happens happens.

"Hey, Kordell gets me excited, too. Some of the things he's done are unreal. Mike gets a bad rap, too. He's one of the most football sound quarterbacks I've known. He might not have the strongest arm, but he's got a great understanding of the game. And he's a great competitor.

"Mike was supportive of Neil, and he was supportive of me and Kordell. Mike is very generous. He holds nothing back. He's positive about himself, and he's been a straight shooter. We'll get more close now because he was closer to Neil before. Neil always treated me like a little kid, because we had a different kind of relationship. Mike treats you as a human being."

Miller thought Chan Gailey would do a great job as offensive coordinator. "I think we'll have a nice offense, with a few new wrinkles, but I think it will basically be the same as what we've been running," said Miller. "I'm getting to know him better.

"I'm not a picture-perfect quarterback by any means, but I have yet — after I've thrown a touchdown pass — had a coach tell me I had the wrong footwork. I know I can do it. For one thing, every scrimmage, every game, I have played well here. I know me. I love to compete."

He looked about the empty locker room, and pointed out some of the name tags.

"Everybody in this locker room was told he wasn't good enough at some point along the way," said Miller.

"I've been excited about being here ever since my first minicamp. I'm taking the snap from Dermontti Dawson, an All-Pro player, and I'm handing the ball off to Barry Foster, one of the best running backs in the league. I kinda had to pinch myself. People had always told me I wasn't good enough to get to this level. I've been told I wasn't athletic enough, or I wasn't this or that. Let's talk about what I can do. I've got a good arm, a quick release, and I know what I need to do to be successful out there.

"One day Neil asked me a question. He said, 'How long do you want to play this game?' And I said, "As long as I can. They're going to have to drag me off the field.' And he said, 'Are you crazy? You don't want to be able to walk away from this game in one piece?'

"I'm in this for the long run. I came in to my first camp here at 240 pounds. I'm down to 210 now and I'm in good shape. I've corralled what I want to be ready for this test. Neil said he did not care about records. I do. I want to be the No. 1 quarterback. I want to set all the records. I want to be one of the best ever to play this game."

On June 5, 1996, the Steelers signed Miller to a new contract that would pay him $6.55 million for four seasons and as much as $11.65 million if he's the starter. The Steelers are in it for the long run, too.

417

Willie Williams
A big brother

"As long as my heart is big,
I'll do just fine."

W illie Williams could easily get lost in the locker room of the Steelers at Three Rivers Stadium. His dressing stall was in the farthest corner from the entrance, pinched in between those of Kordell Stewart and Chad Brown, and he was one of the smallest Steelers at 5-9, 188 pounds. Only Alvoid Mays, another cornerback, might have been smaller, listed at 5-9, 172 pounds. Both were muscular, with taut physiques, and looked more like boxers than football players, especially when they were standing around the locker room in gray shorts.

One day, Leon Searcy was screaming at Williams about something, and Searcy, 6-3, 304 pounds, was bullying his little buddy in a playful manner. "Quit picking on me," pleaded Williams, rolling his bright eyes. Then, in a near whisper, he muttered, "I don't get no respect around here."

Williams came through for the Steelers in a big way during the 1995 season, starting at right cornerback in place of Deon Figures after two seasons as a tackling demon on the special teams. He gained great respect, even AFC Defensive Player of the Month honors for December, and came up with many big interceptions and touchdowns. Mays moved into the left corner spot when Rod Woodson was injured in the opening game, but was found wanting after five games and eventually gave way to Carnell Lake, who was moved over from his safety spot. The only member of the previous season's secondary still in position was free safety Darren Perry.

When the under-sized Williams and Mays manned those critical corner slots, the Steelers were thought to be quite vulnerable, but Williams proved that he was big enough to meet the challenge. Williams was able to defend passes against taller receivers, and he made a critical solo tackle in the late going to help preserve the American Football Conference title game victory over the Indianapolis Colts. The Steelers could have been crippled by the loss of Woodson and the reduced effectiveness of Figures, so Williams was a key contributor to the Steelers' comeback from a 3-4 start that could have undermined teams with less heart.

"We started off real slow because we lost Rod Woodson and had to make some changes," Williams said. "I think the whole defense has confidence in the secondary right now. Once we played a couple of games together, we got used to each other. We started playing with real confidence."

Steelers defensive back Willie Williams

Willie and wife Melissa with daughter Dominique. Melissa earned master's degree in human resources management in spring of 1996 from the University of South Carolina.

Jim O'Brien

Williams, left, chats with Kordell Stewart in Steelers' clubhouse during minicamp in May, 1996.

This was a stout-hearted fellow. He still bore some scars from his past, two of them self-inflicted during some crazy fraternity induction ceremonies during his days at Western Carolina University in Cullowhee, North Carolina. Others were tucked away in his sometimes heavy heart.

He had two inverted "S" brands on his muscular body, one on his right bicep, and one over his left breast. Both were about two inches long. He branded himself — that's the only way to explain what he did — by pressing twisted hot coat hangers to his flesh during Phi Beta Sigma initiation ceremonies. He told me the coat hangers had been held over the flame on a stove until they were red hot. Some fraternity fun...

Many of the Steelers had tattoos on their bodies, but only a few had anything approaching what Williams had, a swelling of skin in an inverted "S" shape.

Such marks were once put on slaves with hot irons by their masters to show ownership, so it seemed incredulous that college students in a black fraternity would do such a thing. Why would anyone scar themselves permanently in such a manner? "I wish I hadn't done it," said Williams. "I wouldn't do it now." But the shenanigans of sailors and college students have never made a great deal of sense, and have long baffled better minds than mine.

Williams may have been unique in another way. He was the only Steeler to disclose that he had spoken to a brother in prison during the playoffs and right up to Super Bowl XXX. He said he had been talking over the telephone with his kid brother, Clyde, a year younger at 24, who was imprisoned at the Bennettsfield (S.C.) Correctional Institute. "The day after Christmas, he called my mother, and she called me," said Williams, "and we had a three-way conversation. He'll call once a week."

Two brothers who had grown up in the same home were worlds apart in so many ways. Willie realized that he walked a tight wire when it came to staying out of the kind of trouble that led his brother in the wrong direction. Willie was on his way to Tempe, Arizona for the biggest football game of his life, and Clyde was trying to convince the authorities that he had cleaned up his act and could be released from prison. "He's very proud of me," said Williams. "I wish he hadn't gotten involved with bad stuff in the first place."

Clyde was coming up for parole, and he was pleading with Willie to help him, saying he was ready to return to school, and would do so if Willie would help him financially. That was no problem with Willie, but Clyde had conned him and his family before with promises to repent and turn his life around, only to disappoint them once more. People who have drug or alcoholic problems have a habit of telling people, especially loved ones, what they want to hear, but often betray those who care most about them. It's typical behavior for those whose lives have been enslaved by chemical dependency.

"I want to believe him, but I don't know...," said Williams. "He called me yesterday. We stay in touch. It seems like he's changing. We talk about what he's going to do when he gets out. I want to help him. I'm in a position financially now where I can do something for him and my family."

Their father was a minister, and they were brought up in a rigorous religious environment in Columbia, South Carolina. But the marriage broke up, leaving a splintered family. Willie thought he would be joining the Marines until he was offered a scholarship to play football at Western Carolina. He had a younger sister, Monika, 21, who was a student at Florida A&M, and an older sister, Bernadette, 27.

Clyde was his greatest concern.

"When I was in fifth grade, our house burned down. We lost everything."
— Willie Williams

Willie James Williams Jr. was a big handle for a little guy, but he grew into it. His father, Willie Sr., was a real estate agent and a Baptist minister. His mother's name was Eliza.

"He was real strict; there were a lot of rules in our house," said Williams. "We could not go out and stay out all night. He made us go to church. He pushed a lot when we were kids to go to church. And my mother supported him in that regard.

"My dad being a minister, I enjoyed it. But it made him upset when we couldn't go to church or wanted to do other things on Sunday. He'd say 'That's not the right thing to do.'

"I'm glad I was raised in a home like that. I love my father to death. He carried on for us when things were real difficult. He didn't agree with some of the things we wanted to do, but I think I have benefited from his guidance in the long run.

"I'm a religious man. I go to church at the Macedonia Baptist Church by the Civic Arena. I was baptized there last summer."

He credited Chuck Sanders, a former Steelers running back (1986-87) from Slippery Rock University, with leading him to that church on Bedford Avenue in the Hill District. Sanders was a frequent visitor to the Steelers' locker room.

The Rev. Jason Barr said he baptized Williams in August of 1995, and that Sanders, in a personal ministry, not only brought athletes to the church, but also underpriviledged kids from Northview Heights, a project near Three Rivers Stadium. "Sanders is the president of the Men of Macedonia," he added.

Williams is welcome wherever he goes. He is a "Yes, sir," and "No, sir" kind of guy, a throwback to another generation in that respect. He's overcome many obstacles in his bid to be successful in life.

"When I was in the fifth grade, our house burned down," said Williams. "We lost everything. We were struggling. My father and mother were so concerned about us. We had no clothes. My mother's father took us in. We came out of it OK. But there were some tough times.

"I remember my father going back into the home, looking for his Bible. He couldn't find it. It was the first time I ever saw my father cry. The next day he found his Bible. He told us, 'Keep believing in God, things will work out.'

"I wasn't so sure at the time. It was a real setback. I lost my first football trophy in that fire. I was playing quarterback for a local football team and two weeks earlier I got that trophy. I found it in the ruins of the fire. I found it and it was no good, it was all melted, and it brought tears to my eyes. My brother Clyde cried, too."

Willie was playing for a peewee football team at the local recreation center called the Greenview Eagles, he recalled, when he lost that trophy in the fire.

"At first, my mother didn't like the idea of us playing football. We were so small; she thought we were going to get hurt. We went to North Carolina to play in a championship game. It was the first trip I ever went on. I was so excited. And I could see that football could bring good things in my life. I was the smallest kid; my younger brother was getting bigger than me. He's taller than I am."

He said the Steelers were one of his favorite teams when he was a little kid. He was ten years old when the Steelers won their fourth Super Bowl in January of 1980.

"I liked Lynn Swann because he was small, too. I loved Terry Bradshaw and Franco Harris. Last year, I got Franco's autograph when he came into our dressing room. I hollered out, 'Oh, my, that's Franco Harris!' I went over and shook his hand. He said, 'What's your name?' And I told him. Then I asked him to sign something for me. 'Who am I writing this out to?' Franco asked me. And I said, 'You're making it out to me.' He just smiled."

"He got in with the wrong crowd. Now he's paying the price."
— Willie on his brother Clyde

"I don't feel terrible about some of the bad stuff my family has encountered," said Williams. "I feel good about myself. I can't do anything about my height. It might be easier if I was taller. Only God can control that. I've been playing football for a long time. As long as my heart is big, I'll be OK. I've prayed to God to make sure things would work out. He's done a good job for me and my family."

422

Williams was asked what it was like to be in church as a kid and have his father preaching from the pulpit.

"When I was 15 or 16, I started listening to what he was saying," he confessed. "Before that, all I did was sleep and play around, and he'd see us. We got a little punishment when we'd get home.

"Later on, my father moved out of our house. It was really hard on my mother. I think my brother's problems pulled them apart. Who was to blame?

"My brother and I was real tight. We grew up together and we slept in the same bed. He was smart and he was a good athlete and he could have done whatever he wanted. He got in with the wrong crowd. It caused a lot of problems for our family. Now he's paying the price. He's been in prison for two years."

What for?

"Attempted murder, drug peddling, possession, and anything else you can think of."

When did things go wrong?

"When I was a senior, he started drinking and didn't care about school anymore. He started coming in at night when he wanted to. He got in fights. He'd be in and out of jail.

"When I went to college, things really went bad. He got into drugs. He got addicted to crack cocaine. He started selling. I tried to save him; my parents tried to save him. My brother always brought up things that my mother did. He made it difficult for everyone."

How did Willie manage not to get into trouble like his brother? I had read several books by Pittsburgh-born author John Wideman, a brilliant man, and always wondered what it was like for him to have been so successful as a young athlete, as a writer and as an intellectual voice in the academic world, yet his brother (the subject of a book called *My Brother's Keeper*) and his son were both imprisoned for crimes they had committed. How did that happen?

"I could have been like that; we could have run the streets together," said Williams. "We didn't have any money; it was so hard to see my parents struggling. He could just go out and make some money. I always wondered what I could do.

"I was scared to go out there and do what my brother was doing. I was no angel; I got disciplined at school from time to time for one thing or another. But I drew the line. I got a job at Burger King and at a Bi-Lo super market.

"My father and things I saw in my neighborhood kept me going straight. My brother started living elsewhere, we were never sure where he slept at night. One day I came home from school, and my brother showed up on the front steps.

"He'd been in the street for a month. He was strung out on drugs, and he looked terrible. He didn't look like my brother. It brought tears to my eyes; we had been so close.

"When I go out to talk to kids, I don't talk about football. I tell them, 'If you know it's wrong, then don't do it. If you don't know if it's right or wrong, then ask somebody before you do anything. You just can't do whatever your friends want to do.' You are responsible for yourself."

Williams was asked if he had talked much about his upbringing with Deon Figures, who grew up in a bad neighborhood in southern California, and had been shot in the knee by a stray bullet while driving near his old neighborhood during the off-season. Figures' dressing stall was only two removed from where Williams dressed each day. They were neighbors in the Steelers' locker room.

"He's one of my good friends on the team," said Williams. "My first year here was his first year here. We play the same position and we go to the same meetings and watch the same film, and we're together a lot. I think Deon has changed a lot since he's been here. He saw his friends getting shot and killed back home. He's changed; he's trying to make a difference in his life. I tell him what not to do. I did my share of dirty work, too, when I was in high school. I got suspended from school; I had detention. Everyone did a little something in their school days.

"We didn't have gangs as such; we had friends we ran with. We didn't want anybody coming up to us and giving us a bad time. So we'd get into arguments with kids from other neighborhoods. So I guess we had a gang without knowing it. We didn't wear any special colors, or anything like that. People started carrying weapons. One of my friends turned out for the worse. I've been lucky, I guess."

One of the other guys he grew up with, Tyrone Legette, came out of Columbia and went on to play for the New Orleans Saints. "He went to the University of Nebraska; I wanted to go to the University of South Carolina. They didn't recruit me. They said I was too small. They said I didn't have the necessary SAT scores. Some of the guys they got didn't have such great SAT scores, either."

As a kid, he recalled seeing at least one football game at the University of South Carolina, against Vanderbilt. "I didn't have the money, and no one ever took me," he said.

"I got to see one NFL game in person. My head coach at Spring Valley High School, Jerry Brown, took me to a game in Atlanta between the Falcons and the San Francisco 49ers. He was the one who promoted me to Western Carolina."

With Williams as his star player, Brown coached Spring Valley to a state championship.

Western Carolina Sports Information

Villie Williams during his Phi
Beta Sigma days at Western
Carolina University

Willie James Williams Sr. and his wife, Eliza,
flank Willie during Senior Day at Spring Valley
High School. The couple have since divorced.

Williams family, from left to right, included Bernadette, Clyde in forefront, father
Willie Sr., and Willie Jr.

"I believe life is all about helping other people."
— Willie Williams

"When I first got here, Coach LeBeau told me, 'Willie, you're not too small.' He'd tell other people, 'He can hit; he's got a lot of heart.' Coach Cowher believed in me, too. Tim Lewis, our defensive backfield coach, has helped me a lot. I'm glad God made a way for me. I believe life is all about helping other people. My mother always said, 'Don't forget where you came from.'"

The Steelers selected Williams as a sixth round draft pick in 1993. He was one of three rookies to play in every game that year. He did that even though he suffered a fractured wrist the fourth week of the regular season. That was not going to keep him out of the lineup. He was small, but he had great speed — he was timed at 4.38 seconds in the 40-yard sprint — and he was definitely not afraid to go helmet-to-helmet with much bigger players.

"A lot of people said I was too small to play in the NFL," said Williams. "Now I've got a chance to prove them wrong."

Williams wore eyeglasses during his college days, which made him look even less formidable, but he had demonstrated strong leadership qualities as one of the captains for the Catamounts. He started in every game at Western Carolina and was a three-time all-Southern Conference pick.

But Western Carolina played its home games at E.J. Whitmore Stadium that seated 12,000, and it was never confused with North Carolina or Southern California.

He was a sports management major at Western Carolina and he was the first Western Carolina player ever to play in the Blue-Gray All-Star Classic on Christmas Day in Montgomery, Alabama. He was a late add-on, but grateful to get invited. The game was seen on ABC-TV, which was the first time Williams played in a nationally-televised game.

At the NFL scouting combine in Indianapolis, he was timed in 4.42 seconds for the 40, bench pressed 385 pounds, squatted 515 pounds, and had a 34 1/2" vertical leap.

Draft guru Mel Kiper raved about him, labeling him a super blue chip prospect, comparing him to former Colorado and Rams corner-back Rod Perry.

On draft day, Dick LeBeau, then the defensive backfield coach of the Steelers, said, "Here's a young man who's played in a smaller conference, and probably has been told most of his life, 'You're too short.' Yet, he's found a way to be successful in his athletic career to date."

Tim Beckman, the coach of the defensive backs at Western Carolina, said, "When Willie was drafted, I sent Bill Cowher a little note. I just told him that Willie Williams is a classic Coach Cowher guy. He does things through effort and hard work. He's just like Bill Cowher."

Tom Donahoe, the director of football operations for the Steelers, watched Williams with a keen eye and took note of his steady development:

"Willie's biggest problem was that he didn't have a lot of confidence, even though he always had the skills to play the corner. He's really fast; he can run in the 4.4s consistently, he has good jumping ability, and he's strong for his size. I think by the time we got to training camp this year (1995), we were all confident that Willie just needed to play. Two years ago, he wasn't ready, but by the end of last year he was our best special teams player, and I think the coaches thought he'd be our No. 3 cornerback.

"After Figures got shot and Woodson went down (they were the starting cornerbacks), it was just a matter of putting him out there. Some guys find it's not easy to be embarrassed. It's like Coach Noll used to say, a good corner has to have a short memory."

That quality served Williams in good stead after his opening game performance. He made his first pro start at cornerback against Herman Moore of the Detroit Lions. Moore, who is 6-4, and went on to be the NFL's leading receiver for the season, caught 10 balls on September 3, 1995, at Three Rivers Stadium, and Cowher did not start Williams the following week at Houston.

"Willie had a tough time with his technique in that game," allowed LeBeau, himself a former NFL cornerback. "But with all our guys, we talk to them about that and they correct it, and that's what happened with Willie. As a matter of fact, I think I recall that guy from Detroit beating more than a few guys for touchdowns this season."

Williams was able to look back at that encounter with Moore as a learning experience. "I just have to play taller receivers different than I play guys who are 5-9," Williams said in mid-December of the 1995 season. "Herman Moore is 6-4. I was playing him like I had a 5-10 receiver. I can't do that on the big guys because they're going to use their strength against me. That's what Herman Moore did. But you win some, you lose some. I was just lost in that game. My mind was somewhere else. But I've learned a lot from that game."

Tom Modrak, the Steelers' pro personnel director, came to Williams' defense. "Moore made some plays on him, but a lot of it was just a height thing," said Modrak. "Willie didn't go into the tank. He kept his head with a lot going on around him.

"He's such a good guy and he's so intense that other players like him. He's always focused. You can see at practice, he'll be studying. Other guys will be talking or whatever. You have to give a lot of credit to Rod Woodson and those guys, because they like him, and any time he would make a play at practice you could hear them pumping him up."

Williams had two interceptions against San Diego at Three Rivers Stadium on October 1, 1995, returning one 63 yards for a touchdown. He intercepted another one in the exciting victory at

Chicago. He helped the Steelers get off to a quick start in Cleveland. He intercepted Vinny Testaverde on the Browns' first play, and he recovered a fumble to set up another score on the Browns' second play. Then on December 10, he had two interceptions in the Steelers' 29-10 victory at Oakland.

Cowher became a big fan of Willie Williams. He liked his spirit. "I think his size will always be a factor," said the Steelers' head coach, a former linebacker and special teams performer with the Eagles and Browns. "At the same time, Willie's been able to overcome that, battle that, and not look at it as a minus. It hasn't dampened his confidence at all. He's a tough kid."

Williams was the first to acknowledge that he wasn't as good as Woodson or Lake, two guys he worked out with on a year-round basis.

"I'm happy with the way I'm playing," he said during the playoffs of 1995. "I can't play like Rod and Carnell, they're too big, but I was able to learn enough from them that I can play. I feel real good the way I'm playing. I feel fortunate to be part of the Steelers defense.

"I was always tired of people telling me I was too small. That's one thing that has kept me going. I've pretty much been playing with a chip on my shoulder."

"I told them to never sell themselves short, to be a fighter." — Mrs. Eliza Williams

It was May 1, 1996, and Clyde Williams was watching TV at his mother's apartment in Columbia, South Carolina. Clyde had come home after being incarcerated for three years at the Bennettsfield Correctional Institute. He was on probation. He had gone out that day to get some information about a technical school he was checking out. He said he planned on going back to school. He said he planned on preparing himself for a better life. His brother Willie had attended a mini-camp with the rookies and some of the younger players on the Steelers the same week that Clyde had gotten out of prison.

"I have to regain Willie's trust," said Clyde. "I'm trying to make a comeback. I've got to convince him that I'm sincere when I say I want his help to turn my life around.

"I was at a parole hearing the same week that Willie and my family were at the Super Bowl. That was like a dream come true. I wish I could have been with them. The trouble I got in kept me from going forward like he did."

I asked Clyde how he could have done what he did, being a criminal, when his father was a minister, his mother a hard-working woman who did her best to bring up her four children to be successful, and his older brother a big-time star with the Steelers.

"Rebellion, that's why," Clyde came back. "I always had a hard head, ever since middle school. I had a bad attitude."

"Do you think you can change?" I asked him.

"I don't *think*; I know I can," he said. "Most definitely. What I was doing is a dead end."

Mention of the Super Bowl brought something to mind. "The way I see it, I felt like Neil O'Donnell sold us out."

Chalk up another critic for Neil O'Donnell. This one was watching the game on TV with his cellmate at Bennettsfield Correctional Institute. And everybody there knew that Clyde's brother was starting at defensive back for the Steelers.

I asked Clyde if he felt a sense of pride seeing his brother in the Super Bowl.

"Not really," he said. "It was not me making money. It was not me there. But I'm proud of my brother."

I mentioned that his brother wanted to be proud of him, too, that Willie was willing to help him out financially if he was sincere about going to school. "I was checking out a technical college today," said Clyde. "I'm not able to leave the state, so I'm looking at something close to home."

When asked what he had done to get himself jailed, Clyde said, "Do you want a list of them? Drug trafficking. Accessory with intent to kill. Strongarm robbery."

He told me like a kid reading a good report card to his parents.

"I need to do this for my brother as well as for myself," Clyde continued. "My brother has been the biggest factor in my life for the past three years. I never had a hero. I didn't believe in Superman or Batman. I just looked up to my brother. I'm going to try and follow in his footsteps. The fruit doesn't fall too far from the tree."

Asked what his relationship was like with his father, Clyde said, "We're not as close as we used to be. Some things happened, which I don't want to talk about. I'm with my mom now and she's trying to help me as best she can. It's up to me now."

Eliza Williams was working two jobs. She had been working for 27 years as an analytical service technician with Allied/Signal Fiber Division, which used to be Allied Chemical. She sold real-estate part-time in Columbia.

"I used to tell them all to get the education, and to be the best you can be," said Mrs. Williams. "I told them to never sell themselves short, to be a fighter."

She mentioned that her daughter Bernadette managed a Pizza Inn, and was preparing to take the LSAT test to go to law school. Her other daughter, Monika, was a junior at Florida A&M, majoring in math, and was working part-time for an attorney in Tallahassee.

"That's another thing that's motivating Clyde," said Mrs. Williams. "His sisters and brother are doing well. He doesn't want to be the only one who's not. Clyde is on the road to recovery. Clyde has to prove himself to Willie if he wants his help.

"Willie being in professional football has had a great impact on Clyde. Clyde can see how he could be farther along if he'd done what Willie did. The coaches all felt Clyde had great ability. He sees now where he's made his mistakes, and he's working on a comeback. He went out on his own today to get something going regarding his education.

"Clyde has really changed and improved himself. He realized he has thrown away some years that could have been very beneficial to him. Willie has had an important impact on him. I don't think Clyde is going to disappoint him anymore."

Then she turned her attention to her older son, Willie. "He always had the dream to be a professional football player," she said. "When they were young, they were both on the small side, and I didn't want them playing football. I was afraid they'd get hurt. Their father talked me into letting them play.

"When I got involved and learned to enjoy the games, then I felt more comfortable. I don't know if you know this, but when Willie was two years old his legs were very crooked. Did he tell you about that? The doctor said they could be straightened out. He put braces on his legs. The more he wore them, though, the worse his legs got. He wore them for about six months when I decided to take them off. I just didn't feel any confidence in them. I just took them off and tossed them in the closet. And I said some prayers for him. In time, his legs got straighter.

"He ended up running on the track team at Spring Valley High School. He holds the record for the 100 yard dash. He still holds it, from what I know. There was nothing in his real early days that indicated he could ever be a pro football player some day. But he came on strong in his sophomore and junior years, and we felt more confident about his chances then. I believe Willie has come a long way.

"I always taught them to pray and respect other people, and to believe there is a God. Today, Willie will always say that all he has came from God."

Willie Williams tackles Cleveland receiver Andre Rison.

George Gojkovich

Ernie Mills
He knew what he wanted

*"I never felt like I was
at school to play football."*

Ernie Mills remembered his best day at the University of
Florida. It came at the Stephen C. O'Connell Center, the 14,000-
seat arena where he usually sat in the student section and
rooted ardently for the Gators' basketball team. It was not at the Ben
Hill Griffin Stadium at Florida Field, the 72,000-seat stadium where
he enjoyed some magnificent games as a wide receiver for the Orange
and Blue football team.

It was on December 22, 1990, when Mills received a bachelor of
science degree at graduation ceremonies. "It felt very good," said
Mills, drawing it out, stretching one syllable words into two syllable
words. "It was a most satisfying day."

Mills flashed an engaging gap-toothed smile to punctuate his
proud reflections. There was not a sweeter smile in the Steelers
locker room. He wore a mustache and sometimes he would sport a
light beard. Often, he would wear rose-colored sunglasses. It was fitting because Mills seemed to look at the world through rose-colored
glasses. And that does improve the picture. He was talking about his
developmental years, taking a breather after a voluntary off-season
workout with some of his teammates on the Pittsburgh Steelers at
Three Rivers Stadium back in mid-May, 1995, before his fifth pro
season.

He was one of the smallest of the Steelers, listed at 5-11, 191
pounds, and appearing even smaller — like a boxer — but he also had
demonstrated, especially during the 1994 playoffs, that he had a big
heart and inner strength. He was fast becoming one of the Steelers'
most sure-handed pass-catchers, and was particularly adept at going
across the middle — no man's land — and braving the bruised ribs
that go with such derring-do.

The best was yet to come. Mills would come up with many clutch
catches during the 1995 season; the biggest one in the closing minutes
of the AFC title game with the Indianapolis Colts would set up the
winning score and send the Steelers to Super Bowl XXX. During a
torrid two-year period, Ernie Mills would become the Steelers' big-
play guy. It was fun to watch his progress up close, to see him get
better and better, to see him get respect after being looked upon only
two years earlier as one of the wide receiver group thought to be a
weak link in the Steelers' armada.

He wore No. 89, which in Pittsburgh will always be associated
with Mike Ditka, a Hall of Fame receiver from Aliquippa, who starred

as an All-American at Pitt, and with the Chicago Bears, Philadelphia Eagles and Dallas Cowboys. Mills was the kind of gutsy competitor that the demanding Ditka would adore.

Talking to Ernest Lee Mills III in May of 1995, it quickly became evident that this young man had a mission to make something of himself, in every respect. He was a cool customer, who could shift from an assassin's stare to an ambassador's smile in a short span, and was proud of his accomplishments. He wanted to be a star, he wanted to be special. It had been that way since his earliest schooldays in Dunnellon, Florida, a beautiful little community about 15 miles from the Gulf of Mexico.

"I was playing in the Blue-Gray All-Star Game in Montgomery, but I told them I had to get back to school for the graduation ceremony," said Mills. "They flew me by private jet to Gainesville, and I returned to Montgomery afterward by commercial flight in time to play in the game on Christmas Day.

"I had been red-shirted as a defensive back in my freshman year at Florida, so I was there for four-and-a-half years and graduated at mid-year, following the fall semester. It was a big day in my life.

"I had been a good student going back to my grade school days, and I knew then I wanted to go to college. My parents wanted me to get an education. As far as football goes, it was paying my way. I had planned on going to college before I got a football scholarship. I think I looked at it a little differently than some of the other athletes at Florida. I never felt like I was at school to play football."

His mother said he shed tears of joy at his college graduation ceremonies.

"I'm very proud of my college degree," said Ernie Mills. "I even take offense when someone puts down my degree. It was in sports administration. But it wasn't a Mickey Mouse program. They (the critics) weren't there and they don't know what it was all about. I had to take a lot of business and accounting classes, science, nutrition and anatomy courses. College was more challenging for me than what I'd experienced in school before that."

I mentioned to Mills that I had taught sports information and public relations classes in the sports management major at Robert Morris College in Pittsburgh, and thought the required curriculum, top-heavy with business-oriented classes, was quite challenging. I had taught some young people who had successfully chased their dreams to have a sports-related career. They often defied doubters.

There had been doubters in Dunnellon about the sports and school challenges that awaited Mills when he matriculated to the University of Florida, and again when the Steelers selected him in the third round of the 1991 National Football League draft.

There had been boosters, too, and Mills preferred to dwell on the Dunnellon people who pushed and prodded him to take on challenges and be the best he could be, the ones who have stayed with him all the way.

432

Ernie Mills

Bill Amatucci

George Gojkovich

Mills remembered John Pruitt, a gentleman who once owned a supermarket in his hometown, and gave him and his brother Tony, a year younger, a chance to work and make some spending money during their high school days.

Mills was 17 and had just finished playing basketball at Dunnellon High School when he started working at Pruitt's supermarket. "I was on the track team, but that was no big deal at our school; I'd go to practice and work out for maybe a half hour, and then go to work," said Mills.

"Mr. Pruitt was a positive influence in my life. He was positive with all the guys in our neighborhood. He was good to my family.

"When word got out that I was going to Florida on a football scholarship, Mr. Pruitt would assure me, 'There's no doubt you're going to play. Just make sure you get an education. Take advantage of this opportunity.' Every time I went back there, when I was going to college, he'd ask me how my grades were. He always had faith in my ability.

"He was always happy for me, and he was especially happy when I graduated.

"I was taking a math course in middle school. I had a teacher who was very good at it. She wanted me to take an advanced math class, so I did. When I was a freshman in high school, I took algebra. I wasn't afraid to take myself seriously in school. I learned a lot of different things in school, and I got some super support. I never acted like I was smarter than my friends, but I didn't duck tough courses to run with the pack, either."

The math teacher who taught him in eighth grade became Congresswoman Karen Thurman, and has since served as a marshal along with Mills of the Dunnellon Little League Parade.

He was looking beyond Dunnellon, as much as he loved his hometown. "I didn't want to stay there and make my life there," said Mills. "I loved the place, and the people, and I wouldn't trade my early days there for anything. I just didn't feel there were opportunities for me to be successful. And I wanted to be successful."

"There's a feeling of lost opportunity."
— Ernie Mills

Ernie Mills was one of the main targets for Neil O'Donnell in the AFC championship game against the San Diego Chargers at the end of the 1994 NFL season, and he performed brilliantly. He caught eight passes for 106 yards altogether, and several of those came in a late drive that brought the Steelers within three yards of the Super Bowl. But the Steelers came up short, of course, and lost a heartbreaker to the Chargers, 17-13.

No one took it any harder than Mills. He was looking forward to having his family and friends from Dunnellon see him at work in a Steelers uniform at Joe Robbie Stadium in Miami, in his native Florida, against the San Francisco 49ers in Super Bowl XXIX.

"I've been back home since then," said Mills in mid-May of 1995, "and everyone tries to be nice about it. Some people say, 'It's too bad, but you played a great game. Don't worry about it.' It's nice of them to say that, but it does bother me. There's a feeling of lost opportunity. Going back to Florida for a Super Bowl would have been very special. People from my hometown said, 'We were ready to go there with you.' It would have been great. They try to be nice and they say, 'Well, you saved us some money.'"

Opportunities and money were not always easy to come by in Dunnellon.

Mills came to that conclusion when he was in eighth or ninth grade. "It seemed to me," he said, "that either you were going to have a nine-to-five job in the town, not making much money, or you could be in the Army, or be selling drugs. There are a lot of good, hard-working people in the community, but I didn't want to grow up in that type of atmosphere.

"My mom and dad both pushed me. Even though they got a divorce, they both worked hard at whatever they did, and they taught me how to do the same. It was just a dream for me to play football and be able to help my mom do some things.

"She wanted me to get an education. She's very smart, but she wasn't able to go to school. Her name is Maxine, and she's a secretary-dispatcher for the Dunnellon police department. My father, Ernest Jr., is a lineman for Florida Power. He lives in Tampa now, and has his own family."

Mills had much in common with many of his teammates on the Steelers, with parents frequently splitting up, but he was among the lucky ones in that his father continued to be involved in his upbringing.

His maternal grandparents, Nathaniel and Johnie Mae Daniels, both deceased, were always a positive influence in Ernie's young life. Nathaniel and Ernie's other grandfather, Ernie Mills Sr., attended most of his activities.

"I was nine when my parents split up," explained Ernie. "It was a struggle. Me and my brother Tony had to go through some tough times. With my mom working, my brother and I alternated washing dishes, washing clothes, preparing meals, chopping wood for the fireplace."

He and his mom remained close. She told me in a telephone conversation that she sometimes kidded Ernie by saying, "E.T., call home. I need to know what you're doing." There were not too many parents of the Steelers players who demonstrated their pride as much as the mother of Ernie Mills. She was a most faithful correspondent on this book project.

435

"He's not one of those players who's gotten too big to remember where he came from."
— James Corne of Dunnellon

The biggest day in Ernie Mill's life, except for his college graduation day, certainly came on January 28, 1996, when he started at wide receiver and returned kickoffs for the Steelers against the Dallas Cowboys in Super Bowl XXX.

A rally was held in his hometown of Dunnellon on January 25, 1996, three days before the big game. A banner was unfurled in his honor and money was being raised to erect a permanent billboard declaring Dunnellon as "the hometown of Ernie Mills." Pittsburgh was spelled without an "h" — the way it was originally spelled. Mrs. Williams wrote "oops" over the picture in the local newspaper clipping she had sent me.

Ernie Mills Sr., his grandfather, was there, wearing a large cowboy hat which could have confused some people about which team he was rooting for. The Rev. Michael Warren was offering up prayers on behalf of the Mills Family at the First Bethel Missionary Baptist Church.

Ernie Mills had played as a kid in the Marion County Youth Football League, and on a youth basketball team. At Dunnellon High School, he ran track, played basketball and football and played in the school band. He was graduated from Dunnellon High in 1986, and he had become an even bigger hero in his hometown because of his outstanding play at Florida and with the Steelers.

"Ernie hasn't changed one bit since the day he left Dunnellon," said James Corne, a former high school teammate who attended the public rally in Dunnellon. "He's never been too good for anybody else and it's great to see all his hard work pay off for him .

"Back in high school, he was shy and you never heard much from him. He's not so shy now, but he's not one of those players that's gotten too big to remember where he came from. Ernie still comes around and still takes time to talk to everybody he comes in contact with."

Dunnellon's football team went 10-2 in Ernie's senior year, going as far as the state semifinals. He was not a big star, so some were surprised when he got a scholarship to play football at Florida.

He was seriously recruited by only two schools: Florida and Florida State.

Tommy Williams, who was the coach of the defensive backs at Dunnellon, remained a big fan. "When the Steelers were driving in the AFC Championship, I knew they'd go to Ernie," said Williams. "That's his spot. It's a shame the pass was a little behind him, or it would have been six points.

"Ernie didn't even play football in his freshman year in high school. I think he was in the band or something. Basketball was more his thing then. But he came out for football as a sophomore and things just took off for him.

"Ernie's speed wasn't overwhelming and he wasn't a Parade All-American or anything like that. He didn't get much notice until his senior year. But one night scouts from Florida came to see him play and he intercepted two passes and forced a fumble on defense and made a couple of catches, and they offered him a scholarship."

Maxine Williams always taught her children about persistence and patience and hoped they would grow up to be sources of pride. They did not disappoint her.

"I feel so full of pride and so thankful that so many good things have been happening," said Mrs. Williams. "Every time I see Ernest on television, I just think to myself, 'that's my baby.'"

Mrs. Williams wrote to me following Super Bowl XXX.

"Ernie cried at his college graduation ceremonies, he felt so good. I did the same thing when I saw Ernie running onto the field for the Super Bowl. I just said, 'Thank you, Jesus,' because he'd done so many great things for Ernest.

"Words cannot express how thankful and proud I am of Ernie's success, that the Lord has truly smiled on him. And he knows the importance of a mother's love. Ernie has not forgotten his roots, and his love for his family shines through. I am also proud of my son, Tony, who has also been a special blessing from The Lord. It has not been easy for either of them, but they have made things work for them, through their efforts and their faith in God."

Ernie was not an instant star at Florida or with the Steelers. It took time for him to develop in both places.

"I've always taught Ernest and all the children that if you want something enough, you'll be willing to work hard for it," said Mrs. Williams in a telephone conversation. "I always knew he could do anything he wanted to do. I knew it wouldn't be easy, but he's worked hard at it. He's always been a man and always stayed focused.

"I'm even more proud when I see how the local kids look up to him. And he just goes his own quiet way and hasn't changed much.

"I was really surprised when he opened up on television (when interviewed after the 1996 AFC championship). He's no Deion Sanders when it comes to talking, but he was talking about telling Neil O'Donnell to 'throw it up and I'll go get it.' You could tell he was really excited. That was nice to see."

She said her younger son, Tony, was more of a talker and demonstrative person. Tony went to Sterling College and Southeast Oklahoma State University on a partial scholarship for football, and was playing college ball at the same time as his brother. Tony, who was 27 at the time and living in Charlotte, went to the Super Bowl with his mother, his kid brother, Roberto, 13, and sister, Renata, 9. Tony and Roberto had both visited and stayed with Ernie in Pittsburgh during the 1995 season.

Mills' father, Ernest Mills Jr., went to the game, too, with his second wife and their three children. "Ernie's father and I divorced when he was nine and Tony was eight," said Mrs. Williams. "I retained custody, but their father always remained close to them."

"I want to try and give something back to the town that gave me my start."
— Ernie Mills

A lot of sportswriters from Florida interviewed Mills at the pre-Super Bowl XXX media sessions. One of them was Hubert Mizell, the sports columnist of the *St. Petersburg Times*, an old friend of mine from the year, 1969, when I worked at *The Miami News*, and he was the sports editor for the AP's Miami bureau.

Mills harkened back to the days when he used to walk along the railroad tracks in Dunnellon. Mizell described it as "a little Florida town known for its clear-blue streams and old-fashioned values."

Mills said of his hometown: "It's a small place where everybody knows everybody. But it's home, where Mom and my past are located. I want to try to give something back to the town that gave me my start."

To that end, Mills had gone home five or six times to serve as the grand marshal of the annual Little League Baseball parade through downtown Dunnellon. He was the title sponsor of a new high school track and field event — the Ernie Mills Relays — and he said he was launching a project to build a youth recreation center there.

According to a pamphlet published by the Chamber of Commerce, Dunnellon is a community of less than 2,000 residents. It's known as the "Gateway to Florida's Nature Coast." The Withlocooche River and Rainbow River run through it, as do the railroad tracks. It was once a mining boom town — after the discovery of some of the purest phosphate deposits in the world — but that didn't last. Nowadays its economy is based more on agriculture, logging, livestock and tourism. There are lots of lakes and gardens, and the locals boast that the fishing, especially for bass, is as good as it gets in Florida. It's a pretty place.

"We'd get to dreaming," Ernie recalled, "wondering about our future." Wondering what would lie ahead if they followed those railroad tracks.

Even when he had idle time as a teenager, Mills knew better than to get into any kind of trouble.

"My brother, Tony, and I always knew to avoid getting into trouble when we were kids," he recalled. "Mama was the police dispatcher, so she *absolutely* would be the first to know if her boys got sideways with the law."

438

He and his brother Tony spent a lot of time watching sports on TV, and playing their own games. "We would watch the big-leaguers on TV," Ernie said, "but almost never saw the end of their games. By then, we were outside, trying to emulate the pros.

"O.J. Simpson was a boyhood hero of mine. When I first got started in football, everybody wanted to be O.J. We'd play football and say we were O.J. when we were carrying the ball. For a lot of people who grew up watching him, they definitely don't want him to be guilty of that murder. I can't even watch it. I still can't believe he's going through this. It would've hurt more if I were younger. It just shows that anybody can do anything.

"Another one of my boyhood heroes was Tony Dorsett (Mills' teammate Erric Pegram also idolized Dorsett). I wanted to be a running back like them. Later on, when I was playing defensive back at Dunnellon High School, my main men were NFL cornerbacks like Mike Haynes."

Mills didn't get many pass-catching opportunities in high school, but he was named to the all-state team as a senior. "We didn't need much in the way of wide receivers," he said. "Our coach, Richard Kennedy, loved running the football. If we could've gone through entire games without ever putting the ball in the air, Coach Kennedy would've been very pleased."

Ernie was recruited to Florida by assistant coach Mike Heimerdinger as a defensive back. Galen Hall, a former Penn State quarterback, was the head coach then at Florida. "I was redshirted as a freshman, then had trouble cracking the lineup," said Ernie. "But my time in the 40 was 4.2, which was by far the fastest on the team. Our wide receivers coach convinced Coach Hall to move me over. To this day, though, I love playing cornerback."

Mills made some big plays, but was hardly a star. That title belonged to running back Emmitt Smith, who went on to be one of the NFL's finest runners with the Dallas Cowboys. (Smith, by the way, returned in the spring of 1996 to complete his studies and get his degree because he had promised his mother he would when he left school early to turn pro. It was a shame that story did not draw headlines as big as teammate Michael Irvin's drug problems.) After Ernie's junior season at Florida, Hall was fired and replaced by Steve Spurrier, who lived by the pass. Mills was ready-made for Spurrier's sophisticated pro-style offense in which he played multiple receiver positions. It was that one year that attracted the attention of pro scouts.

The Steelers drafted him on the third round, right after they had selected Jeff Graham of Ohio State.

"Things changed," said Mills, smiling at the memory. "Spurrier brought a wide-open passing game. At the end of my senior year, I caught seven against Kentucky and then eight passes against Florida State. It greatly enhanced my NFL possibilities."

Emmitt Smith was still a fan of Ernie's. They got together before Super Bowl XXX in Arizona, and Smith said some kind things about his former teammate: "Ernie's a big-play guy. I just hope he doesn't make one against us.

"Ernie's definitely come a long way. I saw him out here and we embraced. It's nice to see him have a heck of a year. He's made a lot of plays, but he's just now getting his share of recognition."

"Ernie's a big-play guy."
— Emmitt Smith
Dallas Cowboys

Ernie Mills had to be patient to get his due in Pittsburgh. Just before the AFC championship contest with the Indianapolis Colts, Mills was musing over his situation in the Steelers' locker room.

"There'd be times I'd think I wish I was catching this many passes or that many passes," he said. "But you know what? You learn real quickly that winning is the most important thing. So many guys come into the league, catch a lot of balls and never play on a winning team. We're winning here. I'd rather have it this way."

The Steelers had used a rotation system among four receivers most of the previous season, but abandoned that scheme. All the receivers seemed to benefit from the change. "I can't explain why we're catching the ball better," said Mills. "It's probably just a confidence thing. It's easy to lose confidence when you drop a couple. That's something we've all learned to fight through.

"I love big games. You hear players say a playoff game is just another game, but that's not true. Take that Buffalo game. I was so nervous I couldn't stop shaking before the game. Doing that well that day gave me a lot of confidence."

Speaking of Cris Carter, who was among the leaders of the NFL in receptions at the time, Mills said, "He can have the receiving title. I'll take the Super Bowl. I'd make that trade any day."

Going to the Super Bowl became a goal once he started to get his act together in Pittsburgh.

"I've always had fantasies about playing in the Super Bowl. But more than just getting here, I've wanted to play well in the Super Bowl and to win," he said the week before the big game. "We don't want to just get to the Super Bowl, we want to win the Super Bowl."

He knew the Cowboys were favored by 13 1/2 points, but this did not dismay Mills.

"Our offense has blossomed since we opened up in the second half of the season, spreading the field with four and even five receivers," said Mills during a media event at the Scottsdale Doubletree Resort where the Steelers were staying.

Ernie, his mother Maxine, sister Renata, and brothers Tony and Roberto

Ernie's mother holds his trophy as top defensive back at Dunnellon High sports banquet.

Ernie is joined at his 1986 high school graduation by Tony, Roberto and their mother, Maxine.

Ernie in 11th grade

at U. of Florida

Tony at Sterling College

Ernie in kindergarten

"Neil has become a much more dominating quarterback. Behind that beard, he's having some real fun now.

"We have some surprises planned for the Cowboys. Our goal is to make it almost impossible to defense all our offensive weapons, especially Yancey, Kordell, Andre and me as pass receivers. Dallas is a great team, but nobody in this league is anywhere close to being unbeatable."

Mills had been a third-down specialist for much of his five-year pro career. He became a starter when Charles Johnson was injured in October, 1995. Johnson did not dress for the Super Bowl because of a knee injury. In the end, Ernie topped the Steelers with eight touchdown catches. He set a team record with a 24.2-yard average on 54 kickoff returns.

In the AFC title game against Indianapolis, Mills had three receptions for 54 yards, including a sideline tip-toeing acrobatic reception at the Colts' one-yard line that led to the Steelers' game-winning touchdown. It was a highlight catch for the ages.

It wasn't the "Immaculate Reception," but it came close, and will be remembered by Steelers' fans forever. He ran an up-and-out pattern, hauling in a Neil O'Donnell pass over his left shoulder. He planted his right foot, dragged his left and couldn't avert going out of bounds because of his momentum after a 37-yard gain that gave the Steelers first-and-goal at the Colts' one-yard line with 1:51 left in the AFC championship game. Mills remembered what preceded the play:

"In the huddle before the play, I said, 'Just give me the chance.' Neil put it right there. It was a great throw."

Bam Morris barreled into the line twice and 13 seconds later the Steelers were ahead. The Colts almost came up with an immaculate reception of their own at the last second, but the Steelers survived the scare and were on their way to the Super Bowl. For the second year in a row, it came down to the last play before the outcome in the AFC championship game was decided.

"We started the season at 3-4," Mills said, "and we knew we were better than a 3-4 team. It's like we wrote off the first seven games as a separate season and began a new one from there."

The Steelers went on to win eight straight before a 24-19 loss to Green Bay in the regular season finale. In the playoffs, the Steelers knocked out Buffalo 40-21 and Indianapolis 20-16.

Ernie was having an outstanding game in Super Bowl XXX before he suffered a knee injury in the fourth quarter. "My first thought was, 'Lord, please let it not be a serious injury.' I thought it was a neck injury at first; that's always a fear," said Mills' mother.

It was diagnosed as a torn anterior cruciate ligament in the knee, the same injury that sidelined Rod Woodson for most of the season. Mills went to the dressing room for medical attention. He managed to come out on crutches and waved to his mother in the stands. It was reassuring for her.

His absence in the closing minutes of the game was a big factor in the Steelers' coming up short. When they most needed it, they didn't have their complete passing package. If Mills had been on the wide flank to the right side it would have changed the strategy of the Steelers and the Cowboys. Mills would have commanded more respect than Corey Holliday from both O'Donnell and Cowboys' defensive back Larry Brown.

"Ernie said the loss wasn't as bad as when they lost to San Diego last year," said Maxine Williams. "I wish we'd have won, but I enjoyed just being there for such a big event. The halftime show was worth it; I just love Diana Ross. It was breathtaking."

And Ernie enjoyed seeing his mother and his family in the stands. "My mother has always supported me in everything I've done," said Ernie Mills. "She's always been there for me. She was never a huge football fan, but she's always been behind me if she knew I was interested in something."

"We had plenty of dirt and plenty of grass to play ball every day."
— Ernie Mills

At the outset of 1995, Mills spoke about his meteoric career. He believed it started because he laid a good foundation, going back to his earliest schooldays.

"I was serious, but I did have fun," he said. "School was easy. I didn't have to study. I had a God-given gift. I got my work done before I went home. College was tougher, because of the kinds of courses I took. But I always took care of business.

"I was usually pretty busy. There was always some type of activity after school. It definitely kept me out of trouble. We all played sports. Whatever the season was, we had plenty of dirt and plenty of grass to play ball every day. We even played basketball on dirt."

Ernie was a good basketball player, and played on the high school basketball team a year before he went out for football as a sophomore. "I've been able to dunk a basketball since I was in 10th grade. Now I think I'm more into football. More of a student of the game," he said.

"We all had guys we looked up to. There were a lot of people I tried to emulate in sports. Dr. J was one of my favorites. He was the guy I wanted to be like the most. Every time I stepped on the court, I wanted to be Dr. J. I never met him, but I always liked him."

I had not only met Dr. J, but I covered him and the New York Nets for several seasons when I was writing in the Big Apple in the '70s. Dr. J was one of my all-time favorites, too, and I told Mills some stories about his hero that he seemed to enjoy hearing.

443

"Just looking at his mannerisms on television, I had a special feeling about him," said Ernie. "I never saw him lose his temper. The thing that really got your attention was his dunking. He never seemed cocky or boastful, he was unselfish."

Mills had emulated Dr. J well in his approach to the game and to the people he met. Both of us had met Michael Jordan and shared some stories about the Chicago Bulls' great star.

"He seems like a very down to earth person," said Mills. "To be a person of that magnitude — his competitiveness is so great — and handle it as well as he does is most impressive. I met him through Larry Griffin, who used to play here (defensive back, 1987-1993) and knew Jordan from the University of North Carolina. We went to see the Bulls play in Chicago, right before our game. Griffin took me and Dwight Stone."

Ernie Mills thought there were more gifted athletes at Dunnellon High School when he was there, but they all didn't realize their dreams.

"One guy in high school could do it all...he was short, about 5-7, but he scored 29 touchdowns my senior year," recalled Mills. "He ended up going to play baseball, with the Yankees organization, but he hurt his shoulder. To see him play baseball you'd think of Ricky Henderson. But things didn't work out for him. I heard he's living in Tampa these days.

"We had an offensive lineman who was the only player on our team to play in the Florida-Georgia all-star game, but he didn't make it beyond that.

"Sometimes you're just blessed. You have to have the will to do things....it's a lot of hard work...you have to do both. I wasn't banking on just sports. I wanted to make it on my own. I got strong support regarding my school work when I was in middle school and in high school. I took the ACT exam after my junior year, so I could get in on my own.

"I've got a little brother who's 13 and a sister who's 8. I always ask them how they're doing in school. When they get their report cards they have so much pride in their grades."

He had indicated earlier that his father and mother expected him to perform well in school. What sort of an influence was his father on his work ethic? Did he ever see his dad at work as a lineman for Florida Power?

"When I was eight or nine, I went out with him on a highway in the woods," said Mills. "He was working on a large metal power line, one of those monstrous jobs. He was cutting a wire that wasn't necessary anymore. He was so high up there. I knew that I was scared of heights. It looked scary to me. I have a healthy respect for electricity. It's a very tough job. My father works hard; he's that type. He'd get up at 6:30 or 7 in the morning and work all day. At night he'd be working on one of his cars or trucks. He was very hard working. I used to look at him and wonder how he could do it. He instilled that in all of us.

444

"There was no doubt I had a father in my life. It bothered me. The back and forth stuff, going from one home to another, the arguments they had. It would bother any kid. But there was always family and friends around to make sure I wasn't so sad."

Were marital split-ups the norm in his neighborhood?

"There were a lot of strong marriages around the area where I came from," said Mills. "I think it had a positive influence. That's one of the reasons I don't have a kid and that I'm not married. When I decide to get married, I want to be ready for that. I want to be there all the time.

"Right now, that responsibility would be tough. It's a responsibility my mom has talked to me about. The wives are the ones who have to deal with it. There's a lot of stress. You have to have a strong woman."

Mills was asked what sort of stress he felt, and if he had ever worried about being cut, about having it all end, or being traded before he established himself. Even at the outset of the 1995 schedule there was talk that Mills might be traded to the New York Jets. Dick Haley, the Jets' personnel director, had drafted Mills when he was with the Steelers, and really liked him.

"There's always the thought," said Mills. "What stresses me out is the constant demand to perform to your ability. Everything is filmed. You have an expectation for yourself to perform at a certain level, and the coaches have an expectation as well.

"You don't have control as to whether or not you're going to get the ball. You rely on the offensive line and the quarterback to get you the ball. The quarterback touches the ball every time.

"I'd like to be a sociable person, where you can get along with everybody. I take football very seriously. I didn't always. But I do now. But it has to be fun, too. Fun is what got you started in the first place. You don't want it to be just a job.

"I never judged anybody in the locker room. I figure it's up to them, and the coach knows how to deal with each individual. There are a lot of different personalities."

Who helped him find his way in the locker room when he first reported to the Steelers?

"Dwight Stone, he was always the guy. I never saw him upset or down or doubting. He always was upbeat, even when he had cause to be down, when he wasn't getting used much."

Did it bother him when Stone left to go to the Carolina Panthers?

"It doesn't bother you as much now because of free agency, and more people going from one team to another," Mills said. "But Dwight was a good friend. He helped me settle in quickly. He was a guy, an older receiver, who helped me learn the ropes. There was Dwight and Louis Lipps. Dwight was outgoing. Louis wasn't as outgoing in the beginning, but after you got to know Louis, he was sociable, too. At first, Louis was a little more reserved and to himself. It was hard to get to know Louis. Once you did, he was fine.

"Myself and Jeff Graham, we were together a lot. I thought Jeff had a lot of ability. I don't think anyone doubted his ability. It just didn't work out for him here.

"I'm a different person now than I was when I first got here. I'm able to deal with guys being here and with guys being gone. It doesn't affect friendships."

The Steelers' wide receivers from the 1994 and 1995 seasons seemed to have a strong bond, and met socially at least once a week at each other's places.

"Yancey is more hyper. I'm more laidback. My calm relaxes him. We support each other. Charles and Andre are the same way. We say different things to encourage each other. 'That was a big-time play. We're on the move now.' We know when we're on the field that we've got to get it done. I've been able to keep the same focus."

Why did it take so long for him and the rest of the receivers to gain respect?

"At wide receiver, you have to wait for your opportunities. As opposed to running backs, the ball is not in your hands initially. So many things have to happen before that ball gets there.

"Sometimes you can run a super route and the quarterback is looking a different way. Sometimes you run a perfect route and they run the ball.

"As much as I like what Lynn Swann did, I didn't like the Steelers....I was a Cowboys fan. The older I got, the more I became aware of the Steelers. Once I started playing more, I started realizing how amazing Swann and Stallworth were.

"My scholarship for Florida was at defensive back. I could run pretty good routes because I had played receiver in high school. Halfway through my first season I was switched to wide receiver. If I worked hard, I knew I could be good at it. And I'm still working hard to get better. And it's paid off."

"Ernie is the type of person every parent wants to have as their son."
— Principal Bobby James, Dunnellon High School

In late April, 1996, while Ernie Mills was rehabilitating himself at the Steelers' complex at Three Rivers Stadium, he was being honored at the House of Representatives in his home state. His mother and father were both on hand for the occasion.

"It was such a great feeling," his mother said. "Words alone can't express what I feel about so many positive things happening the last few years in our lives."

State Representative Helen Spivey (a Democrat from Crystal River, Florida) read a resolution commending Mills for his accomplishments before the entire House. It not only lauded Mills for his athletic feats, but particularly noted his active participation in his hometown.

"He's always come back and worked with us, we are very pleased that a young man of his caliber hasn't forgotten what it's all about," said Dunnellon High School Principal Bobby James. "He always manages to come back, in rain or shine, and give back.

"We have this thing that people still say we don't have a lot in terms of role models. But Ernie is an exemplary figure. Ernie is the type of person every parent wants to have as their son. We look and hope we can have other kids give back to their communities once they have also been successful."

An excerpt from the resolution read: "That the Florida House of Representatives hereby commends Ernest Lee Mills III for his remarkable achievements on the football field and expresses its sincere appreciation and admiration of him for using his great success as a catalyst to inspire young people."

Ernie Mills had reunion with former Florida teammate, Emmitt Smith, in Phoenix restaurant on Friday night, Jan. 26, prior to Super Bowl XXX meeting. Ernie's brother, Tony, and Tracey, Tony's girlfriend, joined in the fun.

"You really cannot step into the same river twice. Each time it is different, and so are you."
— Alice Walker,
The Same River Twice

Neil O'Donnell
Jack's boy makes good

"There is more to life than football."

W hen Neil O'Donnell was a student at the University of Maryland he was reputed to have the largest dorm room on the campus at College Park, Maryland, and he had it all to himself. He liked the privacy, the isolation, the 30-inch TV set. He was 23 years old and in his fifth and final season with the Terrapins, was taking graduate level classes, and pointing toward a future in pro football and, eventually, the education or business world. There were no distractions when he wanted to do his schoolwork or review his playbook. He wanted to be alone.

When O'Donnell was playing for the Pittsburgh Steelers, he spent less time in the team's locker room than any other player. He was always somewhere else. At midday, when most of the players ate their lunches at their dressing stalls, and some retreated to the players' lounge if they wanted to check out the TV, play some dominos or simply escape the media rush, O'Donnell seldom showed his face. This was a time frame in which the players were supposed to be available for interviews by the media. More often than not, O'Donnell was taking his lunch and making business calls in the office of trainer John Norwig. At lunchtime, Norwig's office became O'Donnell's office. "He was a good guy," said Norwig, "and I will miss him."

Once a week, at best, O'Donnell would drift into the dressing room for ten or fifteen minutes and favor the media with a few sound bites before begging off and disappearing into the training room area once again. "No doubt about it," he often said in response to questions. He was much better after ballgames, but he made everybody's job more difficult with his reluctant manner.

As far as he was concerned, he wanted to be judged on his performance, on wins and losses, not on what he had to say. O'Donnell was the youngest of nine children, which might also explain why he wanted to be alone once in a while. O'Donnell's background was different from most of the players on the Steelers, or pro football at large.

Both of his parents had master's degrees and his father had worked hard in the auto sales business to develop his own dealership. It was quite successful and the O'Donnells were financially well off. All of O'Donnell's brothers and sisters were well educated and successful in their own right. O'Donnell graduated with a degree in economics within his first four years at Maryland — that was one of his main goals when he went there — and he was eight credits shy of a master's degree. He went to school during the summer. One of his friends on the Steelers thought he was insecure, which was one of the reasons he went his own way. There's a strong possibility he just had different interests, was smarter than most of the players and the sportswriters, and showed signs of having a superior attitude.

"Football's not my whole life," he told me one day when we were hiding out in a hallway together. "There are other things I can do and do well. I have other interests."

He agreed to talk to me from time to time, but not in the dressing room, not where everyone else could see us, or where others might want to get at him. He said he had read my earlier books on the Steelers and he was willing to help.

He wasn't enamored with most of the media. Had I been on the beat every day, he might have felt the same way about me. "You've been around," he said. "You can understand what I'm saying. Did they ever play? I've been burned by some of them more than once. I don't trust them." Like most ballplayers, O'Donnell didn't suffer sportswriters or criticism very well. I'd been held in similar disdain by other athletes during my career as a sportswriter. Any sportswriter who thought athletes genuinely cared about them was a fool.

The hallway where we were hanging out was painted with black and gold and white stripes. It was a hallway where the likes of Roberto Clemente and Willie Stargell and Barry Bonds had passed through on their way to play, where Terry Bradshaw and Franco Harris, Jack Ham, Jack Lambert, Mel Blount and Joe Greene had passed. I told O'Donnell he was playing in a place, in a city, where the standards were pretty high, where it was often hard to gain acceptance, where quarterbacks, in particular, were fair game.

But it was a good place where great athletes had achieved much success, I assured him, and that it was hard to do better. There was talk at the time, in the second half of the 1995 season, that the New York Jets or New York Giants, or perhaps the Philadelphia Eagles, were going to come after O'Donnell at season's end, when he became an unrestricted free agent. He would be able to play someplace even closer to home. That and more money might be a hard parlay to pass on. The Steelers had taken a big gamble by not getting O'Donnell's signature on a contract before the start of the 1995 season. They were rolling the dice...

"I love Pittsburgh," O'Donnell declared during the 1995 season, before he thought seriously about going to New York. "It's a great city. It is a great place to play. The funny thing is that the people are still living in the '70s, and want a championship right away. It's a tough place to play."

"Life is about change."
— Leslie O'Donnell

O'Donnell had grown up in Madison, New Jersey, and had gone back to that area during the off-season, and he knew what sports in the New York metropolitan area were all about. He had gone to the New

York Giants' games and training camp near his home in his youth, and dreamed of playing for them some day. The Jets, in time, also came to play at the same stadium in East Rutherford, New Jersey.

I offered O'Donnell a few words of advice, based on working nine years at *The New York Post* and covering all the New York area sports teams at one time or another. I had been there from 1970 to 1979, and it was a period when many of the New York teams won, or had just won, league championships, and it was a great decade in New York as well as back home in Pittsburgh. New York is a city that can generate a great deal of excitement and electricity.

It started in 1969, the year before I got to New York, when the Mets and the Jets both won it all. I got there in time to cover the New York Knicks in the 1970 playoffs when they won the first NBA title in the history of the franchise. They did it again in 1972. I covered the Muhammad Ali-Joe Frazier fights, and that was as good as it gets in sports.

I covered the New York Nets who won two ABA titles in the early '70s with Julius "Dr. J" Erving as the team's star, and the New York Islanders who were putting the pieces together that would eventually win them four Stanley Cup championships. I covered the New York Apples when they won the World Team Tennis title. It was heady stuff.

I was missing out on something back home, though. I was lucky enough to get back to Pittsburgh in 1979 in time to cover the Steelers when they won their fourth Super Bowl in the decade. The Pirates had won the World Series twice, in 1971 and 1979, and Pitt won the national college football championship in 1976. So I knew about the attraction of working in New York as well as the pull of one's hometown. There were pluses and minuses in the equation, either way. "Neil, you know there is no greater place to be than New York if you are on a championship team," I told him, "but, if you are in the middle of the pack or bringing up the rear, there is no worse place to be than New York. It's either heaven or hell."

As a good Irish Catholic from New Jersey, O'Donnell knew the difference. It is important, however, to know where O'Donnell comes from, what kind of family and background and upbringing, to understand the man, what makes him tick, and what prompted him to depart Pittsburgh in favor of New York. I liked O'Donnell. I thought he was bright, decent, aware and a real competitor. He should have been more popular in Pittsburgh. Despite the Joisey accent, he was a Pittsburgher. He wasn't as available, approachable and quotable or nearly as great a quarterback as the Terry Bradshaw of four Super Bowl victories. That was his biggest flaw, his real failing. He didn't know how to make fun of himself the way Bradshaw did. And he could have gone out on a high note, and not looked back, but he chose to offer some critical remarks about the direction the Steelers' organization was taking, and that didn't go down well in Pittsburgh. After all, the Jets had been a joke in the league the last few years. In what direction were they going?

il O'Donnell sets to throw.

O'Donnell sets up behind
Dermontti Dawson.

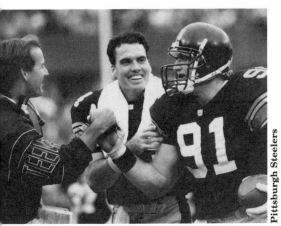

Donnell joins coach Bill Cowher and Kevin
eene in celebrating opposing team's turnover.

O'Donnell in huddle

eil and Leslie at Children's Hospital press
onference

Some people I have a high regard for in the business insist that it was simply a matter of economics that drove O'Donnell to depart Pittsburgh in favor of New York, that the Jets' offer was worth $7 million more than the Steelers' final offer. He went for the money, they said, just the money, and they urged him to come clean on that issue.

The difference in the money was significant — he didn't have to check with his brothers at their Wall Street offices to recognize that — but there were other factors that figured in his decision.

He was a gritty quarterback who always came up short with the Steelers and their fans. He was a good quarterback, but Pittsburghers knew a great quarterback when they saw one. They had Bradshaw, who led the Steelers to four Super Bowl titles. The city and the nearby western Pennsylvania communities had turned out more great quarterbacks perhaps than any other area of the country.

There was Dan Marino, Joe Montana, Joe Namath, George Blanda, John Unitas, Terry Hanratty, Tommy Clements, Jim Kelly and Babe Parilli. And the Steelers had a few good ones, most of them for too few years, such as Bobby Layne, Jim Finks, Lenny Dawson, Jack Kemp, Earl Morrall and Bill Nelsen.

The standards were high in New York — they had enjoyed Bennie Friedman, Charlie Conerly, Y.A. Tittle, Joe Namath, Fran Tarkenton, Phil Simms and Jeff Hostetler — and O'Donnell knew that, but the good quarterbacks never lack self confidence and O'Donnell felt he could deal with the challenge. Going back home, being closer to his family, taking advantage of the opportunities afforded a high-profile athlete in the Big Apple, and the money — yes, the money — all made it quite appealing. Economically, the numbers were numbing for those of us not used to such rarefied financial air: $25 million over four years. He might have been turning his back on a chance to go back to the Super Bowl and of leading a championship team, but the pro sports scene simply was not the same as it once was, and such motivation, such loyalty, was no longer as important as it once was, in football or in the business world. He was comfortable in Pittsburgh, but he was catching flak for his failure to direct the Steelers to a Super Bowl triumph.

Plus, he was getting a push from his wife. "Life is about change," Leslie told him.

His agent, California-based Leigh Steinberg, had been assuring Steelers' officials from the start that Neil did not want to go elsewhere. In the end, however, Steinberg told Neil during negotiations, "If you have one life to live as an athlete, why not live at least a part of it on center stage?"

The Steelers simplified the decision for him when Bill Cowher chose not to rehire his offensive coordinator of his first four years with the Steelers, Ron Erhardt, and tight ends coach Pat Hodgson, whom Erhardt had brought with him from the Giants when he came to the Steelers. O'Donnell knew Erhardt's offensive system, liked working with him and trusted his judgment, and it added to his comfort level.

"When I heard Ron was offered the job here as offensive coordinator," said O'Donnell, when he addressed the New York media during his visit to check out the Jets, "my interest really came up a lot to come here to New York."

Then, too, the Jets' director of player personnel was Dick Haley, who had been with the Steelers when they selected O'Donnell in the draft.

If, indeed, O'Donnell was a little insecure in some areas, this had to make him feel a little more secure, as did the presence of his family — they were all rooting for him to join the Jets — and the chance to go home again. O'Donnell seemed intrigued by the idea of playing near his home.

"It's like a homecoming for me," O'Donnell said before he even signed to play for the Jets. "I know New York very well. I know the media. I know the people around here. I'm excited. I really am."

"The bottom line is wins and losses in this business."
— Neil O'Donnell

O'Donnell didn't show up for the annual Dapper Dan Dinner, Pittsburgh's biggest sports awards banquet, at the end of March, 1996. He was one of the finalists for Man of the Year in Sports in Pittsburgh. But he knew he wasn't going to win — Jaromir Jagr of the Penguins was announced as the winner at the dinner — and he figured he would be booed because he had abandoned the Steelers in favor of the Jets. When his name was mentioned during the program, he was booed. So he didn't miss anything. Earlier, he had been ripped on TV and radio sports talk shows, in letters to the editor of the city's newspapers, and by the local media for taking the money and running off to New York. He was mentioned in the same breath as Barry Bonds and Bobby Bonilla and Doug Drabek, villified Pirates of the past who had done the same. Another Steeler stalwart, right tackle Leon Searcy, had signed a contract making him the highest-paid offensive lineman in the league, with the Jacksonville Jaguars, but he didn't catch nearly as much criticism as O'Donnell.

While O'Donnell may not have been a Bradshaw, surely he had been a major contributor to the Steelers' success. His own teammates, indeed, had named him the Steelers' MVP in 1995. But he came up short of everyone's championship aspirations in his final two seasons as the Steelers' quarterback.

The 1994 season ended with O'Donnell misfiring on his final pass to Barry Foster in the end zone against the San Diego Chargers in the AFC championship game at Three Rivers Stadium. The Steelers came up three yards shy of the Super Bowl. Overlooked was how O'Donnell had driven the Steelers the length of the field in an exciting passing drill during the last minutes of that game to give the Steelers a shot at the big dance.

O'Donnell had overcome disabling injuries early in both the 1994 and 1995 seasons to come back and direct the Steelers to near-championship status. He made it exciting. O'Donnell didn't come up short in the final minutes of the AFC title game the second time around. He fired a long pass to Ernie Mills that set up the game-winning touchdown burst by Bam Morris in a nail-biter with the Indianapolis Colts. O'Donnell had his ups and downs in Super Bowl XXX, but he will best be remembered, and cursed, for the two ill-directed passes he put into the hands of Cowboys' defensive back Larry Brown that absolutely killed whatever chances the Steelers had of winning their fifth NFL championship. Most fans were not interested in the complexities involved, how there was a breakdown in communication between quarterback and receivers, or whatever. O'Donnell had come within one unsuccessful drive of directing the Steelers to a Super Bowl title, and few offered him any praise for the great effort.

It is much easier to be a quarterback from high in the stands or in the press box. All the receivers and possibilities are so much easier to pick out from above. At field level, one wonders how a quarterback can see anything, how they can breathe, or how they survive the thundering herd that is always rushing their way, hell-bent on destruction. "A lot happens in a hurry out there," O'Donnell said. "You have no idea of what it's like out there."

I have seen enough football games in my life, and scrambled for my life as a near-sighted sandlot Unitas-wannabe, however, to appreciate what O'Donnell did for the Steelers during his six seasons with them, and he can take pride in his performance. He gets passing marks. O'Donnell was just 29 when he signed with the Jets. He had just come into his own with the Steelers. His timing with the receivers took a long, trying time to develop. He and his receivers had grown to the point where the coaches could install a sophisticated offense that made the Steelers one of the most exciting clubs to follow in the NFL. Like him or not, it appeared that O'Donnell would be difficult to replace.

The Jets beefed up their receiving corps and offensive line to go with the addition of O'Donnell in their bid to become respectable once more, if not assuring themselves of a return to the days when Joe Namath directed them to an upset victory over the Baltimore Colts in the Super Bowl at the end of the 1969 season. Remember the excitement when Namath signed a multi-year contract calling for $400,000 when he came out of Alabama and turned his back on the NFL in favor of the AFL? "I wouldn't compare anyone to Joe Namath — he was one of the greatest quarterbacks to ever play," said O'Donnell at the Jets' camp.

O'Donnell didn't make a lot of sense with some of the things he said when he signed with the Jets, but he was doing his best to justify his action. He had mixed emotions about what he was doing. Asked why he was interested in joining the Jets, he said, "Winning. I've been to the glory part of the NFL, starting in the NFL. Now the commitment is winning games. I know and everyone else knows the bottom line is wins and losses in this business."

If that were truly the case, how could he have left a strong Steelers' team that looked capable of getting back to the Super Bowl in favor of a franchise that had been a league joke for years? Who had a better chance of winning in the near future — the Jets or the Steelers?

The Jets' deal was for $1.25 million more per year than Pittsburgh was offering him to stay. It was for five years for a reported $25 million, including a $7 million signing bonus. "I'm still Neil O'Donnell, and I'm still going to play the same game I always have," said O'Donnell.

O'Donnell said there was a part of him that was frustrated by the Steelers "lack of aggressiveness" during the negotiations. He questioned the direction in which the Steelers were going, and his remarks riled up former teammates and sports media back in Pittsburgh. His best friends on the Steelers were somewhat miffed by the message he was offering for public consumption. In a sense, they screamed back at O'Donnell, "Take the money, but keep your mouth shut about the Steelers and their situation!"

"Sometimes people describe it as being in a zone."
— Neil O'Donnell

If O'Donnell enjoyed his privacy at Maryland and with the Steelers, how was he going to deal with the greater demands on his time and innermost thoughts that he would find in New York?

"I know the media in Pittsburgh isn't as big, but I find ways to get away from that," O'Donnell told the New York media at their first meeting."I don't need my name in banners. I just stick close to my family. I don't need my name in the paper every week. I look at wins and losses. My job is to win football games."

O'Donnell had directed the Steelers to eight wins in their final nine games of the regular season schedule in 1995. O'Donnell deserved to be a winning pitcher in the finale at Green Bay as well, but Yancey Thigpen, the team's most sure-handed receiver, had dropped a pass when he was wide open in the end zone on the Steelers' final play. It should have been a game-winner. Bill Cowher smiled through the disappointment; some day he will wish the Steelers had won that season finale as well as the regular season finale in San Diego the season before. His career record would have looked better with both of those victories. There were, in truth, no meaningless games in the NFL, not as long as they're keeping score.

O'Donnell discussed his situation in the hallway outside of the Steelers' weight room on New Year's Day, 1996. Teammate Carnell

Lake was lifting weights in the background. Norm Johnson and Donta Jones were adjusting barbells, about to do the same. O'Donnell spoke above the heavy metal clatter.

"It's the momentum, something I've worked at, so long to get to this," said O'Donnell, relating to how he felt about his effectiveness at quarterback, even though the pinkie on his throwing hand had been permanently curled when he broke his hand in the opening game of the season. There were titanium pins put in his hand to hold it together, and you could see them jutting through the pink-blotched skin on the back of his right hand. His hand looked like it would be difficult for him to type, let alone throw a football, but he had never been more accurate than he had been in the second half of the season.

"That was a difficult experience," said O'Donnell of his early-season setback. "It's something you have no control over. Finally, when I had a chance to put it together on the field, I get hurt like that. But I've overcome that. I'm playing with a lot of confidence. Sometimes people describe it as being in the zone."

Here he was playing the best football of his life, looking forward to the playoffs, yet disappointed that his dad didn't live long enough to enjoy it. Jack O'Donnell died before the start of training camp for the 1994 season. I brought up the subject.

"He's always in my prayers," said Neil. "He's one of the reasons I play this sport. He has the best seat in the house now. He was always sending me to the camps. My toughness; I get it from my father. Everyone else went to the beach, and I was out at some football camp somewhere."

Jerry Olsavsky passed us in the hallway. His father had died at age 66 a month earlier, on December 1, 1995, and it stole much of the steam from Olsavsky's miraculous comeback from what had been viewed as a career-ending injury two years earlier. I asked O'Donnell if he had spoken to Olsavsky and offered his condolences.

"I spoke to Jerry right after," said O'Donnell. "I told him I was there and I know what it's like, how it feels. If Jerry wants to tell you about our conversation, he can. But I went to him right after I heard about it.

"It's something that you are never prepared for. I watched my father struggle for so long. When it comes so quickly it kills your whole insides. There's no one who can tell you what to do or how to deal with it.

"My father was so interested in us. When I was a child and playing sports, my father never missed a game. It couldn't have been easy for him and my mother, raising nine kids. He worked nine to nine six days a week. He put in plenty of hours. He came home every night for dinner at six. If we weren't there, we got an earful. If he didn't do that, he wouldn't have known what was going on in our lives. He'd say, 'How was your day?' I sit down every night with my wife and dog. We have a sitdown meal. That's the way I was brought up. Our friends tell Leslie, 'You don't have to do this.' But I feel that we do need to do this. If you don't have a time, you'd never know what was going on in your partner's life. 'How was your day?' Otherwise, you could go along a whole week without finding out how they felt.

"I still talk to my mother all the time, and I call my brothers and sisters. We still want to know what is going on in each other's lives. That's very important to me. I don't need all the business of pro football; I love my privacy.

"I'm very consistent in my ways. I'm not flashy. I'm not interested in a lot of hoopla. I felt I was an adult at 17. My dad wouldn't put up with any bullshit on my part. He didn't want to hear any excuses.

"I'm living the dream. I wish my father could be here. He would enjoy it more than anyone. When he retired, it would have been nice if he could just come and live with us during the season, just hang around. But he got sick."

"Some of the great ones do it differently."
— Neil O'Donnell

O'Donnell's parents sound like the kind of people who would have gotten along well with Art Rooney, the late owner of the Steelers. Neil O'Donnell sat across from me on the other side of a desk that had been Mr. Rooney's in what had been his office in the Steelers' complex at Three Rivers Stadium, and which since his death at age 87 in August of 1988 had been used as a library/museum. I was sitting in a chair once occupied by "The Chief." One of the perks of being a sportswriter on the Steelers beat was spending time with Mr. Rooney. He would always offer a huge cigar and stories and thoughts and warmth that made moments with him something special and precious.

It was a Friday afternoon, September 15, 1995, three days before the Steelers were scheduled to play the Dolphins in Miami in a nationally-televised Monday Night Football offering. One of Art Rooney's dearest friends, Baldy Regan, once known as "The Mayor of the North Side," had passed away the day before. Two of Mr. Rooney's closest associates, secretary Mary Regan, and Ed Kiely, the former publicity man for the Steelers, were swapping stories and reflections about Baldy Regan.

"He knew all the guys on the team," said O'Donnell, picking up on the observations he had just heard outside Mr. Rooney's old office. "Baldy Regan was one of the first people I met when I came here. He was always hustling, getting after us to play for the Steelers basketball team. I did that for a while."

It's no wonder he was after O'Donnell. As a high school player back in Madison, New Jersey, O'Donnell averaged 28 points a game on the basketball team. His nickname in those days was "Supe," short for Super.

O'Donnell felt less than super as he spoke, however. He was nursing a hand injury and was not going to be able to play at Miami.

I talked to O'Donnell about Dan Marino, the quarterback of the Dolphins, who had been a favorite of Mr. Rooney when Marino was playing at the University of Pittsburgh. "We've got to find a way to keep that kid in Pittsburgh," Mr. Rooney remarked to me one day when Marino was starting his senior season at Pitt.

O'Donnell knew Marino well, and liked him a great deal. "I respect Danny," said O'Donnell. "I've been going down to Marino's golf tournament for about six years. We've developed the kind of relationship where I stay over for a few days, and we just go out golfing.

"What amazes me is that he's able to do what he does despite all the physical problems he has. He's got a bum shoulder. He's had a problem with his Achilles tendon. He has so many problems. Yet he waddles back five to seven yards and fires the ball better than anyone. I don't think he has the strongest arm, but he's got the quickest release.

"If anyone tries to critique his throwing motion they could pick him apart. He carries the ball too low. He pats the ball; they tell you not to do that. He does it his way. I remember at the Pro Bowl that someone just told him, 'Just complete the pass. I don't care how you do it.'"

I mentioned to O'Donnell that Jackie Sherrill, who had coached Marino early in his career at Pitt before giving way as coach to Foge Fazio, told Marino not to let anyone fool around with his throwing mechanics.

"Some of the great ones do it differently," O'Donnell said. "Look at Barry Sanders. He never gets hit. He just goes down. If he weren't so successful, he'd be criticized for that."

I mentioned that Franco Harris had been criticized for running that way and evading unnecessary punishment, despite his success with the Steelers of the Super Bowl era. "I told you those Steeler fans were tough," said O'Donnell.

"How about Montana?" I asked.

"I don't really know Joe," he said. "But guys like John Elway, whom I personally know, I admire. Elway and Marino have great confidence in themselves. So does Montana; you can see that.

"Look at Danny, he's so competitive, even when you play him in golf. He has that aura about him. He's the man. And he knows it. Last year when he came back from the Achilles tendon problem, he was struggling at camp to come along, and he was getting heat in the papers. I asked him, 'How are you dealing with this?' He said, 'It doesn't bother me one bit. I've done it every year.'"

O'Donnell paused. "Did they have a chance to get him here? Did he go on the second round?"

Yes, the Steelers had a shot at Marino. He was the fifth quarterback taken, late in the first round of the 1983 draft. The Steelers had the 21st pick on the first round, and they went with a defensive lineman from Texas Tech named Gabe Rivera. He was injured in an auto accident in his rookie season and never walked again. He had been drinking and he shot through the rear window in a head-on collision with a car driven by a devout Steelers fan.

458

I told O'Donnell I thought Marino benefited from the change of scenery and an opportunity to play right away for Don Shula.

"Miami is a great place to be a quarterback," said O'Donnell. "Throwing in that weather is an advantage. You can throw all year round. That heat is great for the arm. It's tough sometimes to throw the ball here in December. It's cold and it's windy. The wind blows it four yards to the left, and they're on your case. The fans don't want to hear about the conditions. You just do it."

I asked O'Donnell if he felt badly about being sidelined for a Monday night game?

"I've been undefeated on Monday night," he said. "I'm 4-0 as a starter. I never missed watching or playing in a Monday Night game. There's something special about it. You sit around all day thinking about it. If you don't feel it as you get older then you should get out.

There's something about it, just like opening day. You can't sleep the night before. I don't get nervous; I get anxious. You can only look at game film so many times. You're thinking, 'Let's go.'

"Lot of people watching; guys back in my home town. Families who are busy on the weekend and may not watch a game will sit down together on Monday Night. I can remember how special it was when I was a kid. I watched it all the time.

"As a player, you get a feeling. It's awesome. You're on stage. It's the only game in town."

O'Donnell was looking around the room at all the photos on the wall. He caught sight of one showing the Steelers squad of the previous season. "So many guys are missing now," he said. "Who'd have thought so many guys would be gone. Look what's happened to Barry Foster. There's a guy who had a difficult life. Foster was one of 13 children. He told me about how there were times when he went to bed at night without having anything to eat. When he was real hungry. People don't talk about stuff like that, but it might help you understand Barry a little better."

He spotted some squad photos from the '70s. How did O'Donnell feel about the legacy those guys had left, winning four Super Bowls the way they did? Did he feel that the Steelers of today would always be measured by the achievements of those teams?

"We're worried about winning one for ourselves," said O'Donnell. "We're not trying to continue their tradition. You talk to Franco and those guys and they'll tell you the same thing. We're different teams."

> *"Much of the devastation in our country*
> *has originated in the realm of lost values.*
> *Do people really care anymore? I wondered.*
> *We need firm standards, yet daily there are*
> *reminders that our standards have slipped, or*
> *never were. What happened to the common sense*
> *notion that two parents are better than one?*
> *What happened to making the effort of teaching*
> *pride in a job well done?"*
> — *Times Present, Times Past*
> A Memoir by Bill Bradley

"We are a very proud family."
— Barbara O'Donnell

In the basement of their home in Madison, New Jersey, there is a glass case which contains trophies, medals and all manner of memorabilia from the athletic triumphs of all members of the O'Donnell family.

There were nine children in the house, six boys and three girls. Neil O'Donnell was the youngest. There were five brothers who played college football at Michigan, Duke, New Hampshire, Penn State and Boston College. All of them were now working with Wall Street firms.

Rosemary was an executive with Calvin Klein. Florence was vice-president for marketing with a division of AT&T. Patty was an independent television producer with four Teddy awards to her credit.

"They are quite good role models," said Barbara O'Donnell of her children. "There is a tremendous sense of pride. We don't settle for just anything. It sounds hokey, but we are a very proud family."

Barbara and her late husband, Jack, both had graduate level degrees. Jack grew up outside of Philadelphia, played football and was graduated from West Chester University and received a master's degree from Temple. She graduated from Immaculata and the Teachers College at Columbia University, where she earned a degree in institutional management.

Jack O'Donnell helped instill a strong work ethic in his sons by putting them to work at his auto dealership, O'Donnell Buick, washing and polishing cars and cleaning up.

Jack had worked his way up from mechanic to wealthy owner of O'Donnell Buick. "If they needed extra money, they had to work for it," Jack said. "None of them wanted a dealership. That's why I retired."

Barbara said football once monopolized the dinner table conversation, but it also started drifting toward discussions about the prime rate, municipal bonds and zero coupons as the kids got older and went to work.

There was always a brother ahead of Neil. Jack was the oldest. One year Mike, Steven and Peter played on the same high school team. Matt was a senior on the Madison High team that included Neil as a freshman.

"The ages were spaced, though there was always healthy competition," said Mike, the former Penn State wide receiver who was working with Smith Barney. "But in a big family you share close quarters. Neil might be a little more reserved, a little more demure than the rest of us. He would rather lead by example than by expressing it. He'll set his mind to do something and do it first, versus the more vocal person, who would say they're going to do this or that. Being the baby, you would think he would be more vocal. But he speaks his piece when it's necessary, and we're very proud of him."

460

George Gojkovich

Pittsburgh Steelers/Michael F. Fabus

Neil O'Donnell looks downfield for receivers, and gets set to take snap from Dermontti Dawson while directing Steelers' attack. Below, he is flanked by his father, Jack, and mother, Barbara, while older brother Jack Jr., stands behind him during his days at the University of Maryland campus.

Neil might be the next one in his family to get a graduate degree. In a notable accomplishment in major college athletics in this era, he graduated in four years.

"Coming out of high school, I didn't know if I would be a starter in college," he recalled, "but one of my goals was to graduate in four years, no matter what I had to do. I gave up a lot of summers to stay at school and take two classes. I never failed a class at Maryland. The goal was to graduate in four years and I did it."

Ken Baron, who was O'Donnell's advisor in the student support service of the athletic department at the University of Maryland, offered these thoughts: "Neil looked after himself and then let others help him. He was also really good about going to class and doing the work, and we didn't have anything to do with that."

O'Donnell didn't get off to a good start in his first term at Maryland. "I remember my father saying, 'If you don't get the grades up, you'll be back home in a community college,' " said O'Donnell.

Bobby Ross was the coach at Maryland when O'Donnell decided to go there, but Ross left for the pros before O'Donnell began playing. He played for Coach Joe Krivak at Maryland.

O'Donnell didn't have the kind of strong arm that Boomer Esiason, one of his predecessors at Maryland, possessed, and pro scouts always offered faint praise for O'Donnell as a prospect, but everybody cited his strong competitive spirit.

George Young, general manager of the New York Giants, said of him, "I think he's very interesting. He has a good enough arm and a lot of savvy."

O'Donnell had a reputation for nervous feet. He scrambled a lot. He was sacked a lot. He worked at his craft. He put in long sessions studying film, preparing for games.

Steve Axman, his quarterback coach at Maryland, had coached Troy Aikman at UCLA, Of O'Donnell, he said, "He's an excellent quarterback, in that he poses so many threats. He can run, he can sprint out and throw and he can go deep."

O'Donnell liked Maryland because they had sent a lot of quarterbacks to the pros. He competed with sophomore Scott Zolak for a starting position, and fell behind Zolak at one point, but later reclaimed his job. Zolak ultimately became a backup quarterback with the New England Patriots.

"I came to this school because I knew they would put the ball in the air and they were sending quarterbacks to the pros," said O'Donnell. He left Maryland as the second-ranked passer in history, behind Esiason, with 4,8989 yards and 26 touchdowns.

O'Donnell dared to dream. He wanted to play in the NFL one day. "I lay in bed and I think about making the big plays — the long score for a touchdown," he said during his last season at Maryland. "But mostly I think about winning and how we can win. I think of big plays because I am a big play quarterback."

462

Maryland coach Joe Krivak said of O'Donnell: "You never had to worry about him being ready to play and being ready to compete. He had a lot of athletic ability, and he was a very intense guy. He had all the physical tools and developed a great deal of mental toughness and mental discipline. I always thought he made good decisions. The players knew who was in control."

"I just want to play my game and go home."

O'Donnell admitted he felt pressure in 1993 after signing a 3-year deal worth $2.725 million per season. After the Steelers signed O'Donnell, they got Mike Tomczak for $2.55 million for three years and later extended that contract. O'Donnell and Tomczak were a much more complementary pairing than O'Donnell and Bubby Brister.

O'Donnell went from being the lowest paid starting quarterback in the league to one of the higher paid ones. He had been making $271,000 in base salary, more than Bradshaw ever made before he got into network TV.

Everything is relative, of course. After O'Donnell departed Pittsburgh, the Steelers tore up the final year of Jim Miller's contract, in which he was to make $196,000, and signed him to a new four-year deal that could pay him more a year than O'Donnell ever made, and one that could end up paying him twice as much as O'Donnell made with the Steelers if he became a starter. And this was a guy who had been the No. 3 or No. 4 quarterback the previous season and whose total NFL game experience was three quarters of actual playing time.

"Most quarterbacks want all that glamour and stuff like that," said O'Donnell during an interview on January 6, 1996. "But that's not my style. The media's job is to write stories and sell papers. I know that. I know the media sometimes looks for dirt and tries to find out more about Neil O'Donnell and what he's doing. That's your job and I respect that. My job is to win football games. I'm really not a strong believer in reading the newspapers.

"I'm more concerned about my relationship with the players on our team," O'Donnell declared. "I try to find a way to keep everybody out there having fun and being cool. You can't be a cheerleader out there. That's not my style. I know there are some people a lot more emotional, but I just try to do my job. I think they look up to me to keep everybody calm and focused on what we have to do. I just want to play my game and go home."

O'Donnell said his poise under pressure was the result of growing up the youngest of nine children.

"I think it's my nature, coming from such a large family," he said. "I try to look at everything the same way and not get up or down. I'm not the rah-rah type of guy.

"I guess you could say I got that from my mother. We had all those kids in our family, yet I never saw her get angry. I never heard her raise her voice. That rubbed off on me. And when you're in a big family like I was, you just have to stay calm.

"I believe my toughness came from my father. He never let anything stop him if he wanted something or set a goal."

His father suffered a stroke one day in 1991 after a pre-season opener in his first year with the team.

"Knowing how tough my dad was, I always believed no one could hurt him," said O'Donnell.

Jack never missed one of Neil's games at Maryland, home or away. Ironically enough, Jack even took Neil, when he was only six years old, to the Steelers' 1972 playoff victory over the Oakland Raiders when Franco Harris made the "Immaculate Reception."

His father was ill and could not attend the wedding when Neil and Leslie were married on May 21, 1994. The couple honeymooned in Bermuda before the Steelers' mini-camp. "The wedding was so hard on us," said Neil. "It was such an emotional day. Everyone in my family was there except my dad."

Neil said he spent as much time as possible with his father when he was in failing health. "All I can do is let him know how much I love him and care about him," said Neil at the time.

It wasn't long after that his father died. "It's been an up and down year for me," O'Donnell said late in the season. "My father died in June, and then we won the division. But the coaches stayed with me, and we're getting better as a team.

"One thing you have to do is not agree with your critics. That's the one thing I learned very early, especially here in the small town of Pittsburgh. You have to believe in yourself because everybody is going to tell you how bad you are."

While he lost his greatest fan, he found a new one in his wife, Leslie. "I got a great girl in Leslie; I was lucky," he said. She was a health and physical education teacher for kindergarten through 12th grade. She had degrees in physical education/health education and sports management.

She did her best to point up her husband's best side. They both went to Children's Hospital, and got involved with a visitation program there. "Sometimes this football world can be crazy, with the way the players are perceived, the game is perceived. The game is the thing," allowed Leslie. "Getting involved in something like this, it helps Neil realize there is so much more going on besides who the Steelers are playing this week."

"One week you're a hero, the next week you're a zero."
— Neil O'Donnell

Looking back, O'Donnell said some things when he won MVP honors on the Steelers at the end of the 1995 season, and when he appeared at press conference sessions at Super Bowl XXX that would leave a Steelers' fan shaking his or her head in the wake of his leaving Pittsburgh for New York.

When he was named the team's MVP, O'Donnell said if he stayed with the Steelers he thought he could erase almost all of Terry Bradshaw's records. It was unlikely, though, that he would have ever equalled Bradshaw's record of directing the Steelers to four Super Bowl victories.

When O'Donnell went to the Jets, Bradshaw was critical of the move. He questioned O'Donnell's motives. "At least I don't have to worry about my records being broken," Bradshaw said, sarcastically. "I never lost a Super Bowl, and that's the only record I really care about."

O'Donnell was pleased, however, to have his teammates name him the team's MVP:

"I think it means a great deal. It's the guys you practice with every day, you shower with every day, you see them every day. You do everything with them. They see the type of person and the type of football player you actually are because they spend so much time with you. It's an honor to be voted the MVP. I'm proud of it. I worked very hard to get it. But it's a team effort. I can never do my job without the other 10 guys on the field."

As for his love-hate relationship with the fans, he insisted the criticism didn't bother him. "I think it's the nature of the business," he said. "It changes every week. One week you're a hero; the next week you're a zero. I really don't get caught up in that. I really don't. What the fans think, I can't let bother me, as long as I have the respect of the guys in this locker room. And I have that.

"I've heard the heat, but I always kept my mouth shut, did my talking on the field and worked hard at what I did. You go to Pittsburgh nowadays and there are a lot of people behind Neil O'Donnell.

"I still have some unfinished business as a Steeler. I'm happy in Pittsburgh. I really am. I enjoy playing there. I think it's something special, also, to stay with one team your whole career. It's a business, I understand that. There won't be any hard feelings. I'll just have to see what happens."

O'Donnell didn't really change his feelings in that regard, so some might suspect, when he signed with the Jets soon after Super Bowl XXX.

I spoke with O'Donnell in mid-May after he had come off the field at a Jets' practice session during a mini-camp in Hempstead, New York. "I had a great run in Pittsburgh," he said. "I didn't badmouth anybody, no matter how the media might have presented it. I have nothing but good feelings about that city and that organization. I had a chance to come home and play ball and I'm excited about that. But Pittsburgh is a great place to play ball and I'll be rooting for those guys. Give the 'Burgh my best."

New York Jets

Neil O'Donnell flashes his new Jets' jersey with assist from head coach Rick Kotite at New York press conference.

O'Donnell addresses New York media as newest member of New York Jets.

Ron Erhardt, Jets' offensive coordinator, oversees Neil's workout at Hempstead, N.Y. practice facility.

Yancey Thigpen
A survivor

*"I wasn't worried about football,
I was worried about living."*

It was an alarming night Yancey Thigpen won't soon forget. He can remember the scene, even though it was dark and hard to see, as vividly as all that he experienced in the bright desert sun at Tempe, Arizona for Super Bowl XXX.

It happened outside a townhouse where he was living at the time, near Allegheny Center on the city's North Side, not far from Three Rivers Stadium where he would emerge as a star receiver for the Steelers during the 1995 season.

To hear Thigpen tell it, there were scary moments when he did not know if he would be around for the 1995 football season. Frankly, he feared for his life.

It was about 11:30 p.m. on a Monday night, May 23, 1995, when Thigpen was robbed at gunpoint outside his apartment on West North Avenue. Two men wearing hooded sweatshirts and black ski masks accosted him and a woman friend as they were getting out of his car.

The men forced Thigpen to lay face down on the pavement with a gun pointed at his head. How frightening that must have been. The sidewalk was rough and cold. The streets where Art Rooney loved to roam, in the First Ward of Old Allegheny, as Rooney often referred to it, weren't as safe as they had once been. The North Side had always been a rough neighborhood, even when its mansions were the homes of rich men and women, but it had gotten worse.

One of Thigpen's teammates, Deon Figures, had caught a stray bullet in the knee while driving his car through Los Angeles less than two weeks earlier, on May 13, and Steelers officials were concerned about Figures' future in football.

Later on during the season, other Steelers would run into one difficulty or another on the streets of Pittsburgh. Jonny Gammage, the cousin of Steelers defensive lineman Ray Seals, was killed in an altercation with suburban police in a case that drew national media scrutiny. Thigpen knew Gammage from working with him at Christmas visits to area malls to distribute gifts to underprivileged children. Seals was sitting on a stool nearby in the Steelers' clubhouse, separated from Thigpen by Ernie Mills, as Thigpen talked about that night in May when he thought he was going to be shot in the head by strangers on a North Side street.

It was seven months from that incident, and the knowledge of all that had gone down in Pittsburgh since then — headline stories about homicides in the city, drive-by shootings, people getting killed in

George Gojkovich

Yancey Thigpen

George Gojkovich

robberies, or simply for being in the wrong place at the wrong time —
had to be sobering stuff for Thigpen, and put that night into an even
different light. How lucky he had been to survive that night and to
be able to become one of the most respected receivers in the National
Football League, indeed, a first-time Pro Bowler.

"Without a doubt, football was the farthest thing from my mind
that night," recalled Thigpen, with a little prodding. "I'm thinking
this guy is going to shoot me. I wasn't worried about football, I was
worrying about living.

"The only thing in my mind was me. No, I didn't think about
Deon, and how he was shot in the leg. Deon Figures didn't cross my
mind. I was wondering whether these guys wanted to make a reputation by taking out a professional athlete, a Steeler. I have no doubt
in my mind they knew me."

The robbers went through his pockets and his car, taking his
keys, $400 in cash, credit cards, two gold watches, a diamond ring, a
gold chain, and some personal items of "sentimental value." A second
man took a gold chain, a gold watch, and a purse containing an
unknown amount of cash and credit cards from Thigpen's companion.

The men then drove off in Thigpen's car, a pricey white 300
Nissan ZX. The car was later recovered, a short distance from the
scene. It was undamaged, but the keys and luggage in the trunk were
missing. Thigpen had arrived at Pittsburgh International Airport
that evening after a flight from Charlotte. He had been back home in
North Carolina visiting family and friends.

"Of course, I'm still very upset about it," he said. "I have tried to
get involved in the community in a positive way. The Steelers stress
that. And I have talked to kids, and have played in a lot of basketball
games and stuff to help raise money for neighborhood projects. I don't
want this to turn me off about the kids.

"You have to realize who people are. One, two or three people
don't speak for everybody. You can't change your mentality by the
actions of others, but it left a bitter taste. You feel real vulnerable.
You're trying to be a role model for young people and then this type of
thing happens."

What did he remember about the robbers?

"One of them had a gun on him," said Thigpen. "He was younger
than me. I'm not sure about the other guy. They don't have much life
ahead of them, though, if they keep up that kind of behavior.

"I tried not to let one or two bad apples ruin my outlook on
things. I just have to be more careful. That was on a Monday night
and two nights later, at the other end of town, I was with Ernie Mills
and we came out of a place and Ernie's stereo had been ripped out of
his car. So this stuff goes on everywhere. It's just everywhere. It's
one of those things. You can't let it turn you off, or change your
attitude, about working with young people."

It did prompt Thigpen to take an apartment on Grandview
Avenue atop Mt. Washington, a somewhat safer neighborhood, where

he had a view of Downtown Pittsburgh and Three Rivers Stadium, as well as the streets where he was mugged.

Thigpen was the picture of health as he spoke about his May Day dilemma. There wasn't a more attractive figure in the Steelers' locker room than Thigpen. He was handsome with thick dark eyebrows and his mustache and beard were always trimmed just so. He had a sleek look about him. He was a well-muscled 6-1, 206 pounds. There were always gold chains dangling around his neck, a gold watch on his wrist, and he had a wardrobe of many warm-up coordinates. He was a cool-looking dude, and he was always friendly, and readily available to the media. He spoke softly, but willingly.

He realized things could have been worse. "I think about it all the time," he said. "I've seen how things have come down for Ray Seals with his situation, losing his cousin and best friend in such a crazy manner. Ray knows he has the support of all the guys. Ray has handled his situation well, and we're all with him.

"If something is on my mind, I don't have to go around bothering everyone with my problem. But there's so much camaraderie in this clubhouse. There's good communication. We're all in this together."

"He's always been a good kid."
— Yancey Thigpen's mother

Minnie Thigpen had been on her feet all day, and her back was starting to stiffen, as it did every day around quitting time.

She was in her 15th year as a beautician — that's what she called herself, though hair stylist has become a more fashionable term for what she does — at the Nu-Vision Hair Studio by Minnie in Tarboro, North Carolina, about ten miles east of Rocky Mount.

This was early March, 1996. She said she was scheduled for back surgery in two weeks. Sometimes we don't think of it, but beauticians, barbers, hair stylists and shopkeepers stand on their feet constantly, and it's hard on a body. She was in her shop from 8 a.m. to 6 p.m., Tuesday through Friday and from 8 a.m. to 3 p.m. on Saturday.

Soon, she would be leaving the shop and going home to Conetoe, a small community about eight to ten miles from Tarboro. There were factories and farms and about 2,000 citizens in Conetoe. It's where Yancey Thigpen comes from.

"He's the youngest of my six kids," said Minnie Thigpen. "He's always been a good kid. I never had any problems with him. He always was one of those kids who thought he could get whatever he wanted. His dad always tried to please him. Yancey could be mean to his sisters and brothers and beat on them from time to time, but it was all playful stuff."

Minnie Thigpen remembers that fateful night on the North Side, too, because her son called her on the telephone right after it happened to tell her about his harrowing experience.

"He said he'd never been as scared," recalled Minnie Thigpen. "He said he could see himself dying right there on that sidewalk. He said the man held a gun to his head. There was nothing he could do. He thought it was all over for him. When he told me about it, I was just as scared as if I'd been there."

Minnie was so proud of her son, of all her children, and was thrilled by all the good things that happened to her Yancey after his scary brush with a gun-toting robber.

"I always told them to stay in school, to get an education," remembered Minnie. "They all did real good."

The Thigpens had been challenged in another way in 1995, as Yancey's father, Edward, found himself out of work when he was laid off at Black & Decker, where he had been employed for 25 years. "I'm carrying the load right now," she said, "but we're hoping things will improve. I'm hoping my back surgery will give me some relief, and that things pick up for my husband." She and Edward were separated 13 years earlier, and later divorced, but they still cared about each other's welfare.

"I was a Lynn Swann fan before I was a Steelers fan."
— Yancey Thigpen

Yancey Thigpen knew about the Steelers from his earliest days in football. "As a kid, I was a Pittsburgh Steelers fan," he said. He was sitting in the left corner of the locker room, next to Brentson Buckner, and Buckner nodded when he overheard Thigpen's remarks because he, too, was a big Steelers fan as a youngster growing up in Georgia. "But I was a Lynn Swann fan before I was a Steelers fan."

He saw Lynn Swann on TV and tried to copy his style, even practicing acrobatic catches. Thigpen was ten years old when Swann starred in the Steelers' fourth Super Bowl victory, against the Los Angeles Rams in Super Bowl XIV. While he emulated No. 88, he was still satisfied when Steelers' equipment manager Tony Parisi gave him No. 82. He knew that was John Stallworth's number.

"I loved Swann and Stallworth," continued Thigpen. "I was a big fan of theirs, so I'll always respect them. Every day, I was either Lynn Swann or John Stallworth when we played on the sandlots. We didn't have any cable TV back then, so it seemed like every game that was on TV had either the Cowboys or the Steelers. Either you loved the Cowboys and Steelers or you hated them. I picked the Steelers over the Cowboys mostly because they were in the same region of the country.

"Looking at Lynn Swann as a kid was something of an incentive for me. I always wanted to make those kind of grabs. I started young trying to make incredible catches.

"I played football, basketball and baseball and, when I went to high school, track and field. I knew I could get a college scholarship, but I wasn't sure whether it was going to be for football or basketball. George Gervin, number 44, was my favorite basketball player. My football skills started to be superior during my sophomore year. I was so much better than everybody else on the field."

Gervin and David Thompson, another high-flyer from Thigpen's native North Carolina, headed the 1996 Class for induction into the Basketball Hall of Fame. Stallworth and Swann were among five Steelers who had been under consideration for the 1996 Class for the Pro Football Hall of Fame. So Thigpen picked his heroes well when he was a kid back in Tarboro. Gervin and Thompson both ran into problems with drugs during their careers, but cleaned up their acts and were representing NBA teams in community service with young people.

And now Thigpen was wearing the same number (82) Stallworth wore when he was playing for the Steelers. Swann was his idol, but Stallworth was a close second. I shared stories about Gervin and Thompson, whom I met and interviewed during my days on the pro basketball beat at *The New York Post*, and about Swann and Stallworth with Thigpen, because I had gotten to know them both when I was on the Steelers' beat as a writer with *The Pittsburgh Press*, and he seemed eager to learn more about them.

"It's a pleasure to wear the number," said Thigpen, who had met Swann, who still lived in the Pittsburgh area, but not Stallworth, who was back home in Huntsville, Alabama. "The guy was one of the greatest receivers to ever play the game. For me to even be compared to him or considered close to achieving some of the things he achieved, it's a pleasure. It's an honor to be associated with the organization and wear his number and to have him be the one I'm striving to even come close to.

"I don't know of any wide receivers who came from Winston-Salem State and accomplished what I've accomplished," Thigpen said, without a hint of bragging in his soft voice. "Being a hero in a city as big as Pittsburgh...I'd never imagined it."

He always knew this is what he wanted, to have a shot at succeeding in the big time.

"My successes in football made my decision easier when it came time to concentrating on one sport as a career choice," said Thigpen. "As a kid, I always wanted to be a professional athlete. My goal was to get a college scholarship.

"I was a very competitive person. Coming out of high school, I had no doubt in my mind I would start for my college football team as a freshman. I went to an organization, at Winston-Salem State, that didn't believe in playing freshmen. Only three freshmen made the traveling squad and played any. I was one of the three. One was the quarterback Cornell Maynard. He had tunnel vision for me. He only saw me. He eventually was the starter, but he left when the coach went elsewhere. I started as a sophomore.

As 16-year-old hoopster

Thigpen family, from left to right, are Yancey, Vickie, mother Minnie, father Edward, Keith and Valerie. Carolyn and Timothy were missing when photo was taken.

With Santa Claus at 3

At age 8

As 5-year-old

Young biker

"I was very confident. I was so consistent. If I hadn't done any-thing after three quarters, and wasn't having a good game, I always competed till the end because I expected to turn things around.

"I've never been a cocky player, but I have always been a confi-dent player. I don't talk a lot of trash. That's not my style. I think our team was definitely mischaracterized in that regard during the playoffs last year (1994 season). We were very confident. We were having fun. Laughing. Joking. On the field, at practice, we were really having fun.

"Our season went by so fast. We were winning, and we didn't mind the bad weather or the winter cold. Snow or rain, it didn't matter. The last third of the season we were winning and having fun. No one complained. We just went out and did it. We were very confi-dent, playing as a team. We got a bad rap.

"The cockiness or assumptions about winning didn't come out of this locker room. No one here predicted that we were winning, not that I was aware of it.

"I saw guys laughing and joking, but I didn't see or hear anybody putting anybody down. Even Barry (Foster) was laughing and talking, and you know that's not like him. He was working hard and joining in the fun.

"I saw it. I could see it in the guys' eyes before the Cleveland game. I could see emotions and enthusiasm. I knew we were going to play well, but I just said that to myself. I didn't say it to any writers or TV guys.

"The guys who are here, and who have experienced that situa-tion, will benefit from it. I think if you put us in that same situation again I don't think it would happen again. There was a lot of hurt in here. It will help us.

"Every year since Coach Cowher's been here, we've taken another step forward. If we'd gone to the Super Bowl and lost it, we'd have more drive to get back. To lose that game (with San Diego in the AFC championship) the way we lost it really hurt. The way we were playing before that game, we would have played till April, and there'd have been no sense of tiredness.

"Looking at the strides I made last year, what I did bad and what I did good, I'm trying to look at myself with a critical eye. Everyone should look at themselves and see how they can get better. Then the team will get better."

What steps did Thigpen plan to take during the 1995 season to improve his performance?

"As far as I'm concerned, I'm looking at more film, looking at dif-ferent schemes, critiquing myself," he said. "We have a great group of wide receivers on this team. We're trying to play as a group. No one's pouting. We try to be helping each other.

"A couple of years ago, we had a couple guys complaining about playing time, contracts, making more money and not getting their number called. There wasn't a lot of that last season. But you're always going to have selfish people."

"It's like walking
through a jewelry store."

It was two weeks away from Super Bowl XXX, and Thigpen was talking by his dressing stall in the Steelers' locker room. He wore wedding band sized diamond-studded earrings — I later learned they cost about $2,000 while visiting a jewelry store in the Clark Building downtown — and a gold necklace chain that contained diamond-studded YT initials in the middle.

How did it strike him, he was asked, when he saw the four Lombardi Trophies in the lobby of the Steelers' complex when he came to work and left to go home each day?

"It's like walking through a jewelry store," said Thigpen, who has obviously spent some time in jewelry stores. "I like seeing all that stuff. It's more of an incentive. You know what it took to get those and you want some of your own."

Who would he like to be if he continued to catch passes with the same consistency as he had during the 1995 season.

"Jerry Rice; he's a great player," said Thigpen. "He made plays. Does it week after week and in the Super Bowl."

I told Thigpen that Hal Hunter, a former Steelers assistant coach who had worked more recently with the San Francisco 49ers, had told me at the AFC title game party at the Hyatt that Rice was a classy individual off the field.

"I'm not surprised to hear that," said Thigpen.

In Super Bowl XXX, Thigpen would be matched against Dallas Cowboys cornerback Deion Sanders much of the time.

"It's a team thing," he said, "and I'm a team man. It's not me against Deion. If I don't make any catches and we win, I'll be happy. If I make ten catches and we lose, I won't be. You want to walk in that door one day and actually see a trophy that you put in there.

"The Steelers are 4-0 in Super Bowls. You don't want to be the one that when people say the Steelers went to the Super Bowl five times and this was the team that lost. You don't want to be associated with the team that lost."

As it turned out, Andre Hastings made ten catches and he was hardly happy. Thigpen was limited to one catch. It was a two-yard touchdown catch directly in front of Sanders, who shoved him toward the ground as he grabbed the ball.

But the Steelers lost a heartbreaker.

The Steelers were heavy underdogs going into the game with the Cowboys, so Thigpen put a positive spin on his prospects, no matter the outcome.

"It's special," he said, "to go to the Super Bowl and the Pro Bowl, all in one year. Nothing came easy for me. I'll work even harder."

As it turned out, he scored a touchdown pass in both the Super Bowl and the Pro Bowl — streaking 65 yards after making a one-handed catch of a pass over the middle from Cincinnati's Jeff Blake.

I told him it was interesting and satisfying for me to have seen him and his next-door neighbor, Ernie Mills, as well as C.J. Johnson and Hastings, come into their own over a two-year stretch, to see them blossom and mature. The best seemed ahead of them, if they could overcome some nagging injuries. Thigpen had stubbed two toes, for instance, and they would still be bothering him when he reported to the Steelers' mini-camp in June of 1996.

"Me and Ernie, we're as close as anybody on the team, and we care about C.J. and Andre and the other guys," said Thigpen. "Back then (two years earlier), we were a group of guys who didn't get much respect. Our success hasn't changed us at all. We're still doing the same things together.

"We had to stick together. At the time, basically, it was us against the world. We weren't making a lot of plays. But we weren't getting a lot of opportunities, either. We tend to stick together."

"Those six weeks were my hell."
— Yancey Thigpen

When the Steelers held off the Indianapolis Colts in the AFC Championship Game, Thigpen sat on a stool in the locker room long after nearly everyone else had left, to go out and celebrate the biggest victory of their pro careers. Thigpen thought his feet were frozen to the floor. He couldn't move. He felt drained.

"I just sat there and could see myself wandering off into space," he said. "I had come so far."

He found himself thinking about his football-playing days at Winston-Salem State, a Division II school, and some of the four-hour bus trips for road games.

"Sometimes they didn't have enough room on the bus," Thigpen said. "Guys had to follow us in school vans.

"We practiced on a field you wouldn't dream about falling down on. It may have looked great at the start of camp. But a week later, it was all dirt and full of holes."

Thigpen said the school's athletic budget was so skimpy that he often had to buy his own tape for spatting his shoes, and his own gloves.

But Thigpen pulled in passes with a flair. Pete Richardson, his former coach at Winston-Salem who later became the head coach at Southern University, said of Thigpen: "He had unusual jumping ability. He would go up and take it away from people. You put the ball around him, he'll find a way to come down with it."

Thigpen thrived as a receiver at Winston-Salem, however, and caught the eye of many pro scouts, especially San Diego Chargers general manager Bobby Beathard, who picked him in the fourth round in 1991.

476

But by his second training camp, Thigpen was put on waivers.

"It was some lame story about, 'You were the toughest decision. We were up all night. It was just a numbers game,' and stuff like that," said Thigpen.

"I had never been in that position before, where someone thought of me as not being good enough. It was a letdown. I never got a chance out there. I was devastated. There have been others who've been cut and had the ability, but got lost in the shuffle. It happens all the time. If someone doesn't see something in you right away, you may never get the opportunity you need to prove yourself.

"I played with guys in high school and in college who were as good as me. They might not have gotten the opportunity where they came from. Some guys are better prepared for the pros coming from bigger programs in college."

Thigpen continued to work out with a friend and lived at the home of that friend's grandmother. "Those six weeks were my hell," he recalled. "I was worried my career was over. When somebody says you can't do something, you always want to show them you can. You want to prove it. And you want to prove it over and over. I never lost faith in myself. I knew I had talent. I knew I could play in San Diego. I knew I had as much talent as the people they were playing."

Then the Steelers called and invited him to come to Pittsburgh for a tryout. "He had a monster workout," said Tom Donahoe, Steelers director of football operations. "It was unbelievable. He's a phenomenal athlete. You talk about workout warriors. Yancey could test with anybody. In terms of running, jumping, changing directions, he's as good as anybody we've got."

He signed as a free agent with the Steelers in 1992 and became a starter for the 1994 season. He caught only one pass in 1992 and nine in 1993. But he turned three of those nine catches into touchdowns.

Thigpen became a starter in 1994 and one of the AFC's best receivers during the 1995 season. He finished the regular season with a team-record 85 catches for 1,307 yards, the second most in the AFC. He shattered some of the records set by John Stallworth, one of his boyhood favorites. Stallworth had caught 80 passes in 1984 to establish the club record for one season. Both records were set in 16-game seasons.

"As a kid, out in the backyard, in sandlot football, everyone was somebody," Thigpen said. "You had a Tony Dorsett in the backfield and a Terry Bradshaw at quarterback. I imitated Lynn Swann."

The regular season ended on a strange note for Thigpen. He dropped a potential game-winning touchdown pass in the end zone — he was so wide open — on fourth down against Green Bay with 11 seconds left on the clock. Neil O'Donnell put it right in his hands, but it didn't stick.

That play kept the Steelers from winning their last nine games of the regular season, but Bill Cowher hugged Thigpen and forced a smile when he came to the sideline. Cowher didn't want to dwell on anything negative. The Steelers had already clinched the division and a bye in the first round of the playoffs and would open at home. Cowher's forgiving manner only reinforced the feelings Thigpen had about the team.

"Nobody's been pointing fingers around here lately," said Thigpen. "I was in San Diego before I came to Pittsburgh, and we had groups there, maybe 15 different groups, who each did their own thing. Here in Pittsburgh, we have more of a team. Every time somebody posts a notice to get together at some place after practice we always have a good response. The guys show up to socialize, like at the Clark Bar. There will be 15 or 20 guys there when you get there, and another 15 or 20 guys will have been there before you arrived. We have a lot of fun together."

"Yancey is an excellent blocker."
— Chan Gailey

Thigpen totaled only 10 receptions in 1992 and 1993, but became a special teams ace for the Steelers and was named a Pro Bowl alternate in 1993.

"Yancey came up the hard way," said Chan Gailey, the coach of the wide receivers when Thigpen became a starter. "To play special teams, you have to be tough and you have to be able to block. Yancey is an excellent blocker. To me, that is something that separates him from a lot of other receivers."

The top pro receivers were still named Rice, Michael Irvin and Herman Moore, but Thigpen thought he was about to join them. "I'm not in awe of them at all," he said. "Those guys are being thrown the ball a lot more than I am being thrown the ball. I feel if I am given the opportunity I can be right up there with those guys.

"When I was at San Diego, the receivers weren't thought to be that good, either. The San Diego receivers had the same rap as the receivers did here when I first got here. Then they got a quarterback in Stan Humphries, and all of a sudden the receiver problem was solved. All of a sudden their wide receivers looked pretty good. It's all a matter of opportunity. We were forced to pass more this year, and Neil O'Donnell and I had a lot of success. I believe he has a lot of confidence in my ability to get open and catch the ball.

"If I'm on top, I want to stay on top, and if I'm not on top, that's where I want to be. I'll work until I get there, no matter how long it takes or how much work it takes.

"I knew I could make big plays, but it's a matter of being in the right place at the right time. Coming to Pittsburgh and doing the things I've done to get into this position, I've finally put myself in the right place at the right time.

"I'm a big receiver. I'm strong. I have speed, size and the will to compete. I have a strong sense of urgency when it comes to getting the job done."

Thigpen became O'Donnell's "go-to" guy — the first Steeler since Louie Lipps 10 years earlier to compile 1,000 yards receiving, with an AFC second-best 1,307 yards.

"Neil O'Donnell has begun to play really good, and now our passing offense is a strength," said Thigpen. "Neil has a lot of confidence in us. He knows I'm going to put out every Sunday. If I drop a pass, he's not going to quit looking my way. And if a guy drops a pass on this team, now the rest of the receivers will say, 'Hey, it happens. It's over. Forget it.' That's what we have here now. If a guy has a bad game, we'll go straight to that guy and let him know we care. And if they do well, we'll tell him how great that is.

"I've always been a person who worked real hard and was persistent to be the best I could be," said Thigpen. "I'm not content with things. If I get 100 catches this year, I won't be happy to settle for 99 next season. I always want to progress. I have a really strong sense of urgency when it comes to getting a job done. I'm the type of person who can't stand to be behind someone. Whatever it takes for me to rise to the top, that's what I want to do.

"Some people approach things differently. Some people in this league don't believe they're supposed to play special teams. But I look at it differently. If this is what I was brought in to do, that's what I've got to do. Regardless of what I'm asked to do, I will take it upon myself to do it and do the best I can."

That was why he had been Cowher's kind of player. "Yancey has really worked at it," said the Steelers' head coach. "He's had some success, but he keeps it all in perspective. It's not like this has come to him, and he's gloating over it. Being the best is very important to him, and it couldn't happen to a better person. He's working at it."

Coach Bill Cowher embraces ace receiver Yancey Thigpen.

Sketch by LeRoy Neiman

"Jim O'Brien was one of a group of young sports writers of the 1970s in New York who were more than journalists. This new breed — Jim, along with Larry Merchant, Vic Zeigel, Stan Isaacs, Bob Lipsyte — treated the readers of the *New York Times*, *The New York Post* and *Newsday* to a new investigative look at the total sports scene from ownership to management through the athletes on to the fans. It was great stuff."

— *LeRoy Neiman*

37
#33
Charles Johnson
55
#95
Willie J Williams Jr